INTERNATIONAL DEVELOPMENT IN FOCUS

The Long Road to Inclusive Institutions in Libya

A Sourcebook of Challenges and Needs

HEND R. IRHIAM, MICHAEL G. SCHAEFFER, AND KANAE WATANABE, EDITORS

WORLD BANK GROUP

Contents

CHAPTER 4   Setting the Stage for Public Sector Reform   49

Michael G. Schaeffer, Zied Ouelhazi, Maroua Lassoued, Wesal Ashur, and Kanae Watanabe

CHAPTER 5   Institution Building: Lessons from World Bank Engagement in Libya   71

Francesca Recanatini

CHAPTER 6   Causes of Instability and Local-Level Capacity for Peace   89

Rani Daoud

Figures

Maps

Tables

Foreword

In some countries, designing and implementing major reforms, especially after prolonged levels of conflict, is made more difficult due to externally imposed circumstances. This is especially true for Libya, where the prolonged level of conflict has adversely impacted the relationship between the central public administration and subnational governments. To make things more challenging, the competing public administrations between East, West, and other areas of the country have led to a web of public institutions with unclear or overlapping mandates accompanied by a limited technical capacity to execute fundamental primary tasks of government. According to the World Governance Indicators for Libya, between 2012 and 2018, the negative effects of these multiple challenges are evidenced by declines in public sector effectiveness, political stability, regulatory quality, and the rule of law.

The decade-long dynamic of crisis and conflict since the 2011 revolution has come at a devastating cost for the Libyan people. In addition to significant insecurity, displacement, degradation of infrastructure and basic services, and reductions in the people's well-being, the conflict has reduced social cohesion, fracturing relationships between communities.

The early enthusiasm around the country's political and economic potential turned lukewarm as it became clear that political wrangling was derailing Libya from a path of sustainable growth. The unified executive authority, tasked with leading Libya to national elections by the end of 2021, ultimately postponed the election. Not having a constitutional framework to work from has also created a vacuum that fuels continued conflict. However, the process of drafting and agreeing on a new constitution has remained stalled and the country today risks sliding back into a deeper division.

Against this background, the purpose of this collaborative sourcebook, *The Long Road to Inclusive Institutions in Libya*, is to provide information and reflections for larger debates on and in Libya, for colleagues in the country's government and administration as well as civil society, academia, and partner organizations alike. This sourcebook compiles analytical work that has been conducted over the past several years by World Bank teams as well as many partner organizations of Libya. As one crucial element for public policy making, namely reliable and regular available data, is scarce in the country, teams have been utilizing several analytical techniques (phone surveys, nighttime data, qualitative surveys) to ground their work, and many of the resulting studies shed new light on Libya's medium- to long-term challenges.

Sincere thanks go to the editors of this volume; the dozens of contributing authors from the European Union (EU), Deutsche Gesellschaft für Internationale Zusammenarbeit (GIZ), the United Kingdom's Department for International Development (DFID), the United Nations Children's Fund (UNICEF), the United Nations Development Programme (UNDP), the United Nations Support Mission in Libya (UNSMIL), the World Bank, and the World Food Programme (WFP); as well as to the many colleagues and Libyan officials who have supported this work.

Strong institutions are one crucial dimension to helping Libya build back a stronger and more resilient economy. Libya will emerge from this difficult period with the international community, including the World Bank, standing ready to help, not only to meet the short-term needs, but also to enhance institutions that will help usher in brighter years ahead.

Jesko S. Hentschel
Country Director for the Maghreb and Malta
Middle East and North Africa Region
The World Bank

Acknowledgments

The Long Road to Inclusive Institutions in Libya is a collaboration led by the World Bank. It greatly benefited from contributions from bilateral and multilateral partners, including the European Union (EU), Deutsche Gesellschaft für Internationale Zusammenarbeit (GIZ), the United Kingdom Department for International Development (DFID), the United Nations Children's Fund (UNICEF), the United Nations Development Program (UNDP), the United Nations Support Mission in Libya (UNSMIL), and the World Food Programme (WFP).

The team wishes to extend its gratitude to our Libyan colleagues from the Central Bank of Libya, the General Authority for Water Resources, the General Electric Company of Libya, the Ministry of Finance, the Ministry of Health and Primary Care Institution, the Ministry of Planning, and the Ministry of Social Affairs for their collaboration.

At DFID and the Foreign & Commonwealth Office, we acknowledge Steph Trinci's assistance. At the EU, we acknowledge the assistance, advice, and contributions from Mary Hovers and Antonis Tsamoulis. At the German Embassy in Libya, we thank Denis Sertcan. At UNDP, we thank Gerardo Noto and Peter Rundell. At the United Nations Economic and Social Commission for West Asia, we thank Tarik Alami, Mohamed Hedi Bchir, Hakim Ben Hammouda, and Mohamed Abdelbaset Chemingui.

We also thank Patricia Morales (US Embassy in Libya) and Russell Bauer, John Pennell, Joseph Scheibel, Sara Werth, and Clinton White, all from the US Agency for International Development. We acknowledge the assistance of Hilary Childs-Adams (government of Canada) and Jan-Jaap Sas (Netherlands Embassy in Libya) and comments by Claudia Gazzini (International Crisis Group).

This book was developed under the overall guidance of Jesko Hentschel (World Bank Country Director for the Maghreb and Malta, Middle East and North Africa Region). We are grateful to the valuable advice and support provided by Kevin Carey. We acknowledge the valuable comments provided by many colleagues from the World Bank Group Libya country team, including Ebrahim Al-Harazi, David Bernstein, Anush Bezhanyan, Fadila Caillaud, Javier Diaz Cassou, Moez Cherif, Stephane Dahan, Heba Elgazzar, Erik Fernstrom, Tendai Gregan, Johannes G. Hoogeveen, Djibrilla Adamou Issa, Henriette von Kaltenborn-Stachau, Jens Kristensen, Luc Laviolette, Olivier Lavinal, Eric Le

Borgne, Carole Megevand, Rekha Menon, Harriet Nannyonjo, Harun Onder, Jean Pesme, Sixto A. Requena, Elena Segura, Lia Sieghart, Lili Sisombat, Abdoulaye Sy, and Laura De Castro Zoratto.

A very special thanks go to Marouane El Abassi, former Libya Resident Representative of the World Bank, and Marie Francoise Marie-Nelly, former Maghreb Country Director, for their long-term and steadfast engagement in Libya, which in many ways laid the groundwork for much of the material and research included in this sourcebook.

About the Editors and Authors

ABOUT THE EDITORS

Hend R. Irhiam is the Operations Analyst for the World Bank's Maghreb and Malta Management Unit, where she covers Algeria, Libya, Malta, Morocco, and Tunisia. She has over 10 years of extensive operational, strategy and policy experience in complex fragile, conflict, and violence settings. She is a Fulbright Scholar, and she holds an MA in international development from Ohio University.

Michael G. Schaeffer is a former Libya Country Representative for the World Bank and former Public Sector Adviser for the World Bank in Libya. He has more than 30 years of experience in governance, decentralization, public finance, and public investment management, gained in more than 70 countries. He holds an MA in economics and an MSc in natural resource management from the University of Michigan.

Kanae Watanabe is a Senior Partnership Specialist at the World Bank. She has 25 years of strategy and policy experience in fragile and conflict-affected states. She holds an MA in international law and economics and a PhD in international conflict management from the Johns Hopkins University School of Advanced International Studies and a certificate of public international law from The Hague Academy of International Law.

ABOUT THE AUTHORS

Samer Abdeljaber is the Palestine Representative and Country Director of the World Food Programme (WFP), where he has worked for 20 years, including in Iraq, Sudan, and the Syrian Arab Republic. Formerly, he was the Country Director of the WFP operation in Libya. He is a strong advocate for the change in food security wrought by enhancing community resilience, stimulating local economies, and supporting social safety nets. He holds an MA from Princess Sumaya University.

Ehtisham Ahmad is a Consultant affiliated with the London School of Economics' Grantham Research Institute and Asia Research Center, the University of Bonn, Zhejiang and Sun Yat-Sen Universities, and the Chinese Academy of Fiscal Science. In 20 years at the International Monetary Fund, he served as a Senior Adviser to the executive board (representing Pakistan) and Adviser to and Division Chief of the Fiscal Affairs Department. He holds a PhD in economics from the University of Sussex.

Erica Aiazzi is an Education Specialist with UNICEF Libya. She has worked on the inclusion of refugee and migrant children in national education systems, education data, and education management information systems. She holds an MS in research methods in education from Oxford University.

Dalia Al Kadi is a Senior Economist in the Macroeconomics, Trade, and Investment Global Practice at the World Bank. As a Country Economist working on the Middle East and North Africa since 2013, she has led research, provided policy advice to governments, and engaged in operations in 10 countries. She holds a BA in economics from the American University of Beirut and an MPA in international development from Harvard University.

Ali Ibrahim Al Melhem is a Consultant in the Macroeconomics, Trade, and Investment Global Practice at the World Bank, focusing on the Middle East and North Africa Region. He joined the World Bank in 2020, where his research has been on applying tools from big-data and remote sensing to economic monitoring in Fragility, Conflict, and Violence countries. His expertise focuses on the economics of culture, macroeconomic development, and the application of machine-learning techniques in social sciences. He has a PhD in economics from the University of Colorado-Boulder.

Mansour Faisal Alrumayyan is a Health Specialist in the World Bank's Health, Nutrition, and Population Practice. He holds an MD from King Saud University and a post-doctoral degree in public health and health care management from Johns Hopkins University.

Wesal Ashur is a Public Sector and Governance Specialist at the World Bank, where he has worked on public financial management reforms, public investment management, and broader public sector governance reforms. Before joining the World Bank, he worked at the Libyan Investment Authority, a sovereign wealth fund, and as a Nonexecutive Director of one of its main subsidiaries. He holds an MS in accountancy and finance from the University of Dundee.

Narine Aslanyan is Deputy Representative at the UNICEF Lebanon Country Office. She has more than 20 years of experience in international development and humanitarian action. She holds an MA in humanitarian assistance from Tufts University and an MA in teaching foreign languages from the Gjumry Pedagogical University.

Matthew Brubacher is an Economic Adviser to the UN Support Mission in Libya, where he uses conflict dynamics to facilitate the energy transition and promote the sustainable management of water resources. For 20 years, he worked in various UN peace operations in Africa. He holds a BA from the School of Foreign Service at Georgetown University, an MSc in climate change and development from SOAS, University of London, and an LLM in public international law from the London School of Economics and Political Science.

Matteo Caravani is a Political Economist at the Makerere Institute for Social Research. He worked as an International Consultant for the United Nations Food and Agricultural Organization in both Palestine and Rome, for the World Food Programme in Uganda (Karamoja region), for the Overseas Development Institute in London, and for the Institute of Development Studies (IDS). Overall, his research interests include social change, agrarian transformation, and pastoralism in Sub-Saharan Africa. He holds PhD in development studies from IDS, University of Sussex, Brighton.

Andrew Cheatham is a Conflict Prevention Adviser with the United Nations Development Programme and a Senior Consultant to the United Nations Institute of Peace. A lawyer and former UN official with a history of problem solving in highly complex conflict and crisis environments in the Middle East and North Africa, he is a regular guest lecturer on crisis response and diplomatic communications at the Department of War Studies at King's College London. He holds a JD from City University of New York School of Law and an MA in war studies/counterterrorism from King's College London.

Fadel Daoud is a Program Officer and Cash Coordinator for the World Food Programme in Libya. He holds a bachelor of business administration in Finance from American University of Beirut.

Rani Daoud is a Decentralization and Local Governance Expert with more than 15 years of experience in the Middle East and North Africa Region. He currently heads the Deutsche Gesellschaft für Internationale Zusammenarbeit decentralization project in Libya, which supports the development and implementation of the local governance architecture and the devolution of functions to the municipal level.

Carlo del Ninno is a Lead Economist in the social protection unit of the World Bank's Middle East and North Africa Region. Over the past 19 years, he has worked on analytical and operational issues on safety net programs in Sub-Saharan Africa and South Asia. In the Africa Region, he worked on safety net policies and programs and managed the Sahel Adaptive Social Protection Program. He holds a PhD in economics from the University of Minnesota.

Michele Di Maio is a Professor of Economics at Sapienza University in Rome, and a World Bank Consultant. An expert on the analysis of the relationship between conflict and economic activity, he has published in the *Journal of the European Economic Association*, the *Economic Journal*, the *Journal of Development Economics*, and others. He holds a BA in economics and social sciences from Bocconi University and a PhD in economics from the University of Siena.

Denizhan Duran is a Health Economist in the World Bank's Health, Nutrition and Population Global Practice, where he works on health financing, quality of care, pandemic preparedness, and health systems in the Middle East and North

Africa Region. Before joining the World Bank, he worked at the World Health Organization, the Clinton Health Access Initiative, and the Center for Global Development. He holds a doctor of public health in health systems from Harvard University.

Tim Eaton is a Senior Research Fellow in the Middle East and North Programme of Chatham House, London. His research focuses on the political economy of the Libyan conflict. In 2018, he authored a report on the development of Libya's war economy that illustrates how economic activities have become increasingly connected to violence. He holds a BA in history from Nottingham University and a diploma in Arabic from SOAS, University of London.

Uche Eseosa Ekhator-Mobayode is a Young Professional in the Poverty and Equity Global Practice at the World Bank. Before joining the World Bank, she was an Assistant Professor of Economics at the University of Pittsburgh-Bradford. She has published articles on the socioeconomic impacts of armed conflict. She holds a PhD in economics from Northern Illinois University.

Donna Espeut is a Consultant to UNICEF Libya. She has worked extensively on issues related to the well-being of children and women. She holds a PhD in public health from the Bloomberg School of Public Health at Johns Hopkins University.

Ibrahim Farah is Chief Education Officer, UNICEF Libya. He has worked extensively on education in Syria and Libya. He holds an MA in education from Saint Josef University.

Lars Flocke Larsen is a Political and Economic Adviser to the European Union's External Action Service. He was an Economic Analyst at the European Union's Delegation to Libya, where he was Co-chair of the Economic Working Group (part of the UN–facilitated Berlin Process for Libya). He holds an MA in international business and development studies from Copenhagen Business School.

Mohamed Fortia is a Governance Officer for the United Nations Development Programme in Libya. A lawyer by training, he holds an LPC and bachelor of laws degree from the University of London.

Valeriya Goffe is a Senior Financial Sector Specialist in the Finance, Competitiveness, and Innovation Global Practice at the World Bank, where she leads the financial sector work in Libya and Saudi Arabia. She holds an MBA degree from the Kogod School of Business at American University, Washington, DC, and a PhD in finance from the Kiev National University of Economics. She is also a certified financial analyst charter holder.

Afef Haddad is the World Bank's Country Program Coordinator for the Maghreb and Malta and the leader of the Women's Economic Empowerment Initiative in the Maghreb. The recipient of a 2019 Excellence in Leadership Award, she has published on human capital and international trade. She holds a PhD in international economics from the Sorbonne.

Rawad Halabi is the Country Director of the World Food Programme in Libya, where she works to ensure the continuation of services in support of the international humanitarian community, particularly the United Nations Humanitarian Air Service, the Emergency Telecommunication Cluster, the Logistics Cluster, and the UN Hub in Benghazi. She holds an MBA from Robert Kennedy College.

Maya Hammad is a Research Consultant at the International Policy Centre for Inclusive Growth, where she works on social protection in the Middle East and North Africa. She holds an MA in international social and public policy from the London School of Economics and Political Science.

Mariam M. Hamza is a Health Economics Consultant in the Global Health, Nutrition and Population Practice of the World Bank, where she works on health system performance, health system financing, human capital, and human resources for health. She is a candidate for a PhD in economics at American University, Washington, DC.

Arian Hatefi is a physician and Senior Health Specialist at the World Bank, with more than 10 years of experience in health service delivery, policy, financing, and governance. He is also an Associate Professor at the University of California San Francisco. He hold an MS of international healthcare management, economics, and policy from SDA Bocconi School of Management and an MD from Emory University.

Christopher H. Herbst is a Senior Health Specialist in the World Bank's Health, Nutrition, and Population Global Practice and the Co-leader of the World Bank's Libya Health Sector Support Program. He has worked in more than 25 countries in Africa, Asia, and the Middle East. He holds an MSc in health policy and economics from the London School of Economics and a PhD in health labor markets from Lancaster University.

Yukinori Hibi is a Program Unit Head with the World Food Programme (WFP). He has designed and implemented food assistance projects using conditional and unconditional schemes in Libya and is responsible for extending capacity strengthening assistance to WFP's partners and involved communities. He holds an MA in law from Meijo University.

Mohini Kak is a Senior Health Specialist in the World Bank's Health, Nutrition and Population Global Practice and the Co-leader of the Libya Health Sector Support Program. She has technical and operational experience working on health systems and service delivery, particularly related to maternal and child health, nutrition, and noncommunicable diseases in South Asia and more recently the Middle East and North Africa. She holds an MSW from TATA Institute of Social Science and an MSc in public health nutrition from University of London.

Deeksha Kokas is a Consultant to the World Bank's Poverty Global Practice. Her research covers trade, poverty, jobs, and digitization. She has also worked on finance and private sector issues as part of the World Bank's Development Research Group and Trade and Competitiveness Practice. She holds an MA in economics from University College London.

Adea Kryeziu is a Social Protection Specialist at the World Bank. She has published extensively on social protection matters over the past 10 years, including their links with climate change, disaster risk management, and energy subsidy reform. She serves as Co-chair and Task Team Leader of the Intra-Agency Social Protection Assessments Partnership, playing a key role in managing relations with donors and partner organizations.

Maroua Lassoued is a World Bank Governance Consultant specializing in institutional governance, decentralization, and improvement of service delivery. She has contributed to several publications, including the World Bank's "Proceedings of the Libya Local Government Forum" (2021). Originally trained as a civil engineer, she is completing her MA in governance and public policies at the European University of Tunisia.

Victor B. Loksha is a Senior Energy Consultant active in Africa, the Middle East and North Africa, and Europe and Central Asia. He has led operational, analytical, and knowledge-generating and exchange activities and reviewed grant proposals on energy sector governance, markets, and planning. He holds an MA in public administration from Columbia University's School of International and Public Affairs and a PhD in environmental economics from Moscow State University.

Jesse D. Malkin is a Consultant based in Colorado Springs, Colorado, with expertise in health services, health policy, and health outcomes research. He worked in the pharmaceutical industry for several years. He holds an MA in philosophy, politics, and economics from University of Oxford and a PhD in public policy analysis from Pardee RAND Graduate School.

Vasco Molini is a Senior Poverty Economist for the Sahel region at the World Bank. His main interests are income distribution, inequality, and conflicts. He has published in international peer-reviewed journals, including *World Development*, the *Journal of Development Economics*, the *Review of Income and Wealth*, and *Food Policy*. He holds a PhD in development economics from the University of Florence and a postdoctoral degree from the Free University in Amsterdam.

Amr S. Moubarak is a Social Protection Economist. Previously, he worked as the acting Operations Team Lead for the Global Partnership for Social Accountability as part of the Social Sustainability and Inclusion Global Practice in the World Bank, working on projects across sectors in health, climate change, social protection, and gender, among others. He holds an MA in international development from Georgetown University and a BS in economics (secondary concentration in statistics).

Grace Namugayi is the Vulnerability Analysis and Mapping Specialist with the World Food Programme, where she specializes in food security analysis, monitoring and evaluation, and the identification of populations in need of assistance and the cause of their vulnerability. She holds an MS in information systems and technology from City University in London and a BS from Makerere University, Uganda.

Minh Cong Nguyen is a Senior Data Scientist in the Poverty and Equity Global Practice of the World Bank, where he leads the Middle East and North Africa Team for Statistical Development. His research interests include poverty, inequality, welfare measurement, small area estimations and imputation methods, and data systems. He holds a PhD in in applied microeconometrics from American University, Washington, DC.

Yuko Osawa is the Chief of the Child Protection Section of UNICEF Libya. She holds an MA in international affairs from the School of Public and International Affairs of Columbia University.

Zied Ouelhazi is a Public Sector Specialist and a Consultant to the World Bank working on Tunisia and Libya. His work focuses on macrofiscal issues, public financial management, local governance, and the health sector. He holds a PhD in economics from the Institut des Hautes Études Économiques et Commerciales de Carthage, Tunisia.

Barbara Pellegrini is a Child Protection Specialist with UNICEF Libya. She has worked extensively on children on the move and child protection in emergencies. She holds an MA in international cooperation and development from the Institute of Advanced Studies in Pavia and a postgraduate degree in political science from the University of Pavia.

Remy Pigois is Social Policy Manager for the Maghreb at UNICEF. He has worked extensively on public finance management, social protection, and social policies. He holds a predoctorate diploma in mathematics and econometrics from the Sorbonne University.

Mohammed Qaradaghi is a Senior Energy Specialist and Team Leader for Iraq and Libya in the World Bank's Energy and Extractives Unit. He holds an MS in project management from the George Washington University School of Business and a PhD in energy and environmental management from the George Washington University School of Engineering and Applied Science.

Aminur Rahman is a Lead Economist in the Finance, Competitiveness, and Innovation Global Practice at the World Bank. He has advised governments and policy makers in countries around the world. He holds an MA in development economics from Oxford University, where he was a Laila Hirani Memorial Scholar, and a PhD in economics from University College London.

Severin Rakic is a physician with extensive operational and analytical health system reform experience in the Middle East and North Africa and Europe and Central Asia Regions. He holds an MBA in health, population, and nutrition in developing countries from Keele University of Staffordshire, and a PhD in health care and nursing faculty from Pan-European University Apeiron, Banjaluka, Bosnia and Herzegovina.

Iyad Rammal is a Senior Water Specialist in the World Bank's Water Global Practice, where he leads water supply and sanitation projects, including the construction of wastewater treatment plants, capacity-building and sector reform, and utility aggregation efforts. He has taught at Palestinian universities and provided training for public employees. He holds an MSc in management engineering from FEATI University and a PhD in public administration from University of Santo Tomas.

Francesca Recanatini is a Lead Economist at the World Bank. In her more than 20 years at the World Bank, she has worked in Eastern Europe, Sub-Saharan Africa, Latin America, and the Middle East and North Africa. She has published papers on corruption, governance indicators, and transition; coauthored *Building for Peace in MENA*; and contributed to the *Oxford Handbook on Quality of Government, Anticorruption Policy: Can International Actors Play a Role?, The Global Handbook on Research and Practice in Corruption*, and *The International Handbook on the Economics of Corruption*. She holds a PhD in economics from the University of Maryland, College Park.

Sixto A. Requena is a Water Sector Consultant who has worked in more than 40 countries. His areas of expertise include investment project design, project appraisal, project implementation, water sector strategic planning, and public-private partnerships. He holds an MA in economics from Boston University and an MA in public administration from the Harvard Kennedy School.

Anna Ressler is a Consultant to UNICEF Libya. She has worked extensively on issues related to child rights and international law. She holds an MA in international human rights law and is a PhD candidate at the Law School of the University of Reading.

Valerio Leone Sciabolazza is an Assistant Professor of Economics at the University of Naples Parthenope. He is an Associate Editor of the *Journal of Economic Geography* and a Consultant to several international agencies. He holds an MS in economics and social sciences from La Sapienza University and a PhD in international economics and finance from La Sapienza University.

Almoataz Bedin Allah Shikhy is a Consultant who joined the World Bank Group under the Voice Secondment Program. He provides operations support to technical teams across sectors working in Libya. He holds an MA in public procurement from the University of Rome, Tor Vergata.

Daniel Stroux is the Chief Technical Adviser with the United Nations Development Programme Libya. Previously, he has worked in various positions, including Chief Electoral Adviser with the United Nations Support Mission in Libya and Director for Institutional Reform and Democracy at BiRD (Bureau for Institutional Reform and Democracy) Gmbh.

Eleanor Swingewood is a Communications Officer for the World Food Programme in the Libyan Country Office.

Tarik M. Yousef is a Nonresident Senior Fellow in the Foreign Policy Program at the Brookings Institution and was Director of the Brookings Doha Center. Tarik is an Economist who has worked at the International Monetary Fund, the World Bank, and the UN, and was on the faculty of Georgetown University's School of Foreign Service. He specializes in the economies of the Arab world. He holds a PhD in economics from Harvard University.

Abbreviations

ACLED	Armed Conflict and Location Event Data Base
BEA	US Bureau of Economic Analysis
BPC	Basic People's Committee
capex	capital expenditure
CBL	Central Bank of Libya
CCMCE	Central Commission of Municipal Council Elections
CDA	Constitution Drafting Assembly
CEDAW	Convention on the Elimination of All Forms of Discrimination against Women
CIT	corporate income tax
COVID-19	coronavirus disease
CPI	Consumer Price Index
CRA	Civil Registry Authority
CRC	Convention on the Rights of the Child
CSO	civil society organization
DALY	disability-adjusted life year
DCIM	Department of Combating Illegal Migration
DMSP	US Air Force Defense Meteorological Satellite Program
DPOC	Decentralization Process Organizing Committee
DSM	demand-side management
DTM	Displacement Tracking Matrix
DTM FM	Displacement Tracking Matrix Flow Monitoring
DTM MT	Displacement Tracking Matrix Mobility Tracking
EC	European Commission
ECCE	early childhood care and education
ECD	early childhood development
ECE	early childhood education
EIA	US Energy Information Administration
EITI	Extractive Industries Transparency Initiative
EMIS	education management information system
EPSC	exploration and production-sharing contracts
ERW	explosive remnants of war
ESCWA	Economic and Social Commission for Western Asia

ESWG	Education Sector Working Group
FAO	Food and Agriculture Organization
FCV	fragility, conflict, and violence
FDI	foreign direct investment
FM	financial management
FMP	Financial Management Program
FMP	flow monitoring points
FSI	Food Security Index
FTP	first tranche petroleum
FY	fiscal year
GAWR	General Authority for Water Resources
GB	gigabyte
GBV	gender-based violence
GCC	Gulf Cooperation Council
GCWW	General Company for Water and Wastewater
GDC	General Desalination Company
GDP	gross domestic product
GECOL	General Electric Company of Libya
GER	gross enrollment ratio
GFA	general food assistance
GFMIS	government financial management information system
GIA	General Information and Documentation Authority of Libya
GIZ	German Development Cooperation (Deutsche Gesellschaft für Internationale Zusammenarbeit)
GMRP	Great Man-Made River Project
GNA	Government of National Accord
GNC	General National Congress
GNI	gross national income
GNU	Government of National Unity
GPI	gender parity index
GRM	grievance and redress mechanism
GW	gigawatt
GWh	gigawatt hour
ha	hectare
HCC	Higher Committee for Children
HCS	High Council of State
HIC	Health Information and Documentation Centre
HNEC	High National Election Commission
HNO	Humanitarian Needs Overview
HoR	House of Representatives (Tobruk)
HRP	Humanitarian Response Plan
ICT	information and communications technology
IDP	internally displaced person
IED	improvised explosive device
ING	Interim National Government
IOM	International Organization for Migration
ISIS	Islamic State of Iraq and Syria
JENA	Joint Education Needs Assessment
JMMI	Joint Market Monitoring Initiative
kV	kilovolt
kWh	kilowatt hour

LAAF	Libyan Arab Armed Forces
LD	Libyan dinar
LES	Libya Enterprise Survey
LIA	Libyan Investment Authority
LNA	Libyan National Army
lng	liquefied natural gas
LPA	Libyan Political Agreement
LPDF	Libyan Political Dialogue Forum
LPDFA	Libyan Political Dialogue Forum Agreement
LRP	local and regional procurement of food aid
MARA	monitoring, analysis, and report arrangements
MCMD	million cubic meters per day
MEB	Minimum Expenditure Basket
MENA	Middle East and North Africa
MHPSS	mental health and psychosocial support
MIA	Military Investment Authority
MIS	management information system
MMR	Man-Made River
MMRP	Man-Made River Project
MODA	multiple overlapping deprivation analysis
MoE	Ministry of Education
MoF	Ministry of Finance
MoH	Ministry of Health
MoHESR	Ministry of Higher Education and Scientific Research
MoLG	Ministry of Local Government
MoP	Ministry of Planning
MoSA	Ministry of Social Affairs
MRM	monitoring and reporting mechanism
MRRM	migrant resource and response mechanism
MSME	micro, small, and medium-size enterprise
MSNA	Multi-Sector Needs Assessment
MSO	Medical Supply Organization
MSU/FSG	Food Security Group at Michigan State University
MT	metric tons
mVAM	mobile Vulnerability Assessment and Mapping
MW	megawatt
MWh	megawatt hour
n.a.	not available
NASA	National Aeronautics and Space Administration
NATO	North Atlantic Treaty Organization
NCD	noncommunicable disease
NCDC	National Centre for Disease Control – Libya
NGO	nongovernmental organization
NNPC	National Nigerian Petroleum Company
NOAA	National Oceanic and Atmospheric Administration
NOC	National Oil Corporation
NO$_2$	nitrogen dioxide
NSAS	Nubian Sandstone Aquifer System
NTC	National Transitional Council
NTL	nighttime light
O&M	operations and maintenance

OCHA	United Nations Office for the Coordination of Humanitarian Affairs
OHCHR	Office of the United Nations High Commissioner for Human Rights
OLS	Operational Linescan System
PAPFAM	Pan Arab Project for Family Health
PFG	Petroleum Facilities Guard
PFM	public financial management
PHC	primary health care
PIM	public investment management
PM	prime minister
PSA	production-sharing arrangement
PSC	production-sharing contract
PV	photovoltaic
PWD	person with disabilities
RDD	random digit dialing
RPBA	Recovery Peace Building Assessment
RTGS	real-time gross settlement
SARA	Service and Availability and Readiness Assessment
SDG	Sustainable Development Goal
SDI	service delivery indicators
SDR	special drawing rights
SGBV	sexual and gender-based violence
SJC	Supreme Judicial Council
SLAC	Supreme Local Administration Council
SME	small and medium-size enterprise
SOE	state-owned enterprise
SOL	sum of lights
SOP	standard operating procedure
SPRI	Social Policy Research Institute
SSecF	Social Security Fund
SSF	Social Solidarity Fund
SWF	Sovereign Wealth Fund
TSA	Treasury Single Account
TVET	technical and vocational education and training
UASC	unaccompanied and separated children
UIS	UNESCO Institute for Statistics
UN	United Nations
UNDP	United Nations Development Programme
UNESCO	United Nations Educational, Scientific and Cultural Organization
UNHCR	United Nations High Commissioner for Refugees
UNICEF	United Nations Children's Fund
UNSMIL	United Nations Support Mission in Libya
UO	unexploded ordinance
UPR	universal periodic review
URL	uniform resource location
USAID	United States Agency for International Development
USIP	United States Institute of Peace
VAC	violence against children
VAM	vulnerability assessment and mapping

VAT	value added tax
VIIRS	Visible Infrared Imaging Radiometer Suite
WASH	water, sanitation and hygiene
WBG	World Bank Group
WB-WFP	World Bank-World Food Programme
WDR	World Development Report
WEF	World Economic Forum
VIIRS	Visible Infrared Imaging Radiometer Suite
WFP	World Food Programme
WTP	water treatment plant
WWTP	waste-water treatment plant(s)

Note: All dollar amounts are US dollars unless otherwise indicated.

Introduction

The Long Road to Inclusive Institutions in Libya: A Sourcebook of Challenges and Needs is a sourcebook that contributes to the collective understanding of challenges and needs in Libya. As this book was being developed, the Berlin Process was coming to a conclusion (mid-2022), significant parts of the country remained under the control of militia groups and foreign fighters, and two rival political administrations continued to spar for political control. However, there remains a glimmer of hope that a unified government may succeed in bringing the country back together.

This sourcebook compiles analytical work that has been cultivated over the past several years by the World Bank and partner organizations of Libya. Utilizing a number of analytical techniques (including phone surveys and nighttime data), the authors make a unique contribution to the discussion on Libya's medium- to long-term challenges. The book covers areas that the World Bank and partner organizations have engaged in over the past few years.

The objective of this sourcebook is to provide information and reflection for larger debates on Libya for the government, civil society, and academia. This book is organized into five parts: State Institutions: From Legacy to Reform, Tracking the Economy during Conflict, The Impact of Conflict on People, Services during Conflict, and Toward New Institutions.

Some important findings that emerge from the chapters in this book are the following:

1. The decade-long dynamic of crisis and conflict since the 2011 revolution has come at a devastating cost for the Libyan people. In addition to significant insecurity, displacement, degradation of infrastructure and basic services, and reductions in their well-being, the conflict has reduced social cohesion, fracturing relationships between communities.

2. One of the fundamental challenges Libya faces is the need to pull the economy out of crisis and restore the macroeconomic framework in a way that is sustainable. As Libya begins to transition to a more stable political and security environment, it will be critical to secure hydrocarbon production and to increase the efficiency, transparency, and effectiveness with which such revenues from it are used. Libya's budget structure remains largely fragmented, driven by an approach that is largely disconnected from an explicit policy or

development strategy. Priority should be given to establishing a clear macrofiscal policy framework with consistent fiscal rules reflecting the country's economic objectives.

3. Top-down approaches need to be combined with local- and community-based bottom-up approaches to enhance the likelihood of sustainable peace. The traditional reconstruction approach that follows the decisive ending of a conflict and focuses primarily on the central government as the key counterpart for implementing reconstruction will not ensure sustainable peace in Libya. A dual approach is needed that simultaneously develops decentralized governance that is closer to the local level in a nuanced way so as to not contribute to the country's further fragmentation.

4. The most urgent need is to improve infrastructure and basic service delivery. The scale of investments required for energy, water, health, education, and social protection in the near to medium term and the inherent complexities of infrastructure investment (the long-term nature, interconnectedness, social impacts, and externalities, positive and negative) make progress in this area especially challenging. Investments in social and physical infrastructure require robust and transparent policy and institutional settings, as well as effective governance.

5. Libyan households face four ongoing and interrelated shocks that are severely affecting the welfare of the population, especially among vulnerable groups, such as the displaced, migrants, and refugees. These shocks include (1) protracted conflict; (2) the reduction of reliable import routes; (3) food and commodities crises exacerbated by the exchange rate devaluation, which have made essential goods prohibitively expensive; and (4) the COVID-19 pandemic, which has slowed economic activity and had devastating effects on the informal labor economy. The pandemic also exacerbated food insecurity. The increase in prices is especially acute in the southern parts of the country, where the distance from the coast adds logistical and cargo costs to the price of products.

6. Improving service delivery as quickly as possible would help reduce fragility and increase well-being. In the preliminary stages of recovery, immediate needs be addressed include (1) restoring and stabilizing electricity and water supply; (2) restarting schools safely; (3) improving health service delivery, including addressing the COVID-19 pandemic; (4) establishing effective and efficient social safety nets; and (5) repairing key infrastructure, such as housing and other buildings, broadband internet, and transport and logistics networks.

Libya needs to assess the situation on the ground across all key sectors and regions and develop a reconstruction strategy and vision for bringing the country together. The current situation can be used to develop a near- and medium-term vision for a political, economic, and socially inclusive Libya while acknowledging the need to adapt as the circumstances evolve. A vision will have to be based on the analysis of alternative short-, medium-, and long-term interventions and the sequencing of related reforms, all while considering realities on the ground. If peace and stability are to take hold, Libya's partners must stay the course, sustain engagement, and support Libya's efforts to rebuild equitably and inclusively.

The views expressed in the different chapters are those of the authors. The findings and opinions expressed do not necessarily reflect those of the World Bank Group or its Board of Directors.

1 Overview

MICHAEL G. SCHAEFFER, HEND R. IRHIAM, AND KANAE WATANABE

World Bank

CONTEXT

Libya has been plagued for the last decade by a destabilizing and deadly conflict between warring factions, and despite mediation efforts by the international community, these conflicts persisted well into 2020–21. Armed confrontations began with the collapse of Muammar Gaddafi's forces in 2011, who ruled the country since 1969. Fighting was initially between forces loyal to Gaddafi and opposition groups supported by the North Atlantic Treaty Organization (NATO); however, a new and broader conflict emerged in 2014. There were legislative elections that year, however, and the Supreme Court ruled that the elections were unconstitutional and that the newly elected assembly should be dissolved. Divisions in the country then gave rise to a civil war between forces in the East, based in Tobruk, and forces in the West, based in Tripoli. Each had the support of armed militias and was aided by foreign elements. The Libyan civil war is usually dated from July 2014 to October 2020 (figure 1.1).

In 2015, the United Nations initiated the Libyan Political Agreement (LPA), which created the Government of National Accord (GNA). In 2015, the UN Security Council unanimously endorsed the LPA, welcoming the formation of a Presidential Council that recognized the GNA as the sole legitimate executive government of Libya (Daoud 2021). The agreement was initially accepted by both sides; however, the Tobruk-based House of Representatives withdrew its acceptance in summer 2016, leaving the GNA under the control of the factions based in Tripoli. The GNA claimed to be the sole legitimate authority in Libya and was recognized as such by the United Nations. The House of Representatives continued to advance its own claim to be the legitimate political authority in Libya.

In 2017, foreign initiatives and other external factors shifted the power balance in a manner that reduced the revenue stream of some armed groups. The UN-backed GNA was struggling to exert control over territory held by rival factions, intensifying geographical and political divisions between the East, West, and South. Armed groups exploited the turmoil, using the country as a

FIGURE 1.1

Timeline of political events in Libya

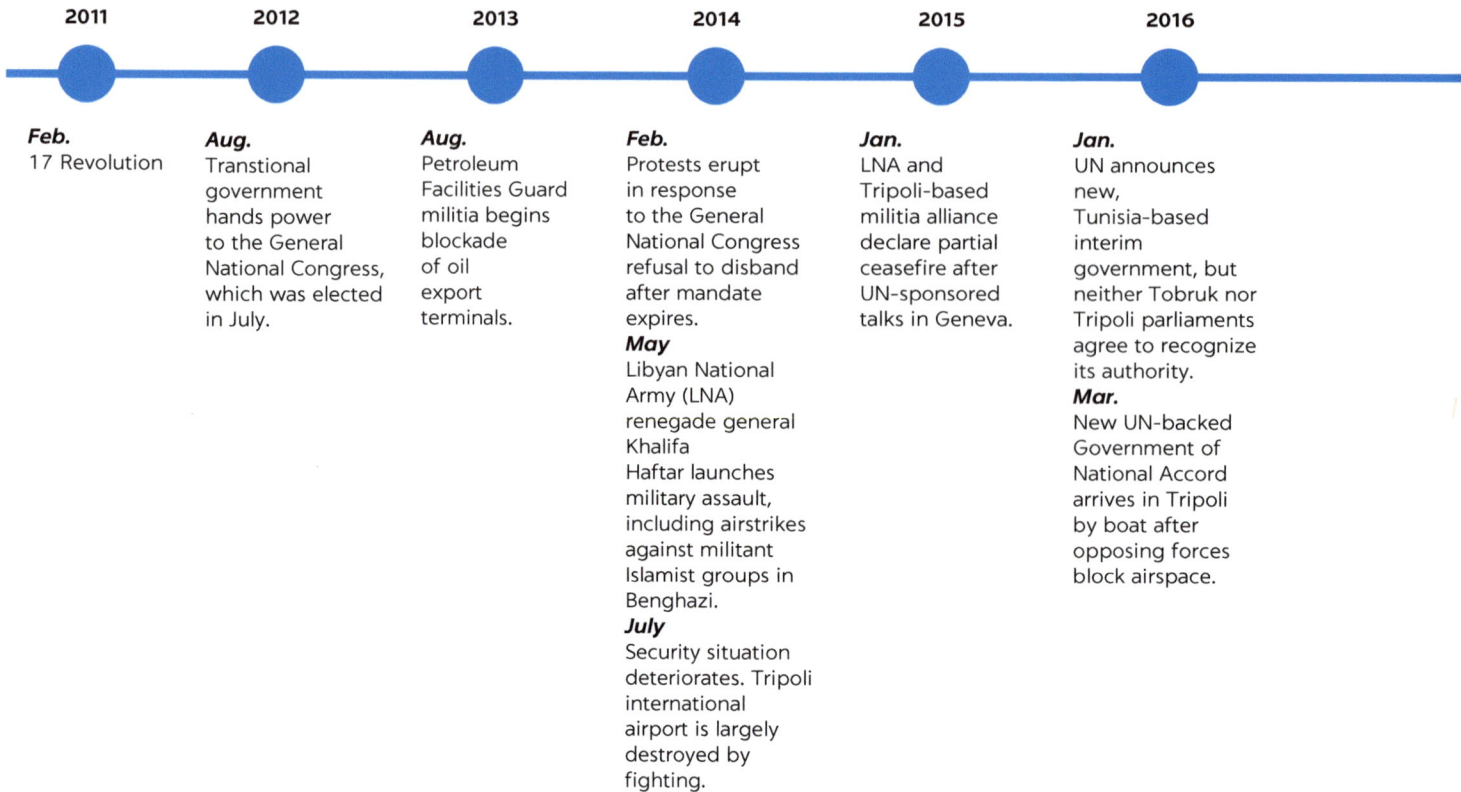

2011	2012	2013	2014	2015	2016

Feb.
17 Revolution

Aug.
Transtional government hands power to the General National Congress, which was elected in July.

Aug.
Petroleum Facilities Guard militia begins blockade of oil export terminals.

Feb.
Protests erupt in response to the General National Congress refusal to disband after mandate expires.

May
Libyan National Army (LNA) renegade general Khalifa Haftar launches military assault, including airstrikes against militant Islamist groups in Benghazi.

July
Security situation deteriorates. Tripoli international airport is largely destroyed by fighting.

Jan.
LNA and Tripoli-based militia alliance declare partial ceasefire after UN-sponsored talks in Geneva.

Jan.
UN announces new, Tunisia-based interim government, but neither Tobruk nor Tripoli parliaments agree to recognize its authority.

Mar.
New UN-backed Government of National Accord arrives in Tripoli by boat after opposing forces block airspace.

Source: World Bank.
Note: HoR = House of Representatives; HSC = High Council of State; UNSMIL = United Nations Support Mission to Libya.

base for organized crime. Tribal violence added another layer of fragility (Eaton 2018; World Bank 2021). Fighting continued intermittently in the following years, with Haftar's Libyan National Army (LNA) bringing much of central and southeast Libya under the control of the House of Representatives government. GNA supporters and anti-LNA groups retained control of the capital, Tripoli, and the northwest of the country. The conflict has unfolded in several phases, leading to a state of protracted conflict defined by high levels of fragility and insecurity.

In 2019, a process of consultation on Libya was initiated by the German government and the Special Representative of the UN Secretary-General. On January 19, 2020, the launch of political talks, known as the Berlin Process, established a three-track process on security, economic, and political affairs. The political track created the Libyan Political Dialogue Forum (LPDF). The 74-member LPDF, which included representatives from across the political spectrum, culminated in the selection of a new unified interim executive authority in February 2021.

By early 2020, most fighting was concentrated in and around Tripoli and other large cities (including Sirte, in the Central region), as well as in the South, which witnessed a largely unopposed push by the LNA to consolidate power in Sabha and the El Sharara oil fields. The situation was complicated by the presence of foreign fighters. Risks include the increased presence of the Islamic

2017 **2018** **2019** **2020** **2021** **2022**

July
Islamic State group ejected from Benghazi after three years of fighting.

July
LNA takes control of Derna, the last Islamist control hold in the East.

Apr.
LNA advances on Tripoli.

Jan.
Berlin Conference on Libya
June
UN-backed government drives LNA forces out of Tarhouna, last stronghold in the West.

Mar.
UN-backed Government of National Unity (December) Election of presidential and parliament election postponed.
June
Berlin Conference on Libya.

Jan.
Libya's elections postponed.
Feb.
HoR endorses Bashagaas Prime Minister-designate.
Mar.
UNSMIL starts consultations with HoR and HSC Joint Committee.
May
Bashagha bases his government in the city of Sirte.
June
Libyan Political Dialogue Forum expires 22 June.
Jan.–June
Ongoing consultation between HoR and HSC to reach an agreement.

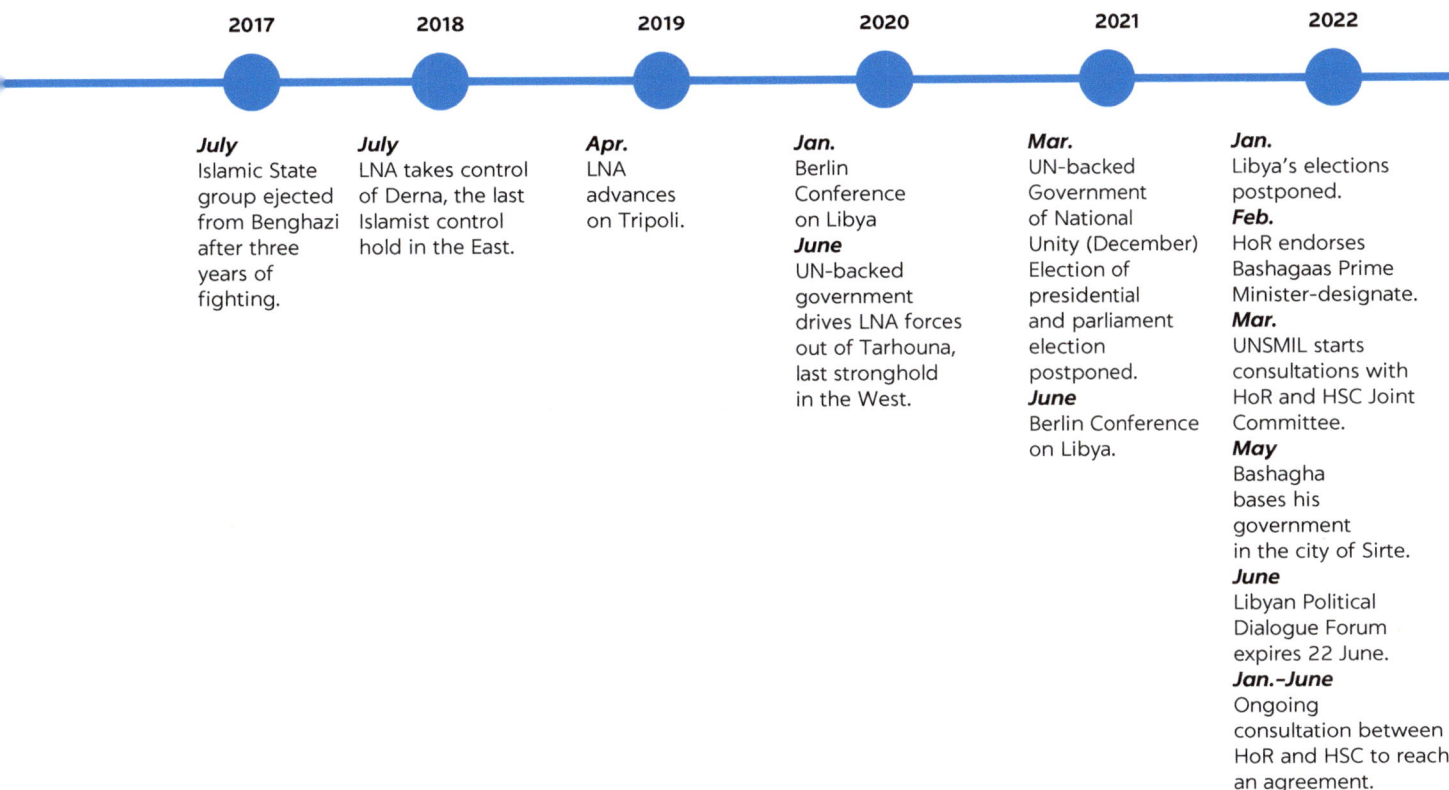

State of Iraq and Syria (ISIS), insecurity posed by a highly porous southern border, and the presence of foreign mercenaries and criminal groups that target citizens and migrants. The situation has resulted in attacks against Southern water pipelines and oil facilities on which the North depends (Eaton 2018; World Bank 2021).

Attempts to bring the warring parties together and create a government of national unity were unsuccessful as both sides consolidated their positions and established their own governing institutions. It was only in October 2020 that a permanent ceasefire in all areas of Libya was accepted by all parties. Foreign fighters were given three months to leave the country. A designated interim Government of National Unity (GNU) was primarily tasked with leading to national elections for December 2021.

Persistent disagreements over the legal framework for elections passed by the House of Representatives, political and legal disputes related to the eligibility of several presidential candidates, and reported security threats against the High National Election Commission resulted in the commission delaying the release of the final list of eligible presidential candidates, effectively postponing the elections. The political scene in 2022 has been stalemated, with two rival administrations, led by Fathi Bashagha in Sirte and Abdulhamid al-Dbeibah in Tripoli. With the end of the LPDF in June 2022, the political road map has largely been hindered by the lack of agreement on national elections.

For nearly a decade, the Libyan people have paid a high cost of war. The governments are under pressure to respond to the pressing needs of the population, made more urgent by the COVID-19 pandemic. To respond to the situation, they would need to embark on a process of conciliation and reform against a backdrop of weak national institutions, increasing regional political instability, and deepening polarization.

Every Libyan government since 2011 has been transitional in nature, and no post-Gaddafi government has built consensus around a national agenda or vision. Several interrelated layers of conflict coexist today, with localized groups and militias fighting one another—some because of alignments with competing political camps, some in support of or in opposition to extremist groups, and others over access to resources, such as oil. Various militia actors hold considerable power, which they use to influence state institutions, siphon off public resources, and divert political processes to further their own interests, ensuring that their demands are met through the use—or threat of use—of violence.

Violence and economic instability in Libya have become increasingly correlated. One of the drivers of fragility and conflict is control over oil resources—upstream from oil fields to downstream corruption in the use of public resources. Macroeconomic crisis loomed as fighting damaged oil infrastructure and militias took over oil facilities, reducing oil exports and the foreign exchange and government revenue that those revenues generated. The plummeting of international oil prices that began in June 2014 led to a sharp decline in foreign exchange revenues. The subsequent increase in oil prices during 2021–22 has provided economic relief, but substantial structural adjustments in the Libyan economic environment still should be encouraged.

The lack of adequate and legitimate national- and local-level public service institutions, and the absence of coordination between the levels, has both eroded the state's legitimacy and provided space for nonstate actors to fill the government's role. Widespread corruption and public frustration have been key drivers behind the conflict. Subsequent administrations have failed to break this legacy and demonstrate a commitment to transparency and accountability, thus fueling further frustrations and grievance.

Conflict in Libya has significant implications for the region. Strong economic, social, and security ties between Libya and its neighbors Algeria, the Arab Republic of Egypt, and Tunisia mean that instability in Benghazi and Tripoli is felt in Algiers, Cairo, and Tunis as well. One example is the flow of highly subsidized Libyan goods, including gasoline, to neighboring countries, through illicit trade run by militias. Another is the human trafficking that has continued channeling migrants to Europe, despite its horrors and dangers.

As this book was being written, the Berlin Process was coming to a conclusion (mid-2022), significant parts of the country remained under the control of militia groups and foreign fighters, and two rival political administrations continued to spar for political control. However, there remains a glimmer of hope that a unified government may succeed in bringing the country back together.

OBJECTIVE AND STRUCTURE

The Long Road to Inclusive Institutions in Libya is intended to serve as a sourcebook of the challenges and needs that exist in Libya today. This sourcebook should be used as a foundation to inform technical work and partner dialogue that can be undertaken in advance of, and as an input into, an eventual planning process with the government, civil society organizations, and the Libyan people. The hope is that the book will inform Libyan and international policy makers on the status of various sectors and provide ideas for the way forward to define appropriate actions and reforms that will support peace and stability. This book builds on the World Bank's (2019) *Supporting Peace and Stability in Libya* and other partners' publications that have been cited throughout the book.

The authors that helped formulate and develop this book were opportunistic in their approach, writing to specific areas that they or their various institutions engaged. As such, this book provides an umbrella view of the situation in Libya, based on information, data, and lessons informed from domestic and international experiences. However, this book does not presume to be exhaustive. The authors draw on the data collection, analyses, and extensive experience of the international community gathered in recent years, including the experiences of Deutsche Gesellschaft für Internationale Zusammenarbeit (GIZ), the European Union, the Organisation for Economic Co-operation and Development (OECD), the United Kingdom's Foreign and Commonwealth Office (FCO), the United Nations Children's Fund (UNICEF), the United Nations Support Mission to Libya (UNSMIL), the United States Agency for International Development (USAID), the World Bank, and the World Food Programme (WFP). The book also benefits from contributions and comments by authors from Chatham House, the International Crisis Group (ICG), and the Brookings Institution. The book should therefore be looked at as a stock-taking exercise. The views expressed in the various chapters are those of the authors.

Why prepare and present this book now? After almost ten years of political instability, the Libyan transition process has entered a new phase and this team of authors viewed this moment as an opportunity to develop a sourcebook of material that can be used not only for Libya's future program considerations and also inform international engagement in middle-income countries (MICs) in conflict more broadly. This sourcebook includes a combination of innovative hybrid analytics (phone surveys, nighttime lights) and opportunistic technical assistance. The higher-level political economy chapters—combined with details on what fiscal federalism might look like in Libya and attention paid to the inertia of legacy institutions—cover areas not often encountered in fragile, conflict, violent (FCV) constituencies. By providing a sourcebook of the challenges confronting Libya, the authors hope that the international community can avoid slipping into more technocratic and supply-driven approaches.

The 21 chapters are organized into five parts. Setting aside the Introduction and Overview, they are part I, "State Institutions: From Legacy to Reform"; part II, "Tracking the Economy during the Conflict"; part III, "The Impact of the Conflict on People"; part IV, "Services during Conflict"; and finally, part V, "Toward New Institutions." Rather than reading all the chapters, readers may want to go directly to a specific subject of interest.

State institutions: from legacy to reform

Tim Eaton (Chatham House) provides in his chapter 2, "The Battle for Control of State Institutions," that there are substantial state-building challenges (political and institutional). Libya is a divided country without a cohesive unifying territorial or organizational ("state") structure. Following the revolution, the prospect of more inclusive and transparent institutions has not been realized, and state institutions have struggled to function and secure legitimacy. Coordination between central and local levels of government is missing, weakening the effectiveness of the state at the municipal level. The absence of an independent and accountable justice system is a significant obstacle to peace and stability. The author provides that the unresolved tensions between reformist elements and the institutions that were created in the 2000s and the socialist type entities of the 1970s and 1980s remain unresolved. The result is a transactional system in which institutions have become part of the conflict rather than delivering results for citizens.

In chapter 3, "Beyond Power Sharing: Long-term Economic and Political Stability," Tarik M. Yousef offers that given the challenges facing Libya's unity government, the limited progress made over its life span, and the vulnerability of the power-sharing arrangement to domestic and geopolitical spoilers, it is easy to take a dark view of the prospects for the current power-sharing agreement's ability to maintain peace and begin the task of rebuilding the country. Viewed as a short-term bridge to long-term stability, however, the power-sharing agreement may provide a singular opportunity to end the conflict, build a shared vision for development, and lay the foundations for a new social contract. Securing this bridge requires that Libyans and their international supporters avoid reducing the problem to the realization of holding national elections by any set date. Even when elections take place, Libya will continue to struggle with issues left unaddressed during the formation of and by the GNU.

Michael Schaeffer, Zied Ouelhazi, Maroua Lassoued, Wesal Ashur, and Kanae Watanabe provide chapter 4, "Setting the Stage for Public Sector Reform." To drive economic growth and support economic stabilization, they note, Libya could use this moment to modernize the structure of its economy, diversify away from near-total oil dependency, foster the development of the private sector (with support of the financial sector), and use it to drive job creation. The authors also provide that even during this extended period of political conflict, it was crucial to try to advance structural governance and public financial management (PFM) reforms.

Francesca Recanatini offers in chapter 5 "Institution Building: Lessons from World Bank Engagement in Libya," that many lessons emerge from the ongoing World Bank's engagement in FCVs and from the governance program in Libya, including the importance of (1) focusing on building institutions and governance through a flexible, multisectoral approach that takes into account the incentives of the parties involved in and affected by the conflict; (2) building capacity while promoting social cohesion and collaboration; (3) remaining engaged with the broadest group possible of state and nonstate actors—local, national, and international—to understand local dynamics and develop an integrated vision for institution building; (4) recognizing that there are no one-size-fits-all solutions; and (5) thinking more strategically and in terms of a longer-term vision, with an openness to risk, learn, and adapt.

In chapter 6, "Causes of Local Instability and Local Level Capacity for Peace," Rani Daoud affords that Libya is an extremely challenging political economic environment, because of the divide in national-level governance and many unresolved security issues. The nature of Libyan fragility, particularly at the local level, is complex, context specific, and protracted. Local governance is a critical arena for peace-building and nation-building efforts because local institutions, systems, and processes represent the daily interface between state and society. Inclusive and accountable local governance can help restore social cohesion in Libya's divided communities, facilitate participation in public life, and distribute resources and opportunities equitably while also blending formal and informal processes of representational and participation.

Tracking the economy during conflict

Libya's private sector is characterized by unique features as provided by Aminur Rahman and Michaele Di Maio in chapter 7, "Libyan Private Sector: Difficulties, Challenges, and Perspectives." Tracking economic activity during conflict can be an extremely challenging activity. The economic consequences of conflict are devastating. At the aggregate level, violent conflict is associated with lower output, lower investment, and lower growth. The authors posit that understanding the specific mechanisms through which aggregate negative effects materialize is critical for the design of effective policies that can unlock the potential for economic growth in the conflict-ridden regions of the world. Post-conflict Libya needs to create conditions conductive to the expansion of the private sector market also by limiting the role of the state-owned enterprises.

Valeriya Goffe's "State of the Financial Sector," chapter 8, provides that the split in the central banks' stymied control over monetary and fiscal policy and performance of full bank supervision, because both central banks printed money and issued currency without coordinating. The central bank remains the majority shareholder of public banks, which hold 90 percent of deposits and loans in the system, while being the regulatory agency of the banking sector. However, banks have neither sufficient information nor capacity to make informed credit decisions. Initiatives and progress in the financial sector beyond banking have all but frozen. Despite these difficult conditions, there is still a possibility to support the financial and private sector in Libya.

In an innovative approach, night-time lights (NTL) were used by Dalia Al Kadi and Ali Ibrahim Al Melhem and presented in chapter 9, "Nowcasting Economic Activity Using Night-Time Lights," to estimate gross domestic product (GDP) and oil production in Libya at a high frequency and granularity. NTLs provided an important source of information on economic activity in Libya, expanding the information set that policy makers can rely on. NTL benefits from being data that are high frequency, granular, and are insulated from human error or malfeasance. Interestingly, in a conflict-affected setting, NTL provides more reliable information than official national accounts data, which can be subject to bias, manipulation, and measurement error.

The impact of conflict on people

Uche Eseosa Ekhator-Mobayode, Vasco Molini, Grace Namugayi, and Valerio Leone Sciabolazza in chapter 10, "Fragility, Livelihoods and Migration Dynamics," provide that Libyan households face four ongoing and interrelated shocks that are severely affecting the welfare of the population, especially among vulnerable groups, such as the displaced, migrants, and refugees. These shocks include (1) protracted conflict; (2) the reduction of reliable imported goods routes; (3) food and commodities crises exacerbated by the exchange rate devaluation, which have made essential goods prohibitively expensive; and (4) the COVID-19 pandemic, which has slowed economic activity and had devastating effects on the informal labor economy. The pandemic has exacerbated food insecurity. The increase in prices is especially acute in the southern parts of the country, where the distance from the coast adds logistical and cargo costs to the price of products.

Samer Abdeljaber, Fadel Daoud, Rawad Halabi, Yukinori Hibi, Grace Namugayi, and Eleanor Swingewood, all from the World Food Programme (WFP), in chapter 11, "Food Insecurity," provide that food insecurity persists in Libya, with an estimated 604,000 people food insecure, a number that dramatically increased following the onset of the COVID-19 pandemic. The main drivers are the prolonged instability caused by the armed conflict, reliance on imports, stark economic fluctuations, and the impact of the COVID-19 pandemic. With needs on the rise, humanitarian support in Libya must move toward a need's-based approach, supporting vulnerable populations in a conflict-sensitive, communal way.

In chapter 12, on "Impacts of the War, Conflict, and COVID-19 on Gender in Libya," Afef Haddad, Minh Cong Nguyen, Hend Irhiam, and Deeksha Kokas provide that many Libyan women suffer from widespread social, political, and economic exclusion as well as gender-based violence (GBV). The Constitutional Declaration of 2011, as well as the draft constitution finalized in July 2017, provide for gender equality; however, there is no associated implementing legislation, and social norms continue to accord greater power and rights to men. Women in Libya face discrimination regarding inheritance, opportunities to participate in public life, and personal freedom and mobility. Legal and societal barriers also negatively affect women's employment opportunities. From a physical and psychological standpoint, the civil war impacted most Libyans in the form of violence: loss of a relative or a friend, destruction of properties, or being forced to leave home. In addition, women and children have been, however, often targets of armed groups, which were tools for extorting money from their families.

Services during conflict

The decade's long conflict has provided that the most urgent need is to improve infrastructure and basic service delivery. The scale of investments required for energy, water, health, education, and social protection in the near to medium term and the inherent complexities of infrastructure investment (the long-term nature, interconnectedness, social impacts, and externalities, positive and negative) make progress in this area especially challenging.

Donna Espeut, Remy Pigois, Anna Ressler, Narine Aslanyan, Yuko Osawa, and Barbara Pellegrini in chapter 13, "Advancing a Child Protection System," stipulate that violence against children has been pervasive in Libya since 2011. In 2018, a stunning 90 percent of boys and 88 percent of girls reported having experienced physical, psychological, or sexual violence at school, at home, or in their community in the previous 12 months. Combating the problem is difficult because Libya lacks a comprehensive child protection system. Unclear delineation of roles and responsibilities between local government institutions involved in child protection has resulted in disjointed leadership and coordination. The way forward will require (1) aligning existing child protection—including child and juvenile-justice-related legislation, standards, and procedures—with international standards and conventions; (2) strengthening the child protection system and ensuring that the requisite human and financial resources are available for subnational and community service delivery; (3) changing norms and behaviors; and (4) creating good data systems.

Victor Loksha and Mohammed Qaradaghi, in chapter 14, "The Electricity Sector," point out that energy—Libya's main economic sector—has taken a major hit during the past decade. Estimates provided by the National Oil Corporation (NOC), Libya's state-run oil company, provide that the war has cost Libya $100 billion in damage to oil fields and the closures of oil terminals. Additional losses from oil smuggling since 2011 are estimated at $750 million a year (Barltrop 2019). No similar estimates of damage are available for the electric power sector, but some relevant data are available from the set of studies completed by the World Bank's Middle East and North Africa (MENA) energy team in 2017–18. This chapter reviews the studies on Libya's electricity sector and attempts to quantify the burden of the conflict and political instability since the onset of political instability (in 2011).

In chapter 15, "Degradation of the Water Sector during the Armed Conflict," Iyad Rammal and Sixto A. Requena point out that water infrastructure has suffered considerable damage, including because of targeted attacks, impairing its productive and service capacity, and increasing its operating costs. Before the armed conflict, about 95 percent of the population had good-quality water services; today, only 64 percent of people have access to safe drinking water. In addition, budget allocation for maintenance and for critical inputs, including chemicals and energy, have been significantly reduced, resulting in diminished services and deterioration of infrastructure assets from lack of proper maintenance. The way forward will require a strategic phased approach to recover and develop the water sector: (1) short-term response—keeping on and protecting the main service delivery through the rehabilitation of existing facilities, enhancing capacity building and water sector data; (2) medium-term response—recovery of damages and system enhancement; and (3) long-term response—water security development program and financial sustainability of the water sector.

In chapter 16, "A Health Sector in Intensive Care," co-authors Mohini Kak, Severin Rakic, Jesse D. Malkin, Mansour Alrumayyan, Denizhan Duran, Mariam M. Hamza, Arian Hatefi, Almoataz Shikhy, and Christopher H. Herbst provide that the Libyan health sector is in crisis. The conflict has deepened problems that existed before 2011, including lack of preparedness for a shift toward noncommunicable diseases, poorly functioning primary health facilities that resulted in an overreliance on hospitals, limited and poor-quality services in remote areas, weak health information systems, and limited and inefficient use of health financing. Various international organizations have stepped in to fill gaps, by helping health authorities carry out timely responses to disease outbreaks, including for COVID-19, and stock essential medicines and medical supplies. Systematic interventions are needed to improve the primary health system, the health workforce, pharmaceutical and supply chains, and health financing.

Donna Espeut, Remy Pigois, Narine Aslanyan, Anna Ressler, Ibrahim Farah, and Erica Aiazzi in chapter 17, "Education Reform in the Context of Conflict, Migration, and COVID-19," note that the Libyan education sector has been devastated by the conflict and by changing migration flows. A decentralization reform that capacitates subnational actors, along with effective multistakeholders and multisectoral coordination mechanisms at all levels, must be prioritized. Improving the education sector requires (1) introducing education and learning opportunities for all children in a way that addresses learning interruptions; (2) optimizing the content, structure, and quality of education systems; (3) incorporating psychological-social support, life-skills training, and prevention of violence activities; and (4) enhancing the management of qualified, motivated teachers to maximize children's ability to learn.

In chapter 18, "Creating Conditions for Low Carbon Pathways during Conflict," Matthew Brubacher examines how conflict dynamics might allow for promoting initiatives and reforms that could mitigate carbon emissions. Brubacher shows that with the requisite technical and political skills, interventions such as subsidy reform, energy transition, and water rationalization are often easier to implement during rather than after conflict. Implemented properly, these interventions can not only mitigate emissions but enhance resiliency and sustainability.

Co-authors Carlo del Ninno, Amr S. Moubarak, Adea Kryeziu, Matteo Caravani, Remy Pigois, and Maya Hammad in chapter 19, "Social Assistance Programs and Their Effectiveness in Responding to Crises," provide that numerous ongoing and interrelated shocks have severely affected Libyan households and the poorest segments of the population, including the displaced. The combination of fuel shortages, significant water and electricity cuts, and economic deterioration in 2020 had devastating consequences for children and families in Libya. Approximately 1.3 million people in Libya—about 18 percent of the population—needed humanitarian assistance in 2019. About 35 percent of the population in need were children, and 371,700 were displaced persons or refugees (UNHCR 2019). The co-authors provide that the major challenge ahead is for the national government of Libya to launch a concerted effort toward reform of the current social protection system, as part of its short-term strategy to support the recovery efforts. Reforms of the social protection system, and the social assistance programs, will play a crucial role in providing the necessary support to Libyan households in a more systematic and transparent way. Those interventions should address the needs of a larger proportion of the poor and vulnerable population, and their challenges, due to volatility in prices of the Minimum Expenditure Basket, and COVID-19-induced economic shutdown; these have left a substantial portion of the population with diminished assets, declining purchasing power, and mounting debts. These government interventions will also be necessary to help cement peace across different regions in Libya.

Toward new institutions

Ehtisham Ahmad and Lars Flocke Larsen argue in chapter 20, "Equitably Managing Petroleum Resources to Help Resolve Conflict," that in the medium term the development of a system of transparent and fair management system of oil revenues will involve significant reforms of allocation of petroleum revenues to ensure adequate levels of public spending on core functions in all parts of the country. This will involve strengthening regional and local governance (multilevel governance). Stronger public finance management systems will be needed to increase accountability and the efficiency of spending and reduce waste and leakages, and greater local accountability will also require own-source revenues and nondistorting transfers. Improving multilevel governance will require an agreement on an intergovernmental finance framework, beginning with an agreed distribution of revenues from the national to regional and/or local levels of government. The intergovernmental finance framework could usefully include a system for distributing a share of oil revenues to oil-producing regions (revenue sharing). It should also include other transfer mechanisms for both producing and nonproducing regions and the development of local own-source non-oil tax revenues at the margin (such as a surcharge or piggyback on a national tax base) for enhanced accountability. Revenue-sharing arrangements have been critical in reducing conflict and creating a national identity in both Nigeria and Indonesia.

Andrew Cheatham, Daniel Stroux, and Mohamed Fortia in chapter 21, "Subnational Governance," argue that 10 years after its revolution, Libya is still struggling to transition to a functioning democracy with local governance systems and administrations that meet the needs of the population. One of the major frustrations that brought about the revolution was the heavily centralized rule of the Gaddafi government. Since 2011, successive interim governments and legislative bodies have tried to remedy the problem with legal reforms that set out a decentralized authority with shared competencies and responsibilities among central, provincial, and local authorities. In practice, only a few responsibilities have been transferred to local municipalities. Legal ambiguity has caused confusion between the central authority and the local administrations, leaving room for lasting concentration of power at the national level. Mayors and local councilors have been extremely frustrated by the complete failure to transfer responsibilities and distribute budget allocations, as prescribed by law. The authors provide that there is a real risk of repeating and relying on technocratic approaches that are delinked from, and do not fully recognize, the political economy of engagement in Libya. Mechanistic interpretations of the principles of national ownership were at the center of international support in 2011–20 and have failed the international community. It is essential to integrate political economy considerations in a manner that begins to understand the prevailing economic incentives and helps to address the tensions and unresolved conflicts.

THE PATH FORWARD

If Libya is to achieve lasting peace, it must develop a near- to medium-term vision for political, economic, and social inclusivity that addresses concerns over the division of power. Such a strategic visioning exercise ought to be based on participatory dialogue with traditional and nontraditional actors, including youth and women. Some elements to consider include the distribution of wealth, the transition from a state-led to a private-sector-driven economy, and economic diversification away from oil.

Libya also needs to build a state that has legitimacy. As it lacks a history of accountable public administration or sectoral management, it needs to build foundational technical skills—such as basic administration, evidence-based policy making, and policy implementation—so that institutions function effectively, as pointed out by authors in section II. Doing so needs to be prioritized for institutions vital to recovery and reconstruction and basic services, such as the ministries of finance, planning, health, and education; the General Electricity Company of Libya (GECOL); and the water authority. Accountability and transparency in policy reforms and administration need to be mainstreamed, so that citizens can see that the state is functioning and delivering results equitably. The perception of the citizenry is critical to creating a virtual cycle of legitimacy and stability.

As the economy is very central to the political stability and long-term prosperity of the country, Libyans deserve stronger attention to the public discourse, especially with the prospect of elections being held. A public discourse should be launched about the costs of inaction, the size and scope of trafficking/smuggling, the deteriorating macroeconomic situation, rampant corruption, and the lack of diversification and options for young people, all of which impact Libya's future. This could help establish a shared narrative and the need to prioritize a sustainable national economic governance system and its institutions. This would need to be matched with prioritized support to establishing effective, transparent, and accountable public institutions, processes, and mechanisms as enabling conditions for improved national and local service delivery and state legitimacy. As such the ongoing political dialogue should accompany the focus on elections with a more explicit elaboration of what a widely accepted social contract might look like, including associated economic institutions.

The case of Libya strongly reflects the interplay between the political and the economic sphere. Antagonism between diverse groups (political groups, armed groups, and informal economic networks) for access to and control of the country's rich natural resources is an undermining factor for national reconciliation, prolonging any conflict or frictional dynamics. Economic recovery could become a national plan capable of reuniting Libyans and could lend useful support to the political process of national reconciliation. In this context, it is important to consider strengthening the economic dialogue as on ongoing lever to inform the political dialogue. Such integration is also key to ensuring that economic reform does not impede efforts to advance the tender political process, and that economic decisions and interventions do not harm political stabilization prospects (for instance, economic reforms that cause a sudden drop in living standards might seriously threaten the standing of the interim government).

The conflict in Libya has created the space for a thriving war economy. This includes human trafficking and the extortion of migrants going into Europe. There is also an active market for the smuggling of goods and a black market. This is all in the context of an emergent private sector. Libya needs to transition from a centrally planned economy to an enterprise culture, and from a hydrocarbon economy to a diversified one that can absorb the available workforce into qualified jobs.

Libya also continues to face numerous challenges in establishing a robust, efficient, and transparent PFM system and in ensuring sustainable use of its hydrocarbon revenues. A clear macrofiscal framework with consistent fiscal rules that reflects the country's economic objectives in an environment of volatile oil prices has yet to be established. The formulation of Libya's budget remains fragmented, that has been disconnected from explicit policy or development strategy and lacks a medium-term perspective to inform the annual budget. Weak public economic management and procurement systems in Libya make it extremely difficult to provide effective accountability and financial controls at both national and subnational levels.

Improving service delivery for citizens as quickly as possible is key to changing public perceptions and increasing the legitimacy of the state. In the early stages of recovery, immediate needs are likely to include restoring and stabilizing electricity and water supply; improving health service delivery (including addressing the COVID-19 pandemic); establishing effective and efficient social safety nets; and repairing key infrastructure, such as broadband internet, roads, buildings, and transport networks. Geographic areas and groups of people that have been neglected, such as the South, youth, women, and internally displaced persons (IDPs), must be included. After years of crisis and conflict, people desperately need to see that peace is possible, and people who have taken up arms need to see that there are dividends to peace.

There is a danger that Libyan women's and girls' needs and priorities will be shut out of reconstruction and recovery efforts due to a rollback on gender equality. Gaddafi's Libya had been progressive in terms of education and women's representation in employment. With the dissolution of his rule in 2011, the resulting competing political and military contestants have marginalized women. As the political process appears to be moving forward, the exclusion of women in the process poses a key risk for Libya's long-term progress. Therefore, analysis that can form the basis of advice to support gender equality needs to be very specific, given that Libya's gender situation is somewhat unique among the countries in the region.

Libya's South risks being further isolated and decoupled from development. Consideration needs to be given to Libya's unique geographical and sociopolitical features. A tyranny of distance impacts development opportunities in all remote areas in Libya's vast South, but there is also the challenge to integrate those who have historically been excluded from full citizenship.

There is a real risk of repeating and relying on technocratic approaches that are delinked from, and do not fully recognize, the political economy of engagement in Libya. Such mechanistic interpretations of the principles of national ownership were at the center of international support in 2011–20 and have failed the international community. It is essential to integrate political economy considerations in a manner that begins to understand the prevailing economic incentives and helps to address the tensions and unresolved conflicts.

Given the continuing fluidity of the environment, international institutions need to maintain a flexible and adaptive approach to their country's programming and operations. Libyans need to prioritize activities that improve the functioning of institutions by improving accountability frameworks, building capacity, and reducing corruption; delivering basic services that improve the lives of the Libyan people; and building trust between the government and citizens. These steps will be possible only if Libyans decide that the cost of war and a destabilized political economic environment has become too high.

Reunification and peace are likely to come in fits and starts. The task may appear daunting. But Libya is not alone. It has international partners that want to support a stable, peaceful, and inclusive Libya.

REFERENCES

Barltrop. 2019. "Oil and Gas in the New Libyan Era: Conflict and Continuity." OIES Paper 22, Oxford University for Energy Studies, Oxford. https://www.oxfordenergy.org/publications /oil-gas-new-libyan-era-conflict-continuity.

Daoud, Rani. 2021. "History and Evolution of the Subnational Government System of Libya." In *Libya: Proceedings of the Libya Local Government Forum*, edited by Michael Schaeffer, Maroua Lassoued, and Zied Ouelhazi. Washington, DC: World Bank.

Eaton, T. 2018. *Libya's War Economy: Predation, Profiteering and State Weakness*. London: Chatham House.

UNHCR (United Nations Commission on Human Rights) 2019. "Global Trends: Forced Displacement in 2019." UNHCR, https://www.unhcr.org/5ee200e37.pdf.

World Bank 2019. *Supporting Peace and Stability in Libya: A Compilation of Existing Analysis on Challenges and Needs*. Washington, DC: World Bank.

World Bank. 2021. *Libya: Socio-Economic Monitor*. Washington, DC: World Bank.

RELATED READINGS

Eaton, T. 2017. "An Impediment to Peace: Libya's Lucrative and Destabilizing War Economy." *War on the Rocks*, June 15, 2017. https://warontherocks.com/2017/06/an-impediment-to -peace-libyas-lucrative-and-destabilizing-war-economy/.

IMF (International Monetary Fund). 2012. "Libya Beyond the Revolution: Challenges and Opportunities." Departmental Paper 12/03, IMF, Washington, DC.

Lacher, W. 2011. "Families, Tribes and Cities in the Libyan Revolution." *Middle East Policy Council* 18 (4): 140–54. http://www.mepc.org/families-tribes-and-cities-libyan-revolution.

Lacher, W. 2016. "Libya's Local Elites and the Politics of Alliance Building." *Mediterranean Politics* 21 (1): 64–85. https://www.tandfonline.com/doi/full/10.1080/13629395.2015.1081451.

Lacher, W. 2018. "Tripoli's Militia Cartel: How Ill-Conceived Stabilization Blocks Political Progress, and Risks Renewed War." SWP Comment 20, Stiftung Wissenschaft und Politik, Berlin. https://www.swp-berlin.org/fileadmin/contents/products/comments/2018C20 _lac.pdf.

Lacher, W., and A. al-Idrissi. 2018. "Capital of Militias: Tripoli's Armed Groups Capture the Libyan State." Briefing Paper, Small Arms Survey, Graduate Institute of International and Development Studies, Geneva. https://www.smallarmssurvey.org/resource/capital -militias-tripolis-armed-groups-capture-libyan-state.

World Bank. 2013. *Doing Business 2014 Economy Profile: Libya*. Washington, DC: World Bank.

World Bank. 2016. *Libya's Economic Outlook*. Washington, DC: World Bank. https://www .worldbank.org/en/country/libya/publication/economic-outlook-fall-2016.

World Bank. 2018. *Doing Business 2019 Economy Profile: Libya*. Washington, DC: World Bank.

World Bank. 2020a. *Libya: Economic Monitor (2020)*. Washington, DC: World Bank.

World Bank. 2020b. *Worldwide Governance Indicators* (WGI). Washington, DC: World Bank. http://governanceqa.worldbank.org/wgi/.

State Institutions: From Legacy to Reform

2 The Battle for Control of State Institutions

TIM EATON

Chatham House

The author provides that there are substantial state-building challenges (political and institutional). Libya is a divided country without a cohesive unifying territorial or organizational ("state") structure. Following the revolution, the prospect of more inclusive and transparent institutions has not been realized, and state institutions have struggled to function and secure legitimacy. The absence of an independent and accountable justice system is a significant obstacle to peace and stability. The author provides that the unresolved tensions between reformist elements and the institutions that were created in the 2000s and the socialist-type entities of the 1970s and 1980s remain unresolved. The result is a transactional system in which institutions have become part of the conflict rather than delivering results for citizens. A decade after the overthrow of Muammar Gaddafi, the institutions of the post-revolutionary Libyan state display more continuity than might initially have been anticipated. Government structures have evolved and fragmented, but key state institutions such as the Central Bank of Libya (CBL), the National Oil Corporation, and the Libyan Investment Authority remain largely unchanged. This chapter explores the evolution of Libyan state institutions and how the battle for their control has affected the Libyan people.

INTRODUCTION

This chapter is organized as follows. It begins by assessing the status of Libyan state institutions on the eve of revolution. The chapter then reviews attempts of post-revolutionary leaders to manage the state. The chapter subsequently assesses the unsuccess of Libyan leaders to establish a functional unified government between 2014 and 2021, exploring the myriad of governance challenges, as rival governments emerged, and institutions were divided. Finally, the chapter assesses the challenge before the Government of National Unity (GNU), Libya's first unified government since 2014, to reverse these trends.

JAMAHURIYA INSTITUTIONS ON THE EVE OF REVOLUTION

On the eve of revolution, Libya's system of governance remained tightly under Muammar Gaddafi's control. Official lines of reporting and oversight were secondary to the real ways in which Gaddafi and his "men of the tent" exerted power and authority.

Over 42 years, Gaddafi's government embarked upon a series of administrative reorganizations. In the 1970s and 1980s, political institutions were created to facilitate "direct democracy" in the Jamahuriya (state of the masses). The private sector was abolished in favor of state- (and supposedly, people-) run business, and foreign ownership was "Libyanized." State dominance of the economy translated into the creation of myriad committees, agencies, holding companies, and monopolies (Pack 2021). The Jamahuriya could point to major advances for its population in these two decades. Literacy became near universal, reaching 94 percent in the 1950s (Martinez 2007). The standard of living of most Libyans improved significantly thanks to the implementation of state investment in redistributive policies.

The application of international sanctions on Libya from 1993 placed significant strain on the Libyan economy and highlighted the deficiencies of the Jamahuriya's system of governance. Gross domestic product (GDP) per capita fell from $6,700 in 1993 to $4,900 in 1999, and the population increased from 4.3 million to 5.6 million (Martinez 2007). Consumer prices increased 200 percent between 1992 and 1997, leading to a deterioration in the standard of living. The government also had to contend with coup attempts from Warfalla tribesmen in 1991, the army in 1993, and an Islamist insurgency in Eastern Libya in 1995–98, as public sentiment turned against the government. It had become clear during the period of sanctions that the government had become increasingly reliant on its security organs—its intelligence network and loyalist elite military units—to maintain its rule (Laessing 2020).

Libya's reemergence on the international scene following the lifting of international sanctions in 1999 prompted moves to introduce market-based reforms. In 2003, reforms were undertaken to liberalize the economy. Major shifts soon took place, with 360 state-owned enterprises targeted for privatization or liquidation in 2003, a large-scale development strategy launched in 2004, and the renegotiation of a series of major oil contracts with international oil companies (St. John 2010).

The Libyan Investment Authority (LIA), the state's sovereign wealth fund, was formed in 2006. A 2010 law consolidated the state's other overseas investment vehicles—the Libyan African Investment Portfolio, the Libyan Foreign Investment Company, the Long-Term Portfolio, and the Libyan Local Investment Development Fund—under the LIA (Eaton 2021a), which had an estimated value of $65 billion at that time (Spittaels et al. 2017). The same year, new legislation was passed that provided a legal basis for greater powers for local administrations and increased freedoms for the private sector to seek foreign investment. These shifts caused tensions with the governments' old guard, who preferred the maintenance of the expansive socialist architecture of the state, but also with other power centers, notably the CBL, over who should spearhead reform processes. Critically, this period would also see competition ramp up between Gaddafi's sons over who would succeed their father. Gaddafi's heir apparent, Saif al-Islam, was closely associated with the reformist trend.

This battle remained in progress and essentially unresolved on the eve of the Libyan revolution, with new and old institutions coexisting uncomfortably (Boudreaux and Delmar-Morgan 2011).

The result was that Libya in 2011 was a hodgepodge of sprawling political institutions created in different eras, with hundreds of state-owned entities with unclear or overlapping mandates. Many of these entities had long been rendered redundant. The competing visions for the structure of the state that they represented were incompatible. The relative stability of the Gaddafi system was ensured through the security apparatus rather than the coherence of the Jamahuriya's formal state structures, providing a huge challenge for post-revolutionary leaders and their governments, which have lacked the security apparatus to keep the system in check (Mattes 2008).

CHANGE AND CONTINUITY: REVOLUTION AND THE STRUGGLE FOR THE STATE (2011–14)

Libya's opposition coalesced in the early weeks of the 2011 uprisings against the Gaddafi government to build a political platform that could manage the country's transition and avert state collapse. The specter of events in Iraq loomed large for the opposition, which, over the course of February and March 2011, created the National Transitional Council (NTC). By July 2011, the NTC was recognized as the legitimate authority of the Libyan people by most of the international community, even as fighting continued. It formulated a constitutional declaration in August 2011, organized elections in July 2012, and handed power over to the newly elected General National Congress (GNC), the legislative authority, in August 2012. The GNC subsequently appointed a president and a prime minister and was tasked with establishing a permanent constitution within 18 months.

The NTC comprised a broad array of former Gaddafi's government insiders, technocrats, and domestic and internationally based opposition elements. Critically, the NTC—and political leaders in general—had limited relations with the rebel forces fighting on the ground, a disconnection that would have long-term implications for the consolidation of the security sector. The inclusion of figures that had operated in high-profile positions within the Gaddafi government cast doubt among many over their revolutionary credentials. Business and opposition figures that had—or at least were believed to have had—close relations with the Muslim Brotherhood led to portrayals of an Islamist capture of the state's institutions.

The NTC's approach to taking over the reins of Libya's key institutions began while the civil war still raged. Key actors within the three vital financial organs of the Libyan state—the CBL, the National Oil Corporation (NOC), and the LIA—soon abandoned Gaddafi (Boudreaux and Delmar-Morgan 2011). The rebels did not wait for the conflict to be decided to appoint their own officials: an NTC NOC chief and CBL governor were appointed as early as March 2011 (*Financial Times* 2011).

NTC negotiations with the international community over access to Libya's overseas accounts were crucial. UN Security Council Resolution 1970, passed on February 28, 2011, announced an asset freeze on specific members of the Gaddafi family. It was expanded in March, through Resolution 1973, to include designated assets and resources controlled by the Libyan authorities, including the CBL, the Libyan Foreign Bank, the LIA, and subsidiaries of the Libyan Arab Investment Portfolio and the Libyan Foreign Investment Company. Gaddafi's forces lost Tripoli to the rebels in August 2011, and Gaddafi was killed in October 2011. At the NTC's request, the UN Security Council authorized the release of the assets of the CBL and the Libyan Foreign Bank (LFB), which is 100 percent owned by CBL, on December 16, 2011. Overnight, Libya's new administration had gained access to over $100 billion of cash, deposits, government bonds, and stocks (Blas 2011).

The new authorities were quick to distribute funds to Libyans. On the first anniversary of the uprising, in February 2012, the transitional authorities gave LD 2,000 to every Libyan family (Reuters 2012). The move would have been justifiable as a one-off approach to helping Libyan families navigate the financial implications of the war and the dysfunction it caused. But it also set the trend for the continuation of Gaddafi-era approaches to the distributive state.

The approach to paying off Libyans in return for compliance has been a defining feature of the post-revolutionary period, perpetuating the transactional relationship between state and citizen (Badi 2021). The opportunity to reform Libya's system of government in the immediate aftermath of the revolution to make it serve the people more effectively was missed. Successive prime ministers replicated Gaddafi-era policies of free or state-subsidized social services, circumventing legal restraints on public spending to do so, expanding the budget, and accumulating mounting debts.

The effects of this process were reflected in the state budget (figure 2.1). Salaries rose from 17 percent of public expenditure in 2010 to 63 percent in 2015.[1] The most problematic aspect of this process was the distribution of payments to *thuwwar* (revolutionary fighters). An estimated 25,000 fighters participated in the uprising against Gaddafi; 10 times that figure was believed to have received payments as of May 2012. In 2013, the government confirmed that it would continue making the payments (St. John 2015).

FIGURE 2.1

State revenues, expenditure, and public debt, 2000–20

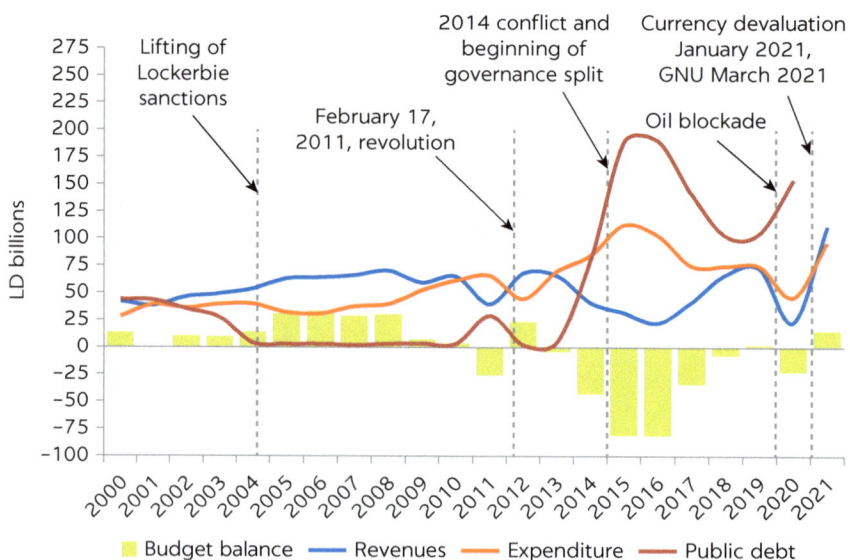

Source: Libyan authorities, World Bank staff estimates.
Note: GNU = Government of National Unity. Expenditures from 2015 are combined estimates of expenditure by Libya's Western and Eastern authorities.

Beyond the creation of the new government, the post-revolutionary leaders were presiding over the same distributive system created by Gaddafi, without the support of coherent security institutions, as the army and intelligence services had been eviscerated. The post-2011 "revolutionary" sector comprised a vast array of locally based armed groups and their constituencies, over whom political leaders and state officials could exert limited authority. Rather than the state absorbing and demobilizing these armed groups into a unified chain of command, as envisaged by classical security sector reform doctrine, the inverse took place, with armed groups using their state affiliation to co-opt the state and continuing to arm, mobilize, and integrate themselves into the state's security apparatus without becoming subservient to it (Eaton 2020b).

These dynamics greatly affected the ability of Libya's institutions to function. The oil sector was subjected to growing demands from the Petroleum Facilities Guard. A blockade of Libya's oil crescent from 2013 to late 2016 cost Libya over $100 billion in lost revenues (Ghaddar, George, and Lewis 2016).[2] Such developments contributed to the establishment of a vicious cycle in which local constituencies resorted to extortion to obtain services and resources from the state, which further reduced the state's ability to obtain those resources and provide the services. The fact that processes of institutional capture were well under way meant that the institutions themselves, and their resources, were part of this conflict.

The GNC displayed promising early progress in reaching elections and embarking upon a defined constitution-building process. But rifts expanded significantly in 2013. Although most GNC members were technically independents, the elections of July 2012 saw two principal blocs emerge. The National Forces Alliance included many liberals who had held positions within the former Gaddafi government. The Justice and Construction Party emerged as the political arm of the Muslim Brotherhood. The passing of a Political Isolation Law in May 2013, which barred people who had held positions under the Gaddafi government from holding office, represented a critical inflection point. It effectively put individuals who had defected from the Gaddafi government and supported the revolution, in the same category as people who had fought on the side of the Gaddafi government (Bloomberg 2011).

The Political Isolation Law reflected a clear desire for retribution and reflected tension over the degree of continuity that should be permitted from the Gaddafi era. These political disputes were reflected in mounting social polarization and tensions in the security space. The GNC's 18-month mandate elapsed in January 2014, and the constitutional process remained stymied. The results of the parliamentary elections of June 2014 were contested and would prove the spark for a further round of violence. By the close of 2014, rival legislatives emerged. The House of Representatives—elected in June 2014—relocated to Tobruk in Eastern Libya. In Tripoli, the rump of the GNC reconstituted itself. Both legislatives appointed new governments. Thus, by the close of 2014, the unwieldy architecture of the Jamahuriya remained effectively untouched, with an added degree of complexity as rival administrations claimed legitimacy. Post-revolutionary leaders delivered little for the population beyond a continuation of distributive policies. Power sharing and the absence of a constitutional settlement meant that constructive debate over the future shape of state remained absent.

Battles for control of institutions centered on who would be appointed to leadership positions—and therefore be placed on the payroll—rather than policy-based discussions over reform of those institutions. Few of the institutions functioned according to their mandate, and it was difficult to tell which had become moribund, although in most cases, the state continued to pay their salaries whatever their status. The runaway expenditure on state-sector salaries proved increasingly unaffordable. International oil prices were falling, and Libyan oil production was hampered by the blockade of Eastern oil fields. In response, the state drew down its foreign currency reserves to cover the deficit between government spending and state revenues.

THE GOVERNANCE SPLIT AND THE EMERGENCE OF INSTITUTIONAL AUTONOMY (2014–20)

Internationally mediated attempts to resolve the governance split in Libya failed to halt the process of administrative bifurcation and ensuing chaos in 2014–20. The signing of the UN–mediated Libyan Political Agreement in the Moroccan city of Skheirat in December 2015 provided for the formation of a Government of National Accord (GNA).[3] The GNA never emerged as the unity government it was intended to be, however. Members of the Presidency Council aligned with Khalifa Haftar soon boycotted it, and the House of Representatives failed to ratify the Libyan Political Agreement, meaning that the GNA had no basis in Libyan law. The result was that the "Interim Government" appointed by the House of Representatives continued to operate in Eastern Libya and the GNA operated in Western Libya, with Southern Libya almost entirely ignored by the two sets of rivals.

The governance split contributed to a steady deterioration in due process. The inability of the GNA to work with the House of Representatives meant that the Presidency Council was unable to follow procedures as laid out in Libyan law, leaving the GNA reliant on the provisions of the Libyan Political Agreement. The House of Representatives was increasingly reduced to a rump of a limited number of deputies, and violations of due process were widespread. Over the course of the governance split, the GNA and the House of Representatives issued decrees and legislation that is of contested legitimacy. The terms of the GNA and House of Representatives expired.[4]

The governance split caused corresponding splits in state institutions as the rival administrations sought to make their own appointments and run their own operations. These splits placed Libya's institutions in an impossible situation. At the CBL, members of the board of directors who backed the House of Representatives established the CBL branch in al-Bayda as its new headquarters. The House of Representatives sought to remove the sitting CBL governor, who remained in Tripoli and sided with the Tripoli-based authorities. The result was that the sitting CBL governor remained in his post and operated without a functioning board (there was no board meeting for six years) and therefore little in the way of formal oversight.

At the NOC, the chair of the board of directors appointed by the Tripoli-based authorities in May 2014 negotiated the so-called Vienna Agreement with the chair of the Eastern-based board, to unify the NOC boards and agree to distribution rights in May 2016. However, a dispute over the failure to move the NOC's headquarters to Benghazi led to the collapse of the agreement later that year. The Eastern-based Interim Government replaced the board in

February 2017, with the intent of creating a mechanism through which the Eastern-based authorities could export oil to the international market and bypass Tripoli.

The LIA was subject to a highly complex set of legal wranglings.[5] In October 2014, the Interim Government appointed a new chair and CEO to LIA's board, which was operating from Malta because of security concerns. In April 2015, the LIA board of trustees—made up of the executive members of the Tripoli-based Government of National Salvation—actioned a decision by the Libyan court to overturn the ruling of the Political Isolation Committee that sought to reinstate former Gaddafi aides as chair and CEO of the LIA. The decision meant the Tripoli headquarters of the LIA was under the leadership of GNA and the Malta office was controlled by the Eastern-based Interim Government.

In 2016, the GNU appointed another member to LIA's board. Meanwhile, the Interim Government appointed its own successor. To complicate matters further, legal action in London between the two former LIA CEOs representing both sides over who should be recognized as the legal representative of LIA assets was expanded to include the new appointees. The result was a bizarre spectacle in which a British judge sitting in a British court was asked to rule on the procedural validity of LIA appointments as laid out in Libyan law. The judge eventually ruled in favor of GNU appointee.[6] The LIA has been so consumed by internal battles, however, that it has been unable to prove its ability to manage its assets and therefore unable to make the case for the lifting of the asset freeze applied in 2011.

Few institutions escaped the division. Those that did, such as the attorney general's office, had to tread carefully to navigate the widening gaps in local operating conditions, work with local forces, and be judicious in their operations. The GNA's decision to continue to provide salaries to all on the payroll before 2014 increased the ability of Libya's institutions to continue to cooperate—even if not on a senior management level—and to maintain relations with colleagues. Some institutions that were technically split remained functionally unified. The NOC is a good example, with the Eastern NOC largely relegated to an empty office block and a series of attempts to broker sales contracts. The effect on other state institutions was stasis, making many of Libya's institutions moribund, mirroring the effect of the Jamahuriya, in which old institutions remained in existence even after they were no longer relevant.

The battles for control and distribution of patronage extended throughout these organizations. The LIA, which has five major subsidiaries and an estimated 500 companies, was a major site of such competition. The government wielded significant influence, as its board of trustees comprises government ministers and appoints the LIA's board of directors. The board of directors could in turn replace the boards of directors of the subsidiaries and so on throughout the LIA pyramid. Appointments to these boards can be lucrative, and the opacity of the activities of LIA's myriad companies—most of which are not subject to sanctions and are registered outside of Libya—means that there is little accountability. Some of these companies, formed in the Gaddafi era, appear to have retained the same management teams, another indication of continuity.

The schism in the CBL has proved especially damaging to Libya's economy. The Tripoli CBL continued to hold a monopoly over access to Libya's foreign exchange reserves and continued to distribute salary payments to people who were listed on the payroll in 2014, before the governance split. Denied these resources, the Bayda-based CBL underwrote the expenditures of the Interim Government, which expanded its public sector payroll significantly by issuing debt via commercial banks headquartered in the East (Eaton 2020b). By 2021, the World Bank estimated the accumulated debt of the CBL Bayda at LD 71 billion (World Bank 2021). Starved of liquidity, the CBL Bayda printed a cumulative total of approximately LD 14.5 billion in banknotes and minted coins in Russia by October 2019 (Sagdiev and Lewis 2019). These problems contributed to a significant expansion of the black market, as Libyans became increasingly reliant on it for access to foreign currency. Many traders were forced to use the black market to import goods. A significant margin developed between the official and unofficial rates of exchange, and a liquidity crisis set in (Harchaoui 2018).

International support has helped mitigate the impacts of the governance split on the CBL and NOC, thereby reducing the threat of partition. If the CBL Bayda had obtained access to the international financial system and the rival NOC had been able to obtain income directly from oil sales, Libya would likely have faced an existential threat as the prospect of widespread conflict would have become almost inevitable. International support to the CBL and the NOC has also granted these institutions an unparalleled degree of autonomy.

The inability of the GNA and the House of Representatives to work together inadvertently empowered the CBL. Its management of liquidity, payment orders, and trade finance has seen the CBL emerge as the dominant force in economic decision-making. Bitter disputes developed between the CBL and the GNA, with the CBL governor emphasizing the need to safeguard reserves and accusing the GNA of incompetence and the GNA prime minister accusing the governor of overstepping his mandate. The CBL has adopted this position with increasingly limited oversight.

The NOC has become increasingly interventionist in political disputes, seeking to pressure political decision-makers to reach a political settlement. Operating across Libya, the NOC must maintain good relations with local communities to continue to function. Oil blockades have repeatedly been used as a means of extracting concessions from political decision-makers since 2013. In a brazen act of political maneuvering, the oil crescent was blockaded by locally based forces in January 2020, only two days before a major international summit. The head of Libyan Arab Armed Forces (LAAF) contended that the blockade was because of a tribal decision, but it was clear that his forces determined whether the blockade was implemented or not. By September 2020, the cost of lost revenues of the continuing blockade was estimated at $5 billion. The NOC lamented its need to import expensive foreign fuel to compensate for production losses just when it had a record low budget, accruing what it dubbed "historic financial debts" (NOC 2020).

The NOC subsequently decided to overstep its mandate. Amid acrimony between the chair of NOC and governor of CBL over funding for the NOC, the NOC announced that it would be withholding oil revenues and not passing them on to CBL "until the Bank has a clear transparency in front of the Libyan people regarding the mechanism of spending the oil revenues."[7] The funds would be retained in the NOC's account with the Libyan Foreign Bank. Although it is likely that the NOC saw no alternative to adopting an interventionist stance, withholding oil revenues set a dangerous precedent. The incident also illustrated the extent to which Libya's institutions are active players in, rather than simply victims of, Libya's conflict.

Lack of control over the security sector continued to constrain the ability of Libyan authorities to govern. The GNA's arrival in Tripoli in March 2016 had to be secured through accords with armed groups based in the capital. Bereft of security forces over which it could exert command and control, the GNA found a modus vivendi with Tripolitanian armed groups nominally affiliated with the Ministry of Interior.[8] This emerging settlement allowed for a degree of stability and improved security for Tripoli's citizens, but it also enabled predation of (mainly state) economic resources, which sustained grievances of actors based outside of the capital, who saw the wealth of Tripoli militia nouveau riche (Eaton 2020a).

After consolidating their control in the capital, Tripoli's armed groups graduated from coercive forms of revenue generation to more complex financial schemes and institutional infiltration to maintain their interests.[9] In the business sector, armed groups used their leverage over financial institutions (garnered through the provision of security) to enter into partnerships with established traders. Many soon entered business on their own after learning the ropes. Political leaders sought allegiances with Tripoli's armed groups in order to continue to operate on the ground. Armed group members, or their acquaintances, obtained state positions in the Foreign Ministry and key positions in the Ministry of Finance, among others. Armed groups sought to infiltrate rather than replace state institutions (Eaton 2021b).

Throughout this period, Eastern authorities came to be increasingly dominated by the LAAF, as Haftar strengthened his hold over the political, economic, and security spheres. Strengthened by significant materiel support from international actors, Haftar thrived despite being ostracized by the Libyan Political Agreement. The House of Representatives, increasingly reduced to a rump as more of its members boycotted it, passed a raft of legislation that enabled the LAAF to acquire powers to overtake the competencies of the Interim Government, access significant revenue, and increasingly cannibalize the public and private sectors.[10] In 2016, a defense committee, comprising key decisionmakers from the Interim Government, House of Representatives, LAAF, and the CBL Bayda, was established with the sole purpose of funding the LAAF.[11] In a 2019 interview, the head of the Eastern CBL noted that about a third of the Eastern CBL's spending had gone to the LAAF in 2016–18.[12] In subsequent years, Haftar made it clear that he was seeking to usurp civilian authorities through progressive encroachment into their mandates. This process culminated in an April 2020 address to the nation in which Haftar claimed a popular mandate for military rule (LAAF 2020).

In the private and public sectors, the LAAF developed its Military Investment Authority (MIA) as a vehicle for economic expansion. The law, passed by the House of Representatives in 2016, facilitated the development of the MIA, providing significant commercial advantages to the LAAF. The legislation exempts the LAAF from taxes and allows it to open offices and accounts overseas.[13] Following its creation, the MIA engaged in a wide variety of fields, from agricultural projects to road and infrastructure building and export of scrap metals, on a basis that is at best quasi-legal. In some cases, the LAAF simply requisitioned state projects. In September 2017, Haftar unilaterally announced his intention to bring 96 projects under the "protection" of the LAAF.[14] In other cases, the LAAF has sought to supplant state agencies. For example, in September 2019 the LAAF created a parallel version Brega Fuel and Marketing Company to sign contracts with its Military Investment

Authority for the distribution of subsidized fuel. The MIA in turn signed a contract with a company based in the United Arab Emirates (UAE) for the onward sale of the fuel, which would have allowed the MIA to sell state-subsidized fuels at a commercial rate to international customers had it proved successful (Eaton 2021c).

Internationally led peace attempts struggled to break through the bifurcation of Libya's political system. The incumbents of the political institutions had no personal incentive to reach a settlement, as it would likely mean the end of their authority. As political negotiations dragged on, the expansion of Haftar's forces into Southern Libya in January 2019 was followed by the launch of a LAAF offensive on Tripoli in April 2019. The ensuing war brought significantly greater involvement from foreign mercenaries and foreign powers, as Haftar drew heavily on support from foreign mercenaries. In response, Turkish intervention following the conduct of memorandums of understanding with the GNA ultimately led to a return to the status quo before the launch of the Tripoli offensive.

The result of these dynamics was a crisis of legitimacy and the creation of an elite that seemed more interested in maintaining its hold on power than improving the daily life of the Libyan people. At the close of 2020, almost no actor on the Libyan political scene or in a leadership position at a state institution could claim an uncontested mandate.[15] The toll of the patterns of elite competition and self-interest on the Libyan people was high. The war for Tripoli caused another wave of displacement of Libyan families and further eroded social cohesion. A culture of impunity was sustained by armed actors committing crimes without fear of accountability. In the city of Tarhuna, mass graves were found following the ouster from the city of the Kani militias along with other LAAF-aligned forces (Sommerville 2021).

The services provided to Libyans deteriorated significantly. Electricity blackouts of up to 22 hours a day became a regular feature. The General Electricity Company of Libya (GECOL) blamed its operating environment, among other factors, for the predatory activities of criminals who stole equipment and armed groups who refused to comply with staged blackouts. Subsidies for goods—on which government expenditure was significant—became increasingly unavailable. In many parts of Libya, fuel sold at more than five times the official subsidized rate (Eaton 2019). The liquidity crisis was accompanied by a banking crisis, as the CBL Tripoli sought to insulate itself from the debt-fueled spending of the Eastern authorities.

As state spending on salaries and handouts increased, investment in the maintenance of infrastructure and development slowed to a near halt. The legally mandated processes for determining development spending and the budget more broadly were no longer followed, leading to warnings that the electricity grid was on the verge of collapse and the Great Man-Made River in dire need of maintenance. The Libyan authorities' response to the COVID-19 pandemic was heavily criticized, with allegations of corruption leveled at the GNA's health ministry. These developments left an increasing number of Libyans vulnerable. A December 2020 assessment by the United Nations Office for the Coordination of Humanitarian Affairs (OCHA 2020) found that 17.5 percent of Libyans needed humanitarian assistance.

Reforms to address these problems were not forthcoming, leading to increasing frustration among Libyans. Between August and October 2020, protests emerged across the country, from Tripoli, Zawiya, and Misrata in the West to

Benghazi in the East and Sebha in the South, criticizing the inadequate provision of services and widespread corruption in the respective political administrations. In Tripoli, protests were dispersed by force, with a number of protestors arrested (Zaptia 2020b).

CONCLUDING REMARKS

The opening months of 2021 delivered unexpected political progress, likely spurred by the deteriorating domestic situation and the willingness of external players to support dialogue. On February 5, 2021, a new GNU was selected through the auspices of the UN-led Libyan Political Dialogue Forum.[16] The GNU was approved by the House of Representatives on March 10, making it the first unified Libyan government since 2014.

The GNU was charged with reunifying Libya's institutions and preparing the country for elections in December 2021. Yet that elections timetable has since broken down, as familiar disputes over procedures and debates over who should be allowed to run—particularly following the declaration by Saif al-Islam Gaddafi that he would stand—derailed the process. In its time in office, the GNU has found that fully fledged reunification is more difficult to achieve than ever before. The GNU inherited a convoluted system of government institutions (the House of Representatives and the High State Council have been retained) replete with vested interests and an increasingly fragmented set of state institutions that operate with fewer and fewer checks and balances. It also has little—if any—influence over security actors. Moreover, the GNU appears to have added to these problems through attempts to centralize power—and government spending—through the auspices of the prime minister's office.

At the time of writing, reforms to the system of governance are required yet remain elusive. Restoring the status quo ante of the Jamahuriya—albeit without the pervasive security sector—will not deliver the improved governance the Libyan people need. Such reforms are not addressed by the political process (they are presumably left to the government set to be elected) or even discussed in meaningful terms by political rivals. As a result, the policy debates of the last years of the Jamahuriya remain unresolved, and no consensus over the future shape of the state has emerged. The battle remains for control of its existing elements.

NOTES

1. Figures for 2010 are from Chami et al. (2012); figure for 2015 comes from estimates by Libyan authorities and World Bank estimates.
2. The oil crescent covers a region stretching along the coast from Sirte to Ras Lanuf. It extends to the Jufra district.
3. The GNA sought to replace the two governments and combine the rival legislatives. The rump GNC became the High State Council, a consultative body, and the House of Representatives was retained as the legislative body. A nine-member Presidency Council, comprising members representing Libya's three historic regions, was created to form the executive.
4. The Libyan Political Agreement envisaged a maximum two-year term for the GNA; the House of Representatives resolved the problem of its own term expiry by tabling a vote among the active rump to unilaterally extend it.

5. For a detailed account of events relating to the LIA, see Eaton (2021a).

6. See Mohamed v Breish & ORS, Casemine database, March 25, 2020, https://www.casemine.com/judgement/uk/5e7d88762c94e071a16f2fb3.

7. The exact connection between the NOC's position and an unofficial deal reached between GNA Deputy Prime Minister Ahmed Maiteg and Haftar over agreed conditions for the lifting of the oil blockade (reached in September 2020) is unclear. See Zaptia (2020a).

8. Four principal Tripolitanian armed groups—the Special Deterrence Forces (popularly known as Rada, from its name in Arabic), the Nawasi Brigade, the Tripoli Revolutionaries Brigade, and the Abu Slim Matryr's Brigade—established what has been dubbed a cartel in the capital, forcing out opponents. See Lacher and Idrissi (2018).

9. See Eaton et al. (2020) for a detailed analysis of these dynamics.

10. Key legislation includes the January 2015 creation of the post of general commander of the Armed Forces (to which Haftar was appointed in March 2015), the antiterrorism law of the same year, and two laws on military investment passed in 2016 and 2018. Eaton (2021b) provides a detailed account of these laws.

11. The committee was formed as a result of an agreement between Haftar and the prime minister of the Interim Government, Abdullah al-Thinni. It was headed by the LAAF's chief of staff, Abdulrazaq al-Nadhouri. Other members included the prime minister, the governor of the Eastern CBL, the minister of finance, and the head of the House of Representatives' National Security and Defense Committee.

12. This spending accounted for 43 percent of the budget in 2016, 27 percent in 2017, and 20 percent in 2018, for a total of about LD 9.5 billion over three years. For details of Hibri's interview, see Alwasat (2019).

13. Each provision is, however, qualified by stating that the activity must remain within the bounds of "the legislation in force." It is on this ground that the Interim Government has objected to the activities of the MIA, noting that they violate the legislation in force, most notably Commercial Law 20.

14. For a copy of the letter, see Choudhury et al. (2021).

15. Many of the members of the High State Council were working from the mandate of elections in 2012, which had expired in January 2014. Members of the House of Representatives were operating from their mandate of elections of contested validity in 2014. The Interim Government was formed in 2014 for a period envisaged at two weeks. Haftar was appointed as general commander of Libyan armed forces by a small number of House of Representatives deputies in 2015. The GNA was not elected at all; it was selected. Its mandate ran out in 2018 and it had never operated as the LPA envisaged. The CBL governor was appointed by unelected transitional authorities in October 2011. The main reason for his survival appears to have been the inability of his opponents to agree on a replacement. The NOC chairman has been in place since May 2014, operating without an elected counterpart as oil minister, as his predecessor had.

16. The Libyan Political Dialogue Forum (LPDF) agreed on the selection criteria on January 18, 2021, and voting for the new government took place February 5. Seventy-three votes were cast, with one LPDF member abstaining.

REFERENCES

Alwasat. 2019. "Al-Hibri: One-Third of the Budget over the Last Three Years Has Been Allocated to the Army," February 19, 2019 [in Arabic]. http://alwasat.ly/news/libya/236465.

Badi, E. 2021. "Of Conflict and Collapse: Rethinking State Formation in Post-Gaddafi Libya." *Middle East Law and Governance* 13: 44–45.

Blas, J. 2011. "Colossal Task ahead for Libya's New Oil Chief," *Financial Times*, September 5, 2011. https://www.ft.com/content/9a8b610a-d7b4-11e0-a06b-00144feabdc0.

Bloomberg. 2011. "Gaddafi's Money Man in Vienna Loses Funds, London Friends," April 26, 2011.

Boudreaux, A., and A. Delmar-Morgan. 2011. "Oil Chief Leaves Libya as Regime Is Targeted." *Wall Street Journal*, May 18, 2011. https://www.wsj.com/articles/SB10001424052748703421204576328542926545706?mod=asia_home.

Chami, R., A. Al-Darwish, S. Cevik, J. Charap, S. George, B. Gracia, S. Gray, and S. Pattanayak. 2012. *Libya beyond the Revolution: Challenges and Opportunities.* Washington, DC: International Monetary Fund. https://www.imf.org/en/Publications/Departmental -Papers-Policy-Papers/Issues/2016/12/31/Libya-Beyond-the-Revolution-Challenges -and-Opportunities-25784.

Choudhury, L. M., A. Aoun, D. Badawy, L. A. de Alburquerque Bacardit, Y. Marjane, and A. Wilkinson. 2021. *Final Report of the Panel of Experts on Libya Established Pursuant to Security Council Resolution 1973 (2011) (S/2021/229).* New York: United Nations. https:// www.undocs.org/en/S/2021/229.

Eaton, T. 2019. *Libya: Rich in Oil, Leaking Fuel.* London: Chatham House. https://chathamhouse .shorthandstories.com/libya-rich-in-oil-leaking-fuel/index.html.

Eaton, T. 2020a. "As Conflict Escalates in Libya, the Economy Veers towards Crisis," *War on the Rocks,* May 19, 2020. https://warontherocks.com/2020/05/as-conflict-escalates-in-libya -the-economy-veers-toward-crisis/.

Eaton, T. 2020b. *The Development of Libyan Armed Groups since 2014: Community Dynamics and Economic Interests.* London: Chatham House. https://www.chathamhouse.org/2020/03 /development-libyan-armed-groups-2014.

Eaton, T. 2021a. *Libya: Investing in the Wealth of a Nation.* London: Chatham House. https:// www.chathamhouse.org/2021/02/libya-investing-wealth-nation.

Eaton, T. 2021b. *The Libyan Arab Armed Forces: A Network Analysis of Haftar's Military Alliance.* London: Chatham House. https://www.chathamhouse.org/2021/06/libyan -arab-armed-forces.

Eaton, T. 2021c. *An Unwieldy Alliance.* London: Chatham House.

Financial Times. 2011. "Libyan Cash May Be Hidden in Desert." Video, May 16, 2011. https:// www.ft.com/video/3f953443-437e-3e70-b2d5-2d3c7dae2445.

Ghaddar A., L. George, and A. Lewis. 2016. "Libya Oil Exports Threatened as NOC Warns against Port Deal," Reuters, July 24, 2016. https://www.reuters.com/article/us-libya -oil-exports-exclusive/exclusive-libya-oil-exportsthreatened-as-noc-warns-against -port-deal-idUSKCN1040DO.

Harchaoui, J. 2018. "Libya's Monetary Crisis." *Lawfare,* January 10, 2019. https://www .lawfareblog.com/libyas-monetary-crisis.

LAAF (Libyan Arab Armed Forces). 2020. "Speech of the General Commander of the Libyan Armed Forces Khalifa Haftar to the Libyan People" [in Arabic], YouTube, April 27, 2020. https://www.youtube.com/watch?v=ZRcWEuUeVGQ.

Lacher, W., and A. Idrissi. 2018. "Capital of Militias: Tripoli's Armed Groups Capture the State," SANA briefing paper July 2018. Geneva: Small Arms Survey, Graduate Institute of International and Development Studies. https://www.smallarmssurvey.org/resource /capital-militias-tripolis-armed-groups-capture-libyan-state.

Laessing, U. 2020. *Understanding Libya Since Gaddafi.* London: Hurst.

Martinez, Luis. 2007. *The Libyan Paradox.* London: Hurst.

Mattes, H. 2008. "Formal and Informal Authority in Libya since 1969." In *Libya Since 1969: Qadhafi's Revolution Revisited,* edited by D. Vandewalle. New York: Macmillan.

NOC (National Oil Corporation). 2020. "The Illegal Oil Blockade Blights the Life of Every Libyan Citizen." September 11, 2020. https://noc.ly/index.php/en/new-4/6117-the-illegal -oil-blockade-blights-the-life-of-every-libyan-citizen.

OCHA (Office for the Coordination of Human Affairs). 2020. *Humanitarian Needs Overview: Libya.* New York: United Nations. https://reliefweb.int/sites/reliefweb.int/files/resources /hno_2021-final.pdf.

Pack, Jason. 2021. *Libya and the Global Enduring Disorder.* London: Hurst. https://www .hurstpublishers.com/book/libya-and-the-global-enduring-disorder.

Reuters. 2012. "Libya PM Promises Families' Cash to Quell Discontent," February 18, 2102. https://www.reuters.com/article/us-libya-pm-idUSTRE81H0O320120218.

Sagdiev, R., and A. Lewis. 2019. "Supplies of Banknotes from Russia to East Libya Accelerated This Year: Data," Reuters, October 29, 2019. https://www.reuters.com/article/libya -economy/update-1-exclusive-supplies-of-banknotes-from-russia-to-east-libya-accelerated -this-year-data-idUKL8N27E3HN?edition-redirect=uk.

Sommerville, Q. 2021. "Libya's City of Ghosts," BBC, March 30, 2021. https://www.bbc.co.uk/news/world-africa-56574424.

Spittaels, S., N. Abou-Khalil, K. Bouhou, M. Kartas, D. McFarland, and J. Alberto Pintos Servia. 2017. *Final Report of the Panel of Experts on Libya*. New York: United Nations Security Council. https://documents-dds-ny.un.org/doc/UNDOC/GEN/N17/116/23/PDF/N1711623.pdf?OpenElement.

St. John, R. B. 2010. "The Libyan Economy in Transition: Opportunities and Challenges." In *Libya Since 1969*: *Qadhafi's Revolution Revisited,* edited by D. Vanderwalle. New York: MacMillan.

St. John, R. B. 2015. *Libya: Continuity and Change*. Oxford, UK: Routledge.

World Bank. 2021. *Libya Economic Monitor* (Spring 2021). Washington, DC: World Bank. https://www.worldbank.org/en/country/libya/publication/libya-economic-monitor-spring-2021.

Zaptia, S. 2020a. "The CBL–NOC Tug-of-War on Authority over Libya's Oil Revenues Continues." *Libya Herald*, November 27, 2020. https://www.libyaherald.com/2020/11/27/the-cbl-noc-tug-of-war-on-authority-over-libyas-oil-revenues-continues/.

Zaptia, S. 2020b. "Serraj Speech to the Nation: Attacks CBL and Treasonous Media, Says International Community Concerned Purely with Self Interest." *Libya Herald,* April 9, 2022. https://www.libyaherald.com/2020/04/09/serraj-speech-to-the-nation-attacks-cbl-and-treasonous-media-says-international-community-concerned-purely-with-self-interest/.

RELATED READING

Eaton, T. 2018. *Libya's War Economy: Predation, Profiteering and State Weakness*. London: Chatham House. https://www.chathamhouse.org/2018/04/libyas-war-economy-predation-profiteering-and-state-weakness.

3 Beyond Power Sharing: Long-Term Economic and Political Stability

TARIK M. YOUSEF

The Brookings Institute

Given the challenges facing Libya's unity government, the author provides the limited progress made over its life span, and the vulnerability of the power-sharing arrangement to domestic and geopolitical spoilers, it is easy to take a dark view of the prospects for the current power-sharing agreement's ability to maintain peace and begin the task of rebuilding the country. Viewed as a short-term bridge to long-term stability, however, the power-sharing agreement may provide a singular opportunity to end the conflict, build a shared vision for development, and lay the foundations for a new social contract. Securing this bridge requires that Libyans and their international supporters avoid reducing the problem to the realization of holding national elections by any set date. Even when elections take place, Libya will continue to struggle with issues left unaddressed during the formation of and by the Government of National Unity (GNU).

INTRODUCTION

After a decade of political division, violent conflict, and economic instability, the weary Libyan population cheered the February 2021 announcement of a breakthrough power-sharing agreement by representatives of the Libyan Political Dialogue Forum (LPDF). Under the UN-brokered agreement, the LPDF voted to appoint a new prime minister and Presidency Council, and one month later, parties from both sides of Libya's long-standing conflict formed the country's first unified government since 2014. The challenges before the GNU were daunting. However, at its inception, the unity government offered a unique opportunity to ensure the cessation of armed conflict and to lay the foundation for long-term political and economic stability.

A year later, whether Libya's warring factions and political leaders will fully seize the opportunity offered by the establishment of the unity government remains an open question. While the power-sharing agreement remains in place, the elections initially planned for the end of December 2021 were postponed, and no agreement on a new timeframe for holding them has been reached. As a result, a new legitimacy crisis has enveloped the country, with the House of Representatives seeking to replace the GNU prime minister, arguing that his tenure, set originally to end with the elections, has expired (Fishman 2022). The prime minister and his political allies have countered that the legislature lacks the power to replace him and that doing so would trigger a return to war.

Beyond these acute crisis points, the GNU's power-sharing agreement has proved vulnerable on many levels. Its formula, which focuses on distributing power among representatives of various regional and political camps, complicates the tasks of political and economic stabilization, undermining the government's attempts to deliver on policy priorities while incentivizing policy dysfunction, corruption, and even a return to violence (Megerisi 2021). Going forward, the GNU may well replicate Libya's troubled history with transitional governance in the post–Muammar Gaddafi era, echoing the experiences of many conflict countries that have adopted similar power-sharing arrangements in the pursuit of peace.

Drawing on lessons learned from Libya's transition over the past decade and broader international experience with power-sharing agreements, this chapter discusses prospects for the country's political and economic stability. This chapter is organized as follows. The second section provides an overview of international experience with post-conflict power-sharing arrangements. The third section reviews international efforts at securing a power-sharing agreement in Libya. The fourth section details the initial challenges posed by the implementation of the most recent power-sharing agreement, while the fifth section discusses how those challenges have materialized over the past year. The sixth section identifies ways to maximize positive outcomes for Libya under the agreement. The seventh section provides some concluding remarks.

THE EFFICACY OF POWER-SHARING AGREEMENTS

Over the past few decades, power-sharing agreements have become a widely used mechanism for an international community seeking to bring conflict actors to the negotiating table. In the low-trust environments that characterize civil wars, these agreements dissuade opposing sides from conflict by granting them shared control over policy making and access to state resources while providing them with a means of signaling their commitment to peaceful reconciliation (Bell 2018; Gates et al. 2017; Mattes and Savun 2009). These arrangements also provide the basis for the realization of renewed citizen trust in government and trust between fragmented social groups, laying the groundwork for new social contracts and more sustainable efforts to secure peace and prosperity (Furness and Trautner 2020).

In practice, power-sharing agreements are often blunt instruments, rapidly pieced together and more focused on the immediate cessation of violence than on longer-term objectives, such as developing a national vision, pursuing reconciliation, or promoting sustainable development. Rather than enabling long-term peace, these agreements often enable state capture by existing elites and war profiteers, fostering clientelism and corruption (Heydemann 2018). Resultant unity governments are often ineffective at delivering public services or rebuilding the economy, undermining their ability to build citizen trust in government. At worst, poorly executed power-sharing agreements can galvanize popular grievances, providing fodder for spoilers and those inclined to return to violence to secure their goals (Haass and Ottman 2017).

The modern history of power-sharing agreements demonstrates that their underlying structure is key to long-term success. In this regard, Graham, Miller, and Strøm (2017) provide a useful typology for power-sharing arrangements and their respective risks. These include inclusive arrangements, dispersive arrangements, and constraining arrangements. Inclusive arrangements are structured to provide governmental representation to opposing parties by offering them positions or decision-making power over resources or specific portfolios. Dispersive arrangements distribute power by devolving decision-making authorities to specific geographic territories or groups, such as states, regions, ethnic groups, or tribes. In contrast, constraining arrangements do not guarantee conflict actors direct influence over government, but use institutional mechanisms such as constitutional provisions, independent courts, and civil society to provide oversight and constrain governmental power.

While inclusive arrangements may more rapidly secure the commitment of conflict actors to an immediate resolution of the conflict, they tend to benefit and reinforce existing elites. Both inclusive and dispersive arrangements are particularly fragile because of their inability to guarantee equity with respect to security, public services, and political participation, and, by extension, their inability to foster citizen trust in government (Furness and Trautner 2020). As such, they are prone to conflict relapse, as those left out of power-sharing arrangements realize the cost of exclusion and reconsider violence as a means of securing their interests. In contrast, constraining arrangements are generally more successful in promoting broader trust by ensuring that governments are accountable to independent oversight and that citizens are protected from governmental abuses (Graham, Miller, and Strøm 2017). In turn, they have a better track record of preventing the reemergence of conflict once an agreement is secured.

While international peace negotiators would favor more effective design of power-sharing arrangements, the choice of selected approaches more often comes down to a range of practical factors, including the balance of power between stakeholders, existing legal systems and institutions, progress in negotiations, and the need to secure buy-in from disparate parties (Forster 2019). They also come down to broader geopolitical considerations, including the role of external actors in conflict, the scope for international cooperation to facilitate conflict resolution, and the attention span of the international community to support mediation efforts. All of these factors ultimately shaped the choice, timing, and outcomes of Libya's power-sharing agreements.

EFFORTS TO SECURE A POWER-SHARING AGREEMENT FOR LIBYA

Since the 2014 political crisis that ushered in a period of heightened civil conflict and economic instability in Libya, the United Nations Support Mission in Libya (UNSMIL) has worked assiduously with involved political factions, militias, and foreign powers to contain emerging conflicts, limit institutional fragmentation, and facilitate negotiations toward a peaceful settlement. These efforts have resulted in two power-sharing agreements: the Libyan Political Agreement (LPA) reached in Skhirat, Morocco, in December 2015 and the current agreement, the Libyan Political Dialogue Forum Agreement (LPDFA), reached in Geneva in February 2021. Although these agreements were reached under strikingly different circumstances, they share broad similarities in how they were structured. Importantly, while the LPDFA has remained in place for over a year, it includes many of the vulnerabilities that ultimately led to the unsuccess of the LPA with respect to longer-term economic and political prospects.

Both the LPA and the LPDFA were structured as inclusive power-sharing arrangements, designed to distribute control over government policy and state resources among the various parties to the conflict. Arguably, Libya would have been better served by a constraining power-sharing arrangement that provided for the formation of a government with members aligned by political vision coupled with institutional constraints and protections for opponents, unrepresented constituencies, and ordinary citizens (Graham and Lupu 2016). However, the country's weak institutional environment, fragmented conflict actors, and low level of citizen trust in government (figure 3.1) would have rendered such an arrangement daunting and time consuming. For its part, a dispersive arrangement would likely have faltered on issues related to the equitable distribution of oil resources, not to mention concerns about unchecked corruption and fears that decentralization initiatives could pave the way for the country's partition, even though polling data show that local government enjoys more trust than the national government (Arab Barometer 2020; Center for Insights in Survey Research 2019).

The LPA had aimed to end the dispute between the General National Congress (GNC), the elected legislature seated in 2012, and the House of Representatives (HoR), the legislature seated following the narrow mandate of 2014 elections, the results of which were rejected by many in the GNC (ICG 2016). The agreement created a Presidency Council tasked with forming a government in Tripoli, led by HoR member Fayez al-Sarraj and several deputies and ministers, an arrangement intended to provide regional balance while securing the buy-in of various factions and communities. Under the agreement, the GNC would become the High Council of State (HCS)—an advisory body—while the HoR would continue as Libya's sole legislature, approving appointments to Al-Sarraj's unity government, the Government of National Accord (GNA). The agreement recognized the need to protect the integrity of Libya's sovereign economic entities, including the Central Bank of Libya (CBL), the National Oil Company (NOC), and the Libyan Investment Authority (LIA), and specified mechanisms of cooperation between the HoR and the HCS for appointing heads of economic, judicial, and oversight institutions (UNSMIL 2015).

Although the GNA was seated with UN recognition as Libya's legitimate government, the agreement was not ratified by the HoR. Support from Eastern

FIGURE 3.1

Trust in public institutions in Libya, 2018–19

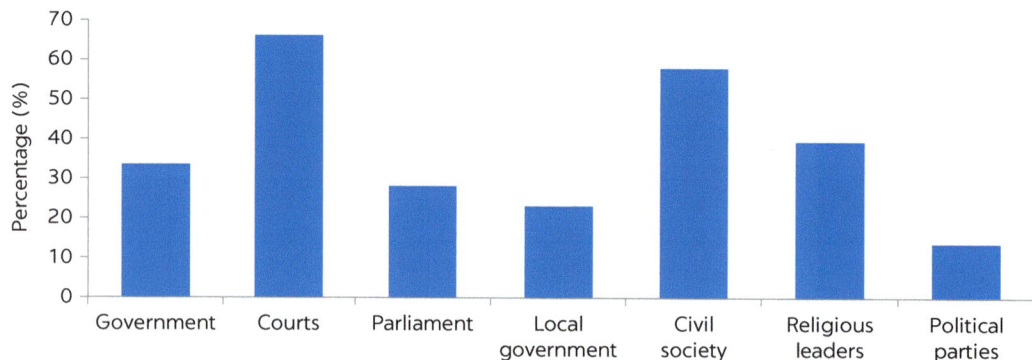

Source: Arab Barometer 2020.
Note: Figure shows percentage of respondents who indicate that each institution can be trusted a great deal or to some extent.

political factors dissolved under continued disputes about control over the CBL, the NOC, and the LIA, and, more importantly, a provision of the LPA empowering the GNA to designate the leaders of a united Libya's armed forces and security services (ICG 2016). Faced with such constraints, the HoR-backed Libyan National Army (LNA) rejected the agreement and, with significant diplomatic, military, and financial support from abroad, escalated efforts to seize territory and control over oil production and export terminals between 2016 and 2018 (Winer 2019). In the process, the LNA and the parallel government institutions under its control reinforced Libya's fragility (figure 3.2) and ushered in a pronounced period of instability and conflict.

Although oil production and export capacity began to recover in 2016, this took place amid a significant decline in international oil prices. Faced with tightening budget constraints, both the GNA and the parallel government in the East resorted to uncoordinated financing of a ballooning national fiscal deficit through the CBL (Harchaoui 2019; ICG 2019). The introduction of a Russian-printed parallel dinar through the CBL's Bayda branch and continued disruption of the national payment system fragmented the banking sector geographically, compounded recurring liquidity shortages (see chapter 2), and accelerated the depreciation of the dinar on the black market, all as the informal economy expanded and highly subsidized imported fuel was smuggled across the border.

Meanwhile, the CBL's efforts to protect international reserves by rationing foreign exchange through officially administered letters of credit and allowances for personal international transfers—all at the overvalued official exchange rate—incentivized widespread abuse and corruption by traders, militias, and politicians (Eaton 2018; Noria Research 2019).

In turn, the standard of living for ordinary Libyans declined, as did policy coherence. Efforts by the international community to facilitate institutional unification and budget consolidation between Tripoli and Bayda yielded few tangible benefits. Even within the GNA, policy formulation and execution were

FIGURE 3.2

Fragile states index for Libya and regional comparators, 2006–21

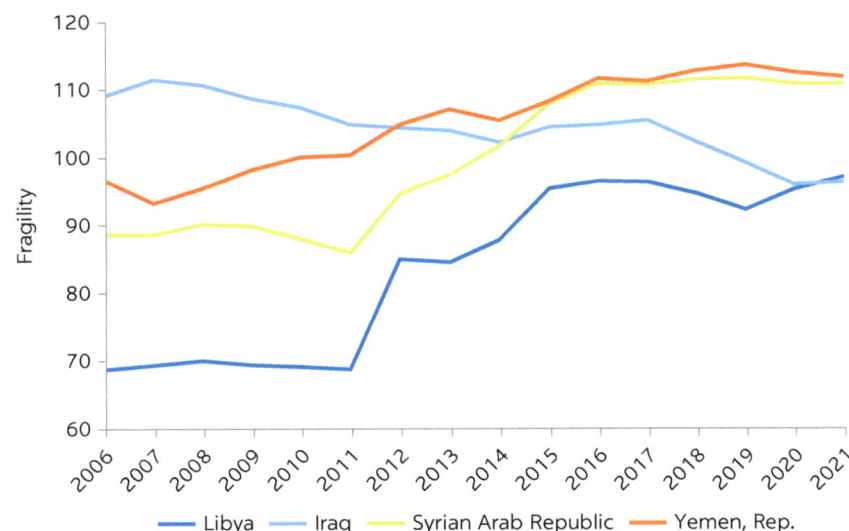

Source: Fund for Peace 2021.
Note: The index ranges from 0 to 120, with higher values indicating greater fragility.

haphazard, and long-standing reform proposals to the costly public sector pay-roll and subsidy programs were repeatedly shelved, notwithstanding available technical support from international financial institutions (Mezran and Melcangi 2020). The GNA became increasingly preoccupied by the need to shore up support from fragmented political constituencies, on the one hand, and the recurring crises that came to typify its relationships with independent bodies, including the Administrative Control Authority, the Audit Bureau, and the CBL, on the other. Extended delays to salary payments, chronic power cuts, periodic shortages of fuel products, and a decline in the provision of basic public services became the norm, reflecting a general deterioration in the quality of governance (figure 3.3).

As UNSMIL prepared to hold a national conference on April 2019 to deal with the crisis of legitimacy and agree on a new roadmap for the country, the conflict witnessed its most intensive and dangerous escalation as the LNA, with robust foreign military support, attacked and laid siege to Tripoli with the declared goal of unseating the UN-backed GNA. After months of brutal fighting, opposing forces under GNA command, having secured military support from abroad in early 2020, launched a counterattack that eventually drove the LNA out of the Western region of the country. While active hostilities continued after June 2020, forces on both sides (and their international supporters) increasingly recognized the rising costs of conflict and the futility of efforts to secure a military victory. Meanwhile, the country faced economic collapse, driven by another massive fiscal crisis after the suspension of oil production and exports by the LNA, as well as growing fears over the potential impact of the COVID-19 pandemic (World Bank 2021).

UNSMIL seized on this opportunity to push for a new agreement in 2020. Learning from its experience with the unsuccess of LPA, UNSMIL prioritized engagement with the external powers backing each side in Libya's civil war to secure their buy-in and preclude any derailment of an agreement on their part (Williams and Salamé 2021). In January 2020, it convened representatives of key foreign governments and international institutions in Berlin, securing an agreement in support of Libyan dialogue (UNSMIL 2021a). At the same time, UNSMIL negotiators began working with Libyans to put in place three parallel working groups: the Libyan Political Dialogue Forum, the Libyan Economic Dialogue,

FIGURE 3.3

Selected governance indicators, 2009–19

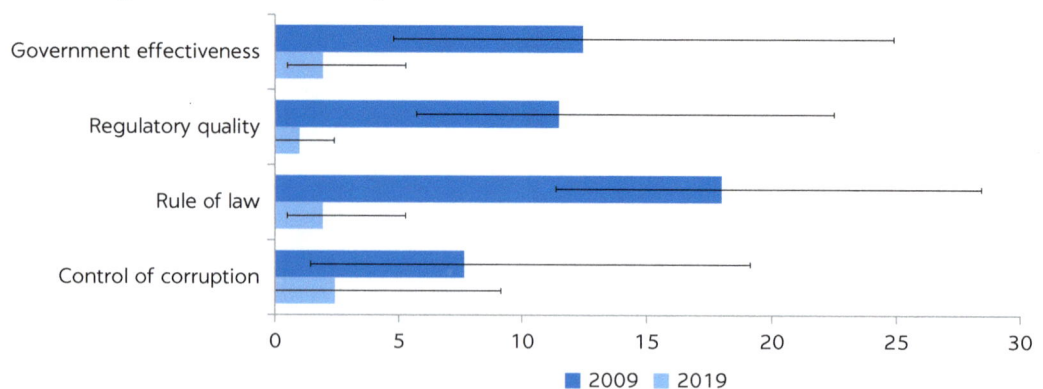

Source: Worldwide Governance Indicators, various dates.

and the Joint Military Commission. While progress on these three fronts was halting, the Joint Military Commission was able to secure a ceasefire agreement and monitor its implementation. The Economic Dialogue worked on several proposals to establish national spending priorities and unify government institutions. After several rounds of difficult deliberation, the LPDF announced in February the agreement that would establish the GNU.

INITIAL PROSPECTS AND CHALLENGES FOR THE 2021 AGREEMENT

Under the LPDFA, the initial transition from GNA to GNU was orderly. The prime minister put forward an early plan to stimulate the economy and to begin rebuilding basic public services, laying the groundwork for building broader public trust in and support for government. And, at least on the surface, the power-sharing agreement resulted in a government broadly representative of Libya's diverse political factions and social groups. The tripartite Presidency Council included representatives from Libya's historic regions of Tripolitania, Cyrenaica, and Fazzan. Both the LPDF and the GNU include former government leaders, academics, activists, technocrats, and businesspeople from a variety of political, regional, and tribal backgrounds. The two groups also include individuals associated with the Gaddafi administration, who were excluded from previous post-revolution governments.

The vulnerabilities of the power-sharing agreement nevertheless became evident in the early stages of the transition as the GNU attempted to tackle critical issues, such as finalizing the government budget, appointing ministers and heads of public sector companies, and managing the competing agendas of international actors (including foreign forces remaining inside the country). The prime minister and the three members of the Presidency Council do not share a clear political vision. Moreover, the prime minister had little to no influence over the selection of ministers, as he emphasized following the seating of the Cabinet. This, and the explicit agreement on securing consensus on major issues within the Presidency Council and with the speaker of the HoR, has limited his ability to move his policy priorities forward (Al-Wasat 2021). Notably, the GNU's Cabinet structure, with 35 ministers appointed based largely on whom they represent over their personal capabilities, has left the government with little cohesion to formulate, coordinate, and implement policy.

In addition to these challenges, there is evidence that positions in the GNU were doled out more cynically than implied by the representative façade of selected members. As has been observed elsewhere with inclusive power-sharing agreements, entrenched elites and powerful political actors in Libya played a decisive role in the appointment process (Lacher 2021). Many of the new government leaders have held positions in past governments or maintain links to patronage networks that have fostered clientelism in the past. As Lacher (2021) notes, "The agreement rehabilitated this very elite, reshuffling access to spoils among the political class." At the same time, perhaps as important as who is in the GNU is who is not: granting positions on the (partial) basis of tribal, regional, and political affiliation invariably leaves many constituencies underrepresented, which may feed into existing grievances and distrust.

Importantly, Libya's power-sharing agreement was reached by avoiding some of the most politically contentious issues. This avoidance may reflect learning from the unsuccess of the LPA, which had specified the unity government's control over these sensitive matters. To date, the country's leadership has yet to agree on difficult questions associated with the military and economic aspects of the conflict, including the following:

- *Armed forces, foreign fighters, and public security:* The continued presence of militias and private armies, as well as the government's dependence on some of these forces to provide local security and policing, ensure that potential spoilers maintain the capacity to disrupt the political process. At the same time, the departure of foreign military forces, agreed to under the terms of Libya's ceasefire, has not occurred. Efforts to unify the military command, put in place a national military, and support local governments in establishing police forces are essential to enhance security and undermine spoilers. There has been no agreement to date on how to move forward in this regard. Political actors have deferred to the standing Joint Military Command, but it has focused on monitoring the ceasefire.

- *Control over independent government agencies:* Since the country fragmented in 2014, legislators and government officials in Tobruk and Tripoli have grappled over the leadership of Libya's key independent agencies (most notably, the CBL and the Audit Bureau, but also the NOC and LIA, technically under the GNU's control). Governance of these institutions is highly contentious because of their control over Libya's financial resources and government spending. Any near-term resolution to appoint individuals to positions of leadership over these institutions, as sought unilaterally by the HoR in April and May 2021, will likely come down to regional representation rather than technocratic expertise, exposing the institutions to political manipulation and undermining their ability to protect Libya's resources.

- *National oil resources and equitable redistribution:* Libya's oil wealth has been the grand prize for competing conflict actors. Without a common national vision for how oil resources are redistributed, political reconciliation will continue to be undermined by actors who tap into population grievances about how revenues are spent to further their own political ambitions (El Krekshi 2020). Meanwhile, prospects for Libya's oil industry remain uncertain, as its oil infrastructure deteriorates, oil prices remain volatile, and developed countries invest more heavily in green alternatives (Barltrop 2019). The challenge has only increased with the recent surge in international oil prices, an increase that will bolster revenues in the short term but does not necessarily change the fundamentals defining long-term prospects for the sector.

FAILED ELECTIONS, POLITICAL FALLOUT, AND INCREASED UNCERTAINTY

The LPDFA has offered Libya a new path toward permanent, sustainable governance arrangements after a decade of political transitions that were interrupted by crisis and violence. However, like its predecessor the LPA, the LPDFA rests on a fragile foundation, one that has proven vulnerable to the machinations of political rivals and the lack of trust among Libya's fluid and fractured ruling coalitions (Lacher 2018). This vulnerability is heightened by the inclusive nature of the power-sharing arrangement, the lack of institutional constraints on political leaders in Libya, and heightened public expectations of a return to normalcy.

Even more unpredictable is the behavior of external actors and the direction of regional geopolitics. Both factors were favorable to securing the power-sharing agreement within the broader context of the COVID-19 pandemic, the global economic slowdown, and renewed US commitment to international cooperation under the Biden administration, all of which fostered a mode of de-escalation among regional rivals toward Libya (Dalay and Yousef 2022).

The fragility of the power-sharing agreement became more pronounced in the run-up to the planned national elections on December 24, 2021, and the political crisis that ensued after their postponement. Libyans had taken a more skeptical view of the GNU over the summer of 2021, turning to elections as a means of addressing political divisions and the challenges facing the country. However, the HoR and HSC could not reach an agreement on the constitutional basis for elections as envisioned by the LPDFA (UNSMIL 2021b). Likewise, UNSMIL's efforts to facilitate a legal basis through the LPDF fell through. Political leaders began floating proposals on the timing and sequencing of presidential and parliamentary elections as well as the referendum to ratify the constitution. Not surprisingly, political rivals seized on the opportunity to influence the process so as to eliminate potential challengers. The election law forced through by the speaker of the HoR in September 2021 proved too polarizing and controversial to provide a consensual basis for elections (Ahmed 2021). As such, the decision by the Libyan Elections Board to effectively postpone the December elections was unsurprising.

While the stipulation that elections be held in December was critical to securing support for the LPDFA agreement and the birth of the GNU, it always seemed impractical that a country emerging from a violent conflict and lacking strong institutions would be able to organize free and fair elections in less than a year. With a limited tradition of party politics, weak civil society, and an HoR election law forbidding party lists, the vote likely would have perpetuated the dominance of tribal, regional, and transactional politics in recent years. Moreover, without an agreement on the constitutional basis, the legitimacy of any election outcomes would be subject to question, aggravating political divisions and institutional fragmentation and perhaps pushing the country back into war (Fishman 2021). Finally, it has not escaped the public's attention that the incumbent leaders trusted with organizing the vote (HoR, HSC, GNU, etc.) have always had an incentive to prolong their tenure and preserve the status quo, including through the undermining of progress toward holding elections (Badi and Lacher 2021).

The delay in holding elections has triggered a more immediate political crisis. The GNU's tenure had been set to expire once elections were held in December. Now, operating with uncertain legitimacy, the GNU's prime minister intends to stay in office until national elections are held. At the same time, the HoR has moved to place a new prime minister in office immediately while also passing a roadmap calling for elections and a constitutional referendum in 2023, effectively extending the political transition by another 14 months. Both steps by HoR have been challenged by the HSC in Tripoli as well as influential armed groups in the West. As a result, nearly a year into the power-sharing agreement, political actors are once again polarizing the country and raising the prospect of a violent confrontation rather than moving the country closer to permanent governance arrangements. Moreover, while the GNU retains international recognition, the aggressive positioning of the HoR suggests that external actors are once again manipulating the domestic scene for their own ends (Megerisi 2022).

BEYOND THE LIMITATIONS OF POWER SHARING

Given the lack of progress in moving forward on national development priorities and the recent repolarization of the political process in Libya, it is difficult to imagine an optimal solution for the country in the context of the current power-sharing agreement. While it is important to emphasize that the power-sharing agreement has ensured relative stability in the country for nearly a year and has shifted the strategies of power centers in Libya toward political contestation over conflict, the situation remains volatile. In other ways, from the expansion of corruption to the threat of a return to violence, the limits of the inclusive power-sharing arrangement governing Libya's efforts to establish a peaceful resolution to the civil war have become increasingly evident (Jacobs 2022).

Absent a referendum on the controversial draft constitution from 2017 or an agreed upon process and timeline for resolving the ongoing crisis in constitutional legitimacy (Ross 2021), the current power-sharing agreement likely offers the country its best opportunity for moving forward toward a sustainable and stable peace. As such, Libyan leaders and the international community should continue to support efforts to hold elections as quickly as possible, bearing in mind that the proposed timeline of June 2022 is likely not possible. As a matter of priority, this also means that the international community should help diffuse the escalating rift between the incumbent GNU prime minister and the HoR–appointed successor, which threatens to unravel the LPDFA without providing Libyans a consensual pathway forward that balances the need for political legitimacy through elections with sustaining public trust and maintaining stability (Forster 2019).

In tandem with efforts to contain the immediate crisis and others that will surely arise in the coming period, there are areas in which domestic and international actors can shore up political support for the fragile LPDFA and bolster its durability. International experience with post-conflict transition arrangements has emphasized the importance of viewing transition agreements as a process that requires regular maintenance, interventions that adapt to changing conditions and contexts, and mediation efforts between the political interests of various parties (Forster 2019). In Libya, there are several means for doing so, including through support for institutions that constrain political actors, efforts to combat corruption, and investments in government capacity for service delivery.

SUPPORTING CONSTRAINING INSTITUTIONS

Libya's current power-sharing arrangement does not constrain the actions of political leaders enough to enforce the rule of law and avoid exacerbating popular grievances and distrust in government. Institutions are weak, and the bodies vested with providing checks and balances are themselves either parties to the conflict or paralyzed. However, it may not be too late to implement institutional constraints, as follows:

- *Empowering the judicial system to provide oversight*: Constraining agreements often depend on the judicial system, especially a supreme court, to limit overreach by executives and legislatures. Although Libya's judiciary has suffered post-revolution, it has largely escaped fragmentation and enjoys more public trust than any other governmental or civilian institution (figure 3.3). The

Supreme Judicial Council (SJC), for example, could be empowered to provide checks on abuses by the legislature and government and ensure protection of citizen rights. Although the absence of an active constitution may limit the SJC's powers, the 1951 constitution, the 2011 draft constitution, and existing legislation provide a basis for judicial action. UNSMIL could work through the LPDF to create such a role for the SJC, and international actors could provide technical support.

- *Protecting the integrity of independent economic institutions*: Libya's sovereign economic institutions, which perform a crucial role in generating, managing, and monitoring public funds, are critical to the country's current economic recovery and future prosperity. As it did consistently during the conflict, the international community needs to make explicit its commitment to supporting the integrity and independence of these institutions and, to the extent possible, neutralize attempts to politicize their management during the period leading up to national elections. Political leaders should focus on unifying the parallel structures and enhancing the governance of these institutions, to strengthen policy making, provide transparency, and rebuild public trust (Bell 2018).

- *Protecting and building capacity for civil society*: Independent civil society organizations (CSOs) play an essential role as constraining watchdogs in the context of power-sharing agreements, while offering new governments an instrument for community engagement and the provision of equitable public services (Barnes 2006). Although CSOs proliferated in Libya after the revolution, many have failed or have been politicized; others suffer from capacity constraints. The ability of CSOs in Libya to play their role in stabilizing the country's political and economic transition depends on the GNU leadership and the judicial system taking steps to ensure freedom of association and protecting CSOs from threats of political retribution or physical violence from militias (Cairo Institute for Human Rights Studies 2019; Romanet Perroux 2015).

IMPROVING GOVERNANCE AND FIGHTING CORRUPTION

Libya has one of the lowest levels of trust in government within the Middle East and North Africa region (figure 3.4), and the public believes corruption is endemic in the public sector. Domestic and international actors should prioritize anticorruption efforts to rebuild citizen trust in government and enable sustainable policy implementation. Successful anticorruption initiatives in post-conflict environments depend on cooperation between the government, courts, civil society, and international organizations (Fenwick 2011). Such efforts will be challenging, given Libya's weak institutions, low absorption capacity, and large government expenditures (Chene 2012; Dix and Jayawickrama 2010).

Libya's Office of the Attorney General and the Audit Bureau have a mandate to pursue cases of corruption, and both entities have demonstrated their willingness to bring charges against government officials for corruption among GNU ministers (Asharq Al-Awsat 2022). Their ability to continue playing this role effectively will require concrete commitments from government and legislative leaders in support of the anticorruption effort. International organizations can support anticorruption efforts by providing technical assistance and employee training, as well as by facilitating coordination between government agencies. The LPDF also could amend the power-sharing agreement to create anticorruption

FIGURE 3.4

Perceptions of corruption in government in the Middle East and North Africa, 2018–19

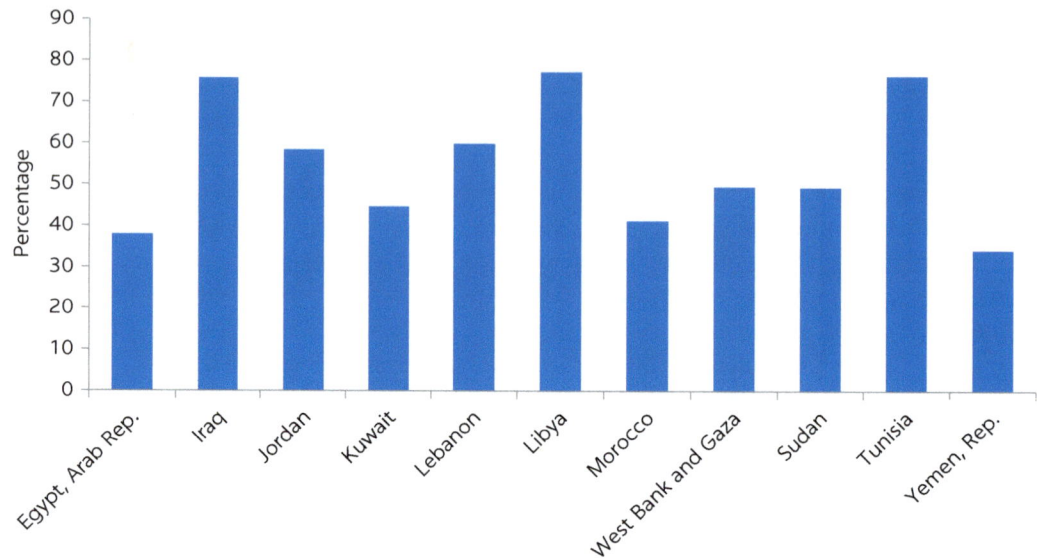

Source: Arab Barometer 2020.
Note: Figure shows percentage of respondents who believe there is corruption to a large extent in government.

provisions and mechanisms of oversight. CSOs play an important role in monitoring and reporting suspected corruption; to do so in Libya, they must be protected by law and supported by external funding (Dix and Jayawickrama 2010).

BUILDING GOVERNMENT CAPACITY FOR PUBLIC SERVICE DELIVERY

The government's ability to build popular trust and citizen buy-in will depend primarily on its ability to improve basic public services. Long-standing under-investment and overregulation have limited and misdirected the capacity of Libya's ministries, subministerial agencies, and local governments. The public sector also has experienced a steady exodus of talent and expertise during the past decade of instability and mismanagement. Although the GNU may not have the mandate to engage in long-term development planning, bureaucratic upskilling can lay the foundation for sustained international technical assistance to guide the work of Libya's civil servants and enable them to deliver at a higher level. Even in the short term, international technical experts can work with Libyan counterparts to formulate quick wins and develop initiatives that do not undermine reforms, limit future options, or trigger political tensions within the power-sharing structure (Bell 2018).

The GNU's economic policy decisions must be made with an eye toward future sustainability. Many policy initiatives adopted by the GNU and other proposed populist measures do not meet this criterion. They include public sector salary increases, which add to mounting fiscal burdens, and rapid implementation of large public investment schemes, which are susceptible to capture by vested interests. As Wittes, Saba, and Huggard (2020) note, "Ill-informed or inadequate approaches to stabilization and development might recreate or reinforce drivers of conflict and fragility." A municipal- or city-based development strategy that includes small- and medium-size enterprises can deliver tangible results in the short term and provide an alternative to centralized planning and service delivery (Allen et al. 2019). Such an approach also would help reframe regional disputes over resource distribution as technical problems, enable better economic planning, and encourage policy makers to understand the long-term costs of poor policy decisions. Ensuring that Libya's political leaders understand the international consequences of corruption can help improve transparency in decision making and public financial management.

CONCLUDING REMARKS

Given the challenges facing Libya's unity government, the limited progress made over its life span, and the vulnerability of the power-sharing arrangement to domestic and geopolitical spoilers, it is easy to take a dark view of the prospects for the current power-sharing agreement's ability to maintain peace and begin the task of rebuilding the country. Viewed as a short-term bridge to long-term stability, however, the power-sharing agreement may provide a singular opportunity to end the conflict, build a shared vision for development, and lay the foundations for a new social contract.

Securing this bridge requires that Libyans and their international supporters avoid reducing the problem to the realization of holding national elections by any set date. Even when elections take place, Libya will continue to struggle with issues left unaddressed during the formation of and by the GNU. Moreover, elections in the context of a corrupt political system dominated by identity politics will likely reproduce the existing government structure rather than bringing together an impactful coalition of aligned political actors and technocrats.

International experience with conflict resolution suggests that domestic actors and external parties, while continuing to support the GNU and the power-sharing agreement, can enable a transition to a sustainable political resolution. This can be accomplished by empowering constraining institutional structures, building broader government capacity, promoting good governance, and working with Libyan communities to advance a shared national vision. While such efforts will take time and will not provide a panacea for the myriad challenges facing Libya, they provide the foundations for institutionalization, civic engagement and the rebuilding of public trust that will ensure greater citizen engagement and sustainable governance going forward.

REFERENCES

Ahmed, Nada. 2021. "Libya's Elections and Stability." Washington, DC: Tahrir Institute for Middle East Policy. https://timep.org/commentary/analysis/libyas-elections-and-stability/.

Allen, John, Hady Amr, Daniel L. Bryman, Vanda Felbab-Brown, Jeffrey Feltman, Alice Friend, Jason Fritz, et al. 2019. *Empowered Decentralization: A City-Based Strategy for Rebuilding Libya*. Washington, DC: Brookings Institution.

Al-Wasat. 2021. "جريدة «الوسط» :تحديات تنتظر حكومة الدبيبة: الخدمات و«كورونا والانتخابات»" (Challenges await Dabaiba government: services, corona, and elections), *Al-Wasat*, March 12, 2021. http://alwasat.ly/news/ibya/313930.

Arab Barometer. 2020. *Arab Barometer V*. Ann Arbor, MI: Inter-University Consortium for Political and Social Research.

Asharq Al-Awsat. 2022. "Third Libya Minister Detained over Alleged Graft," *Asharq Al-Awsat,* January 27, 2022. https://english.aawsat.com/home/article/3439491/third-libya-minister -detained-over-alleged-graft.

Badi, Emadeddin, and Wolfram Lacher. 2021. "Agree to Disagree: Libya's New Unity Government." *Sada* (blog), February 8, 2021. Carnegie Endowment for International Peace, Washington, DC.

Barltrop, Richard. 2019. "Oil and Gas in the New Libyan Era: Conflict and Continuity." OIES Paper 22, Oxford Institute for Energy Studies, UK. https://www.oxfordenergy.org /wpcms/wp-content/uploads/2019/02/Oil-and-Gas-in-a-New-Libyan-Era-Conflict-and -Continuity-MEP-22.pdf.

Barnes, Catherine. 2006. "Agents for Change: Civil Society Roles in Preventing War and Building Peace." Issue Paper 2, Global Partnership for the Prevention of Armed Conflict, The Hague. https://www.gppac.net/files/2018-11/Agents%20for%20Change.pdf.

Bell, Christine. 2018. *Economic Power-Sharing, Conflict Resolution and Development in Peace Negotiations and Agreements.* Scotland: Political Settlements Research Programme, University of Edinburgh. https://www.politicalsettlements.org/publications-database/economic-power -sharing-conflict-resolution-and-development-in-peace-negotiations-and-agreements/.

Cairo Institute for Human Rights Studies. 2019. "Libya: CSOs Must Challenge Executive Authorities' Denial of Freedom of Association." Press Release November 25. https://cihrs.org /libya-csos-must-challenge-executive-authorities-denial-of-freedom-of-association/?lang=en.

Center for Insights in Survey Research. 2019. *Public Opinion Survey: Fifteen Municipalities of Libya, December 31, 2018–January 31, 2019.* Washington, DC: Center for Insights in Survey Research.

Chene, Marie. 2020. "Lessons Learned in Fighting Corruption in Post-Conflict Countries." U4 Expert Answer 355, December 17, 2020, Transparency International, London. https://www .u4.no/publications/lessons-learned-in-fighting-corruption-in-post-conflict-countries/pdf.

Dalay, Galip, and Tarik Yousef. 2022. "Making Sense of the Great Reset," *National Interest,* January 9, 2022. https://nationalinterest.org/feature/making-sense-middle-east%E2 %80%99s-%E2%80%98great-reset%E2%80%99-199065.

Dix, Sarah, and Nihal Jayawickrama. 2010. *Fighting Corruption in Post-Conflict and Recovery Situations: Learning from the Past.* New York: United Nations Development Programme. http://content-ext.undp.org/aplaws_publications/2594849/Fighting%20corruption%20 in%20post-conflict%20and%20recovery%20situations.pdf.

Eaton, Tim. 2018. *Libya's War Economy: Predation, Profiteering and State Weakness.* London: Chatham House. https://www.chathamhouse.org/2018/04/libyas-war-economy-predation -profiteering-and-state-weakness.

El Krekshi, Maruan. 2020. "Libya: Before Power-Sharing Deals, Libyans Must Define a National Vision." *Africa Report,* October 26, 2020. https://www.theafricareport.com/47311/ibya -before-power-sharing-deals-libyans-must-define-a-national-vision/.

Fenwick, Luke. 2011. "Counter-Corruption Reforms in Post-conflict Countries: Metrics, Indicators and Impact in Rwanda, Liberia, and Serbia." Back Papers/Reform Experience, Transparency International UK, London. https://ti-defence.org/wp-content/uploads /2016/03/2011-10_CounterCorruptionReforms_PostConflict.pdf.

Fishman, Ben. 2021. "December Elections in Libya Risk a Return to Civil War." *National Interest* November 21, 2021. https://nationalinterest.org/feature/december-elections-libya -risk-return-civil-war-196702.

Fishman, Ben. 2022. "Libya's Renewed Legitimacy Crisis," PolicyWatch 3577, February 14, 2022, Washington Institute for Near East Policy, Washington, DC. https://www.washingtoninstitute .org/policy-analysis/libyas-renewed-legitimacy-crisis.

Forster, Robert. 2019. "Interim Governance Arrangements in Post-Conflict and Fragile Settings." Presented at the International Institute for Democracy and Electoral Assistance's "Sixth Edinburgh Dialogue on Post-Conflict Constitution-Building." Scotland: University of Edinburgh. https://www.idea.int/sites/default/files/publications/interim-governance -arrangements-in-post-conflict-and-fragile-settings.pdf.

Fund for Peace. 2021. Fragile States Index, database. Washington, DC: Fund for Peace.

Furness, Mark, and Bernhard Trautner. 2020. "Reconstituting Social Contracts in Conflict-Affected MENA Countries: Whither Iraq and Libya?" *World Development* 135: 1–12. https://doi.org/10.1016/j.worlddev.2020.105085.

Gates, Scott, Benjamin A. T. Graham, Yonatan Lupu, Håvard Strand, and Kaare W. Strøm. 2017. "Power Sharing, Protection, and Peace." *Journal of Politics* 78 (2): 512–26. https://doi:10.1086/684366.

Graham, Benjamin A. T., and Yonatan Lupu. 2016. "What's the Best Path to Peace in Libya?" *Washington Post*, March 3, 2016. https://www.washingtonpost.com/news/monkey-cage/wp/2016/03/03/whats-the-best-path-to-peace-in-libya/.

Graham, Benjamin A. T., Michael Miller, and Kaare Strøm. 2017. "Safeguarding Democracy: Power-Sharing and Democratic Survival." *American Political Science Review* 111 (4): 686–704. https://www.cambridge.org/core/journals/american-political-science-review/article/safeguarding-democracy-powersharing-and-democratic-survival/D31FFD5C1EE8DF14FA2C9BB8E73536EB.

Haass, Felix, and Martin Ottman. 2017. "Profits from Peace: The Political Economy of Power-Sharing and Corruption." *World Development* 99: 60–74. https://www.sciencedirect.com/science/article/pii/S0305750X17302401.

Harchaoui, Jalel. 2019. "Libya's Looming Contest for the Central Bank." *Clingendael Magazine*, April 2, 2019. https://www.clingendael.org/publication/libyas-looming-contest-central-bank.

Heydemann, Steven. 2018. "Civil War, Economic Governance and State Reconstruction in the Arab Middle East." *Daedalus* 147 (Winter): 48–63. https://direct.mit.edu/daed/article/147/1/48/27180/Civil-War-Economic-Governance-amp-State.

ICG (International Crisis Group). 2016. *The Libyan Political Agreement: Time for a Reset*. Report 170. Brussels: ICG. https://www.crisisgroup.org/middle-east-north-africa/north-africa/libya/libya-political-agreement-time-reset.

ICG (International Crisis Group). 2019. *Of Tanks and Banks: Stopping a Dangerous Escalation in Libya*. Middle East and North Africa Report 20. Brussels: ICG.

Jacobs, Anna. 2022. "Libya Backslides as Two Governments Vie for Power, Again." The Arab Gulf States Institute in Washington blog. February 22, 2022. https://agsiw.org/libya-backslides-as-two-governments-vie-for-power-again/.

Lacher, Wolfram. 2018. "Libya: The Gamble that Failed." In *Mission Impossible? UN Mediation in Libya, Syria and Yemen*, edited by Muriel Asseburg, Wolfram Lacher, and Mareike Transfeld. SWP Research Paper 8, Stiftung Wissenschaft und Politik, German Institute for International and Security Affairs, Berlin. https://www.swp-berlin.org/en/publication/mission-impossible-un-mediation-in-libya-syria-and-yemen/.

Lacher, Wolfram. 2021. *Libya's Flawed Unity Government: A Semblance of Compromise Obscures Old and New Rifts*. SWP Comment 29, Stiftung Wissenschaft und Politik, German Institute for International and Security Affairs, Berlin. https://www.swp-berlin.org/10.18449/2021C29/.

Mattes, Michaela, and Burcu Savun. 2009. "Fostering Peace after Civil War: Commitment Problems and Agreement Design." *International Studies Quarterly* 53 (3): 737–59. https://www.jstor.org/stable/27735119.

Megerisi, Tarek. 2021. "Libya Crisis: The Unity Government's Success Hides Serious Dangers Ahead." *Middle East Eye*, April 13, 2021. https://www.middleeasteye.net/opinion/libya-new-unity-government-dangers-ahead.

Megerisi, Tarek. 2022. "The Man from Misrata: Why Libya Has Two Prime Ministers (Again)," Commentary, February 16, 2022, European Council on Foreign Relations, Berlin. https://ecfr.eu/article/the-man-from-misrata-why-libya-has-two-prime-ministers-again/.

Mezran, Khalid, and Alessia Melcangi. 2020. *Economic Interests, Political Conflicts, and External Interferences: The Complex Interlocking of the Libyan Crisis*. Philadelphia, PA: Foreign Policy Research Institute. https://www.fpri.org/wp-content/uploads/2020/11/economic-interests-political-conflicts.pdf.

Noria Research. 2019. *Predatory Economies in Eastern Libya: The Dominant Role of the Libyan National Army*. Geneva: Global Initiative against Transnational Organized Crime.

Romanet Perroux, Jean-Louis. 2015. "Libya's Untold Story: Civil Society Amid Chaos." Middle East Brief 93, Brandeis University, Waltham, MA. https://www.brandeis.edu/crown /publications/middle-east-briefs/pdfs/1-100/meb93.pdf.

Ross, Simona. 2021. "Lost in Translation: Constitutional Legitimacy in Libya," *Journal of Constitutional Law in the Middle East and North Africa* (December 2021). http://jcl-mena .org/article.php?aid=9&iname=7.

UNSMIL (United Nations Support Mission in Libya). 2015. "The Libyan Political Agreement, as signed on 17 December 2015." Tripoli: UNSMIL. https://unsmil.unmissions.org/libya -political-agreement.

UNSMIL (United Nations Support Mission in Libya). 2021a. *Berlin International Conference on Libya: 19 January 2020.* Tripoli: UNSMIL. https://unsmil.unmissions.org/berlin -international-conference-libya-19-january-2020.

UNSMIL (United Nations Support Mission in Libya). 2021b. "UNSMIL Is Pleased to Announce the Convening of a Two-Day Virtual Meeting of the LPDF to Finalise the LC Proposal on the Constitutional Basis for Parliamentary and Presidential Elections." Press Release, May 19, 2021. https://unsmil.unmissions.org/unsmil-pleased-announce-convening-two -day-virtual-meeting-lpdf-finalise-lc-proposal-constitutional.

Williams, Stephanie, and Ghassan Salamé. 2021. "Why There's Hope for Libya." *Newlines*, April 22, 2021. https://newlinesmag.com/argument/why-theres-hope-for-libya/.

Winer, Jonathan. 2019. *Origins of the Libyan Crisis and Options for Its Resolution.* Policy Paper 2019-4, Middle East Institute, Washington, DC.

Wittes, Tamara, Joseph Saba, and Kevin Huggard. 2020. *Stabilization and Human Development in a Disordered Middle East and North Africa: Lessons from a Joint Brookings–World Bank Project.* Washington, DC: Brookings Institution.

World Bank. 2021. *Libya Economic Monitor—Spring 2021.* Washington, DC: World Bank. https:// www.worldbank.org/en/country/ibya/publication/ibya-economic-monitor-spring-2021.

World Bank, various dates. Worldwide Governance Indicators database. Washington, DC: World Bank. http://info.worldbank.org/governance/wgi/.

4 Setting the Stage for Public Sector Reform

MICHAEL G. SCHAEFFER, ZIED OUELHAZI, MAROUA LASSOUED,
WESAL ASHUR, AND KANAE WATANABE

World Bank

*The authors provide that to drive economic growth and support economic
stabilization, Libya could use this moment to modernize the structure of its
economy, diversify away from near-total oil dependency, and foster the
development of the private sector (with support of the financial sector) and use it
to drive job creation. In providing a very detailed overview of Libyan public
finances during the period of two competing public administrations, the authors
maintain that it is crucial to try to advance structural governance and public
financial management (PFM) reforms. Libyans need to prioritize activities that
improve the functioning of institutions by improving accountability frameworks.*

INTRODUCTION

Libya's economic decline has been universal, affecting everyone. Following the
revolution, state institutions have struggled to function and to secure legitimacy. The fall of Muammar Gaddafi engendered the prospect for more inclusive and transparent institutions to emerge that could manage public resources
fairly and accountably.[1] Despite these initial hopes, the weak institutional environment and the poor quality of service delivery have further undermined citizens' trust in the state.

The situation in Libya continues to remain fragile. Actors competing for space
within the illicit economy continue to fuel domestic tensions. These militias
have grown into sophisticated criminal networks that straddle business, politics,
and the administration (Lacher 2018). Over the past decade, state resources were
plundered to the benefit of a narrow group of actors, leading those excluded
from the current status quo to build alliances aimed at forcefully altering the
balance of power. Meanwhile, rent seeking and war profiteering continue, as the
illicit economy has evolved into a multibillion-dollar business based on smuggling, predation, and extortion. Most of the violence stems from criminal activity
and attempts to maintain and expand revenue from smuggling and extortion.

Prerevolution economic policies—including the introduction of state control
over the economy and the private sector's neglect—weigh heavily on Libya today.

The authors thank Dr. Marouane El Abassi, the former World Bank Group Country
Representative for Libya and current Central Bank Governor of Tunisia, for his excellent
professional guidance.

In the late 1980s, restricted privatization was permitted in some areas. However, state monopolies and policies to protect government-owned company interests caused huge market distortions, and large numbers of skilled workers—particularly from the well-educated upper class—have left the country to work abroad. The oil rentier state has resulted in a social contract based on public service without the need for taxation.

Unemployment has risen sharply, and public sector wages remain the sole source of income for many families. The non-oil economy accounts for a negligible part of total exports, accounting for only a minor percent of gross domestic product (GDP). With the steep decline of the non-oil economy over the past decade, many jobs have been lost and most families depend on public sector wages. To compensate for the economic decline and inflation, public salaries have increased multifold since 2012.

This chapter provides a brief economic and public financial explanatory overview of the Libyan economy over the past decade. We then provide a set of forward-looking public financial and policy recommendations.

EFFECT OF THE CONFLICT ON THE ECONOMY AND GOVERNANCE

As rival authorities competed for power during 2014–20, the resulting divisions and dysfunctional administrations became fertile ground for a pervasive war economy to develop, with militias taking control of the fragmented state (Lacher and Al-Idrissi 2018). The continuing crisis and conflict created perverse incentives for security and short-term gains over national stability. Militia groups were able to thrive by grabbing control of parts of the state apparatus.

Despite the installation of the international and domestically recognized Government of National Unity (GNU) in March 2021, militias continue to control many aspects of the economy, a reality that has evolved over the past 10 years and has deeply entrenched graft and corruption in all areas of the Libyan economy (Lacher 2018). A return to well-functioning central governance that is accountable and fully transparent is inimical to the major beneficiaries of the militia-based economy. As long as these underlying pressures and polarizing dynamics continue to fester, it will be extremely difficult for Libya's economy and society to regain stability and reimpose the rule of law.

AN UNBALANCED ECONOMY AND FISCAL SYSTEM

Heavy dependence on oil

Hydrocarbons—which account for about 75 percent of GDP, 95 percent of exports, and more than 97 percent of government revenues (figure 4.1)—have long dominated the Libyan economy (figure 4.2) (World Bank 2021). Much of Libya's fuel is smuggled outside the country, diverted directly from refineries, ports, and warehouses using falsified paperwork. Access to international criminal networks is required to sell the smuggled fuel (UNSC 2017). These networks cooperate with a variety of political actors in a classic case of state capture. The existence of international fuel-smuggling activities involving nearby countries is another indicator of the maturity of Libya's illicit economy (World Bank 2017).

With about 3.5 percent of the world's proven crude oil reserves, Libya has been in a prominent position in international oil markets. The economic impact

FIGURE 4.1

Real GDP, 2010–21

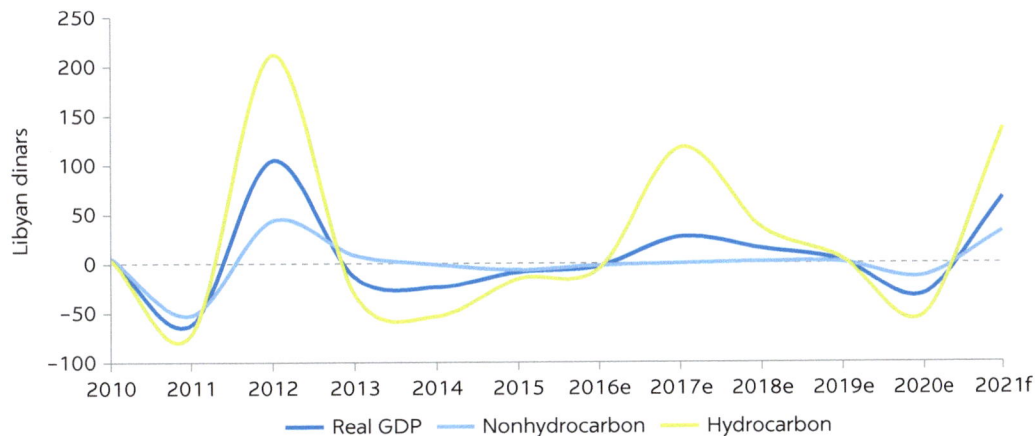

Source: Libyan authorities, World Bank, and International Monetary Fund (IMF) staff estimates.
Note: e = estimate; f = forecast; GDP = gross domestic product.

of the hostilities was felt in 2019 and 2020 as real GDP growth slowed sharply to 2.5 percent, down from what seemed a promising steady recovery during 2017–18, when it averaged 20.8 percent a year. Cross-border smuggling of refined fuel is well established with Tunisia, where the official price at the pump was 580 percent above the cost in Libya during 2017–19.[2] The fact that Libya's fuel remains heavily subsidized has contributed to the vibrant fuel-smuggling business (World Bank 2017).

The most common smuggling scheme involves ghost gasoline stations, which exist only on paper.[3] Loaded fuel trucks are diverted to the border or fuel is pumped into boats to ship to nearby countries (Ezzeddine 2018; Lacher 2018). Cross-border fuel smuggling consists mainly of relatively small-scale smugglers crossing the Tunisian border, using modified cars and vans fitted with oversized fuel tanks or series of jerrycans. To operate smoothly, the fuel-smuggling rings need to pay off border guards and local security forces on both sides of the border, thereby weakening institutions and contributing to fragility (Eaton 2018). The heavy dependence on and volatility of oil revenues as well as the rigidity of expenditure structure hinders Libya's fiscal sustainability. The importance to Libya of the hydrocarbon sector will continue for the short to medium term, as world energy demand increases (IEA 2019).

This petro-economy dependence is reflected not only in Libya's GDP but also in its public finances. In 2021, revenues from the hydrocarbon sector accounted for 97.9 percent of total revenues (Central Bank of Libya 2022). Oil supply and price shocks have adversely affected the ability of the government to cover wages/salaries and subsidies during the 2015–20 period. The 2020 current account deficit was estimated at 51.4 percent of GDP. With a currency devaluation and increasing oil revenues, the current account deficit has eroded in 2021.

Although demand for fossil fuel energy sources will continue over the near to medium term, Libyan policy makers would be well advised to diversify Libya's economic and revenue base, because demand for fossil fuel consumption is expected to slow markedly over the next few years, thanks to rising motor fuel efficiency and the transition to electric vehicles (IEA 2019). This trend toward lower fossil fuel dependency is especially relevant for Libya, most of whose exports (crude oil, refined petroleum products, natural gas, and chemicals) go to developed economies (Italy, Germany France, China, and Spain), which are likely to be part of the new fuel efficiency era and can readily adapt to wind, water, and/or solar energy.

Budgeting

Reflecting the presence of two governments that claim to be the legitimate central authority, Libya had two separate budgets throughout much of the 2014–20 period. The Government of National Accord (GNA) managed all revenues and expenditures that it handled before the start of the current conflict,[4] including the wages and salaries of public employees on the central payroll. The Interim Government operating in Bayda manages its own "extra spending," generally by financing with government bonds and treasury notes (World Bank 2020b).

Foremost among these problems is that petroleum is a highly volatile and unpredictable revenue source. This reality undermines the central government's ability to carry out an effective macrostabilization policy, a fundamental revenue-assignment function of any central authority. A perverse outcome is that Libya's stabilization strategy comes down largely to a policy of additional government employee hiring, resulting in a high and ever-increasing wage bill, with the result that spending on all other public functions is largely ignored.

Between 2014 and 2021, the budget was continuously reallocated to address the fluctuations in oil production (and revenues) and the changing demands of an economy under stress (see figure 4.8). Public sector finances focused primarily on salaries/wages and humanitarian needs, with substantial and offsetting declines in capital expenditures. Data for 2020 from Libya's two central banks (in Tripoli and Bayda) reveal more than $12 billion of lost revenue from the oil blockade. This loss has had a knock-on effect on government spending, with virtually all capital expenditure projects scrapped for 2020 (figure 4.3). Total 2020 aggregate revenues could not cover aggregate expenditures (wages and salaries), subsidies and transfers, or capital and contingency expenditure (box 4.1). Although oil production is estimated at 1.2 million barrels a day in 2021, subdued

FIGURE 4.2

Oil revenues unable to cover wages and salaries, and humanitarian expenses

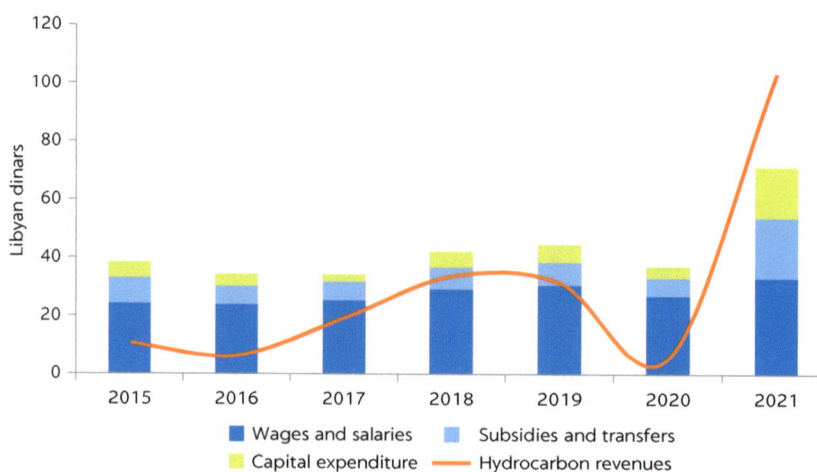

Source: Libyan authorities and World Bank staff.

FIGURE 4.3

Capital expenditure scrapped in 2020

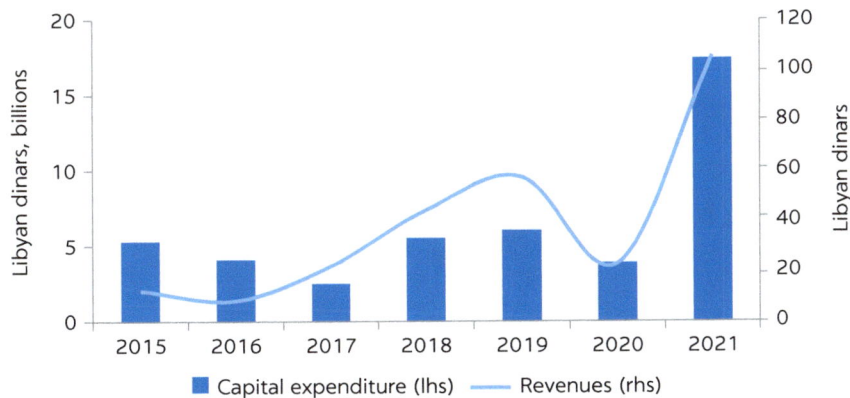

Source: Libyan authorities and World Bank staff.
Note: lhs = left-hand side; rhs = right-hand side.

BOX 4.1

Composition of the Libyan budget

The Libyan budget consists of four chapters:

- Chapter 1, wages, and salaries: Wages and salaries, along with subsidies and transfers, are the fastest-growing component of the budget. It counted for 48 percent of GDP in 2020[a]. These expenses represent the primary threat to near-term budget sustainability.
- Chapter 2, goods, and services: Goods and services represent nonlabor recurrent expenditures. They increased only because some conflict-related expenses were switched to this chapter.

- Chapter 3, development expenditures (capital expenditures): After 2014, capital expenditures virtually collapsed. According to technical experts in the Ministry of Planning, several reform measures are necessary to improve public investment spending, including improved project prioritization and reclassification of line items that should be allocated to chapter 2 recurrent expenditures.
- Chapter 4, subsidies: Chapter 4 includes oil, fuel, and other subsidy programs. As of January 2021, it represented the second-largest expense category in the budget.

a. World Bank 2021.

oil prices will continue to weigh on the fiscal account. As oil output and prices increase, the fiscal deficit should narrow, or close, significantly (see annex 4A).

Framing these two government/two budget arrangements, the Tripoli–based Central Bank of Libya (CBL) played the role of the Treasury, centralizing revenues from taxes, fees, and oil sales and paying the expenditures of the GNA. Its budget suffered from wide swings and systematic deficits during 2014–20, with double-digit deficits in four out of those six years. Despite the expected collapse of most of the major revenue sources (oil, foreign exchange fees), the GNA was unable to adjust expenditures, which remain high.[5] Given the shutdown of the oil fields through September 2020, export revenues dwindled to $3.3 billion in 2020 and Libya suffered from a deep recession in 2020 (figures 4.4 and 4.5).

FIGURE 4.4

Consolidated (East and West) budget, 2015–20

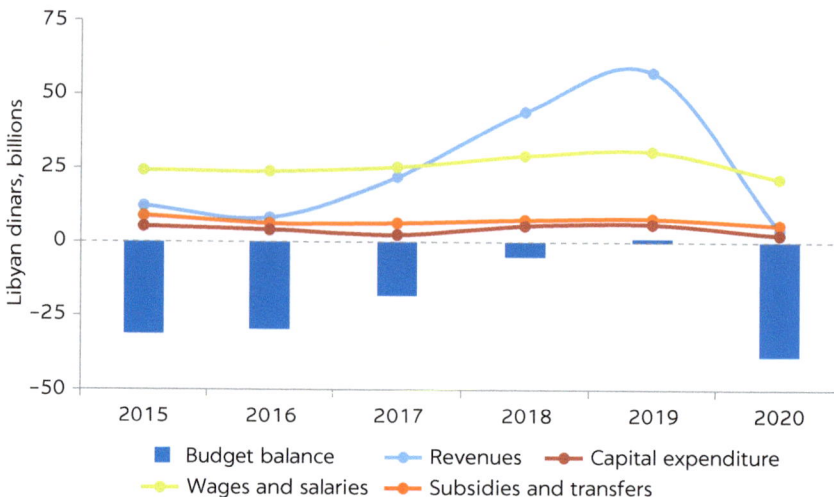

Source: Libyan authorities and World Bank staff estimates.

FIGURE 4.5

Key fiscal indicators in the West and East, 2015–20

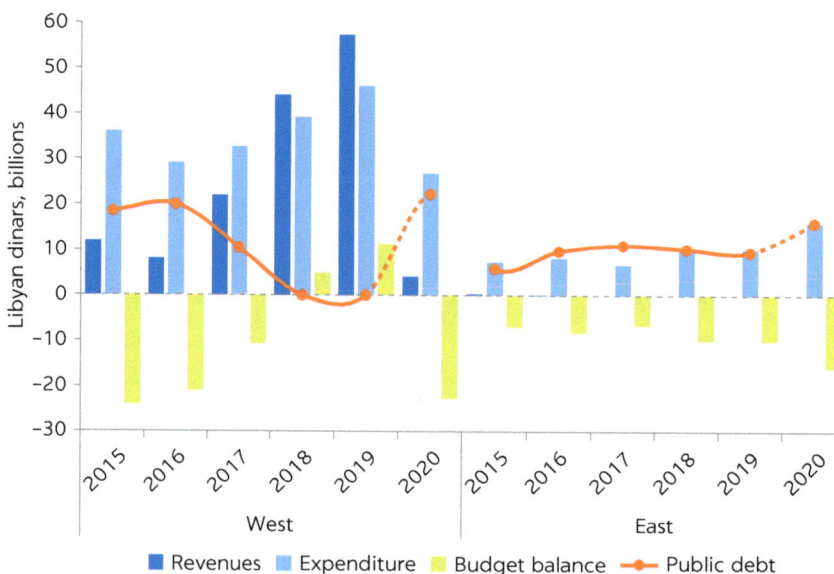

Source: Libyan authorities and World Bank staff estimates.
Note: Government of National Accord (West) budget is from January to November. Eastern Interim Government budget is through December 2020 (estimate).

Development (capital) spending

Much of Libya's extensive infrastructure has fallen into disrepair and needs major rehabilitation or replacement. For example, in FY08, the actual/budget development spending execution ratio rose to 92 percent. Investment spending averaged about LD 20 billion a year between 2008 and 2014. Public investment spending dropped to about LD 2.4 billion in 2020. Weaknesses in public investment management before the revolution and through 2021 include the lack of sector policies to guide investment decisions, weak and unenforced public investment procedures, and a proliferation of contracts that leads to uncoordinated execution of investment projects. Creating fiscal space—and improving project prioritization, preparation, and development—are critical. A constrained fiscal space, together with the use of investments as a stimulus for growth, call for more efficiency in public investment management practices. Table 4.1 summarizes the conditions underpinning ineffective investment spending.

Government domestic debt

Revenues covered barely a fifth of government expenditures in the West, forcing the government to turn to the CBL for deficit financing of LD 26.7 billion.[6] With the Bayda Interim Government lacking access to state oil revenues, spending in the East was financed almost entirely by bond issuance in 2015–20, in the amount of LD 9.7 billion. Total debt stock stood at LD 154 billion at the end of 2020 (figure 4.6).[7]

Government debt in the West is placed at LD 84 billion, following deficits in 2013–17 and again in 2020. Government debt in the East is estimated at LD 71 billion (it has run annual deficits since 2015). In addition, the government owes LD 26 billion in accrued family benefits, LD 19 billion in delayed benefit payments, and LD 8 billion in dues to the Social Security Fund. Total liabilities inclusive of these payables are estimated at LD 207 billion at the end of 2020. Government debt is almost completely domestic; public obligations to third parties are unknown. The devaluation of the LD-$ exchange in early January 2021 (to LD 4.48 per dollar) brought the value of Libya debts to $34 billion.

TABLE 4.1 Conditions that underpin poor performance in investment spending

ISSUE	EXPLANATION
Inadequate procurement planning	• Spending units do not prepare for procurement before the start of the fiscal year. • Spending units do not make procurement commitments against future budgets.
Inadequate procurement law and procedures	• Requirements for three bidders cannot always be met. (Many projects are single-source selection.)
Project delay because of external factors	• Deliveries of imported goods are delayed because local firms hold low inventories. • Delivery of goods and materials are delayed; standard contracts do not penalize late delivery.
Weaknesses in project planning	• Spending units lack strategic vision. • Projects are developed to satisfy budget call circulars rather than business planning requirements. • Planning is focused on single year, with few spending units engaged in multiyear planning.
Weaknesses in project management	• Program managers are not always responsible for authorizing expenditure. • Financial reporting to central administrative offices (such as the Ministry of Finance) is limited. • Central administration may not track implementation progress.
Cash-based appropriations	• It is difficult to estimate annual expenditure on a cash basis. • Flexibility to carry forward unspent appropriations is not clear.
Inappropriate project coding structure	• Treasury control of expenditure on project codes limits funding availability; it takes time to reallocate funds between projects (if needed).
Failure to follow expenditure rules	• Planning of cash flow forecasts does not adequately take account of the capital (development) spending program. • Planned expenditure commitments may not be used in the planning of funding allocations.

Source: World Bank.

FIGURE 4.6

Domestic debt by the West and East, 2014–20

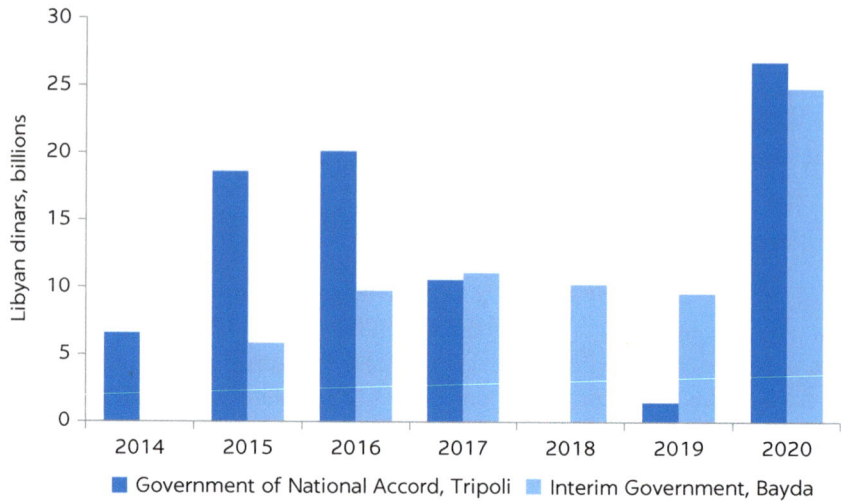

Source: Libyan authorities, World Bank and IMF staff estimates.

BANKING AND PRESSURE ON THE DINAR

The split in the government impaired normal central bank functioning and adversely affected the financial sector by preventing the authorities from gaining control over monetary and fiscal policy. Government spending was partially financed by foreign exchange reserves, foreign exchange fees,[8] the printing of currency, and borrowing independent of Tripoli through the CBL (Tripoli).

Full supervision of banks headquartered in the East was not possible. Ad hoc supervision was pervasive over the past decade. Management of foreign currency decisions was very challenging because of the lack of control of funds and the inability to reach formal decisions (for example, on dinar devaluation). Accordingly, a dual payment system was created, in which banks in the West process payments via the real-time gross settlement system (RTGS) through the Tripoli-based CBL, while banks in the East, which act as a branch of the CBL, perform transactions manually, as the Eastern branches are disconnected from the RTGS.[9] The convergence of political uncertainties and weak economic fundamentals put pressure on the Libyan dinar, leading to its depreciation by 50 percent since the beginning of 2020, which led to a wide divergence between the official LD-dollar exchange rate and the parallel rate (box 4.2).[10]

Fraudulent use of letters of credit

Among the most damaging schemes affecting the Libyan economic environment during the past several years has been the fraudulent use of letters of credit.[11] Such letters are used when importing goods; they provide access to foreign currency at the official import rate for goods into Libya.[12] Letters of credit issued between July 1 and July 15, 2020, were denominated in US dollars (81.4 percent) and euros (18.6 percent). Private banks issued 52.5 percent of the total number of letters of credits. A contributing factor to the ongoing conflict is illustrated by the breakdown by region, which shows that 86 percent of letters of credit were issued to banks based in the West and just 10 percent and 4 percent issued to banks based in the East and South, respectively.

Exchange rate dynamics of the official and parallel markets

Libya's currency peg came under severe pressure from the drastic oil production and export cutbacks in 2020. The Libyan dinar had been pegged to Special Drawing Rights (SDR) at an official exchange rate of LD 1.00 = SDR 0.5175 since 2003. Meeting on December 16 for the first time in five years, the board of directors of the Central Bank of Libya (CBL) divided between Western and Eastern branches, agreed to devalue the currency and apply the new single rate across the country. The decision followed the "economic dialogue" held in Geneva, convened by the United Nations, and co-presided by the Arab Republic of Egypt, the United States, and the European Union. The United States and the European Union cochair the Economic Working Group on Libya of the Berlin Process, through which parties discuss currency reform (among other issues), including the unification of the exchange rate. The new official exchange rate was set at LD 1.00 = SDR 0.156 effective January 3, 2021. The equivalent dollar is LD 4.48 = $1.00, based on the current SDR-dollar exchange rate (figure B4.2.1). The new rate applies to all governmental, commercial, and personal foreign exchange transactions.

In the parallel market, where the rate diverges significantly from the official rate, the Libyan dinar was highly volatile throughout 2020. That volatility was fed by uncertainties in the political and military talks in Morocco, Switzerland, and Tunisia; continuing liquidity problems in the banking sector; the demand for import financing; and the decision by the National Oil Company (NOC) to suspend the deposit of oil revenues at the CBL in Tripoli, which manages the dollar accounts where all sales by the NOC are collected. The parallel market rate in the Western areas, which stood at LD 4.19/$1 at the beginning of the year, depreciated to LD 6.50 in May, as fighting between Government of National Accord (GNA) and Libyan National Army (LNA) forces intensified. It appreciated to LD 5.52 on September 26, after the NOC resumed exports from safe ports; depreciated to LD 6.38 on November 12, as the NOC stopped deposits of oil revenues at the CBL in Tripoli; and appreciated to LD 5.96 on December 17, the day after the CBL agreed to devalue the official rate beginning in January 2021.

The devaluation of the official exchange rate in January 2021 effectively eliminates the need for the surtax on foreign exchange transactions. First imposed in September 2018, the surtax aimed to narrow the difference between the parallel market rate and the official rate on commercial and personal

FIGURE B4.2.1

Exchange rate LD per US$, January 1, 2020–January 31, 2022

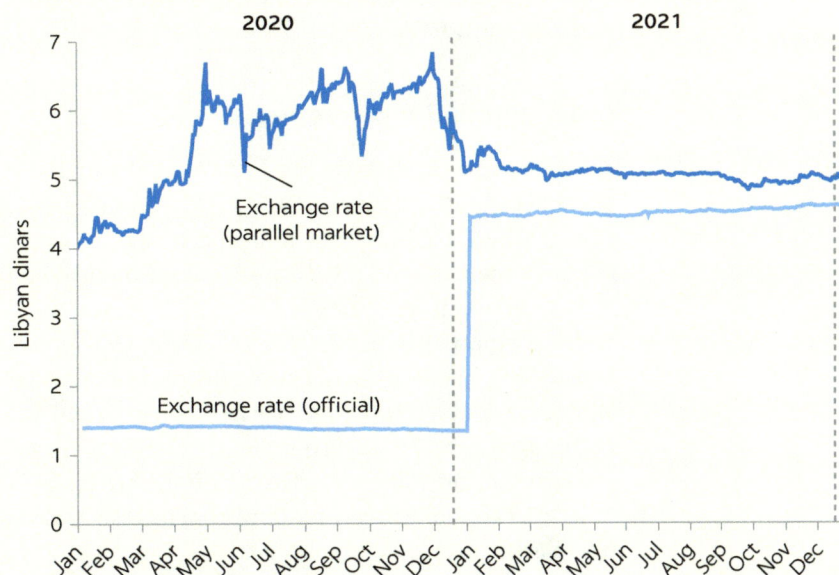

Source: World Bank 2021.

continued

Box 4.2, *continued*

transactions covered by the tax. The redundancy of the surtax implies that there will not be any foreign exchange fee revenues in 2021. The devaluation is also expected to have other effects on the economy. The dollar equivalent value of the LD 154 billion government debt, which would have been $110 billion before the devaluation of the Libyan dinar, stands at $34 billion at the new exchange rate. Although all government debt is domestic, the debt is still effectively serviced with external receipts (oil revenues), making the debt less costly to the government. The devaluation is also expected to increase the inflation rate, both by stimulating domestic demand and by increasing the price of imports.

In emerging market and developing economies, the median value of the exchange rate pass-through rate—the percentage increase in consumer prices associated with a 1 percent depreciation of the effective exchange rate after one year—was 0.08 between 1998 and 2017[a]. The increase in prices in Libya from the 220 percent devaluation of the dinar in January 2021 will likely be less than implied by this ratio. Libya has had sizable parallel foreign exchange market for some period; rate changes in the parallel market pass through to domestic prices over time. Moreover, the surtax on foreign exchange transactions effectively devalued the currency in 2018, at least for commercial and personal transactions; there would have been price effects since then.

a. Ha, Stocker, and Vilmazkuday 2019.
Source: World Bank 2021.

Often, the amount of goods procured is smaller (or nonexistent) than the amount agreed in the letter of credit, leaving a criminal group with excess dollars that can be sent to partners or shell companies overseas. When the shipment arrives in Libya, bribes ensure that the customs paperwork is falsified to indicate that the correct amount of goods has been delivered. The criminal group has a further opportunity to profit from the transaction by selling the goods at a price closer to the black-market price. In some cases, no goods arrive at all, and the criminal group uses the letter of credit to launder money overseas. In 2016, the Libyan Audit Bureau identified more than $570 million in fraudulent letters of credit involving 21 banks and 23 companies, half of which were foreign (Libyan Audit Bureau 2017).

Gross international reserves

Gross international reserves reached $79.8 billion at the end of 2020, down from $124 billion in 2012) (figure 4.7). Recent estimates by the International Monetary Fund (IMF 2021) indicate that foreign exchange reserves slumped to $49.0–$57.7 billion at the end of FY20. Government instability and internal conflict since 2013 and the war on Tripoli led by the LNA since 2019 have severely affected crude oil exports. The decline in gross international reserves reflects the holding of dollars by households as a haven instrument after the family hard currency allowance doubled to $1,000 per person a year in FY19. The high allowance encouraged speculation, given that the family allowance is exempt from the foreign exchange transaction fee, which further fueled black-market activities. The CBL (Tripoli) had to withdraw from its cash reserves to cover import bills, pay salaries, and maintain subsidies.

Growth of money outside the banking sector

The financial situation of the public sector has been precarious over the past several years, with government financing expenditures by borrowing from the CBL and drawing down on deposits at the CBL. The money supply increased as a result of the monetization of the budget deficit, causing currency in circulation to increase substantially over the past decade. As of mid-2021, over LD 35 billion remained outside the banking system as cash in circulation (figure 4.8).

FIGURE 4.7

Gross international reserves and crude oil imports, 2006–20

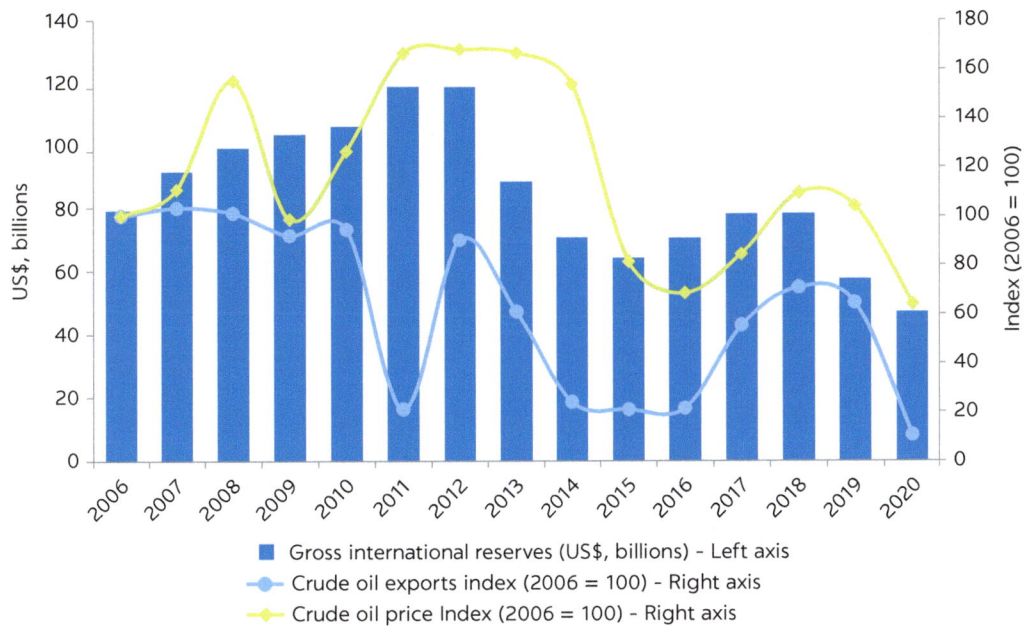

Source: Central Bank of Libya (Tripoli), World Bank and IMF staff calculations.
Note: Data for 2020 are for January–August.

FIGURE 4.8

Currency outside banks, 2012–21

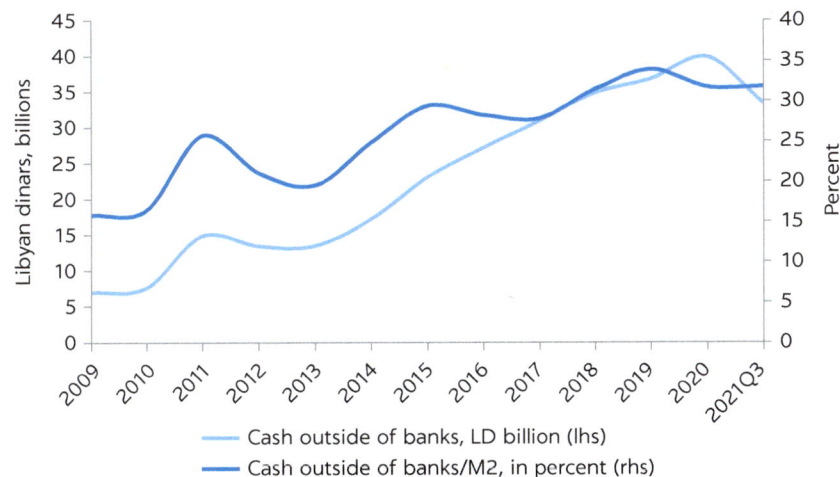

Source: Central Bank of Libya (Tripoli) and World Bank staff calculations.
Note: lhs = left-hand scale, capital expenditure; rhs = right-hand scale, revenues.
M2 = Money Supply.

By comparison, in FY12, LD 15 billion remained outside the banking system. Demand deposits are estimated at LD 75 billion.

Although currency in circulation increased substantially between 2014 and 2020, the demand for cash increased even more, resulting in sporadic shortages of liquidity in the banking system, which the CBL addressed by imposing limits on cash withdrawals by individuals. Indeed, following five years of frenetic demand for cash by customers—which almost tripled the amount of cash outside banks between 2013 and 2010—currency in circulation increased by an estimated 3.5 percent in 2020.

DETERIORATING GOVERNANCE INDICATORS

The initial upheaval that swept Libya in 2011 and initially gave civil society a stronger voice in demanding fiscal transparency and political accountability has to some extent been silenced by the ongoing "no war, no peace" conflict over the past decade. The gradual fragmentation of political and military groups since 2014 has complicated attempts at peace and reconciliation and had impacts that extend beyond Libya's borders. Key institutions and PFM arrangements continue to exist, but they have been seriously degraded.

Post-Gaddafi governments have largely been unable to end armed conflict, stop the deterioration of the security situation, and impose authority. Libyan society lacks even weak, partially independent social institutions that can help manage a peaceful transition (World Bank 2021). Civil society groups have been active, however, as have the newly independent media.

Evidence of this deterioration is sobering:

- **Development indicators**. The 2020 Human Development Index places Libya 105th out of 187 countries (World Bank 2020b). The World Bank (2016) lists Libya as one of the world's four high-intensity, conflict-affected states (the other three are Afghanistan, Somalia, and the Syrian Arab Republic).
- **Transparency and corruption**. The 2019 Transparency International Corruption Perception Index ranks Libya 168th out of 190 countries. Despite the strengthening of the National Audit Bureau and the introduction of a National Anti-Corruption Commission in 2012 and the Administrative Control Authority in 2013, results remain negligible (World Bank 2020). Libya's ranking fell from the 23rd percentile in 2000 to the lowest percentile in 2020 with respect to control of corruption. In terms of accountability, Libya fell from the 10th percentile in 2000 to 8th in 2019 (figure 4.9). However, there have been several recent initiatives by the attorney general that resulted in the arrest of several officials on allegations of corruption.
- **Public accountability**. Public accountability in Libya is weak, and key institutions perform poorly in relation to their role in combating corruption.[13] According to the 2020 Global Corruption Barometer, 48 percent of Libyans perceive public officials and civil servants to be either corrupt or extremely corrupt. The health and oil sectors are perceived to be the most corrupt institutions in the country (Transparency International 2020). The fragmentation of the country's institutions has adversely affected the performance of each institution and resulted in power struggles and fostering of deep mistrust among actors.

FIGURE 4.9

World Governance Indicators on Government Effectiveness and Corruption, 1995–2019

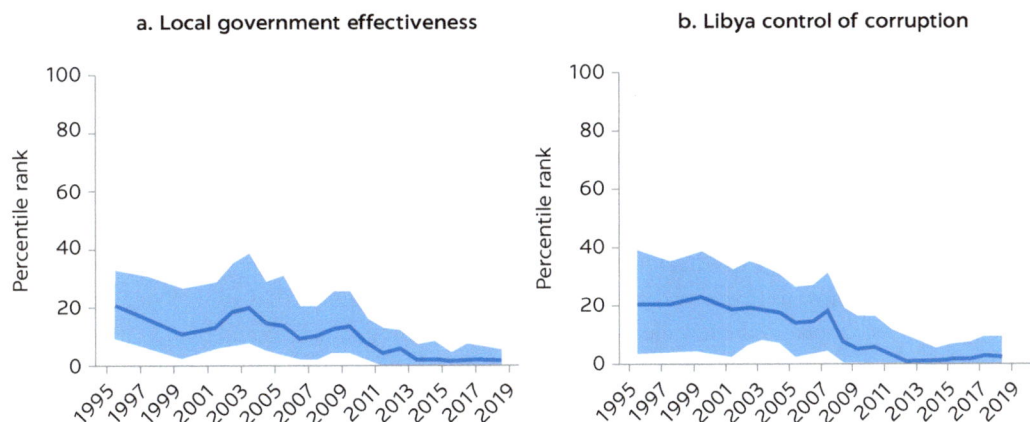

a. Local government effectiveness

b. Libya control of corruption

Source: World Bank 2020c.

REGIONAL SPILLOVERS FROM THE CONFLICT

The economic upheaval in Libya has had significant global and regional spillovers. Before the conflict, Libya accounted for about 2 percent of global oil production and hosted a large number of migrant workers (more than 1.5 million in 2014). The abrupt exodus of foreign workers added to the already large pool of unemployed workers in Tunisia, the Arab Republic of Egypt, and Chad and drastically reduced the remittances they once sent home (World Bank 2021).

Libya's instability has directly affected Egypt, Sudan, Chad, Niger, and Algeria. It has had impacts on European states and on conflicts from Syria to Mali. Libya's fragmented security scene has made it an attractive operating environment for organizations that have ambitions to increase their influence in Libya and to use it as a base to strike abroad. The collapse of state authority has sparked rapid growth and competition within Libya's illicit marketplace, making Libya the key transit hub for irregular migration to Europe and a hub of the illegal arms trade.[14]

Libyan subsidies of fuel and basic foodstuffs such as wheat have led to arbitrage opportunities for cross-border trade. For example, fuel obtained at the Libyan subsidized rate can be sold for a significant profit in Tunisia. Reduction of this trade poses a significant threat to livelihoods in southern Tunisia. Removal of subsidies by the Libyan government would exacerbate these dynamics.

STRENGTHENING PUBLIC FINANCIAL MANAGEMENT

Libya faces a number of challenges to establishing a robust and efficient PFM system.[15] As it begins to transition toward a more stable environment, there is a need to ensure efficient and more effective use of its hydrocarbon revenues and to establish a clear macrofiscal policy framework with consistent fiscal rules reflecting the country's economic objectives. The United States Agency for International Development (USAID) has supported a macrofiscal policy unit at the Ministry of Finance. This unit should enhance fiscal policy formulation and help make the budget a strategic policy tool linking national policy objectives to macroeconomic performance.

The World Bank and IMF held a number of macrofiscal and budget consultations with Libyan authorities over the 2014–21 period. However, the budget structure remains largely fragmented and largely disconnected from an explicit policy or development strategy. Libya would benefit from introducing reforms on ensuring a unified budget process, including full integration of recurrent and capital (development) budgets, introducing a medium-term (three- to five-year) perspective to inform the annual budget, and strengthening the policy context of budgeting.

The current budget structure is straightforward, with four chapters (on wages and salary, recurrent spending, development spending, and subsidies), but the budget lacks a clear and comprehensive style. There does not appear to be any clear linkage between policy priorities and budget allocations.

However, even in the midst of conflict, there is an emerging agenda for making the intersection between policy priorities and PFM work. Eight tasks need to be addressed:

1. **Enhance the functionality of the Ministry of Finance.** The Ministry of Finance is the core institution for fiscal management. It needs to be at the center of Libya's economic policy making, to ensure that capital and current expenditure decisions are fully integrated, particularly in light of the parallel Ministry of Planning, whose sole tasks are to manage and monitor development spending. A more integrated project prioritization and medium-term development spending plan must be developed.

2. **Establish a clear macrofiscal policy framework.** Libya needs a clear macro-fiscal policy framework with a consistent fiscal rule reflecting the country's economic objectives and the volatile (and unstainable) nature of hydrocarbon-based revenue. Key among the problems to be addressed is the formulation of a budget policy that incorporates a long-term development strategy. A first step toward accomplishing this goal is to pursue reforms focused on ensuring a unified budget process, including full integration of recurrent and capital budgets; introducing a medium-term perspective to inform the annual budget; strengthening the policy context of budgeting; and adopting a comprehensive and clear budget presentation. The linkage between policy priorities and budgetary allocations should be strengthened and a budget preparation calendar established that specifies the roles and functions of different agencies. Capital spending—subject in the short term to financial and human capacity constraints—will have to be reassessed given urgent reconstruction needs, efficiency considerations, and the need to assess the limits of the economy's absorptive capacity.

3. **Improve budget classification and accounting practices.** Libya's accounting system is based largely on manual (or semimanual) single-entry reporting structures. As a result, there are substantial delays in the production of quarterly and annual accounts. Cash receipts and payments are recorded manually in cash books against respective budget chapters. The lack of mechanisms to record and account for payment arrears undermines the transparency of Libya's PFM system.

   To increase transparency and accountability and better inform economic policy making, future reforms should focus on developing and implementing an internationally accepted budget classification structure and chart of accounts. The World Bank has provided a draft multidimensional segment chart of account structure that could serve as a starting point. Once agreed to, it is essential that the government establish a Government Financial Management Information System (GFMIS). Efforts should be made to establish and integrate the GFMIS to complement the proposed accounting and financial controls upgrade.

4. **Establish a Treasury Single Account (TSA).** Efficient management of the government's liquid financial assets will require development of a TSA at the CBL that will consolidate all cash resources. All cash should be consolidated in a "top" account; subaccounts can enable accounting and control mechanisms required for budget execution. It is necessary to close noncore Treasury accounts and link the TSA to the Libyan Investment Authority, Libya's primary sovereign wealth fund.[16] Excess cash balances at line ministry commercial bank accounts, including trust and escrow monies, should be brought under the TSA and swept daily into the TSA. The payments system should become more dynamic and centralized. Once a GFMIS accounting system is implemented, the payments system can become fully centralized and integrated with the accounting and control system.

5. **Recognize that cash flow planning and forecasting are essential.** To ensure effective government cash planning, the authorities need to build capacity at the ministries of planning and finance and in-line ministries for cash flow forecasting. As cash planning becomes more accurate and systematic, the Treasury will be able to identify cash flow forecasting errors and develop methodology to calculate TSA cash buffer requirements. As part of the general improvement in cash management, it will also be important to develop the Treasury-bill market over the medium term.

6. **Reform the wage bill.** Measures that have been introduced in other countries include reducing reliance on the public sector as the primary employer, decompressing the wage structure, (re)aligning civil service remuneration with that of the market, monetizing allowances to make the total compensation package more transparent, and professionalizing and strengthening the recruitment system.

7. **Enforce a commitment control system.** Under Libya's legal and regulatory framework, budget expenditures cannot exceed the ceilings specified in the annual budget law, but the rule is not enforced. A commitment control system should be introduced to keep track of commitments in the "appropriation book" and enforce them through the financial controllers in spending units. To eliminate overlaps between the financial controller, the internal auditor, and the Audit Bureau and develop a proper internal audit function over the medium term, a working group should be set up to review and devise a plan to enhance the internal control system.

8. **Improve project appraisal and selection.** Better project preparation would lead to better project outcomes. Improvements can be made across all stages of the public investment management chain. Strengthening the upstream appraisal and selection of projects and monitoring their execution could result in immediate improvements in the quality of investment projects. Efforts currently being considered by the Ministry of Planning should be accelerated in support of these objectives. In particular:
   - **Project implementation guidelines for budget preparation by ministries, departments, and agencies should be developed** to include standard provisions on institutional arrangements and procedures for capital budgeting.

    – **Policy guidelines should be established** to ensure the full integration of a public investment plan in the medium-term budget framework (and debt management strategy). Public investment plans, including feasibility studies, should be required, and made public.

CONCLUDING REMARKS

Without a resolution of the underlying internal power divisions, a stable political environment, and regulatory frameworks, prospects for durable peace and stability in Libya and regional cooperation may be limited. The current peace settlement provides an opportune moment to engage in the development of a near- and medium-term vision for a political, economic, and socially inclusive Libya, with an openness to evaluating risk as the situation evolves. A vision should be built on the careful analysis of alternative short- and long-term interventions that are sequenced based on a long-term plan, considering realities on the ground (World Bank 2020c).

The lack of unified vision can derail any political transition process very quickly and produce new violence. Libya suffers from a fundamental lack of agreement on a shared national vision to guide the institutional, economic, and territorial transformation. There have been active efforts to foster this agreement, but the path has been difficult. Even as progress is made at the national political level, a top-down approach to peacebuilding will unlikely yield the desired results unless significant engagement of civil society and private sector actors takes place.

The challenge is to build a state with legitimacy in a context of weak public administration and institutions. It is imperative that foundational technical skills—such as basic administration, evidence-based policy making, and policy implementation—be introduced and normalized to ensure that key institutions can function effectively. Such skills are particularly important for institutions vital to recovery and reconstruction, such as the ministries of finance, planning, health, and education; the General Electricity Company of Libya; and the Water Authority. Mainstreaming accountability and transparency in administration and reforms and doing so in a way that fosters inclusion so that citizens see that the state is functioning and delivering results equitably is critical to creating legitimacy and stability.

Effectuating long-term change through economic reform is not yet within the government's reach since it does not have the adequate policy toolkit and must deal with still divided economic institutions. Moreover, the short-term mandate of the GNU has defeated any purpose of its ministers' long-term plans for the economy, and their economic vision oscillated between the necessities of economic diversification, which calls for privatization as well as renewables, and the traditional rentierism of the oil state.[17] In fact, the structural weaknesses of Libya's economy require long-term planning and implementation, which has so far not been possible due to the continuous political instability and divided institutions.

Improving fiscal sustainability is a key ingredient of stability and durable peace. Doing so requires a package of interlinked and mutually reinforcing reforms. One higher level of reform that can be beneficial is a medium-term fiscal assessment. Libya's dependence on oil has fostered an undiversified economy that lacks access to significant non-oil income. Volatile international oil prices and frequent interruptions to domestic oil production have adversely impacted the country's fiscal health.

Although budget preparation is less important than budget execution in the immediate post-conflict period, there needs to be a focus on where the fiscal situation is headed. The government should establish realistic, affordable priorities, which it is in a better position to achieve than many countries characterized by fragility, conflict, and violence thanks to the country's vast oil resources. A bifurcated public administration combined with weak public financial management systems allowed the proliferation of rogue economic activity and enabled a predation economy to take hold. Fiscal transparency and financial accountability mechanisms should be enhanced to stem corruption.

Libya has an opportunity to modernize the structure of its economy and create substantial private sector employment opportunities. It is crucial to advance structural reforms to support economic diversification and improve the ease of doing business to enable private sector growth. Doing so could create much needed employment for its young and growing workforce rather than employment in the public sector, which is currently far beyond sustainable. Enhancing access to finance for small and medium-size enterprises and entrepreneurs by developing the financial sector would go a long way toward generating new employment opportunities.

Peaceful and stable reunification is likely to come in fits and starts. It remains to be seen whether the GNU can reinstate civilian control over militias and the LNA. Strengthening government capacity will be critical to address gaps at the technical and operational levels to manage or address needs as they evolve. Libya is not alone. It has partners that support a stable, peaceful, and inclusive Libya.

ANNEX 4A: BUDGET EXECUTION BY REGION

TABLE 4A.1 **Government revenues and expenditures, 2017–21**

Libyan dinars, billions

	2017			2018			2019			2020			2021
ITEM	WEST	EAST	TOTAL	WEST	EAST	TOTAL	WEST	EAST	TOTAL	WEST	EAST	TOTAL	TOTAL
Total revenue	21.9	—	21.9	44.1	—	44.1	57.4	—	57.4	23.0	—	23.0	65.3
Hydrocarbon	19.2	—	19.2	33.5	—	33.5	31.4	—	31.4	5.3	—	5.3	62.7
Nonhydrocarbon	2.7	—	2.7	2.4	—	2.4	2.5	—	2.5	2.5	—	2.5	2.6
Tax revenue	1.0	—	1.0	1.5	—	1.5	1.2	—	1.2	1.3	—	1.3	1.4
Own income	0.8	—	0.8	1.1	—	1.1	0.9	—	0.9	1.1	—	1.1	1.2
Customs duties	0.2	—	0.2	0.4	—	0.4	0.3	—	0.3	0.2	—	0.2	0.2
Nontax revenue	1.7	—	1.7	0.9	—	0.9	1.3	—	1.3	1.2	—	1.2	1.3
Foreign exchange fee	—	—	—	8.2	—	8.2	23.4	—	23.4	15.2	—	15.2	—
Total expenditure	32.7	6.7	39.4	39.3	9.9	49.2	46.1	10.0	56.2	36.2	9.7	45.9	77.0
Current expenditure	30.8	6.1	36.9	35.9	7.8	43.6	41.5	8.7	50.1	31.0	7.6	38.7	60.0
Wages and salaries	20.3	4.9	25.2	23.6	5.5	29.1	24.5	6.0	30.5	21.9	5.0	26.9	32.0
Goods and services	4.5	0.8	5.3	5.7	1.4	7.0	9.7	2.0	11.7	3.5	2.0	5.6	11.0
Subsidies and transfers	6.0	0.4	6.4	6.6	0.9	7.5	7.2	0.7	7.9	5.6	0.6	6.2	17.0
Capital expenditures	1.9	0.6	2.5	3.4	2.1	5.5	4.6	1.4	6.0	1.8	2.1	3.9	17.0
Contingency reserves	0.7	—	0.7	—	—	—	—	—	—	3.4	—	3.4	—
Balance	−11.5	−6.7	−18.2	4.9	−9.9	−5.0	11.3	−10.0	12.0	−13.2	−9.7	−22.9	−11.7

Source: Libyan authorities and World Bank staff estimates.
Note: — = not available.

TABLE 4A.2 Budget execution by region, 2015–19 (percent of GDP)

BUDGET ITEM	2015 WEST	2015 EAST	2015 TOTAL	2016 WEST	2016 EAST	2016 TOTAL	2017 WEST	2017 EAST	2017 TOTAL	2018 WEST	2018 EAST	2018 TOTAL	2019 WEST	2019 EAST	2019 TOTAL
Total revenue	30.9	0.7	31.6	22.3	0.1	22.4	41.5	0.0	41.5	61.5	0.0	61.5	78.8	0.0	78.8
Hydrocarbon	27.6	0.0	27.6	17.0	0.0	17.0	36.4	0.0	36.4	46.6	0.0	46.6	43.1	0.0	43.1
Nonhydrocarbon	3.3	0.7	4.1	5.3	0.1	5.4	5.2	0.0	5.2	3.4	0.0	3.4	3.5	0.0	3.5
Tax revenue	1.9	0.0	1.9	2.1	0.0	2.1	1.9	0.0	1.9	2.1	0.0	2.1	1.7	0.0	1.7
Taxes on income and profits	1.7	0.0	1.7	2.0	0.0	2.0	1.6	0.0	1.6	1.5	0.0	1.5	1.3	0.0	1.3
Customs duties	0.1	0.0	0.1	0.2	0.0	0.2	0.3	0.0	0.3	0.6	0.0	0.6	0.4	0.0	0.4
Nontax revenue	1.5	0.7	2.2	3.2	0.1	3.3	3.3	0.0	3.3	1.3	0.0	1.3	1.8	0.0	1.8
Foreign exchange fees							11.5		11.5	11.5		11.5	32.2		32.2
Total expenditure	93.7	18.9	112.5	80.1	22.5	102.6	61.9	12.7	74.6	54.7	13.7	68.4	63.3	13.8	77.1
Current expenditure, of which:	83.6	15.1	98.8	75.3	16.1	91.4	58.3	11.6	69.9	50	10.8	60.8	57.0	11.9	68.8
Wages and salaries	52.8	9.9	62.7	52.4	12.9	65.3	38.4	9.4	47.8	32.9	7.6	40.5	33.7	8.2	41.9
Good and services	9.4	3.6	13.0	6.8	1.9	8.7	8.6	1.5	10.1	7.9	1.9	9.8	13.4	2.8	16.1
Subsidies and transfers	21.4	1.7	23.1	16.0	1.3	17.4	11.3	0.8	12.1	9.2	1.2	10.5	9.9	0.9	10.8
Capital expenditure	1.0	3.7	13.8	4.8	6.4	11.2	3.6	1.1	4.7	4.7	2.9	7.7	6.4	1.9	8.3
Contingency reserve				1.0		1.0	1.4		1.4						
Balance	-62.7	-18.1	-80.9	-58.8	-22.4	-81.2	-21.8	-12.7	-34.5	6.8	-13.7	-7.0	15.5	-13.8	1.7

Source: Libyan authorities and World Bank staff estimates.

NOTES

1. Libya has a history of social inequality, youth unemployment, and gender and regional disparities. The 2017 Gender Inequality Index rates Libya at 0.170, reflecting a relatively low level of inequality.
2. The official subsidized rate for fuel in Libya is LD 0.15 ($0.11) per liter (for vehicles). In Tunisia, gasoline costs TD 1.8 ($0.75) per liter.
3. In late 2017, a team from the National Oil Company sent to spot-check 105 gas stations believed to be receiving regular deliveries of fuel found that 87 of them were nonoperational.
4. This section covers the conflict from the 2014–21 period.
5. A surtax on foreign currency sales for commercial and personal purposes, introduced in 2018 and accounting for 40 percent of all revenues in 2019–20, earned LD 15.2 billion in 2020 and about two-thirds of the total revenue of LD 23.4 billion in 2019. Some LD 13.7 billion of the foreign currency surtax was allocated upfront to pay off public debt in 2019–20.
6. Data on expenditures in the West cited in this report are from the Ministry of Finance. The Central Bank of Libya also reports expenditures data in the West, which are slightly different from those of the Ministry of Finance.
7. Debt data are based on estimates by government authorities, the IMF, and the World Bank.
8. First imposed in September 2018, the surtax aimed to narrow the difference between the parallel market rate and the official rate on commercial and personal transactions covered by the tax.
9. The CBL does not recognize the manual clearing procedure adopted in the East and disconnected the RTGS for Eastern banks.
10. The parallel exchange rate market refers to the nonofficial (black-market) rate; the official exchange rate is set by the CBL. For background on parallel versus official exchange rates, see Kiguel and O'Connell (1995).
11. Global Witness. 02/2021. "Global Witness reveals fraudulent Libyan Letters of Credit money entering international financial system via London."
12. CBL figures indicate that $11.2 billion in letters of credit were issued in 2019/20.
13. This section is derived largely from World Bank (2019).
14. The International Organization for Migration Libya identified a total of 610,128 migrants from over 44 nationalities in the 100 Libyan municipalities during round 38 of data collection (July–September 2021).
15. At the request of the Libyan authorities, the World Bank has provided technical assistance in public financial management and governance. The bank has recommended measures to improve accountability and transparency.
16. The Libyan Investment Authority has approximately $68 billion in managed assets.
17. A rentier state is where key agents use both oil wealth and coercion to keep the population happy, by, for instance, offering generous subsidies or artificially maintaining prices low through price caps.

REFERENCES

Central Bank of Libya. 2022 (various). *Economic Bulletin*. Tripoli: Central Bank of Libya.

Eaton, T. 2018. *Libya's War Economy: Predation, Profiteering and State Weakness*. London: Chatham House.

Ezzeddine, Nancy. 2018. *Libyan Tribes in the Shadow of War and Peace*. Clingendael, Netherlands: Institute of Internal Relations, The Hague. https://www.clingendael.org/publication/libyan-tribes-shadow-war-and-peace.

Ha, Jongrim, M. Marc Stocker, and Hakan Yilmazkuday, 2019. "Inflation and Exchange Rate Pass-Through." Policy Research Working Paper 8780, World Bank, Washington, DC. https://openknowledge.worldbank.org/handle/10986/31406.

IEA (International Energy Agency). 2019. *World Energy Outlook*. Paris: IEA. https://www.iea.org/reports/world-energy-outlook-2019.

IMF (International Monetary Fund). 2021. *Libya Economic Update*. Washington, DC: IMF. https://www.imf.org/en/Countries/LBY.

Kiguel, Miguel, and Stephen A. O'Connell. 1995. "Parallel Exchange Rates in Developing Countries." *World Bank Research Observer* 10 (1): 21–52. www.jstor.org/stable/3986565.

Lacher, W. 2018. "Tripoli's Militia Cartel: How Ill-Conceived Stabilisation Blocks Political Progress, and Risks Renewed War." SWP Comment 20, Stiftung Wissenschaft und Politik, Berlin. https://www.swp-berlin.org/fileadmin/contents/products/comments/2018C20_lac.pdf.

Lacher, W., and A. Al-Idrissi. 2018. "Capital of Militias: Tripoli's Armed Groups Capture the Libyan State." Briefing Paper, Small Arms Survey, Graduate Institute of International and Development Studies, Geneva. http://www.smallarmssurvey.org/fileadmin/docs/T-Briefing-Papers/SAS-SANA-BP-Tripoli-armed-groups.pdf.

Libyan Audit Bureau. 2017. *Libya National Audit Report*. Tripoli, Libya.

Transparency International. 2020. *Global Corruption Barometer*. Berlin: Transparency International. https://www.transparency.org/en.

UNSC (United National Security Council). 2017. "Resolution on Libya." New York: UNSC.

World Bank. 2016. *Libya's Economic Outlook*. Washington, DC: World Bank. https://www.worldbank.org/en/country/libya/publication/economic-outlook-fall-2016.

World Bank. 2017. *Republic of Tunisia: Impact of the Libya Crisis on the Tunisian Economy*. Washington, DC: World Bank.

World Bank. 2019. *Supporting Peace and Stability in Libya: A Compilation of Existing Analysis on Challenges and Needs*. Washington, DC: World Bank.

World Bank. 2020a. Human Developmet Index Database. Washington, DC: World Bank. https://databank.worldbank.org/Human-development-index/id/363d401b.

World Bank. 2020b. *Libya: Economic Monitor (2020)*. Washington, DC: World Bank.

World Bank. 2020c. Worldwide Governance Indicators (WGI) Database. Washington, DC. World Bank, September 16, 2020. http://governanceqa.worldbank.org/wgi/.

World Bank. 2021. *Libya: Socio-Economic Monitor*. Washington, DC: World Bank.

RELATED READINGS

Daoud, Rani. 2021. "History and Evolution of the Subnational Government System of Libya." In *Libya: Proceedings of the Libya Local Government Forum)*, edited by Michael Schaeffer, Maroua Lassoued, and Zied Ouelhazi. Washington, DC: World Bank.

Eaton, T. 2017. "An Impediment to Peace: Libya's Lucrative and Destablizing War Economy." In *War on the Rocks*, June 15. https://warontherocks.com/2017/06/an-impediment-to-peace-libyas-lucrative-and-destabilizing-war-economy/.

ICG (International Crisis Group). 2020. Updates #1 and 2. https://www.crisisgroup.org/middle-east-north-africa/north-africa/libya.

IMF (International Monetary Fund). 2012. "Libya Beyond the Revolution: Challenges and Opportunities." Departmental Paper 12/03. Washington, DC: IMF.

IMF (International Monetary Fund). 2013a. *Libya: Selected Issues*. Country Report 13/151. Washington, DC: IMF. https://www.imf.org/external/pubs/ft/scr/2013/cr13151.pdf.

IMF (International Monetary Fund). 2013b. *Libya: Technical Assistance Report: Public Financial Management Reform Priorities in the New Environment*. Country Report 13/36. Washington, DC: IMF.

IMF (International Monetary Fund). 2013c. *Libya: 2013 Article IV Consultation*. Country Report 13/150. Washington, DC: IMF.

Lacher, W. 2011. "Families, Tribes and Cities in the Libyan Revolution." *Middle East Policy Council* 18 (4): 140–54. http://www.mepc.org/families-tribes-and-cities-libyan-revolution. Libya's Local Elites and the Politics of Alliance Building." *Mediterranean Politics* 21(1): 64–85. https://doi.org/10.1080/13629395.2015.1081451.

Rahaman, Aminur, and Michele di Maio. 2021. *Libya: Private Sector Amid Conflict*. Washington, DC: World Bank.

REACH. 2020. *Libya: 2019 Multi-Sector Needs Assessment*. Tunis: Libya Inter-Sector Coordination Group.

Salamé, G. 2019. "Remarks of Special Representative for the UN Secretary General Mr. Ghassan Salamé to the United Nations Security Council on the Situation in Libya." United Nations Support Mission in Libya, January 18. https://unsmil.unmissions.org/sites/default/files/srsg -salame-briefing-unsc-libya-18-january-2018-english.pdf.

Schaeffer, Michael, Maroua Lassoued, and Zied Ouelhazi, eds. 2021. *Libya: Proceedings of the Libya Local Government Forum*. Washington, DC: World Bank.

Schaeffer, Michael, and Zied Ouelhazi. 2021. "Intergovernmental Fiscal Concepts and Best Practices: Lessons for Libya in Libya." In *Libya: Proceedings of the Libya Local Government Forum*, ed. Michael Schaeffer, Maroua Lassoued, and Zied Ouelhazi. Washington, DC: World Bank.

Tosun, Mehmet Serkan, and Serdar Yilmaz. 2009. "Centralization, Decentralization, and Conflict in the Middle East and North Africa." *Midddle East Development Journal* 2 (1).

UNDP (United Nations Development Programme). 2015. *Towards National Reconciliation in Libya*. http://www.ly.undp.org/content/libya/en/home/projects/Toward-National -Reconciliation-in-Libya.html.

World Bank. 2013. *Doing Business 2014 Economy Profile: Libya*. Washington, DC: World Bank.

World Bank. 2018. *Doing Business 2019 Economy Profile: Libya*. Washington, DC: World Bank.

5 Institution Building: Lessons from World Bank Engagement in Libya

FRANCESCA RECANATINI

World Bank

The author provides that many lessons emerge from the World Bank's engagement in fragility, conflict, and violence (FCV) situations and from the governance program in Libya, including the importance of (1) focusing on building institutions and governance through a flexible, multisectoral approach that takes into account the incentives of the parties involved in and affected by the conflict; (2) building capacity while promoting social cohesion and collaboration; (3) remaining engaged with the broadest group possible of state and nonstate actors—local, national, and international—to understand local dynamics and develop an integrated vision for institution building; (4) recognizing that there are no one-size-fits-all solutions; and (5) thinking more strategically and in terms of a longer-term vision, with an openness to risk, learn, and adapt.

INTRODUCTION

The World Bank's long experience in countries affected by FCV has revealed the importance of strengthening governance and institutions in a more holistic and integrated way in such settings. This chapter offers an overview of the World Bank's experience in Libya, particularly its efforts to build capacity and engage with different stakeholders while promoting inclusive governance during the multiple political crises that Libya has experienced since 2011. It also provides some reflections on what policy makers and practitioners should continue to do and what they should be doing differently going forward by embracing a fresh approach to reconstruction and development that complements the existing approaches and focuses on the people affected by the conflict and their role in creating and supporting sustainable peace.

The chapter is organized as follows. The first section examines the challenges faced by FCV countries, introduces a new approach to breaking the cycle of violence, and examines the role of governance in FCV settings. The second section describes governance and the conflict in Libya and World Bank engagement there. The last section provides some concluding reflections.

THE PERSISTENCE OF FRAGILITY, CONFLICT, AND VIOLENCE

Ten years after the Arab Spring, several countries in the Middle East region are still facing significant destruction, displacement, and disorder. The breakdown of state institutions and governance systems, coupled with economic and social losses inflicted by conflict, have had a major impact on regional and international security and humanitarian, social, and economic affairs. The absence of the state in conflict areas has opened space for nonstate actors, including extremists, terrorists, and armed groups, competing for power and resources. These conflicts have also drawn in various international and regional powers competing either directly or through proxies and spinning a complex web of intersecting conflicts that threaten regional stability.

Despite significant efforts by a diverse set of actors over the past decades, several countries and communities in the region have not been able to break the cycle of "stabilization and conflict" and have instead seen their level of fragility increase. Efforts in some of these countries to break the cycle of violence have been perceived to lack a vision for sustainable peace and a focus on inclusion and job opportunities that can allow people to provide for themselves and their families. This failure has led to a decline in integrity and a loss of hope for the future (figure 5.1).

A NEW APPROACH TO BREAKING THE CYCLE OF VIOLENCE

To break the cycle of violence, practitioners and policy makers have started to explore how to move toward a more integrated and nuanced long-term approach. The past decade has witnessed a growing understanding of the social, economic, and human impact of conflict on countries and their citizens—of the importance

FIGURE 5.1

The impact of conflict in Iraq, Libya, and the Republic of Yemen

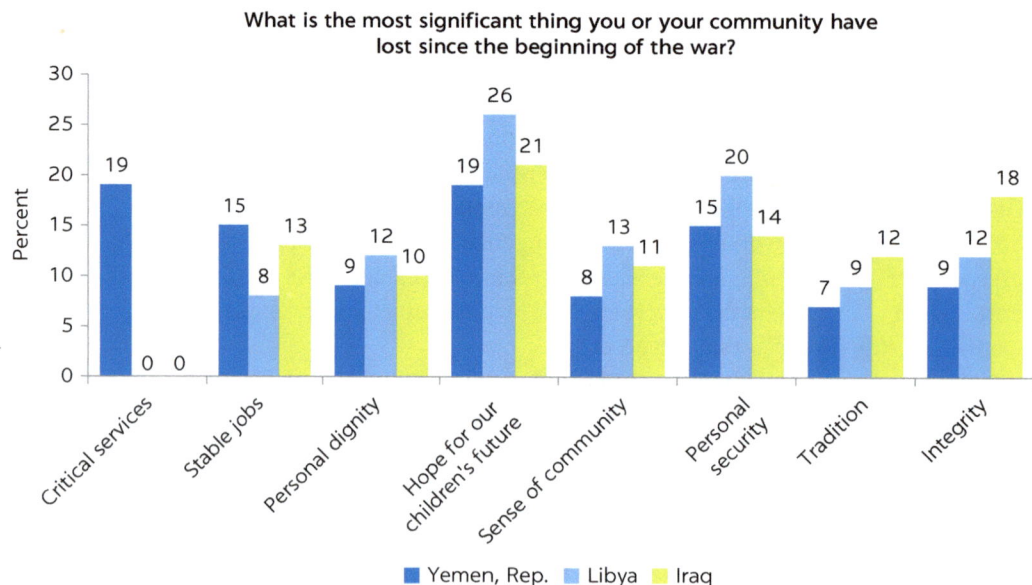

What is the most significant thing you or your community have lost since the beginning of the war?

Legend: Yemen, Rep. | Libya | Iraq

Source: RIWI 2019.
Note: Sample size = 21,230.

of addressing the root causes behind the conflict to prevent relapses—and the complexity associated with the transition from conflict to sustainable peace and inclusive growth.

Over the past decade, the World Bank has renewed its efforts and sharpened its focus on understanding how to engage more effectively in situations of FCV. The World Bank's *World Development Report* (WDR) 2011, on conflict, security, and development, stressed the importance of thinking differently about operational engagement in and financial assistance for FCV countries in order to build confidence, respond flexibly, and commit to establishing legitimate institutions for the long term. The WDR 2011 led to additional work in this area, from evaluations by the Independent Evaluation Group in 2014 and 2016 to the World Bank reports *The Toll of War* (World Bank 2017a) and *Pathways for Peace* (UNDP and World Bank 2018). These reports, especially *The Toll of War*, emphasize the importance of governance and institutions as a way to break the cycle of violence while taking into account the human, social, and economic consequences of conflicts, not only the destruction of infrastructure and other physical capital.

The WDR 2011 led to additional work in this area, from evaluations by the Independent Evaluation Group in 2014 and 2016 to the World Bank reports, *The Toll of War (2017)* and *Pathways for Peace (2018)*. These reports, especially *The Toll of War*, emphasize the importance of governance and institutions as a way to break the cycle of violence while taking into account the human, social, and economic consequences of conflicts, not only the destruction of infrastructure and other physical capital.

The focus on human, social, and economic causes and the consequences of conflict and fragility culminated in a new strategy for engagement in FCV situations, which the World Bank Group released on February 27, 2020, and a World Bank policy on "Development Cooperation and Fragility, Conflict, and Violence," which articulates the legal framework for bank engagements in FCV settings. Box 5.1 summarizes the strategy's main principles.

BOX 5.1

Core principles of the World Bank Group FCV strategy

Building on progress over the past decades, the fragility, conflict, and violence (FCV) strategy articulates a framework for the World Bank to adapt its interventions to different types of FCV situations and the local context—and to make its instruments more agile, flexible, and FCV sensitive. It identifies four key areas for engagement:

1. Preventing violent conflicts and interpersonal violence by addressing the drivers of fragility and the long-term risks, including natural resource degradation and depletion exacerbated by climate change, demographic shocks, and gender inequality

2. Remaining engaged in crisis situations and active conflicts to support countries mired in high-intensity crises

3. Escaping the fragility trap by helping countries build capacity and strengthen the social contract to support them as they transition out of situations of FCV

4. Mitigating the impacts of FCV to support countries and communities, especially the most vulnerable ones, in dealing with cross-border challenges and spillover shocks.

Source: World Bank.

In parallel, the World Bank's Governance Global Practice has increasingly focused on the role of governance and institution building in FCV contexts, producing several analytical efforts that have helped build a body of knowledge based on its work on building institutions in FCV situations.[1] What has emerged is a sobering view of past efforts to address conflict and support transition toward long-term stability and inclusive institutions. The traditional approach focused on rebuilding physical infrastructure and top-down interventions appears unable to foster inclusive and effective institutions. In fact, this approach led to further exclusion, a rebuilding of the past status quo, and the emergence of complex local and regional dynamics that have supported illicit activities and war economy. It does not appear to support the rebuilding of trust within the communities affected by the conflicts or the emergence of a more inclusive social contract. This chapter builds on this body of collective knowledge and focuses on the importance of strengthening governance and institutions in an integrated way while engaging in FCV countries.

GOVERNANCE AND INSTITUTION BUILDING IN SETTINGS OF FRAGILITY, CONFLICT, AND VIOLENCE

As highlighted in the 2011 WDR on conflict, security, and development, governance is at the heart of the challenges confronted in many countries affected by FCV: weak governance systems promote conflict and instability and undermine peace and reconstruction efforts. Conflict and poor governance go hand in hand, obstructing inclusive and sustainable development. Violent internal conflicts pose a major challenge to sustainable development, divert scarce financial and physical resources, and weaken a country's social fabric and human capital. On average, countries coming out of war face a 50 percent chance of relapsing in the first five years of peace according to *Pathways for Peace* (UNDP and World Bank 2018).

Poor governance and corruption have an adverse impact on economic growth, access to basic services, and social development, penalizing especially the most vulnerable citizens. Corruption and grievances resulting from the lack of the rule of law, elite rent seeking, perceived injustice, unfair treatment, and marginalization in society are considered central factors in contestation, unrest, and violent conflict. Poor governance also reduces the effectiveness of investment and international aid. Effective governance systems are also critical to ensure commitment, coordination, and cooperation among actors and promote effective policies (World Bank 2017b). Building resilient governance systems that encompass institutions capable of addressing past and current grievances and of delivering services is therefore critical for FCV countries to be able to break the cycle of violence and transition toward sustainable peace and inclusive development.[2]

Institution building is critical to breaking the cycle of violence, promoting social cohesion, and addressing past grievances. At the same time, sustainable and inclusive peace can occur where institutions are resilient and more responsive to society's needs and governance systems are able to create the environment for the nonviolent resolution of grievances, as emphasized in the *Global Peace Index Report 2020* (IEP 2020).

Over the past decades, practitioners and policy makers have produced extensive knowledge and tools for building institutions and strengthening governance in countries with weak but functioning governments and relative stability. They have been less successful in establishing effective governance systems and inclusive institutions in FCV countries and communities breaking the cycle of violence and relapse into conflict. Because of the challenging circumstances and pressure to act quickly, policy makers have often used approaches similar to those used in low- and middle-income settings, with limited success and inadequate acknowledgment of the unique challenges FCV countries face with respect to breaking the cycle of violence.[3]

Although each FCV situation has its own characteristics and history, most countries share a number of common challenges that affect the challenge of strengthening governance and building institutions (UNDP and World Bank 2018):

- **Low levels of trust and social cohesion**: Trust in government institutions is the first casualty of violent civil conflict, especially when parts or all the government participate in the conflict. Low levels of trust in government negatively affect compliance with government rules and decisions. Government officials and employees in FCV settings may have few incentives to respond to the needs of certain communities and citizens. The lack of trust between individuals and communities also leads to low levels of social cohesion, creating space for new exclusionary institutions to emerge.
- **High levels of uncertainty and insecurity**: Fear of the resurgence of violence and limited social cohesion promote lack of predictability and, in turn, insecurity.
- **Low technical and organizational capacity within the government**: Violent conflict may disable or displace civil servants and policy makers or force them to emigrate to safety; basic and advanced training facilities may have been destroyed; and institutional memory may have been lost through the destruction or theft of data, records, and archives, resulting in lack of access to accurate information. The weak leadership and organizational skills in FCV settings further undermine the ability of governments to coordinate responses and interventions across agencies and ministries.
- **Inadequate government infrastructure and resources**: The ability of governments to conduct their core functions and establish constructive relations with their citizens is usually very weak in FCV settings. The destruction of government buildings, facilities, and equipment further weakens the limited government's capacity and often prevents it from being able to reach out to citizens and provide services. The destruction of transport and communication networks can isolate regions and limit the territorial reach of the state.

A review of reconstruction efforts by the Institute for State Effectiveness (2019) highlights the challenges and risks policy makers face when engaging in FCV contexts and supporting reconstruction:

- Engagement is often articulated through silo-driven projects that can promote mismanagement and corruption.
- The vision and approach used is fragmented, leading to incoherent government systems and institutions.
- Practitioners have limited understanding of the nature of the regime, the character of the state, and the incentives of interest groups that shape the political dynamics within the FCV context.
- Often these efforts facilitate the introduction of flawed incentive structures—such as failures to manage disarmament, demobilization, and reintegration

appropriately—that will take decades to undo, as institutional inertia and incentives for violence continue.

- Uncoordinated interventions with limited understanding of the political landscape can inadvertently support illicit criminal economy, not only thwarting the potential for the legitimate economy to grow but also ripening conditions for corruption.
- The distorted system of incentives created by uncoordinated interventions promotes elite capture, preventing the redistribution of wealth and power, perpetuating inequalities and grievances.

To respond to these challenges, policy makers and development practitioners increasingly recognize the importance of concentrating their efforts on building legitimate, inclusive institutions at all levels to promote social cohesion. In practice, this has been implemented through programs and interventions focused on rebuilding core institutions for service delivery, strengthening domestic resource mobilization, and promoting transparency accountability and participation. To be successful in establishing inclusive institutions and governance systems, however, these programs need to be articulated through a long-term, multi-sectoral approach that takes into account the incentives of the people involved in FCVs and affected by the conflict and focuses on promoting social cohesion while creating opportunities for all. Such an integrated approach is more likely to yield sustainable results and generate greater impact than the sectoral, or siloed, approaches often used. The need for an integrated approach is especially pressing in FCV contexts because resources are limited, needs are great, state institutions and control instruments of public goods are extremely weak, and civil society voice is limited.

Building for Peace (World Bank 2020) recognizes the importance of an integrated approach for rebuilding institutions and governance in FCV settings. It is anchored in two of the pillars of the World Bank's FCV strategy: remaining engaged in conflicts and helping countries escape conflict traps. By focusing on these two pillars, the report develops an integrated approach that is grounded in understanding the powers and incentives of all actors and how they can evolve and interact before, during, and after conflict. Such an approach offers an alternative way of thinking for policy makers and practitioners interested in inclusive and sustainable peace. In particular, it articulates the importance of the time dimension when thinking about transition toward sustainable peace by linking past, present, and future:

- **Understanding the past** involves understanding the past allocations of power and resources among actors, past dynamics, and economic interests that may have contributed to conflict, institutional distortions, and unaddressed grievances.
- **Making sense of the present** involves understanding the power and incentives of existing actors, the existing allocation of resources, and the political and economic interests revolving around war. It requires assessing existing assets, including not only physical assets but also institutional, human, and social capital, to build on them—and to see them as starting points, not gaps.
- **Mapping the future** involves developing a shared long-term vision that maps out alternative policy options and specifies how they could affect actors' incentives, power, resource distribution, and institutions in the future. It requires identifying the spoilers and enablers of sustainable peace,

their political and economic incentives, and their values, norms, and commitments.

By focusing on people and explicitly articulating how actors and incentives can change over time, this integrated approach can help policy makers and practitioners develop policies and interventions that can respond more effectively to conflicts and violence while avoiding relapses into instability. Focusing on the long-term objective of sustainable peace and mapping the alternative roads to that future can also increase awareness of the risks and unintended consequences associated with reconstruction efforts.

Considering not just the past or the present but also the future—how the design of policies today may affect the future shape of institutions and the society of a country—is key for sustainability. Unlike siloed strategies for reconstruction, programs developed through the integrated approach and analysis of policy options can increase the benefits of peaceful contestation over the use of violence, reducing the risk of renewed conflict and offering a way out of the conflict trap.

The *Building for Peace* report also helps synthesize a few key messages for policy makers that some practitioners working on the front line have begun to recognize (table 5.1):

- **Engage earlier and stay engaged**, using a broad set of tools available, since today's conflicts commonly lack a clear end.
- **Understand the context and the actors involved.** Without understanding history, past grievances, and the evolution of institutions and economic interests during the conflict, it is easy to rebuild the past, including the sources of past grievances.
- **Put people at the center.** Populations in conflict-affected contexts need to be engaged in determining all aspects of the reconstruction process, from local priorities to a long-term vision.
- **Use a broad concept of security that encompasses not just physical security but also economic and social security.**
- **Remember the displaced.** Displaced populations have been profoundly and directly affected by conflict. They include people who do not wish to go back to where they came from.
- **Identify assets and local resources, not just damage.** When engaging, the focus should be not only on what has been damaged by the conflict but also on what has remained and is working. Communities can help us understand the elements that contribute to resilient societies.

TABLE 5.1 Building for peace to break conflict traps

THE WHAT	THE HOW
Build inclusive institutions and strengthen communities to promote social cohesion.	Develop a long-term strategy to address grievances and evaluate trade-offs.
Create sustainable economic opportunities for all.	Engage flexibly with a diverse set of actors, and allow for adaptation.
Build on resilient assets while addressing damages.	Conduct assessments without blinders.

Source: World Bank 2020.

- **Think local,** balancing top-down support and reconstruction of major infrastructure with bottom-up and locally based support that generates local jobs, supports local infrastructure, and rebuilds communities and social fabric.
- **Be mindful of the effects of policy decisions and interventions made today on the institutions of tomorrow.** A careful evaluation of trade-offs can steer a country toward sustainable peace.

THE CONFLICT IN LIBYA AND WORLD BANK ENGAGEMENT

Since 2011, Libya has been struggling to break the cycle of violence and conflict and build inclusive institutions that can support sustainable peace. The World Bank has engaged on the ground through an innovative and comprehensive program that has made some progress and forged relationships of trust between the World Bank team and Libyan counterparts.

HISTORY OF GOVERNANCE AND CONFLICT IN LIBYA

Libya's history and development since the 19th century led to a governance system that was weak and fragmented. After 1969, the Muammar Gaddafi era promoted the dismantling of national institutions in favor of a chaotic and "popular" government model in which real power was personalized and held by Gaddafi and a small group around him. Piecemeal attempts between 2000 and 2010, led mainly by Gaddafi's son Saif al-Islam, to pivot back toward a more conventional constitution and organizing bureaucratic and economic life met resistance from the old guard and bore little fruit before the rebellion in 2011. Unlike neighboring Tunisia and the Arab Republic of Egypt, Libya had no robust national state institutions to survive the Gaddafi government; when Gaddafi's government collapsed, so did the institutions he had established.

The fragmented administration of the Gaddafi system and its weak state institutions fostered very low levels of social cohesion across communities and regions and a high level of distrust in state institutions. Political life under Gaddafi did not promote social cohesion on a national scale. It rather increased distrust not only between institutions and people but also between tribes and communities. The system also undermined the growth of a civil society that might have created networks of social capital within and across regions. The absence of a private sector discouraged the growth of economic enterprises and business networks—outside of state ownership or control—that could have served as a basis for social capital.

The discovery of oil in the late 1950s undermined the development of a diversified and potentially competitive economy and created a very high dependence on oil, which accounted for as much as 80 percent of gross domestic product. As the oil sector was government owned and run, very little private sector expertise was developed. Despite efforts in the 2000s to diversify and partially privatize economic enterprise, Libya entered its recent era with an economy with little non-oil sectoral capacity or private sector entrepreneurship. These historical and institutional challenges were exacerbated by the 2014 crisis and the prolonged instability and conflict among militias and groups that have plagued the country since then.

In the summer of 2019, the World Bank completed a phone survey of about 5,000 Libyan citizens to assess the situation on the ground (RIWI 2019).

The data collected, although possibly partial because of the reliance on phone accessibility, provide a picture of the growing challenges and constraints across the country. They underscore the complexity of the situation and the need for a comprehensive and integrated engagement.

What emerged, eight years after the fall of Gaddafi, is a picture of a country that has further been divided, where most of the citizens feel that economic and social opportunities have not yet materialized and where trust in the government is low and declining. Respondents indicated a strong desire to build their own society, without foreign involvement (figure 5.2). The call for less foreign involvement is strongly felt across the entire county. The sense of vision that Libyans are calling for is, quite pragmatically, to empower themselves with better education, and to start working in newly created jobs.[4] Collectively, more than half of respondents say that peace, and this vision, has been hindered by corrupt leaders and international involvement.

Libyans feel they have lost many things since the beginning of the conflict, especially hope for their children's future and personal security (figure 5.1). A core group of Libyans focuses on employment and education, reflecting the fact that half of the sample was unemployed and about half lacked a post-secondary degree. Respondents living in more difficult circumstances prioritized more fundamental needs, such as stability and community cohesion.

The survey responses also reveal a critical additional issue: the existence of significant differences across the country, which should be taken into consideration when thinking about institution building. The change in the Gaddafi government and the subsequent unrest and conflict have affected different parts of Libya differently, weakening nascent institutions and creating

FIGURE 5.2

Survey respondents' assessment of governance and institutional challenges in Libya, by region, 2019

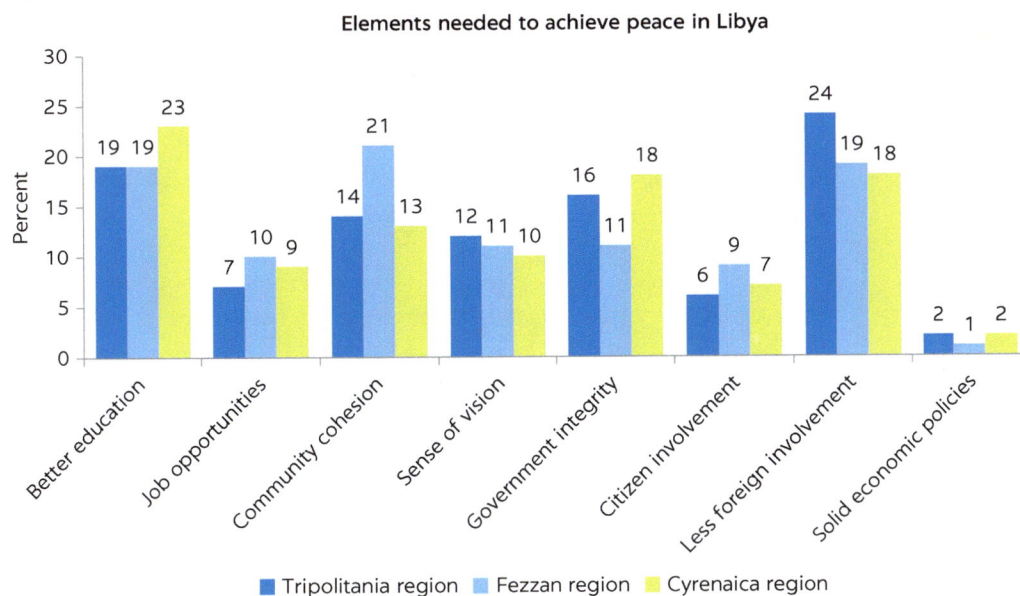

Elements needed to achieve peace in Libya

Source: RIWI 2019.
Note: Sample size = 2,437.

MAP 5.1

Survey respondents' assessment of financial situation in Libya, by location, 2019

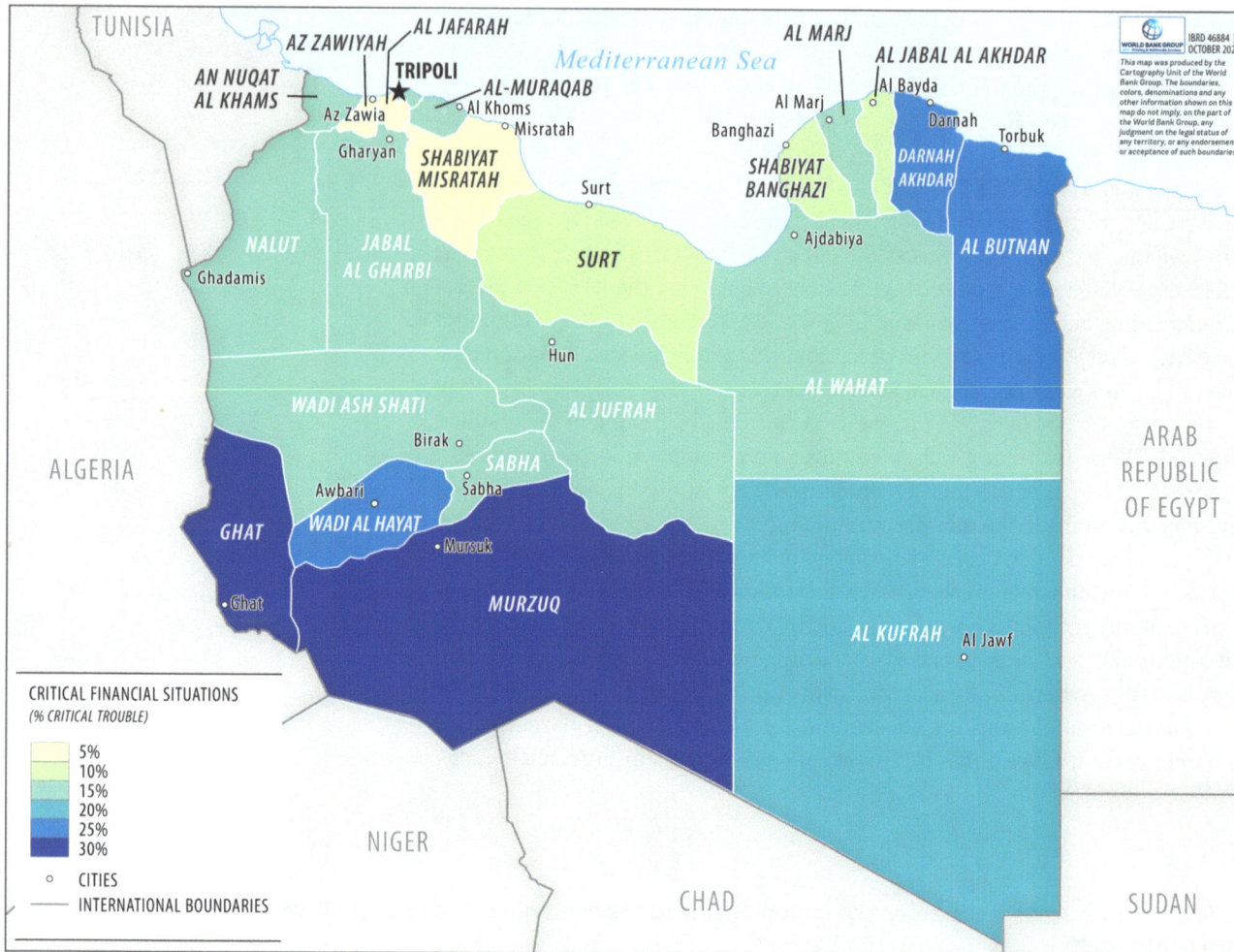

Source: RIWI 2019.
Note: Sample size = 11,804.

the space for illegal economic activities and interests. Respondents evaluate differently their financial situation differently, as shown in map 5.1.

Trust and social cohesion also differ across the three main regions of Libya. People in the Cyrenaica region perceive themselves to be the most secure. They have more trust in local leaders to deliver change for both Libya and their communities, and the highest degree of social cohesion. This region also has the highest trust in the armed forces to improve their economic situation. According to respondents in Cyrenaica, the most important way to establish peace is to improve education (identified by 23 percent of its respondents).

The Fezzan region appears to be the least socially integrated, safe, and secure. There is a slightly lower degree of trust in the armed forces and national society to improve people's situations, as more people in Fezzan still look to international organizations and civil society organizations for support. According to respondents in Fezzan, the most important way to establish peace is to increase community cooperation and education (identified by 21 percent of its respondents).

The Tripolitania region falls in between Cyrenaica and Fezzan in terms of safety, security, and financial health. People in this region reveal the highest level of trust in national society to improve people's economic situation. The share of people calling for less foreign involvement (24 percent) is the highest of Libya's three regions (only 18 percent of residents in Cyrenaica and 19 percent in Fezzan called for less foreign involvement). Relative to the other regions, people in Tripolitania have less trust in local leaders to deliver effective change for Libya and the local communities.

These differences across regions are also apparent in the type of business interactions respondents report to be willing to have with other Libyans (figure 5.3). The deterioration of trust and decline in social cohesion are evident across districts, signaling the importance of focusing on local challenges in order to rebuild social cohesion and create stronger institutions.

FIGURE 5.3

Level of business interactions in Libya, by region and district, 2019

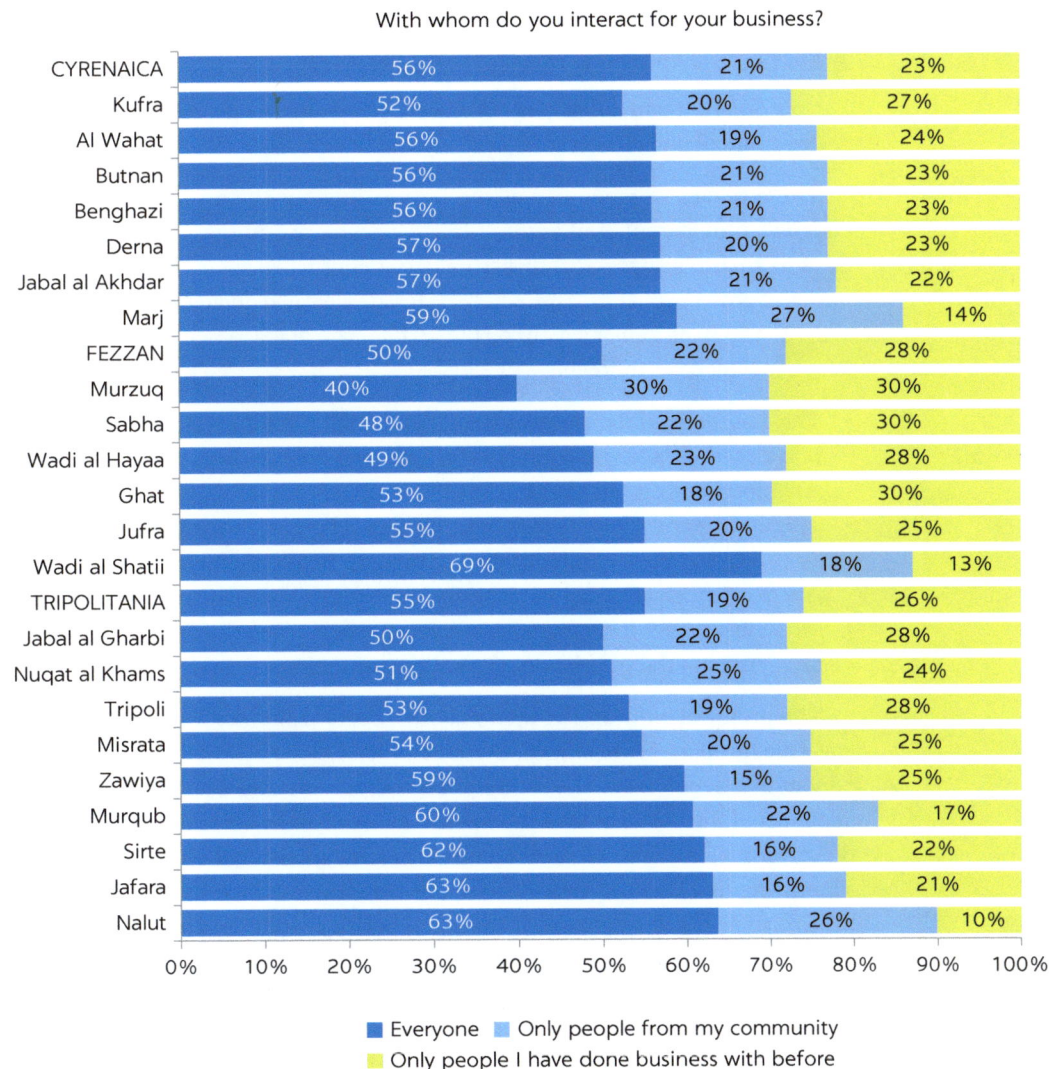

With whom do you interact for your business?

District	Everyone	Only people from my community	Only people I have done business with before
CYRENAICA	56%	21%	23%
Kufra	52%	20%	27%
Al Wahat	56%	19%	24%
Butnan	56%	21%	23%
Benghazi	56%	21%	23%
Derna	57%	20%	23%
Jabal al Akhdar	57%	21%	22%
Marj	59%	27%	14%
FEZZAN	50%	22%	28%
Murzuq	40%	30%	30%
Sabha	48%	22%	30%
Wadi al Hayaa	49%	23%	28%
Ghat	53%	18%	30%
Jufra	55%	20%	25%
Wadi al Shatii	69%	18%	13%
TRIPOLITANIA	55%	19%	26%
Jabal al Gharbi	50%	22%	28%
Nuqat al Khams	51%	25%	24%
Tripoli	53%	19%	28%
Misrata	54%	20%	25%
Zawiya	59%	15%	25%
Murqub	60%	22%	17%
Sirte	62%	16%	22%
Jafara	63%	16%	21%
Nalut	63%	26%	10%

Legend:
■ Everyone ■ Only people from my community
■ Only people I have done business with before

Source: RIWI 2019.
Note: Sample size = 6,925.

Given such a challenging, diverse, and evolving context, what can policy makers and development practitioners do in Libya to support transition toward sustainable and inclusive peace? The next section begins to answer this question by providing an overview of the multisector, multiyear program developed and implemented by the World Bank governance team for Libya starting in 2012.

WORLD BANK ENGAGEMENT IN LIBYA

The World Bank has been working to support Libya since the fall of Gaddafi. Support provided in the early stages of the transition grew into a multiyear program focused on building sustainable and inclusive institutions while addressing the long-standing institutional challenges highlighted in the previous section. From the very early stages of engagement, the principal objective of the program was to spur the emergence of a governance system that could support effective and accountable government functioning while building capacity and fostering social cohesion.

The program was based on three pillars:

1. Management of public financial resources

2. Management of information and human resources

3. Coordination and collaboration among government agencies and between government and citizens.

These pillars were viewed as the foundations for the establishment of an effective, transparent, and accountable government and the necessary conditions to ensure a successful transition from conflict to sustainable peace and inclusive growth. They also reflected the lessons learned during implementation of the World Bank's engagement on public financial management started in 2012, which included the following:

- The basic public financial governance and public administration structures in Libya needed to be considerably strengthened in order to establish a modern and functioning government.
- There was a considerable lack of technical and organizational skills at all levels of Libyan public administration to manage financial and human resources and to establish an effective relationship between the state and its citizens.
- Medium- to long-term engagement was needed, given the complexity of the problems and the volatility of the political situation.

The program built on the idea that an effective and accountable center of government, along with political accountability and the rule of law, is a key component of a democracy—the aspiration of Libya's Interim Constitution of 2011 and most of the participants in the peace process. To be effective, the center of the government (from the president to the prime minister, the Cabinet, and the supporting civil services) needed to be able to address critical strategic and public service needs through a well-managed policy process and well-established channels of communication with citizens and business to adjust its policies and interventions to the evolving situation.

Establishing the foundations for an effective and citizen-centric center of government is particularly important in a post-conflict state. Stability and legitimacy require relatively decentralized government, as regional interests are met with strong local inputs. The government also has to be sensitive to diverse political forces and responsive to the needs and concerns of citizens in the early post-conflict days. These competing priorities call for a reliable and effective policy decision-making process at the very center, strong technical and organizational capacity throughout government agencies and entities, and an integrated and adaptable strategy.

Under each pillar, the team designed a series of activities, from targeted technical assistance to multistakeholder dialogues, in-depth assessments, functional reviews, traditional training activities, and exchanges with policy makers from other countries (figure 5.4). The diverse set of tools allowed the team to be more responsive to the needs of counterparts and to establish a solid base for long-term collaboration. It also helped facilitate collaboration among Libyans from different government agencies and locations. Regular budget dialogues with government authorities and collaborative leadership training are examples of this approach (box 5.2).

The program was guided by three principles that have now been fully integrated into the World Bank FCV Strategy. First, governance and institution building are cross-sectoral issues that require an integrated and collaborative approach to reconstruction. This principle ensured that each pillar of the program included activities focused not just on traditional public sector areas but also on other sectors to create synergy and ensure an integrated vision for the country. These activities were coordinated and implemented in a collaborative way, creating opportunities for Libyan counterparts to engage across sectors. For example, the focus on fiscal stabilization was complemented by an emphasis on data collection by the government and its newly established National

FIGURE 5.4

The World Bank's program on governance and institution building for Libya

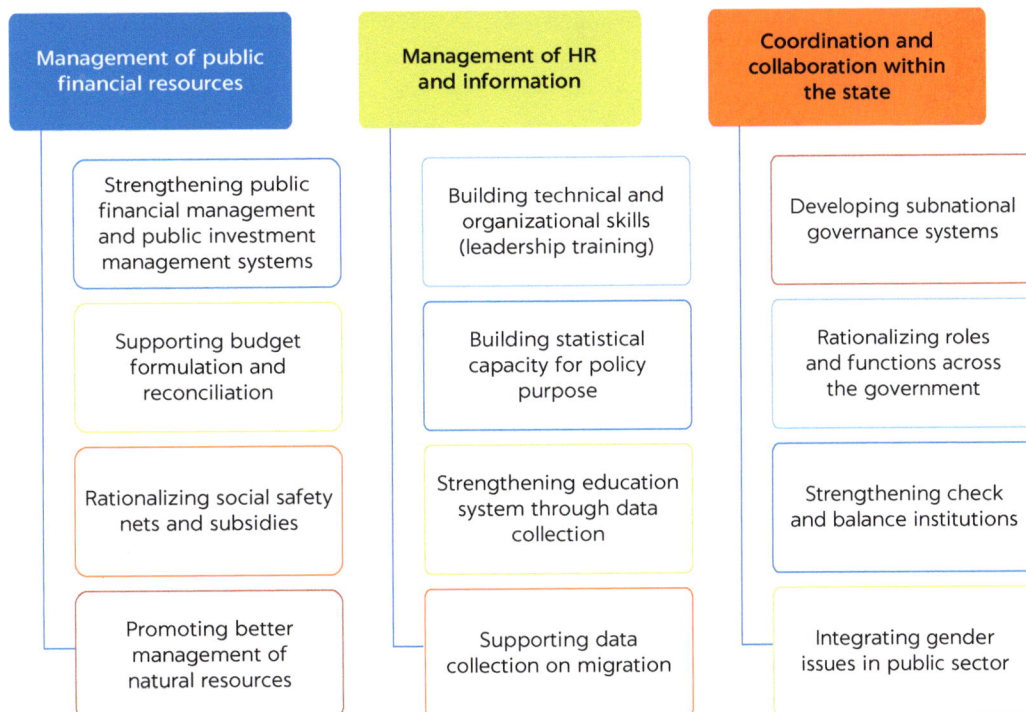

Management of public financial resources	Management of HR and information	Coordination and collaboration within the state
Strengthening public financial management and public investment management systems	Building technical and organizational skills (leadership training)	Developing subnational governance systems
Supporting budget formulation and reconciliation	Building statistical capacity for policy purpose	Rationalizing roles and functions across the government
Rationalizing social safety nets and subsidies	Strengthening education system through data collection	Strengthening check and balance institutions
Promoting better management of natural resources	Supporting data collection on migration	Integrating gender issues in public sector

Source: World Bank.
Note: HR = human resources.

BOX 5.2

World Bank efforts to build capacity and promote collaboration

The World Bank developed a Collaborative Governance Leadership Development Program that it delivered in six modules over a period of 18 months. Forty civil servants participated, coming from the ministries of interior, finance, justice, transportation, local governance, social affairs, labor, foreign affairs, economy, education, and health; the General Information Authority; the Anti-Corruption Authority; the National Oil Company; the General Electric Company of Libya; the General Authority for Water Resources; and the Social Security Fund. The program focused on developing leadership skills that could help address cross-cutting technical challenges that civil servants face while working in a volatile environment. Training was tailored to the Libyan context and offered participants the opportunity to work together to identify solutions to common challenges and objectives. In addition to the formal training sessions, participants were provided with Tripoli-based coaches, who helped them apply the techniques learned during the training to their individual situations. Trainees met at regular intervals in Tripoli, allowing them to interact with one another and with the coaches to discuss and help resolve day-to-day challenges.

Statistical Agency and on accountability through the support of the Supreme Audit Agency.

Second, the introduction of new governance systems was complemented by capacity-building activities that focused on both technical and organizational skills. These activities not only helped build capacity in different parts of the government, they also allowed working relationships with Libyan counterparts to be established that helped the program continue to deliver despite the difficult political circumstances on the ground.

Third, the program aimed at bringing together local actors and stakeholders from different parts of the country and the political spectrum to begin to address past grievances and rebuild social cohesion.

In designing and implementing different activities, the team created opportunities for dialogue and exchanges by stakeholders. Doing so also allowed the World Bank team to inform and shape its engagement by listening to the points of view of everyone affected by the conflict. An example is the capacity building delivered in early 2016 through a four-day workshop attended by 35 Libyan civil servants. The open and frank discussion that took place during the workshop highlighted some of the priority areas for additional capacity building. It also stressed the importance of integrating gender issues in the program. Figure 5.5 summarizes the discussion that took place and the main messages that emerged.

These principles made the program innovative for FCV contexts and allowed the team to build in flexibility and adaptability while taking risks. The political circumstances on the ground required a flexible approach that could adapt to the evolving local dynamics. The program was therefore articulated along two levels of engagement, depending on the political and security situation on the ground. In Scenario A (ongoing local conflict and unclear central authority), the program proposed targeted technical assistance. The program was supposed to continue implementing capacity-building activities and knowledge sharing in the broad areas of institutional development and governance. Proposed activities focused on the basic technical skills and knowledge necessary to make the transition to an effective, transparent, and accountable government. Scenario B (clear

FIGURE 5.5

Summary of outcomes of collaborative workshop on rebuilding institutions in Libya

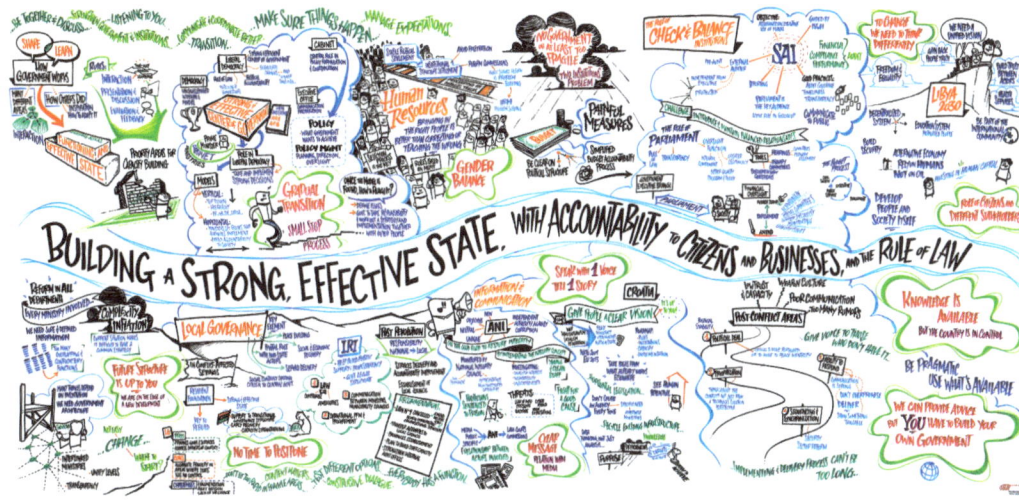

Source: World Bank Governance Global Practice Libya team.

counterpart and a stable political solution) articulated a more comprehensive program that included implementation of integrated institution-building activities by a team based in the country with a diverse set of counterparts.

The two-scenario approach allowed the program to continue to operate and stay engaged after the 2014 crisis, which led to increased fighting among militia and the formation of two rival political administrations claiming legitimacy. The unstable security environment stalled any activity by any political administration and forced international partners to leave Libya in August 2014. Although a constructive policy dialogue was not possible, the World Bank team continued to support the transition process. It continued to support public administration staff at the Ministry of Finance, the Ministry of Planning, the Central Bank of Libya, and the National Audit Bureau, principally in the areas of public sector accountability.

Despite the difficult circumstances, the World Bank team remained engaged, thanks to its relationships with counterparts, in an attempt to prevent a dangerous hiatus in the transition process that could cause a resurgence of conflict and instability. The capacity-building and technical assistance activities provided were viewed as a means to produce stability, especially by strengthening intra-government coordination and enabling "quick wins" in social services and the resumption of public investment on a new and efficient basis.

Implementation of this program since 2014 has enabled the World Bank to establish a strong working relation with technical staff and public administration from the East and the Central Bank of Libya. Three lessons emerge from its experience:

1. In a fragile and unstable environment, technical assistance can be used not only to build capacity but also to bring together actors from different sides of the conflict and to lay the foundations for trust between the state and citizens and better service delivery. The technical assistance on public financial management, for example, while focusing on highly technical issues. helped bring actors from different political sides into inclusive economic and policy

discussions over the course of several years, laying the foundations for future collaboration for a unified state and public administration.

2. Balancing technical issues with capacity building on organizational and managerial skills can help local counterparts apply the knowledge they acquire. As the team began to implement the program, it became clear that Libyan counterparts needed not only technical knowledge but also the organizational and managerial skills to ensure the use and implementation of the technical skills the World Bank was building. In response, the bank expanded the original program to include collaborative leadership skill training for mid-level civil servants.

3. Inclusion of a diverse group of counterparts is critical, and a flexible and adaptable approach is needed. During program implementation, the team regularly reprioritized activities to accommodate the needs of the political context, expanding the work program to include a component on women's issues and challenges within the public administration, for example. Such flexibility and adaptability have enabled the program to continue over the years despite the challenging conditions on the ground.

CONCLUDING REMARKS

Many lessons emerge from the ongoing World Bank engagement in FCVs and from the governance program in Libya. They include the importance of (1) focusing on building institutions and governance through a flexible, multisectoral approach that takes into account the incentives of the parties involved in and affected by the conflict; (2) building capacity while promoting social cohesion and collaboration; (3) remaining engaged with the broadest group possible of state and nonstate actors—local, national, and international—to understand local dynamics and develop an integrated vision for institution building; (4) recognizing that there are no one-size-fits-all solutions; and (5) thinking more strategically and in terms of a longer-term vision, with an openness to risk, learn, and adapt.

The World Bank's governance program will continue to evolve, as Libya is still struggling for unity and stability. Four challenges are especially pressing for the next phase of governance and institution building in Libya:

1. The widespread presence of militias after the collapse of the Gaddafi system has created a culture of violence. To strengthen the nascent governance systems, policy makers will have to integrate or disarm these militias, build trust and political engagement with new national political institutions, and make sure that the emerging national rulers and authorities do not revert to rule through violence.

2. A decade of instability and the historical legacy have widened fractures across regions and communities. To ensure a sustainable transition toward peace, governance systems will have to balance the tension between central and local forces and interests, finding ways to support the emergence of institutions that are inclusive and effective in managing resources for all citizens.

3. The institutional vacuum of the past decade has allowed illicit and illegal economic interests to enter in Libya. Libya has become a trade route for

weapons, illicit drugs, contraband, and migrants en route to Europe. Any effort to strengthen governance and institutions will have to take into consideration these new economic interests and their power on the formal political actors.

4. Because of the political crisis, rule of law institutions have not emerged. The recent positive developments toward a political solution and unity are beginning to create the conditions for the emergence of functioning legal institutions. Without such rules of the game and the systems to implement them, tension and conflict will continue to dominate the political, economic, and social life of Libya.

NOTES

1. These studies include *Strengthening Public Financial Management Reforms in Post-Conflict Countries* (2012); *Institutions Taking Root: Building State Capacity in Challenging Contexts* (2014); *Securing Development, Public Finance and the Security Sector* (2017); *Social Service Delivery in Violent Contexts: Achieving Results against the Odds* (2017); *Paths between Peace and Public Service: A Comparative Analysis of Reform Trajectories in Post-Conflict Countries* (2019); *Building for Peace in MENA: Reconstruction for Security, Sustainable Growth and Equity* (2020); and recent research on procurement and domestic revenue mobilization in FCV settings.
2. For analysis and data on the link between institutions and fragility, see the discussion of positive peace in the *Global Peace Index Report 2020* (IEP 2020).
3. Brinkerhoff (2005) provides a comprehensive overview of the literature on how to reestablish governance in FCV and post-conflict countries. He also provides a critical discussion of the terminology used by practitioners.
4. About half of respondents do not have a post-secondary degree, and about half are unemployed.

REFERENCES

Brinkerhoff, David. 2005. "Rebuilding Governance in Failed States and Post-Conflict Societies: Core Concepts and Cross-Cutting Themes." *Public Administration and Development* 25: 3–14.

IEP (Institute for Economics and Peace). 2020. *Global Peace Index Report 2020: Measuring Peace in a Complex World.* Sydney: IEP. https://www.visionofhumanity.org/wp-content/uploads/2020/10/GPI_2020_web.pdf.

Institute for State Effectiveness. 2019. "Lessons from Peacebuilding and Reconstruction Experiences." Background paper, *Building for Peace: Reconstruction for Security, Equity and Sustainable Peace in MENA,* World Bank, Washington, DC.

Kaufmann, Daniel, Aart Kraay, and Pablo Zoido-Lobatón. 1999. "Governance Matters." Policy Research Working Paper 2196, World Bank, Washington, DC.

RIWI. 2019. "Building For Peace in Iraq, Libya, and Yemen." Background paper for *Building for Peace Report (2020),* World Bank, Washington, DC.

UNDP (United Nations Development Programme) and World Bank. 2018. *Pathways for Peace: Inclusive Approaches to Preventing Violent Conflict.* Washington, DC: World Bank and UNDP. https://www.worldbank.org/en/topic/fragilityconflictviolence/publication/pathways-for-peace-inclusive-approaches-to-preventing-violent-conflict.

World Bank. 2011. *World Development Report 2011: Conflict, Security, and Development.* Washington, DC: World Bank. https://openknowledge.worldbank.org/handle/10986/4389.

World Bank. 2017a. *The Toll of War.* Washington, DC: World Bank. https://www.worldbank.org/en/country/syria/publication/the-toll-of-war-the-economic-and-social-consequences-of-the-conflict-in-syria.

World Bank. 2017b. *World Development Report 2017: Governance and the Law*. Washington, DC: Worled Bank. https://www.worldbank.org/en/publication/wdr2017.

World Bank. 2020. *Building for Peace: Reconstruction for Security, Equity and Sustainable Peace in MENA*. Washington, DC: World Bank. https://www.worldbank.org/en/region /mena/publication/building-for-peace-reconstruction-for-security-sustainable-peace -and-equity-in-the-middle-east-and-north-africa.

6 Causes of Instability and Local-Level Capacity for Peace

RANI DAOUD

Deutsche Gesellschaft für Internationale Zusammenarbeit

The author provides that the nature of Libyan fragility, particularly at the local level, is complex, context specific, and protracted. Local governance is a critical arena for peacebuilding and nation-building efforts because local institutions, systems, and processes represent the daily interface between state and society. Inclusive and accountable local governance can help restore social cohesion in Libya's divided communities, facilitate participation in public life, and distribute resources and opportunities equitably while also blending formal and informal processes of representation and participation.

INTRODUCTION

This chapter summarizes the results of a comprehensive peace and conflict assessment conducted by the German Development Cooperation (GIZ) in 16 Libyan municipalities in 2020. It identifies the core factors of instability as perceived by the stakeholders who participated in the assessment process, including municipal elected councilors, municipal officials, representatives of civil society organizations (CSOs), representatives of government offices, private sector actors, and other local stakeholders. It also identifies potential capacities that could contribute to more peaceful local settings during the transitional stage.

The chapter is organized as follows. The first section describes the methodology used in this analysis. The second section provides a historical overview of the factors that helped create the current political and social dynamics. Section three looks at the challenges facing Libya today. Section four examines the sources of instability and peace capacities in Libya. Section five offers some possible solutions. The last section provides some closing remarks.

METHODOLOGY

The analysis is based on information collected in participatory peace and conflict analysis workshops conducted during the second half of 2020 with community leaders representing municipal councils, civil society, and other stakeholders.

Workshops took place in 16 municipalities. A total of 301 participants took part in the 16 workshops, including 227 men and 74 women.

The assessments were conducted in a participatory process over three days in each municipality. Each workshop was facilitated by a trained facilitator, and discussions were guided using participatory working aids and analysis tools. Workshop results were documented and then analyzed to capture common causes of instability cited by the participants, and potentials for peace

HISTORICAL OVERVIEW

The rule of Muammar Gaddafi has had a profound impact on the social, political, and economic landscape of Libya. Gaddafi built a highly centralized state, and tribal leaders held greatest power. The first government elected after the revolution (the National Transitional Council) passed Law 59 of 2012 on the local administration system, the basis for establishing municipalities in Libya (box 6.1). In 2013, 99 municipalities were established; in 2014, the first round of local elections took place.[1] This newly established local system partly embodied the change called for by the revolutionary forces and answered the demands of local elites and regions that were yearning for influence. The stark contrast with the highly centralized system under Gaddafi meant that institutions had to be built from scratch.

Law 59 of 2012 devolves some authorities to municipalities and gives legal and financial responsibilities to local administrations. However, the process of decentralization has been stunted by national political and armed conflict. Voter turnout of only 18 percent in the 2014 elections both reflected and further entrenched the persisting national divisions (USIP 2019).

The national parliament split into two factions in the wake of the election, one based in Tripoli and the other in Tobruk, in the East of Libya. An estimated 1,600 militias were in operation in pursuit of their tribal, Salafist, Islamist, political, and/or economic interests (USIP 2019). The internationally recognized Government of National Accord,[2] based in Tripoli, was established in December 2015, upon the signing of the Libyan Political Agreement following a process mediated by the United Nations Support Mission to Libya. Staunch political opposition and questions of legitimacy catalyzed the rise to power of the

---

BOX 6.1

Law 59 on local administration

Law 59 outlines the competencies as well as the financial resources of municipalities. According to the law, the municipality is responsible for direct provision of services to its citizens—enforcing municipal regulations, establishing and managing public utilities, and developing investment projects within the municipality.

The municipality must also establish and manage the institutions within its jurisdiction that it deems

necessary to execute the functions in line with a standardized organizational structure as laid out in Law 59. In most municipalities, these structures had to be developed from scratch, as local entities did not play a key role in the centralized Gaddafi system. Conflicting decrees issued since 2014 have created confusion regarding roles and responsibilities of local level governments.

Libyan National Army, setting the stage for armed conflict between the two major political factions of Libya that continued through 2020 (ICG 2019). Violent conflicts between population groups, geographic regions, and both state and nonstate actors have led to the large-scale destruction of infrastructure and a deterioration in living conditions. Libya's core governance, human development, and related indicators have significantly declined over the past decade (box 6.2).

CHALLENGES FACING LIBYA TODAY

Libya faces multiple challenges related to territorial fragmentation and the reemergence of subnational identities that further social exclusion (World Bank 2019). Power is held primarily by local elites who have created loyalties and secure their interests by controlling or collaborating with armed militia groups.

BOX 6.2

The nexus between human development and conflict

Since the events of 2011, Libya's position in the Global Peace Index has plummeted, falling from 68th in 2010 to 157th in 2020 (figure B6.2.1). Its Human Development Index (HDI) ranking fell from 53rd in 2020[a] to 105th in 2020[b].

Most of the decline in the HDI took place following the outbreak of the Libyan civil war in 2014. This event appears to have had a more drastic impact on human development than on the peace situation, partly because the peace situation was already bad before the war. The HDI also shows the close link, and adverse impact, between human development and conflict.

a. UNDP 2010.
b. UNDP 2020.

FIGURE B6.2.1

Libya's global peace index and human development index rankings, 2010–20

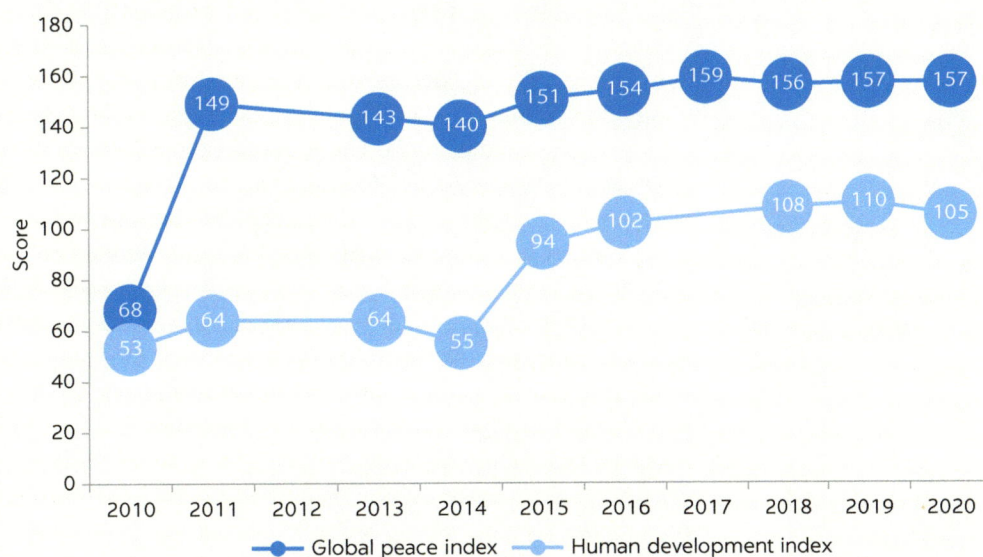

Source: Global Peace Index (database), 2010–20, Institute for Economics and Peace, Sydney, https://www.economicsandpeace.org/report/global-peace-index-2022/; World Development Indicators (database), 2010–20, World Bank, Washington, DC, https://databank.worldbank.org/source/world-development-indicators.

Tribalism and ethnicity play a limited role in localized conflict and the ways in which affiliations between different armed groups are shaped, particularly in rural areas (World Bank 2019). Political parties and CSOs remain weak and lack clear profiles and mandates.

Libyan society is fractured and excludes many groups—including women, youth, and internally displaced persons (IDPs)—from public, social, and economic life. The lack of inclusion has increased the socioeconomic marginalization of local communities. It remains a fundamental obstacle to maintaining social stability in Libya. Social bonds are being forged across the country's local (municipal and tribal) identity groups. Today's Libya resembles a nation of city-states shaped by local identities (World Bank 2019). During the conflict, groups convened, largely by international agencies, for the purpose of maintaining links at the technical level and developing some technical expertise for Libya's future. Local agreements forged between communities have strengthened local and subregional institutions and created pockets of reasonably effective local governance and stability.

In most urban areas, tribal identities play a secondary role, as personal identities are shaped by political affiliation and local clans.[3] Tribes, subtribes, and other groups have a variety of leadership structures; they have rarely functioned as monolithic blocks, because of rapidly changing positions and affiliations with armed groups (Lacher 2016). Most group identities are shaped by local leaders who are in control of resources (El Kamouri-Janseen, Shadeedi, and Ezzeddine 2018). Tribal alliances play a role in localized conflicts in the Western and Southern regions of Libya.

The heart of the conflict is control over resources, including oil fields, transit routes, and smuggling networks (Lacher 2016). Local militias or their surrogates, some shaped around tribal identities, administer small cities and provinces that are not completely under the control of the central authorities. Particularly in Libya's Western mountain region and parts of the Southern desert, local leaders have been successful in leveraging tribal and ethnic identities to build up armed groups (El Kamouri-Janseen, Shadeedi, and Ezzeddine 2018).

One survey found that local conflicts are perceived of in tribal terms (in the South); as part of a struggle against Islamist extremists (in the East); or as a combination of competitions among tribes, militias, and cities (especially in the West) (Altai Consulting 2018). The general population strongly desires a legal framework (a transparent and fair justice system), however, and accountability that is not solely determined by an offender's relationship to the political elite.

The conflict has significantly hampered the development of effective and legitimate governance structures at the local level. As a result, municipalities have not been able to fulfil their responsibilities in delivering services, improving living conditions, and contributing to social cohesion. Rather than contributing to the resolution of conflict, malfunctioning local governance structures are directly contributing to it, as citizens feel pressured to compete for limited resources. This failure has created a vicious cycle in which the conflict constrains local governance development, and the fragmented local governance structure fuels the conflict.

Unfortunately, elections were not scheduled for June 2022. The merger of two separate government systems would be complicated even under the best scenarios. In Libya, it is further complicated by continuing political competition and the structural challenges faced by the Tripoli and Bayda administrations.

Libya continues to face several structural challenges at the national and subnational levels:

- **Limited support to municipalities**. The limited emphasis on strengthening elected municipal governments continues to constrain the ability to improve local service delivery, the local economy, local security, and civil society, with adverse effects on inclusion and social cohesion.
- **Absence of women in local governance and reconciliation processes**. Because of social norms and security concerns, it is largely unacceptable in Libya for women to attend consultations, negotiations, or events that are regarded as appropriate only for men (Obeidi 2017). However, women play a significant role in civil society initiatives and national-level dialogue (Altai Consulting 2018).
- **Governance structures**. Governance structures at central ministries and the local level vary in size, have overlapping mandates, lack quality control, and do not follow due process (UNESCWA 2015; World Bank 2019). The fragmentation of the country's institutions has affected all public bodies and resulted in significant (ongoing) power struggles, which continue to foster mistrust among many actors.
- **Collapse of administrative structures**. Since 2014, administrative structures have collapsed, because of cycles of violence between the two rival governments. The mass exodus of senior public sector employees during the conflict resulted in a wide technical capacity gap (UNDP 2016, 2018).
- **Relationship between the central public administration and municipal governments.** As a result of the conflict, many regions and municipalities have decentralized and learned to govern themselves.

SOURCES OF INSTABILITY AND CAPACITIES FOR PEACE

This section summarizes the findings of the 16 municipal assessments conducted in 2020. The analysis identified five domains across which sources of instability and peace capacities seem to be spread: municipal governance and services, land and territory, the economy, social cohesion and diversity, and security and armed groups.

Municipal governance and services

Weak municipal leadership
Many of the assessments noted weak municipal leadership. It reflects several factors, including the following:

- The greater relative strength of tribal leaders
- Militia control over resources
- Inability to properly manage resources and ensure that basic needs of municipality residents are met
- The incomplete decentralization process that was supposed to occur as the result of the passage of Law 59 of 2012
- Political divisions at the national level, particularly as they affect decisions about decentralization process and municipalities
- Lack of coordination and communication between the municipality and other state entities and institutions, predominantly the security forces.

However, some participants recognized the positive impact of local mayors having the authority to influence policy as a peace capacity.

Leadership is perceived to be much weaker in rural municipalities than in urban ones (figure 6.1). Residents of municipalities farthest from Tripoli appear least content with their leadership; municipalities in Tripoli seem to perceive their leadership as more effective and powerful. These differences reflect several factors. Mayors who are physically closer to the seat of the national government may enjoy more direct exchanges and leverage when representing their constituent's interests at the national level. Municipalities in Tripoli are also more likely to be familiar with local governance tasks, as many of the civil servants worked in similar fields before the revolution. The effectiveness of these municipalities may also have a positive impact on the legitimacy of the municipality, benefitting both the institution and its leadership.

Weak municipal leadership and corruption are the dominating themes prevalent in most assessments. Both give nonstate actors the space to establish themselves in the political arena. Their power affects various areas of municipal responsibility, such as the delivery of basic services, control over resources, and the resolution of conflicts. It can often lead to further mismanagement and polarization of society, reducing efficiency. Municipalities in which these entities are successful in fulfilling these responsibilities are losing their legitimacy and further weakening the trust in democratic processes.

Poor service provision

Most municipalities perceived poor service provision and destroyed physical infrastructure as sources of instability. In some municipalities, such as in Nalut, services could not be delivered because of security issues and roadblocks. In other municipalities, such as Janzour, strained budgets and inability to generate local revenues prevented municipalities from providing adequate electricity and waste collection. Residents of most municipalities perceived lack of services and infrastructure—including lack of access to affordable, good-quality health care (figure 6.2)—as a driver of conflict.

FIGURE 6.1

Weak leadership and corruption as drivers of instability, by region, 2020

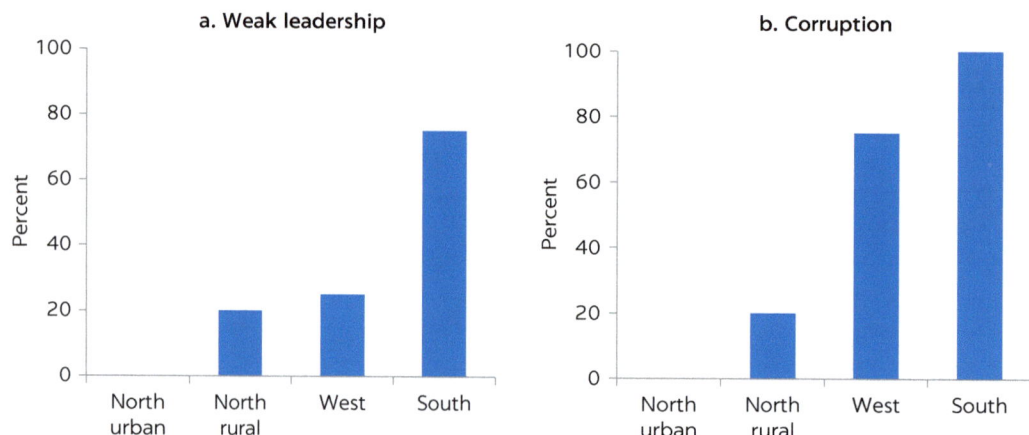

Source: GIZ 2021.

FIGURE 6.2

Health care–related factors as drivers of instability, by region, 2020

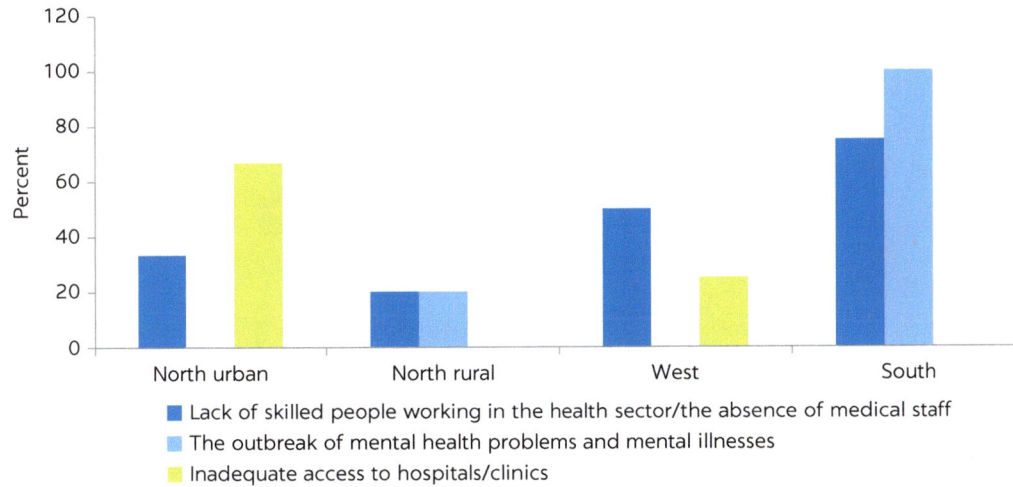

■ Lack of skilled people working in the health sector/the absence of medical staff
■ The outbreak of mental health problems and mental illnesses
■ Inadequate access to hospitals/clinics

Source: GIZ 2021.

FIGURE 6.3

Service delivery factors as drivers of instability, by region, 2020

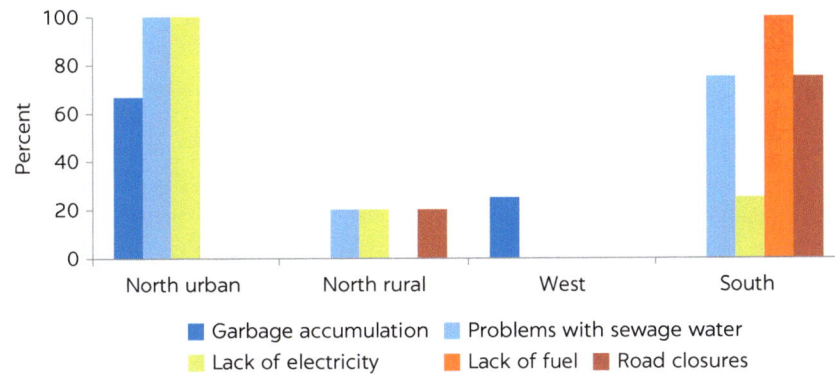

■ Garbage accumulation   ■ Problems with sewage water
■ Lack of electricity   ■ Lack of fuel   ■ Road closures

Source: GIZ 2021.

Municipalities in the South and the urban North cited lack of infrastructure as the primary factor in the conflict; they also identified garbage accumulation and lack of fuel as key factors (figure 6.3). The assessment was not able to identify whether these services had degraded more in these areas than elsewhere.

The influx of IDPs—which has caused overcrowding, traffic congestion, and garbage accumulation—has put further strain on municipal resources. Some respondents viewed the fact that IDPs had fled to their areas as an indication of its relative peacefulness. Respondents in Garabulli noted that their municipality's "socially and politically peaceful stance" led many IDPs to come to their area.

Land and territory

Libya's Law 4, adopted in 1978, limits "property ownership to one residence or plot of land on which to construct a residence for each male head of a household" and permits government seizure of land if the owner owned more than a single plot. In many cases, multiple people have deeds to the same piece of land, leading to disputes. Residents in major urban municipalities such as Janzour, Hay Al Andalus, and Tarhonah cited such disputes as a key destabilizing factor.

The inability of the police to protect ownership and the ineffective judicial system were also cited. The police are generally unable to prevent land occupation, and there is a lack of a fatwa against trespassing. The location of municipalities was one of the few widely recognized peace capacities. Residents in municipalities such as Al Zintan and Nalut viewed proximity to other municipalities or to Algeria and Tunisia as enhancing peacefulness because it enhanced trade opportunities.

Location was also seen as a strategic peace capacity, because its sometimes enabled municipalities to establish relationships with other municipalities and to strengthen the social fabric between them. One way this has happened has been through reconciliation committees. Participants in Al Zintan and Tarhonah noted the positive role of reconciliation committees, with one resident of Al Zintan mentioning that the committee had convinced conflicting parties to come to agreement about opening a road. Tarhonah participants noted that such committees facilitate communication with neighboring cities and help "resolve disputes and bridge points of view." Local stakeholders tended to identify sources of instability, identify goals, and provide recommendations; they rarely mentioned peace capacities.[4]

Economic conditions

Residents in nearly all municipalities noted weak economic conditions as a source of instability. Across municipalities, respondents cited the liquidity crisis,[5] high unemployment, and low wages (figure 6.4). Participants reported that the liquidity crisis has caused people to turn to crime to meet basic needs. Residents in Al Zintan and Misrata noted that young people are unable to marry because of lack of financial means to support themselves. Some participants connected the liquidity crisis to the split of the central bank in Libya and noted the lack of confidence in the banking system. The presence of adequate capital was understood to be a peace capacity. In Hay Al Andalus, Janzour, Al Zintan, and Nalut, residents noted that high rates of youth unemployment are leading to riots and protests as well as increases in extremism.

Social cohesion, diversity, and identity

In several municipalities, the presence of different racial groups—as well as both IDPs and permanent inhabitants—was cited as both a source of instability and a peace capacity. Residents in some municipalities mentioned tribal identities as a source of instability. Residents in most municipalities reported tribalism and/or racism as having adverse impacts on the stability of their municipalities.

Discrimination has led to social grievances and violations of rights. Participants in Nalut, for example, noted that the municipality fails to take into consideration cultural differences. Tribalism and racism have led to unequal distribution of services and utilities, exacerbating an already immense source of tension in communities, as reported in Nalut and Janzour. Religion has also contributed to marginalization or instability in both municipalities.

FIGURE 6.4

Economic factors as drivers of instability, by region, 2020

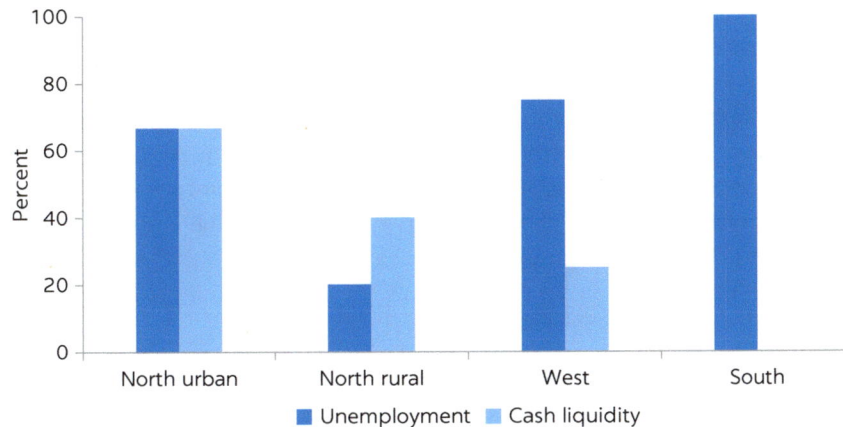

Source: GIZ 2021.

Tribalism and reported fanaticism around it have led to corruption, impunity, salary differences, and unequal opportunities and access to jobs. Tribalism has also proven to be an obstacle in the consolidation of state legitimacy in the post–civil war period and decentralization processes. Participants in Tarhonah highlighted concerns over a lack of Libyan national identity because of tribalism. The power of tribal leaders in Tarhonah and Zliten has become a source of instability, participants from those municipalities said, because it led to the impairment and marginalization of state security institutions, which have little control over tribal leaders. Disputes over the assignment of political and administrative positions—particularly tribal-based quotas in Zliten—have contributed to instability in some municipalities. In Msalatta, participants noted that tribal authority has created instability by fueling conflicts over land, blocking economic investments and local production, contributing to social problems within families, blocking the equitable distribution of positions of power, and leading to impunity for people with tribal affiliations.

Nevertheless, the assessment noted that diversity is an important peace capacity potential. Participants in Hay Al Andalus, Janzour, and Msalatta pointed to diversity as a peace capacity; all three municipalities are home not only to Arabs but also to people of Amazigh, Tawaregh, and Tabo ethnicity. Residents of Janzour noted the history of intermarriage between Amazighs and Arabs as a capacity for peace. Residents of Msalatta highlighted its history and capacity for receiving IDPs as a peace capacity. People in Janzour highlighted the municipality's welcoming attitude to IDPs as a peace capacity.

Presence of security and armed groups

Participants in almost all municipalities reported that the presence of armed groups and weapons in their communities has had a destabilizing effect on the stability of the community. Participants from every municipality noted that armed groups, arms, and lack of security were sources of instability. Violent clashes with armed groups have reduced economic productivity. Residents in most municipalities noted increases in crime (including bank robberies, muggings, and stealing of electric cables) and the spread of illegal drug use as sources of instability.

Participants cited unemployment (particularly of youth), the inability of the police to control criminals, corruption, and the presence of militias as sources of instability. Participants in Nalut mentioned the lack of municipality participation and communication with security forces to develop a joint plan for the municipality, failure to implement the security law, the poor training and authority of security forces, and the lack of monitoring and surveillance. Participants in Janzour pointed to a lack of effective security forces, arms proliferation, and violent clashes with armed groups as sources of instability but also noted that Al-Forsan Brigade had secured the area and had chosen not to go to war with other militias, making it a peace capacity.

BRIDGING THE GAP BETWEEN PROBLEMS AND SOLUTIONS

Recognition of sources of instability or peace capacities did not lead to the identification of corresponding or responsive recommendations or goals. In a few municipalities, participants cited explicit goals related to tribalism; most respondents noted it as a source of instability, however. Given the historical and influential role that tribal and ethnic structures have played in Libyan society, further investigation into goals and recommendations may be useful. It is possible that recommendations aimed at addressing social reconciliation may have been implicitly intended to address factors related to tribalism. Suggestions to increase transparency and integrity in municipal processes may also have been intended to address concerns about tribalism.

Many recommendations were assigned to civil society without great clarity about what participants meant or understood by the term. No specific CSOs were cited. Developing a greater understanding of what levels of community and society are considered responsible for the realization of goals would aid in implementation efforts.

CONCLUDING REMARKS

Libya is an extremely challenging political economic environment, because of the divide in national-level governance and many unresolved security issues. It remains a very difficult environment at the municipal level, for different—and much more nuanced—reasons. The nature of Libyan fragility, particularly at the local level, is complex, context specific, and protracted. There is a growing consensus that multidimensional approaches to the Libyan context can help restore the social contract between the state and its people, which will serve as the essential foundation for sustainable peace and development.

Local governance is a critical arena for these efforts because local institutions, systems, and processes represent the daily interface between state and society. Inclusive and accountable local governance can help restore social cohesion in Libya's divided communities, facilitate participation in public life, and distribute resources and opportunities equitably while also blending formal and informal processes of representation and participation.

A survey of municipal-level participants revealed a long list of factors undermining the stability of their communities. It also uncovered some peace capacities. For example, some participants saw ethnic diversity as a threat to stability, while others expressed pride in the diverse nature of their municipalities and framed it as a strength. Participants in this assessment identified goals and actionable recommendations for the months and years ahead, which fell into nine categories: comprehensive national reconciliation, decentralization; municipal administration and service provision, community participation, social cohesion and reconciliation, the economy, opportunities for youth, a focus on women, and armed conflict and criminal actors. Taken together, these goals appear to serve as the raw material for a roadmap to the future.

NOTES

1. In September 2021, Libya consisted of 121 municipalities. In 2014, elections of municipal councils commenced. Elections took place in 95 municipalities that had already concluded their first term of office (2014–18). A second round of elections started in 2019 and have not concluded to date. Around 25 municipal councils were reelected and the process is still ongoing.
2. Refer to chapter 3, "Beyond Power-Sharing: Long-Term Economic and Political Stability."
3. This section is based on the analysis of family, tribe, and leadership identities by Al-Shadeedi, and Ezzeddine (2018).
4. Participants' tendency to focus on sources of instability rather than peace capacities was not unexpected. As Anderson (1999, 23) writes, "Local people in conflict settings . . . tend to focus on divisions and tensions. The newness of the violence and the constant danger it poses overwhelm them. Even though they may maintain 'normal' actions (which often represent connectors, as we discuss later), they see everything as 'abnormal' because of the conflict. They often fail to recognize the many ways they continue to act and think in non-war ways." Nevertheless, Anderson notes, "in all civil war situations, some things connect the people who fight. In all societies there are capacities for peace."
5. Refer to chapter 2, "The Battle for Control of State Institutions," and chapter 4, "Setting the Stage for Public Sector Reform."

REFERENCES

Altai Consulting. 2018. *National Reconciliation in Libya: A Baseline Survey*. Final Report. Paris: Altai Consulting.

Anderson, M. B. 1999. *Do No Harm: How Aid Can Support Peace—or War*. Boulder, CO: Lynne Rienner.

Al-Shadeedi, Al-Hamzeh, and Nancy Ezzeddine. 2018. *Libyan Tribes in the Shadow of War and Peace*. Clingendael, Netherlands Institute of Internal Relations, the Hague. https://www.clingendael.org/publication/libyan-tribes-shadow-war-and-peace.

GIZ. 2021. *GiZ Libya Subnational Survey*.

ICG (International Crisis Group). 2019. *Addressing the Rise of Libya's Madkhali-Salafis*. Middle East and North Africa Report 2020. Belgium: ICG. https://www.crisisgroup.org/middle-east-north-africa/north-africa/libya/addressing-rise-libyas-madkhali-salafis.

Lacher, Wolfram. 2016. "Libya's Local Elites and the Politics of Alliance Building." *Mediterranean Politics* 21 (1): 64–85. https://www.tandfonline.com/doi/full/10.1080/13629395.2015.1081451.

Obeidi, A. 2017. "Local Reconciliation in Libya: An Exploratory Study on Traditional Reconciliation Processes and Mechanisms since 2011." Working paper, United Nations Development Programme, New York.

UNDP (United Nations Development Programme). 2010. *Human Development Report 2010: The Real Wealth of Nations. Pathways to Human Development.* New York: UNDP http://hdr.undp.org/en/content/human-development-report-2010.

UNDP (United Nations Development Programme). 2016. *Core Government Functions Assessment—Critical Emerging Issues and Priorities for (Re)Building Government Employment and Public Administration Institutions in Libya.* New York: UNDP.

UNDP (United Nations Development Programme). 2018. "Tripoli's Militia Cartel: How Ill-Conceived Stabilization Blocks Political Progress, and Risks Renewed War." SWP Comment 20, Stiftung Wissenschaft und Politik, Berlin. https://www.swp-berlin.org/fileadmin/contents/products/comments/2018C20_lac.pdf.

UNDP (United Nations Development Programme). 2020. *Human Development Report 2020: The Next Frontier: Human Development and the Anthropocene.* New York: UNDP. http://hdr.undp.org/en/content/human-development-report-2020.

UNESCWA (Economic and Social Commission for Western Asia). 2015. "Annual Report 2015." UNESCWA, Beirut.

USIP (United States Institute of Peace). 2019. "Libya Timeline: Since Qaddafi's Ouster." USIP, Washington, DC. https://www.usip.org/libya-timeline-qaddafis-ouster.

World Bank. 2019. *Supporting Peace and Stability in Libya: A Compilation of Existing Analysis on Challenges and Needs.* Washington, DC: World Bank.

RELATED READINGS

Altai Consulting. 2013. *Key Informant Interviews with Businessmen in Benghazi and Misrata in July 2013.* Paris: Altai Consulting.

Altai Consulting. 2015. *Libya Civil Society Mapping.* Paris: Altai Consulting. https://www.altaiconsulting.com/insights/libya-civil-society-mapping.

Altai Consulting. 2017. *Libyans: A Media Mapping Research Survey.* Paris: Altai Consulting.

Ben Lamma, M. 2017. *The Tribal Structure in Libya: Factor for Fragmentation or Cohesion?* Paris: Observtoire du monde arabo-musulman et du Sahel, Fondation pour la Recherche Stratégique. https://www.frstrategie.org/sites/default/files/documents/programmes/observatoire-du-monde-arabo-musulman-et-du-sahel/publications/en/14.pdf.

Ezzeddine, Nancy. 2018. *Libyan Tribes in the Shadow of War and Peace.* Clingendael, Netherlands: Institute of Internal Relations, The Hague. https://www.clingendael.org/publication/libyan-tribes-shadow-war-and-peace.

Gender Concerns International. 2017. *Countries in Focus: The Situation of Women in Libya.* The Hague, Netherlands: Gender Concerns International. http://www.genderconcerns.org/country-in-focus/libya/the-situation-of-women-in-libya/.

Lacher, Wolfram. 2011. "Families, Tribes and Cities in the Libyan Revolution." *Middle East Policy Council* 18 (4): 140–54. http://www.mepc.org/families-tribes-and-cities-libyan-revolution.

Lacher, Wolfram. 2020. *Libya's Fragmentation: Structure and Process in Violent Conflict.* London: I. B. Taurus.

Tracking the Economy during Conflict

7 Libyan Private Sector: Difficulties, Challenges, and Perspectives

AMINUR RAHMAN AND MICHELE DI MAIO

World Bank

The authors posit that understanding the specific mechanisms through which aggregate negative effects materialize is critical for the design of effective policies that can unlock the potential for private sector development and economic growth in Libya. Post-conflict Libya needs to create conditions conductive to the expansion of the private sector market also by limiting the role of the state-owned enterprises and expanding the legal, regulatory, and economic conditions for private enterprise to flourish. Libya's private sector is in desperate need of help to overcome the challenges it faces. There is no time to "wait and see" what develops. Urgent actions need to be taken to enable the private sector to survive the conflict era and create a solid foundation for post-conflict growth.

INTRODUCTION

The conflict in Libya has profoundly, and adversely, affected the private sector. It has increased firms' production and distribution costs, exacerbated investment risk, made access to foreign labor more difficult, and reduced access to finance, as shown by a survey of 400 firms across Libya—the Libya Enterprise Survey (LES)—and interviews with a range of stakeholders conducted by the World Bank between May and December 2018. Informal and illegal economic activities and rent seeking have also increased. Nonetheless, Libya's private sector shows resilience and a sense of optimism about Libya post-conflict.

This chapter examines the private sector. It is structured as follows. The first section provides an overview of the sector. The second section highlights the key features of the business environment amid conflict. The third section documents the conflict's effects on firm performance. The fourth section discusses resilience and expectations about a post-conflict Libya. The fifth section provides concluding remarks, identifying possible actions for consideration during the conflict and post-conflict periods.[1]

OVERVIEW OF THE PRIVATE SECTOR

Dominance of the public sector and lack of competitiveness

The Libyan economy has been for years dominated by a large public sector fueled by oil production and oil revenue. Porter and Yergin (2006) describe Libya in the early 2000s as divided into a high-value, low-employment energy sector and a low-value, high-employment nonenergy sector, both led by the state. This economic system—and the absence of a private sector–led diversified economy—dragged down productivity.

In the pre-conflict era, several factors restrained the emergence of a dynamic private sector. These factors included the dominance of state-owned enterprises, the lack of competition, the unpredictability of policy, red tape, poor governance, and lack of access to finance, skills, and good-quality infrastructure, a set of features that make Libya like several transition economies.[2] Pre-conflict Libya ranked near the bottom in various dimensions of competitiveness, placing 110th out of 111 countries on the Global Competitiveness Index.[3] Competitiveness suffered from lack of a skilled workforce (110th of 111 in educational quality), poor-quality infrastructure and telecom networks run by the state (Libya ranked as one of the lowest across all dimensions of infrastructure quality), barriers to entry for foreign and domestic firms, lack of financial sector development (last out of 111), a small domestic market, lack of business innovation and sophistication, lack of an industrial base, and widespread corruption and favoritism.

Difficulty attracting foreign direct investment

Even before the 2011 revolution, foreign direct investment (FDI) inflow was impeded by a poor business environment and an anti-FDI approach. FDI approvals were subject to long delays, and work permits and visas for foreign company personnel were restricted and delayed. The existence of a minimum threshold for FDI excluded many foreign investors who wished to invest smaller amounts. The uncertain business environment and policy instability weakened the confidence of investors and hindered investment by the Libyan diaspora. On all Worldwide Governance Indicators—control of corruption, regulatory quality, government effectiveness, rule of law, voice, and accountability—Libya lagged behind the Middle East and North Africa region average by a substantial margin in 2004 (Porter and Yergin 2006).

Emergence of the private sector

In the pre-conflict era, the private sector was just emerging. A survey of small and medium-size enterprises (SMEs) in Libya by Porter and Yergin (2006) indicated that 70 percent of them were small (less than 25 persons). The majority were either supplementary entrepreneurs (people who had a government job and a small business activity) or necessity entrepreneurs (people who could not find a public sector job). Of the entrepreneurs surveyed, 46 percent stated that they would prefer a public sector job.

The dominance of the state and the lack of competition badly hindered the development of the private sector in the pre-conflict era. Decades of state dominance in production and distribution and the lack of competition eroded incentives for innovation and business sophistication. Further, isolation from the international community, the lack of FDI in the non-oil sector, and import dependency impeded Libyan firms' ability to be international suppliers. An important feature of the private sector in Libya is the substantial level of informality. Before 2011, the informal economy was estimated to account for about 40–50 percent of official gross domestic product (GDP); the cumbersome business environment was viewed as a key underlying reason for the high level of informality (Porter and Yergin 2006). Several factors can drive informality amid conflict. Among these, the most important are that conflict may damage trust in state institutions and that it may erode the benefits of formalization, such as access to credit and markets.

At the time of the 2011 conflict, Libya was still one of the least diversified oil-producing economies in the world, with most firms being micro or small (World Bank 2011). The composition of the private sector has changed little since then. In the LES 2018, most Libyan firms (84 percent) are micro or small, with fewer than 20 employees. Only 14 percent of firms declared themselves not registered with any institution, and 59 percent stated they were registered at the local Chamber of Commerce, where registration is compulsory by law. Only two in five declared being registered with the government or the municipality.[4]

Underrepresentation of women and youth

Women and young people are underrepresented in Libya's entrepreneurship space. According to the LES 2018, just 6 percent of company owners are women, and only 8 percent of owners are under 34. Family ownership is one of the most common business ownership structures in Libya, and most Libyans taking over family businesses are men. Youth-owned businesses are most likely to be in services and trading sectors, where the initial capital needed is generally lower than in sectors such as construction and manufacturing. Services and trading sectors are also more exposed to innovation and new technologies, possibly giving educated youth a comparative advantage over older generations.

Reliance on foreign workers

Libyan firms have for a long time relied on a foreign workforce. The out-migration because of the 2012–20 conflict has adversely impacted Libyan firms. Before the 2011 uprising, there were an estimated 1.2–1.5 million foreign workers in Libya, nearly half its labor force. During the uprising, an estimated 1 million foreign laborers fled Libya (World Bank 2015). According to the LES 2018, Libya's private sector continues to rely heavily on foreign workers, with 17 percent of workers not Libyan nationals.[5] For high-skilled jobs, the disconnect between the Libyan workforce's skills and market needs leads employers to recruit foreign workers (Expertise France 2016). Many foreigners are also hired for low-skilled and manual jobs (mostly in an informal manner) that Libyans are reluctant to take.

Dependence on oil and imports

Libya's oil dependency contributes to its import reliance. An overvalued exchange rate during the 2015–20 period, fueled by oil revenues, made Libya heavily import dependent at the expense of export competitiveness. According to the LES 2018, 46 percent of firms import. Many firms in the Western and Eastern regions import goods or services (66 percent and

56 percent, respectively), a much larger share than in the South (10 percent). These geographical differences are related to the fact that import costs correlate negatively with geographical proximity to import markets and that firms located in the Western and Eastern regions are larger (and thus more likely to import). The conflict has posed a serious threat to the import-dependent economy through a combination of factors, including increased transportation costs, security threats, lack of access to letters of credit, and manipulation of foreign exchange rates.

Outside of the oil and gas sector, very few firms export. Most of Libya's non-oil and gas industries are underdeveloped and cannot compete in global markets with high-quality products at competitive prices (OECD 2016). According to the LES 2018, other than oil, Libya exports a very limited range of products, including cosmetics and honey. Fewer than 3 percent of private Libyan firms exported goods or services in 2017. Those that did were mostly medium-size firms concentrated in the Western region.[6] Increased production and distribution costs induced by the conflict further dampen Libyan firms' cost competitiveness in international markets.

Domestic market orientation

Libya's private sector is oriented predominantly toward the domestic market. Most businesses (88 percent) sell to the public, according to the LES. One-third of businesses sell to other businesses,[7] which has an important bearing on the need to reduce information failure and search costs for suppliers finding buyers and vice versa. These costs, which are likely to have increased during the conflict, are generally higher for micro and small firms, which represent most of Libya's private sector. Digital technology, through online platforms and digital marketing media, could reduce these costs, particularly when the conflict makes face-to-face interactions costlier and less secure. Online platforms and e-commerce are increasingly becoming important instruments for the facilitation of international trade as well.

Public procurement

Public procurement can be a critical vehicle for private sector development in Libya. In the pre-conflict era, the state was the dominant consumer of goods and services produced in Libya. However, nontransparency and corruption in public procurement, along with delays in processing payments, hampered the potential of using public procurement as a vehicle to promote SMEs' access to domestic markets and growth (Porter and Yergin 2006). According to the LES 2018, about 17 percent of businesses have the Libyan government as a client. In post-conflict reconstruction, the volume of public contracts is likely to increase, making it possible for public procurement to become a significant source of domestic demand for the private sector.

THE BUSINESS ENVIRONMENT AMID THE CONFLICT

The conflict has further distorted Libya's pre-conflict noncompetitive business environment. The majority of firms report macroeconomic uncertainty, political instability, limitations on letters of credit, low domestic demand, corruption,

FIGURE 7.1

Change in key constraints in the business environment between 2013 and 2018

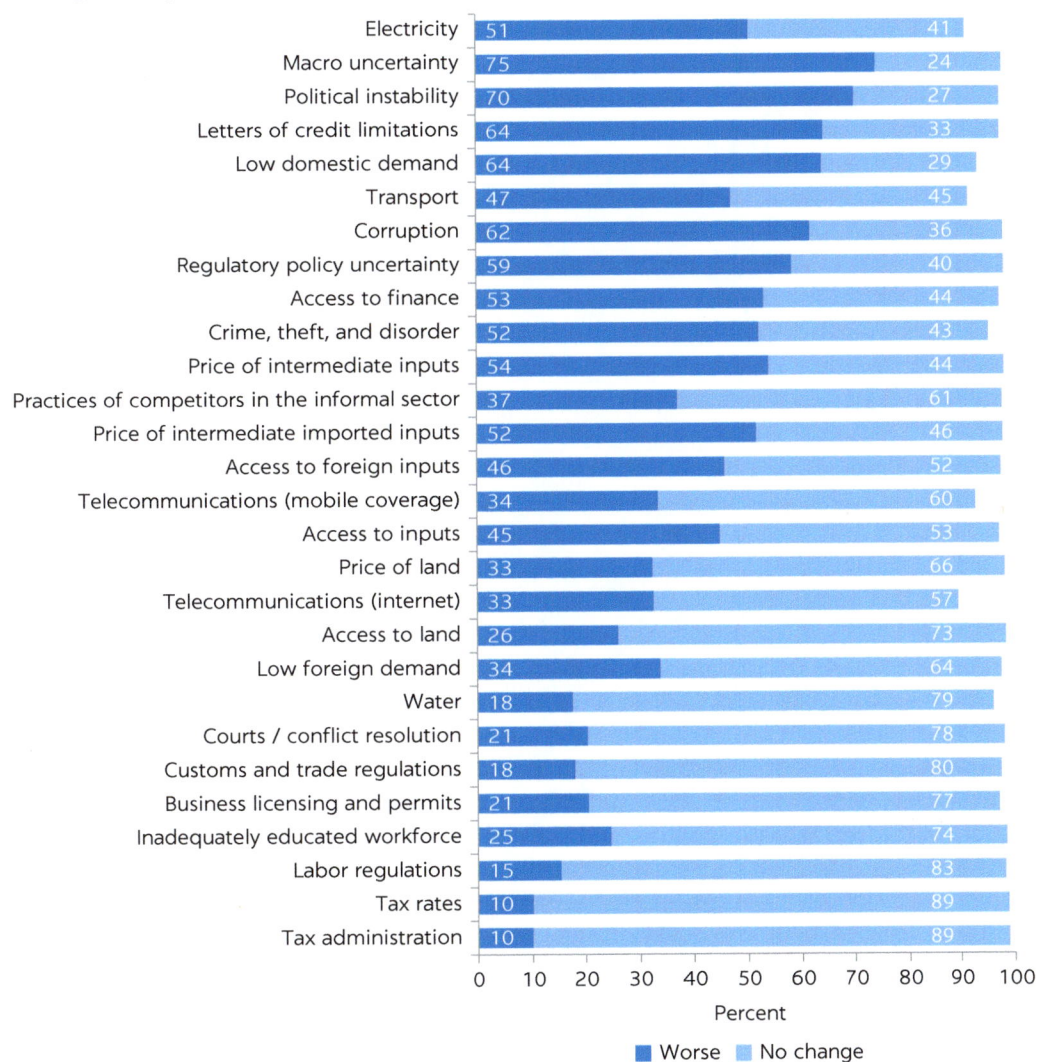

Constraint	Worse	No change
Electricity	51	41
Macro uncertainty	75	24
Political instability	70	27
Letters of credit limitations	64	33
Low domestic demand	64	29
Transport	47	45
Corruption	62	36
Regulatory policy uncertainty	59	40
Access to finance	53	44
Crime, theft, and disorder	52	43
Price of intermediate inputs	54	44
Practices of competitors in the informal sector	37	61
Price of intermediate imported inputs	52	46
Access to foreign inputs	46	52
Telecommunications (mobile coverage)	34	60
Access to inputs	45	53
Price of land	33	66
Telecommunications (internet)	33	57
Access to land	26	73
Low foreign demand	34	64
Water	18	79
Courts / conflict resolution	21	78
Customs and trade regulations	18	80
Business licensing and permits	21	77
Inadequately educated workforce	25	74
Labor regulations	15	83
Tax rates	10	89
Tax administration	10	89

Percent

■ Worse ■ No change

Source: LES 2018.

regulatory policy uncertainty, intermediate input prices, inadequate access to finance, inadequate availability of electricity, and crime, theft, and disorder as top constraints, noting that they have worsened since 2013 (figure 7.1). At the same time, some of the top pre-conflict-era constraints, such as access to land and tax rates, have become less relevant during the conflict.

MACROECONOMIC UNCERTAINTY AND THE LIQUIDITY CRISIS

The Libyan conflict disrupted the economy and cut oil output, weakening the Libyan dinar. Until the last quarter of 2018, this situation fueled inflation by increasing the prices of imported production and consumption goods. In the absence of fiscal adjustment, the fall in oil revenues between 2013 and 2017 forced Libya to use its net foreign currency reserves to finance deficits, causing its balance of payments to deteriorate.[8] The weakening economy has also weakened the already fragile trust that economic actors had in the banking system, leaving them reluctant to deposit their money in banks and thus generating the liquidity crisis.

Measures to stave off the depletion of reserves over the 2015–19 period worsened the liquidity crisis and fueled a currency black market and elite capture.[9] Restrictions imposed by the Central Bank of Libya (CBL) on letters of credit and access to domestic cash and foreign exchange at the official exchange rate fueled a currency black market. CBL measures also added to inflationary pressure (and contributed to a drop in domestic purchasing power) by making it harder and costlier for the private sector to import inputs and finished products. The gap between the official and black-market foreign exchange rate promoted capture of letters of credit and foreign currency at the official exchange rate by influential and connected firms, creating unfair competition that crowded out firms that badly needed access to imported inputs and raw materials for their production process or finished products for trading. It also allowed militias to pursue several fraud schemes. Manipulation of letters of credit was a serious problem in Libya: of the $1.6 billion of them granted to 2,159 firms in 2017, more than 20 percent appear to have been fraudulent, according to the 2017 Libya Audit Bureau Report. More than 80 percent of firms in the LES 2018 reported being heavily affected by restrictions on letters of credit and foreign currency.[10]

The liquidity crisis has been a serious bottleneck for the private sector. The LES 2018 indicates that 88 percent of firms reported that restrictions on obtaining letters of credit were significantly tighter than they were in 2013, and 86 percent of enterprises considered these restrictions to have had a major or very severe impact on their business. The impact has been felt heavily by firms in the manufacturing and construction sectors: 91 percent of firms in the manufacturing sector and 86 percent of firms in the construction sector stated that restrictions on letters of credit had a major or very severe impact on their businesses. On average, the value of imports of firms in the manufacturing and construction sectors dropped by 75 percent and 67 percent, respectively, between 2013 and 2017. Eighty-three percent of firms also reported significantly more restrictions on obtaining foreign currency than in 2013. This constraint had a major or very severe impact on the business of 80 percent of firms. The impact was greatest for trading firms (89 percent), followed by manufacturing firms.

Access to finance

The conflict has further complicated access to finance, which was already a key constraint in the pre-conflict era. Eighty-two percent of firms in the LES 2018 report that restrictions on obtaining credit had increased since 2013, a problem that hindered 64 percent of firms. The conflict significantly increased the difficulty private firms experience in obtaining loans, which reflects low and uncertain profitability, insufficient collateral and financial transparency, and the unfinished transition to Islamic finance.

Infrastructure and public services

Inadequate public services, especially electricity, make conducting business difficult in Libya. Access to electricity is a top constraint, with 69 percent of enterprises in the LES 2018 viewing it as a major or very severe obstacle to growth, up from less than 50 percent during 2013–14. Power cuts are frequent across the country; electricity is a more severe constraint to firms operating in the South (16 percentage points above the average) than in Tripoli and the Western region (22 percentage points below the average). Half of all firms and 100 percent of firms in the South report the constraint to have worsened since 2013.

Transport is also a significant constraint to growth. In the LES 2018, 52 percent of firms consider transport to be a major or very severe constraint. This perception is more significant in the Southern region (33 percentage points above the average), where roads were damaged by clashes, leaving them unfit for transit. Because of conflict-related impacts on transport infrastructure, 47 percent of firms overall and 99 percent of firms in the South consider transport constraints to have worsened since 2013.

Transport of goods throughout the country has been subject to predation and extortion by militias. Weakened state institutions, lack of security, and the increasing power of nonstate armed groups in Libyan territory have led to various types of illegal payments and extortion. Entrepreneurs are forced to pay to cross checkpoints, both legal and illegal, and to ensure security for transported goods, which are important revenue sources for militias. Increased transportation and security costs increase input prices, and victims of continuous extortion episodes may relocate or abandon their businesses.

Among Libyan firms, 30–42 percent report additional costs (beyond official or regular costs) incurred because of the ongoing security and political crisis. These unofficial costs in the South are up to 31 percentage points above the average. Trade and construction firms seem to experience such additional costs more than firms in other sectors. Most of these illegal payments are associated with transport costs, which are highest in the South.

Regulatory and institutional issues

Since 2011, the policy and regulatory framework for private investment has been unclear. This has created uncertainty over regulatory policy, which 51 percent of firms surveyed in the LES 2018 report as a major or very severe obstacle to growth. Over the years, Libya has introduced various policies and measures to support the development of the private sector, but all remain incomplete or were halted because of the prolonged conflict. These measures include the creation of offshore free zones to attract FDI to support the export and manufacturing sectors, efforts to join the World Trade Organization (initiated in 2004 and given a fresh push in 2010), the signing of a Trade and Investment Framework Agreement with the United States in 2013, a cooperation agreement with Morocco to strengthen trade, and a draft law on public-private partnerships.

In its current form, the foreign investment law discourages FDI. It limits foreign ownership to 49 percent and includes a LD 1 million ($715,000) capital requirement, which represents a high barrier to entry for smaller firms. The stipulation that firms must have 10 years of experience to set up a joint stock company is prohibitive for most firms. Although the government is, in theory, open to foreign investment in eight sectors (transportation, health, education, industry, agriculture, maritime, tourism, and public utilities), significant opacity surrounds bidding processes and awards.

Corruption and illegal activities

Political instability greatly affects the rule of law and levels of corruption. Together with conflict-induced risks and uncertainty, the lack of government able to control the territory created a breeding ground for informal and illegal activities. During the conflict, corruption increased (OECD 2016). This has had a negative effect on the development of the private sector because corruption reduces market competition by favoring the growth of businesses that resort to bribery or informal and illicit practices and that evade taxes, registration, and license costs.

Among firms included in the LES 2018, 46 percent view corruption as a major or very severe constraint to growth. Interviews with business leaders and entrepreneurs suggest that corruption seems to be present at various stages of business transactions. Payment of bribes is reported as common, especially to obtain loans, letters of credit, or to ensure the safe transport of inputs or goods. About 62 percent of firms report this constraint to have worsened since 2013.

Forty percent of firms report that crime, theft, and disorder are major or very severe constraints to growth. The issue seems most severe in the construction sector (16 percentage points above the average) and for firms in the South, where 86 percent describe it as a major or very severe constraint (in contrast, 25 percent of firms in the Eastern region rate the issue as major or severe). For the majority (52 percent) of firms, the constraint has worsened since 2013.

One of the most important consequences of weakened state institutions is the lack of state control over the borders. Lack of control over the borders has contributed to the proliferation of smuggling. Smuggling in Libya concerns two main types of products. The first is products Libya subsidizes, such as fuel. Fuel smuggling has several negative impacts, the most important of which are large losses for the Libyan government, increases in the exchange rate with the dollar, fuel shortages in the local market, and increased black-market prices. The second type of product(s) that are smuggled are goods that are imported into Libya at the official exchange rate, such as wheat flour, and then resold in the black market at much higher prices (Eaton 2018).

EFFECT OF THE CONFLICT ON FIRM PERFORMANCE

The conflict affected every region of Libya, albeit with different intensity. During 2013–18, the Eastern region had the largest number of violent events and fatalities, followed by the West.[11] The firms most affected by Libya's conflict were not necessarily located in regions where fatality rates were the highest, however. Firms in the South, followed by those in the West, report the greatest negative effects from the conflict, implying that conflict can affect firms more profoundly than is revealed by measures of conflict intensity such as number of fatalities, physical destruction, and material damages and operation site closures. Less visible impacts include loss of markets and destruction of networks and distribution channels.

Material damage

Material damage and operation site closure are two direct effects of the conflict. Consistent with the geographic variation in fatalities, the LES 2018 shows that the largest share of firms affected by material damage and site operation closure was in the Eastern region (59 percent) (map 7.1).

Revenues, demand, and competition

The conflict has led to a decline in revenues for 51 percent of firms, according to the LES 2018, but this average conceals substantial heterogeneity. Although a majority of firms (53 percent) in the LES 2018 report that annual revenues declined over the preceding five years, 41 percent report revenue increases. This increase could be attributed to the changing nature of market competition, to an increase in informal activities, to a change in the access to letters of credit (and their manipulation in the black market), and other means of elite capture.

Declines in revenues are linked to firm size, with large firms suffering most (figure 7.2). However, the link with firm size could be biased if conflict makes it more likely that smaller firms exit the market, as seems to have been the case in the Syrian Arab Republic (Salmon, Assaf, and Francis 2018). Firms located in the middle region of Libya are more likely to experience lower revenues (79 percent of the sample) than were those in other regions.

Market demand and competition are key channels affecting firm revenues. The crisis had a negative impact on market demand for many firms (59 percent), but sales volume increased for 21 percent of firms. The decrease in demand is likely the consequence of the population being forced to use their limited income for only essential goods, thereby increasing the demand for these products at the expense of others.

MAP 7.1

Percentage of firms reporting material damage and site closures, 2018

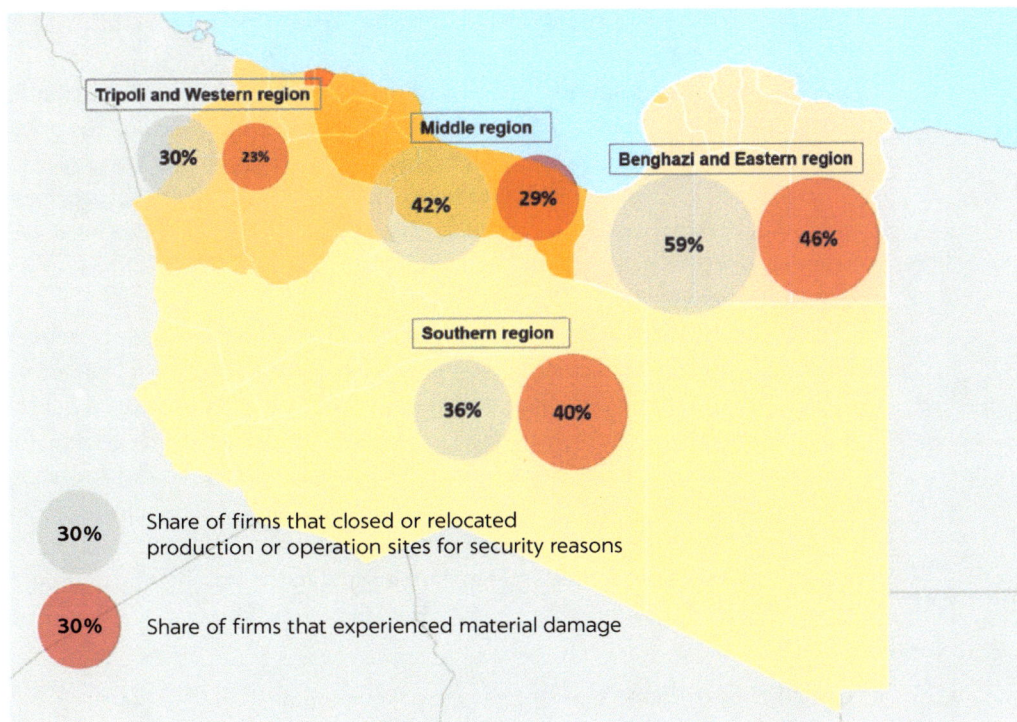

Tripoli and Western region
30%   23%

Middle region
42%   29%

Benghazi and Eastern region
59%   46%

Southern region
36%   40%

30% — Share of firms that closed or relocated production or operation sites for security reasons

30% — Share of firms that experienced material damage

Source: LES 2018.

FIGURE 7.2

FIGURE 7.2

Firms reporting lower revenue, 2018

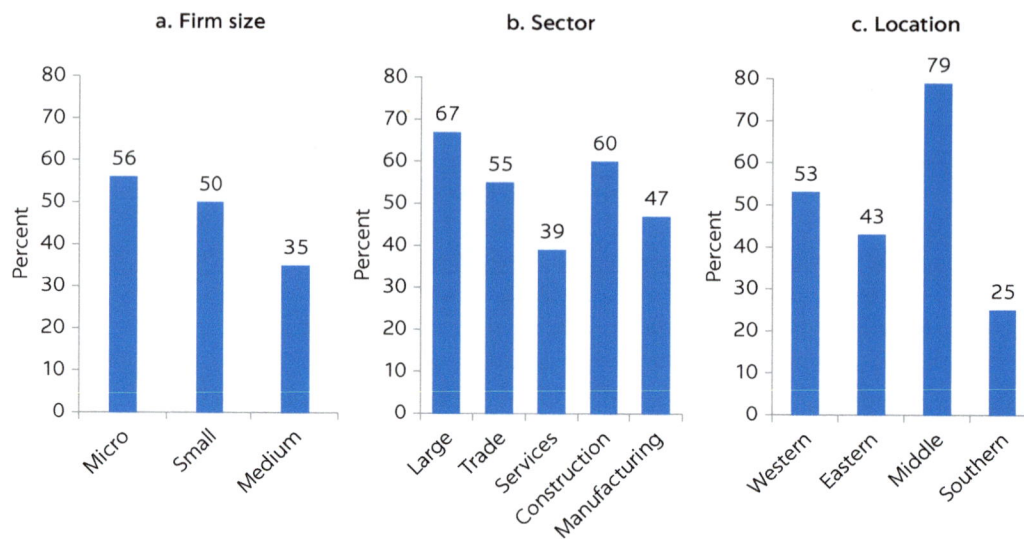

Source: LES 2018.

Conflict has reduced domestic competition. About 43 percent of firms in the LES 2018 report that at least one main competitor had stopped operation since 2013. Among the reasons for exit, firms report the lack of revenue, direct damage to their operation sites, inability to compete with the firms benefiting from black-market rates, or lack of access to letters of credit. Other firms exited because they or their main clients had to leave the country, an effect felt particularly by oil service companies. Many firms reporting a decrease in the number of competitors are in the trade and services sectors (35 percent and 38 percent, respectively, of the sample of firms). The number of competitors that exited is highest for firms in the manufacturing sector (22 on average during the crisis period). Most firms reporting a decrease in the number of competitors are micro or small firms (42 percent and 39 percent, respectively), a finding that is consistent with the conjecture that conflict may cause smaller firms to shut down whereas larger firms experience losses but stay in business. The Eastern region saw the largest number of competitors exit.

The changing dynamics of competition tend to mirror the change in market share for firms across sectors, sizes, and location. Of the firms in the LES 2018, 79 percent report that their market share declined during the crisis, and 21 percent reports an increase in market share. Most of the firms reporting an increase in market share are in trade and services sectors (39 percent and 41 percent, respectively). Firms reporting an increase in market share are also mostly micro and small firms (40 percent and 42 percent, respectively). Most of the firms reporting an increase in market share are located in the Eastern and Southern regions.

Conflict and jobs

The crisis has led to job losses in the private sector, with 30 percent of enterprises reporting a decrease in the number of employees between

2013 and 2017. Firms in the LES 2018 report a 10 percent net loss in jobs over this period. Job loss is most prominent among microfirms (29 percent loss), followed by small firms (15 percent loss), large firms (12 percent loss), and medium-size firms (2 percent loss). Job loss is most prominent in the construction sector (28 percent reduction), followed by the trading sector (16 percent loss).

The reduction in employment is more pronounced in large firms (21 percentage points above average) and construction and manufacturing firms (13 and 7 percentage points above average, respectively). Overall, 15 percent of firms report Libyan staff abandoning their positions because of the crisis; among large firms, the figure is 28 percentage points above average. One-fifth of firms report foreign employees leaving the country. This problem is particularly acute among construction firms (12 percentage points above average), historically the largest employers of foreign workers. However, a nontrivial share of firms increases the number of employees (figure 7.3).

Employment losses occur because of shedding of jobs by firms, displacement of domestic workers, and out-migration of foreign workers. Firms report the lack of both unskilled and skilled workers, pointing to a significant loss in the supply of human capital. Accumulating human capital takes a long time, making these results particularly worrisome with regard to the capacity of the Libyan economy to recover from the conflict in the short term.

The top three constraints affecting firms' hiring of additional workers are the general economic situation, wage inflation, and the security situation. About 63 percent of firms rate the general economic situation as a major or very severe obstacle, about equally across sectors; it is a more significant issue for hiring in the Southern region (29 percentage points above average). The general economic situation seems to affect fewer large firms (27 percentage points below average). Wage inflation affected 45 percent of enterprises, particularly in the South (48 percentage points above average). The general security situation affects the hiring decisions of 43 percent of firms.

FIGURE 7.3

Impact of the conflict on jobs, by sector, 2018

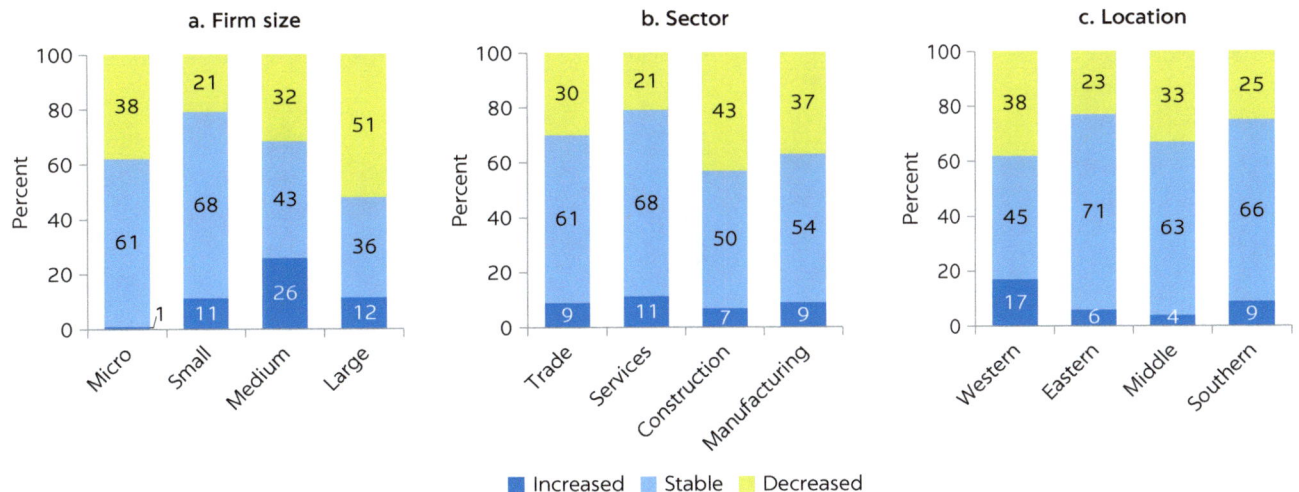

Source: LES 2018.

Firm operations

The conflict has disrupted firms' production and operations in several ways, including by increasing costs, disrupting supply lines, creating shortages of intermediate inputs, and reducing days of production (figure 7.4). About 68 percent of firms report higher costs. Larger firms tend to feel the burden the most, primarily because they are easier targets for illegal activities, operate in sectors for which the crisis-induced unavailability of inputs is more relevant, and have suffered more from lost days of production. Firms in the South face higher costs than firms elsewhere. Because this region is landlocked, firms have likely experienced higher transport and additional informal or illegal insurance costs because of the lack of security. The damage to infrastructure in the South is also significant. Firms in the services sector seem to be less affected by crisis-induced cost increases than other firms because the effects of high prices for raw materials, intermediate inputs, and consumption goods are less for them than for firms in other sectors, such as manufacturing and construction.

The negative effect of the crisis on production and operations has been greatest for manufacturing firms (72 percent of the sample), especially manufacturing firms in the South (17 percentage points above average) and for micromanufacturing enterprises (11 percentage points above average). Manufacturing firms are also more likely to have seen their imports decrease between 2013 and 2017 (29 percentage points above average), mostly because of the restrictions imposed on imports of raw materials as opposed to food products.

The crisis affects both the availability and the price of intermediate inputs. Some 78 percent of firms report a negative effect on the availability of inputs, and 42 percent consider the prices for intermediate inputs to be a major or very severe obstacle. As expected, the problem seems to be most acute for manufacturing firms. About 41 percent of firms experience extra losses from looting, theft, or vandalism since the onset of the crisis. Generally, large firms in the construction trade and construction sectors (44 percent and 41 percent, respectively) are more likely to be affected.

FIGURE 7.4

Share of firms reporting crisis-related impacts, by type of impact, 2018

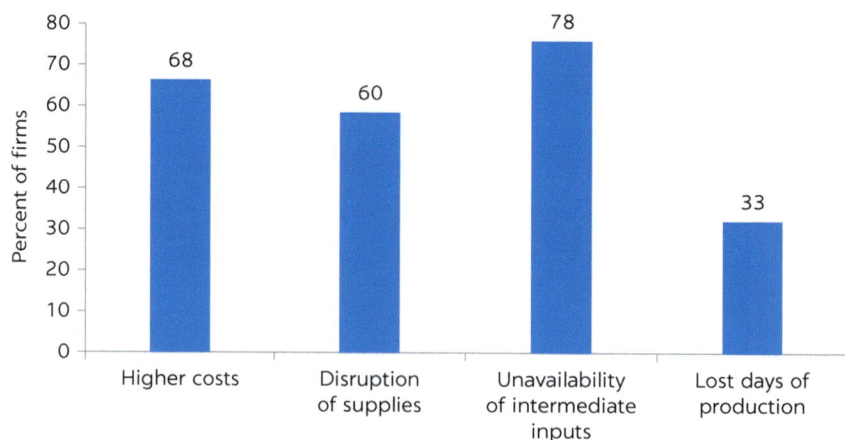

Source: LES 2018.

RESILIENCE AND EXPECTATIONS ABOUT LIBYA FOLLOWING THE END OF THE CONFLICT

To survive during the conflict, many firms have become resourceful and creative. Surviving firms needed to adapt and innovate to navigate the challenges created by the conflict. For many firms whose main businesses have been heavily affected by the crisis, doing so has meant developing new product lines or offering new ways of delivering services when conventional ways become unfeasible. The pressure to survive has made Libyan businesses more resilient and innovative, providing the economy with a good foundation for post-conflict growth.

The conflict has created some space for the private sector. The collapse of government services made room for private enterprises, and the government's failure to pay salaries provided individuals with incentives to leave the government payroll and look for income in the private sector. Because of the crisis, the state has neglected several public services, including health (failing to provide medicines to hospitals and medical centers) and education (failing to maintain schools, pay salaries, or supply materials), clearing a path for private investment. The departure of foreign firms has also left an empty space that Libyan private firms can fill. Overall, 5 percent of firms in the LES 2018 state that the ongoing crisis created new opportunities for their firms. This share is larger among manufacturing firms and firms in Tripoli and the Western region (figure 7.5).

Anecdotal evidence suggests that small-scale private businesses have multiplied since 2014, including cafes and catering and retail businesses. Interviews with stakeholders also suggest that the number of women entrepreneurs in trade and food processing has increased, particularly in the municipality of Benghazi.

Youth have turned increasingly to entrepreneurship because of the collapse of the public sector. According to Expertise France (2016), 71 percent of Libyan

FIGURE 7.5

Percentage of firms reporting that the crisis created new opportunities, 2018

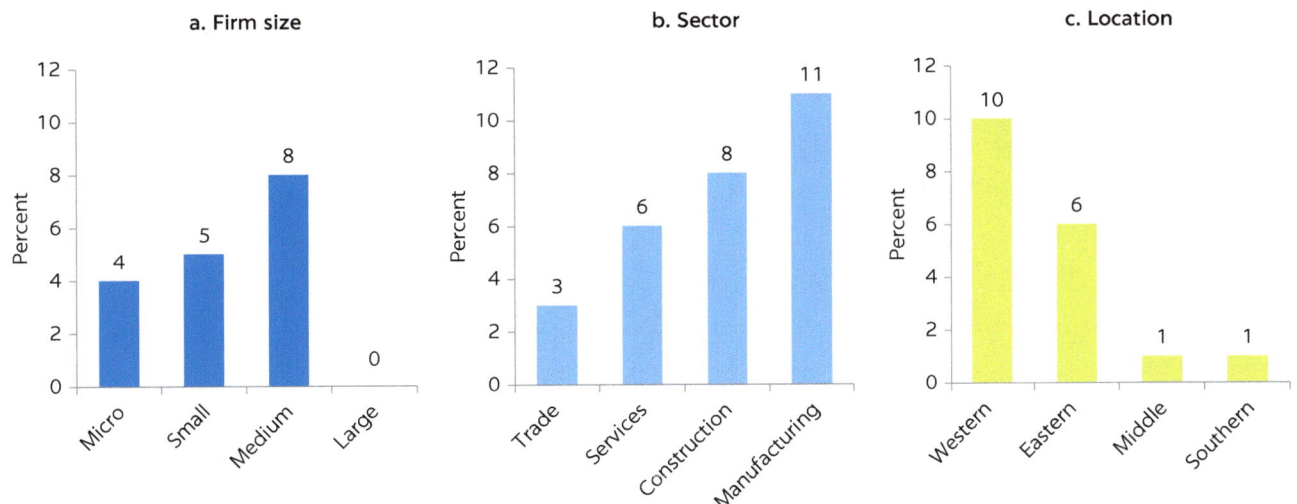

Source: LES 2018.

youth are attracted to entrepreneurship. Employed youth are more likely to be entrepreneurs than wage earners. They use their revenues to invest in their projects and generate more income. Unemployed youth also turn to entrepreneurship because of the lack of other opportunities. Youth have responded to innovative ideas and business opportunities to address different market failures generated by the conflict.

Overall, the private sector shows optimism, with 78 percent of firms in the LES 2018 believing the end of the crisis would trigger significant growth. Firms in sectors such as construction and manufacturing and in locations such as the Southern region, which have seen the most negative impacts from the conflict, show the highest optimism (figure 7.6). About 97 percent of firms in the South express optimism about Libya once the crisis ends. Asked about their behavior in the next two years, 78 percent of firms in the 2018 LES report planning to increase production, 49 percent report planning to increase investment, and 41 percent report planning to increase the number of people they employ. All large firms report planning to increase production, 87 percent report planning to increase investment, and almost half report planning to increase hiring.

Interviews with stakeholders suggest that growth sectors include construction, private health services, and fast-moving consumer goods. A number of other sectors also have potential, including the information and technology sector, which is still underdeveloped but is likely to attract youth as well as, possibly, foreign investors; the manufacturing sector, if restrictions on importing machinery and raw materials are eliminated; services, especially e-services and financial services; and high-value agricultural products, especially in the South.

FIGURE 7.6

Firms' views of post-conflict impact, 2018

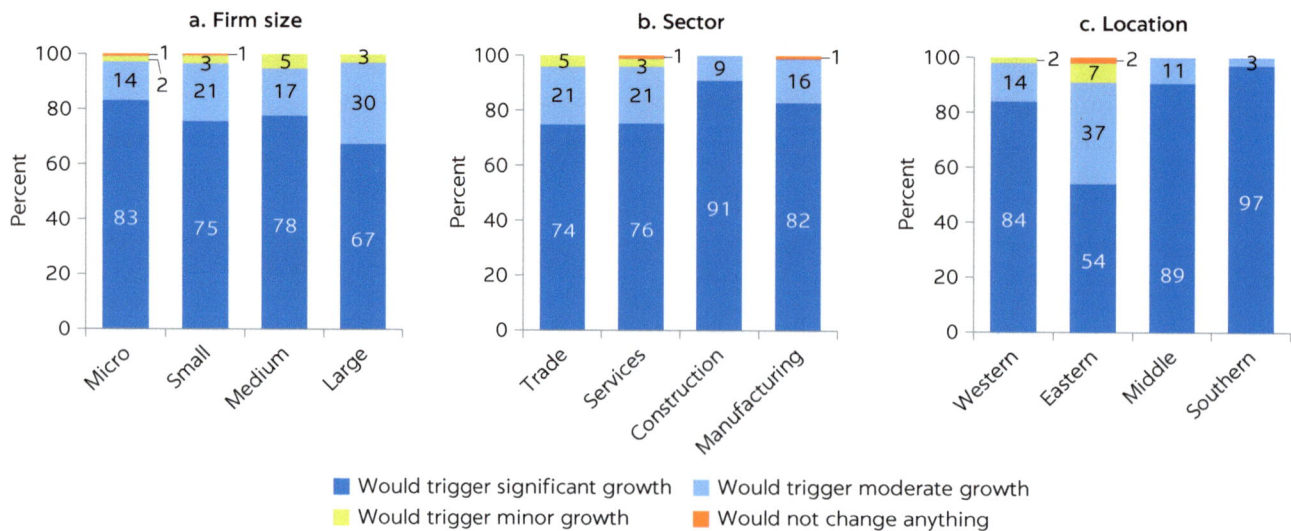

Source: LES 2018.

CONCLUDING REMARKS

Libya's private sector is in desperate need of help to overcome the challenges it faces because of the conflict. There is no time to "wait and see" what develops. Urgent actions need to be taken to enable the private sector to survive the conflict era and create a solid foundation for post-conflict growth.

Immediate actions are needed to tackle fraudulent letters of credit. Difficulties in obtaining letters of credit keep businesses from accessing a wide range of production inputs and finished products. Many sectors, including the construction and fast-moving consumer goods sectors, are badly affected by letter of credit fraud, which contributes to the inflation that hurts Libyans at large.

A fair and transparent public procurement system could contribute to post-conflict economic growth, particularly in sectors such as construction. Promoting access to public procurement by SMEs could be key to promoting their development in Libya. It could also be an important way to reduce informality.

Post-conflict reform priorities need to focus on attracting private investment in reconstruction by completing the unfinished business regulatory reforms of the past 15 years. These reforms need to provide a predictable and transparent regulatory environment conducive to foreign FDI and public-private partnerships; easier entry, exit, and business operation; trade; and a transparent and efficient public procurement system free of elite capture. Building on successful public-private partnerships in contexts of fragility, conflict, and violence, such as Afghanistan and Liberia, this agenda is critical to drive private investment in post-conflict reconstruction and in fast-moving consumer goods, health, education, and other sectors and to promote export competitiveness.

Post-conflict Libya also needs to create conditions conductive to the expansion of the private sector market by limiting the role of the state-owned enterprises. Possible policy actions to consider include creating transparent tax and incentive regimes that treat private and public economic actors similarly; enhancing corporate governance of state-owned enterprises; and passing and implementing competition law and regulations that set up a competent competition authority that can effectively tackle monopolies, cartels, and other anticompetitive behaviors.

Measures will be also needed to channel the rents generated during the conflict into productive uses instead of losing them to capital flight. Although accurate estimates are unavailable, rents generated through illicit economic activities, such as smuggling of subsidized fuel, letter of credit fraud, and accessing foreign currency at the official exchange rate and selling it on the black market, are worth billions of dollars a year (DRI 2019). Imposing more effective international sanctions on offenders, freezing their assets overseas, and channeling their overseas assets back to Libya could be effective.

Libya also needs to adopt a private sector development strategy focused on promoting an entrepreneurship ecosystem that supports youth and women, SME development, and export competitiveness (given Libya's small domestic market). Priority actions to consider include stock taking, harmonizing, and coordinating various public sector and donor activities and programs begun before and during the conflict; identifying gaps; and designing and implementing a sustainable strategy (with specific roles for the public sector, the private sector, and development partners).

A pre-condition for effective support to the Libyan private sector is joint action by external partners to curtail the financial channels that enable elite capture and militia control of economic activities. In the Libyan war economy, vast wealth has been generated through distortions in foreign currency, price subsidies for fuel and other basic products, smuggling, and weak controls over the disbursement of public funds. Much of this wealth is reportedly flowing through the financial systems of neighboring and other countries. Although these distortions originate in policy inconsistencies and institutional fragmentation within Libya, their impact is magnified by these international financial flows. Libya's development partners can commit to using existing mechanisms such as United Nations sanctions (especially related to finance and oil trade), anti-money-laundering and know-your-customer practices, and the sharing of tax information, which would tighten the enforcement net. These measures will contribute to make it more difficult to extract resources from the Libyan economy to fuel the conflict.

NOTES

1. This chapter is based on Rahman and Di Maio (2020).
2. Pre-conflict describes the period prior to 2011–12.
3. Libya was not originally one of the 110 countries in the *Global Competitiveness Report* (GCR) of 2005–06. Porter and Yergin (2006) constructed indexes for Libya and compared them with the 110 countries covered in the GCR.
4. It is difficult to estimate the share of informal activities in Libya's private sector as a whole: the informal economy accounts for 30–40 percent of GDP, according to the African Development Bank (AfDB 2011), and informal employment represents 40–60 percent of total employment (ETF 2014).
5. The Libyan Enterprise Survey (LES) was undertaken in 2018.
6. The concentration of exporting firms in the Western regions is likely related to the cost advantage of geographical proximity to destination markets and the availability of a port and an airport, which have continued to operate, albeit with difficulty, during the crisis.
7. These percentages do not sum to 100 because firms sell to more than one type of buyer.
8. Foreign currency reserves increased in 2018 and 2019 (compared with 2013–17), as oil production increased and domestic demand fell.
9. Elite capture refers to the capture of state resources (primarily oil resources), public expenditure, and institutions; favorable access to foreign currency and letters of credit; and capture of public contracts by individuals or groups.
10. To address the letter of credit and foreign exchange crisis, the government introduced a 183 percent fee on foreign currency in September 2018. On March 5, 2020, the CBL proposed increasing that fee to 200 percent. Since the announcement by the CBL board of directors regarding the establishment of a unified exchange rate starting January 3, 2021, the gap between the parallel market rate (LD 5.10 per dollar) and the official rate (LD 4.48) has narrowed.
11. Data on conflict events are drawn from the PRIO/Uppsala Armed Conflict and Location Event Data Project (ACLED), https://www.prio.org/data/4, which covers conflict events between 1997 and 2018.

REFERENCES

AfDB (African Development Bank). 2011. "Libya: Post-War Challenges." Economic Brief, September. Abidjan, Côte d'Ivoire: AfDB.

DRI (Democracy Reporting International). 2019. "At a Glance: Libya's Transformation 2011–2018: Power, Legitimacy and the Economy." Berlin: DRI.

Eaton, T. 2018. *Libya's War Economy: Predation, Profiteering, and State Weakness*. London: Chatham House, Royal Institute of International Affairs.

ETF (European Training Foundation). 2014. *Labour Market and Employment Policy in Libya*. Turin, Italy: ETF.

Expertise France. 2016. *Youth Motivations to Entrepreneurship*. Paris: Expertise France.

LES (Libyan Economic Survey) "Libyan Economic Survey—Private Sector Analysis" Tripoli: World Bank.

OECD (Organisation for Economic Co-operation and Development). 2016. *SMEs in Libya's Reconstruction: Preparing for a Post-Conflict Economy*. Paris: OECD Publishing.

Porter, Michael E., and Daniel Yergin. 2006. "National Economic Strategy: An Assessment of the Competitiveness of the Libyan Arab Jamahiriya." Tripoli: General Planning Council of Libya.

Rahman, Aminur, and Michele Di Maio. 2020. *The Private Sector amid Conflict: The Case of Libya*. International Development in Focus. Washington, DC: World Bank. https://openknowledge.worldbank.org/handle/10986/34818.

Salmon, K., N. Assaf, and D. Francis. 2018. "Surviving Firms of the Syrian Arab Republic: A Rapid Assessment." Policy Research Working Paper 8397, World Bank, Washington, DC.

World Bank. 2011. *Libya Investment Climate: Enhancing Private Sector Performance for Diversification and Employment*. Washington, DC: World Bank.

World Bank. 2015. *Labor Markets Dynamics in Libya*. Washington, DC: World Bank.

RELATED READINGS

Libya Herald (Sami Zaptia). 2018. "750m Worth of Libyan Fuel Is Stolen: Sanalla," April 20, 2018. https://www.libyaherald.com/2018/04/20/750-m-worth-of-libyan-fuel-is-stolen-sanalla/.

WTO (World Trade Organization). 2020. "Trade Set to Plunge as COVID-19 Pandemic Upends Global Economy," News Release, April 8, 2020. https://www.wto.org/english/news_e/pres20_e/pr855_e.htm.

8 State of the Financial Sector

VALERIYA GOFFE

World Bank

The split in the Libyan central banks during 2013–22 stymied control over monetary and fiscal policy and performance of full bank supervision because both central banks printed money and issued currency without coordinating. The central bank remains the majority shareholder of public banks, which hold 90 percent of deposits and loans in the system, while being the regulatory agency of the banking sector. However, banks have neither sufficient information nor capacity to make informed credit decisions. Initiatives and progress in the financial sector beyond banking have all but frozen. Despite these difficult conditions, there is still a possibility to support the financial and private sector in Libya.

INTRODUCTION

This chapter analyzes developments in Libya's financial sector, identifies key constraints to its growth, and makes recommendations on enhancing financial intermediation. It is organized as follows. First, the history and development of financial sector in Libya are presented, including a discussion of the main players and key statistics. Second, challenges to the development of the financial sector are discussed. Third, developments outside the banking sector are elucidated. Finally, recommendations for enhancing financial sector development in Libya and concluding remarks are offered. This chapter is a snapshot of the banking sector from 2017 to this period. We draw conclusions from this period, as teams were not able to draw data for the report.[1]

LIBYA'S FINANCIAL SECTOR

Libya's financial sector was never sufficiently developed. Decades of central planning and the dominance of oil revenues led to a highly centralized economy, with the banks, predominantly state owned (with the main shareholder the central bank), essentially acting as intermediaries to finance government projects with depositors' funds. As a result of this structure, Libyan banks did not develop modern banking tools or approaches, especially in client strategy and risk management. Nonbank financing was particularly limited, with few alternatives to bank financing and almost no capital markets. Private property was severely limited during the revolutionary period and formal financing of private sector activities almost nonexistent.

The government tried to shift the economy in the years preceding the 2011 civil war, but reforms in the financial sector have had minimal impact. The resolution of sanctions, declines in oil prices, and other factors encouraged the government to seek a more open economy. Private banking was introduced and other avenues of financing, such as the stock market, were launched. However, in view of the years of legacy weaknesses, many of these reforms had only minimal impact; by the time of the 2011 civil war, the private sector remained weak and disorganized and the banking sector, which still overwhelmingly dominated national finance, remained heavily under the influence of the poorly managed state banks.

Today, the five state banks hold over 90 percent of Libya's deposits, thanks to both the channeling of government salaries mainly through state banks and the many hidden advantages given to state banks, including the broad perception of implicit deposit guarantees. Box 8.1 describes the sector.

The Central Bank of Libya (CBL) is the main shareholder of public banks and the regulatory agency of the banking sector. These dual functions create obvious conflicts of interest, including potential forbearance to the benefit of state-owned banks and the granting of credit to well-connected beneficiaries. Libya is one of the few countries in the world in which the state owns financial institutions through a central bank.

BOX 8.1

Libya's banking sector at a glance

The banking sector

- The split in the central bank results in two central banks (in Tripoli and Bayda).
- Most banks are headquartered in the West and report to the Central Bank of Libya (CBL), Tripoli. Banks headquartered in the East control about a third of banking activity and report to the central bank in Bayda. All banks have operations in both the East and the West of the country and hold reserves at both central banks.
- The banking sector controls over 80 percent of financial sector assets. It includes 19 banks, 5 of which are state owned. Public banks are owned by the CBL. They control approximately 90 percent of deposits.

- Banking system assets totaled LD 124 billion in 2018 and made up 51 percent of gross domestic product (GDP). Loans and credits represented LD 16 billion (13 percent). Short-term deposits accounted for 87 percent of total deposits.
- The National Deposit Guarantee Fund, established in 2005, oversees the CBL. It covers up to LD 250,000 for current accounts. No payout has been made since its inception.
- In 2013, Libya adopted Law No. 1, which prohibits interest on all civil and commercial transactions. The law led to reduction in credit extension.
- Specialized credit institutions include the State Savings and Real Estate Investment Bank, the Agricultural Bank, the Libya Development Bank, and Rifi (Rural) Bank.

continued

Box 8.1, *continued*

Nonbanks

- Libya has 22 insurance companies. The top two control 60 percent of industry assets.
- The Libyan Stock Market was founded in 2006. It has been inactive since 2014 because of political instability.
- Libya has one leasing company, focused on automobile leasing.
- Libya's first microfinance institution was established, with donor funding, in 2019.
- Law No. 4 of 2016 established the legal basis for sukuk (Islamic bond), but none has yet been issued.
- State-owned funds include the Libyan Investment Authority (Libya's sovereign wealth fund), the Libyan Economic and Social Development Fund, and the Libyan Internal Investment and Development Fund.

Financial and payment infrastructure

- The Libyan Credit Information Center was created in 2009. It provides limited information, and quality is a concern.

- Libya's land registry is dysfunctional. There is no movable assets registry.
- The national switch has been instituted, but not all banks are yet connected. The volume of transactions processed through the national switch has been increasing. It includes 7,095 points of sale and over 500,000 customers.

Financial inclusion and access

- Credit to the private sector as share of GDP stood at 17.7 percent in 2018. In 2015, only 2 percent of private firms reported having a loan or credit from a bank.
- Two-thirds of Libyans have a bank account; most accounts are limited to receiving wages. Savings and borrowing rates are high (60 percent and 50 percent, respectively) but largely informal.
- Refugees and migrants are excluded from formal financial services.

In the past decades, the number of banks has increased. Toward the end of the Muammar Gaddafi era, the government liberalized its inadequate banking laws. New, private banks began to enter the system. Several banks were opened to foreign ownership, a trend that was halted and largely reversed by the political crisis.

In 2020, Libya had 19 banks (table 8.1). Most of the new entrants are very small and have so far not had significant impact on financial intermediation. Several of the private banks have already demonstrated poor lending capacity and consequent high rates of loan losses. For most of the rest, income comes largely from transactional businesses, such as foreign exchange trading and transfers.

The increase in the number of players did not translate into greater financial intermediation; inefficient state banks overwhelmingly dominate the sector. The four large predominantly state-owned banks—Jumhouria, National Commercial, Sahara, and Wahda—held 90 percent of deposits as of 2017 and about the same share of loans. The two largest state-owned banks, Jumhouria and National Commercial, together controlled 72 percent of risk-weighted assets (mainly loans) as of 2017, down from 75 percent in 2010 but still representing overwhelming dominance, thanks mainly to financing large state firms (figure 8.1).

TABLE 8.1 **Ownership and location of banks in Libya**

TYPES OF OWNERSHIP/BANK	LOCATION
State owned	
Jumhouria Bank	Tripoli
Libyan Foreign Bank	Tripoli
National Commercial Bank	Bayda
Mixed ownership	
North Africa Bank	Tripoli
Sahara Bank	Tripoli
Wahda Bank	Benghazi
Private ownership	
Alejma'a Alarabi Bank	Benghazi
Al Waha Bank	Tripoli
Al Yaqin Bank	Tripoli
Aman Bank for Commerce and Investment	Tripoli
Arab Commercial Bank	Tripoli
Assaray Bank Trade and Investment Bank	Tripoli
Bank of Commerce and Development	Benghazi
First Gulf Libyan Bank	Tripoli
Libyan Islamic Bank	Tripoli
Mediterranean Bank	Benghazi
Nuran Bank	Tripoli
United Bank for Commerce and Investment	Tripoli
Wafa Bank	Tripoli

Source: Central Bank of Libya.

Specialized credit institutions

Like many emerging economies, Libyan set up state-owned banks to facilitate credit to targeted economic sectors. Table 8.2 describes the four specialized credit institutions.

The specialized credit institutions were set up as extensions of the government to provide support to the targeted sectors. Although called banks, they do not take deposits and are therefore outside the supervisory purview of the central bank. They played an outsized role in the expansion of credit in Libya, reaching more than two-thirds of outstanding loans by end 2010 (IMF 2013).

Because of low financial literacy of the population and lack of financial education initiatives, credits issued by the specialized credit institutions were widely viewed as government grants rather than loans. Some other countries of the world (for example, in Africa) also faced similar problems because their populations expected free assistance from the government and were not sufficiently educated on the nature of assistance being provided. In most cases, loan losses were high and funds had to be replenished on a regular basis, effectively becoming wealth transfer mechanisms to targeted segments of the population. The social impact that each was allegedly sustaining was not well measured to the cost of the subsidy and wealth transfer was hard to calculate and difficult

FIGURE 8.1
Risk-weighted assets of Libyan banks, 2017

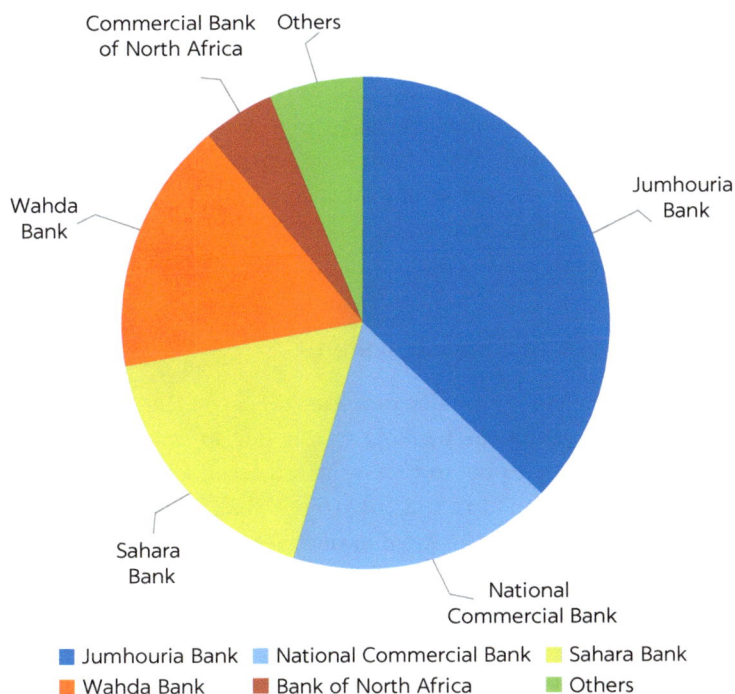

Source: Central Bank of Libya.

TABLE 8.2 **Target areas of specialized credit institutions**

NAME	MAIN TARGET AREA
Savings and Real Estate Investment Bank	Residential housing
Agricultural Bank	Farmers and agriculture
Libya Development Bank	Industry and manufacturing
Rifi (Rural) Bank	Rural development

Source: Central Bank of Libya.

to justify, other than to meet some broad political objectives. The Agricultural Bank and Rifi Bank appeared particularly troubled; both banks are currently effectively suspended.

The Agricultural Bank has essentially frozen operations. It granted loans mainly to farmers for agricultural support, including equipment and working capital, and longer-term investments, such as on-site housing and food processing. Interest rates were far below costs, in terms of both funding and risk. Because of high loan losses and low repayments, the bank suffered liquidity shortages and is likely to have severe negative capital.

The Savings and Real Estate Investment Bank was set up to provide retail property finance services to the public. Owned by the Ministry of Finance, the bank was established in 1983 with a capital of LD 100 million. The bank has effectively ceased new lending, except when granted specific funds to do so.

The Savings and Real Estate Investment Bank relies primarily on government salaries for repayment. Real estate development loans have suffered high losses. These loans are secured not by individual salaries but by the real estate itself.

The choice of land for development was made by an independent unit, the General Authority for Housing and Utilities, and the bank often perceived the land supplied as inappropriate (for example, lacking needed infrastructure).

Libya's Development Bank focuses on industry and manufacturing. It is perceived as one of the stronger special credit institutions. Founded in 1980, with original capital of LD 626 million, it lends to projects of various sizes, organizing them into portfolios by size. The total outstanding portfolio reached LD 1.3 billion in 2019. Bank management reports that default rates remain low, even in the current crisis, and that information management appears to be better than at other specialized credit institutions.

Capitalization of the banking system

The banks are sufficiently capitalized, at least on paper. Despite the high level of nonperforming credits, the banking system has appeared to have booked sufficient capital, with capital to risk-weighted assets hovering comfortably above 15 percent between 2012 and 2017 (figure 8.2), at least partly thanks to the high proportion of funds invested in relatively low-risk CBL assets (up to 70 percent by 2017).[2]

At the same time, most observers believe that even with the relatively small portion of funds in loans, the banking system is undercapitalized and likely largely insolvent, especially the state banks, given the very high rates of loan losses. Some state banks have capitalization levels significantly below the industry average. Only a full audit will reveal the extent of any systemic shortfall. Given the CBL's inability to conduct rigorous reviews; the overall poor information management within the banks, especially the state banks; and the great shocks to the banks' income flows and asset quality since the current crisis, it is almost certain that the CBL's estimates of bank capital are no longer realistic.

The state-owned banks have particularly questionable asset value. For many years, they have been obliged to finance ailing state-owned firms and to support social objectives, such as affordable housing, with little hope of repayment. A realistic valuation of the state banks' assets, and therefore their capital value, would necessitate a full audit by an independent firm, which has not occurred for many years.

FIGURE 8.2

Risk-weighted assets to total capital, 2012–17

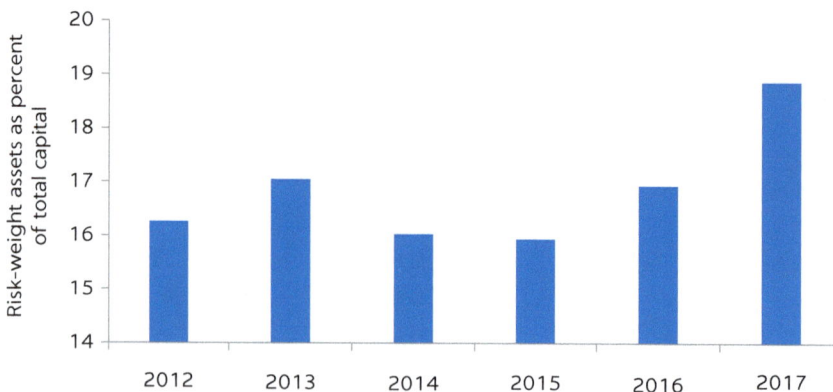

Source: Central Bank of Libya.

CHALLENGES FACING THE SECTOR

Corruption

The banking sector has greatly suffered from the decline in the rule of law. The financial sector is widely viewed as corrupt, with market distortions such as the gaps between checks and cash and between exchange rates, leading to opportunities for extralegal arbitrage. The Tripoli-based Libyan Audit Bureau, appointed by Parliament, has warned that corruption in the banking system is damaging the economy, highlighting six specific types of corruption:

1. Growth of cross-border smuggling of money through manipulation of letters of credit

2. Import of fake and phantom goods to access subsidized foreign currency

3. Widespread money laundering resulting from fraudulent letters of credit

4. Fraudulent manipulation of debit cards

5. Fake deposits through manipulation of the clearing system

6. Misuse of guaranteed checks (Zaptia 2017).

Lack of trust in the banking system and the split of the central banks

The political and financial crises have led to a lack of trust in the banking system. The trust crisis has led to a flight out of the banking system, with most Libyans holding financial assets in cash. From 2004 to 2017, cash outside banks rose from less than LD 3 billion to over LD 27 billion, reaching about a third of the money supply.

The split in the central banks has impaired normal central bank functioning and affected the financial sector in many different ways. Most importantly, it has stymied control over monetary and fiscal policy as the Eastern branch of the central bank prints money and issues bonds without central authority. Spending of the Eastern authorities on salaries, goods and services, and other items is partially financed by the government in Tripoli; the rest is funded through money printing and borrowing independent of Tripoli. Performance of full bank supervision of banks headquartered in the East is not possible. The three banks headquartered in Bayda represent up to a third of banking activity. Management of foreign currency decisions has become very challenging because of both lack of control of funds and the inability to reach formal decisions (on dinar devaluation, for example). A dual payment system has also been created: banks in the West process payments via the real-time gross settlement system (RTGS), and banks in the East perform transactions manually, as the Eastern branch of the central bank has been disconnected from the RTGS.[3]

Cash withdrawals and hoarding

Difficult access to foreign currency at the official rate and lack of trust in banks led to a massive systemic withdrawal. By 2018, up to a third of Libyans' cash was outside the banking system. The dramatic decline in the value of the Libyan dinar led to hoarding of hard currency and unequal access, with profit-seeking by more powerful forces and corrupt individuals and entities further damaging confidence in the banking sector. Devaluation of the dinar would help solve the problem, but it is currently not possible, given the CBL board's lack of authority caused by the central bank split.

As a workaround solution, the CBL moved to narrow the gap between the formal and informal markets with a 183 percent fee on foreign exchange transactions.[4] This action enabled wider access to foreign currency and a rapid narrowing of the gap between the black market and official rate. It also created significant inflow of funds into the budget: the foreign exchange tax was the second-largest revenue item in Libya's budget in 2019 (after oil revenues). However, it is only a partial solution to the underlying problem. As a result of gaps in its application, there are currently three exchange rates: the CBL rate, the rate with the tax, and the parallel market rate. In addition, easier access to foreign exchange has exposed vulnerabilities at some poorly governed banks, with the volume of foreign exchange sales increasing rapidly in 2019 without sufficient due diligence performed by the banks on their clients. The CBL implemented enhanced due diligence of several banks that started facing liquidity problems as a result of massive sales of foreign exchange their clients.

Inadequate credit extension

Several supply- and demand-side factors hinder firms' access to finance. On the demand side, the conflict has directly affected many firms, making it difficult for them to repay bank loans. Key players in the real economy have suffered loss of income and assets through direct harm to their operations, loss of clients, or collapse of supply and distribution channels. A significant share of the Libyan private sector was in the business of commerce, primarily import and redistribution. These activities have been hit hard by the loss of civilian income, the decline in the value of the Libyan dinar, its volatility, and the unreliable availability of foreign exchange.

The credit risk environment remains weak. The broader business environment stymies credit extension, given weak or absent collateral laws, lack of protection of secured creditors' rights through bankruptcy laws, and weak credit information. Credit information suffers from a lack of reliable client financial information along with a poor audit and accounting infrastructure. Avoidance of taxes discourages transparency, and independent auditors or rating agencies, which would encourage financial transparency, have yet to make headway in Libya. The CBL has set up a credit bureau, the Libyan Credit Information Center, but its data set is limited and hampered by systemic information weaknesses.

Financial intermediation continues to decline. The pace of banking intermediation, already low by global standards, has recently dropped even further, almost to a standstill, as a result of the ongoing military conflict, which depressed economic activity and directly destroyed assets in the real estate sector; the split between Western and Eastern factions; the imposition of an Islamic banking law (Law No. 1 2013), which overnight forbade interest on loans and deposits; the lack of foreign currency and the wild swings in LD values; and the increase in corruption linked to the overall decline in the rule of law.

The poor quality of financial intermediation has led to high rates of nonperforming loans. The state banks, which historically served primarily as distributors of state-directed financing, never evolved modern methods of credit risk management. Dominating the banking sector, their weak capacity distorted credit allocation, with poor-performing firms benefiting from underpriced risk funds. The consequent ripple effect echoed distortions throughout the system, precluding the evolution of modern tools to correctly measure and price risk. The most recent evaluation of bank portfolio quality dates from 2010, and even at that time, over 20 percent of loans were nonperforming, which would normally threaten system solvency. At that time, two private banks were particularly at risk, with more than three quarters of their loans in default. The situation was almost certainly much worse, as supervision was weak, with noncapture of restructured credits and overdue interest, for example. Moreover, Libyan banks may not write off overdue loans without court agreement, leading to long-dead loans sitting on the balance sheet and exaggerating asset size. Since the time of the last supervisory review, the proportion of nonperforming loans has risen dramatically at all banks, especially state banks, threatening systemic capital and liquidity.

Credit extension as a share of banking assets has dropped dramatically. The combination of high credit risk, liquidity volatility, and uncertainty regarding the rules and processes of shari'ah-compliant financing has slashed the extension of bank credit. Banks' assets have increasingly fled from lending to both other banks and final customers to the relative safety of placement with the CBL. Loans—which were already a small proportion of total assets by global and regional standards—have continued to shrink (figure 8.3). Banks have become less intermediaries and more safe deposit boxes—and not fully reliable ones at that.

Systemwide, most customer deposits are placed in liquid assets, mainly CBL deposits, with little lending. As credit extension has collapsed, the vast majority of customer deposits are recycled into very liquid assets, overwhelmingly bank deposits with the CBL (table 8.3). Loans rebounded very slightly in 2019, but not enough to change the loan-to-deposit ratio of 18 percent. The state remains the largest holder of deposits, with 44 percent of total.

Few firms, public or private, have access to formal lending. The decline in credit allocation has squeezed financing for businesses and corporations. Lending represented only 13 percent of bank assets in 2018 (EU 2018). Most of

FIGURE 8.3

Lending as share of total assets, 2015–17

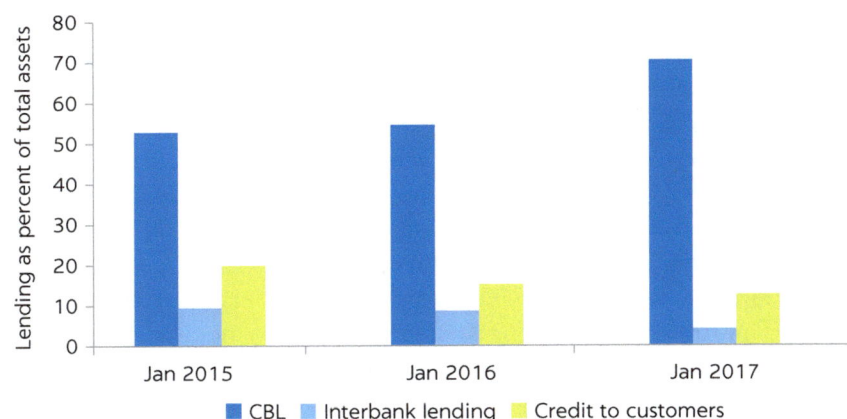

Source: Central Bank of Libya (CBL).

TABLE 8.3 **Systemic balance sheet of the banking system, 2018**

ASSETS			LIABILITIES		
TYPE	LD, BILLIONS	PERCENT OF TOTAL	TYPE	LD, BILLIONS	PERCENT OF TOTAL
Liquid assets	92	74	Deposits	101	82
of which deposits at CBL	84	68			
Deposits and investments	9	7			
Loans and credits	16	13	Capital and reserves	4	3
Other	7	6	Other	19	15
Total	124	100		124	100

Source: Central Bank of Libya.

the credit that is being extended goes to large companies. Small and medium-size enterprises are largely frozen out of the formal financial system and tend to self-finance or seek informal financing sources.

The financing of private firms is far below levels in high-income economies. Domestic credit to the private sector as a share of gross domestic product (GDP) averaged 21 percent from 2010 to 2017—far lower than the 51 percent among countries in the Middle East and North Africa (MENA) region and the 99 percent among upper middle-income countries (figures 8.4 and figure 8.5).

Credit extension to private firms has been particularly hard hit by the crisis. By 2015, only 2 percent of private firms in Libya reported having a loan or credit from a bank—far lower than the 52 percent in Lebanon and 32 percent in Morocco (World Bank 2018). Figure 8.6 shows the proportion of credit to private, public, and foreign firms.

The low level of credit allocation to the private sector can be traced to multiple causes. The poor enabling environment discourages lending, and banks have low internal competence for risk discrimination. Libya suffers from very low levels of credit risk management capacity, including credit analysis. The problem is especially acute at the state banks but is a systemwide problem. It is widely believed that the banks, especially state banks, grant loans based more on personal connections than on rational risk versus reward analysis (Alrafadi, Kamaruddini, and Yusuf 2014). Moreover, the state banks did not typically face incentives to preserve capital and were given mixed, and typically poorly measured, social impact goals.

Poor credit risk management leads to disproportionately higher demand for collateral. Even poorly managed banks eventually run into pressure to limit loan losses. Without proper credit risk-management tools, the usual mitigation approach is to raise collateral coverage requirements in an often-false belief that collateral will offset default risk. Libya stands out in its reliance on collateral, even by high MENA standards, with essentially no credit extension relying solely on cash flow strength. This finding is not surprising, given the difficult economic environment in Libya and the lack of knowledge of cash flow lending techniques by the banking sector.

Firms in Libya that want to borrow must thus already have substantial collateralizable assets. In the best of times, this requirement would limit lending to an

FIGURE 8.4

Domestic credit to the private sector in Libya, the Middle East and North Africa Region, and upper-middle-income countries, 2010–17

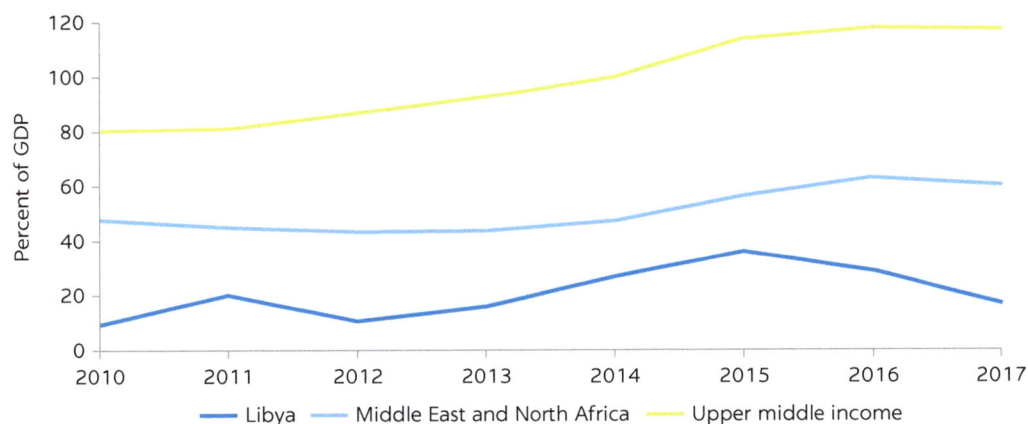

Source: World Development Indicators (database), World Bank, various years.
Note: GDP = gross domestic product.

FIGURE 8.5

Domestic credit to the private sector in the Middle East and North Africa

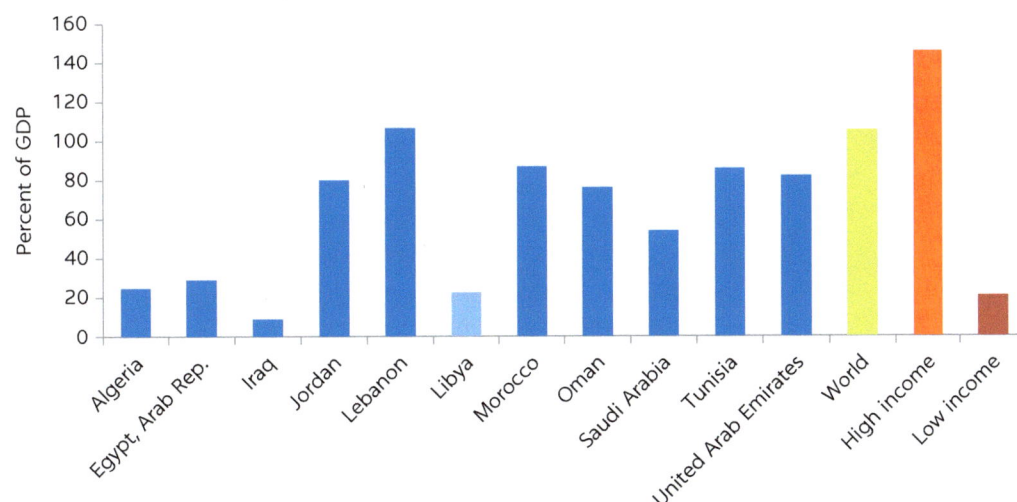

Source: IMF, International Financial Statistics databank and data files, https://www.imf.org/en/Publications /International-Financial-Statistics/Issues/2016/12/31/International-Financial-Statistics-20151; and World Bank and Organisation for Economic Co-operation and Development GDP estimates, 2017.
Note: GDP = gross domestic product.

elite subset. However, given Libya's weak property regime, including a dysfunctional land registry and a poor legal and judicial environment, credit extensions are limited to all but the largest and/or best-connected borrowers. This reliance on connections and name lending also increases the risk of corruption.

A new initiative aims to reactivate Libya's partial credit guarantee program. A donor-funded project is helping relaunch Libya's partial credit guarantee scheme, which has been renamed the Credit Guarantee Fund. The Government of National Accord has approved the fund's restructuring, with a new board, and a memorandum of understanding has been signed with six Libyan banks to offer

FIGURE 8.6

Proportion of credit to private, public, and foreign firms, 2015–17

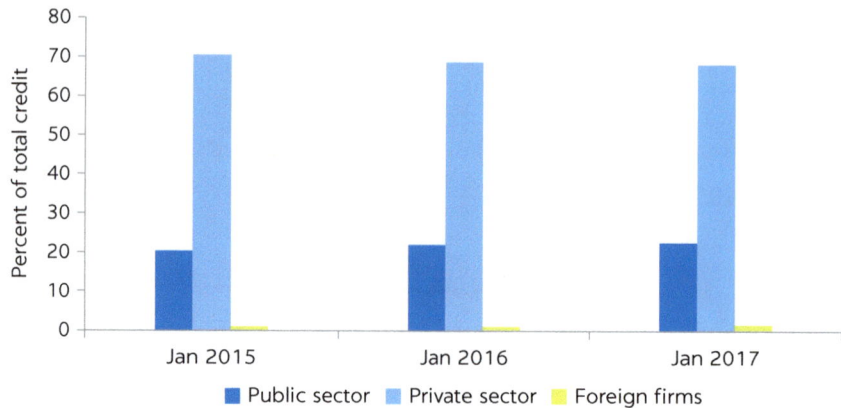

Source: Central Bank of Libya.

LD 150 million worth of credit to be guaranteed. The consulting team is working on risk and operating policies and building information technology systems. It is expected that the fund will help banks provide loans to creditworthy businesses that lack collateral.

Informality of savings and borrowing

Savings rates in Libya are high but informal. Over 60 percent of the population reports having saved in the past year (figure 8.7). However, the distribution of saving is much less formal than in other MENA countries. Although the rate of formal saving in Libya (17 percent) exceeds the regional average of 12 percent, 44 percent of Libyans resort to informal means of saving.

Most borrowing is informal. Although more than half of Libyans report having borrowed money in the past year, only 8 percent reported have done so formally, through a financial institution or credit card. The majority of Libyans who borrow do so from family or friends (figure 8.8). This pattern is not uncharacteristic of other MENA countries, where informal borrowing accounts for the largest share of loans. In other countries, borrowing from retail stores is also common. In some countries, savings clubs are also used, although they are much more common in Sub-Saharan Africa.

Financial inclusion

On the surface, Libyan households appear to have a high level of access to financial services. Banks are (largely) functioning and rates of account ownership relatively high. Approximately two-thirds of Libyans hold an account at a financial institution—a larger share than in the Arab world (37 percent) or MENA (48 percent) (map 8.1). A key reason for the relatively high account penetration is the large share of government jobs, which pay salaries directly into pay accounts.[5] However, most of these accounts are limited to receiving wages, with very little financial intermediation. Almost two-thirds of Libyans save and borrow, but only about one-fifth save and one-tenth borrow through formal channels. Libya is a

FIGURE 8.7
How individuals save in six countries in the Middle East and North Africa, 2019

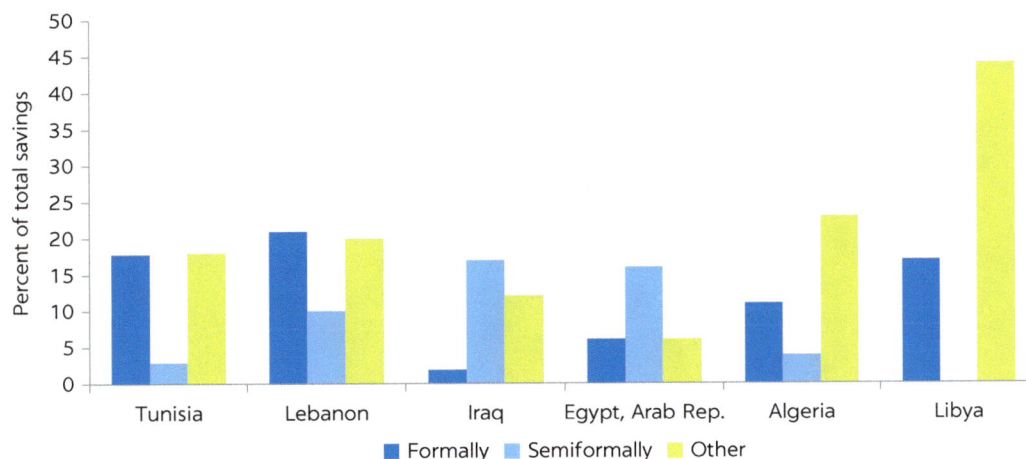

Source: Global Findex Database, World Bank, 2019.

FIGURE 8.8
Source of loans in six countries in the Middle East and North Africa, 2018

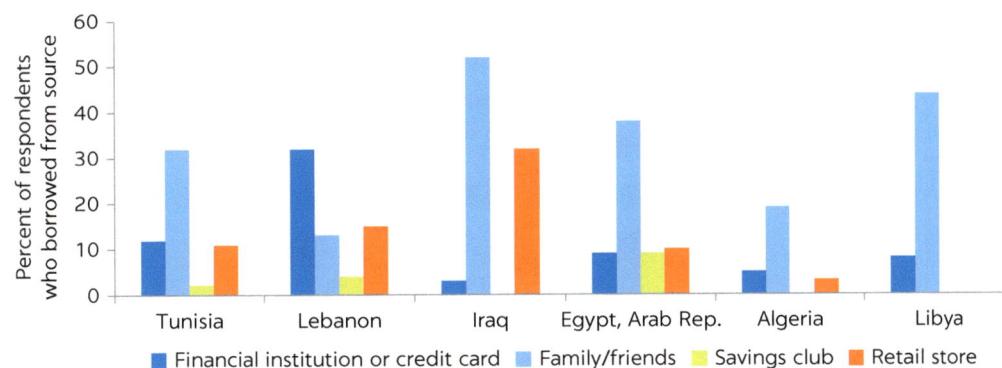

Source: Global Findex Database, World Bank, 2018.

primarily cash-based economy when it comes to payments for goods and services, as well as wages, especially in the private sector.

A common reason for initially opening a bank account in MENA is to receive a government transfer (figure 8.9). Bank accounts also allow individuals to take advantage of the government allowance to purchase $500 each annually at the official exchange rate. These purchased funds are disbursed via a Visa or MasterCard issued by the bank at which the recipient maintains an account (Danish Refugee Council 2018). The banking relationship in Libya is overwhelmingly for the purpose of cash disbursal, with most account holders withdrawing cash and then acting as if in an otherwise cash-based economy.

Private sector workers, in contrast, receive wages in cash. Overall, only 43 percent of adult workers in Libya receive wages through an account at a financial institution. The remaining workers are paid in cash. The figure is more than 70 percent in the public sector and just 21 percent in the private sector.

MAP 8.1

Share of the population over 15 holding an account at a financial institution in the Middle East and North Africa, by country

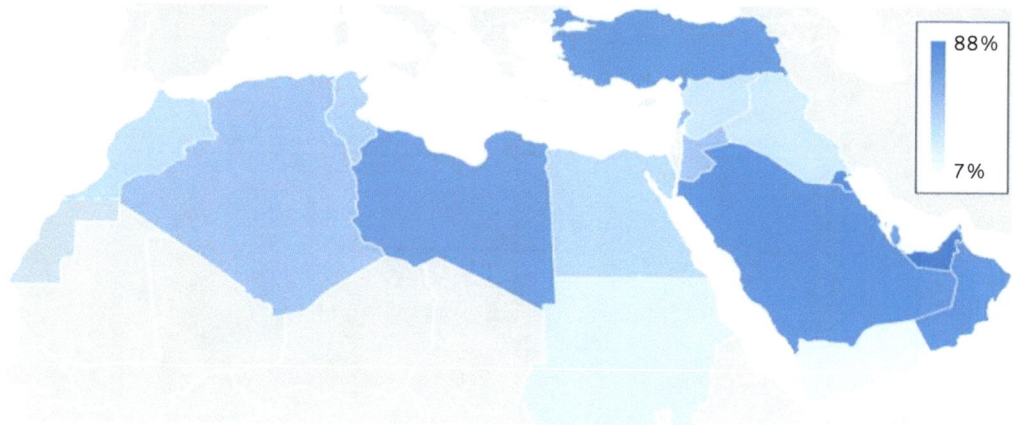

Source: Global Financial Inclusion Data Bank (World Bank 2018).

FIGURE 8.9

Share of individuals 15 and over who opened their first account in order to receive a government transfer (percent)

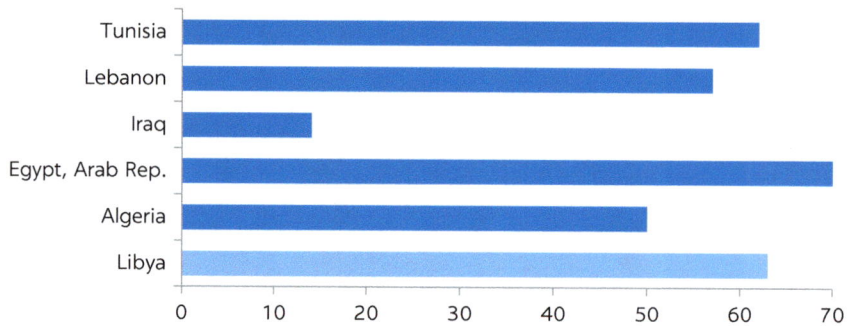

Source: Global Findex Database, World Bank.

Gender gap

Several inequities in access to finance characterize the financial system, although they are generally less severe than in some of Libya's regional peers. For example, the gender gap is significant, with an 11 percent difference in account access between men (71 percent) and women (60 percent), but it is relatively low for the MENA region, where the gender gap tends to be higher than global averages. It is 24 percent in Morocco and 27 percent in Algeria.

Income disparity is also reflected in financial access: while 71 percent of individuals from the top three income quintiles hold an account, 58 percent of those from the bottom two income quintiles do so. Despite this disparity, rates of account ownership by income remain far above those of many regional peers. Inequality in account ownership by income is much more pronounced in Lebanon and Tunisia than in Libya, for example.

Use of mobile phones and mobile banking

The share of Libyans using their mobile phones to access their accounts is comparatively low. As of 2017, only 8 percent of Libyans used their phones to access banking services, lagging the MENA average of 12 percent. Regulatory and licensing hurdles have slowed the transition. Banks, telecom companies, and other financial technology providers must acquire a license from the CBL to use electronic payments—and regulations have not kept up with the pace of expansion of these services. Some regulations relating to cards, mobile banking, and electronic payments have been promulgated by the CBL as circulars through the CBL's settlements and payments division. There is no electronic transactions law, despite some efforts initiated as early as 2008–10. There is also no regulation detailing how or whether telecom companies would or should share information with the CBL. Currently, CBL does not oversee telephone transfers that are within a bank, leading to possible money-laundering concerns.

Despite these hurdles, the use of mobile banking and electronic payments is rising quickly. The increase has been spurred partly by the liquidity crisis, as virtual money replaces cash. The most notable player in this space is Watba, a closed-loop service that allows customers of the Bank of Commerce and Development to send money to one another through the use of an app. The volume of transaction of this service is over LD 10 billion—five times the volume of transactions processed through the national switch. A similar service is Sadad, which provides instant transfer capabilities based on an e-wallet system tied to the client's phone number. The functionality is straightforward, but the lack of a fully integrated banking sector has prevented Sadad from becoming a leading player.

Some companies and utilities have begun using electronic bill payments. More sophisticated banks are developing mobile wallet services and products to pay bills and handle other types of transactions. The potential for mobile banking in Libya is significant. Mobile and smartphone penetration is high, especially among young people. The penetration of connections is high, given the geographic concentration of the population in a few main cities along the coast. In addition to a large share of the population owning bank accounts, Libyans are active social media users, with a far larger proportion than other MENA countries outside the Gulf Cooperation Council (GCC) (almost 70 percent versus less than 50 percent) (figure 8.10).

The potential for expanding digital finance is hampered by poor infrastructure and a lack of private suppliers. Libya's 4G coverage (67 percent) significantly lags that of the average for MENA (82 percent); coverage by 3G networks is higher than the MENA average (98 percent versus 93 percent). Connectivity is poor, with connection speeds averaging half non-GCC MENA, as a result of the weak telecommunications infrastructure and intermittent electrical outages.

Poor service and low coverage are largely the result of the dominance of inefficient state companies, in both telecom and electricity, exacerbated by the conflict. Libya has full state ownership in the mobile market; the MENA average is 46 percent. Libya has a high fixed broadband concentration index (8,264 versus 6,804 MENA average).

Libya lacks a legal framework for key drivers of digital growth, lacking regulations on data protection and online privacy, cybercrime prevention, online consumer protection, and electronic transactions or e-signatures. The lack of

FIGURE 8.10

Bandwidth and percentage of social media users in Libya and the Middle East and North Africa

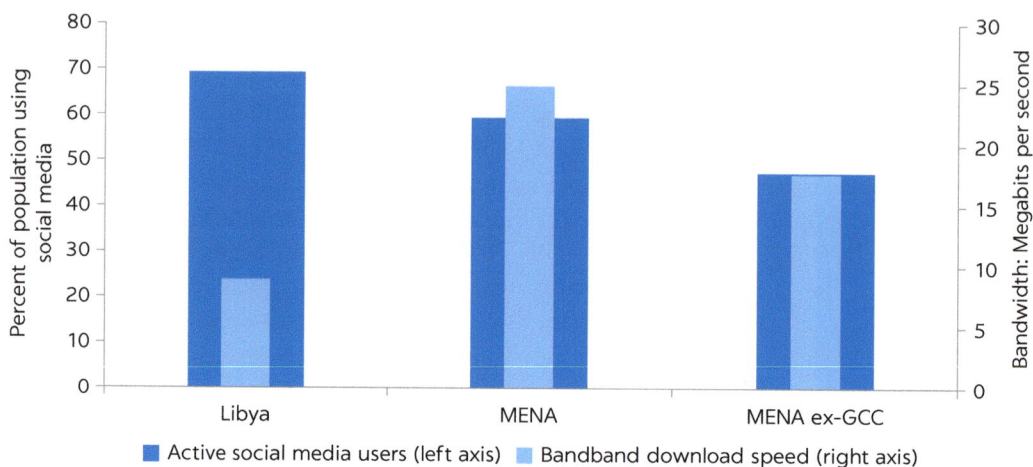

Source: World Bank 2019.
Note: GCC = Gulf Cooperation Council; MENA = Middle East and North Africa.

legal infrastructure hinders private digital service providers (banks or others) from entering the market.

Migrants and refugees

Migrants and refugees constitute a large and growing share of Libya's population, up from 10 percent in 2010 to 12 percent in 2015. Since oil was discovered, in the 1950s, migrant workers have come to Libya from the Middle East, North Africa, and Sub-Saharan Africa. Gaddafi introduced visa-free travel from Sub-Saharan Africa to Libya in the 1990s, making Libya one of the main destinations for migrants in the continent.

Between 2005 to 2015, the number of migrants rose from 625,000 to 771,000, despite the spring uprising and the unrest. Despite the increase, the total value of their remittances out of the country has fallen since 2014 (figure 8.11).

Migrants and refugees are essentially excluded from the financial system, forcing them to rely on cash transactions and exposing them to a variety of risks. Almost half of them save money in a safe place at home, a third transfer part of their savings directly to their home country, and a fifth always carry their savings with them (figure 8.12). Criminal gangs and militias take advantage of the fact that migrants are paid in cash and have limited means to store money safely. Not surprisingly, saving for an emergency situation was identified as the primary reason for savings, followed by returning home and transiting to Italy.

To transfer funds, many refugees and migrants use the parallel market, on which the exchange rate is much costlier than the official rate. Worse yet, migrants in the South lack access to the parallel market and have to rely on their Libyan employer, Libyan friends, or contacts within the refugee community to facilitate transactions. Transactions can take three days, with an average transaction fee of 11–15 percent of the transfer amount.

The greatest cause for financial exclusion is the state of informality. Most migrants and refugees work without contracts, their working hours are long, and their work environments are often precarious. Most work in the service sectors,

FIGURE 8.11

Number of migrants and value of remittances sent from Libya, 2005–16

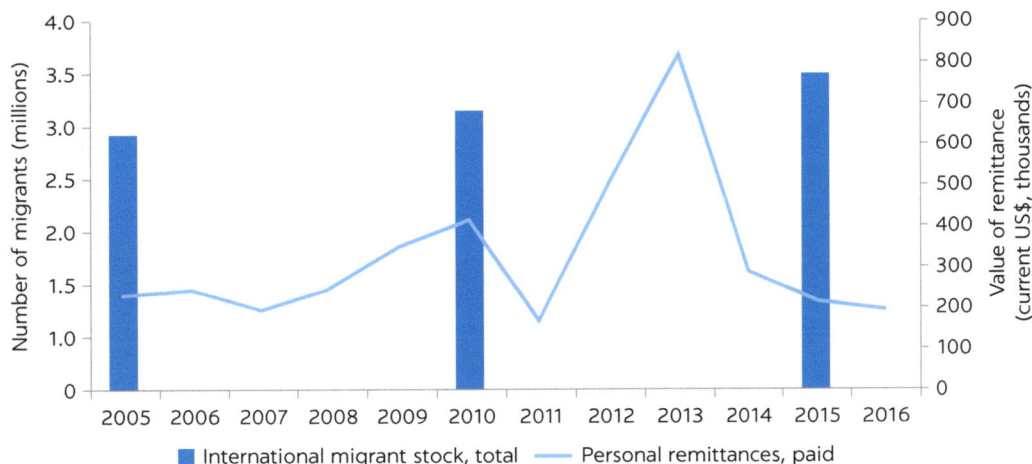

Source: World Development Indicators (World Bank, various years).

FIGURE 8.12

How migrants and refugees in Libya save money

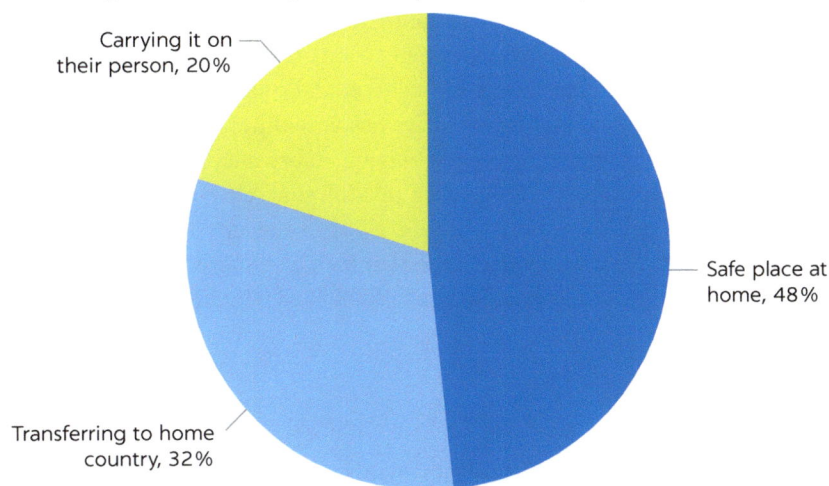

Source: REACH 2018.

followed by construction and agriculture. Wages are paid in cash, because of workers' inability to open bank accounts, their irregular status, and the general practice of paying migrants in cash. Most migrants and refugees seek to work for employers with whom they have established relationships of trust, but not being paid remains a major concern among them. They have little legal recourse in the event of nonpayment. When asked whom they would turn to if not paid, only 11 percent cited the police or nongovernmental organization (Findex data), suggesting a low level of trust in protection from formal institutions.

Small and medium-size enterprises

A draft law on small and medium-size enterprises (SMEs) (Law 2018 7-2) was drafted in 2018, but it has not yet been promulgated. The intent of the law is to streamline SME formation and encourage financing and support. The law defines micro, small, and medium-size enterprises (MSMEs) as follows:

- Micro: Investment or net assets of no more than LD 100,000, with no more than five employees
- Small: Investment or net assets of LD 100,000–1 million, with no more than 25 employees
- Medium: Investment or net assets of LD 1 million–5 million, with more than 25 employees.

A new donor-funded project is supporting the launch of a private fund dedicated to MSMEs. The fund is in its very early stages. Commitments are being sought by the Libya Stock Market and the CBL, and initial discussions are being conducted with target SMEs and investors. The legal and payment infrastructure is not conducive to crowdfunding, especially cross-border. Nonetheless, a self-funded start-up, building on contacts from the second Libya Startups Expo in Tripoli, has launched the first crowdfunding website. The site takes a 5 percent fund-raising fee and remains small, with only a few dozen backers.

DEVELOPMENTS OUTSIDE THE BANKING SECTOR

Initiatives and progress in the financial sector beyond banking are essentially frozen. The stock exchange has essentially been on hold with very little public trading. A few private placements, both shares and sukuk, have been proposed, but the lack of political and legal clarity has stifled progress. Other forms of finance, such as leasing and insurance, remain embryonic. Insurance is further hobbled by the lack of experience with takaful, shari'ah-compliant insurance approaches. Nevertheless, there has been a positive recent development in the microfinance sector—the opening of the country's first microfinance institution, which is a subsidiary of the existing bank established with donor funding.

RECOMMENDATIONS

Any initiatives to strengthen the Libyan financial sector are invariably tied to the evolving political situation in Libya, including but not limited to the division between Tripoli and the Eastern region. In particular, reforming/stabilizing the monetary regime is a precondition to any progress in financial intermediation but can only be accomplished following the unification of CBL with its Eastern branch. Resolution of the political crisis is beyond the scope of this report, but many initiatives could be launched, to varying degrees, even under the current circumstances in anticipation of an eventual peaceful outcome. In particular, the international audit of the central banks in Tripoli and Bayda is essential to a potential unification of central banks in the future. Preparations for asset quality review of the leading banks to determine capital shortfall and analysis of legal and regulatory framework for mergers and acquisitions and banking resolution are also some of the immediate priorities. There would also be significant benefits from initiating the groundwork on (1) rebuilding the land registry, (2) starting to develop the legal and regulatory framework for microfinance and leasing, and (3) building the capacity of financial institutions in SME finance to achieve greater financial inclusion.

CONCLUDING REMARKS

The financial sector of Libya is characterized by several unique features. First, the split in the central banks has stymied control over monetary and fiscal policy and performance of full bank supervision because both central banks print money and issue currency without coordinating. Second, the central bank remains the majority shareholder of public banks, which hold 90 percent of deposits and loans in the system, while being the regulatory agency of the banking sector. Third, banks have neither sufficient information nor capacity to make informed credit decisions. Fourth, initiatives and progress in the financial sector beyond banking have all but frozen.

Despite these difficult conditions, there is still a possibility to support the financial sector in Libya. However, the political environment creates significant challenges that need to be taken into consideration.

NOTES

1. The technical analysis in this chapter is based on the material in the *Libya Financial Sector Review* (World Bank 2020).
2. Inconsistencies in the recorded capital data as well as the likely undercounting of distressed credits make these results unreliable, but they are indicative of the CBL's formal view of systemic capital levels.
3. The central bank does not recognize the manual clearing procedure adopted in the East.
4. The fee was reduced to 163 percent in July 2019.
5. Almost 85 percent of Libyans worked for the government in 2019.

REFERENCES

Alrafadi, Khalad M. S., Badrul Hisham Kamaruddini, and Mazila Md Yusuf. 2014. "Efficiency and Determinants in Libyan Banking." *International Journal of Business and Social Science* 5 (5): 156–68. https://ijbssnet.com/journals/Vol_5_No_5_April_2014/18.pdf.

Danish Refugee Council. 2018. *Libya: Delivery Mechanism Mapping for Cash-Based Interventions.* Copenhagen: Danish Refugee Council.

EU (European Union). 2018. *Identifying Action to Improve Access to Finance for SMEs and Private Sector Development in Libya.* May 28, 2018. Brussels: European Commission. https://www.developmentaid.org/organizations/awards/view/113686/identifying-action-to-improve-access-to-finance-for-smes-and-private-sector-development-in-libya-lot.

IMF (International Monetary Fund). 2013. *Searching for the Finance-Growth Nexus in Libya.* Washington, DC: IMF.

REACH. 2018. *Access to Cash and the Impact of the Liquidity Crisis on Refugees and Migrants in Libya.* Tunis: REACH. https://reliefweb.int/report/libya/access-cash-and-impact-liquidity-crisis-refugees-and-migrants-libya-june-2018.

World Bank. 2015. *Labor Market Dynamics in Libya.* Washington, DC: World Bank. https://documents1.worldbank.org/curated/en/967931468189558835/pdf/97478-PUB-PUBLIC-Box-382159B-9781464805660.pdf.

World Bank. 2018. "Country Engagement Note for the State of Libya." Washington, DC: World Bank.

World Bank. 2019. "MENA Digital Economy Benchmarking Libya (9/19)." Washington, DC: World Bank.

World Bank. 2020. *Libya Financial Sector Review.* Washington, DC: World Bank. https://openknowledge.worldbank.org/handle/10986/36789.

World Bank. Various years. Global Financial Inclusion Data Bank, Washington, DC. https:// databank.worldbank.org/source/global-financial-inclusion.

World Bank. Global Findex Database, Washington, DC. https://www.worldbank.org/en /publication/globalfindex.

World Bank. World Development Indicators (database), Washington, DC. https://databank .worldbank.org/source/world-development-indicators.

Zaptia, Samia. 2017. "Corruption in Libyan Banking Sector Threatens Whole Economy—Audit Bureau 2016 Annual Report," *Libya Herald*, May 4, 2017. https://www.libyaherald .com/2017/05/04/corruption-in-libyan-banking-sector-threatens-whole-economy-audit -bureau-2016-annual-report/.

9 Nowcasting Economic Activity Using Night-Time Lights

DALIA AL KADI AND ALI IBRAHIM AL MELHEM

World Bank

Using high-frequency granularity, the authors estimated gross domestic product (GDP) and oil production in Libya. Night-time lights (NTLs) provided an important source of information on economic activity in Libya, expanding the information set policy makers can rely on. NTL benefits from data that are high frequency, granular, and insulated from human error or malfeasance. Especially in a conflict-affected setting, NTL provides more reliable information than official national accounts data, which can be subject to bias, manipulation, and measurement error.

INTRODUCTION

Like many developing countries, Libya struggles with tracking basic economic activity to support the effective design of public policies. It faces the typical challenges of data availability, reliability, and timeliness. These challenges, however, are compounded by conflict that results in limited state capacity and resources, impediments to data collection, and lower economic integration and price equalization across regions, which distorts the true level of economic output. Official data on annual gross GDP—arguably the most used macroeconomic indicator—has not been published since 2014. Quarterly GDP and subnational GDP data are not available either. Libya, like other fragility, conflict, and violence (FCV) settings, is also characterized by rapidly evolving demographic, social, and economic contexts and a complex landscape of domestic and international actors and interests. This heightens the need for tracking economic activity at a high temporal and spatial granularity, which is challenging to do with standard data sources.

This chapter develops a big data tool to nowcast GDP and oil production in Libya at a high frequency using satellite data on night-time lights. *Nowcasting* is the process of predicting the present (in contrast to forecasting, which is aimed at predicting the future). Following the literature on the use of NTLs in economic nowcasting, we build linear regression models to predict real GDP by including variables on oil prices and conflict in addition to NTLs. We show that our model is useful for nowcasting not only GDP but also oil production. This result is largely due to the high share of the oil sector in the Libyan economy and the direct channel between oil production, gas flaring, and NTLs. Thus, we find that NTLs are a particularly promising big data source for the study of economic activity in Libya in the absence of high quality and high frequency standard data sources.

Nowcasting GDP and oil production in Libya at a high temporal and spatial granularity would significantly improve the ability of stakeholders (for example, domestic policy makers, the private sector, humanitarian agencies, and development partners) to monitor the economic and distributional impact of conflict events, and internal and external shocks and associated policy responses, on economic and welfare outcomes. These data would enable stakeholders to better plan for short-term humanitarian interventions, rapid policy responses, and medium- to long-term reconstruction efforts. They could also serve as an example for the use of NTLs for economic monitoring in other FCV or data-poor environments.

NTLs have become a widely accepted proxy for economic activity at both national and subnational levels and have been shown to correlate strongly with annual movements in real GDP (Henderson, Storeygard, and Weil 2012). Production and consumption of most goods and services in the evening requires lights. Under the assumption that light is a "normal" good: as per capita income rises, so does per capita consumption and production, thereby raising per capita lights. This hypothesis has been confirmed in the literature, both within and across countries, and is increasingly used as a proxy for economic activity (Donaldson and Storeygard 2016). In the economics literature alone, over 150 papers have used NTLs since 2012, thanks partly to platforms such as Google Earth Engine, which make it easy to access the data (Gibson, Olivia, and Boe-Gibson 2020).

NTL data benefit from high frequency, high spatial granularity, broad coverage, and credibility, all of which are lacking in FCV contexts. The high-frequency nature of NTL data is perhaps the most attractive feature, as it allows researchers to study the immediate impact of a shock. Satellites capture data from the same location at weekly or even daily frequencies, offering substantial temporal coverage. For example, a number of recent papers study the impact of COVID-19 containment measures on NTLs in India (Beyer, Franco-Bedoya, and Galdo 2020), China (Elvidge et al. 2020), and Morocco (Roberts 2021).

Another advantage of NTL data over standard data sources is the high spatial granularity, which allows drilling down into subnational areas and a much wider cross-section of areas. This is particularly relevant in conflict situations like Libya's where the geography of conflict can have a stark impact on economic activity and welfare, so much so that averaging across a country of large regions might hide large inequalities. NTLs benefit from being collected uniformly and consistently, without regard to natural disasters or political strife, thereby allowing for broad data coverage across space and time. Coming directly from impartial satellites, NTL data are also insulated from intervention by national statistical agencies or other data collection actors, which can sometimes be inefficient or biased.

The use of NTL data for economic monitoring has its limitations, however, including heavy computing and disk-space requirements, the need to develop specific statistical techniques to extract macroeconomic-relevant signals from often unstructured datasets, and the risk of erroneously picking up on noisy responses from real-time data, among others. NTL data also suffer from issues related to top-coding and image saturation. These challenges are compounded in FCV settings by the unavailability of ground-truth economic indicators that models can rely on to learn better relationships in the data.

This chapter is structured as follows. The first section tests the usefulness of NTL data to nowcast economic activity in Libya. The second section discusses the results and implications. The last section provides some concluding remarks.

PILOTING THE USE OF NIGHT-TIME LIGHTS DATA FOR ECONOMIC MONITORING IN LIBYA

Data

We use the Visible Infrared Imaging Radiometer Suite (VIIRS) and Defense Meteorological Satellite Program (DMSP) satellites as sources for our NTL data. These estimates come from imaging satellite data collected by the US National Aeronautics and Space Administration and National Oceanic and Atmospheric Administration. The VIIRS began collecting data in 2012. It measures brightness from artificial light emissions observed from space. The US Air Force's DMSP Operational Linescan System produced an NTL time series from 1992 until 2013.

The VIIRS dataset is provided at a high spatial resolution of less than 500 square meters. It provides nightly, monthly, and annual estimates. The DMSP data provide annual estimates only. The VIIRS satellite provides a wider detection range, finer quantization, lower detection limits, and in-flight calibration, which help correct for saturation of images and improve temporal comparability (Elvidge et al. 2013).

Using data from both VIIRS and DMSP, we estimate the annual and monthly sum of lights (SOL) as our measure of national NTL output. We use monthly data from the VIIRS satellite for the period April 2012 to December 2020. For earlier years, we use annual data from the DMSP satellite that extend as far back as 1992. Map 9.1 shows the map of NTL's Libya in 2019 as an example.

Each dataset is essentially a collection of pixels on a map, where each pixel is labeled with a corresponding radiance value. This radiance value is the average recorded luminosity (in nano-watts/cm^2/sr) over all cloud-free nights for the period in question. In Libya, cloud coverage is extremely low, which limits distortions to satellite radiance estimates (in northern countries, cloudier weather can provide material limitations on the use of NTLs). To compute an overall measure of total luminosity, we use SOL, which sums all pixel-radiance values in a given administrative area. Using the VIIRS monthly data, we compute the SOL for Libya for all 105 months between April 2012 and December 2020 (figure 9.1).

By exploiting the overlapping year between VIIRS and DMSP, we construct an annual time series of NTLs from 1992 through 2020 (figure 9.2). Using the annual DMSP dataset, we construct national SOL estimates for 1992–2013. To aggregate the monthly VIIRS estimate to an annual frequency, we select the median value from all monthly SOL estimates for each year (Liu et al. 2017). When combining the two annual datasets, we apply annual DMSP growth rates for 2012 (the overlapping year) to the VIIRS time series in order to extend the dataset from 2012 to 2011. We repeat this procedure for the following years to continue extrapolating the VIIRS time series backward using DMSP growth rates for 1992–2012. We extrapolate the VIIRS time series backward to 1992 instead of forecasting the DMSP series from 2013 onward because the VIIRS

MAP 9.1

Night-time lights map of Libya, 2019

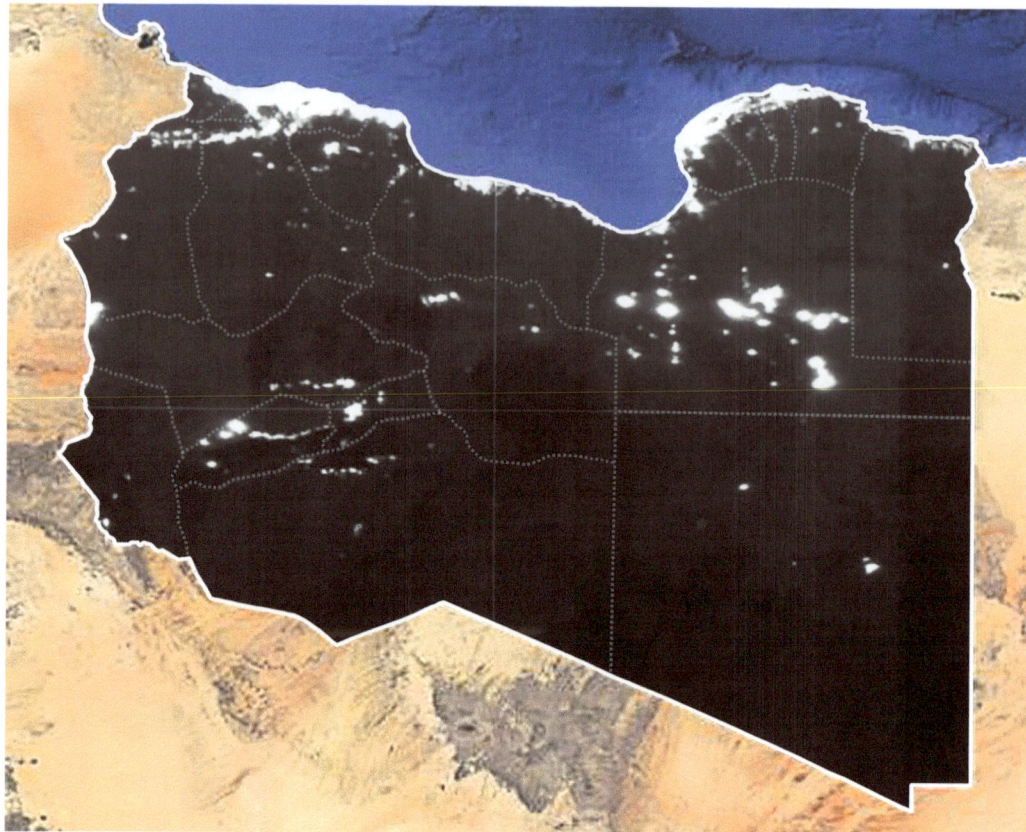

Source: Visible Infrared Imaging Radiometer Suite.

FIGURE 9.1

Monthly night-time lights data, 2012–20

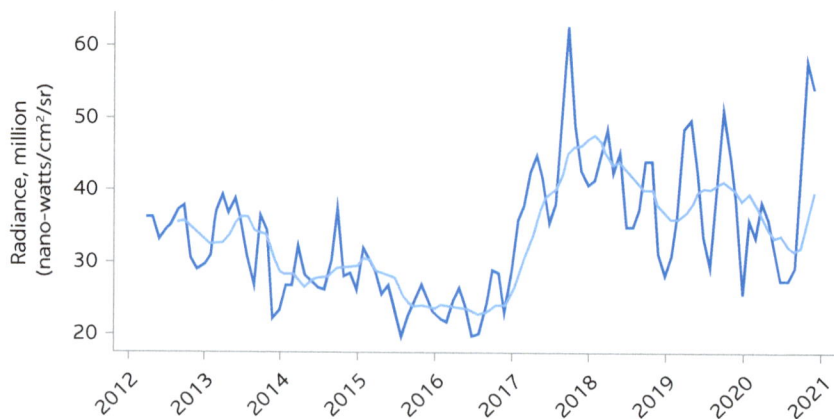

Source: Data from Visible Infrared Imaging Radiometer Suite.

FIGURE 9.2

Combined night-time lights time series from DMSP and VIIRS, 1992–20

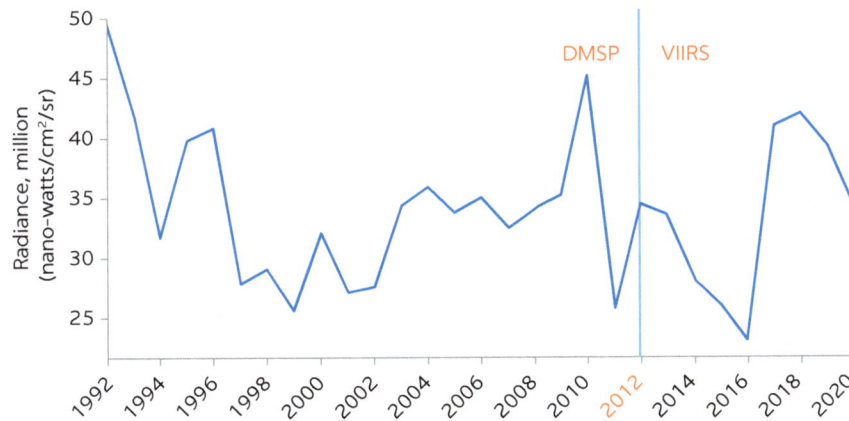

Source: Calculations based on data from the VIIRS and DMSP satellites.
Note: DMSP = Defense Meteorological Satellite Program; VIIRS = Visible Infrared Imaging
Radiometer Suite.

satellite is considered more accurate than the DMSP and does not suffer from issues of top coding.[1] (For the procedure used to construct the NTL time series, see annex 9A.)

Analysis

To establish whether NTLs have a meaningful relationship with economic activity, we regress them against real GDP and real GDP growth rates, using the procedure outlined by Henderson, Storeygard and Weil (2012). Annual GDP data for Libya were obtained from the World Bank's World Development Indicators data repository, which relies on data from the authorities for the pre-conflict period and estimates by World Bank staff and the authorities for the conflict period. We test the inclusion of additional specifications from publicly available sources—namely, the intensity of conflict and the price of oil—to enhance the predictive power of the regression.

We also control for variation in conflict events and oil prices. To measure the intensity of conflict, we rely on the Armed Conflict Location and Event Database (ACLED), which has recorded and geotagged every conflict event since 1997. We use the monthly and annual total number of conflict events recorded by ACLED in Libya. Because of the dominant role oil plays in the economy, all else equal, a change in oil prices will lead to a direct change in the value added of hydrocarbon production (even for a constant volume of oil production) and thus will affect GDP, even when measured in real terms.[2] The intensity of NTLs would pick up changes in the volume of oil production that are driven by changes in oil prices; it would not pick up the arithmetic change in the dollar value of GDP resulting from a change in oil prices. Thus, including a control variable for oil prices in the regression provides additional information that allows the model to produce an incrementally better prediction of real GDP. Data on annual and monthly oil prices were collected from the US Energy Information Administration. We did not include time effects in our final specification because the evolution of Libyan GDP (and NTLs) has not followed any obvious long-run trend (figure 9.3).[3]

FIGURE 9.3
Night-time lights and real GDP, 1992–2020

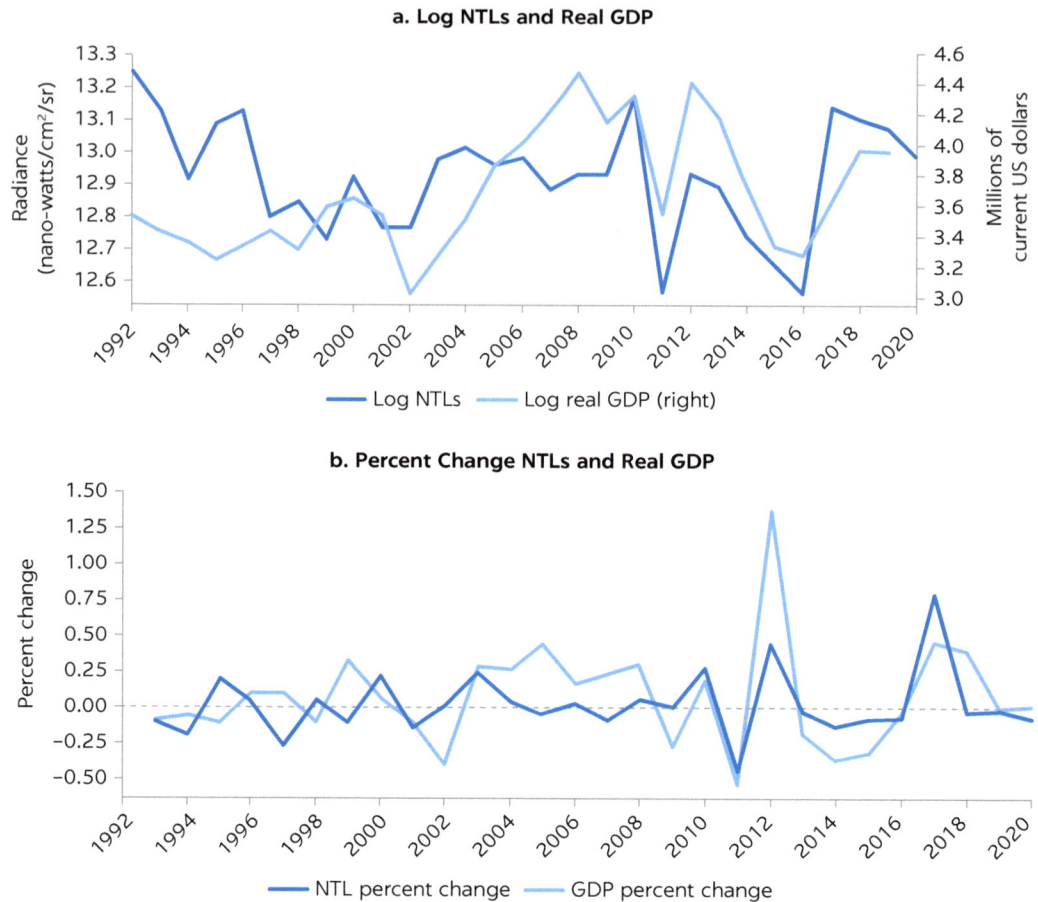

a. Log NTLs and Real GDP

b. Percent Change NTLs and Real GDP

Source: Based on NTL data from VIIRS and DMSP satellites and GDP data from World Bank World Development Indicators.
Note: DMSP = Defense Meteorological Satellite Program; GDP = gross domestic product; NTL = night-time light; VIIRS = Visible Infrared Imaging Radiometer Suite.

The equation for the regression of NTLs on the level of GDP is

$$log(RGDP_t) = \beta_0 + \beta_1 log(NTLs_t) + \beta_2 ACLED_t + \beta_3 OilPrice_t + \in_t. \tag{9.1}$$

The equation for the regression of NTLs on the growth rate of GDP is

$$g(RGDP_t) = \beta_0 + \beta_{1g}(NTLs_t) + \beta_{2g}(ACLED_t) + \beta_{3g}(OilPrice_t) + \in_t. \tag{9.2}$$

The coefficients on NTLs are positive and statistically significant across all regression specifications. Results are significant even after the inclusion of ACLED events and oil prices, suggesting that even after taking them into account, NTLs provide additional explanatory power (table 9.1, panel a). The *R*-squared value using only NTLs is 0.364 (column 1), meaning that NTLs alone explain about a third of the variation in GDP. This result is in line with previous research. Interestingly, the price of oil also has strong predictive power, increasing the *R*-squared value to 0.755. The results with respect to growth in GDP show similar results, with the coefficient on NTLs positive and significant across all specifications (table 9.1, panel b).

TABLE 9.1 Regression of night-time lights on GDP and GDP growth

	a. Regression in Log-Form				b. Regression as Percent Change		
	DEPENDENT VARIABLE: LOG(RGDP)				DEPENDENT VARIABLE: RGDP PERCENT CHANGE		
	(1)	(2)	(3)		(1)	(2)	(3)
log(NTLs)	1.389***	1.375***	0.912***	NTL Percent Change	0.877***	0.841***	0.840***
	(0.400)	(0.412)	(0.277)		(0.292)	(0.291)	(0.293)
ACLED-Events		−0.040	−0.141	ACLED-Events Percent Change		−0.141	−0.151
		(0.131)	(0.086)			(0.120)	(0.122)
Oil Price			0.009***	Oil Price Percent Change			0.002
			(0.002)				(0.002)
Observations	23	23	23	Observations	24	24	24
R^2	0.364	0.367	0.755	R^2	0.291	0.334	0.358
Adjusted R^2	0.334	0.304	0.716	Adjusted R^2	0.259	0.271	0.262

Source: World Bank.
Note: ACLED = Armed Conflict Location and Event Database; NTL = night-time light; RGDP = real gross domestic product.
* $p<0.1$, ** $p<0.05$; *** $p<0.01$.

Notably, the coefficient representing the elasticity of NTLs to GDP is near unity, as much of the variation in economic activity relates to variation in oil production that uses gas flaring that is picked up by NTL data. This finding suggests a 1-to-1 relationship between the percent changes in NTLs and GDP—much higher than the average elasticity of 0.277 reported by Henderson, Storeygard, and Weil (2012), who study the relationship between NTLs and GDP using a global panel of 188 countries. However, after accounting for measurement error in true GDP, the authors report an elasticity a little over one. Gibson, Olivia, and Boe-Gibson (2019) find an elasticity of almost 1.0 in urban areas in Indonesia. Both these findings support our results and give additional credence to our estimate.

As we show in the following sections, our elasticity in Libya is higher than average because of the direct relationship between the intensity of gas flaring and oil production. Gas flaring is clearly observable from outer space, hence recorded by satellites and observed in our data. In Libya, large swings in NTLs are directly attributed to gas flaring, which is strongly correlated with oil production, oil exports, and in turn GDP (hydrocarbon GDP accounted for roughly 60 percent of Libyan GDP in 2019). This direct channel between NTLs and GDP in Libya is unique and provides even more rationale to use NTLs in economic monitoring and analysis.

We use our NTL–based tool to estimate high-frequency real GDP. We find a precipitous drop in economic activity during most of 2020 and signs of a rebound late in the year. To construct monthly estimates of real GDP, we use the coefficients for NTLs, the intensity of conflict, and oil prices from the annual regression as parameters for our nowcasting model. These parameters represent GDP elasticities with the aforementioned variables in annual levels and can be applied to monthly data (see equation earlier). The resulting monthly estimates of real GDP show that 2020 was a turbulent year (figure 9.4). The COVID-19 pandemic was partly responsible for the decline in GDP, but more important was the blockade on oil export ports, which persisted throughout most of the year. Observations

FIGURE 9.4

Nowcasting estimates of real GDP using night-time lights, 2012–20

Source: World Bank.
Note: GDP = gross domestic product.

from November and December 2020—following the lifting of the blockade on oil export ports, which lasted from January to mid-September 2020—are exceptionally high, reflecting the ramp-up of daily oil production from 228,000 barrels in January 2020 to 453,000 barrels in October, 1.11 million barrels in November, and 1.25 million barrels in December. If subsequent readings are not mean-reverting and this trend continues in 2021, it could be the first signs of an economic recovery.

We separate NTLs into those from oil and non-oil sources in order to track variation in economic activity at the sector level. We hypothesize that we can estimate oil production by examining NTLs emitted from known gas flaring sites identified by the World Bank's Global Gas Flaring Reduction Program. The program uses satellite data to determine the flaring sites by examining radiant heat levels associated with NTLs. This allows it to identify the exact location of flaring sites and estimate the amount of gas flared for each location. The flaring sites are indeed located in the main producing fields in Libya, from the Sirte and Murzuq basins (map 9.2). We repeat the SOL procedure described in the previous section to produce a measure of oil NTLs that considers only NTLs emitted from the gas flaring sites.

Most of the variation in total NTLs is driven by the volatility of oil activity, which signals that oil NTLs may better predict economic activity in Libya than total NTLs. From 1992 onward, non-oil NTLs gradually climbed, in line with long-run economic growth theories (figure 9.5). The path of oil NTLs has been much more turbulent, particularly since 2012. This trend largely mirrors data on oil production in Libya for that period and is consistent with the observed volatility in oil output and hydrocarbon GDP that many oil producers experience as a result of volatile global oil demand and oil prices. In Libya, this volatility has been compounded by the impact of the conflict and associated blockades on oil export ports.

NTLs from gas flaring have also been in general decline since 2012. During 2020, oil NTLs sharply declined at the beginning of the year and remained depressed for most of the year before rebounding again in November (see figure 9.5), consistent with the timeline of the imposition and lifting of the blockade of oil export ports. These trends suggest that gas flaring associated with oil production in Libya accounts for a large share of variation in NTLs, partly explaining our large parameter estimates in the previous section.

Night-time lights reflecting oil activity, 2015

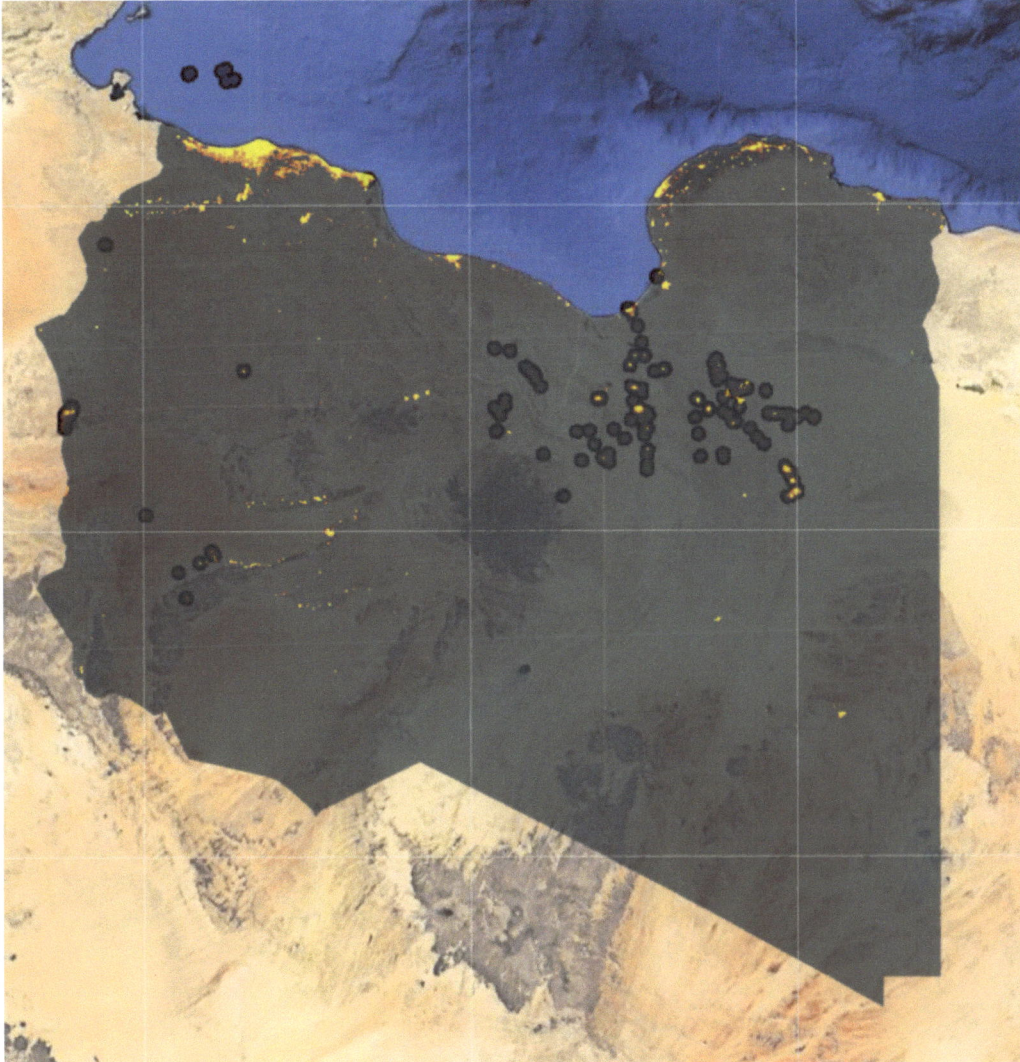

Source: Visible Infrared Imaging Radiometer Suite.
Note: The circles enclose gas flares identified by the World Bank's Global Gas Flaring Reduction Program. Light emissions inside these circles are used to calculate oil-related night-time lights.

Therefore, we posit that isolating the variation of NTLs coming from oil activity will improve the predictive power of economic activity in Libya.

Mapping NTLs in March and December 2020 demonstrates that in 2020, oil activity drove most of the change in NTLs. The NTL maps for those months reveal more gas-flaring activity inside oil-producing regions (indicated by the red circle in map 9.3, panel b) during December 2020, thanks largely to the elimination of the blockade on oil export ports that persisted from January until September 2020. This evidence further confirms that NTLs can reliably estimate oil activity in Libya, providing near real-time information on the state of oil production and in turn GDP.

Monitoring NTLs at the subnational (administrative-1) level reveals a similar story. Although all regions registered a decline in the beginning of 2020 (figure 9.6), the Eastern region experienced the steepest decline. This is largely

FIGURE 9.5

Oil, non-oil, and total night-time lights, 1992–2020

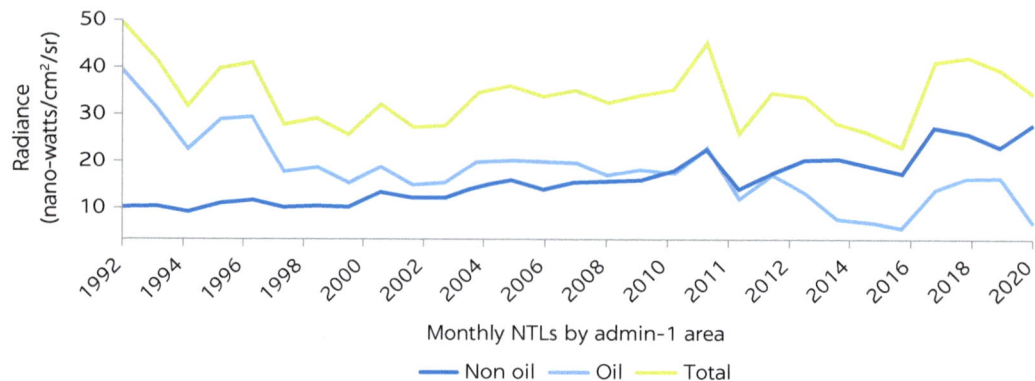

Source: Based on data from Defense Meteorological Satellite Program and Visible Infrared Imaging Radiometer Suite satellites and World Bank's Global Gas Flaring Reduction Program.
Note: NTLs = night-time lights.

because the major oil-producing fields in Libya are situated in the East, and thus economic activity in that region reacted the strongest to the blockade on oil exports. The blockade persisted for much of the year, and when it was lifted and oil production started to recover in the final quarter of 2020, NTLs in the Eastern region rebounded strongly. NTLs in the Western and Southern regions also recovered, albeit to a lesser extent, potentially reflecting the positive economic impact of the improved security situation and the spillover of increased oil production on the rest of the economy.

Looking at the trend in NTLs over the full time series reveals that although the change in NTLs in the different regions follows a similar trend (that is, all regions move together), the Western region shows the least amount of variance. This suggests that the Southern and Eastern regions are more volatile and prone to shocks than the Western region, with potential impacts for policy making. This type of NTL analysis can be replicated at more granular spatial levels, which would allow researchers to track economic developments at the subregional, city, and even neighborhood levels, thereby allowing for a better understanding of the situation on the ground and for more refined policy design.

To investigate whether oil NTLs can predict oil production, we regress monthly oil NTLs on oil production and establish their strong explanatory power. Unlike GDP data, which are available only at an annual frequency, oil production data are available at monthly intervals, providing many more observations for our regression. The correlation between oil NTLs and subsequent production is high (figure 9.7). Monthly oil production data are obtained from CEIC Data. As in the previous section, we regress oil production on oil NTLs alone and include separate specifications that add variables for the intensity of conflict and oil prices incrementally.

The equation for the regression of oil NTLs on (monthly) oil production is

$$log(OilProduction_t) = \beta_0 + \beta_1 log(OilNTLs_t) + \beta_2 ACLED_t + \beta_3 OilPrice_t + \epsilon_t. \quad (9.3)$$

The regression on monthly oil production reveals positive, large, and statistically significant coefficients for NTLs, with a very high R-squared. Without including any variables other than oil NTLs, the model accounts for 71 percent of the variation in oil production, suggesting a very high correlation between the

MAP 9.3

Night-time lights maps, 2020

a. March 2020

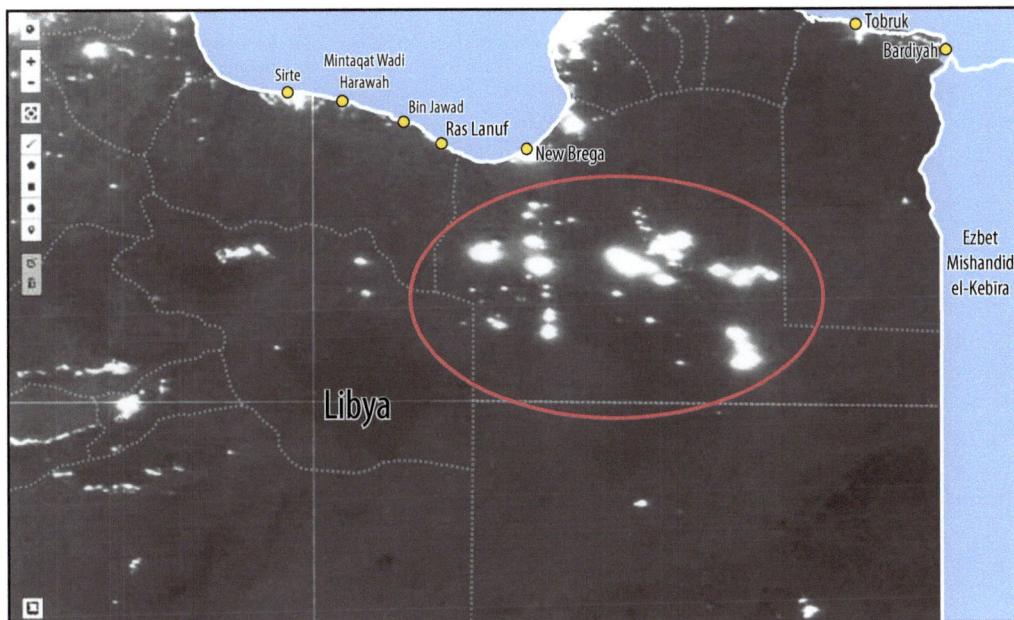

b. December 2020

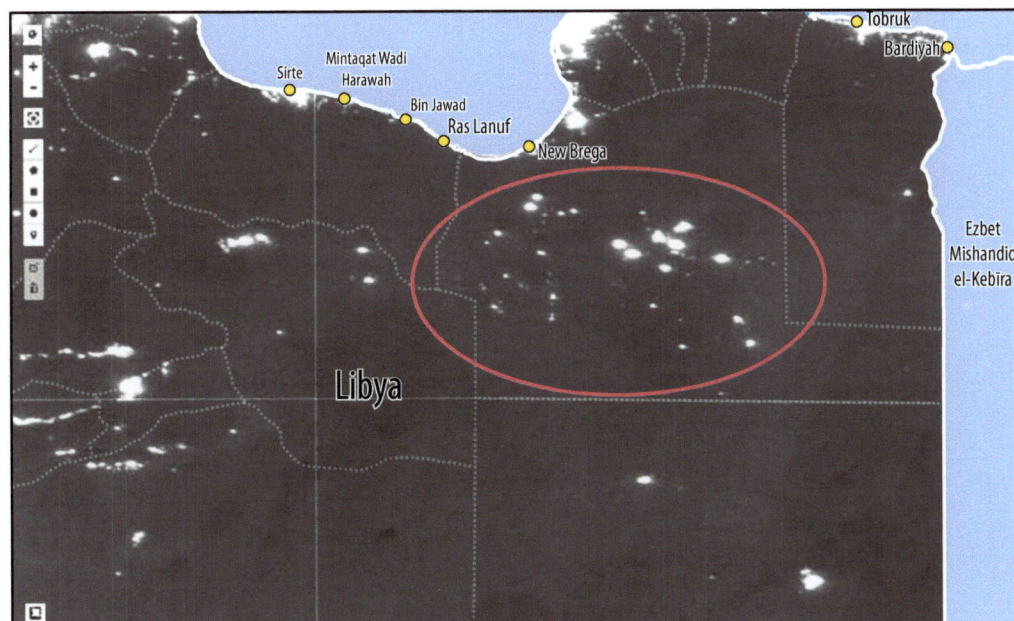

Source: Data from Visible Infrared Imaging Radiometer Suite satellite.

two variables (table 9.2). The coefficient for oil NTLs, interpreted as its elasticity to oil production, is greater than one (1.366), suggesting that this relationship is convex and has increasing returns to scale. Including ACLED events and oil prices does not materially improve the accuracy of oil production estimates. This finding is expected, as the relationship between oil prices and conflict is not as

FIGURE 9.6

Monthly night-time lights for subnational (administrative-1) areas

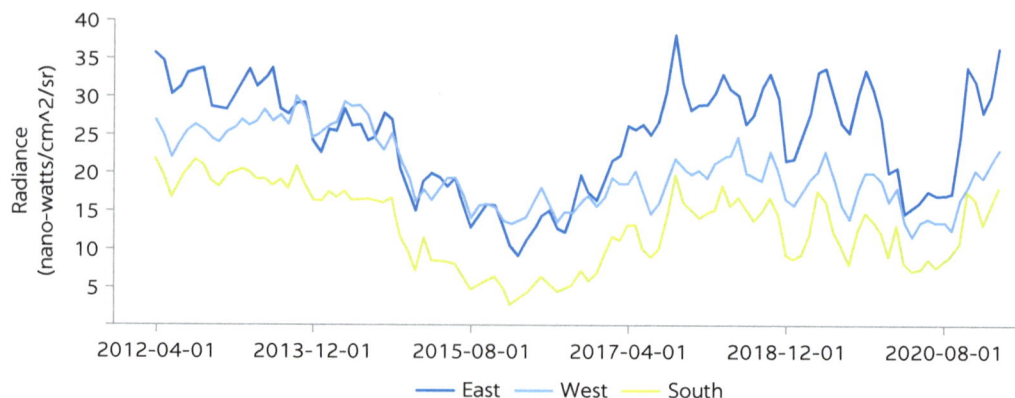

Source: Based on data from Defense Meteorological Satellite Program and Visible Infrared Imaging Radiometer Suite satellites.

FIGURE 9.7

Oil night-time lights and oil production, 2012–20

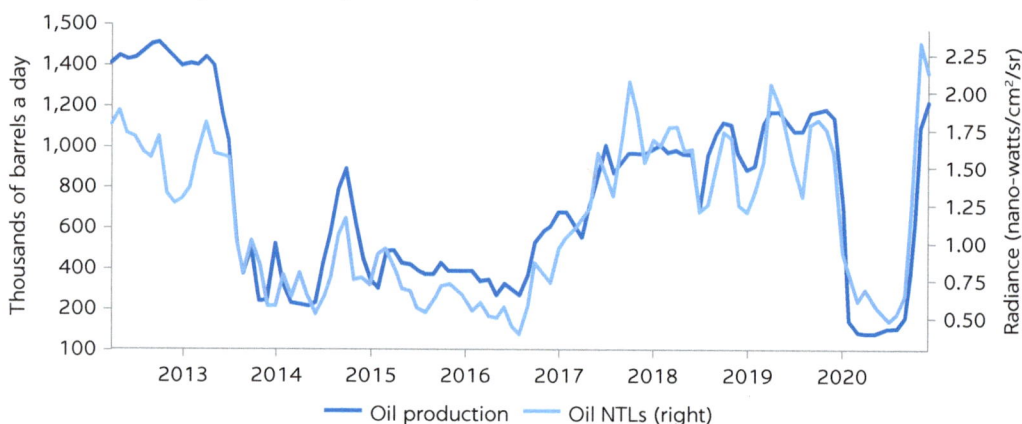

Source: Based on data from Defense Meteorological Satellite Program and Visible Infrared Imaging Radiometer Suite satellites (night-time lights), World Bank's Global Gas Flaring Reduction Program (gas-flaring sites), and CEIC Data (oil production).
Note: NTLs = night-time lights.

TABLE 9.2 **Regression of oil night-time lights on (monthly) oil production**

	DEPENDENT	VARIABLE: LOG (OIL PRODUCTION)	
	(1)	(2)	(3)
log (Oil NTLs)	1.366***	1.280***	1.241***
	(0.086)	(0.087)	(0.086)
ACLED-Events		−2.163***	−1.595**
		(0.709)	(0.724)
Oil Price			0.004**
			(0.001)
Observations	105	105	105
R^2	0.710	0.734	0.751
Adjusted R^2	0.707	0.729	0.743

Source: World Bank.
Note: ACLED = Armed Conflict Location and Event Database; NTL = night-time light.
*p<0.1; **p<0.05; ***p<0.01.

pronounced with respect to production. Furthermore, inspection of ACLED data reveals that few conflict events have occurred in or around oil-producing regions. Although these variables do not provide large marginal additions to statistical goodness of fit, they remain significant across all model specifications.

KEY FINDINGS AND CHALLENGES

NTLs provide an important source of information on economic activity in Libya, expanding the information set policy makers can rely on. They benefit from being data that are high frequency, granular, and insulated from human error or malfeasance. Especially in a conflict-affected setting like Libya, they can provide more reliable information than official national accounts data, which can be subject to bias, manipulation, and measurement error. Data from private companies are subject to their own internal biases and external limitations and are at times delivered with little transparency about what is happening under the hood.

NTLs can be used as a reliable estimator of economic activity in Libya, and this relationship can be strengthened by focusing on oil-related NTLs only. The regression coefficients for NTLs are positive, large, and statistically significant across all model specifications for both GDP and oil production. These coefficients remain significant even after the inclusion of additional parameters that control for key variables that influence the Libyan economy (namely, oil prices and conflict). Combined, these results suggest that NTLs are a strong predictor of economic activity, thanks mainly to the large role the oil sector plays in the Libyan economy and the direct channel between oil production, gas flaring, and NTLs.

Using NTLs as a tool for economic monitoring can be expanded to daily frequencies, providing nowcasting estimates of economic activity in near real time. The Earth Observation Group at the University of Colorado School of Mines has provided daily measurements of NTLs since April 2012, providing researchers with a current and near real time update of changes in NTLs. The daily data are standardized and can be retrieved programmatically, allowing researchers to set up an NTL time series that updates automatically as new data are uploaded to the site. This tool can provide policy makers with daily updates on the state of the oil sector and the economy in near real time, greatly improving their ability to respond and react.

NTLs can be a noisy estimator of non-oil activity, because of the absence of a direct channel. This noise affects the estimation of total economic activity but can be remedied by including additional specifications. As evidenced by the low R-squared values for our regression of NTLs on real GDP (table 9.1, panel a, column 1), we cannot comfortably say that NTLs are a strong predictor of all economic activity. This conclusion is in line with previous research and highlights the various other factors, external and domestic, that affect total income. However, despite the generally low statistical goodness of fit (usually about one-third), the coefficients are large and significant, suggesting that NTLs explain a substantial part of the economy but yield an incomplete picture. With the inclusion of additional specifications for intensity of conflict and prices of oil, we are able to explain about 76 percent of the variation in real GDP using our regression. These data thus allow us to nowcast real GDP with some degree of confidence.

NTLs can also be used to estimate oil production, providing a way to triangulate official oil production data. Being able to do so is particularly important in settings where official figures may not be accurate (where, for example, countries underreport oil production because of sanctions or commitments to limit oil production). NTL data could also be used to estimate oil smuggling, by comparing oil production figures with oil consumption and exports. Interestingly, NTLs have been used to estimate oil production in Iraq and the Syrian Arab Republic by the Islamic State with a high degree of confidence (Do et al. 2018).

In Libya, as in other FCV and data-poor countries, the dearth of reliable observations for models to learn from requires that one take nowcasting results with a grain of salt. Our nowcasting models rely on parameters for NTLs, intensity of conflict, and oil prices that are generated from a regression that uses GDP data from standard data sources. Estimates of real GDP from official national income statistics may have been relatively sound in Libya pre-2011. However, their accuracy during the past decade of conflict is questionable; our nowcasting model provides a way to triangulate the reliability of GDP predictions.

This challenge is less of an issue in the case of nowcasting oil production, as standard data sources for this variable have been more reliable than GDP statistics during the conflict period (unsurprisingly, as collecting data on oil production from a limited number of oil fields is less complex than collecting data on economic activity from myriad economic actors in the country). Oil production data are also collected by a variety of international organizations and private sector firms with strong statistical capacity and reputations for credible and accurate data.

The high spatial granularity of NTL data offers an opportunity to conduct economic monitoring at the subnational level (regional, city, neighborhood, and so forth), which can be very useful to understand the differentiated impact of conflict events or other shocks or policy actions on economic and welfare outcomes in different parts of the country. This would enhance the ability of policy makers to more effectively design policy responses that account for the different needs of populations across the country.

Using NTLs is not without limitations, including heavy computing and disk-space requirements. Each NTL dataset uploaded by the Earth Observation Group averages 3 gigabytes (GB). The entire daily time series starting in 2012 thus totals more than 13,000 GB. Disk space is the main technical limitation for researchers interested in studying daily changes in NTLs, although computing and processing are also challenges. Cloud computing services provide researchers with access to high-powered machines able to store and process such large datasets.

CONCLUDING REMARKS

NTLs are a valuable Big Data source for the study of economic activity in Libya, thanks to the large share of the oil sector in the Libyan economy and the direct channel between oil production, gas flaring, and NTLs. NTLs can also be useful in other data-poor countries that may be in conflict or crisis.

There are many interesting avenues for further research on the use of Big Data sources for nowcasting in Libya and other FCV and data-poor settings. Researchers could test the predictive power of satellite data on atmospheric nitrogen dioxide (NO_2) emissions in estimating economic activity. They could experiment with the use of NTL data, NO_2 data, tanker traffic data, press sentiment, or Google search trends to nowcast a variety of macroeconomic indicators (for example, GDP, exports, consumption, inflation). Doing so could facilitate comparisons of the efficiency and reliability of various data sources and help identify determinants of the variation in predictive power of specific data sources across countries.

Researchers could also use Big Data sources to estimate the economic and welfare cost of war and population displacement at a spatially granular level, by combining NTL or NO_2 emissions data (proxies for economic activity) with data on the frequency, location, and intensity of conflict events using the ACLED database. The results could reveal how the characteristics of conflict (duration, frequency, intensity of conflict events, and so forth) affect economic activity at the national and subnational levels.

Overlaying NTL or NO_2 data and ACLED data with population density maps would allow researchers to study the characteristics of conflict events (frequency, intensity, proximity to population centers) that drive population displacement and in turn to study the impact of this displacement on income and welfare at the subnational level. ACLED provides conflict data at the level of political actors, allowing researchers to study the cost of war at a highly granular level.

Telecom data, if available, would allow researchers to experiment with the construction of poverty and income maps at the individual level, providing high-resolution information on the distribution of welfare within the country. It would also allow them to look at the magnitude and speed of population displacement and income and welfare changes right after the occurrence of key conflict events at a granular geographic level.

ANNEX 9A: PROCESSING NIGHT-TIME LIGHTS DATA

Calibrating the Defense Meteorological Satellite Program (DMSP) data

Because the DMSP data are collected by multiple satellites (F10, F12, F14, F15, and F16), it is necessary to correct the night-time imagery to improve temporal data comparability and accuracy between the DMSP and Visible Infrared Imaging Radiometer Suite (VIIRS) datasets (figure 9A.1). The procedure outlined in the following, suggested by Elvidge (2009), is widely used as a benchmark method that normalizes each DMSP image by a second-order polynomial regression model. When the coefficients of the models are applied to each satellite in the DMSP series, they correct for the sensor variation and allow us to accurately compare data over time.

The equation for the intercalibration is as follows:

$$DN_{\text{rcf}} = C_0 + C_1 \times DN_t + C_2 \times DN_t^2. \tag{9A.1}$$

Once all images in the DMSP dataset have been calibrated, the sum of lights (SOL) is calculated for each of the administrative-0 regions (table 9A.1).

Pre-processing the VIIRS data

We use all available monthly VIIRS estimates for Libya from April 2014 through December 2020. We pre-processed the monthly VIIRS data to remove cloud cover, solar and lunar contamination, background noise, and nonelectric illumination from fires or gas flaring. Libyan NTLs for the summer months are also adversely affected by the summer solstice, because of the phenomenon of stray light, and hence require careful attention. To address these challenges, we filtered the images on the basis of cloud-free coverages and low-radiance levels, to narrow the focus to light emissions that are not contaminated by these factors.

The cloud-free coverage filter determines areas on the map that do not have any cloud-free observations and hence provide noisy estimates of

FIGURE 9A.1

DMSP data before and after calibration, 1992–2012

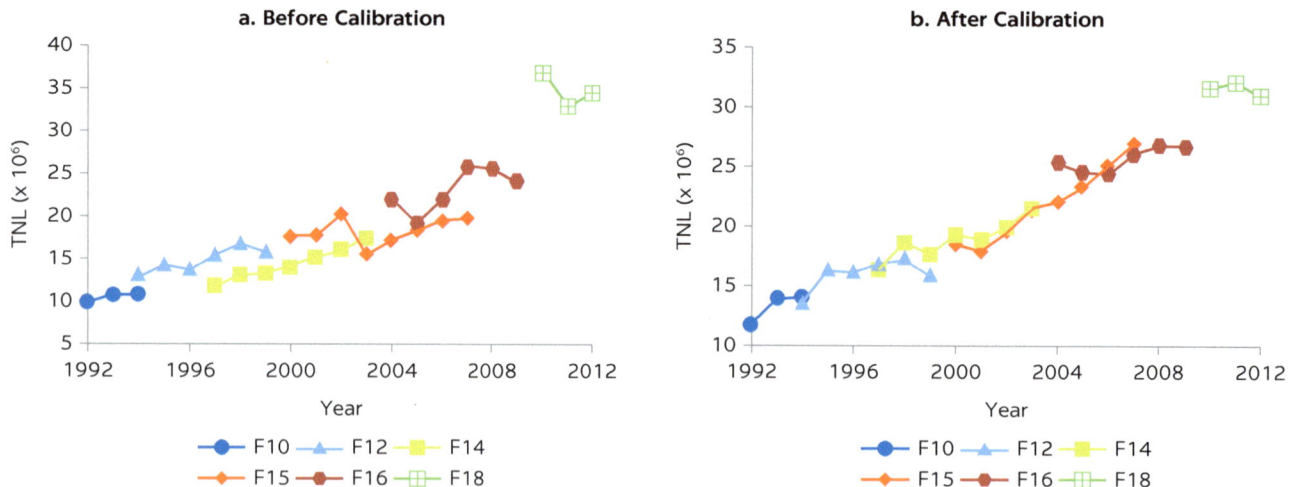

Source: World Bank.
Note: TNL = Total Night Light.

TABLE 9A.1 Sum of lights calculations for DMSP data, 1992–2012

YEAR	SUM OF LIGHTS	YEAR	SUM OF LIGHTS
1992	93,342,424	2003	83,103,853
1993	83,452,214	2004	88,405,558
1994	66,462,456	2005	81,216,498
1995	81,780,585	2006	86,253,499
1996	84,703,109	2007	83,125,969
1997	63,013,259	2008	86,210,502
1998	65,913,307	2009	92,739,589
1999	60,683,763	2010	117,689,664
2000	76,903,127	2011	69,769,306
2001	67,305,574	2012	90,728,685
2002	68,092,784		

Source: World Bank.
Note: DMSP = Defense Meteorological Satellite Program.

light emissions. Any pixel on the map that is consistently cloudy is removed from the dataset and not used in the subsequent analysis. For each month, if a grid cell is cloudy for more than half the time, it is removed from the dataset and replaced with a zero value.

The low-radiance filter eliminates grid cells that have low or inconsistent radiance values. This filter eliminates background noise arising from lunar contamination or solar refraction and removes biomass burning and ephemeral fires. Although the radiance values from background noise are generally low, the spatial extent of the background can dwarf the relatively smaller areas with electric lighting. If the background areas are summed with the lights, the result will be dominated by these, albeit low, radiance values. Biomass typically burns at high radiance values but is often short-lived and does not appear in the same grid cell consistently. Hence, any grid cell that has an average radiance value less than $1 \text{ nW/cm}^2/\text{sr}$ for more than half of the time is replaced by a zero value. The thresholds used in this mask were derived from work using monthly VIIRS conducted by the Earth Observation Group and by visual inspection of the resulting datasets to ensure that they closely resemble the annual products that go through the full pre-processing procedure (Elvidge et al. 2013).

To aggregate VIIRS data from the monthly to the annual level, we select the median value for each grid cell in the 12 months of a given year as the annual value (Chen et al. 2020), in order to avoid using imputation methods for the summer months that are affected by the summer solstice and to avoid using mean or maximum values. A mean value could lower the NTL intensity unfairly, and a maximum value would highlight abnormal readings. The median value is considered more reliable, as it does not assume any value for the affected months or contaminate any calculations (Liu 2017). Table 9A.2 presents a sample of the data after filtering, masking, and aggregating to the annual level.

Creating a combined DMSP and VIIRS dataset for 1992–2020

The final step is to extend the VIIRS time series (2012–20) backward until 1992 by exploiting the overlapping year between the two data sources (2012). We back

TABLE 9A.2 **VIIRS sum of lights data after filtering, masking, and aggregating to annual level, 2013–20**

YEAR	SUM OF LIGHTS
2013	33,531,684
2014	28,063,791
2015	25,911,543
2016	23,039,793
2017	40,947,951
2018	41,963,077
2019	39,352,053
2020	34,300,102

Source: World Bank.
Note: VIIRS = Visible Infrared Imaging Radiometer Suite.

cast instead of forecast because the quality and accuracy of the VIIRS data are considered superior to the DMSP data (Elvidge et al. 2013).

We first calculated the reverse-growth rates for the DMSP series for 2012–1992. These are the annual growth rates of SOL from the DMSP series when moving backward in time (for example, 2012 to 2011). We then determined the 2011 SOL level by applying the DMSP reverse growth rate to the 2012 VIIRS SOL level, applying the procedure recursively until we reach 1992. Table 9A.3 presents the resulting harmonized DMSP–VIIRS time series.

TABLE 9A.3 **Harmonized DMSP-VIIRS time series, 1993–20**

YEAR	SUM OF LIGHTS	YEAR	SUM OF LIGHTS	YEAR	SUM OF LIGHTS
1993	41,817,052	2003	34,245,553	2013	33,531,684
1994	31,637,525	2004	35,874,992	2014	28,063,791
1995	39,710,517	2005	33,715,815	2015	25,911,543
1996	40,743,455	2006	34,948,042	2016	23,039,793
1997	27,713,143	2007	32,496,493	2017	40,947,951
1998	29,014,929	2008	34,018,851	2018	41,963,077
1999	25,592,080	2009	35,218,893	2019	39,352,053
2000	31,946,656	2010	45,212,267	2020	34,300,102
2001	27,071,072	2011	25,779,163		
2002	27,521,229	2012	34,473,950		

Source: World Bank.
Note: DMSP = Defense Meteorological Satellite Program; VIISR = Visible Infrared Imaging Radiometer Suite.

NOTES

1. The DMSP satellite labels pixel-radiances from 0 to 63, which provides a cap on the maximum value. If a pixel-radiance value is at 63 and increases in luminosity, the reading is "top-coded" as 63. This issue is more pronounced at the city level; it is less of a concern at national levels, as the percentage of top-coded pixel falls drastically.
2. Hydrocarbon value added is the volume of oil production times the price of oil.
3. The inclusion of time-trend or year effects does not affect the results substantially.

REFERENCES

Beyer, Robert C. M., Sebastian Franco-Bedoya, and Virgilio Galdo. 2020. "Examining the Economic Impact of COVID-19 in India through Daily Electricity Consumption and Night-time Light Intensity." *World Development* 140.

Chen, Zuoqi, Bailang Yu, Chengshu Yang, Yuyu Zhou, Xingjian Qian, Congxiao Wang, Bin Wu, and Jianping Wu. 2020. "An Extended Time-Series (2000–2018) of Global NPP-VIIRS-like Nighttime Light Data from a Cross-Sensor Calibration." *Earth System Science Data* 13: 889–906.

Do, Q. T., L. N. Shapiro, C. D. Elvidge, M. Abdel-Jelil, D. P. Ahn, K. Baugh, J. Hansen-Lewis, M. Zhizhin, and M. D. Bazilian. 2018. "Terrorism, Geopolitics, and Oil Security: Using Remote Sensing to Estimate Oil Production of the Islamic State. *Energy Research and Social Science* 44: 411–18. https://doi:10.1016/j.erss.2018.03.013.

Donaldson, Dave, and Adam Storeygard. 2016. "The View from Above: Applications of Satellite Data in Economics." *Journal of Economic Perspectives* 30: 171–98.

Elvidge, Christopher D., Daniel Ziskin, Kimberly E. Baugh, Benjamin T. Tuttle, Tilottama Ghosh, Dee W. Pack, Edward H. Erwin, and Mikhail Zhizhin. 2009. "A Fifteen-Year Record of Global Natural Gas Flaring Derived from Satellite Data. *Energies* 2 (3): 595–622.

Elvidge, C., K. Baugh, M. Zhizhin, and F. Hsui. 2013. "Why VIIRS Data Are Superior to DMSP for Mapping Nighttime Lights." *Proceedings of the Asia-Pacific Advanced* Network 35: 62–69. https://doi:10.7125/APAN.35.7.

Elvidge, Christopher D., Tilottama Ghosh, Feng-Chi Hsu, Mikhail Zhizhin, and Morgan Bazilian. 2020. "The Dimming of Lights in China during the COVID-19 Pandemic" *Remote Sensing* 12 (17): 2851.

Gibson, John, Susan Olivia, and Geua Boe-Gibson. 2019. "Which Night Lights Data Should We Use in Economics, and Where?" MPRA Paper 97582, University Library of Munich, Germany.

Gibson, John, Susan Olivia, and Geua Boe-Gibson. 2020. "Night Lights in Economics: Sources and Uses." *Journal of Economic Surveys* 34: 955–80. https://onlinelibrary.wiley.com/doi/abs/10.1111/joes.12387.

Henderson, J. Vernon, Adam Storeygard, and David N. Weil. 2012. "Measuring Economic Growth from Outer Space." *American Economic Review* 102 (2): 994–1028.

Liu, Xiaoping, Jinpei Ou, Shaojian Wang, Xia Li, Yuchao Yan Limin Jiao, and Yaolin Liu. 2017. "Estimating Spatiotemporal Variations of City-Level Energy-Related CO_2 Emissions: An Improved Disaggregating Model Based on Vegetation Adjusted Nighttime Light Data." *Journal of Cleaner Production* 177. https://www.sciencedirect.com/science/article/abs/pii/S0959652617331888.

Roberts, Mark. 2021. "Tracking Economic Activity in Response to the COVID-19 Crisis Using Night-time Lights: The Case of Morocco." Policy Research Working Paper 9538, World Bank, Washington, DC.

The Impact of Conflict on People

10 Fragility, Livelihoods, and Migration Dynamics

UCHE ESEOSA EKHATOR-MOBAYODE, VASCO MOLINI, GRACE NAMUGAYI, AND VALERIO LEONE SCIABOLAZZA

World Bank, World Food Programme, and University of Naples Parthenope

The authors provide that Libyan households face four interrelated shocks that adversely affect the welfare of the population. These shocks include (1) protracted conflict; (2) the reduction of reliable import routes; (3) food and commodities crises exacerbated by the exchange rate devaluation, which have made essential goods prohibitively expensive; and (4) the COVID-19 pandemic, which has slowed economic activity and had devastating effects on the informal labor economy. The pandemic has exacerbated food insecurity. The increase in prices is especially acute in the Southern parts of the country, where the distance from the coast adds logistical and cargo costs to the price of products.

INTRODUCTION

Libya remains largely fragmented and still faces risks and vulnerabilities associated with situations of conflict and fragility. This chapter examines how the fragile setting in Libya affects livelihoods. It is organized as follows. The first section describes the composition of Libya's population and discusses how conflict and COVID-19 affect livelihood. The next section examines the relationship between migration dynamics and economic outcomes in Libya. The last section draws some preliminary conclusions.

THE LIVELIHOOD OF LIBYANS: 2019–21

Demographic profile

According to United Nations estimates for 2021, Libya's estimated population is 6,959,000: 49.5 percent female and 50.5 percent male, with over 80 percent of its overall population living in or around urban areas (UNDESA 2019). As of June 2020, at least 425,714 persons were internally displaced persons (IDPs)—an increase from 221,000 in 2018, 197,000 in 2017, and 304,000 in 2016 (UK Home Office 2020). Armed conflict, insecurity, as well as declining economic conditions and lack of access to basic services is credited as the major reason for displacement, with living conditions for many IDP families worse than their non-IDP counterparts.

Libya has an expanding population pyramid with a substantial proportion of the population below age 15, a majority of which is below the age of 10 (figure 10.1). Although this type of population pyramid is common for developing countries with high birth and death rates, relatively lower life expectancy, and low levels of education, an additional consideration for Libya is the possibility that households in the past 10 years have responded to the uprisings by increasing fertility rates to compensate for loss of life resulting directly from violence and/or conflict and fragility-related hardship; this is not surprising, as it may be a consequence of coping strategies adopted by Libyans.

Evidence from the World Bank–World Food Programme (WB-WFP) Libya Food Security and Nutrition Survey

Three rounds of data collected from the WB-WFP Libya Food Security and Nutrition Survey between September 2019 and December 2020, with results summarized in various editions of the mobile Vulnerability Analysis and Mapping (mVAM) bulletin,[1] aid in understanding of deprivations faced by Libyan households as well as the coping strategies adopted during a time of conflict combined with the COVID-19 pandemic. This provides useful insights into livelihoods in Libya during the period.

The highest proportion of households with inadequate food consumption in the first round of the survey conducted in September 2019 were found in Murzuq, a region with a substantial amount of conflict and airstrikes at the time. Also, 62 percent of respondents in the first round reported facing at least three deprivations while 36 percent reported facing at least four deprivations. Conflict also

FIGURE 10.1

Libya population pyramid, 2021

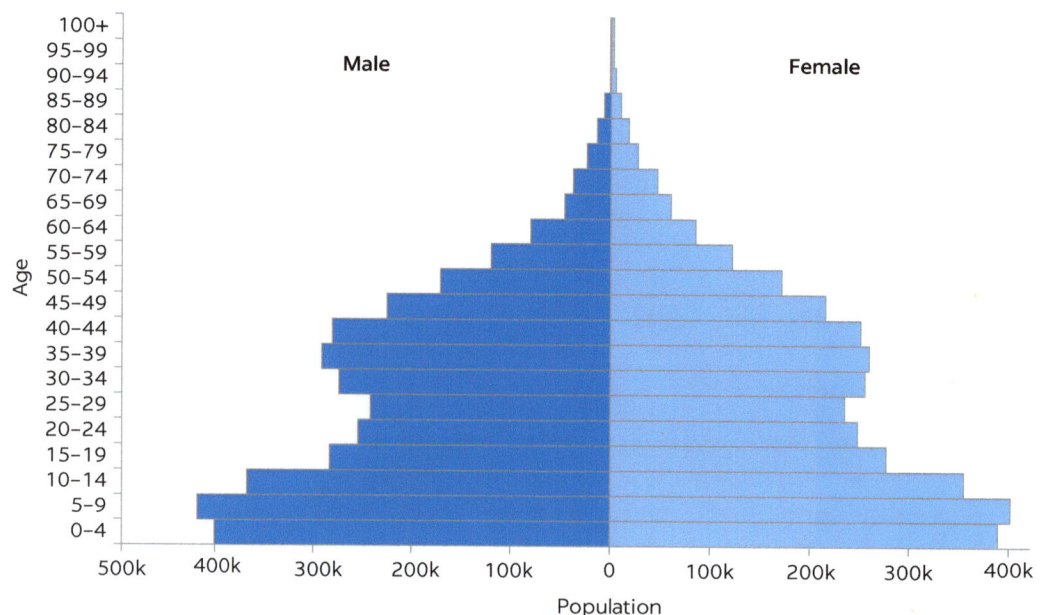

Source: CIA 2021.

appeared to affect prices—while the price of bread decreased, prices in the South of Libya continued to rise. Overall, 88 percent of households reported that there is at least a member in the family who gets a monthly salary from the government. However, this doesn't seem to bring more economic stability or improved access to food to households compared to their counterparts who report not receiving any government salary; the adequacy of the diet is similar for both groups. Finally, the data showed that IDPs have a poorer diet in comparison with host communities. Although both IDP and host community households reported the same share of households with poor food consumption, displaced households reported a higher borderline food consumption (7 percent) in comparison with nondisplaced households (2 percent).

By the second round of the survey conducted between April and May 2020 after the start of the COVID-19 pandemic and continued violence in the country, households were found to have sacrificed diet quality and the quantity of foods consumed to maintain consumption. A majority of households engaged in food-based and other coping strategies to maintain food consumption. Most households adopted food-based coping strategies by consuming less expensive foods (81 percent), reducing the number of meals (73 percent), and reducing meal sizes (71 percent). Additionally, approximately 80 percent of households adopted at least one nonfood coping strategy to maintain food consumption. A substantial amount of the adopted coping strategies was damaging to longer-term household outcomes, including borrowing money, selling productive assets, reducing health and education expenditures, and engaging in illegal or dangerous work. Although nearly all households were affected, food security indicators and reliance on negative coping strategies for both IDP's and women-headed households were worse (figure 10.2). The share of women-headed households that had poor food consumption was approximately four times the share of nondisplaced households with a male head, and the share of IDP households that had poor food consumption was over twice as large.

FIGURE 10.2

Proportion of households with adequate food consumption by residence status

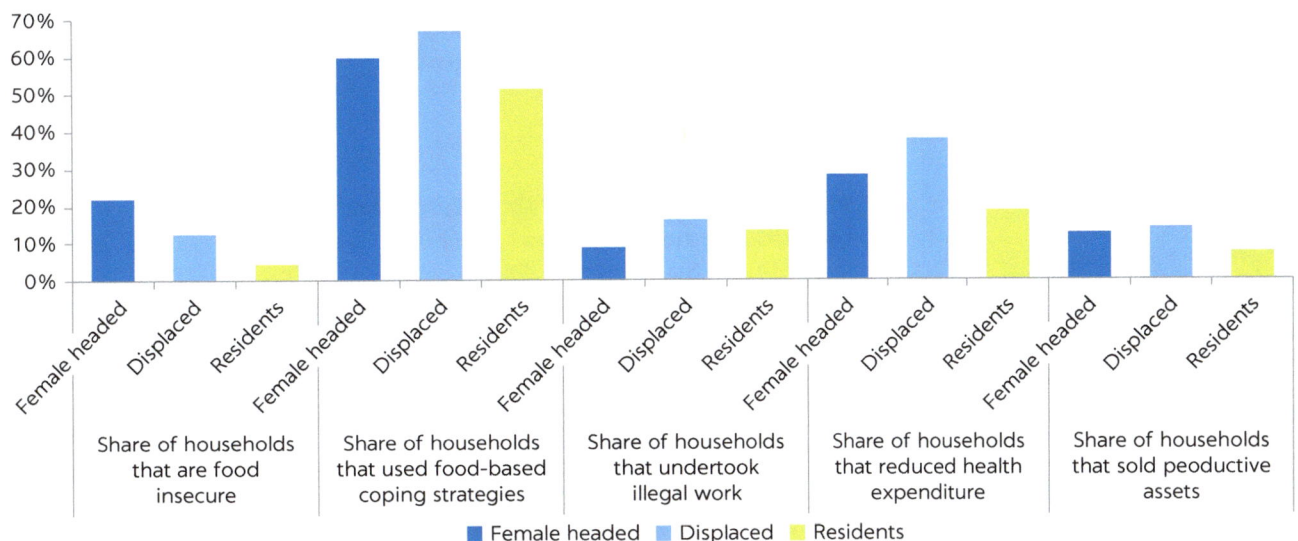

Source: Libya mVAM Bulletin 2.

Finally, the third and most recent round of the survey showed that 10 percent of Libyans had inadequate food consumption (poor and borderline food consumption). Food insecurity was found to be higher in the Eastern and Southern regions where the Libyan National Army—one of the actors associated with the protracted conflict—had significant presence. Also, displaced persons comprised a higher proportion of households with inadequate food consumption (figure 10.3), likely resulting from movement restrictions and curfews implemented to reduce the spread of COVID-19, which led to increased unemployment due to temporary closure of businesses and reduced demand for labor and access to livelihoods.

As in round 2, results from round 3 showed that households heavily relied on coping strategies to maintain food consumption. More displaced households (71 percent) adopted either crisis or emergency coping strategies than nondisplaced households. Loss of livelihoods coupled with high prices forced people to adopt coping strategies to meet food consumption. Displaced households frequently reduced health expenditures (50 percent) and worked in exchange for food (42 percent) or adopted emergency coping strategies including engaging in illegal activities (15 percent) and selling their home (13 percent). Continued utilization of coping strategies could lead to depletion of assets, making households less resistant to further shocks and thus at risk for becoming even more vulnerable. On average, during the month before the survey, households utilized savings (52 percent), bought food on credit (50 percent), worked in exchange for food (36 percent), and borrowed money (31 percent) to maintain food consumption.

Unemployment

Rising unemployment resulting from reduction of demand in labor due to implementation of COVID-19-related movement restrictions and curfews delayed salary payments for government employees and the liquidity crisis were most likely responsible for the high utilization of coping strategies by households to maintain food consumption during this period—a third of the respondents reported not to be working at all. Of those that worked, their employment was mostly not full time. Additionally, the Libyan Joint Market Monitoring Initiative report for the period January 27 to February 4, 2021, shows that the price of the minimum expenditure basket in December 2020 was higher by 12.8 percentage points than

FIGURE 10.3

Proportion of households with inadequate food consumption, by residence status

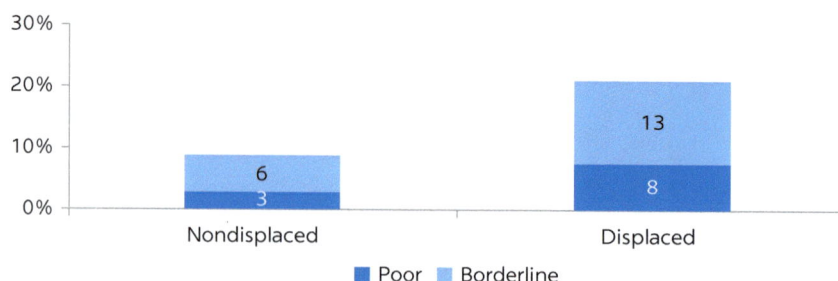

Source: Libya mVAM Bulletin 3.

in the pre-COVID-19 period (REACH 2021). Imported goods were also reported to be more expensive. This could have been because of the near-term effect of the devaluation of the Libyan dinar.

Need for humanitarian assistance

With a high dependency ratio suggested by the expanding population pyramid in Libya, high levels of unemployment and rising prices with continued fragility exacerbates the disproportionate burden on the working age population that must cover expenditures for itself as well as children and the aged population, thus explaining the high rate of need reported in Libya. The Humanitarian Needs Overview (UNOCHA 2021) for Libya published in January 2021 reported that more than 1.3 million people comprising 173, 000 internally displaced persons, 228,000 returnees, 502,000 nondisplaced affected communities, 304,000 migrants, and 46,000 refugees in Libya are in need of multisectoral humanitarian assistance (IOM 2021). This situation, while largely a result of the fragility compounding since 2011, has been exacerbated by the COVID-19 pandemic.

MIGRATION DYNAMICS AND THEIR IMPACT ON ECONOMIC OUTCOMES

In addition to the vulnerabilities Libya faces as a country burdened with conflict, its geographic location along the Mediterranean Sea between North Africa and the Middle East affects migration dynamics. Despite the fragile situation, both legal and illegal migration have flourished because of Libya's proximity to Southern Europe. Migrants make up over 10 percent of Libya's population, making it one of the top countries in Africa for migrants.[2]

Although Libya is far from being an attractive destination for migrants, Libya's instability has been increasingly exploited by transiting migrants as they use the country as a primary departure point routing through the central Mediterranean to migrate to Europe (Di Maio, Sciabolazza, and Molini 2020). Between 2011 and 2016, approximately 630,000 people used the central Mediterranean as the primary route of arrival via irregular migration to reach Italy (EU 2017; IOM 2016). About 90 percent of the over 181,000 people detected on the central Mediterranean route in 2016 departed from Libya (EU 2017). The presence of displaced persons and migrants in Libya is a burden for host communities who absorb the shocks and share their scarce resources and basic services which adversely affects their livelihoods as well as the livelihoods of the IDPs and migrants.

From the Migration Pulse, a web survey conducted by WFP in Libya on migrants from 36 different countries (from West Africa, East Africa, North Africa, and the Middle East) between January to May 2019, migrants were found to compromise their consumption by limiting the amount of food eaten due to the lack of sufficient food (WFP 2019).[3] A third of the migrants were found to have eaten only one meal the day before the survey. Among the migrants, not having enough food to eat or not knowing where their next meal will come from was reported to be a major cause of stress. Fifty-two percent of the surveyed migrants were worried about not having enough food to eat a month before the survey. The primary challenges faced by migrants were insecurity or violence, unemployment, and high food prices. From the Migration Pulse, two-thirds of migrants were found to rely on casual or daily labor (IOM 2021; WFP 2019). To cope with the lack of food or means to buy food, more than a quarter of the of the respondents went a whole day without eating and 15 percent reported to have skipped meals days before the survey.

In May 2020, from a joint survey done in Libya by the UN's International Organization for Migration (IOM) and WFP in which IOM conducted face-to-face interviews with migrants identified by purposive sampling, it was reported that 32 percent of migrants had (poor and borderline) inadequate food consumption and 34 percent were marginally food insecure (IOM 2020). The migrants that were employed as casual laborers and those that had spent less than a year in Libya reported a higher proportion with inadequate food consumption. This was mainly attributed to the deteriorating security situation in the country at the time as well as the threat of COVID-19 pandemic in which the government was forced to implement movement restrictions and curfews that led to reduced employment opportunities, especially among casual laborers. Sixty-three percent were reported to have adopted consumption-based coping strategies due to food shortages. While the most-adopted strategy was consuming less preferred or less expensive food (by 49 percent), migrants also reported limiting meal portions (42 percent) and reducing the number of meals (42 percent). Sixty-five percent of the surveyed migrants reported having adopted livelihood coping strategies, with 31 percent adopting either crisis or emergency coping strategies.

Migrants in Libya have a primary goal of finding employment and sending remittances to their origin countries to help their families. From a study on labor migration dynamics in Libya conducted by IOM in 2019–20, migrants reported being primarily employed in the construction, water supply, electricity, and gas sectors, followed by agriculture, pastoralism, the food industry field, and manual craft (Borgnäs, Cottone, and Teppert 2020). Among surveyed migrants who struggled to find employment, limited job availability was the most cited barrier, followed by insufficient skills for the jobs available. With the impact of the movement restrictions during the COVID-19 pandemic, some businesses were forced to close, increasing unemployment levels, especially in the informal sector. Even with the easing of some restrictions, livelihood opportunities remain constrained and there is increased competition for low-skilled jobs.

Additional data collected by the IOM and recorded in the Libyan Displacement Tracking Matrix (DTM) allow the tracking of the movements and the position of different profiles of migrants and displaced persons present in Libya. Specifically, the DTM provides information about (1) international irregular migrants, that is, those moving outside the regulatory norms of the sending, transit, and receiving country; (2) IDPs, that is, people who have been forced to leave their habitual residence in Libya as a result of or in order to avoid situations of generalized violence; and (3) former IDPs who have returned to their home areas (returnees).[4]

The DTM is organized into two different modules: the DTM Mobility Tracking (MT) and the DTM Flow Monitoring (FM).[5] The DTM MT provides a reliable estimate on the number of international irregular migrants in each Libyan region (mantika) and categorizes them according to their nationality. It also provides information about the quality of the relations of the migrants with the host community, and the impact of their presence on the local labor market and on public services. The DTM MT data are based on interviews with preidentified key informants, composed of local crisis committee representatives or other representatives from national offices. The information collected with the DTM MT is complemented and validated with the DTM FM, which tracks the mobility network of migrants across the Libyan territories. Data for the DTM MT are collected by enumerators who record information about migrants, whether on site or en route, found in predetermined flow monitoring points (FMPs), that is, key points of origin, transit locations, and destination of migrant movements in Libya.[6]

Using data from the DTM MT, we identify the number of international irregular migrants found across the Libyan territory between 2017 and 2020 and complement this investigation with an examination of the relationship between the presence of migrants in Libya and welfare of the host communities. In doing so, we focus on the period between January 2017 and May 2018, that is, the period preceding a major change in the EU policy toward migration flows from Libya[7] and the election of a new government in Italy that began to implement a number of measures to significantly increase the obstacles for migrants trying to reach Europe. This analysis provides a description of the living conditions of migrants in Libya and of the quality of the relation between them and host communities before the action and policies aiming at discouraging migration toward Europe were further tightened up. We also examine the national composition of migrants and its evolution in the most recent years, namely, 2019 and 2020. This investigation allows us to assess if and how migration flows through Libya have been reshaped by the major changes that occurred in the European Union (EU) migration policies since 2018 and by the beginning of the current pandemic. These analyses are conducted using DTM MT data aggregated at the mantika-year level.[8]

Number, location, and density of migrants in Libya

Table 10.1 reports the annual number of migrants registered in Libya during the period 2017–20. Over the period, the average estimated number of migrants is 591,671. The smallest number of migrants is observed in 2017. At the same time, year 2017 has the highest standard deviation in the number of migrants registered across the rounds of the survey conducted during the year.[9] In all the following years, the number of migrants is significantly higher, with 2018 being the year with the highest number of migrants. It is also interesting to observe that the standard deviation in the number of migrants registered between 2018 and 2020 is relatively small, suggesting that migration flows remained fairly constant during the last three years.

TABLE 10.1 **Number of migrants in Libya, 2017–20**

YEAR	AVERAGE	STANDARD DEVIATION
2017	462,356	135.0
2018	677,055	21.1
2019	636,016	37.5
2020	591,258	22.3

Source: World Bank.
Note: Displacement Tracking Matrix Mobility Tracking (DTM MT) data. Average is the average number of migrants recorded in the rounds of the DTM MT conducted during the specific year. Standard deviation is the standard deviation of the number of migrants recorded in the rounds of the DTM MT conducted during the specific year.

We enrich our analysis by looking at the spatial distribution of migrants across the Libyan mantikas by comparing 2017 to 2018. We summarize this information in map 10.1. Some interesting consistent patterns emerge via this figure. Most migrants are located in the Northern regions of Libya, which are in closer proximity to Italy. These regions also host two major cities of the country: Misrata and Tripoli. On the contrary, a smaller number of migrants are consistently located at the Eastern and Western borders, respectively adjacent to Algeria and the Arab Republic of Egypt. At the same time, an increasingly larger number of migrants is registered at the Southern border, close to Chad and Niger. This suggests that a large part of migrants reach Libya from the south, and then they move to the north toward the areas where it is relatively easier to reach Europe.

We conclude this analysis by looking at the number of migrants with respect to the size of the local population.[10] This information is shown in map 10.2. Also, in this case, a consistent pattern emerges. The areas with the highest density of migrant population are those of the Northern regions Zwara, and the regions located in the South. This latter finding is not surprising. Local population in the Southern areas is very small because these are desert zones. Consequently, migrants in these areas account for a larger part of the total population.

The figure also shows that the percentage of migrants in the Southern regions has constantly remained high after 2017. This might suggest that a large population of migrants may have faced increased difficulties to move to the Northern regions and travel to Europe after the change in the EU migration policies, with the results that many may need to spend more time in Libya. This hypothesis would also explain the increasing number of migrants located in Libya after 2017, as reported in table 10.1.

MAP 10.1

Average number of migrants, 2017–20

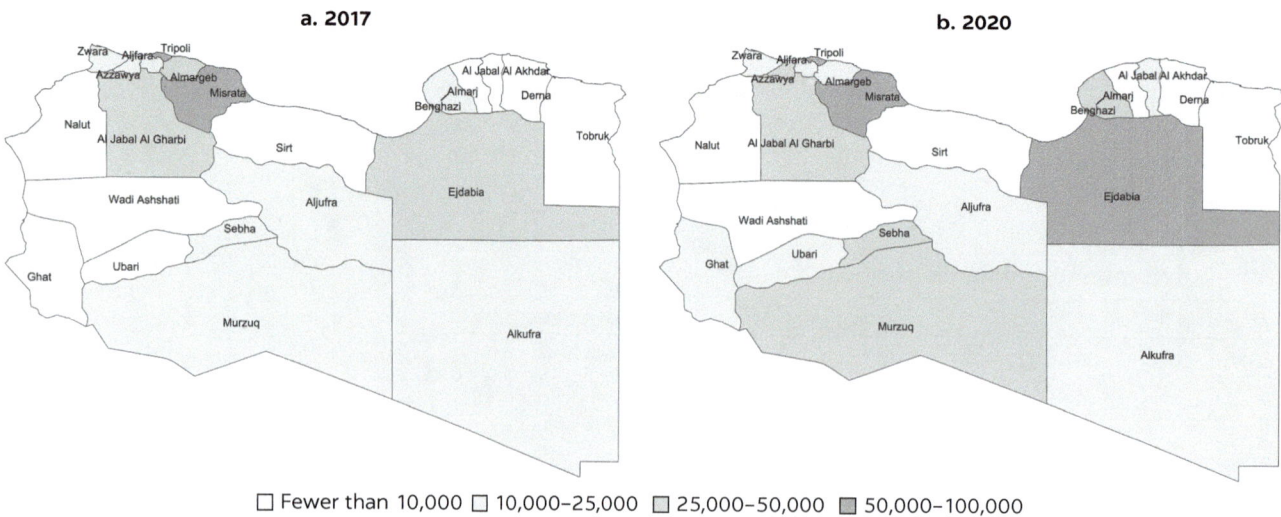

Source: Based on Displacement Tracking Matrix Mobility Tracking data 2017–20.

MAP 10.2

Percentage of migrants in population, 2017–20

a. 2017

b. 2020

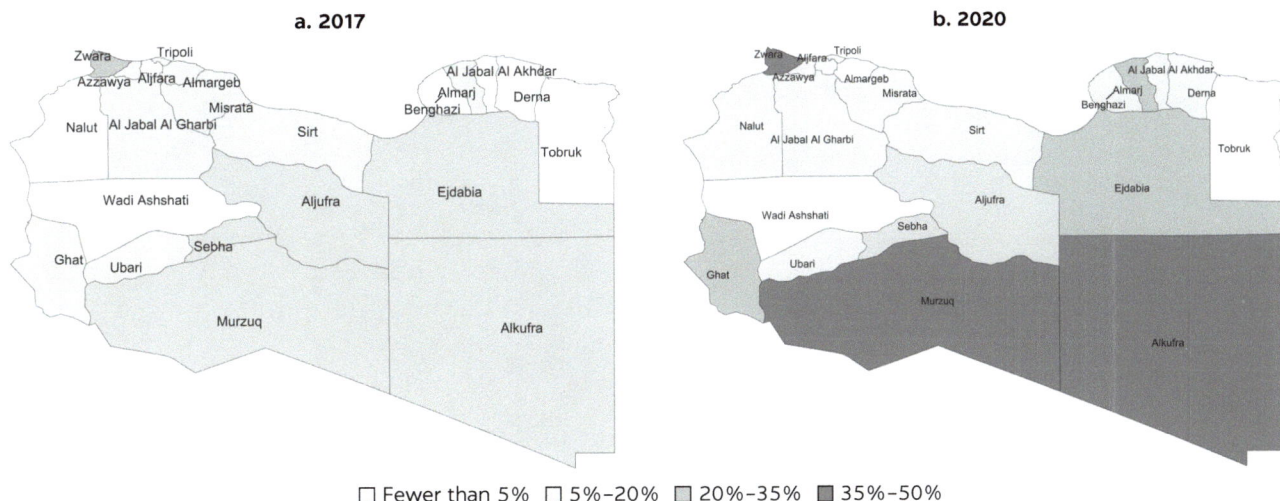

☐ Fewer than 5% ☐ 5%–20% ▨ 20%–35% ▧ 35%–50%

Source: Based on Displacement Tracking Matrix Mobility Tracking data 2017–20.

MAP 10.3

Migrants' relation with host communities, 2017 and 2018

a. 2017

b. 2018

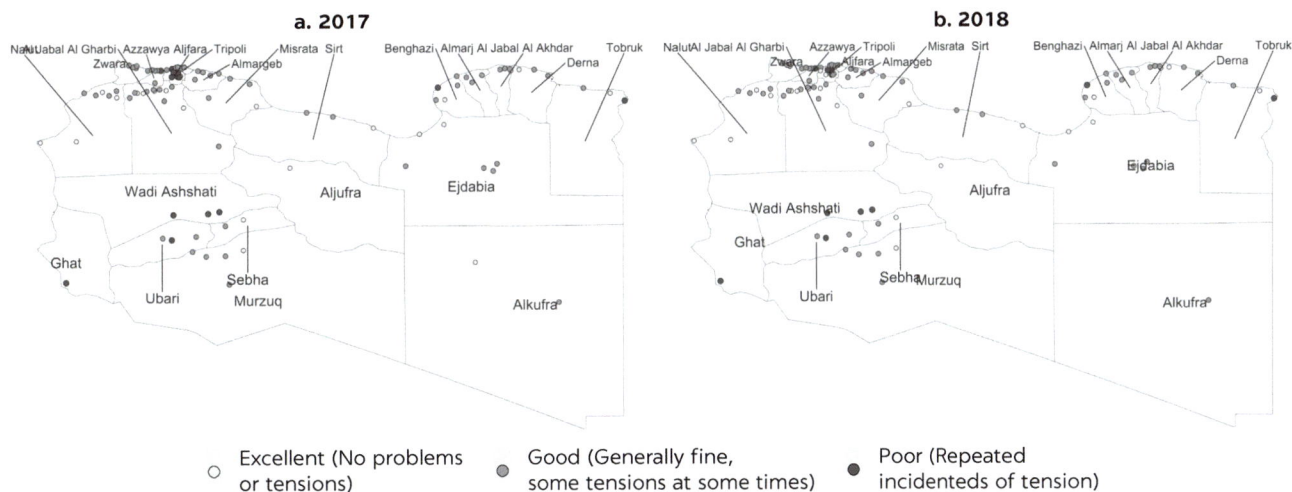

○ Excellent (No problems or tensions)   ◕ Good (Generally fine, some tensions at some times)   ● Poor (Repeated incidenteds of tension)

Source: Based on Displacement Tracking Matrix Mobility Tracking data 2017–20.

Relationship between migrants and host communities

One important aspect to be considered when evaluating the effects of the presence of migrants in Libya is related to their relationship with the local communities and their impact on local economies. The IOM collects data on three different questions: (1) the quality of the relation between the host community and the migrants, (2) the impact of the presence of migrants on the local labor market, and (3) the impact of the presence of migrants on public services. Since answers to these questions are collected at each round of the survey, in map 10.3, map 10.4, and map 10.5, we report, respectively, the most recurrent observation registered for each of the three outcomes in a municipality for a given year.

MAP 10.4

Migrants' impact on the labor market, 2017 and 2018

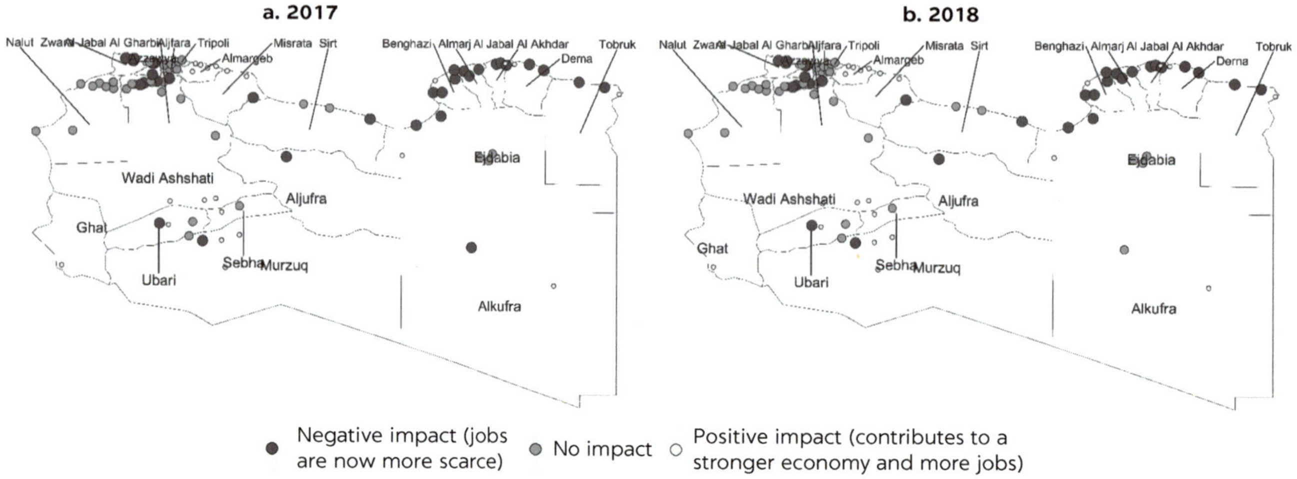

a. 2017

b. 2018

● Negative impact (jobs are now more scarce)   ◓ No impact   ○ Positive impact (contributes to a stronger economy and more jobs)

Source: Based on Displacement Tracking Matrix Mobility Tracking data 2017-20.

MAP 10.5

Migrants' impact on public services, 2017 and 2018

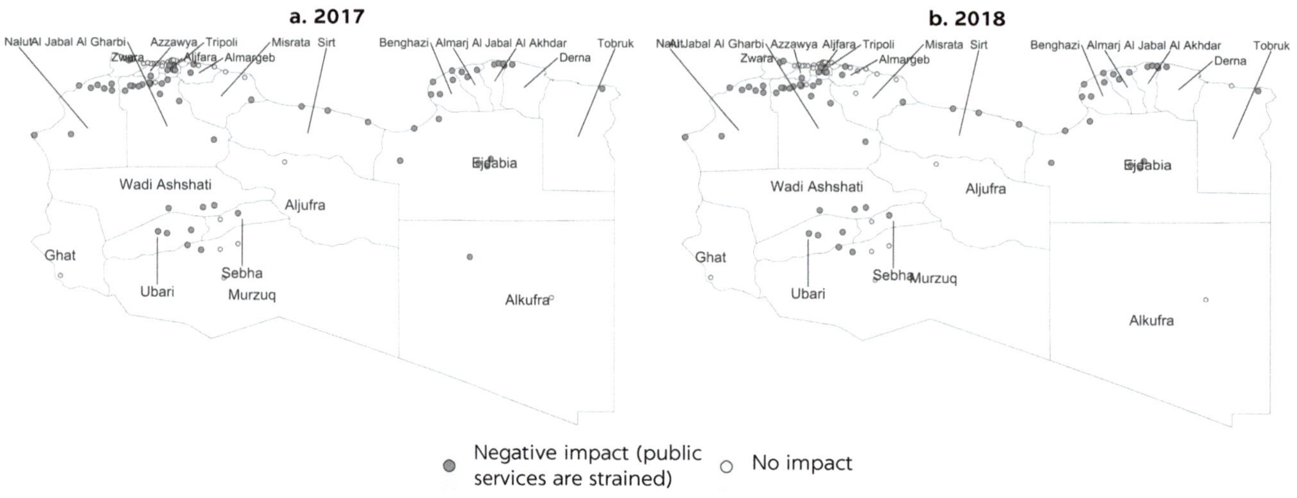

a. 2017

b. 2018

◓ Negative impact (public services are strained)   ○ No impact

Source: Based on Displacement Tracking Matrix Mobility Tracking data 2017-20.

While these measures of impact are inherently subjective and based only on individual perceptions and thus prone to different biases, still they are useful in providing at least a sense of how local communities are experiencing the migration phenomenon from their own perspective. There are four main facts that emerge looking at the results. First, for each of these questions, there is significant heterogeneity in terms of answers in relatively restricted geographical areas. Second, there is a very strong correlation between these measures. This indicates that labor market outcomes, access to and quality of public services, and— in general—the quality of relation with the local community are all aspects that should be considered simultaneously in designing policy interventions.

Third, there are no detectable variations across years in any of these measures. Fourth, based on the comparison between these figures and data reported in map 10.1 and map 10.2, there is no clear correlation between level of presence of migrants (in absolute and relative terms with respect to the population) and the quality of the relation with the host communities.

Evolution in the composition of migrants

The national composition of migrants changed between 2019 and 2020, the years immediately following the implementation of the more restrictive EU and Italian migration policies, which started in 2018. The national composition of migrants in Libya in the two years is summarized in figure 10.4. Two interesting insights emerge by looking at this figure. First, we observe that migrants coming from Niger, Egypt,[11] and Chad represent more than 50 percent of the entire irregular international population in Libya in all considered years. The information about the presence of Egyptians in the top three main nationalities registered, combined with our finding that the Northern regions of Libya host the smallest number of migrants, suggest that most Egyptians travel across the South to reach this country, most likely passing through the desert region of Kufra. This is possible due to the fact that it might be relatively easier to avoid controls in this region.

Second, we register no significant changes that occurred among the most represented nationalities in the migrant population: that is, those accounting for more than 90 percent of the considered population. Both in 2019 and 2020, the main top 11 nationalities are: Nigerien, Egyptian, Chadian, Sudanese, Nigerian, Ghanaian, Malian, Bangladeshi, Syrian, Somalian, and Eritrean. Taken together, these results indicate that the composition of migration flows to Libya remained constant across the past two years, and no relevant fluctuations were registered with the beginning of the pandemics.

FIGURE 10.4

Percentage of migrants by nationality, 2019 and 2020

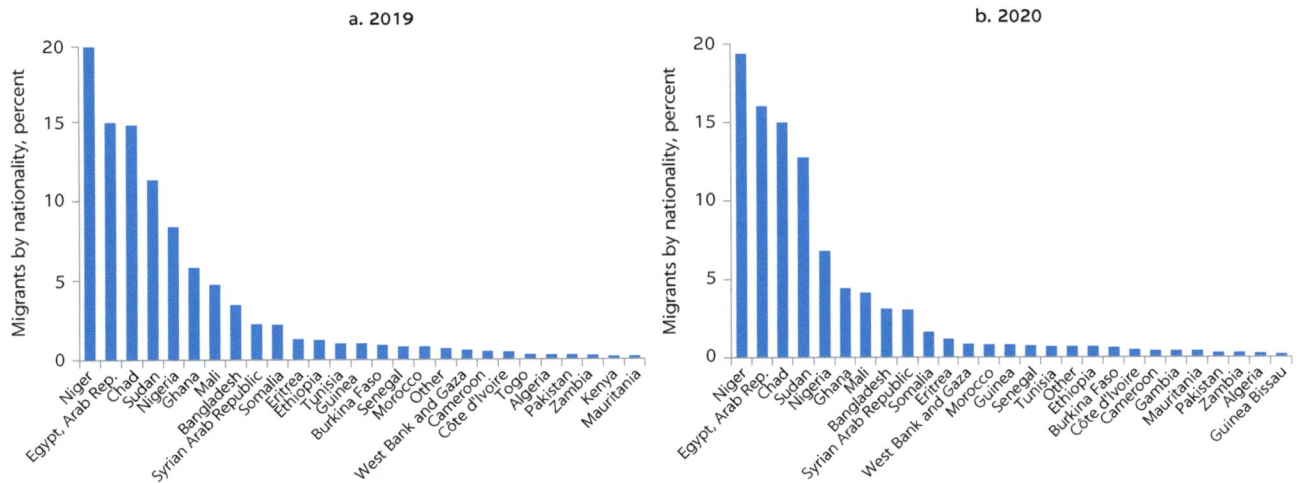

Source: Based on Displacement Tracking Matrix Mobility Tracking data 2019–20.

CONCLUDING REMARKS

The future looks promising for Libya, but the country currently remains fragile. For the first time since 2014, the Eastern and Western governments agreed on a unified budget on February 3, 2021, paving the way for an expansionary monetary policy—allocation of interest-free loans to Libyan commercial banks by the Central Bank of Libya—to increase cash flow in the banking system, support households and business in accessing credit, and boost the economy (REACH 2021). Although this move is impressive, the United Nations Special Mission in Libya has warned that this alone will not address the underlying causes of the economic crisis.

For full economic recovery, the trend of protracted conflict and fragility needs to be permanently reversed. To this end, the interim government that took power in March 2021 had promised to bring together the torn country and oversee a general election on December 24, 2021. However, this election was postponed following the dissolution of the electoral committees across the country, thus dampening the hopes of an immediate reversal in the trend of protracted conflict. The international community has called on Libyan authorities to set a new date swiftly to enhance the focus on rebuilding the country and creating a path toward sustainable economic growth and development. Until then, the available information shows that the combined effect of COVID-19 and protracted conflict in Libya affects livelihoods for everyone, but more importantly, it disproportionately affects the vulnerable population.

Food insecurity remains a concern, especially for migrants and IDPs. Increasing prices, restricted freedom of movement, limited income-generating opportunities, high unemployment, and a high dependency ratio make the prospects of reducing food security without any intervention bleak. Given these facts, it is not surprising that more than 1.3 million people from a country of about 7 million people need multisectoral humanitarian assistance (IOM 2021). This suggests that a sustainable plan aimed at eliminating this high rate of assistance must focus on reversing the trend of protracted conflict and building a country that is resilient to shocks. While the goal for the current interim government, international community, and development actors should be to foster a pathway to sustainable peace, immediate actions are needed in response to the current challenges.

Given the results for three rounds of data collected from the WB-WFP Libya Food, Security, and Nutrition Survey between May 2019 and January 2021, some of these actions should include but not be limited to the interventions that strengthen livelihood especially for food-insecure households affected by the COVID-19 pandemic and conflict, with a view to meeting households' consumption gaps and building their human, social, and financial capital. Other important interventions include monitoring markets, food security, nutrition, and the employment situation to continually assess the impact of conflict and COVID-19-related measures to inform program implementation for all vulnerable groups, including IDPs and migrants.

NOTES

1. Round 1 data were collected from a sample of 1,000 respondents. Round 2 data were collected from a sample of 530 respondents from eight municipalities (Tripoli, Tobruk, Almargeb, Nalut, Aljufra, Murzuq, Zwara, and Alkufra). Round 3 was conducted in eight

Libyan municipalities (Tripoli, Tobruk, Almargeb, Nalut, Aljufra, Murzuq, Zwara, and Alkufra) from 1,000 randomly sampled households consisting of 11 percent displaced persons. In the first two rounds, households were reached via remote data collection through random sampling from a database of phone numbers. In the third round, after the beginning of the COVID-19 pandemic, an attempt to conduct the assessment through random digit dialing saw a high level of nonresponse rates. Because of this difficulty, the third round was conducted face-to-face. See WB-WFP "Libya Food Security and Nutrition Survey: Round 1," September 2019; WB-WFP "Libya Food Security and Nutrition Survey: Round 2," April 2020; and WB-WFP "Libya Food Security and Nutrition Survey: Round 3," December 2020, https://reliefweb.int/report/libya/libya-food-security-outcome -monitoring-round-1-august-2022.

2. See the IOM Libya (n.d.) resources in general at https://www.iom.int/countries/libya (accessed April 12, 2021).

3. See https://docs.wfp.org/api/documents/WFP-0000106917/download/?_ ga=2.192943214.2116615092.1619956764-514092255.1585038251 Accessed April 30, 2021.

4. The definitions for the different profiles of migrants are taken from IOM's "Key Migration Terms," https://www.iom.int/key-migration-terms.

5. For background and details, see IOM, *DTM-Libya, Mobility Tracking Methodology version 11*, https://displacement.iom.int/system/tdf/reports/Mobility%20Tracking%20 Methodology%202017%20V.11%20-%20Mobility%20Tracking%20DTM%20Libya%20 %28E....pdf?file=1&type=node&id=7602.

6. Data are collected on a daily basis but then aggregated on a monthly basis. Data consist of two different layers: (1) the baseline assessment, which records the presence and number of migrants in a specific FMP in a month, and (2) the profile surveys, which collect socio-demographic data about migrants and information concerning the costs, the motives, and the intentions of their journey.

7. Specifically, EU leaders called for further measures to reduce illegal migration on the central Mediterranean route. Among other things, EU leaders agreed to (1) step up efforts to stop migrant smugglers operating out of Libya or elsewhere; (2) continue to support Italy and other frontline EU countries; (3) increase its support for the Sahel region, the Libyan coastguard, coastal and Southern communities, humane reception conditions, and voluntary humanitarian returns; and (4) enhance cooperation with other countries of origin and transit as well as voluntary resettlement. "European Council, 28–29 June 2018: Main Results," http://europa.eu/!xY77py.

8. A challenge inherent to our analysis is the presence of double counting in data registrations. Since data are collected at the FMP level, and migrants can cross multiple FMPs during the same month, using FMP data on a short period of time risks providing an over-representation of the presence of migrants in specific small areas. For this reason, we choose to study trends and patterns at the province level. To this purpose, we average FMP observations at the year level and aggregate them at the province level. This allows us to have a more reliable perspective on the situation of migrants in Libya. Moreover, this approach has also the advantage of making our results easier to interpret and to present.

9. This points to the fact that some significant variations in the passage of migrants occurred over this year: in most of the rounds, the number of migrants is around 400,000, with two peaks in the rounds collected at the beginning and at the end of the year (more than 600,000).

10. Data on mantika-level population are taken from the African Development Bank's Open Data for Africa database, "Libyan Portal," https://libya.opendataforafrica.org/. The last population census in Libya dates to 2006. It indicated a total population of 5,657,692. No further official indication on the population has been given since (Aita 2018).

11. The scope of this chapter is to provide a general overview on the migration flows within Libya. It is beyond our scope to provide a detailed explanation of the different nationalities' scopes and migration trajectories. Future research, based on data that are just becoming available, will deepen this analysis.

REFERENCES

Aita, Samir. 2018. *City Profile of Sebha, Libya*. Sebha: UN Habitat. https://unhabitat.org/sites /default/files/documents/2019-04/rapid_city_profile_sebha.pdf.

Borgnäs, Emma, Linda Cottone, and Tassilo Teppert. 2020. "Labour Migration Dynamics in Libya." In *Migration in West and North Africa and across the Mediterranean: Trends, Risks, Development and Governance*, edited by Phillippe Fargues and Marzia Rango, ch. 24. Grand-Saconnex, Switzerland: International Organization for Migration.

CIA (Central Intelligence Agency). 2021. *World Fact Book 2021*. Washington, DC: CIA. https://www.cia.gov/the-world-factbook/.

Di Maio, M., V. Leone Sciabolazza, and V. Molini. 2020. "Migration in Libya: A Spatial Network Analysis," Policy Research Working Paper WPS 9110, World Bank, Washington, DC. http://documents.worldbank.org/curated/en/707491579010444386/Migration-in-Libya-A-Spatial-Network-Analysis.

EU (European Commission). 2017. "Migration on the Central Mediterranean Route: Managing Flows, Saving Lives." Joint Communication to the European Parliament, the European Council, January 25, 2017. Brussels: European Commission. https://home-affairs.ec.europa.eu/system/files/2020-09/20170125_migration_on_the_central_mediterranean_route_-_managing_flows_saving_lives_en.pdf.

IOM (International Organization for Migration). 2016. "The Central Mediterranean Route: Deadlier Than Ever." Data Briefing Series issue no. 3. Grand-Saconnex, Switzerland: IOM. https://publications.iom.int/system/files/pdf/gmdac_data_briefing_series_issue3.pdf.

IOM (International Organization for Migration). 2020. *Migrant Emergency Food Security Report*. Grand-Saconnex, Switzerland: IOM. https://migration.iom.int/sites/g/files/tmzbdl1461/files/reports/DTMLibya_MigrantFS_May2020_0.pdf.

IOM (International Organization for Migration). 2021. *Libya Crisis Response Plan 2020–2021*. Grand-Saconnex, Switzerland: IOM. https://crisisresponse.iom.int/response/libya-crisis-response-plan-2020-2021/year/2021, accessed April 9, 2021.

IOM (United Nations International Organization for Migration) Libya. n.d. "IOM Libya." Tripoli. https://www.iom.int/countries/Libya.

Libya mVAN (mobile Vulnerability Analysis and Mapping). Various dates. "Bulletin." Rome: Food Security Cluster.

UK (United Kingdom) Home Office. 2020. "Country Policy and Information Note: Security and Humanitarian Situation, Libya." September 2020, vol. 4, London. https://www.gov.uk/government/publications/libya-country-policy-and-information-notes.

UNDESA (United Nations Department of Economic and Social Affairs). 2019. *World Population Prospects 2019*. New York: UNDESA Population Division (accessed April 11. 2021). https://population.un.org/wpp/.

UNOCHA (United Nations Office for the Coordination of Humanitarian Affairs). 2021. *2021 HPC-Libya Humanitarian Needs Overview (HNO)*. New York: United Nations. https://www.humanitarianresponse.info/en/operations/libya/document/2021-libya-humanitarian-needs-overview-hno.

WFP (World Food Programme). 2019. *The Migration Pulse: Understanding the Needs and Food Security Situation of Migrants in Libya*. Rome: WFP. https://docs.wfp.org/api/documents/WFP-0000106917/download/?_ga=2.192943214.2116615092.1619956764-514092255.1585038251.

RELATED READINGS

Barrett, C. B., T. Reardon, and P. Webb. 2001. "Nonfarm Income Diversification and Household Livelihood Strategies in Rural Africa: Concepts, Dynamics, and Policy Implications." *Food Policy* 26: 315–21.

Bundervoet, T., P. Verwimp, and R. Akresh. 2009. "Health and Civil War in Rural Burundi." *Journal of Human Resources* 44 (2): 536–63.

Camacho, A. 2008. "Stress and Birth Weight: Evidence from Terrorist Attacks." *American Economic Review: Papers and Proceedings* 98 (2): 511–15.

Dasgupta, P. 1993. "An Inquiry into Well-Being and Destitution." Oxford, UK: Oxford Academic. https://global.oup.com/academic/product/an-inquiry-into-well-being-and-destitution -9780198288350?cc=us&lang=en&.

Ekhator-Mobayode, U., and A. Asfaw. 2019. "The Child Health Effects of Terrorism: Evidence from the Boko Haram Insurgency in Nigeria." *Applied Economics* 51 (6): 624–38. https://doi .org/10.1080/00036846.2018.1502871.

Eswaran, M., and A. Kotwal. 1989. "Credit as Insurance in Agrarian Economies." *Journal of Development Economics* 31 (1): 37–53.

Fafchamps, M., C. Udry, and K. Czukas. 1998. "Drought and Savings in West Africa: Are Livestock a Buffer Stock?" *Journal of Development Economics* 55: 273–305.

Grimard, F. 1997. "Household Consumption Smoothing through Ethnic Ties: Evidence from Côte d'Ivoire." *Journal of Development Economics* 53: 391–422.

Haggblade, S., P. Hazell, and J. Brown. 1989. "Farm-Nonfarm Linkages in Rural Sub-Saharan Africa." *World Development* 17 (8): 1173–202.

Jones, A., and R. Naylor. 2014. *The Quantitative Impact of Armed Conflict on Education in the Democratic Republic of the Congo: Counting the Human and Financial Costs.* Doha: PEIC.

Justino, P. 2011. "The Impact of Armed Civil Conflict on Household Welfare and Policy." IDS Working Papers 2011, no. 384. https://doi.org/10.1111/j.2040-0209.2011.00384_2.x.

Minoiu, C., and O. Shemyakina. 2012. "Child Health and Conflict in Côte d'Ivoire." *American Economic Review: Papers and Proceedings* 102 (3): 294–99.

REACH. 2021. "Libya Joint Market Monitoring Initiative (JIMMI)." January 27–February 4. https://reliefweb.int/sites/reliefweb.int/files/resources/REACH_LBY_Situation -overview_JMMI_February-2021.pdf, accessed April 10, 2021.

Rosenzweig, M., and H. Binswanger. 1993. "Wealth, Weather Risk, and the Composition and Profitability of Agricultural Investments." *Economic Journal* 103.

Rosenzweig, M., and K. Wolpin. 1993. "Credit Market Constraints, Consumption Smoothing, and the Accumulation of Durable Production Assets in Low-Income Countries: Investment in Bullocks in India." *Journal of Political Economy* 101 (2): 223–24.

11 Food Insecurity

SAMER ABDELJABER, FADEL DAOUD, RAWAD HALABI, YUKINORI HIBI, GRACE NAMUGAYI, AND ELEANOR SWINGEWOOD

World Food Programme

The authors provide that an estimated 604,000 people in Libya are food insecure. Food insecurity has dramatically increased following the onset of the COVID-19 pandemic. The main drivers are the prolonged instability caused by the armed conflict, reliance on imports, stark economic fluctuations, and the impact of the COVID-19 pandemic. With needs on the rise, humanitarian support in Libya must move toward a needs-based approach, supporting vulnerable populations in a conflict-sensitive, communal way.

INTRODUCTION

This chapter examines food security in Libya. The first section examines the severity of the problem in terms of both the availability of and access to food. The second section looks at efforts by the World Food Programme (WFP)[1] to reduce food insecurity in Libya (map 11.1). The last section summarizes the chapter's main findings.

HOW SEVERE IS FOOD INSECURITY IN LIBYA?

Food security is said to exist when all people have physical and economic access to sufficient, safe, and nutritious food that meets their dietary needs and food preferences for an active and healthy life (FAO 1996). Based on this definition, four main dimensions of food security can be identified: availability of food, access to food, utilization of food, and stability of the other three dimensions over time. All four dimensions of food security must be fulfilled simultaneously for food security to be realized.

Armed conflict and reliance on imports have reduced the food security of a large portion of Libya's population. As violence intensified, food prices and requests for food assistance continue to rise. The COVID-19 pandemic has exacerbated the crisis for a population already grappling with conflict and political instability.

The 2021 Humanitarian Needs Overview, produced by the United Nations Office for the Coordination of Humanitarian Affairs (OCHA), estimates that the number of people in need of food, agricultural, or livelihood assistance in Libya doubled in 2020, to 699,000, of whom 604,000 people are food insecure (map 11.1). Nearly half of these households are concentrated in four regions: Tripoli, Ejdabia, Misrata, and Benghazi (OCHA 2021).

The severity of needs and the number of people in need were computed from the data collected from the July 2020 Multi-Sectoral Needs Assessment. The calculation was based on the Consolidated Approach to Reporting Indicators of Food Security, which combines a suite of food security indicators (in this case, food consumption, livelihood coping strategy, and food expenditure share) into a summary indicator, called the Food Security Index (FSI), which represents the population's overall food security status. From the final FSI, the proportion of severely food-insecure households was obtained, from which the severity of needs is derived.

The areas with the most severe food security needs are Alkufra, Benghazi, Murzuq, and Sebha. Among the displaced population, households in Aljufra were the most food insecure. For the country as whole, 14 percent of the population was stressed (had significant food consumption gaps or were able to meet minimum food needs only by adopting irreversible coping strategies), and 18 percent were severely food stressed (had extreme food consumption gaps or suffered extreme loss of livelihood assets that led to food consumption gaps or worse).

MAP 11.1

Scope and severity of food insecurity, 2020

a. People in need

b. Severity of need

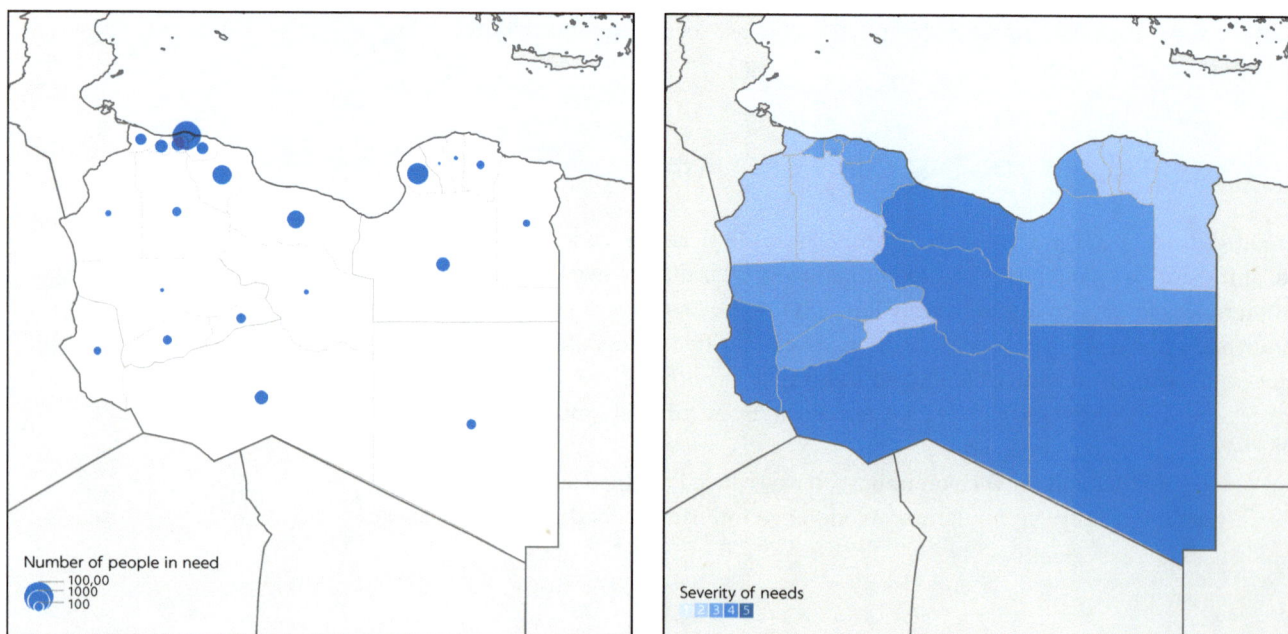

Number of people in need
100,00
1000
100

Severity of needs
2 3 4 5

Source: OCHA 2021.

Table 11.1 gives a snapshot of the relationship between income sources and food security status. Most households have access to income-generation opportunities. Severely food-insecure households are likely to rely more on family support (14 percent) and humanitarian assistance (4 percent) as sources of income.

Availability of food

Under Colonel Gaddafi, the Libyan government provided citizens with free health care and education, public sector jobs, and subsidized food and fuel through an elaborate social safety net system. Libya's subsidy program dates to 1971, when a national institute was created to oversee the provision of essential goods. The system included a range of food and energy products regulated through a compensation fund that set market prices of essential items at affordable rates to protect citizens against global price shocks. For example, from 2001 to 2012, the government increased spending on food subsidies from LD 172 million to LD 2 billion. Most of the increase occurred between 2010 and 2012, when expenditures on subsidies doubled from 2.0 percent to 3.8 percent of public spending and from 1.1 percent of GDP to 2.0 percent. Food subsidies are not currently accessible by all citizens. In July 2020, as many as 65 percent of households were without access to food shops subsidized by the government (World Bank 2020).

Before 2011, Libya imported 80 percent of its consumption requirements, with wheat, oil, maize, and milk comprising the major commodities sourced abroad (FAO and WFP 2011). In 2019, food and beverages represented the bulk of imports. The supply chain consists of private importers and investors, who distribute food to wholesalers and retailers, and the government, which distributes essential commodities to consumer associations sold at subsidized prices. However, importation was done at a reduced capacity, because importers had access to the foreign exchange on the black market, where the exchange rate averaged more than four times the official rate, leading to shortages of commodities such as food.

TABLE 11.1 **Households' main income source, by food security status (percent of total), 2018**

	FOOD SECURITY STATUS			
SOURCE OF INCOME	FOOD SECURE	MARGINALLY FOOD SECURE	MODERATELY FOOD SECURE	SEVERELY FOOD INSECURE
Government salary	83	86	84	73
Own business income	7	5	3	2
Family support	0	2	4	14
Nongovernment salary	2	3	2	2
Government social benefits	1	1	2	2
Remittances	4	1	1	0
Humanitarian assistance	0	0	1	4
Casual labor	1	1	2	0
Zakat (provided during Eid, a small amount of money)	0	0	1	2

Source: WFP 2018.

To put an end to the phenomenon of ghost bakeries,[2] the Central Bank of Libya (CBL) imposed stricter restrictions on obtaining letters of credit. These measures curtailed these fraudulent activities, but they had adverse repercussions on the wheat and bread supply chains, limiting the importation of wheat, raising importation costs, and forcing supply chain actors to obtain currency for imports at black-market rates. The country experienced serious flour shortages and significant increases in prices.

At the end of the first quarter of 2018, the "bread crisis" began. Shortages of wheat flour were severe, many bakeries closed, and the prices of bread and flour soared, causing hardship for consumers and undermining the country's food security. Bread prices rose to nearly twice what they were before 2011, rising from LD 1.13 to LD 1.67 per five pieces of bread between June and September 2018. An amalgamation of factors, especially restrictions on letters of credit, is believed to have triggered the crisis, which continued until November 2018. Libyan authorities and the central bank introduced a series of economic reforms and measures aiming to alleviate the effects of the crisis and improve the country's economy. Among these measures, authorities enforced the use of e-payments for bakeries when purchasing subsidized flour to counter ghost bakeries, funds were allocated to the public mills' companies, and restrictions on the issuance of letters of credit were reduced. Slowly, the Price Stability Fund went back to subsidizing wheat and prices of flour dropped. Bread became more readily available, and many bakeries reopened.

The protracted crisis in Libya has resulted in substantial destruction and disruption to its infrastructure, basic services, and the comprehensive and generous social safety net upon which the Libyan population came to rely. The bread and wheat flour supply chain has come under strain, with wheat flour subsidies for bakers decreasing throughout the country and wheat flour imports falling precipitously. In July 2018, bakeries in Tripoli and Southern Libya closed, and there were reports of bread shortages across the country.

Although the supply chain in 2018 was functional and bread was available to consumers, the reduced capacity of key supply chain actors caused vulnerabilities within the market system. Although subsidized wheat flour is provided to bakeries and a network of jamiyat (consumer associations), the subsidized goods did not always reach the intended location, preventing some vulnerable people from benefiting.

Essential goods and commodities are still available in most places in Libya, most of them still imported. However, COVID–related border closures and import restrictions, government controls on the movement of goods, and militia checkpoints have disrupted the movement of food supplies. Many international agencies, including WFP, report challenges related to access, especially negotiating checkpoints when carrying supplies. Some checkpoints are managed by local militias that do not have clear lines of command. Obtaining official authorizations continues to require significant time and coordination, which delays food distributions.

Fezzan—in the South—is one of the most important areas for agricultural production in Libya. Wheat and barley are the major cereals grown in both the Fezzan region and across Libya, together with vegetables. Other important crops include dates, citrus, olives, grapes, and almonds.

Livestock rearing is also common. During the 1980s, it represented the largest income-generating activity in the agriculture sector. Before 2011, the livestock subsector was highly subsidized, with the government providing agricultural inputs, machinery, and other tools to farmers at reduced cost or free of charge (WFP 2020).

Water scarcity remains one of the major factors limiting the development of the agricultural sector. Rainfall is very limited and occurs primarily along the coast; its volume and distribution vary from year to year. Consequently, agriculture is primarily dependent on irrigation. The agricultural area developed for irrigation was about 470,000 hectares, up from 240,000 before 2011 (FAO and WFP 2011). No reliable estimates are available on the number of hectares currently cultivated.

Power outages and fluctuations in electricity create problems for irrigation and for the storage and conservation of harvested crops. The conflict has also seen the theft and vandalization of private agricultural productive assets, such as large machinery, by armed fighting groups, resulting in major losses for farming communities. All of these factors have contributed to a reduction in the availability of agricultural produce.

Access to food

Most Libyan households face economic challenges in accessing food and essential commodities. According to a 2018 assessment of the food security situation (WFP 2018), the most common sources of income across the entire country were the government or public sector (85 percent), followed by own businesses (5 percent) and family support (2 percent). Most of the population is thus vulnerable to interruptions to or delays in government payments, which reduce the ability to access food and other basic needs in a timely manner.

Low income hinders the ability of Libyan households to meet their basic needs for food and other essential commodities. Among vulnerable groups, returnees and nondisplaced persons are more likely than internally displaced persons (IDPs) to have a low salary. The weighted monthly medium income is about LD 1,000 a month for IDPs and about LD 800 for returnees and nondisplaced persons, according to analysis by REACH Initiative in Libya. Income challenges are particularly pronounced in Sebha, a historically marginalized area, where 97 percent of IDPs are struggling to earn enough money to cover basic expenses. In 2020, the COVID-19 pandemic led to a reduction in employment opportunities, especially for people that rely on casual or informal activities for income. Among people involved in informal economic activities, 59 percent of migrants and 58 percent of IDPs reported a loss or reduction of income, according to the 2020 Migration Pulse report (WFP 2020).

The reduction of foreign exchange revenues from oil exports, combined with the departure of foreign workers and the increased demand for foreign currency, caused foreign reserves to fall from $124 billion in 2012 to $80 billion in 2018, a 35 percent decrease (World Bank 2019), leading to a major liquidity crisis. To contain the situation, the CBL restricted the distribution of cash across the country, which limited access to a fraction of salaries and savings. The liquidity crisis has severely affected the life of vulnerable groups by limiting access to cash in what is a predominantly cash-based economy.

The imposition of a cap on the amount of cash that Libyan households can withdraw from banks—which in some cases had been limited to LD 600 a month—severely affected houschold welfare. The monthly Minimum Expenditure Basket in Libya in September 2018 was estimated to cost LD 864.

Economic access to goods and services is restricted by the inability to withdraw money from bank accounts (78 percent), the irregular payment of salaries and wages (47 percent), and the nonfunctioning of the banking system (13 percent) (WFP 2018). The cash withdrawal limit for customers was estimated to be LD 5,000–10,000 a month as of early 2021, although reports vary.

The Libyan crisis has also prompted an increase in prices. The Consumer Price Index (CPI) increased from 2.5 percent in 2010 to 28.0 percent in 2017, mainly as a result of the ongoing conflict over oil fields, which caused a decline in oil exports and a deterioration of the value of local currency. The rise in prices led to a shortage of goods and services and the emergence of a currency black market. In 2018, the official exchange rate was fixed at LD 1.3 per dollar; the black-market rate reached LD 6–7 per dollar (Hamada, Semen, and Zaki 2020). The Libyan government contributed to the emergence of a second official exchange rate of LD 3.9 per dollar, by imposing a service fee of 184 percent on the official exchange rate for all foreign currency purchases. The creation of two competing central banks, in Tripoli and Bayda, compromised the effectiveness of Libya's monetary policies. These factors caused Libyan households to lose almost 80 percent of their purchasing power between 2014 and 2018.

It was not until January 2018 that the Libyan dinar started to regain more than half of its value, thanks largely to the launch of the family dollar allowance by the CBL. This allowance enabled Libyan citizens to purchase $500 at the official exchange rate. The measures by the government and the CBL to establish a fee on hard currency transactions and ease access to foreign exchange for essential imports led to a further decline in parallel market premia. The improvement in Libya's monetary policy was reflected in an increase in the CPI by 10.7 percent between January and November 2018, up from 28.4 percent in 2017. In 2019, the inflation rate declined to 4.6 percent (World Data Atlas n.d.). In 2020, it averaged –2.8 percent, as parallel market rates continued to converge toward the official exchange rate.

Increases in food prices, coupled with limited access to cash and low incomes, have eroded the spending power of most Libyan households. The increase in prices is generally more acute in the South, where the distance from the coast adds logistical and cargo costs to the price of products. The price of cooking fuel in the South is five times higher than in the rest of the country, for example. As most vulnerable households depend on local markets, they are highly susceptible to rising food prices.

After the first COVID-19 case in Libya was confirmed in March 2020, food prices increased significantly across most provinces, according to the April Joint Market Monitoring Initiative report. The food component of the Minimum Expenditure Basket rose by an average of 26.6 percent since the imposition of COVID-19 restrictions; in the South, it increased by as much as 42.6 percent. Minimum Expenditure Basket prices have been relatively stable but remained 11.3 percent higher than the pre-COVID-19 price as of January 2021 (REACH 2021). The CBL board agreed to a devalued exchange rate across the country of LD 4.48 to the dollar starting January 3, 2021. Currency devaluation is expected to result in an increase in prices of imported goods. Increased import costs will be channeled to traders and wholesalers and will eventually lead to an increase in the retail price of imported goods. Households will eventually bear the burden of the devaluation, as they will pay more for food than they did before the devaluation.

With reduced domestic production, lower imports, and higher food prices, previously food-secure populations are becoming more insecure. This trend is worrisome, given the already high proportion of Libyans (69 percent) that are "marginally food insecure." These people are likely using both food and livelihood coping mechanisms, such as selling their land or homes or engaging in illegal or degrading work. WFP's mVAM[3] April–May 2020 round of data showed weak food security indicators, especially in the South. The largest proportion of households that have inadequate food consumption and rely on food-based coping strategies is in Murzuq. Interviews with displaced households suggest that more than 70 percent of them are adopting either crisis or emergency food strategies.

Prolonged insecurity, coupled with the economic downturn brought on by COVID-19, could erode household resilience. Parallel to intensifying conflict, food prices and requests for food assistance continue to rise, as COVID-19 creates additional turmoil. As noted, the 2021 Humanitarian Needs Overview estimates that, in 2021, the number of people in need of food, agricultural assistance, or livelihood assistance doubled compared with 2020, to 699,000 people, of whom about 604,000 people are food insecure. A majority showed significantly higher frequency of using negative coping strategies to adapt to food scarcity (reducing the number of meals per day or limiting the size of portions). During the previous month, 77 percent of respondents could not access supermarkets, and 70 percent had no money to buy food.

WFP's assistance targeted 1 million people who fled Libya in mid-2011. Renewed violence following the 2014 parliamentary elections led WFP to resume food distributions, which were operated remotely from Tunisia following the evacuation of all international UN staff from Libya in July 2014. As of April 2021, over 60 people based in Benghazi, Sebha, Sirte, Tripoli, Zwara, and Tunis are working for WFP Libya. Food is distributed to over 100,000 vulnerable people a month in Libya, including migrants, refugees, and asylum seekers. As nutritious food supports a healthy immune system, this support is particularly critical in challenging times like today, when the socioeconomic impact of the COVID-19 pandemic and ongoing armed conflict reduce access to health care services and food.

In urban areas where markets are functioning, WFP distributes general food assistance via cash-based transfers through an e-voucher delivered in partnership with a local technology company. WFP rolled out an e-voucher modality for unconditional food assistance to vulnerable Libyans in April 2020. On average, 10,000 people a month receive food entitlements at WFP-contracted shops, which injected $1.26 million into local markets in 2020. In 2020, WFP locally procured some 665 metric tons of ready-to-eat food rations for its life-saving assistance for vulnerable migrants, refugees, and asylum seekers in Libya. injecting another $1.5 million into the local economy. As well as strengthening the technological capacity of local partners, this modality helps stimulate the local economy with food available in markets through a model that allows for the local procurement and distribution of food through wholesalers and retailers. E-vouchers give families flexibility in choosing the items they need from a range of commodities while maintaining their dignity and returning a sense of normality to their lives.

A longer-term issue in Libya is the mismatch between the jobs needed and the skills of the population. WFP matches the training programs it offers to local job market needs. It implements food assistance for vocational training programs, in which the topics are chosen through community conversations in tandem with the United States Institute of Peace and analyzes local job markets to ensure not only that the most useful skillsets are augmented but also that people are able to develop skills about which they are passionate and which they can use to support their families and communities. Through community conversations, for example, it learned that young farmers in Ubari needed a local market. After some delays caused by COVID-19, it is now building one.

CONCLUDING REMARKS

Food insecurity persists in Libya, with an estimated 604,000 people food insecure, a number that dramatically increased following the onset of the COVID-19 pandemic. The main drivers are the prolonged instability caused by the armed conflict, reliance on imports, stark economic fluctuations, and the impact of the COVID-19 pandemic. With needs on the rise, humanitarian support in Libya must move toward a needs-based approach, supporting vulnerable populations in a conflict-sensitive, communal way.

NOTES

1. The United Nations World Food Programme (WFP) won the 2020 Nobel Peace Prize. It is the world's largest humanitarian organization, saving lives in emergencies and using food assistance to build a pathway to peace, stability, and prosperity for people recovering from conflict, disasters, and the impact of climate change.
2. Ghost bakeries are businesses registered only on paper that are used to gain preferential access to foreign currency and subsidized flour, which is then sold on the black market to benefit from official foreign exchange rates. WFP and REACH Initiative estimate that about 1,200 ghost bakeries exist across Libya.
3. Through its augmented data streams and vulnerability analysis mapping, WFP analyzes and responds to food security and economic conditions across Libya. Its Vulnerability Analysis Mapping (VAM) works with an interactive story map and dashboard that shows the evolution of the cost of the food basket and the prevalence of food insecurity at the national and subnational levels. Mobile VAM (mVAM) is a WFP project that uses mobile technology to remotely monitor household food security and nutrition-, labor-, and food market–related trends in real time, providing high-frequency, gender-disaggregated, and operationally relevant data that support humanitarian decision-making. It was launched in 2019 in Libya, with a small-scale pilot. Since early 2020, the project has partnered with the World Bank in data analysis. WFP works with other agencies to build knowledge on economic conditions in Libya.

REFERENCES

FAO (Food and Agriculture Organization). 1996. *Rome Declaration on World Food Security.* Rome: FAO. http://www.fao.org/3/w3613e/w3613e00.htm.

FAO (Food and Agriculture Organization), and WFP (World Food Programme). 2011. *Food Security in Libya: An Overview.* Rome: FAO and WFP. https://documents.wfp.org/stellent /groups/public/documents/ena/wfp234964.pdf.

Hamada, A., M. Semen, and C. Zaki. 2020. *Investigating the Libyan Conflict and Peace-Building Process: Past Causes and Future Prospects.* ERF Working Paper 1383, Economic Research Forum, Giza. https://erf.org.eg/wp-content/uploads/2020/03/1383.pdf.

OCHA (United Nations Office for the Coordination of Humanitarian Affairs). 2021. *Libya Humanitarian Needs Overview*. New York: OCHA. https://www.humanitarianresponse.info/sites/www.humanitarianresponse.info/files/documents/files/hno_2021-final.pdf.

REACH. 2021. "Joint Market Monitoring Initiative," January 3–11. Geneva: REACH. https://www.impact-repository.org/document/reach/3f0e72e6/REACH_LBY_Situation-overview_JMMI_January-2021.pdf.

WFP (World Food Programme). 2018. *Libya—Food Security: MSNA 2018*. Rome: WFP. https://www.wfp.org/publications/libya-food-security-msna-2018.

WFP (World Food Programme). 2020. *WFP Libya Agriculture and Livelihood Needs Assessment Report: A Study of the Fezzan Region*. Rome: WFP. https://www.wfp.org/publications/libya-agricultural-and-livelihood-needs-assessment-report-study-fezzan-region-2020.

WFP (World Food Programme). 2021. *Socioeconomic Impact of Currency Devaluation, Libya*. Rome: WFP. https://reliefweb.int/report/libya/libya-socioeconomic-impact-currency-devaluation-march-2021.

World Bank. 2015. *The Quest for Subsidy Reforms in Libya*. Washington, DC: World Bank. https://openknowledge.worldbank.org/bitstream/handle/10986/21673/WPS7225.pdf?sequence=2&isAllowed=y.

World Bank. 2019. *Country Engagement Note for the State of Libya for the Period 2019–2021*. Washington, DC: World Bank. http://documents1.worldbank.org/curated/en/750661550977483586/pdf/Libya-CEN-to-Board-final-01252019-636865562772741763.pdf.

World Bank. 2020. *Libya Economic Monitor*, issue 1. Washington, DC: World Bank. http://documents1.worldbank.org/curated/en/121101597261547774/pdf/Libya-Economic-Monitor-July-2020.pdf.

World Data Atlas. n.d. KNOEMA (database). https://knoema.com/atlas/Libya/Inflation-rate.

12 Impacts of War, Conflict, and COVID-19 on Women in Libya

AFEF HADDAD, MINH CONG NGUYEN, HEND R. IRHIAM, AND DEEKSHA KOKAS

World Bank

Libyan women suffer from widespread social, political, and economic exclusion as well as gender-based violence. The Constitutional Declaration of 2011, as well as the draft constitution finalized in July 2017, provides for gender equality; however, there is no associated implementing legislation, and social norms continue to accord greater power and rights to men. Women in Libya face discrimination regarding inheritance, opportunities to participate in public life, and personal freedom and mobility. Legal and societal barriers also negatively affect women's employment opportunities. The authors provide that from a physical and psychological standpoint, the civil war impacted most Libyans in the form of violence: losing a relative or a friend, destruction of properties, or being forced to leave home. Women and children are, however, often targets of armed groups, which were tools for extorting money from their families.

INTRODUCTION

This chapter examines the effects of the civil war and the COVID-19 pandemic on men and women in Libya. It begins by describing the state of gender equality in Libya since the 1950s. It then describes the phone survey conducted in 2021 to assess how the COVID-19 pandemic affected labor and nonlabor outcomes. The results show that the civil war and the COVID-19 pandemic have left adverse effects on all segments of society, especially women. The unemployment rate is high, and female labor force participation is low and mostly in public service sectors. Real labor income has been reduced by half compared to the pre-conflict period, and it declined further due to the pandemic and high inflation recently. The next section describes how the civil war and the pandemic have affected access to services, women's agency, and freedom of movement. The chapter then continues with forward-looking priorities for the government based on survey responses.

This article reflects only the authors' views and not those of the World Bank Group. The authors are grateful to Johannes Hoogeveen, Practice Manager, Poverty Global Practice, World Bank, for his invaluable comments. The survey was conducted by Michael Robbins, Amaney Jamal, and Mark Tessler from the Arab Analytics and Research Associates.

THE STATE OF GENDER EQUALITY IN LIBYA

The position of women in Libya has fluctuated as the political, economic, and social landscape has changed. As early as the 1950s, women could own and dispose of property independently of their husbands, form their own associations, and hold public office; in 1963, they won the right to vote. Women and men lost that right in the 1969 coup led by Colonel Gaddafi that led to the overthrow of King Idris I.

In the 1980s, gender equality was declared a pillar of the state, and Libya ratified international conventions on women's and children's rights. Libya's legislative system has guaranteed gender equality through many laws and decrees (UNDP 2004).[1] In the 1990s, a post equivalent to a deputy speaker of Parliament was created to promote the effective participation of women in the activities of the Basic People's Committee.[2] It is responsible for monitoring activities related to women and their exercise of their rights in government and full participation in society equal to men (UNDP 2004).

Female labor force participation increased, but women's participation remained mostly in the service sector, mainly in the state-led education and health sectors. According to the 2006 census, among women who worked, 70 percent worked in education, 10 percent in health, 12 percent in the general administration, and 5 percent in agriculture (Bugaighis and Tantoush 2017). Although women are paid better in the public sector than in the private sector, female university graduates earn 18 percent less on average than their male counterparts. Women who finished secondary school earn 30 percent less than men in the private sector and 10 percent less than men in the public sector (World Bank 2015b).

A study by UN Women (2020) shows that women are 12 times more likely to be unemployed than men in Libya and that they earn only about a third of what men do. A 2012 Libyan labor force survey conducted (World Bank 2012) revealed that almost half of the population participated in the labor market (61 percent of men and 31 percent of women). The International Labor Organizations estimated that in 2020, about 48 percent of people 15 and older were participating in the labor force.[3]

Libya has made significant progress in reducing illiteracy and achieving gender equality in enrollment. Schools are free.[4] The education system was successful in providing a wide base of free education to the new generations and is considered as one of the fairest and most accessible systems in the world. Nearly 60 percent of Libyan families have a primary school within 600 meters distance. The illiteracy rate has fallen to 14 percent in 2001 after it was 61 percent in 1971[5] (UNDP 2004). It has not, however, been unable to provide human resources that respond to the labor market's needs (World Bank 2015a).[6]

Women's prominence in the revolution led many women and men to believe that the revolution would empower Libyan women. Women participated in everything from documenting and organizing demonstrations to providing medical and logistical support to the armed groups fighting Gaddafi's forces. A survey conducted by the International Foundation for Electoral Systems (IFES 2013) found that nearly one in five women took part in a protest or demonstration (in the Eastern region, the figure was closer to 50 percent). Despite their active role in Libya's revolution in 2011, however, women have enjoyed only very little involvement in the political process. Only 2 women—Salwa Fawzi El-Deghali and Haniyeh al- Ghamati—belonged to the 33-member National Transitional Council (NTC), Libya's de facto government in 2011 and 2012.

In the 2012 national parliamentary elections, held after the NTC term ended, women won 16.5 percent of the 200 seats. In the 2014 elections, their political representation remained low. Women held only 15 percent of the posts in the cabinet of Abdul Hamid Mohammed Dbeibeh, who was elected to lead a temporary unified executive in February 2021. His cabinet included the first female foreign minister and justice minister. Women's representation was largely omitted from political agreements, including the Libyan Political Agreement signed in Skhirat in 2015,[7] the dialogue in Bouznika in 2020,[8] and the Libyan (5+5) Joint Military Commission talks in 2020.[9]

The lack of a strong legal framework leaves women's political representation and rights in a vulnerable state. Following the 2012 and 2014 elections, women's political quotas were low (they remain so today). The Libyan Political Dialogue Forum is still pushing the quota system,[10] but neither the interim constitution nor the new draft constitution explicitly addresses women's rights, which remain under the same threats they faced before the quota system was introduced.

Another example of attempts to limit women's participation is women representation on the Supreme Judicial Council (SJC). In 2011, women were not elected to be part of the SJC, which was a male-only body until 2016, when a woman filled a vacant seat. A 2015 survey indicates that women's participation in the Libyan judiciary is 39 percent. However, women constitute only 14 percent of sitting judges (ICJ 2016).

Since the revolution, Libyan women have faced discrimination in both the law and the way it is implemented. In 2011, the legal requirement of men to obtain consent from their primary wife to marry a second wife was removed. Under the Constitutional Declaration, legal restrictions on polygamy were suspended (Human Right Watch 2013).[11]

The Libyan Nationality Law is ambiguous with respect to women's ability to confer their nationality upon their children if their husbands are nonnationals. (In contrast, the children of Libyan men married to non-Libyan women are Libyan citizens.) The law encourages the stigmatization of women married to foreign nationals (Euro-Mediterranean Human Rights Monitor 2019). According to Human Right Watch (2013), "in April 2013, the Ministry of Social Affairs reportedly suspended issuing marriage licenses for Libyan women marrying foreigners after Libya's Grand Mufti called on the government to ban women from marrying foreigners." Following a campaign led by several women's rights organizations and demonstrations in Tripoli and Benghazi, the article on passing on citizenship to one's children was amended. The draft constitution is still supposed to be voted on by a public referendum (Euro-Mediterranean Human Rights Monitor 2019).

Another example of efforts to restrict the activities of women is the ban issued in 2017 in which authorities in the East prohibited women under the age of 60 from traveling abroad without a male guardian. The ban was repealed several days after it was issued.

A decade of war has brought about adverse consequences for the Libyan economy, infrastructure, and the social fabric, especially for women and children. COVID-19 has exacerbated the already precarious situation, in which armed conflict has resulted in a lack of supplies, food, water, and health and education facilities.

DATA AND METHODOLOGY

The literature on the impact of war on economies, with a focus on women, has expanded in recent years.[12] Analysis for Libya remains limited, however. This chapter attempts to fill this gap, using data from a high-frequency phone survey conducted in 2021.

A nationally representative phone survey of 1,000 women and 523 men was conducted between June and July 2021 in order to better understand the magnitude of the impact of the war, conflict, and the COVID-19 pandemic, with a focus on women in Libya.

Very few official household surveys were conducted in the past decade, because of limited budgets and prolonged conflict. The latest labor force survey was conducted in 2012; the previous household budget survey was conducted in 2007. In a country with ongoing conflict, high levels of insecurity, limited budgets, and movement restrictions, the possibility of conducting face-to-face interviews is limited. In such situations, data collection by phone is often preferred.

To understand and assess the impacts of war and COVID-19 on women and girls and inform debates and efforts to promote the status of women in the country, the World Bank collaborated with Arab Research and Analytics Associates to implement a high-frequency phone survey in Libya. The survey includes three sections. The first section covers basic information about the sampling approach and the demographic characteristics of the respondents. The second section assesses the impacts of war and conflict on women and girls in three periods: the pre-conflict period (2012–14), pre-COVID (January 2020), and 2021. Topics included respondents' access to education, health care, clean water, and electricity; prices and availability of food; women's and girls' agency and freedom of movement; participation in the labor force, community, and political positions; and domestic work distribution, time use, and unpaid labor. The third section captures post-war priorities and questions.

In the absence of a sampling frame or a comprehensive list of phone numbers, a sample of phone numbers for this survey was generated using a random digit dialing (RDD) approach.[13] In this approach, every working mobile number in the country has an equal chance of being contacted. A computer program randomly generated numbers in Libya based on the prefixes associated with the mobile phone carriers operating in Libya. The numbers were randomly selected and dialed using computer software. Only answered eligible numbers were passed on to operators to conduct the interviews.

This survey is unique for several reasons. First, it is one of the most recent phone surveys to focus on women from various aspects and assess how conflict and violence have affected them. Second, the survey provides timely data to evaluate changes in rapidly changing conditions in Libya, from the recent forming of the Government of National Unity to the emergence of COVID-19. Third, it is one of the first phone surveys where attempts are made to reduce survey bias from nonresponse bias and noncoverage bias. Post-collection weighting is applied to the sampled data to ensure survey results match distributions of age, gender, age cohorts, levels of completed education, and mantikas (administrative units) from the 2012 census. Without a proper sampling frame, the census distributions are the only available source, albeit old.

The survey included respondents 18 or older randomly selected from all 22 mantikas. To allow for meaningful and statistically significant comparisons between men and women and different groups of women, the design sample was split between 1,000 women and 500 men. Respondents of both genders were randomly chosen until 500 men were selected. Subsequently, only women were eligible for selection. The survey was administered June 29 to July 15, 2021. The median duration was 23 minutes. On average, 42 calls had to be made for one completed interview. For more details on the survey and methodology, see annex 12a and annex 12b. Throughout the chapter, this high frequency survey will be referred to as the "The Multiple Scars of the War and COVID-19: What Libyan Women Have Endured," or HFS-LW 2021.

RESULTS OF THE SURVEY

More than 75 percent of survey respondents reported having experienced conflict events (figure 12.1). More than half of respondents indicated that they had lost a family member or close friend or been forced to leave home. About 23 percent of respondents had directly experienced violence; 39 percent had had personal property destroyed or stolen. Women tended to be less affected than men by every type of violence, which could reflect restrictions imposed on their movement. Nearly 27 percent of women were never allowed to use public transportation, and 34 percent had to be accompanied if they wanted to commute by public transportation.

Findings from the survey highlight less variation of conflicts across areas of residence, although rural areas and villages/towns experienced more consequences of war than big cities. The data on violence exposure and experience of conflict are consistent with the number of conflict events and number of deaths revealed in the data from the Armed Conflict Location and Event Data (ACLED) database (figure 12.2). In some locations such as Tripoli, Benghazi, and Sirte, exposure to violence is correlated with the large number of deaths.

Women's labor force participation in Libya has been an issue of concern since the beginning of the 2011 crisis because of its low participation rate. Less than half of the survey respondents reported working for pay in the week preceding

FIGURE 12.1

Survey respondents' experience with conflicts

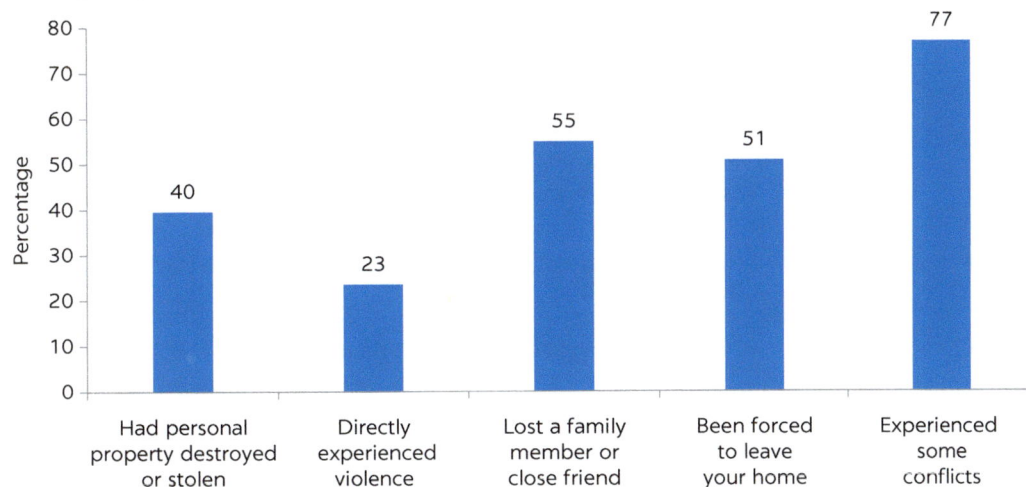

Source: Data from HFS-LW 2021.

FIGURE 12.2

Correlation between experience of conflict and exposure to conflict events and fatalities

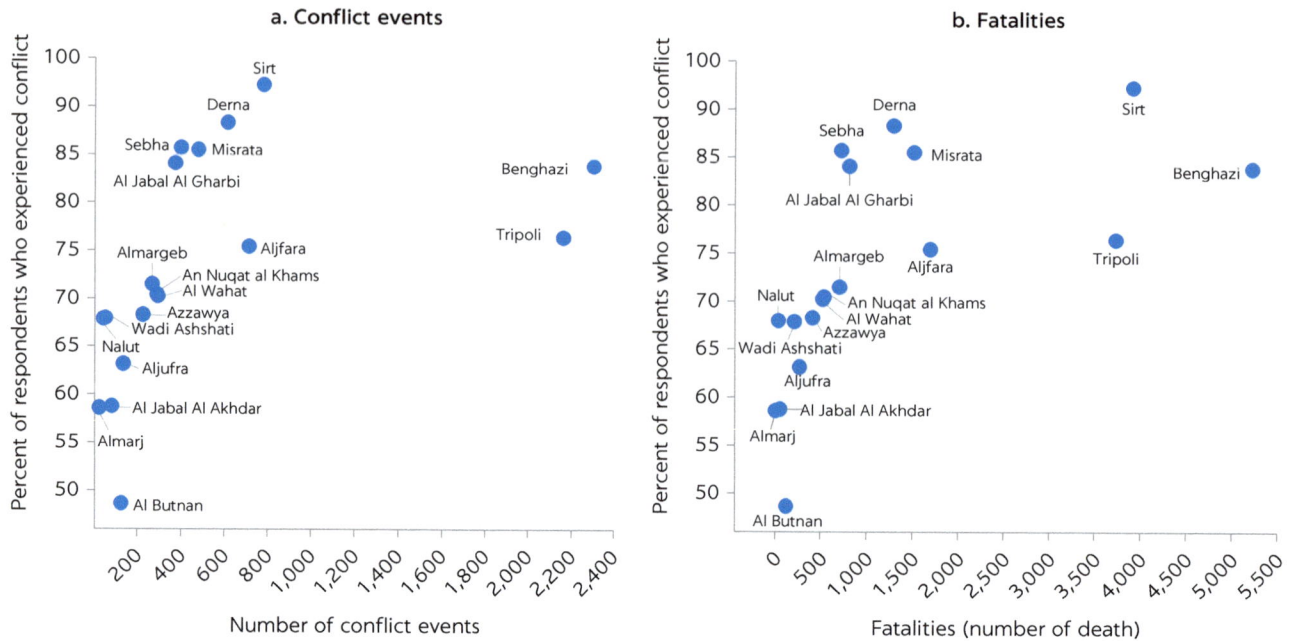

Source: Data from HFS-LW 2021 and Armed Conflict Location and Event Data (database), https://acleddata.com/.

the survey. Working status varied by gender, age cohort, and location. The results revealed the following:

- Nationally, 49 percent of respondents performed any work for pay in the week before the survey interview.
- Women were less likely to be employed than men, with nearly 66 percent of men and only 30 percent of women reporting working in the week before the survey (55 percent of female respondents indicated that they were exclusively housewives). Gender gaps vary across regions. In Almargeb and Tobruk, for example, men were four times more likely to work than were women. In Tripoli and Benghazi, men were just twice as likely to do so.
- Respondents 26–35 years old were more likely to be employed than respondents in other age groups. The share of respondents that were employed was 59 percent among people 26–35, 48 among people 18–25, 45 percent among people 36–45, and 41 percent among people 46 and older.
- Nearly 76 percent of respondents with an educational degree equal to a masters or higher reported working for pay in the week before the survey. In contrast, less than 25 percent of respondents with no formal education did so. This finding contrasts with the situation in other countries in the Middle East and North Africa, such as Tunisia, where unemployment is higher among the better educated.[14]

More people work in wage employment than in self-employment (a classification that usually covers informal self-employed groups and independent workers such as wholesalers, farmers, and construction workers). Sixty percent of respondents reported working for employers in return for wages or some fixed income, and 34 percent reported being self-employed (figure 12.3). The type of employment differs for men and women. Nearly 83 percent of

FIGURE 12.3

Share of survey respondents reporting having worked for pay the week before the survey

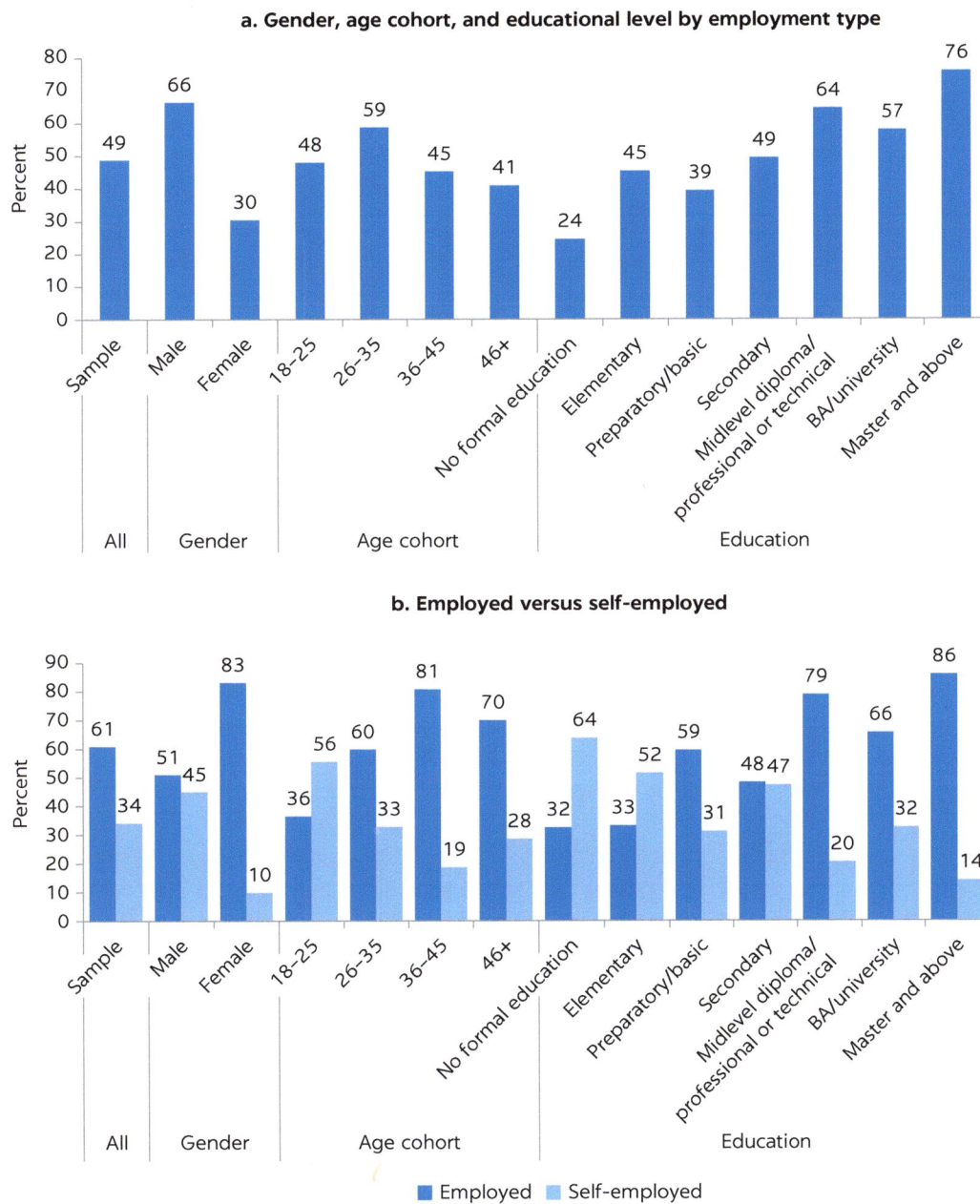

a. Gender, age cohort, and educational level by employment type

b. Employed versus self-employed

Source: Data from HFS-LW 2021.

female respondents reported working for an employer for pay or a fixed income in the week before the survey. Self-employment was dominated by men (45 percent of male respondents were self-employed in contrast to only 10 percent of female respondents). Greater participation of men in informal self-employed work may explain why men work more than women on average (more than 60 percent of employed women worked fewer hours than men).

Consistent with findings from previous studies, the public sector continues to remain the main employer for a large share of Libyan respondents (table 12.1).[15] The HFS-LW survey does not separate employment by public and private sectors. However, the sectoral breakdown of employed respondents reveals that nearly half of respondents that reported working were engaged in public services (23 percent in education, 16 percent in public administration, and 10 percent in health and social work). A larger share of female respondents reported being engaged in public services such as education, health, and social work; male respondents were more likely to be engaged in public administration, defense services, and trade. Nearly 48 percent of female respondents reported working in education, and 15 percent reported working in health and social work. In contrast, nearly 20 percent of male respondents reported working in public administration and defense-related services, and nearly 13 percent reported working in wholesale and retail trading.

All sectors except education, health, and social work are dominated by men, but their dominance is stronger in some sectors (construction, agriculture, wholesale, and trade which are physically demanding) than others (table 12.1). The proportion of men in construction and agriculture is eight times the proportion of women in the sectors. That ratio is about seven in the transport sector and four in the wholesale sector.

At the household level, average per capita monthly income in 2021 was LD 320, with wide gender differences. Monthly household per capita income for female respondents (LD 295) was 14 percent lower than for male respondents (LD 345). Differences are also evident between households headed by men and women. On average, households headed by women earned 25 percent less than households headed by men (table 12.2). Female-headed households earned about LD 188 per capita a month, while male-headed households earned about LD 253 per capita. Household income reported by men is higher than that of women in big cities and lower in villages, towns, and rural areas. This is consistent with the fact that men are more likely to be employed than women and women are reported being engaged in public services.

Although 44 percent of respondents are perfectly satisfied with their life (assessed as 10 on a scale of 10) and about two-thirds of respondents assess their

TABLE 12.1 Sectors of employment of survey respondents, by gender (percent)

SECTOR	MEN	WOMEN	TOTAL
Construction	5.7	0.7	4.0
Agriculture and hunting	10.6	1.3	7.5
Transport, storage, and communications	7.5	1.0	5.4
Electricity, gas, and water supply	6.0	1.5	4.5
Wholesale and retail trade; repair of motor vehicles, motorcycles, and personal and household goods	12.8	3.3	9.7
Public administration and defense; compulsory social security	19.6	7.0	15.5
Other community, social, and personal service activities	3.5	2.8	3.3
Manufacturing	4.1	3.5	3.9
Hotels and restaurants	7.2	8.6	7.7
Health and social work	6.8	15.0	9.5
Education	10.8	47.6	22.9

Source: Data from HFS-LW 2021.
Note: The table shows numbers for sectors with at least 15 observations.

TABLE 12.2 **Monthly per capita income in 2021, by asset tercile, gender, and location (LD)**

CHARACTERISTIC	MEN	WOMEN	TOTAL
Asset tercile			
1 (lowest)	198.6	222.2	210.9
2	271.1	328.9	299.8
3 (highest)	427.4	317.1	375.2
Household head			
No	528.6	314.0	376.1
Yes	253.7	188.5	242.2
Total	344.9	295.2	320.6
Location			
Big city	426.3	339.0	384.0
Village or town	182.8	205.7	194.4
Rural area	221.1	240.2	230.3

Source: Data from HFS-LW 2021.

TABLE 12.3 **Employment rates among survey respondents ages 36–62, by gender and age group**

Percent

	GENDER		AGE GROUP		FULL
ITEM	MEN	WOMEN	36–45	46–62	SAMPLE
Worked last week (2021)	54.0	38.3	45.1	47.4	46.1
Employed	72.2	87.0	80.8	75.5	78.3
Self-employed	27.8	10.3	18.6	22.9	20.6
Worked in January 2020 (pre-COVID-19)	95.0	46.0	73.4	67.0	70.5
Worked in 2012–14 (before the conflict)	93.4	40.2	68.1	65.2	66.8

Source: Data from HFS-LW 2021.
Note: For comparison, table reports statistics for respondents ages 36 to 62 years for all periods.

life as 8 or more on a scale of 10, more than half of the respondents' households cannot cover basic expenses. On average, monthly per capita income for households that can cover basic expenses is twice as large as households that cannot cover basic expenses.

Labor income effects

COVID-19 has had significant employment impacts. Among respondents ages 36–62, the share who reported working was slightly more than 67 percent in 2012–14, 70 percent in 2019, and just 46 percent in 2021 (table 12.3). Real monthly per capita household income decreased from LD 787 in 2012–14 to LD 358 in 2019 and LD 321 in 2021.

COVID-19 led to significant reduction in employment rates for men 36–62, with the share working plummeting from 95 percent just before the pandemic to

54 percent in 2021. The effect was weaker for women, among whom employment fell from 46 percent to 38 percent.

Men were more likely than women to be employed, both before and after the COVID-19 crisis (figure 12.4). Across all three periods, the share of men who worked was about twice that of women. The gender gap in the employment rate is robust to age groups and education levels but varies across area of residence, with a larger gap in rural areas (56 percentage points on average) and villages (42 percentage points on average) than in big cities (33 percentage points on average). Although there was a slight improvement over time, the gender gap in employment status was highest in rural areas, 50 percent in 2021 and 60 percent during the pre-conflict period. This gender gap in employment status appears to be narrowing in town and big city areas.

FIGURE 12.4

Survey respondents' employment status before the conflict, before the pandemic, and in 2021

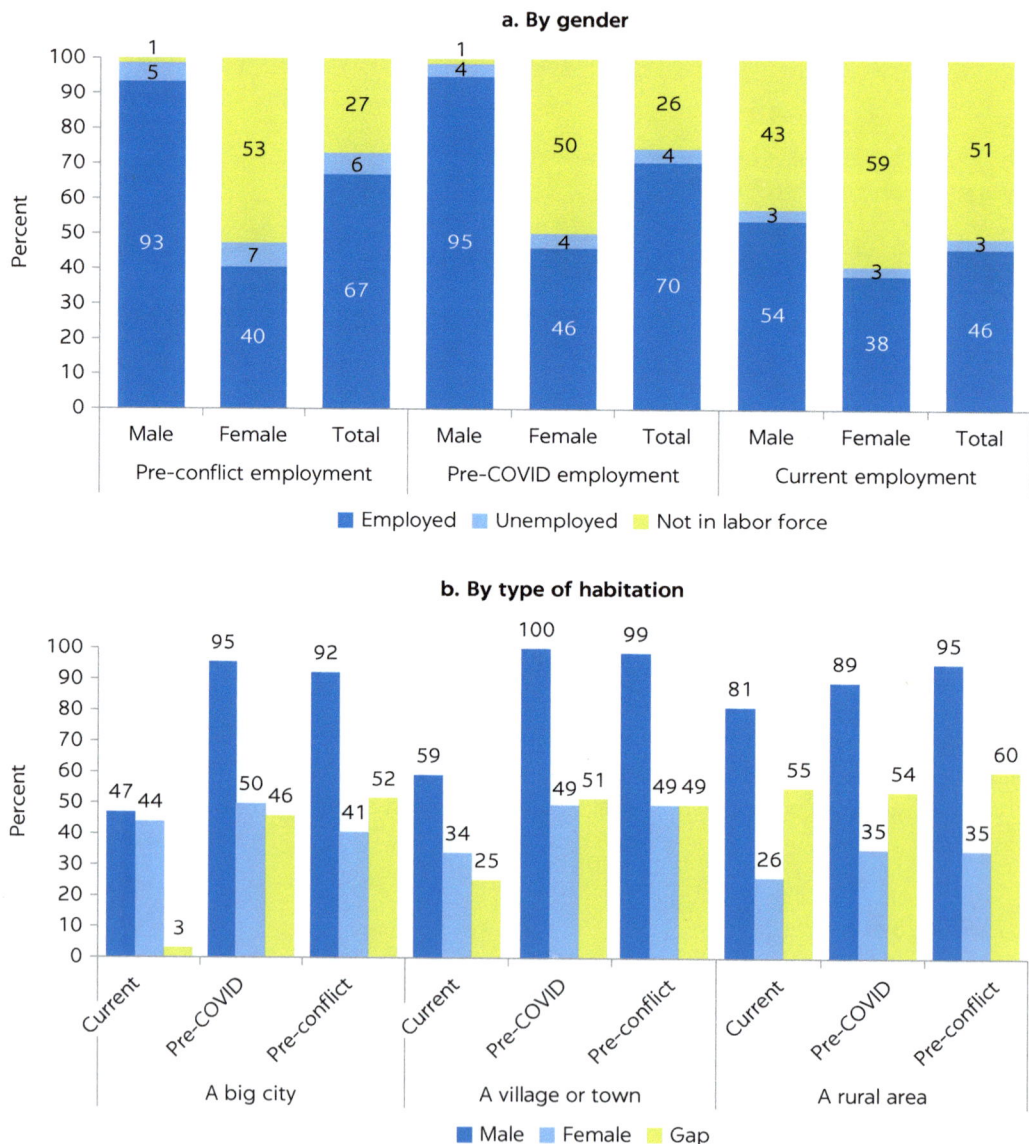

a. By gender

b. By type of habitation

Source: Data from HFS-LW 2021.

TABLE 12.4 Real monthly per capita household income across different periods by gender: Before the conflict, before the pandemic, and in 2021

Libyan dinars

RESPONDENTS	PRE-CONFLICT (2012–14)	PRE-COVID (JANUARY 2020)	2021
All	787.0	358.1	320.6
Men	828.3	366.2	344.9
Women	745.9	349.5	295.2

Source: Data from HFS-LW 2021.
Note: Table shows real income (converted to 2021 price). Outliers (per capita income of more than 99 percentile) were removed for both pre-COVID and pre-conflict periods.

COVID-19 also caused a reduction in real monthly per capita incomes (table 12.4). Real monthly per capita household income decreased from LD 787 in the pre-conflict period to LD 358 in the pre-COVID period and to LD 321 in 2021. For both men and women respondents' household, real monthly per capita income has been reduced in half as compared to the pre-conflict level.

Steep declines in real income reported by respondents in the pre-COVID-19 period can be attributed to high inflation in Libya in recent years. As a result of interregional supply disruptions following the intensification and spread of armed conflict, the prices of local food products rose rapidly. In December 2020, the devaluation in the Libyan dinar raised consumer prices in Libya, where domestic food supply relies heavily on imports for important products such as cereals, leading to a 22 percent increase in prices over 2019 (World Bank 2020).

Nonlabor effects

The armed conflict and the COVID-19 pandemic had direct effects on consumption, service disruption, and changes in other nonlabor outcomes, such as freedom of movement and agency of women (World Bank 2020).

Only 44 percent of respondents reported being satisfied with the current public education service in their area, a smaller share than in earlier periods (table 12.5). There are no significant gender or location differences. Half of respondents think that education was better during the pre-COVID period than in the current period. The percentage is even higher for those satisfied (57 percent) than those dissatisfied (46 percent) with the current education system. When comparing education in the current period, that is, 2021 with pre-conflict outcomes between 2012 and 2014, about 67 percent of respondents think that education was better during the pre-conflict period. Of those respondents who are currently satisfied, another 69 percent indicate that the old education system was better, while these numbers are 65 percent and 72 percent for women and men respondents, respectively.

Only 39 percent of Libyans surveyed report being satisfied with the health care system in the current period, much lower than the share that report satisfaction in pre-COVID and pre-conflict period. More than half of the respondents (57 percent) indicate that the health care system between 2012 and 2014 was in a much better condition in contrast to the current and pre-COVID period. Even for respondents who are currently satisfied with the health care system, most

TABLE 12.5 Survey respondents' satisfaction with selected public services before the conflict, before the pandemic, and in 2021, by gender and age group

Percent

ITEM	GENDER		AGE GROUP		
	MEN	WOMEN	36–45	46+	ALL
Currently satisfied with public educational system	45.3	41.9	44.2	47.1	43.6
Of those satisfied: January 2020 was better or much better than today	56.9	56.9	54.4	59.5	56.9
Of those satisfied: 2012–14 was better or much better than today	72.5	65.5	78.2	76.6	69.2
Currently satisfied with the health care system	37.5	40.0	39.0	38.3	38.7
Of those satisfied: January 2020 was better or much better than today	64.0	50.4	67.0	55.4	57.1
Of those satisfied: 2012–14 was better or much better than today	66.5	57.9	50.1	67.8	62.1
Currently satisfied with access to drinking water	62.4	65.2	69.6	56.5	63.8
Of those satisfied: 2012–14 was better or much better than today	47.2	47.5	37.1	54.0	47.3
Currently satisfied with the reliability of electricity	9.6	8.7	10.3	8.9	9.2
Of those satisfied: 2012 and 2014 was better or much better than today	63.5	47.7	78.8	51.7	55.9
Currently satisfied with the availability of food and necessities	66.1	67.5	68.8	63.5	66.8
Of those satisfied: January 2020 was better or much better than today	47.4	43.7	58.0	33.3	45.5
Of those satisfied: 2012–14 was better or much better than today	66.7	55.9	64.5	59.1	61.3
Currently satisfied with the price of food and necessities	22.9	13.7	26.2	14.7	18.4
Of those satisfied: January 2020 was better or much better than today	63.7	39.2	74.2	43.8	54.6
Of those satisfied: 2012–14 was better or much better than today	78.8	68.2	84.6	64.9	74.9

Source: Data from HFS-LW 2021.

think that the pre-conflict system between 2012 and 2014 was better (57 percent for the pre-COVID period and 62 percent for the pre-conflict period). This is also true for the older respondents (ages 46 and above)—69 percent in this age cohort thinks the pre-conflict system was better. This is not surprising as health care is one of the key sectors that has suffered the most in the last decade due to conflicts, and COVID-19 has only exacerbated these issues.

Libyans have faced painful power cuts as years of chaos and conflict disrupted the electricity grid and facilities. More than 90 percent of respondents reported not being satisfied with access to reliable electricity. Some 56 percent of all respondents and 79 percent of respondents 36–45 years reported that access to electricity in the pre-conflict period was much more stable than in the current period.

Political instability, inflation, border closures, disrupted trade, movement restrictions, and curfews have caused the prices of essential food and goods to spike and reduced availability in Libya. Food and other basic expenditures constitute a major part of the household budget for Libyans, especially among the poor. Only 18 percent of survey respondents reported satisfaction with prices of food and necessities, a much smaller share than in the pre-COVID (55 percent) and pre-conflict (75 percent) periods.

Respondents reported some improvement in freedom of movement, as measured by the ability to visit any place using public or shared transportation, walk to a friend's or family member's home during the day, and participate in a community organization. The 2021 survey results show that 13–14 percent of respondents indicated that they experienced some improvement in freedom of movement in the three activities (figure 12.5).

FIGURE 12.5

Survey respondents' perceptions of changes in freedom of movement between 2012–14 and 2021

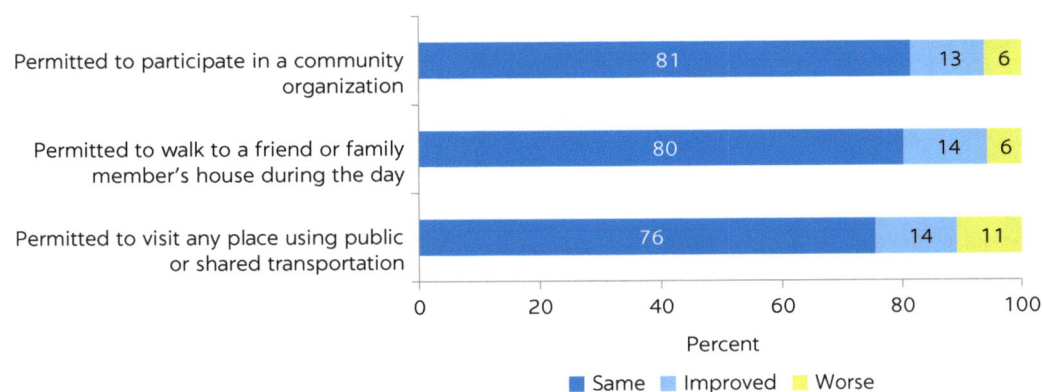

Source: Data from HFS-LW 2021.

However, freedom of movement for women saw little change over the past decade (table 12.6). In 2021, 27 percent of women respondents were not permitted to visit places using public or shared transportation—a very slight improvement over the pre-conflict figure of 29 percent. This type of restriction partly explains the low employment rate for women. About 59 percent of women respondents indicated that they could go alone to a friend's or family member's house with permission, and 18 percent indicated that they could go without permission compared to 57 percent and 13 percent, respectively.

TABLE 12.6 **Survey respondents' assessment of freedom of movement in 2012–14 and 2021, by age**

Percent

	2012–14			2021		
TYPE OF FREEDOM	WOMEN	PEOPLE 36–45	PEOPLE 46+	WOMEN	PEOPLE 36–45	PEOPLE 46+
Permitted to visit any place using public or shared transportation						
Never	28.9	27.7	22.2	27.4	24.7	33.4
Yes, but never alone	35.6	41.0	42.0	33.5	29.3	30.1
Yes, alone but with permission	28.5	24.2	26.1	29.9	35.4	28.3
Yes, alone and without permission	7.0	7.1	9.7	9.1	10.7	8.2
Permitted to walk to a friend's or family member's house during the day						
Never	9.1	6.2	10.3	8.0	10.0	8.8
Yes, but never alone	20.5	26.5	22.6	14.8	14.9	14.9
Yes, alone but with permission	57.6	54.1	51.6	59.4	57.0	51.0
Yes, alone and without permission	12.8	13.3	15.4	17.9	18.1	25.2
Permitted to participate in a community organization						
Never	48.1	58.5	41.1	41.5	53.8	35.5
Yes, but never alone	10.0	10.8	8.5	9.2	7.2	9.0
Yes, alone but with permission	35.3	24.1	44.3	42.0	30.6	47.3
Yes, alone and without permission	6.6	6.6	6.1	7.3	8.4	8.3

Source: Data from HFS-LW 2021.

TABLE 12.7 **Survey respondents' assessment of women's agency in 2012–14 and 2021, by gender**

MEASURE OF AGENCY	2012–14		2021	
	MEN	WOMEN	MEN	WOMEN
Men and women have equal say on family decisions				
Strongly agree	20.7	21.4	21.3	23.7
Agree	50.3	54.7	54.7	56.2
Disagree	14.5	15.6	15.0	13.7
Strongly disagree	14.5	8.3	9.1	6.4
Men and women have equal say on how money is spent in the household				
Strongly agree	19.9	24.1	23.0	25.8
Agree	47.3	53.4	48.4	50.0
Disagree	21.3	12.0	17.2	17.4
Strongly disagree	11.5	10.6	11.4	6.7
Women have complete power over their health decisions				
Strongly agree	24.0	31.2	22.9	34.3
Agree	49.1	50.0	51.5	48.2
Disagree	17.4	12.2	15.3	11.0
Strongly disagree	9.5	6.6	10.2	6.6

Source: Data from HFS-LW 2021.

About 41 percent of women respondents indicated they are not permitted to attend a community meeting; only 7 percent were allowed to do so, while the other 52 percent are permitted to participate either not alone or with permission.

Women's agency remains low but shows some evidence of improvement since before the conflict. Measures of agency include having an equal say in family decisions, having an equal say in household expenditures, and having complete power over decisions affecting one's health. The survey results reveal the following findings about women's agency (table 12.7):

- The shares of respondents who agreed (agreed and strongly agreed) with the statement "Men and women have an equal say on family decisions" were about the same for men (76 percent) and women (80 percent). These figures were slightly higher than in 2012–14 (71 percent for men and 76 percent for women).
- About 75 percent of women (strongly) agreed that men and women have equal say on how money is spent in the household, a lower figure than in 2012–14 (77 percent). Similarly, 83 percent of women agreed that women have complete power over their health decisions, a slightly higher share than earlier (81 percent). These results are indicative of no significant improvements regarding how money is spent in the household or power over health decisions in the current period.

These results are consistent across locations. They vary by age, with older women more likely to report playing a role in deciding how finances are used (figure 12.6). More female respondents (80 percent) in the age group 36 and older agreed that men and women have equal say on money spending than that

FIGURE 12.6

Survey respondents' assessment of women's agency in 2021 and 2012–14, by age cohort

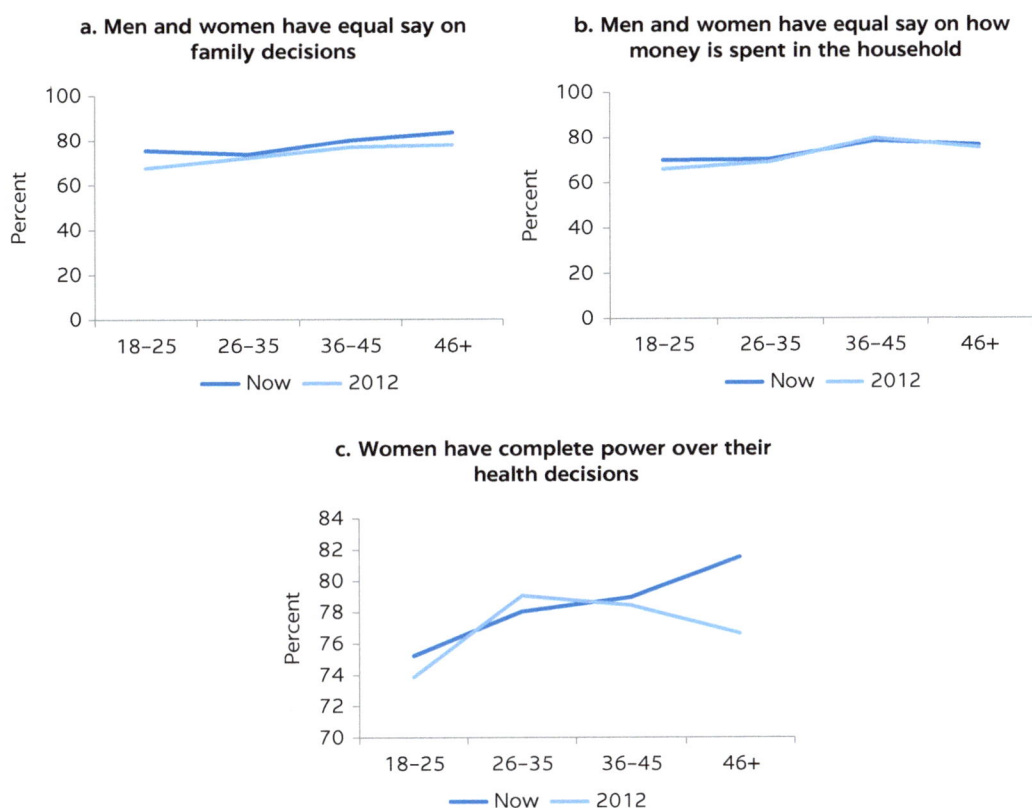

a. Men and women have equal say on family decisions

b. Men and women have equal say on how money is spent in the household

c. Women have complete power over their health decisions

Source: Data from HFS-LW 2021.
Note: Figures shows percentage of respondents who answered "agree" and "strongly agree" to the three questions.

of female respondents in the younger cohorts (ages 18–25 and 26–35, both with 70 percent). For people 18–25, the changes were significant for both having equal say on family decisions and how money is spent in the household. Respondents in the older age cohorts (46+) reported improvements in women's agency on money spending and health decisions.

Both men and women increased their unpaid workload, but women bore more of the burden than men (figure 12.7). Amid COVID-19, household chores and other domestic tasks have been increasingly recognized as a form of essential regular work for both men and women. Chores like cooking, shopping for groceries, and cleaning homes or clothes all take longer than they did before the pandemic. At-home activities and lockdowns increase the burden of cooking and taking care of children and elders.

Relative to 2012–14, the share of respondents that reported spending one to two hours a day caring for children and other family members rose by 3 percent among male survey respondents. An additional 8 percent of female respondents said they spent more than seven hours a day taking care of family. In the survey, 49 percent of women and 24 percent of men reported spending more than seven hours a day taking care of their families.

FIGURE 12.7

Self-reported hours spent caring for family and preparing meals, by gender

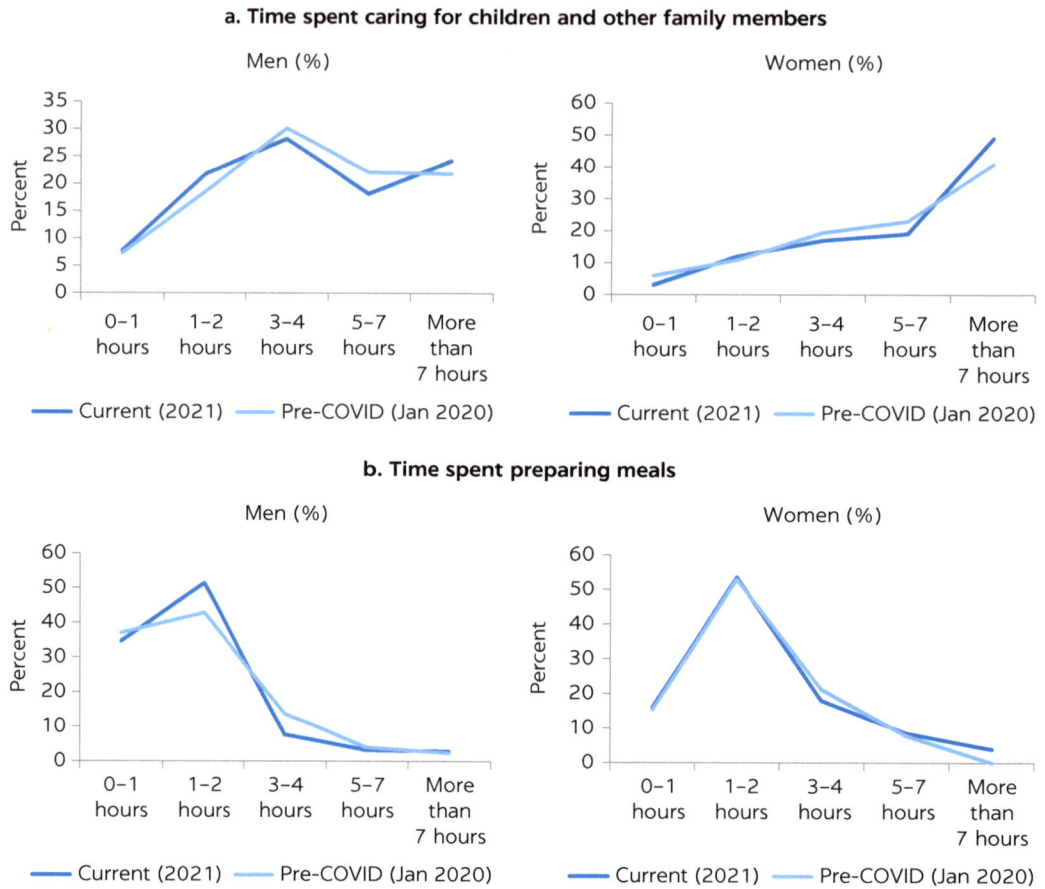

a. Time spent caring for children and other family members

b. Time spent preparing meals

Source: Data from HFS-LW 2021.

LOOKING FORWARD

The third part of the survey focused on the issues respondents believe the government should prioritize to reconstruct the Libyan economy. Nearly 30 percent of respondents cited maintaining internal stability and national security as one of the key areas the Government of National Unity should prioritize, 20 percent cite fighting corruption, 16 percent cite increasing access to and the reliability of electricity, and 11 percent cite improving the education system. Opinions on top priorities for the 2021 transitional government vary by gender and age cohorts (table 12.8). The percentage of men reporting fighting corruption, as an area that should be a priority for the Government of National Accord, is 1.5 times larger than that of women. In contrast, the percentage of women considering electricity and women's rights is larger than men. Across age cohorts, younger cohorts seem to vote for the education system and women's rights, while older cohorts tend to vote for internal stability and national security and fighting corruption. Education system (18 percent), health care system (16 percent), and internal stability and national security (16 percent) are reported in that order as the second top priority that the government should be focusing on. The results on the second top priority are also robust based on gender and age cohorts.

TABLE 12.8 Survey respondents' top priorities for the government of national accord, by gender and age group

Percent

PRIORITY	GENDER		AGE GROUP				ALL
	MEN	WOMEN	18–25	26–35	36–45	46+	
Top priority							
Internal stability and national security	30.8	28.0	23.4	31.9	28.4	33.1	29.4
Fighting corruption	24.4	16.6	20.9	17.8	31.6	13.1	20.5
Electricity	10.9	22.2	17.6	15.7	10.3	22.5	16.6
Education system	12.7	9.8	12.8	13.5	10.1	8.0	11.3
Justice system	9.3	6.0	8.1	5.7	7.6	9.8	7.7
Health care system	5.2	7.8	6.9	5.0	6.9	7.7	6.5
Job creation	3.9	4.2	5.3	3.7	3.7	3.5	4.0
Women's rights	1.0	4.6	4.1	4.5	0.6	1.6	2.8
Improving roads and transportation	1.8	0.7	0.9	2.3	0.8	0.7	1.2
Second-biggest priority							
Education system	14.7	22.0	18.2	14.7	11.6	29.7	18.4
Health care system	15.8	16.4	11.4	14.5	20.7	18.3	16.1
Internal stability and national security	13.9	17.7	17.6	15.8	18.2	11.9	15.8
Electricity	14.5	14.6	16.1	18.8	12.3	9.6	14.5
Fighting corruption	16.6	10.9	11.0	14.7	13.4	15.2	13.7
Justice system	7.5	7.2	13.2	6.1	5.3	5.0	7.3
Improving roads and transportation	9.0	3.3	3.9	3.9	15.3	2.5	6.1
Job creation	5.7	6.2	7.8	6.8	2.6	6.1	5.9
Women's rights	2.5	1.8	0.9	4.6	0.6	1.6	2.1

Source: Data from HFS-LW 2021.

Respondents across demographic groups—including 80 percent of women—expect that women's equality in Libya will improve in the next three to five years (figure 12.8). The top two areas that respondents think the new government should focus on to ensure women's equality are social and economic reforms (figure 12.9). To ensure women's equality, the government should focus on social reforms (33 percent of respondents), economic reforms (28 percent), legal reforms (25 percent), promotion of change within the household (24 percent), and political reforms (16 percent).[16] These priorities are relatively consistent across gender and age cohorts except for legal reforms; based on age, 30 percent of respondents ages 26–35 and just 17 percent of respondents 36–45 think that legal reforms are essential.

Gender-related bias, restrictive social norms, and family responsibilities restrict the lives of Libyan women. About 41 percent of female respondents and 36 percent of male respondents believe that family responsibilities and social norms greatly constrain them from becoming community leaders (table 12.9). For both genders, about a fifth of respondents think there are no constraints to women becoming community leaders. Young respondents seem to think "family responsibilities" and "social norms" are constraints, while older respondents think a "lack of necessary skills" prevents women from becoming community leaders (table 12.10).

FIGURE 12.8

Survey respondents' expectation about women's equality in Libya over the next three to five years, by gender and age group

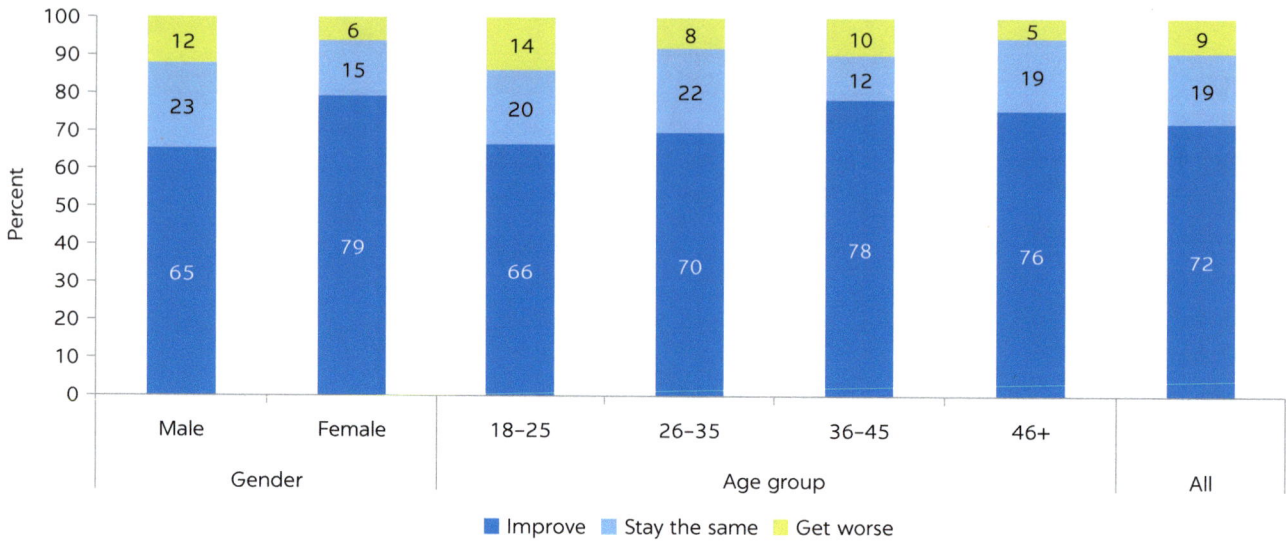

Source: Data from HFS-LW 2021.

FIGURE 12.9

Survey respondents' identification of most important areas to address to ensure women's equality, by gender and age group

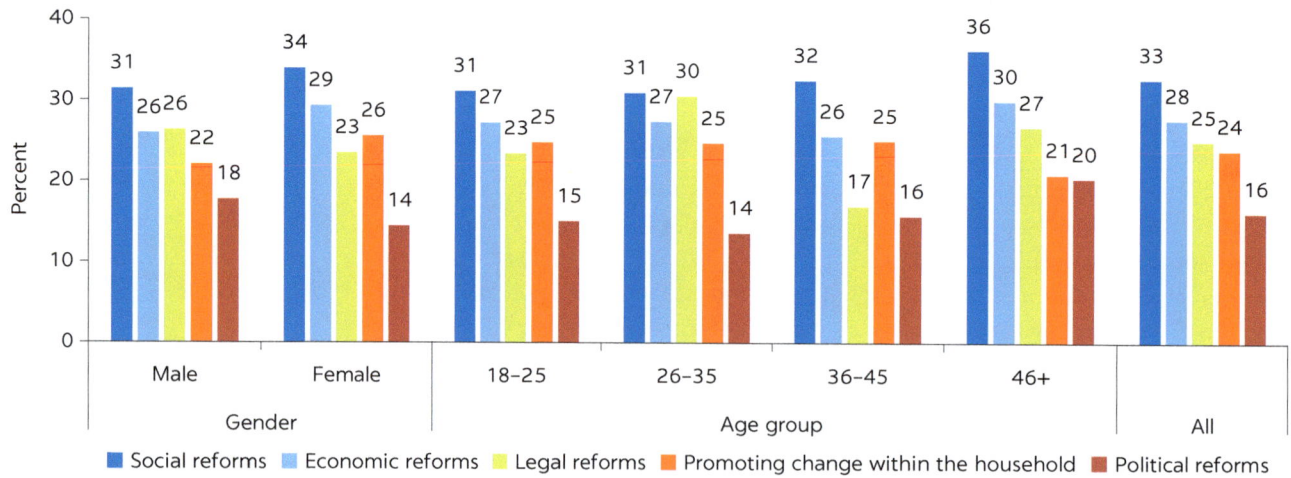

Source: Data from HFS-LW 2021.

TABLE 12.9 **Survey respondents' assessment of constraints women face in becoming community leaders, by gender**

Percent

TYPE OF RESPONSIBILITY AND EXTENT OF CONSTRAINT	MEN	WOMEN
Family responsibilities		
Great	36.4	40.6
Medium	33.7	34.5
Small	8.3	8.1
Not at all	21.6	16.8
Social norms		
Great	38.7	38.2
Medium	34.1	36.8
Small	8.2	7.4
Not at all	19.0	17.6
Lack of necessary skills		
Great	26.9	31.2
Medium	39.5	41.0
Small	11.2	12.4
Not at all	22.4	15.4

Source: Data from HFS-LW 2021.

TABLE 12.10 **Survey respondents' assessment of constraints women face in becoming community leaders, by age group**

Percent

TYPE OF RESPONSIBILITY AND EXTENT OF CONSTRAINT	AGE GROUP			
	18–25	26–35	36–45	46+
Family responsibilities				
Great	34.4	39.8	33.0	31.7
Medium	33.8	32.6	37.4	40.3
Small	9.5	10.2	5.3	6.5
Not at all	22.3	17.4	24.3	21.5
Social norms				
Great	36.0	41.0	37.6	32.5
Medium	34.5	36.3	34.5	37.7
Small	4.4	5.5	5.8	11.3
Not at all	25.0	17.3	22.2	18.6
Lack of necessary skills				
Great	23.8	28.9	35.6	33.5
Medium	42.5	45.6	26.1	33.6
Small	12.5	8.2	6.8	15.1
Not at all	21.3	17.3	31.5	17.9

Source: Data from HFS-LW 2021.

CONCLUDING REMARKS

The civil war and the COVID-19 pandemic have had adverse effects on all seg-ments of Libyan society, especially women. The civil war affected most Libyans in the form of violence. Yet, the particular context of Libya matters for interpre-tation of the results. The public sector was and is the main source of employment for women, and the public sector has continued to receive salaries throughout the conflict—unlike many other conflict contexts. In addition, the overthrow of Gaddafi resulted in contradictory tendencies regarding the rights of women—an opportunity to reflect on the important role of women in the revolution coexist-ing with attempts to roll back the gender equality measures of the Gaddafi era. In the absence of definitive resolution of this tension, the impact of conflict dynamics took over, with generally deleterious effects on women as in other countries.

With conflict almost becoming part of the "baseline" for most Libyans, the pandemic seems to have had a more direct effect, possibly because it is more recent. Our survey found an aggravation of high unemployment rate, low female labor force participation, and a more significant gender gap in the employment rate. The situation has deteriorated further as the gender gap in the employment rate increased, and the employment rate itself decreased when comparing the post- and pre-crisis periods. Measures to mitigate the effects of the crisis are then needed to increase employment and reduce the gender gap in employment. There are two problems: the private sector is small, and women are less likely to be employed than men, potentially due to restrictions on their movement. These problems provide a window of opportunity for the government of Libya and its partners to do more to encourage and empower women to develop income-generating activities, build new businesses, and support existing businesses. Moreover, effective policies should encourage more productive private enter-prises to draw employees from the highly concentrated public sector.

Gender stereotypes and social norms, which curtail women's rights and free-dom of movement, continue to persist, although there has been a slight improve-ment for women since the civil conflict. These issues are not only a significant threat to their freedom of movement but could limit their professional or educa-tional opportunities. Cultural views must evolve to adapt to new economic real-ities, and a gender-supportive framework is critical for an inclusive society. Survey respondents think that social, economic, and legal reforms, promotion of change within the household, and political reforms are the crucial areas the government should address to ensure women's equality.

Both crises have also affected access to essential services, namely, education, health care, electricity, and access to food. Most Libyans are unsatisfied with their current level of accessibility to these services, and a substantial share thinks that the system is getting worse than what they had before the conflict or the COVID-19 pandemic. Electricity is, however, the worst-hit sector, as 90 percent are unsatisfied with the service.

There is little gender discrimination in women's agency (equal say on family decisions, equal say on how money is spent in the household, and complete power over their health decisions). However, although the situation has improved since a decade ago, men tend to disagree more than women in how money is spent in the household and self-control over women's health decisions. Women spend more time caring for children, especially after the pandemic, while working men work longer hours than working women. However, both have increased their unpaid workloads. Women, especially the oldest, expect women's equality in Libya will improve in the next three to five years. However, they think family responsibilities, social norms, and lack of skills are among challenging constraints along the way.

ANNEX 12A: DETAILS OF PHONE SURVEYS DATA COLLECTION

The survey was administered June 29 and July 15, 2021, with a total of about 85,000 calls. Among the eligible phone numbers, about 85 percent of the calls were not answered after three attempted calls and only 2.4 percent answered and completed the interviews. The median duration of completed calls was 23 minutes. On average, 42 calls had to be made for one completed interview. In the end, after the data collection, reviews of interviewed data, and cleaning processes, the final sample ended up with 1,523 respondents (1,000 women and 523 men, ages 18 and older) randomly selected from all 22 mantikas (table 12A.1). The mantikas with the highest number of respondents were Tripoli, Benghazi, and Misrata.

Table 12A.2 shows the basic characteristics of respondents, with and without sampling weights. Statistics with and without sampling weights are similar for all dimensions, except for gender and levels of education. The survey was designed to sample more women than men. However, the gender share is consistent with the 2012 census after applying sampling weight. For respondents' levels of education, literature shows that there seems to be a positive correlation between levels of education and willingness to participate in phone surveys. To reduce this bias, the sample is reweighted to known distributions on levels of education by gender.

Most of the respondents are married, either household head or household head's spouse. Those respondents are highly educated (32 percent held a bachelor/university degree or more) for the whole sample, for both males and females. The average age of the respondents is about 37 years, with more than half of the respondents in younger cohorts such as 18–25 and 26–35 years old.

TABLE 12A.1 **Survey response rate**

	NUMBER OF CALLS	PERCENT
Ineligible numbers		
Not a working number	17,829	21.0
Not in the sample	4,825	5.7
Eligible numbers		
Interview initially granted pending completion	1,499	2.4
No one answered the phone after three attempted calls	52,728	84.8
Respondent was reached but interview was not completed	4,445	7.1
Respondent refused to be interviewed	3,529	5.7
Subtotal of eligible numbers	62,201	100
Total number of calls	84,855	

Source: World Bank.

TABLE 12A.2 **Characteristics of respondents with and without sampling weight (percent)**

		ALL SAMPLE (UNWEIGHTED)	ALL SAMPLE (WEIGHTED)
Gender	Men	34.3	50.7
	Women	65.7	49.3
Age group	18–25	22.1	23.1
	26–35	30.1	29.6
	36–45	24.2	21.9
	46+	23.6	25.4
Location	A big city	66.0	64.8
	A village or town	16.3	15.9
	A rural area	17.8	19.3
Education	No formal education	2.0	8.5
	Elementary	3.0	9.0
	Preparatory/basic	10.1	30.1
	Secondary	17.5	11.0
	Midlevel diploma/professional or technical	16.3	8.9
	BA/university	45.4	28.5
	MA and above	5.8	4.0
Ethnicity	Arab	85.5	80.5
	Amazigh (Berber)	3.7	4.3
	Tourag	1.1	1.3
	Toubou	0.5	1.0
	Alkraghl	0.3	0.3
	Other	9.0	12.5
Marital status	Single/bachelor	28.6	30.6
	Engaged	2.2	3.7
	Married	64.0	58.1
	Divorced	1.2	1.8
	Widowed	3.9	5.4
Relationship to household head	Household head	29.6	40.3
	Spouse	40.3	28.0
	Other	30.1	31.8

Source: Acevedo and Hoogeveen 2021.

The majority of respondents are Arab ethnic (85 percent),[17] with a large share living in big cities (66 percent) and more than 20 percent of respondents in the capital city, Tripoli. The sample respondents are more likely to be married than single (64 percent and 29 percent, respectively). The average household size is six, with a large percentage (77 percent) reporting currently living in a dwelling that their family owns.

The survey instrument was designed to ask respondents about socioeconomic topics in the three defined periods: current period (time of interview), the pre-COVID-19 period (around January 2020), and the pre-conflict period (between 2012 and 2014, right after the fall of the Gaddafi administration, but before the civil war). Since the same respondents were asked about those periods, for some indicators like employment rate, the analysis is done for certain groups of age to ensure respondents were also in the labor force between 2012–14. Respondents were asked about their employment status for the week preceding the interview, in January 2020, and in 2012. Thus, to have comparable statistics, the analysis in this section refers to respondents between 35 and 62 years old.

ANNEX 12B: LIMITATIONS OF PHONE SURVEYS

Phone interviews are a valuable alternative to primary data collection using face-to-face surveys, particularly during a pandemic. In normal circumstances, these surveys would be a useful complement to, not a substitute for, other ways of collecting data, because of the limitations of phone surveys, including the following:

- Areas or groups with limited network coverage or no access to phones, typically the poorest segments of the population, will be undercovered in the sample.
- Indicators measured at the individual level (such as employment and unemployment) may be biased due to respondent selection. Especially in countries where the high-frequency phone surveys are sampled from an existing nationally representative (pre-pandemic) survey, the respondent is often the head of household. Thus, some statistics (such as employment rates) would differ from those estimated by a conventional labor force survey, which collects information from all household members.
- Women tend to be underrepresented because they are less likely to be the head of household, or, in instances where a random digit dialing approach is used, they are less likely to own a phone or respond to an unknown caller.
- The length of a phone interview is limited, making it challenging to design an effective survey. The number of questions that can be asked is small because the questions need to be short and precise for easy comprehension. One implication is that in many instances, the ability to consider distributional impacts is limited. That occurs because the phone surveys cannot generate estimates of poverty (as doing so would require a long list of consumption questions for which these surveys lack sufficient time). To estimate distributional impacts, proxy variables would have to be calculated (such as wealth quintiles) from the (tiny) information on wealth collected in the phone surveys themselves. However, phone surveys that draw their samples from pre-existing welfare surveys could derive the pre-COVID poverty status.
- Sample sizes are typically relatively small—often less than 1,500—to allow for a rapid turnaround. Small sample sizes make it more challenging to infer implications from breaking down results by subgroups.

Despite these limitations, phone surveys have demonstrated their ability to collect high-quality data. Their agility and ability to collect data rapidly without the need for personal presence by an enumerator makes phone surveys a valuable tool for specific situations, such as emergencies, dangerous situations, or situations in which the respondent is mobile.

NOTES

1. In 1988, the Basic People's Committee (BPC) issued the Great Green Charter for Human Rights in the Age of the Masses, which stated that "both men and women in the Libyan Arab society are equal in all that is human and a differentiation of rights between men and women is a gross and unwarranted injustice." The Strengthening of Freedom Act No. 20 of 1991 reiterated that "male and female citizens in the Libyan Arab Jamahiriya are free and equal in right" and that their rights may not be prejudiced. Article 2 asserts that "every citizen (male and female) has the right to exercise their authority and the right to self-determination." It emphasizes that all citizens have the right to self-expression and self-determination through voicing their thoughts and ideas at BPCs.

2. In 1990, Libya ratified the Convention on Elimination of All Kinds of Discrimination against Women and amended its national legislation to reflect the commitment it undertook by signing the convention to abolish all gender-biased legislation. In 1995, however, Libya notified the UN secretary-general of its reservations about the convention. One of them regarded women's inheritance. Because of religious and cultural beliefs, women in Libya do not inherit the same share as men; in most situations, a woman receives half the share of a man. Other developments included Charter on the Rights and Duties of Women in Libyan Arab Society, issued in 1997, which further emphasized the equal rights of women to men.

3. ILOSTAT Explorer (database), "Labour Force Participation rate by sex and age—ILO modeled estimates, November 2021 (%): Annual," International Labour Organizstion. https://www.ilo.org/shinyapps/bulkexplorer43/?lang=en&segment=indicator&id=EAP_2WAP_SEX_AGE_RT_A.

4. Primary, secondary, and university.

5. The Social Economic Survey, 2003, NIDA. This is the most recent information on the illiteracy rate available.

6. Labor regulations (pertaining to contracts, hiring and firing procedures, and migration) remain inflexible in Libya, limiting rather than promoting job creation in the country (World Bank 2012).

7. The Skhirat agreement sought to resolve the dispute between the House of Representatives and the General National Congress (GNC). It created a Presidency Council that took office in Tripoli in 2016 and was tasked to form a unity government and an advisory High State Council of ex-GNC members.

8. The dialogue in Bouznika is a Libyan dialogue between the delegations of the High Council of State and the Parliament of Tobruk, aimed at maintaining the ceasefire and opening negotiations to end conflicts among the Libyan parties.

9. The committee consists of five senior military officers chosen by the Government of National Accord (GNA) and five senior military officers chosen by Khalifa Haftar to discuss a ceasefire, reopening of the coastal road, and withdrawal of all foreign mercenaries.

10. The Libyan Political Dialogue Forum facilitated by the United Nations Support Mission in Libya included of 75 Libyan participants who met to discuss a roadmap for credible, inclusive, and democratic national elections and select a government (the GNA) to lead the country until the December 2021 election.

11. Polygamy is legal in Libya. However, the law has made the explicit consent of the first wife a requirement for any second marriage to take place. It also requires that the husband's financial and health conditions be sufficient to provide for more than one wife.

12. A burgeoning body of literature highlights several channels through which armed conflict can affect economies, infrastructure, and different groups of people. Examples of such studies include Buevnic et al. (2013) and Mueller and Tobias (2016). Mueller and Tobias highlight employment and investment, large outflows of refugees (especially women and children), and service disruption (such as shutting of schools and stalling of medical services) for women and children. Buevnic et al. (2013) identify gendered impacts of armed conflict more carefully. They find that men disproportionately bear the mortality burden of war, whereas women and children constitute a majority of refugees and the displaced. They note that war could lead to intergenerational poverty in households headed by widows. In the long run, however, women can benefit from widowhood by gaining more bargaining power.

13. RDD surveys have several limitations:
    - Response rates can be low.
    - Areas or groups with limited network coverage or no access to phones—typically the poorest segments of the population—will be underrepresented.

- Women tend to be underrepresented, because they are less likely to be the head of household and less likely to own a phone or respond to an unknown caller.
- RDD surveys are nevertheless useful, especially in situations where conditions are rapidly changing, as it takes much less time to prepare and analyze than a standard face-to-face household survey.

14. Kokas et al. (2021) show higher unemployment rates for university graduates (27 percent) than people with no educational certificate (7 percent) in Tunisia, where employment growth has not kept pace with demographic pressures for university graduates and the prime working-age population.

15. Eighty-five percent of Libya's active labor force was employed in the public sector, a large share even by regional standards (World Bank 2015a). The rate for women was even higher (93 percent). Libyans perceive the public sector as an essential source of employment and stability. The private sector is tiny, although it is growing (World Bank 2012). Many respondents prefer lower-paid but secure public sector jobs and remain reluctant to work in the private sector despite higher wages (World Bank 2015b).

16. The team did not examine the reforms and the survey was mainly focused on areas interviewees wish to be reformed. A recommendation for future surveys is to examine each reform.

17. Libya is home to four ethnic groups: Arabs, Amazighs, Touaregs, and Tebous.

REFERENCES

Acevedo, G., and J. Hoogeveen, eds. 2021. *Distributional Impacts of COVID-19 in the Middle East and North Africa Region*. Washington, DC: World Bank.

Buvinic, M., M. Das Gupta, U. Casabonne, and P. Verwimp. 2013. *Violent Conflict and Gender Inequality : An Overview*. Oxford University Press on behalf of the World Bank. © World Bank. https://openknowledge.worldbank.org/handle/10986/19494 License: CC BY-NC-ND 3.0 IGO.

Bugaighis, H., and M. Tantoush. 2017. *Women in the Libyan Job Market*. Berlin and Bonn: Friedrich Ebert Stiftung and Jussor Development and Studies.

Euro-Mediterranean Human Rights Monitor. 2019. *Libyan Women Married to Foreign Nationals: Oppression and Stateless Children*. Geneva: Euro-Mediterranean Human Rights Monitor.

HFS-LW. 2021. Survey conducted for this publication. The Multiple Scars of the War and COVID-19: What Libyan Women Have Endured.

Human Rights Watch. 2013. *A Revolution for All: Women's Rights in the New Libya*. New York: Human Rights Watch.

ICJ (International Commission of Jurists). 2016. *Challenges for the Libyan Judiciary: Ensuring Independence, Accountability and Gender Equality*. Geneva: ICJ.

IFES (International Foundation for Electoral Systems). 2013. *Libya Status of Women Survey 2013*. Washington, DC: IFES.

Kokas, D., A. Rahmen El Lahga, and G. Lopez-Acevedo. "Trends in Growth and Labor Markets in the Last Two Decades: Evidence from Tunisia." IZA Discussion Paper No 14563. IZA, Bonn.

Mueller, H., and Tobias, J. 2016. "The Cost of Violence: Estimating the Economic Impact of Conflict." IGC Growth Brief Series 007. International Growth Centre, London.

UN (United Nations)Women. 2020. *The Economic and Social Impact of Conflict on Libyan Women: Recommendations for Economic Recovery, Legal Reform and Governance for Gender-Responsive Peacebuilding*. New York: UN Women.

UNDP (United Nations Development Programme). 2004. *Common Country Assessment 2004*. Tripoli: UNDP.

World Bank. 2012. *Libya Labor Force Survey (LFS) 2012*. Washington, DC: World Bank.

World Bank. 2015a. *Labor Market Dynamics in Libya*. Washington, DC: World Bank.

World Bank. 2015b. *Simplified Enterprise Survey and Private Sector Mapping*. Washington, DC: World Bank.

World Bank. 2020. *Poverty and Distributional Impacts of COVID-19: Potential Channels of Impact and Mitigating Policies.* Washington, DC: World Bank. https://www.worldbank.org /en/topic/poverty/brief/poverty-and-distributional-impacts-of-covid-19-potential -channels-of-impact-and-mitigating-policies.

RELATED READINGS

Abuhadra, D. S., and T. T. Ajaali. 2014. *Labor Market and Employment Policy in Libya.* Torino: European Training Foundation.

Amnesty International. 2018. *The State of the World's Human Rights.* London: Amnesty International.

Barrett, C. B., T. Reardon, and P. Webb. 2001. "Nonfarm Income Diversification and Household Livelihood Strategies in Rural Africa: Concepts, Dynamics, and Policy Implications." *Food Policy* 26: 315–21.

Bundervoet, T., P. Verwimp, and R. Akresh. 2009. "Health and Civil War in Rural Burundi." *Journal of Human Resources* 44 (2): 536–63.

Camacho, A. 2008. "Stress and Birth Weight: Evidence from Terrorist Attacks." *American Economic Review: Papers and Proceedings* 98 (2): 511–15.

Dasgupta, P. 1993. *An Inquiry into Well-Being and Destitution.* Oxford, UK: Clarendon Press.

Di Maio, M., V. Leone Sciabolazza, and V. Molini. 2020. "Migration in Libya: A Spatial Network Analysis." Policy Research Working Paper WPS9110, World Bank, Washington, DC. http:// documents.worldbank.org/curated/en/707491579010444386/Migration-in-Libya-A -Spatial-Network-Analysis.

Doherty, Megan. 2012. "Libyan Women in the 2012 National Elections." Paper presented at the National Democratic Institute Conference, "Women's Participation in Public Life, Politics, and Decision-Making," Tunis, October 29–30, 2012.

Ekhator-Mobayode, U., and A. Asfaw. 2019. "The Child Health Effects of Terrorism: Evidence from the Boko Haram Insurgency in Nigeria." *Applied Economics* (516): 624–38. https:// www.tandfonline.com/doi/full/10.1080/00036846.2018.1502871.

Eswaran, M., and A. Kotwal. 1989. "Credit as Insurance in Agrarian Economies." *Journal of Development Economics* 31 (1): 37–53.

European Commission. 2017a. "Irregular Migration Via the Central Mediterranean: From Emergency Responses to Systemic Solutions." EPSC Strategic Notes 22, European Commission, Brussels. https://ec.europa.eu/epsc/sites/epsc/files/strategic_note _issue_22_0.pdf.

European Commission. 2017b. "Migration on the Central Mediterranean: Managing Flows, Saving Lives. Joint Communication to the European Parliament, the European Council, 25 January." Brussels: European Commission. https://ec.europa.eu/home-affairs/sites/default/files/what -we-do/policies/european-agenda-migration/proposal-implementation-package/docs /20170125_migration_on_the_central_mediterranean_route_-_managing_flows_saving _lives_en.pdf.

Fafchamps, M., C. Udry, and K. Czukas. 1998. "Drought and Savings in West Africa: Are Livestock a Buffer Stock?" *Journal of Development Economics* 55: 273–305.

Farhart, H. 2017. *The Status of Women Human Rights Defenders in Libya.* Tripoli: The WHRD Coalition.

Grimard, F. 1997. "Household Consumption Smoothing through Ethnic Ties: Evidence from Côte d'Ivoire." *Journal of Development Economics* 53: 391–422.

Haggblade, S., P. Hazell, and J. Brown. 1989. "Farm-Nonfarm Linkages in Rural Sub-Saharan Africa." *World Development* 17 (8): 1173–202.

IOM (International Organization for Migration). 2016. "The Central Mediterranean Route: Deadlier Than Ever." Data Briefing Series Issue no. 3, IOM, Geneva. https://publications .iom.int/system/files/pdf/gmdac_data_briefing_series_issue3.pdf.

IOM (International Organization for Migration). 2021. "IOM Snapshot," July 27, 2021. Geneva: IOM. https://www.iom.int/sites/default/files/about-iom/iom_snapshot_a4_en.pdf.

Jones, A., and R. Naylor. 2014. *The Quantitative Impact of Armed Conflict on Education in the Democratic Republic of the Congo: Counting the Human and Financial Costs.* Doha: Protect Education in Insecurity and Conflict.

Jusoor Center for Studies and Development. 2017. *The Situation of Women in Libya.* Tripoli: Jusoor Center for Studies and Development.

Justino, P. 2011. "The Impact of Armed Civil Conflict on Household Welfare and Policy." IDS Working Papers 2011384, Institute of Development Studies, London. https://onlinelibrary.wiley.com/doi/10.1111/j.2040-0209.2011.00384_2.x.

Make Every Woman Count. 2018. *African Women's Decade 2010–2020: Women's Participation in Decision-Making and Leadership.* London: Make Every Woman Count.

Minoiu, C., and O. Shemyakina. 2012. "Child Health and Conflict in Côte d'Ivoire." *American Economic Review: Papers and Proceedings* 102 (3): 294–99.

OCHA (United Nations Office for the Coordination of Humanitarian Affairs). 2021. *2021 HPC–Libya: Humanitarian Needs Overview.* New York: OCHA. https://www.humanitarianresponse.info/en/operations/libya/document/2021-libya-humanitarian-needs-overview-hno.

Rosenzweig, M., and H. Binswanger. 1993. "Wealth, Weather Risk and the Composition and Profitability of Agricultural Investments." *Economic Journal* 103.

Rosenzweig, M., and K. Wolpin. 1993. "Credit Market Constraints, Consumption Smoothing, and the Accumulation of Durable Production Assets in Low-Income Countries: Investment in Bullocks in India." *Journal of Political Economy* 101 (2): 223–24.

UNFPA (United Nations Population Fund). 2018a. *Gender-Based Violence: Situational Analysis for Libya.* New York: UNFPA.

UNFPA (United Nations Population Fund). 2018b. *The Libyan Youth Today: Opportunities and Challenges.* New York: UNFPA.

UNICEF (United Nations Childrens Fund). 2017. *Libya: Humanitarian Situation Report July–September.* New York: UNICEF.

United Nations Security Council. 2000. "Resolution 1325 2000: Adopted by the Security Council at its 4213th Meeting." New York: United Nations. https://digitallibrary.un.org/record/426075.

WHO (World Health Organization). 2015. *Humanitarian Crisis in Libya.* Geneva: WHO.

IV Services during Conflict

13 Advancing a Child Protection System

DONNA ESPEUT, REMY PIGOIS, ANNA RESSLER, NARINE ASLANYAN, YUKO OSAWA, AND BARBARA PELLEGRINI

United Nations Children's Fund

In 2018, a stunning 90 percent of Libyan boys and 88 percent of girls reported having experienced physical, psychological, or sexual violence at school, at home or in their community in the previous 12 months. The authors provide that combating the problem is difficult because Libya lacks a comprehensive child protection system. Unclear delineation of roles and responsibilities between local government institutions involved in child protection has resulted in disjointed leadership and coordination. The way forward will require (1) aligning existing child protection—including child and juvenile-justice-related legislation, standards, and procedures—with international standards and conventions; (2) strengthening the child protection system and ensuring that the requisite human and financial resources are available for subnational and community service delivery; (3) changing norms and behaviors; and (4) creating good data systems.

INTRODUCTION

Millions of children in Libya under the age of 18 have navigated a plethora of obstacles and child protection threats since the 2011 revolution. Even before 2011, systemic challenges and gaps related to all dimensions of child protection—coupled with long-standing challenges, such as mixed migration flows, social exclusion, and discrimination—created a dynamic that made it difficult to protect all children. The dynamics and systemic structures (including laws and policies) have deteriorated since the revolution, further compromising the protective environment for children. The need is great: in 2021, an estimated 228,000 children and 43,000 adult caregivers were in urgent need of assistance related to child protection (OCHA 2020a).

This chapter synthesizes the evidence and analyzes the impacts of the protracted armed conflict, mixed migration, and COVID-19 on child protection in Libya. It is organized as follows. The first section provides a brief overview of the sector before the 2011 revolution. The second section analyzes the impacts of the ongoing conflict, mixed migration, and the COVID-19 pandemic, first on children and families and then on the child protection system. The third section outlines the way forward in terms of policy reform and action priorities to safeguard children's rights and reduce risks for all children. The last section provides some concluding remarks.

CHILD PROTECTION BEFORE THE 2011 REVOLUTION

Libya acceded to the Convention on the Elimination of All Forms of Discrimination against Women in 1989; the Convention on the Rights of the Child (CRC) in 1993; the Optional Protocol to the CRC on the sale of children, child prostitution, and child pornography in 2004; the Optional Protocol to the CRC on the involvement of children in armed conflict in 2004; and the Convention on the Rights of Children with Disabilities in 2018. It has not yet ratified the 2011 Third Optional Protocol to the CRC on a communications procedure (OHCHR 2011) or the Convention Relating to the Status of Refugees (1951). It is finalizing a combined third and fourth periodic state party report to the CRC.[1] In 2020, it submitted its national report to the Universal Periodic Review. However, Libya's last official state report (the second periodic report) to the CRC was submitted in 2000, and Libya has never reported on either of its two ratified optional protocols or on the Convention on the Rights of Children with Disabilities.

Libya deviates from international standards in many areas. For example, Child Protection Law No. 5 of 1997, the country's primary legal instrument on child protection, sets an age limit of childhood of 16, rather than the international convention of 18. Corporal punishment of children was—and remains—sanctioned in most settings, including home, alternative care settings, and penal institutions; schools are an exception.[2]

Child neglect is criminalized in Libya, but enforcement has historically been limited (NDCC, UNICEF, and Coram 2018). Children 14 and older can be held criminally responsible for all offenses if capable of discernment. According to Articles 80 and 81 of Libya's Penal Code, children between the ages of 7 and 14 cannot be held criminally responsible in the same way as older children, but they can be subject to "preventive measures" that include detention in a juvenile education and guidance center (Libya 2002).

In addition to shortcomings within the legislative landscape, there has been a lack of clear leadership on child protection. The existence of multiple authorities on child protection contributed to a fragmented child protection system. Libya established the Higher Committee for Children in 1998 and a Child Care Administration within the Ministry of Social Affairs in the 2000s to monitor and coordinate actions in childcare and child protection. However, it lacked the requisite institutional frameworks for child protection and child justice to underpin a coherent and well-coordinated multistakeholder child protection system. The environment under the Muammar Gaddafi government also limited civil society participation in child protection (NDCC, UNICEF, and Coram n.d.).

Considering these challenges, full domestication, implementation, and enforcement of the CRC's articles related to child protection was limited. CRC stipulations for child-specific budgeting and specific domestic legislation (Article 13 of the 1997 Child Protection Act No. 5) required annual government allocation of the public budget and provisions in different sectors to address the welfare of children, but financial and human resource constraints have impeded advancement of a national child protection agenda. Libya also lacked a comprehensive, fully functional national management information system (MIS) for the child protection sector, a critical gap that persists today, as well as an accessible complaint mechanism related to child victims of violence (NDCC, UNICEF, and Coram n.d.). It also lacked standard operating procedures on child protection case management, which resulted in inconsistencies and lack of standardization in supporting children.

The child and juvenile justice systems in Libya are very weak. Before 2011, no special department existed within the Ministry of Justice, and there were no specialized units within the Ministry of the Interior (which is responsible for the key child protection actors, such as the police). These shortcomings persist. Child-friendly justice has not been operationalized because of the lack of institutional and human resource capacity, leaving no options for restorative justice, diversion mechanisms, or alternatives to deprivation of liberty (NDCC, UNICEF, and Coram n.d., 24).

Migratory patterns that existed before the 2011 revolution also introduced child protection risks. Libya has had a long history as a transit destination for hundreds of thousands of migrants. In 2011, before the revolution, the International Organization on Migration (IOM) estimated that Libya was hosting 2.5 million irregular migrants and that well-established human smuggling infrastructure and networks existed to bring people into the country (Global Initiative against Transnational Organized Crime 2018). An enabling environment did not exist for child protection before 2011. This lack of preparedness and system functioning has exacerbated risks faced by different groups of children since the 2011 revolution, as shown in the next sections.

IMPACTS OF ARMED CONFLICT, MIXED MIGRATION, AND COVID-19

Impact on families and children

Because of the paucity of data on all dimensions of child protection in Libya, it is not possible to assess trends in child protection outcomes or the full impacts of the protracted conflict and COVID-19 pandemic. It is clear, however, that continued insecurity and challenges related to the enforcement of the rule of law and respect for human rights have threatened child protection in Libya.

Since 2011, adverse child protection outcomes have included psychosocial distress and trauma, family separation, arbitrary detention, child labor, recruitment, association with and use of children by armed groups. and various forms of physical and emotional maltreatment, exploitation, and violence (OCHA 2020a). In 2020–21, the urgent need for child protection assistance is concentrated in certain areas. Tripoli accounts for 30 percent of the estimated 271,000 children and caregivers in need, with child protection needs most severe in the mantikas (districts) of Alkufra, Benghazi, Ghat, Misrata, Murzuq, Sirt, Tripoli, and Wadi Ashshati (OCHA 2020a).

Certain groups of children have been particularly vulnerable to child protection violations since 2011. They include the following:

- Migrant and refugee children, especially children who are unaccompanied by or separated from their families
- Internally displaced children
- Children with disabilities
- Children from ethnic minorities

- Poor children
- Children affiliated with armed groups
- Children with at least one non-Libyan parent
- Abandoned children
- Children born out of wedlock

Compromised resilience of families has directly affected child protection. Reduced household income is associated with the adoption of harmful coping strategies that increase child vulnerability (OCHA 2020a). Vulnerability does not exist in isolation. In 2014, for example, 16 percent of children ages 5–14 were simultaneously deprived of child protection, nutrition, and housing (UNICEF Libya and SPRI 2020).

Schools and health facilities, which should be places of safety for children and communities, have been under siege. As recently as November 2020, the UN Office for the Coordination of Human Affairs (OCHA) documented attacks on institutions in social sectors, as well as civilian attacks targeting migrants, refugees, and asylum seekers (OCHA 2020b). Children are also targets of armed groups, which kidnap them in the hope of extorting money from their families (OHCHR 2018a). In 2020, families in the South were highly concerned about the kidnapping of their children. In contrast, families in the West were most concerned about the risks of their children being injured or killed by an explosive hazard, according to the 2020 multisector needs assessment by REACH (2020).

Over the 10 years of protracted armed conflict, unexploded ordnance, mines (particularly in southern Tripoli), and improvised explosive devices have accumulated, posing threats to children's safety (OCHA 2021b). Risks from the armed conflict were exacerbated by the escalation of violence after the April 2019 offensive by the Libyan National Army to obtain control of Tripoli (Human Rights Council Working Group on the Universal Periodic Review 2020). According to 2020 reporting to the UN Security Council, 77 children (60 boys and 17 girls) ages 6–17 were killed (35) or maimed (42) because of armed conflict, including explosive remnants of war (UN 2020). In 2021, 503,000 people (children and adults) were estimated to need assistance because of the risk from contamination from explosive hazards (OCHA 2021b).

In addition to threats resulting from explosive remnants of war, violence against children is a pervasive threat (figure 13.1). In 2018, 9 out of 10 middle school children (90 percent of boys and 88 percent of girls) reported having experienced physical, psychological, or sexual violence at school, at home, or in their community in the previous 12 months (table 13.1). The higher prevalence of violence in schools relative to home/family settings speaks to the need to mainstream protection in instructional settings.

Teachers are the most common adult perpetrators of physical violence, affecting 67 percent of children; 38 percent of children experienced violence from their parents in the previous 12 months (figure 13.2). Emotional violence against children is also prevalent, with 78 percent of middle school children reporting past experiences with emotional violence.

Children with disabilities are among the subgroups that are most affected by protection violations such as violence, including gender-based violence (OCHA 2020a). Among all children, boys are significantly more likely to experience all types of physical violence than girls (NDCC, UNICEF, and Coram 2018). Other significant predictors of a child's exposure to violence are household wealth quintile (with children from the richest households far less likely to experience

FIGURE 13.1

FIGURE 13.1

Drivers and determinants of exacerbated child protection risks since the 2011 revolution

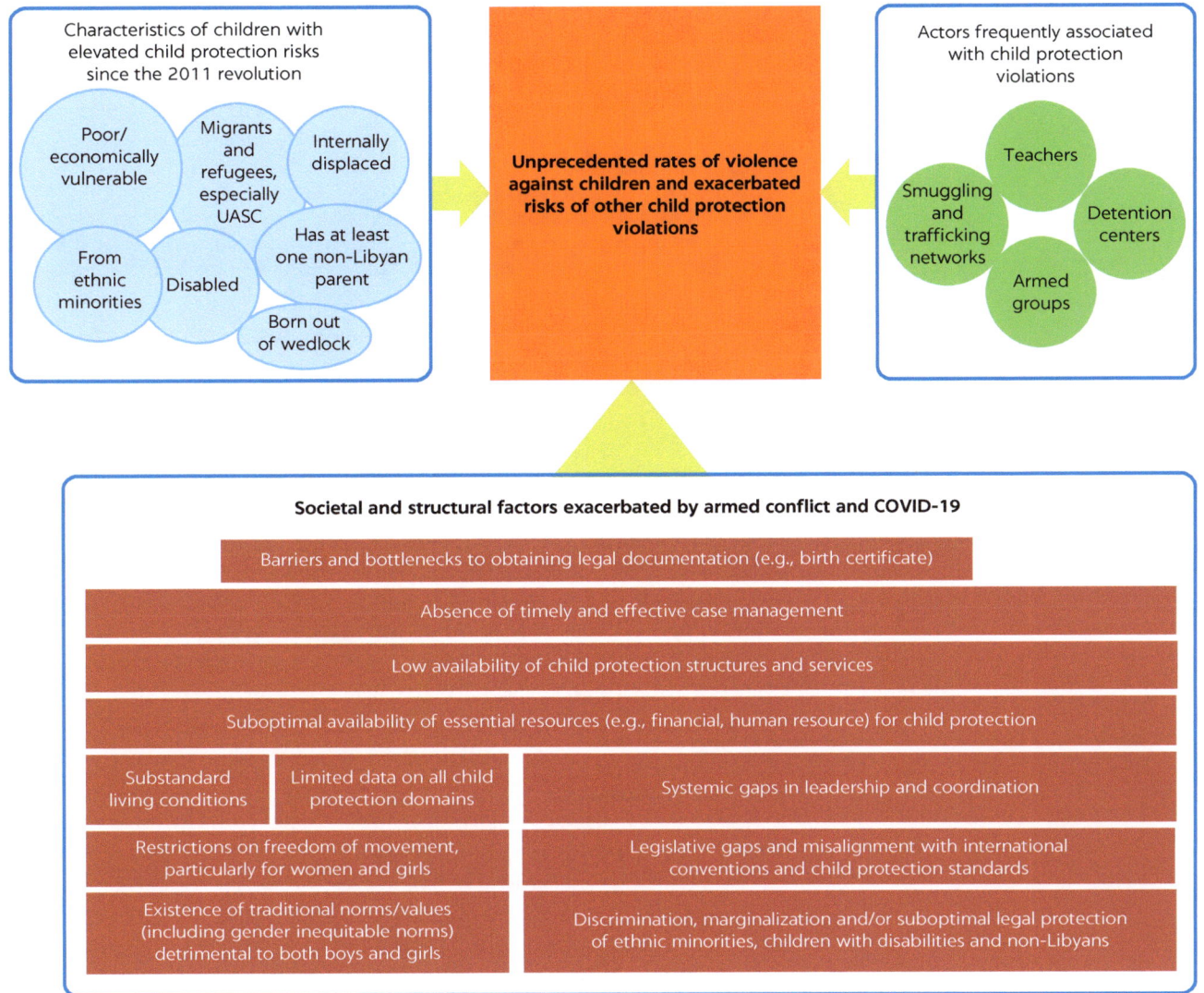

Source: UNICEF.
Note: UASC = unaccompanied and separated children.

TABLE 13.1 **Incidence of violence against middle school children, 2018**

INDICATOR	PERCENT OF CHILDREN REPORTING
Exposed to at least one type of violence	91
Experienced one or more types of physical violence, emotional violence, bullying, or neglect	86
Had past experience of emotional violence	78
Experienced some form of physical violence in last 12 months	73
Was bullied in middle school in last 12 months	36
Was a victim of neglect	15

Source: NDCC, UNICEF, and Coram 2018.

FIGURE 13.2

Perpetrators of physical violence against middle school children in previous 12 months, 2018

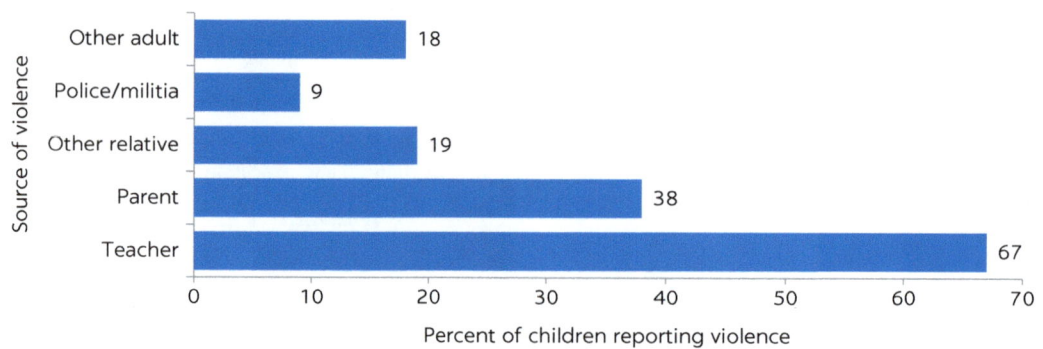

Source: NDCC, UNICEF, and Coram 2018.

violence), being from an ethnic (non-Arab) minority, and having a disability (especially for more severe forms of physical violence).

Support services (legal, medical, psychosocial) for survivors of domestic violence were already sparse before 2011. Restricted movement has particularly limited access to these services by women and girls and exposed them to prolonged periods in their homes with perpetrators of domestic violence (UN Women 2020). Libyans are more likely than non-Libyans to report that there has been an increase in domestic abuse cases since the emergence of the COVID-19 pandemic (NDCC et al. 2020). They are also more aware of where to report domestic abuse cases.

Recruitment and use of children, particularly boys, by armed groups has also occurred since the 2011 revolution. See box 13.1.

There is also evidence that foundational aspects of child protection, such as birth registration, have been compromised, increasing children's chances of mistreatment, exploitation, and abuse. In 2014, the rate of birth registration in Libya was almost universal (99 percent) (PAPFAM 2014). In 2020, about 22 percent of Libyans were reported to be missing some form of legal documentation (OCHA 2020a). Discriminatory laws, stigma, and social norms are contributing factors. Under Libyan law, the presence of a father is required to register a birth. Libyan children born out of wedlock and children born to Libyan women who are married to non-Libyan men are refused Libyan nationality and thus access to a birth certificate, exposing them to exploitation (for example, child labor) because of what is deemed their "illegal" status in the country (Human Rights Council Working Group on the Universal Periodic Review 2020).

Non-Libyans can register a birth at their country's embassy, which makes a formal request to the Ministry of Foreign Affairs to obtain the birth certificate from the appropriate municipality. Information on the specific birth registration challenges and bottlenecks faced by nonnationals is limited. However, most embassies, if still operational, are in Tripoli. There is a lack of clarity and inconsistency on whether birth registration can be done remotely by sending the required documents to an embassy. Additionally, because Arabic is the only language used in Libya's Civil Registry Authority and other public institutions, non-Arabic-speaking migrants and refugees find it difficult to access information about procedures to register a birth.

BOX 13.1

Children recruits and the effects of violence

Child recruitment remains a major threat to child protection. Interviewees for an assessment conducted in four municipalities by the United Nations Children's Fund (UNICEF) and the European Union in 2020 suggested that some children affiliated with armed groups joined for financial reasons, whereas for other children, a desire for family-like bonds is the main pull factor.

People interviewed provided the following insights into what may drive children to join armed groups:

- The financial situation of the family has a huge effect. Those who suffer financially can never fix their situation. . . . The first solution is to join an armed group in order to make money. Sometimes youth want to continue and finish their studies but can't because of their financial situation.

  20-year-old woman from Zentan

- They [armed groups] target youth. They search for young people who are damaged by the war. They target youth who lost their fathers, brothers, and uncles to the war. They try to recruit this type of young male. . . . They tell them that they will have a chance to get their revenge [or they] attract our youth with money. If you tell a teenager that you will give him LD 1,000 per month, he will give up his education.

  –Man from Sebha

Events and threats since 2011 have affected the mental health and psychosocial well-being of children and young people in Libya. According to an assessment conducted in November 2020, 63 percent of Libyans report that the restrictions imposed to slow the spread of COVID-19 have had an impact on their mental health.[a] An alarmingly high number of the young people consulted in another 2020 study report suffering from depression and other mental health issues.[b] They reported references to suicide by peers and the lack of mental health services. As one youth in a focus group discussion explained:

- The war has affected all of us psychologically. Many of us were left as orphans. Many women were widowed. People got sick and others lost their limbs. Some of us witnessed our friends die. This has been happening for years—since 2011. Most of the youth are psychologically destroyed because of the war.

Source: O'Neill and van Broeckhoven 2018.
a. NDCC et al. 2020.
b. UNICEF and EU 2020.

Shortcomings that existed in the enabling environment before 2011 make it very difficult to protect children on the move (migrant, refugee, and asylum-seeking children). The IOM estimates that in 2020, children accounted for 9 percent of the 574,146 migrants and refugees in Libya (7 percent accompanied, 2 percent unaccompanied) (IOM 2020b). Younger migrants and refugees are more vulnerable than older ones (Mixed Migration Centre 2020). Unaccompanied and separated children (UASC) are an especially vulnerable group. UASC girls are sometimes trafficked for sexual exploitation, and UASC boys are more likely to be engaged in harmful child labor (OCHA 2020a). These children and other children on the move also contend with limited access to basic services, including mental health and psychosocial support, education, health care, and legal aid. The fact that the Libyan government still has not ratified the 1951 Refugee Convention complicates the task of addressing the holistic well-being of children on the move.

Migration to Europe, which increased substantially after 2011, also introduces risks to children. According to the UN refugee agency—the United Nations High Commissioner for Refugees (UNHCR)—Libya is a point of departure for up to 90 percent of people crossing the Mediterranean Sea to

Europe (UNHCR n.d.). The number of migrants arriving in Italy and Malta after having crossed the Mediterranean Sea from Libyan and Tunisian shores between April and October 2020 (24,713) is nearly three times that of the corresponding period in 2019 (8,977). A rise in the risk of abduction, arbitrary arrest, and detention that migrants face in Libya has also been well documented (IOM 2020b). The economic downturn, including plummeting income-generating opportunities for migrant workers; tightened security controls, and mobility restrictions imposed because of COVID-19 are among the factors that continue to spur migrants to leave Libya.

Migrants leaving Libya are frequently intercepted at sea, where rescue and return procedures are not child friendly. A 2018 study by UNICEF and IMPACT found that the journeys across Libya of UASC interviewed in Italy lasted 9–10 months on average, with stays of 3 months on average at each stopover site in Libya. Of 152 UASC interviewed in Italy, 93 percent reported having been in captivity at least once during their transit in Libya, and 26 percent reported having spent their entire time in Libya in captivity. The average number of episodes of captivity during transit across Libya was two, although reported frequency ranged from one to seven episodes. The study also noted the presence of unofficial detention centers, most of them filled with children who had been kidnapped; connection houses with no freedom of movement;[3] and detention centers run by the Libyan Department for Combating Illegal Migration (DCIM).

Unlawful and arbitrary detention has exposed children to a range of protection violations and abuses and increased their risk of contracting COVID-19. It also provides them with little or no access to recourse mechanisms and support (OHCHR 2018a). Some detention centers are operated by armed groups rather than the DCIM. Orphans and children whose parent(s) left to join the Islamic State are also sometimes placed in Libyan prisons, because of sociopolitical pressures not to allow them to return to Libyan society (O'Neill and van Broeckhoven 2018). Children in detention are often housed with detained adults, in contravention of international standards (OHCHR 2018b), increasing their vulnerability to sexual abuse, forced prostitution, sexual exploitation, and other violations perpetrated by traffickers or criminal networks reported to be associated with armed groups (Human Rights Council Working Group on the Universal Periodic Review 2020). People from ethnic minorities have increased vulnerability to arbitrary arrest and detention (OHCHR 2018b). Women and children are disproportionately affected by abuse and exploitation in detention (OCHA 2020a).

Impact on the child protection system

Leadership and coordination of Libya's child protection system are suboptimal. Despite some legislative developments since 2011 (such as a draft juvenile justice law), legislative shortcomings compromise the enabling environment. Libyan law still does not adequately protect child victims of sexual abuse, and corporal punishment of children at home and in alternative care settings is still sanctioned (Human Rights Council Working Group on the Universal Periodic Review 2020). Because 16 years is the legal age of majority, a child victim of violence can pursue legal recourse only if his or her legal guardian initiates criminal proceedings against the perpetrator on the child's behalf (the only exception is when the biological parent is the perpetrator of violence) (NDCC, UNICEF, and Coram 2018).

Some legislative measures were introduced to reduce underlying vulnerabilities, but those measures are no longer in effect. For example, according to Law No. 27 of 2013,[4] the Social Solidarity Fund, under the authority of the Ministry of Social Affairs, should pay a family allowance of LD 100 a month to all children under 18 and to single women who have no salary or wage. The law also stipulates that a monthly allowance of LD 150 should be paid to married Libyan women who do not earn any salary or wage. Libya was the only country in the Middle East and North Africa region with a universal child allowance under law. However, this provision was discontinued in 2014 and reactivated only in 2021.

Libya still does not have a protection sector plan that articulates an overarching national vision for child protection. Political conflicts—the existence of the UN-recognized Government of National Accord (GNA) in Tripoli and the House of Representatives (HOR) in Tobruk[5]—have reduced the performance of several line ministries and impeded implementation of a harmonized approach to child protection across the country. The unclear delineation of roles and responsibilities between the Higher Committee for Children and the Ministry of Social Affairs, the lack of a cooperating framework, and the absence of standard operating procedures for case management contribute to a disjointed child protection system (NDCC, UNICEF, and Coram n.d.).

The absence of a functional child protection case management system and referral network compromises the ability to provide timely and effective preventive and response services. Libya still does not have a comprehensive and functional child protection system, and it lacks a mechanism for broadscale community engagement and risk communication for addressing violence against children, including standard operating procedures and a functional information system covering all dimensions of child protection.

The various frontline actors (police, social workers, teachers, health workers, parents/caregivers, community leaders) are not well coordinated or fully sensitized and equipped to contribute to a coherent, effective child protection system. Community-based mechanisms (such as child protection committees and informal justice mechanisms) are lacking. A series of 2016 protection assessments on internally displaced children documented that functional schools in locations such as Bani Walid, Benghazi, and Tripoli did not have child protection mechanisms in place, and teachers were not trained to address protection concerns (Cesvi and UNICEF 2016; Save the Children 2016). Social workers also need better training.

Funding shortfalls for child protection persist. Of the $6.6 million that humanitarian partners estimate is needed to meet child protection needs in 2020, only 68 percent was received (OCHA 2021a). Limited financial resources compromise the full implementation of existing legislation and impede the reach and quality of existing child protection services.

There have been discrete efforts since 2011 to support real-time monitoring of specific protection risks associated with armed conflict situations, driven largely by international resolutions and commitments (OCHA 2020a). However, Libya does not have a formal UN Security Council monitoring and reporting mechanism, as it is considered "situations of concern with no listed 'parties to the conflict' from Libya."[6]

UNICEF and other child protection stakeholders in Libya have been monitoring six grave violations against children during the armed conflict: (1) killing and maiming of children, (2) recruitment and use of children by armed forces or armed groups, (3) attacks on schools or hospitals, (4) rape or other sexual violence against children, (5) abduction of children, and (6) denial of humanitarian access to children.[7] In light of reported violations and abuses against children in Libya, UN Security Council Resolution 2542 extended the child protection mandate of the United Nations Support Mission in Libya (namely, the monitoring and reporting of grave violations) until September 21, 2021.[8] In 2020, Libya's Humanitarian Country Team committed to adopt monitoring, analysis, and reporting arrangements to better monitor, report, and address sexual abuse.

The limited availability of entry points and structures for child protection services, especially for children who experienced violence, abuse, and exploitation, has been an impediment to addressing child protection since 2011. Eroded physical infrastructure and collapsing systems of care have exacerbated child protection risks (OCHA 2020a). According to a 2016 assessment by Save the Children in Benghazi and Tripoli, hospitals were one of the few entry points for formal child protection services. In addition, with disability services limited largely to a small number of locations (Benghazi, Misrata, Sebha, and Tripoli) and mental health services largely absent outside of Tripoli (OCHA 2020a), the system is ill-equipped to address the protection needs of children living with disabilities and/or children in need of mental health and psychosocial support services.

Movement restrictions in response to COVID-19 have further compromised access to safe entry points, particularly for women and girls (OCHA 2020a). UNICEF has introduced online platforms, phone calls, and other mechanisms to extend the reach of child protection and gender-based violence services (including case management and psychosocial support) during the pandemic (UNDP 2020).[9] However, weak recourse mechanisms for violations (in particular, violence) contribute to underreporting of sexual and gender-based violence. Fear of reprisals, widespread stigma associated with violence, and entrenched gender-based discrimination and social exclusion are major deterrents (OCHA 2020a).

The lack of alternatives to detention, coupled with the association of detention centers with smuggling and trafficking networks, continues to compound child protection risks for migrant and refugee children (OCHA 2020a). Substandard shelters and living conditions further compromise child well-being. In response to the lack of child protection services, UNICEF developed the baity (my home) center model as an integrated approach to address the multisectoral needs of vulnerable children and their caregivers in a holistic and inclusive manner. These centers offer Libyan and non-Libyan children improved opportunities to develop, learn, play, and strengthen their resilience. They increase access to social services across age, gender, and status. The centers also act as an entry point for detecting children who are at risk, victims, or survivors of violence, abuse, and exploitation.

Libya's justice system is still oriented toward retribution rather than restoration. Some mechanisms have been introduced to improve child-friendly justice. Since 2014, the Ministry of the Interior has established Family and Child Protection Units (FCPUs), which are one-stop centers for the specialized, child-friendly, gender-sensitive case management of children in contact with the law. There are two FCPUs, in Tripoli and Al Zawiya, and decrees have been issued to establish similar structures in bin Waleed, Misrata, Sorman, and Zwara (NDCC, UNICEF, and Coram n.d.).[10] A 2017 review of the Al Zawiya FCPU documented several strengths, such as the provision of some psychosocial support to children, effective referral mechanisms between the police, the Ministry of Social Affairs, and the FCPU, and the presence of some specialized staff (NDCC, UNICEF, and Coram n.d.). The centers also have several shortcomings, including the "lack of financial and human capacity; staff turnover, particularly of the most highly trained staff; challenges in relation to the ability of women police officers to fulfil their roles due to discriminatory laws; lack of community awareness; weak data collection/analytical systems; and incomplete referral protocols for referral of cases onward for support or further action" (NDCC, UNICEF, and Coram n.d.).

Foundational aspects of child protection, such as birth registration, require intensified focus, particularly given the role of legal documentation in safeguarding child rights and welfare. Although national oversight of birth registration processes, procedures, documentation, and data management is unified under a single authority (the Civil Registry Authority), regional offices have tremendous autonomy. For example, the cost of registering a birth varies across the country, and migrant and refugee families pay higher fees for children born in Libya than do Libyan families.[11]

The coexistence of the GNA in Tripoli and the HOR in Tobruk has compounded the challenge of harmonizing birth registration across the country. Greater vigilance is required to ensure that valid birth certificates are issued for children born in detention and outside of health facilities (OHCHR 2018b). COVID-19 mitigation measures have directly affected Civil Registry Offices in multiple locations, reducing both office working hours and the number of staff who are able to process registrations.[12] Special provisions have been applicable to Libyan children but not to all children living in Libya, for whom the lack of documentation and the possibility of obtaining birth certificates (even when born in Libya) has become increasingly difficult.

The extent of unmet needs for child protection support is substantial. Humanitarian partners exceeded 2020 targets set for case management for boys and girls (table 13.2). However, the targets represented just a tiny fraction of the need.

TABLE 13.2 **Performance of humanitarian partners on selected child protection targets, January–November 2020**

INDICATOR	NUMBER OF CHILDREN IN NEED	2020 ACHIEVEMENT BY HUMANITARIAN PARTNERS	
		NUMBER OF CHILDREN TARGETED	NUMBER OF CHILDREN REACHED
Number of girls and boys receiving age- and gender-sensitive case management services	203,000	1,500	1,800 (121 percent over target)
Number of at-risk girls and boys identified that received or were referred for specialized services	24,000	6,400	9,200 (144 percent over target)
Number of locations with functional referral pathways for child protection in place	—	5	8 (160 percent over target)

Source: OCHA 2021a.
Note: — = not available.

EIGHT PRIORITIES FOR REFORMS

The way forward will require addressing eight priorities.

1. Improve leadership and coordination of child protection

- Bolster legal aspects of the enabling environment in the following ways:
  - Align and harmonize existing child protection, including child-justice-related legislation, standards, and procedures, with international standards. Illustrative legislative actions include revisiting Libya's Child Protection Law and ensuring its alignment with international standards set by the CRC (for example, establishing 18, not 16, years, as the age of majority).
  - Develop a harmonized and comprehensive law on child rights that spans all sectors or domesticate the CRC, which Libya has ratified.
  - Redouble strategic advocacy efforts that encourage the government to (a) enforce the minimum age of criminal responsibility as 14, (b) end arbitrary detention of migrant and refugee children, (c) institute and enforce measures to prevent the mistreatment of children in detention, and (d) resolve any other outstanding legislation (for example, the Mobilization Act No. 21 of 1991) that is inconsistent with the CRC's articles.
- Introduce and operationalize mechanisms to enforce existing legislation (for example, the rule of law related to arbitrary detention, smuggling, and other child protection violations), with requisite resource mobilization and capacity development of the diverse array of protection actors.
- Establish clearly delineated roles, responsibilities, and lines of authority between the Higher Committee for Children and the Ministry of Social Affairs.

2. Strengthen the child protection system

- Enhance the political commitment, accountability, and national/institutional capacity of the social, justice, education, and health sectors to legislate, plan, and budget for scaling up interventions that prevent and respond to violence, abuse, exploitation, and neglect and enhance access to child protection.
- Increase the subnational and community capacity and resources to deliver child protection services (through municipalities, for example, and the promotion of multisectoral service delivery, such as the baity model) to ensure accessible and quality services.
- Facilitate cross-sectoral commitments and contributions to child protection:

  - Strengthen referral mechanisms across entry points/actors, including community-based child protection mechanisms and the adoption of a unified case management standard operating procedure under the leadership of the Ministry of Social Affairs, with compliance of relevant line ministries and civil society organizations.
  - Formalize linkages with the Social Solidarity Fund and other national programs, such as a universal child grant, child allowance, or family allowance, in order to reduce key vulnerabilities (economic vulnerability, discrimination, social exclusion) known to increase risks and to prevent the adoption of negative coping strategies (for example, early marriage and transactional sex and recruitment by armed groups).

- Strengthen the entire data value chain related to child protection and juvenile justice:
  - o Establish a consolidated national MIS for child protection (including juvenile justice), drawing on administrative data systems and MIS in different sectors.
  - o Generate data on priority child protection indicators (aligned with the Sustainable Development Goals, for example).
  - o Facilitate access to data to inform decision making by the full spectrum of stakeholders (government, United Nations, nongovernmental organizations/civil society).
- Institute mechanisms to (a) register vulnerable children (in particular, highly marginalized and/or underserved children, such as children with disabilities, children from ethnic minorities, and children on the move), to facilitate case management and (b) improve birth registration/certification among hard-to-reach, vulnerable populations.

3. Improve mental health and psychosocial support

- Strengthen human resources and structures for identifying and responding to mental health needs, particularly among most-affected children, including children on the move, displaced children, and children from ethnic minorities. Strengthen the capacity of school counselors, social workers, and psychosocial support counselors to deliver mental health and psychosocial support and to better ensure the psychosocial well-being of vulnerable children.
- Ensure the adoption of a child protection/mental health and psychosocial support training of trainer and training manual that has been developed with partners, which the Ministry of Education is reviewing.

4. Address the needs of unaccompanied asylum-seeking children

- Implement formal mechanisms to identify the causes of child separation in a timely manner and take action to prevent separation.
- Increase the availability of suitable, safe, alternative care arrangements and the use of individual case management/care plans.
- Implement and enforce alternatives to juvenile detention.
- Establish partnerships to register, safely reunify, and reintegrate UASC with primary caregivers or other family members.

Strengthen government capacity to safely detect, respond to, and facilitate family tracing and reunification of UASC.

5. Monitor and report on grave violations against children

- Accelerate the rollout of a monitoring and reporting mechanism, as well as monitoring, analysis, and reporting arrangements.
- Ensure that response and support services are available wherever reporting mechanisms are introduced, with linkages to ensure timely response and support services.

6. Enhance community engagement and effect behavior and social change

- Design and scale social and behavioral change strategies that transform social norms and behaviors underpinning child protection risks affecting boys and girls.

- Strengthen the capacities of children, adolescents, young people, families, and communities to implement such strategies and transformative activities.
- Advocate for a rights-based approach to reconciliation and recovery.

7. **Increase prevention of violence against children and improve the response to violations**

- Strengthen the social welfare workforce within the Ministry of Social Affairs and human resource departments at relevant ministries (justice, interior, education) to prevent violence, abuse, and exploitation and respond to children who experience them.
- Integrate violence prevention, mitigation, and response in the development and implementation of national and subnational COVID-19 response plans.
- Redouble child protection in all settings (homes, schools, and communities) through implementation of the five-year plan on violence against children, with a focus on strengthening prevention of and responses to violence against children in institutional settings, particularly schools, where teachers are the main perpetrators.

8. **Design and implement tailored programming to address other widespread impacts** such as recruitment and use of children by armed actors, illegal and arbitrary detention of children, and criminal processing of children, and provide age-appropriate education to communities and at-risk children on the risks of mines and other explosive hazards.

CONCLUDING REMARKS

Violence against children has been pervasive in Libya since 2011. In 2018, a stunning 90 percent of boys and 88 percent of girls reported having experienced physical, psychological, or sexual violence at school, at home, or in their community in the previous 12 months.

Combating the problem is difficult because Libya lacks a comprehensive child protection system. Unclear delineation of roles and responsibilities between local government institutions involved in child protection has resulted in disjointed leadership and coordination. Financial and human resource constraints and the absence of an effective case management system impede child protection efforts. Good-quality, easily accessible services remain limited.

A better response is possible. The way forward will require (1) aligning existing child protection—including child and juvenile-justice-related legislation, standards, and procedures—with international standards and conventions; (2) strengthening the child protection system and ensuring that the requisite human and financial resources are available for subnational and community service delivery; (3) changing norms and behaviors; and (4) creating good data systems.

NOTES

1. The Ministry of Foreign Affairs approved the state party report and submitted it to the secretariat of the Committee on the Rights of the Child in 2020. However, it has not been registered in the treaty body database of Office of the High Commissioner for Refugees,

despite its official submission and confirmation of registration by the secretariat. See the UN Human Rights Treaty Body Database, https://tbinternet.ohchr.org/_layouts/15/treatybodyexternal/TBSearch.aspx?Lang=En&CountryID=99&ctl00_PlaceHolderMain_radResultsGridChangePage=7.

2. Law No. 134 of 1970 on Education permits the minister of education to issue regulations on student discipline. The School Discipline Ordinance for Schools, Regulations Concerning Primary and Preparatory (Basic) Education, the Regulations Concerning Secondary (Intermediate) Education of 1979, and the Regulation Concerning Student Discipline of 1983 also govern corporal punishment in school.

3. Key informants described connection houses as warehouses or large yards managed by smugglers or their partners that are used mostly by refugees and migrants en route to Europe. The cost of using a connection house may be included in the price of the trip or paid on a daily basis.

4. See NATLEX (database), "Libya," International Labour Organization, Geneva. https://www.ilo.org/dyn/natlex/natlex4.detail?p_lang=en&p_isn=96436&p_country=LBY.

5. Refer to chapter 3, "Beyond Power-Sharing: Long-Term Economic and Political Stability."

6. UN Security Council monitoring and reporting mechanisms for addressing the protection of children affected by armed conflict were established with the UN Security Council's adoption of Resolution 1612 on July 26, 2005. https://digitallibrary.un.org/record/554197?ln=en#record-files-collapse-header.

7. For background information on the United Nation's monitoring of the six grave violations, see UN (2018).

8. The Security Council adopted Resolution 2542 on September 15, 2020. http://unscr.com/en/resolutions/doc/2542.

9. Social workers contacted families at risk, mothers, and caregivers of children, and witnesses were able to contact social affairs services.

10. In 2021, the Ministry of Interior Child protection office reported that Libya had 20 FCPUs.

11. Based on November 2020 assessment conducted by UNICEF Libya, spanning seven locations in the East, West, and South (UNICEF Libya and SPRI 2020).

12. Based on November 2020 assessment conducted by UNICEF Libya, spanning seven locations in the East, West, and South (UNICEF Libya and SPRI 2020).

REFERENCES

Cesvi and UNICEF (United Nations Children's Fund). 2016. *IDP Child Protection Assessment in Tripoli and Bani Walid*. Geneva: UNICEF. https://www.humanitarianresponse.info/en/operations/libya/assessment/idp-child-protection-assessement-tripoli-and-bani-walid.

Convention Relating to the Status of Refugees. 1951. United Nations multilateral treaty. Geneva.

Global Initiative against Transnational Organized Crime. 2018. "Responding to the Human Trafficking–Migrant Smuggling Nexus, with a Focus on the Situation in Libya." Policy Note, Global Initiative against Transnational Organized Crime, Geneva. https://reliefweb.int/sites/reliefweb.int/files/resources/Reitano-McCormack-Trafficking-Smuggling-Nexus-in-Libya-July-2018.pdf.

Human Rights Council Working Group on the Universal Periodic Review. 2020. *Summary of Stakeholders' Submissions on Libya Report of the Office of the UN High Commissioner for Human Rights*, 36th session, May 4–15. New York: UN High Commissioner for Human Rights.

IOM (International Organization on Migration). 2020a. *Displacement Tracking Matrix*. Geneva: IOM. https://displacement.iom.int/system/tdf/reports/DTM_R33_Migrant_Report.pdf?file=1&type=node&id=10327.

IOM (International Organization on Migration). 2020b. *Libya's Migrant Report, Mobility Tracking Round 33*. Geneva: IOM.

Libya. 2002. *Second Periodic Report of Libya to the UN Committee on the Rights of the Child*, CRC/C/93/Add.1, September 19, 2002. Libya.

Mixed Migration Centre. 2020. *A Sharper Lens on Vulnerability (North Africa): A Statistical Analysis of the Determinants of Vulnerability to Protection Incidents among Refugees and Migrants in Libya*. Tunis: Mixed Migration Centre. https://mixedmigration.org/resource/a-sharper-lens-on-vulnerability-north-africa/.

NDCC (National Disease Control Center), UNICEF (United Nations Children's Fund), and Coram International. 2018. *Study on Violence against Children in Libya*. Tripoli: NDCC.

NDCC (National Disease Control Center), UNICEF (United Nations Children's Fund), and Coram International. n.d. *Technical Assistance to Support the Strengthening of the Child Justice System: Desk Review*. Tripoli: NDCC.

NDCC (National Disease Control Center), USAID (US Agency for International Development), IOM (International Organization on Migration), UNICEF (United Nations Children's Fund), and Voluntas. 2020. *COVID-19 Behavior Assessment in Libya*. Tripoli: NDCC.

OCHA (UN Office for Coordination of Human Affairs). 2020a. *Humanitarian Needs Overview*. New York: OCHA.

OCHA (UN Office for Coordination of Human Affairs). 2020b. *Libya Situation Report*. New York: OCHA. https://reports.unocha.org/en/country/Libya.

OCHA (UN Office for Coordination of Human Affairs). 2021a. *Humanitarian Response Monitoring Humanitarian Dashboard (Jan–Nov 2020): Libya*. New York: United Nations. https://reliefweb.int/report/libya/libya-humanitarian-response-monitoring-humanitarian -dashboard-jan-nov-2020-issued.

OCHA (UN Office for Coordination of Human Affairs). 2021b. *2021 Humanitarian Response Plan: Libya*. New York: OCHA.

OHCHR (Office of the United Nations High Commissioner for Human Rights). 2011. Optional Protocol to the Convention on the Rights of the Child on a Communications Procedure, New York: OHCHR.

OHCHR (Office of the United Nations High Commissioner for Human Rights). 2018a. *Abuse Behind Bars: Arbitrary and Unlawful Detention in Libya*. New York: OHCHR.

OHCHR (Office of the United Nations High Commissioner for Human Rights). 2018b. *Desperate and Dangerous: Report on the Human Rights Situation of Migrants and Refugees in Libya*. New York: OHCHR.

O'Neill, S., and K. van Broeckhoven, eds. 2018. *Cradled by Conflict: Child Involvement with Armed Groups in Contemporary Conflict*. Tokyo: United Nations University.

PAPFAM (Pan-Arab Project for Family Health). 2014. Cairo: League of Arab States. https:// unsmil.unmissions.org/ceremony-dissemination-results-papfam-survey.

REACH. 2020. *Libya 2020 Multi-Sector Needs Assessment*. Geneva: REACH.

Save the Children. 2016. *Protection Assessment in Libya*. London: Save the Children. https:// reliefweb.int/report/libya/protection-assessment-libya-21-march-2016.

UN (United Nations). 2018. "The Six Grave Violations," New York: United Nations. https:// childrenandarmedconflict.un.org/six-grave-violations/.

UN (United Nations). 2020. *Children and Conflict: Report of the Secretary-General*. A/74/845–S/2020/525. New York: United Nations.

UNDP (United Nations Development Programme). 2020. *United Nations Socio-Economic Framework for the Response to COVID-19 in Libya (UNSEF)*. Draft Final Report, October 2020. New York: UNDP.

UNHCR (United Nations High Commissioner for Refugees). n.d. "Libya." Geneva: UNHCR. https://www.unhcr.org/libya.html.

UNICEF (United Nations Children's Fund) and EU (European Union). 2020. *Vulnerability Assessment of Young People in Four Municipalities in Libya*. New York and Brussels: UNICEF and EU.

UNICEF (United Nations Children's Fund) and IMPACT. 2018. *Solitary Journey of Unaccompanied and Separated Children in Libya*. New York: UNICEF.

UNICEF Libya and SPRI (Social Policy Research Institute). 2020. *Multidimensional Child Deprivation in Libya Brief: A Baseline for Monitoring SDG 1.2 for Children in Libya Based on PAPFAM 2014*. Tripoli: UNICEF Libya and SPRI.

UN Women. 2020. *The Impact of COVID-19 on Gender Equality in the Arab Region*. New York: UN Women. https://www2.unwomen.org/-/media/field%20office%20arab%20states /attachments/publications/2020/04/impact%20of%20covid%20on%20gender%20 equality%20-%20policy%20brief.pdf?la=en&vs=4414.

RELATED READINGS

Capasso, M., J. Czerep, A. Dessi, and G. Sanchez. 2020. *Libya Country Report*. EU-LISTCO. https://static1.squarespace.com/static/5afd4286f407b4a0bd8d974f/t/5df25c4673bd39119 31d2927/1576164430045/Libya+-+Country+Report+Final.pdf.

UNICEF (United Nations Children's Fund). 2011. *Libya MENA Gender Equality Profile: Status of Girls and Women in the Middle East and North Africa*. New York: UNICEF.

UNICEF (United Nations Children's Fund). 2021. *Humanitarian Action for Children Appeal for Libya*. New York. https://www.unicef.org/appeals/libya. New York: UNICEF.

14 The Electricity Sector

VICTOR B. LOKSHA AND MOHAMMED QARADAGHI

World Bank

Over the past decade, Libya's main economic sector—the energy sector—has taken a major hit. Estimates provided by the National Oil Corporation (NOC), Libya's state-run oil company, provide that the war has cost Libya an estimated $100 billion in damage to oil fields and the closures of oil terminals. Additional losses from oil smuggling since 2011 are estimated at $750 million a year. No similar estimates of damage are available for the electric power sector, but some relevant data are available from the set of studies completed by the World Bank's Middle East and North Africa energy team in 2017–18. This chapter reviews the studies on Libya's electricity sector and attempts to quantify the burden of the conflict and political instability since the onset of political instability in 2011.

INTRODUCTION

Energy—Libya's main economic sector—has taken a major hit. The Arab press has quoted the head of the National Oil Corporation (NOC), Libya's state-run oil company, as stating that the war has cost Libya some $100 billion in damage to oil fields and the closures of oil terminals. Additional losses from oil smuggling since 2011 are estimated at $750 million a year (Barltrop 2019). No similar estimates of damage are available for the electric power sector, but some relevant data are available from the set of studies completed by the World Bank's Middle East and North Africa (MENA) energy team in 2017–18.

This chapter reviews the studies on Libya's electricity sector and attempts to quantify the burden of the conflict and political instability since the onset of political instability in 2011. It is organized as follows. The first section describes the central role the energy sector plays in Libya's economy. The second section overviews the main geopolitical milestones in Libya's recent history and their impact on the energy sector's structure and governance. The third section assesses the impact of the continuing civil strife on the electricity sector and identifies the key affected areas along the electricity supply chain; it presents the authors' estimates of the economic value lost as a result of the political turmoil in recent years. The fourth section highlights the detrimental impact of the Libyan government's fossil fuel subsidies. The fifth section presents the authors' estimates of the economic value at risk in the scenario of prolonged conflict in Libya lasting through 2030. The sixth section outlines power sector reform options and priorities for Libya and briefly considers some other countries' successful examples in certain areas of reform. It also highlights some development options for natural gas and renewable energy in Libya.

The chapter applies both retrospective and prospective frames of analysis. The retrospective analysis responds to the questions, "How much better would the electricity sector have performed?" and "How much value would it have saved for the Libyan economy?" absent the instability. The prospective analysis attempts to answer the same questions looking forward. The chapter also reviews the potential reform paths for Libya's electricity sector, including the restructuring of its state-owned power utility General Electricity Company of Libya (GECOL), in relation to post-conflict reconstruction needs where possible and considers the potential for the region of integrating Libya's power system with those of its neighbors.

THE ENERGY SECTOR IN LIBYA'S ECONOMY

Libya has some of the largest proven oil reserves in Africa. Oil revenues have remained Libya's main source of income for decades. Together, oil and natural gas still account for almost three-fourths of Libya's national income and nearly all of its export earnings. Libya's oil and gas sector is under severe stress, however, with the NOC continuing to face security threats from factional fighting (CNBC 2020). From 2013 to 2016, Libya experienced a severe recession, with gross domestic product (GDP) falling by 12.7 percent on average over this period, mostly due to the blockade of several oil production facilities (Policy Corner 2021). The electricity sector, which still mostly uses oil and gas to power its plants, is also exposed to major operational risks caused by fuel supply disruptions.

Resolving the security issues to restore Libya's energy supplies is still the country's most urgent priority, even in the midst of the COVID-19 pandemic. Overall, the Libyan economy contracted by about 31 percent in 2020. However, following this massive contraction, the Libyan economy, including its hydrocarbon sector, is witnessing a significant rebound. After the lifting of the oil blockade in late 2020 and the resilience of global oil prices, hydrocarbon export receipts and in turn the trade balance and current account balance are on an upward swing (World Bank 2021a).

GEOPOLITICAL MILESTONES

The political turmoil has had substantial impacts on the energy sector structure and governance. Figure 14.1 presents the main geopolitical milestones since 2011 and their impact on the country's ability to maintain the integrity of its government institutions.

After the 2011 revolution, the General National Congress established a Ministry of Electricity and Renewable Energy, but it was dissolved by the Government of National Accord in 2016. An energy authority was established in the East. However, it has neither power over nor geographical reach to the West, where consumption and generation are concentrated. Most energy sector reform has been put on hold, and there is an overlap in the role and mission of the different entities under the former Ministry of Electricity and Renewable Energy. No regulatory agency is in place to oversee the operation of the energy sector (World Bank 2017a).

Finally, in the most recent bid by UN-supported Libyan political leaders in the West to reconcile the rival administrations, the new Government of National

FIGURE 14.1
Key events in Libya since 2011

2011	2012	2014	2015	2021
Revolution ends.	An elected parliament, the General National Congress, is established for a transitional period that lasts 18 months.	Elections are held and a new parliament is elected. However, there is conflict over the legitimacy of the elected parliament in Eastern Libya and the expired one in Tripoli, resulting in both parliaments and governments contesting power.	Late in 2015, the UN–led dialogue endorses and later installs as the internationally recognized government of Libya, the Government of National Accord (GNA). (It has not been recognized by the competing governments, prolonging the conflict.)	Early in 2021, the GNA hands over power to the new Government of National Unity (GNU), selected through a UN-supported process, in the latest internationally backed bid to bring political stability to the country.

Source: World Bank 2017a.
Note: UN = United Nations.

Unity assumed power in 2021. Its recent initiatives have encouraged both Libyan citizens and international observers, as well as potential investors in the oil-rich country. An early set of measures for the electricity sector includes a plan for GECOL to reduce power outages by carrying out massive overhauls of the damaged and idling power plants (Libya Herald 2021; UNSMIL 2021).

IMPACT OF THE CONFLICT ON THE ELECTRICITY SECTOR

Electricity access rates for Libya's population were reported to be almost 100 percent as early as in 2000 (IEA 2021)—a remarkable achievement for a country in Africa. Such electrification rates were made possible by the country's heavy investment in electricity infrastructure over the decades before the 2011 revolution[1] through the government's development budget. GECOL, Libya's sole national power utility, oversaw managing these investments. It established a robust power transmission network and adequate generation plant capacity.

GECOL's fortunes took a turn for the worse after 2011, as reflected in the operation of its core business units and state of the country's electricity infrastructure. Insecurity and political instability led to a halt in most projects. GECOL suffered successive assaults on its assets and staff; a large increase in thefts, especially of conductors and electrical apparatus; a significant decline in its ability to carry out maintenance; and severe disruptions in fuel supply to its power plant (box 14.1). These problems resulted in a loss of some infrastructure assets, a decline in the performance of the power network, and—as a result—a severe shortage in power-generation capacity, causing lengthy power cuts in many parts of the country, especially during the summer and winter peak-load periods. GECOL's deteriorating performance, in turn, started a vicious cycle in which rampant commercial losses and nonpayments further contributed to the utility's failure to allocate resources for essential maintenance and investment (World Bank 2017a, 2017b, 2017c).

The level of disruption in planned infrastructure investments is illustrated by the finding (World Bank 2017a) that only 23 percent of the power generation capacity planned for 2010–16 was built (figure 14.2).

Delayed investments in both new and existing infrastructure, as well as continued disruptions to scheduled repairs and ongoing operation and maintenance (O&M), have taken a heavy toll on the operating performance of GECOL and Libya's electricity sector as a whole.

- Of total installed capacity of 10.8 gigawatts (GW), 5.2–6.7 GW was due for overhaul in 2017.
- Fuel supply to GECOL has been unstable.

BOX 14.1

Vulnerability of fuel supplies for electric power generation

Almost all the General Electricity Company of Libya's (GECOL) power stations have been affected by disruptions in the supply of fuel. Insecurity and instability have led to the repeated cutting off of fuel sources supplying power plants. In addition, the ongoing transition from oil to gas in power generation, although well justified on economic and environmental grounds, has been problematic, as the gas pipeline infrastructure and the production of natural gas have not been able to meet demand, forcing some plants to operate on fuel oil. Between 2014 and 2017, the years of the most intense rivalry of competing forces over the oil fields, GECOL regularly lost an estimated 600 megawatts (MW) of its installed capacity because of constraints imposed by the supply of fuel.

Source: World Bank 2017b.

FIGURE 14.2

Planned versus actual capacity expansions, 2010–16

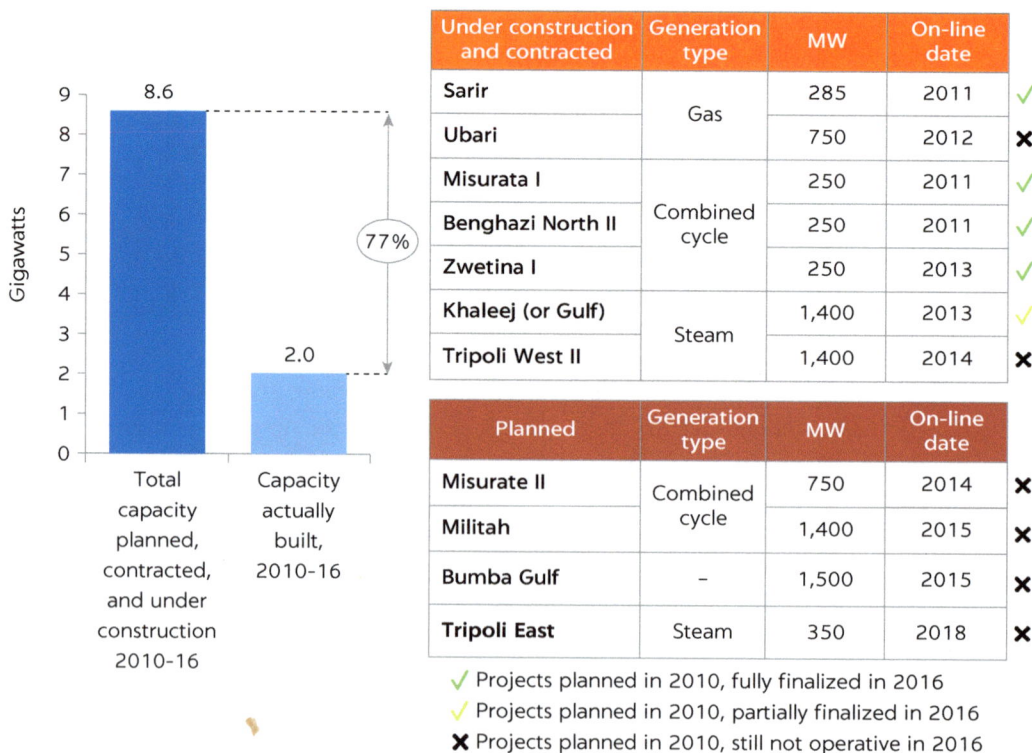

Under construction and contracted	Generation type	MW	On-line date	
Sarir	Gas	285	2011	✓
Ubari		750	2012	✗
Misurata I	Combined cycle	250	2011	✓
Benghazi North II		250	2011	✓
Zwetina I		250	2013	✓
Khaleej (or Gulf)	Steam	1,400	2013	✓
Tripoli West II		1,400	2014	✗

Planned	Generation type	MW	On-line date	
Misurate II	Combined cycle	750	2014	✗
Militah		1,400	2015	✗
Bumba Gulf	–	1,500	2015	✗
Tripoli East	Steam	350	2018	✗

✓ Projects planned in 2010, fully finalized in 2016
✓ Projects planned in 2010, partially finalized in 2016
✗ Projects planned in 2010, still not operative in 2016

Source: World Bank 2017a.
Note: MW = megawatts.

- Available power capacity is far below installed nameplate capacity.
- Low-capacity availability and growing demand have led to negative reserve margin and consequent load shedding.
- Regional differences in generation capacity contribute to supply disruptions. The absence of power generation in the South causes voltage instabilities and prolonged power outages in the region. The Western network is struggling with power shortages, while the East has excess capacity. (See annex 14A for Libya's electricity supply regions and annex 14B for the location of installed generation assets.)
- Damage to transmission substations and overhead lines led to a decrease in grid reliability.

Libya has regularly used load shedding—a technique to avoid systemwide blackouts by temporarily disconnecting some consumers—in recent years. Loss of supply caused by load shedding grew from 2,365 minutes a year in 2010 to a peak of 197,822 minutes a year—38 percent of all the minutes in a year—in 2016, a more than 80-fold increase (World Bank 2017b). Even with load shedding, the country has not been able to avoid blackouts (Reuters 2020b; World Bank 2017b).

Blackouts cause major damage. Their triggers are not always easy to pinpoint. However, of the four blackouts that occurred in 2017, all were triggered by a fault or outage in the transmission network, followed by loss of generating units, as outage of transmission lines reduced the operational reliability of the GECOL power system. In addition to existing line outages, GECOL faces the problem of new transmission line projects that have not been completed. The most critical lines are the East-West interconnections (World Bank 2017b).

Electricity production and consumption

International statistics point to a sharp decline in electricity production in Libya in 2011, followed by an unsteady recovery (figure 14.3).[2]

FIGURE 14.3

Electricity supply and fuel-generation mix, 2000–18

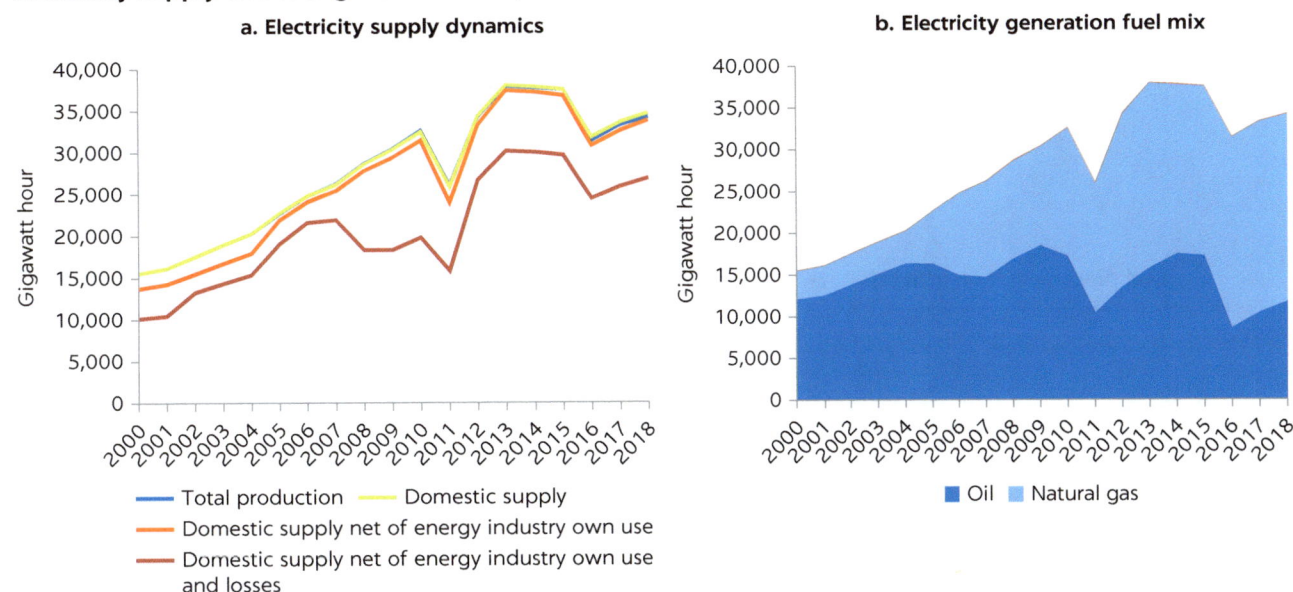

a. Electricity supply dynamics

Total production — Domestic supply — Domestic supply net of energy industry own use — Domestic supply net of energy industry own use and losses

b. Electricity generation fuel mix

Oil — Natural gas

Source: IEA 2020.

International Energy Agency (IEA) statistics on Libya identify the following characteristics:

- The amount of energy traded across borders is very small, making the difference between total production and domestic supply negligible.
- The generation fuel mix is dominated by oil- and (increasingly) natural-gas-fired technology such as simple cycle and combined cycle gas turbine plants. Since the early 21st century, efforts have been made to convert Libya's thermal plants from oil to natural gas in order to maximize petroleum available for export (Britannica 2020). The gas volumes needed to fuel Libya's power plants are about 2 billion cubic meters per year and should be assumed to grow. GECOL's continued substantial reliance on oil products for power generation is uneconomic and an aberration given that generation using natural gas (of which Libya has ample reserves) is cheaper and less polluting. However, the 2011 civil unrest has set back investments in natural gas exploration and production (see annex 14F).
- The solar photovoltaic (PV) generation share is close to negligible.
- Residential consumers account for a large share of consumption.
- Final consumption data became much less reliable after 2011, as seen in the large share of unspecified users in table 14.1.

Available versus nominal capacity

Since about 2016, Libya has had total installed electricity generation capacity of about 10–11 gigawatts (GW) (EIA 2020). A World Bank study reports GECOL's official installed capacity of 10.238 GW in 2017 (World Bank 2017b; see annex 14B for details). The capacity effectively available is much lower than these nominal or nameplate, capacity figures, however. As a result, the country has been facing power capacity shortages since 2011, as shown by the negative reserve margins in figure 14.4.

Recent media reports referencing a review of GECOL by the Libyan Audit Bureau broadly confirm that the capacity shortages have continued through 2021, with available generating capacity of 5,000—5,500 MW falling well short of the demand of 7,000 MW in winter and 8,000 MW in summer (Al Jazeera 2021).

Several factors contribute to the shortage of available power generation capacity in Libya:

- **Overdue maintenance:** GECOL has the technical capacity to carry out much of the needed maintenance work, including overhauls. However, the

TABLE 14.1 **Final electricity consumption, by sector, 2006–18 (percent of total)**

SECTOR	2006	2009	2012	2015	2018
Industry	16	11	8	12	7
Agriculture/forestry	12	11	8	8	7
Commercial and public services	28	44	30	11	11
Residential	37	34	26	36	50
Other unspecified	7	0	28	32	25
Total	100	100	100	100	100

Source: IEA 2020.

FIGURE 14.4

Capacity gap in power generation and (negative) reserve margins, 2010–17

Source: World Bank (2017a, g).
Note: The reserve margin is a percent ratio of capacity surplus over demand. GW = gigawatt.

specialized nature of major overhauls usually means that supervision by the generating units' suppliers is also required. Libya's security and stability situation and advisories by foreign governments have meant that many suppliers have not permitted their personnel to travel to Libya, reducing GECOL's ability to carry out major overhauls.

- **Fuel supply:** Almost all GECOL's power stations have been adversely affected by the supply of fuel. Insecurity and instability have led to the repeated cut-off of fuel sources supplying power plants. In addition, refined petroleum fuels (for example, diesel) as well as gas have been often diverted away from supplying power plants, due to incentives to procure fuel within Libya at subsidized prices and then sell it elsewhere at market prices.
- **Third-party power plants:** In 2017, two power stations owned by third parties were connected to GECOL's power grid. Both plants were old and required major overhauls.
- **Outdated generation expansion plan:** GECOL last carried out a major review of its load forecasts and generation expansion plans in 2007. An updated expansion plan is an important prerequisite to contracting for new generating capacity, in addition to clearing the backlog of generation maintenance requirements. A new least-cost expansion plan will need to reflect reductions in the costs of renewable energy (World Bank 2017d) and possibly include a new assessment of cross-border transmission interconnections opportunities (World Bank 2021b).
- **Staff development:** Despite a large number of staff on its payroll, GECOL lacks sufficient numbers of staff trained to handle O&M of the power-generation units. Staff need to be trained to handle the new generation capacity to be added in the next few years (World Bank 2017b).

Commercial losses

The challenging socioeconomic situation, the absence of a clear governance framework, and poor invoicing and collection practices have led to a dramatic rise in commercial losses and bad debt since 2010, severely affecting GECOL's financial condition. Commercial losses (a proxy for electricity theft) are huge in Libya, both in comparison to the country's own levels a decade ago and to its regional peers. The same is true for receivables, which reflect GECOL's poor collection practices (figure 14.5).

Commercial losses spiked from about 20 percent in 2010 to as much as 75 percent in 2014 before falling to the levels shown in figure 14.5, which are still very high. The increase in commercial losses and bad debt has severely reduced GECOL's ability to cover system costs (estimated at LD 4 billion in cumulated revenue losses for 2011–15).

High commercial losses are related to metering and billing practices (table 14.2). A World Bank report (2017e) estimated that just bringing the level of commercial losses back to their 2010 level could save GECOL LD 1.5 billion between 2018 and 2023.

FIGURE 14.5

Commercial losses and receivables in selected countries in the Middle East and North Africa, 2015

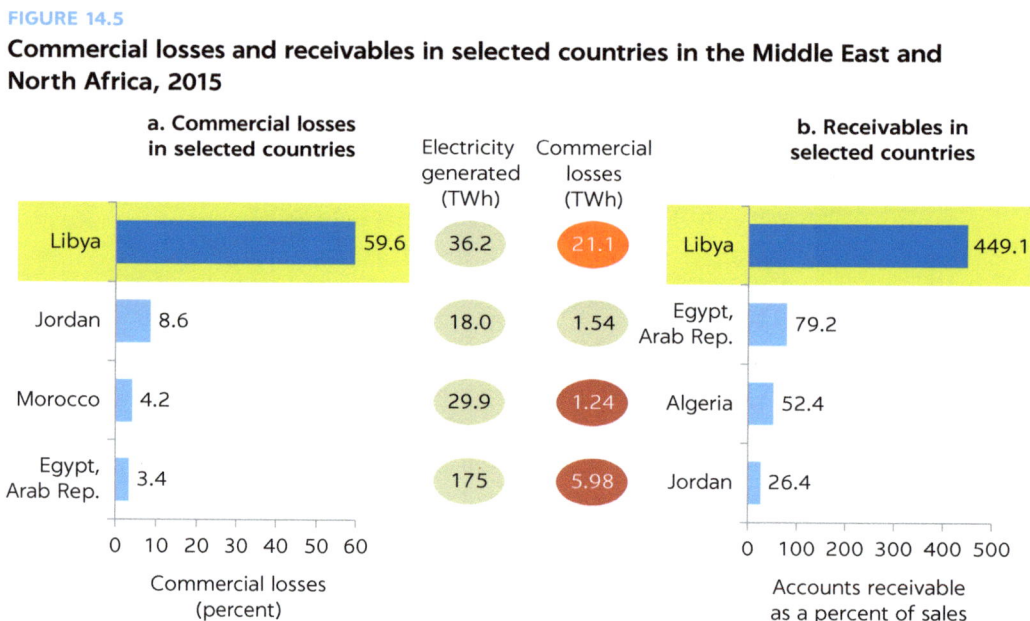

Source: World Bank 2017a.
Note: Receivables data are not available for Morocco. TWh = terawatt hour.

TABLE 14.2 **Factors contributing to high commercial losses in Libya's electricity sector**

FACTOR	DESCRIPTION
Metering	• Large number of nonfunctioning and defective electricity consumption meters in Tripoli and other areas at every voltage level
	• Limited meter coverage outside Tripoli
	• Tampering with meters
	• Illegal connections to electricity network
	• Inaccurate meter readings and wide use of estimations
	• Difficulty accessing some locations, which complicates meter reading and the monitoring of connections and disconnections
Billing	• Lack of regular billing for all customer groups
	• Lack of functioning meters or billing outside Tripoli
	• High financial costs of using traditional method of invoice delivery

Source: World Bank 2017e.

Transmission system

Libya has constructed a strong transmission system, with about 2,300 kilometers of 400 kilovolt (kV) backbone and 14,300 kilometers of 220kV main grid.[3] Stringent design criteria were used to ensure a sufficient level of redundancy. Despite damage to many lines as a result of the armed conflict, vandalism, and theft, the transmission network continued to supply almost all load centers with their power requirements. Major blackouts nevertheless occurred, often triggered by transmission line outages (box 14.2).

Damage to Libya's electricity transmission system caused by armed conflict, vandalism, and theft, 2011–16

Libya's transmission system has suffered many incidents of damage since 2011 as a result of military clashes between factions and acts of vandalism and theft that affected overhead lines and substations. Incidents led to isolation of complete regions until the General Electricity Company of Libya (GECOL) was able to repair or replace the damaged infrastructure. In some cases, repairs took several months or even years.

The most severe and longest-lasting damage was in the south and west of Benghazi city in 2014–15 (yellow circle in map B14.2.1), which led to separation of the network into Eastern and Western sections, load shedding in Benghazi, and shortages in generation in the Western network and consequent load shedding there, too. Damage to the transmission system has also led to prolonged outages in the southwest and southeast, with consequent isolation of power plants or reduction in supplies. In almost every case, GECOL eventually repaired, replaced, or compensated for the damaged parts of the network.

Some parts of the transmission network were reported to be completely out of service in 2017. The total length of overhead transmissions out of service was 819 kilometers at the 220kV level, (5.7 percent of the installed base) and 23 kilometers at the 400kV level (1 percent of the installed base) (World Bank 2017b). Almost all the out-of-service

lines were in the Eastern region, mostly around Benghazi, caused by damage from armed conflict. Besides overhead transmission lines, some transformer substations and switchgear equipment have been damaged.

In addition to existing line outages, GECOL faces the problem of new transmission line projects that have not been completed. GECOL is pursuing plans to reinforce the transmission system with 400kV lines, but the status of implementation is uncertain. The most critical issue may be the 220kV lines of the East-West interconnection. The 220kV link is a bottleneck limiting the amount of power that can be transferred between the Eastern and Western Libyan power networks. This bottleneck is becoming critical, with power shortages faced by the Western network and excess capacity available in the East. This and other transmission line projects will play an important role in improving the transmission system and reducing bottlenecks; resumption of construction works needs to be a priority. GECOL is facing these important challenges at a time when its transmission department is suffering from reduced budgets, difficult and at times dangerous work conditions, scarcities in spare parts and equipment required to maintain key elements of the transmission system, and delays in completing planned additions to transmission infrastructure.

continued

Box 14.2, *continued*

MAP B14.2.1

Transmission network

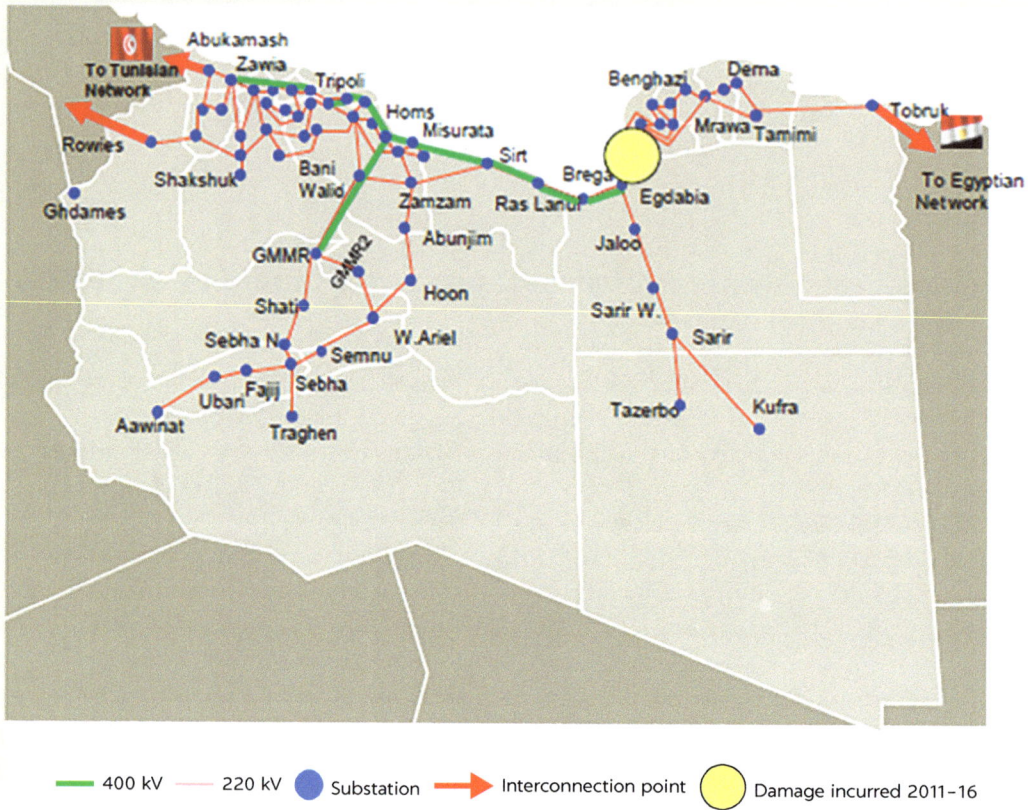

Source: World Bank 2017a.
Note: kV = kilovolt.

Source: World Bank.

Cost recovery, including in distribution and supply

Fuel prices for electricity generation are heavily subsidized, and end-user tariffs for electricity are set at fixed levels far below total production costs (44 percent below system costs in 2015) (World Bank 2017a). In addition, 38 percent of consumption is not invoiced, and 9 percent of potential revenues are lost from poor collection. Of the LD 1.95 billion in system costs incurred in 2015, Libya's electric utility recovered only about LD 170 million, or 9 percent of its system costs (figure 14.6).

It is difficult to isolate factors related to conflict from all others. High commercial losses attributable to poor metering and billing practices may have been exacerbated by the difficult conditions of access to consumers' premises in conflict-prone areas, for example. Within the purview of GECOL

FIGURE 14.6

Share of total system costs collected, 2015

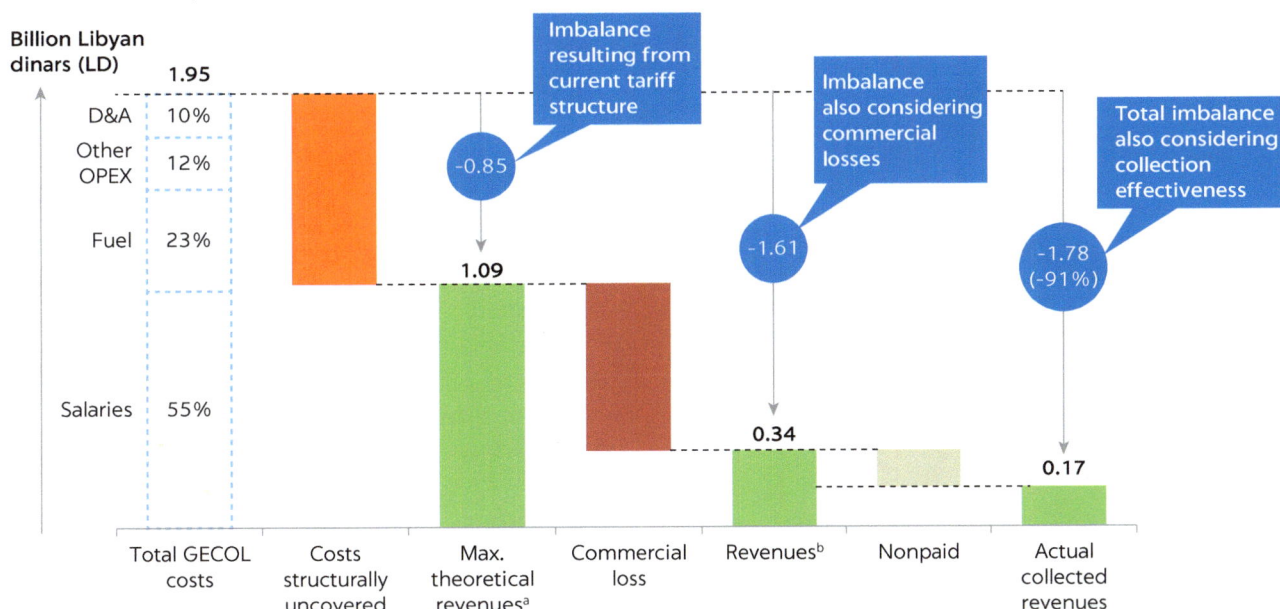

Billion Libyan dinars (LD)

D&A	10%	
Other OPEX	12%	
Fuel	23%	
Salaries	55%	

Total GECOL costs · Costs structurally uncovered · Max. theoretical revenues[a] · Commercial loss · Revenues[b] · Nonpaid · Actual collected revenues

1.95 · 1.09 · -0.85 · -1.61 · 0.34 · -1.78 (-91%) · 0.17

Imbalance resulting from current tariff structure

Imbalance also considering commercial losses

Total imbalance also considering collection effectiveness

Source: World Bank 2017a.

Note: D&A = depreciation and amortization; GECOL = General Electricity Company of Libya; OPEX = operational expenditures.
a. Sum of (tariff by customer type) × (consumption by customer type); based on electricity consumed
b. Sum of (tariff by customer type) × (invoiced energy by customer type)

is a suite of measures that could boost its commercial sustainability (see annex 14B and annex 14D). Box 14.3 shows measures to control illegal connections.

The "costs structurally uncovered" in figure 14.6 are essentially the costs of the government subsidy embedded in the electricity tariff. Subsidizing electricity is a long-standing practice in MENA that predates the 2011 events. The upheaval in Libya since 2011 may have delayed potential reforms in this area.

Lost value of electricity supply

Failure to deliver electricity to consumers willing and able to pay represents a loss for the economy. Despite boasting an electrification rate of close to 100 percent based on technical access of consumers to electricity, Libya suffers from painful power outages (Zaptia 2019a, 2019b). In the calculation presented in figure 14.7 and figure 14.8, the cost of failure to deliver electricity is assessed as the sum of two components: the value of electricity supply not delivered to meet peak demand (a proxy for the cost of load shedding) and the cost of power outages (blackouts). The assessment of losses incurred as a result of political instability requires comparing actual conditions with a retroactive counterfactual scenario of political stability (figure 14.7). The counterfactual scenario assumes a 6 percent annual growth in electricity supply during this period.[4] Annex 14C provides some additional details on the methodology.

BOX 14.3

Regularizing illegal electricity connections

The following measures could help regularize illegal electricity connections in Libya:

- Require a no-objection certificate from the General Electricity Company of Libya (GECOL) to certify that a customer has a regular meter connection in place when applying for any service from a government institution (for example, ID renewal, passport issuance, university registration).
- Impose strict penalties against illegally connected consumers.
- Launch a massive campaign offering free electricity meters for a limited period.

- Implement programs for commercial regularization of old debts.
- Establish direct and open contact with community leaders and local authorities to create awareness that electricity is a commercial good with a price and that electricity consumption should be rational and efficient.
- Design and execute campaigns to create a culture of regular payment of electricity bills, preservation of electric infrastructure, and safe behavior to avoid electrocution.
- Develop educational programs on electricity safety for children.

Source: World Bank.

FIGURE 14.7

Actual versus counterfactual electricity supply, 2000–18

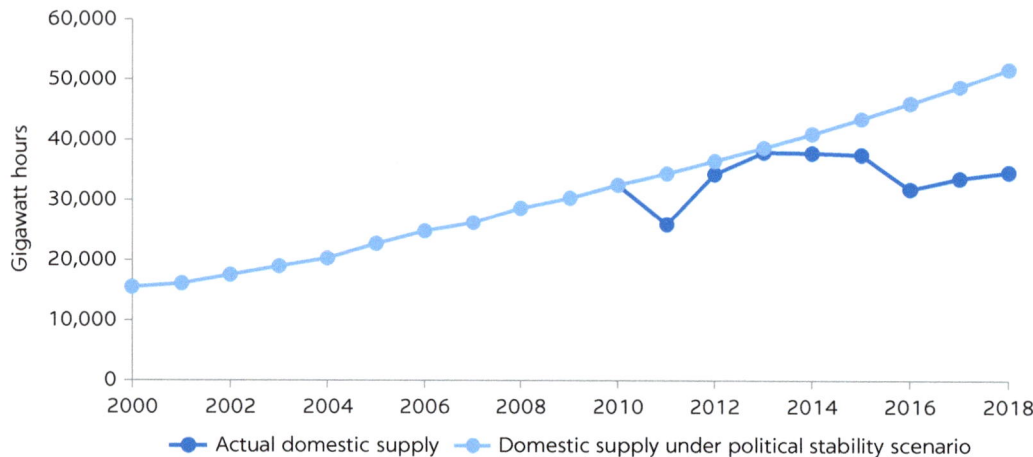

Source: World Bank.

Figure 14.8 shows the estimated economic value lost from Libya's electricity supply shortages potentially attributable to political instability that began in 2011.

The total economic loss caused by electricity supply shortfalls was 7.9 percent of GDP in 2017 and 6.3 percent in 2018. The total present value of the losses discounted back from 2018 (base year) to 2010 is estimated at $15.8 billion.

FIGURE 14.8

Economic losses caused by electricity supply shortages, 2011–18

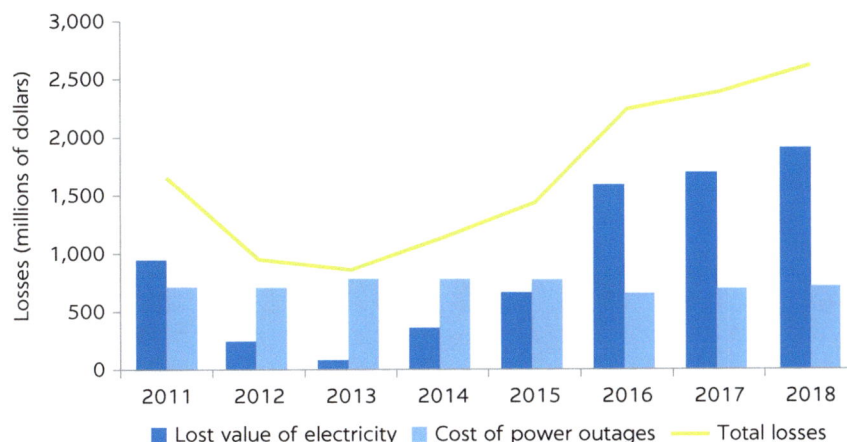

Source: World Bank.

THE LEGACY OF SUBSIDIZED FOSSIL FUELS

The cost of fossil fuel for Libya's electricity generation is almost entirely covered by government subsidies (figure 14.9). The origins of fuel subsidization practices in Libya—and the MENA region as a whole—have been the subject of numerous studies (World Bank 2013, 2021b). Figure 14.9 shows that the price paid by Libya's electric power utility for fossil fuels used to power its plants is a small fraction of the market value of those fuels in the international market for energy commodities.

The political upheaval in Libya following 2011 affected the power sector in several ways. First, the prices of natural gas for electricity generation remained subsidized, despite recommendations to end or reduce the subsidies. Second, in the electricity sector, the fragile political environment disrupted the process of institution building and set the country's clocks back from building a robust governance framework. As a result, measures such as raising electricity tariffs to cost-recovery levels have been delayed. If GECOL increased its tariffs from LD 38 per megawatt hour (MWh) in 2017 to LD 100 per MWh by 2023, it would narrow the gap between its production costs and the revenues collected by an estimated LD 1.4 billion relative to the "do-nothing" scenario (World Bank 2017e; see annex 14D for details). Given the political situation, it has been considered more prudent to slow the electricity tariff increases (to LD 63 per MWh by 2024, for example) (World Bank 2017c, 2017g).

VALUE AT RISK: ECONOMIC LOSSES IF POLITICAL INSTABILITY CONTINUES

Several studies (World Bank 2017a, 2017f, 2017g) try to quantify the extent to which political instability may affect future demand. Demand projections developed through 2030 looked at two scenarios. Scenario A includes a lower

FIGURE 14.9

Subsidized fossil fuel prices paid by GECOL, 2002–16

a. GECOL prices paid versus market levels

b. Fuel price evolution

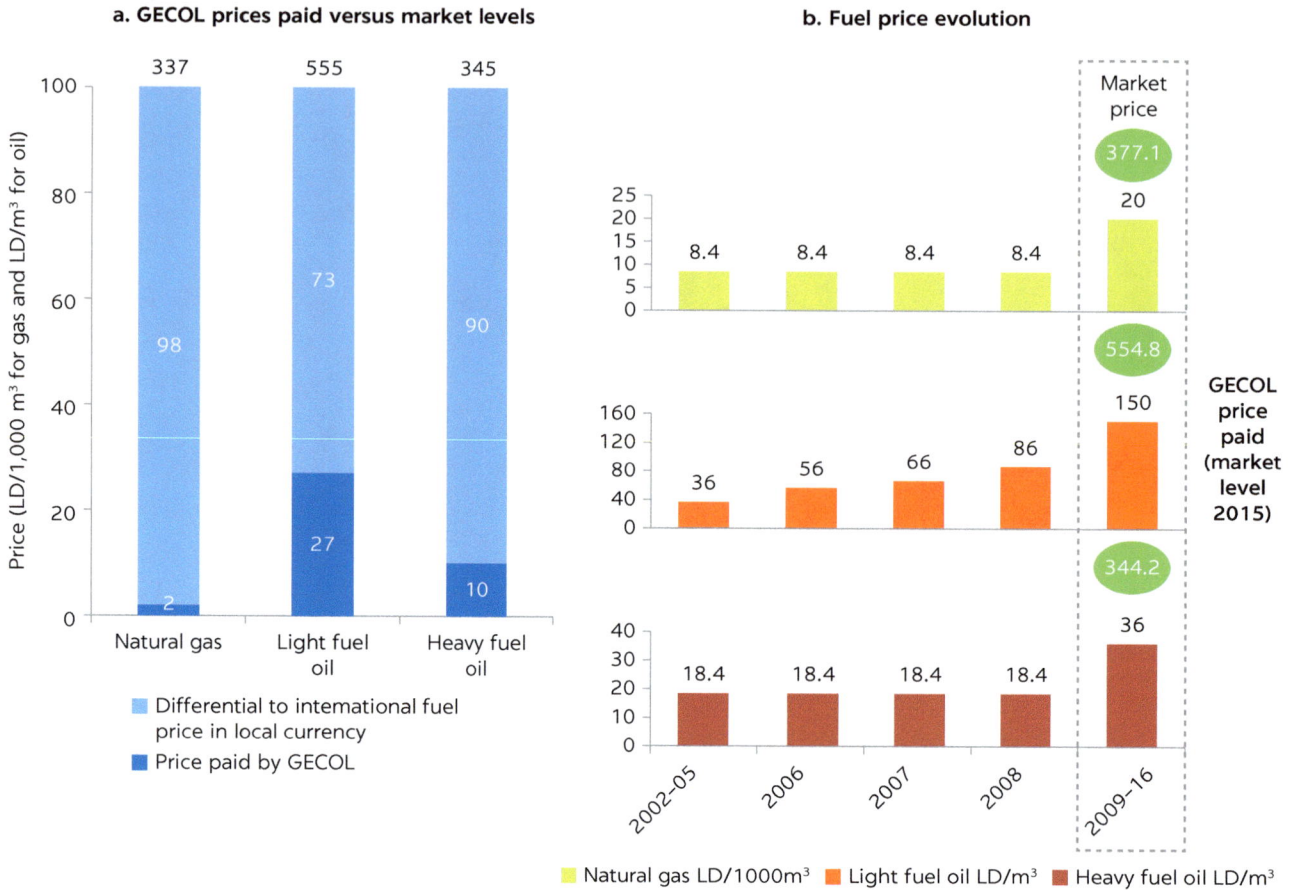

Source: World Bank 2017a.

Note: Prices are international fuel prices in local currency. GECOL = General Electricity Company of Libya; m³ = cubic meter.

growth rate for demand, as a result of continuing political instability. Scenario B, which assumes that political stability is restored, allows rapid development of Libya's electricity consuming sectors (including through megaprojects), leading to greater demand for electricity (World Bank 2017f, 2017g). The trajectories of the two scenarios separate starting in 2022 and then widen (figure 14.10).

On the basis of the electricity consumption gap caused by political instability, it is possible to estimate the corresponding economic value at risk (figure 14.11). Expressed as a present value of unserved electricity for which consumers, under normal circumstances, would have been willing to pay a full-cost-recovering tariff, the economic value at risk is $9.5 billion over 10 years (2020–30). Annex 14C provides additional details.

The cost of power outages is another source of damage to the economy. Its value is highly uncertain and depends on several factors, particularly those affecting Libya's ability to build (or rebuild) enough generation capacity to match growing demand, strengthen the grid, and build transmission interconnections

FIGURE 14.10

Peak demand and consumption projections, 2020–30

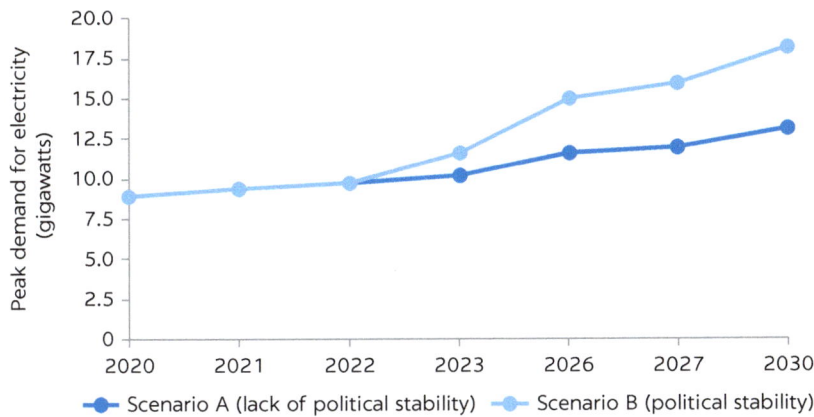

Electricity peak demand (gigawatts)		
Year	Scenario A	Scenario B
2020	8.9	8.9
2025	11.1	13.9
2030	13.1	18.2
Electricity consumption (terawatt hours)		
Year	Scenario A	Scenario B
2020	40.2	40.2
2025	50.5	63.6
2030	59.9	83.1

Source: World Bank (2017a, 2017f, 2017g).

FIGURE 14.11

Projected electricity lost if political instability persists through 2030

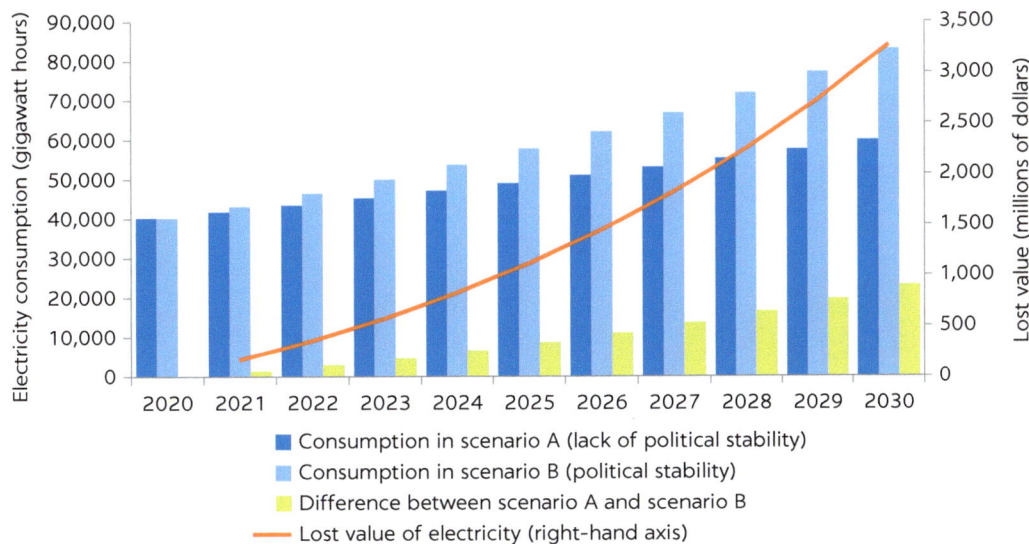

■ Consumption in scenario A (lack of political stability)
■ Consumption in scenario B (political stability)
■ Difference between scenario A and scenario B
— Lost value of electricity (right-hand axis)

Source: Calculation based on World Bank 2017a, 2017f, 2017g.

with other countries as appropriate (see annex 14E on potential transmission interconnections). Interconnection with the Arab Republic of Egypt is particularly important because it could provide interconnection points to Benghazi, which still suffers from power supply disruptions and has the potential to produce renewable energy for export.

RATIONALE AND OPTIONS FOR REFORM

Civil unrest and factional fighting have taken a heavy toll on the Libyan power sector's ability to deliver adequate services for its people. It is therefore critical for the government of Libya to fix the broken sector. This is a worthwhile goal in and of itself, but the additional rationale for having it fixed is to avoid the self-reinforcing vicious cycle where poor service quality causes people to protest, foment violence, and further damage the very infrastructure that can improve their lives. Conversely, the reform-minded government may see the ailing power sector as a source of quick dividends that can unite various parts of the country and society.

Thus, this discussion of the reform options focuses on its initial and most urgent phases, although the path toward a more efficient and competitive power sector for Libya could consist of several stages of reform, each potentially taking several years (figure 14.12).

1. The first stage would focus on the most urgent priorities, including the following:
   - Clarifying sector governance by (1) passing the legislation to establish the policy mandate of the sector governing bodies, notably the Ministry of Electricity; (2) establishing an electricity regulatory agency within the government, with the initial role focusing on supporting accounting unbundling of GECOL's operations; (3) clarifying GECOL's governance framework and implementing reorganization measures as necessary to achieve goals such as separating generation and transmission into different business units; (4) updating the least-cost expansion plans for the

FIGURE 14.12

Stages of reform of Libya's power sector

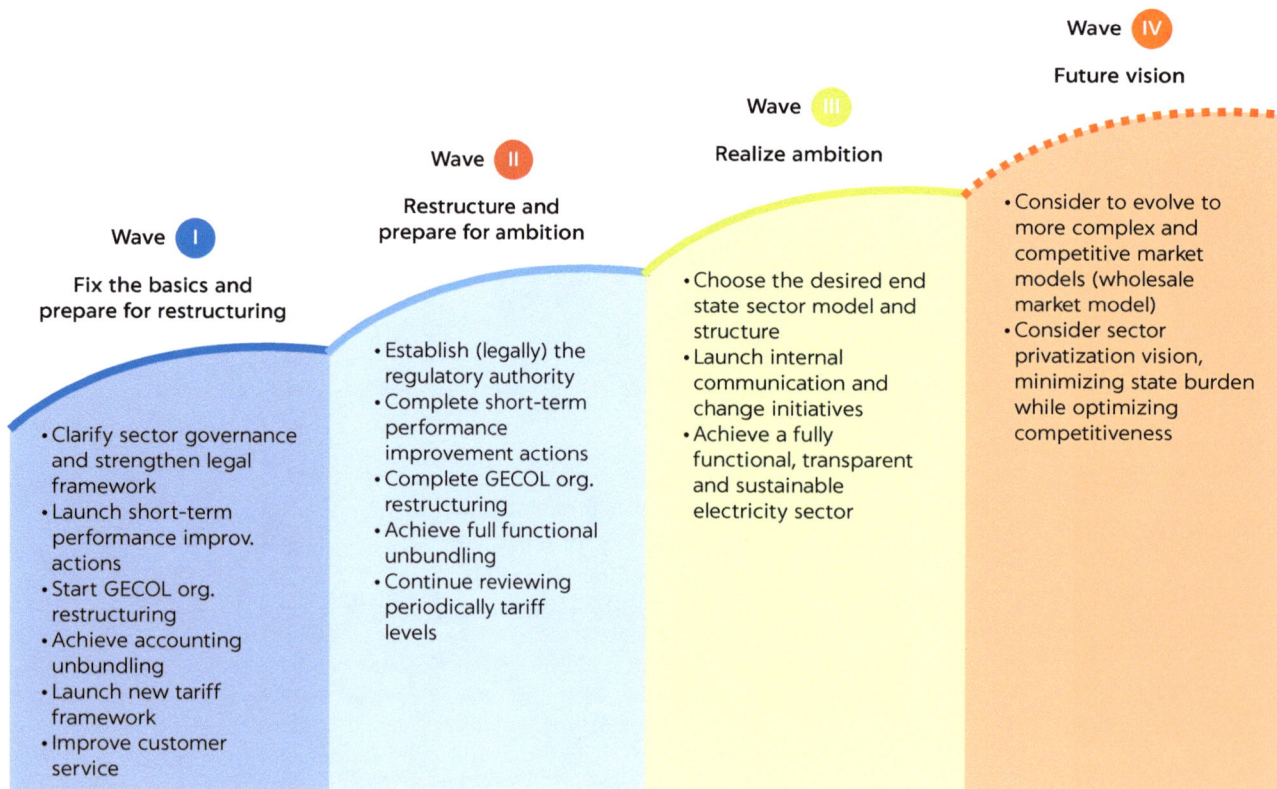

Wave **I**

Fix the basics and prepare for restructuring

- Clarify sector governance and strengthen legal framework
- Launch short-term performance improv. actions
- Start GECOL org. restructuring
- Achieve accounting unbundling
- Launch new tariff framework
- Improve customer service

Wave **II**

Restructure and prepare for ambition

- Establish (legally) the regulatory authority
- Complete short-term performance improvement actions
- Complete GECOL org. restructuring
- Achieve full functional unbundling
- Continue reviewing periodically tariff levels

Wave **III**

Realize ambition

- Choose the desired end state sector model and structure
- Launch internal communication and change initiatives
- Achieve a fully functional, transparent and sustainable electricity sector

Wave **IV**

Future vision

- Consider to evolve to more complex and competitive market models (wholesale market model)
- Consider sector privatization vision, minimizing state burden while optimizing competitiveness

Source: World Bank 2017f, 2017g.
Note: GECOL = General Electricity Company of Libya.

generation and transmission infrastructure based on current information on the energy resources and utilizing appropriate planning techniques; and (5) adopting a National Electricity Strategy within the legal framework for the sector.

- Establishing performance accountability of GECOL, through reorganization as necessary: for example, through a stepped unbundling pathway (focusing initially on accounting unbundling). The operational improvement needs to be achieved across the electricity supply chain in action plans for generation, transmission, distribution, and retail. The most urgent performance improvement targets should include (1) a sharp reduction in commercial losses; (2) closing the gap on available generation capacity by resuming the delayed construction disrupted by war and conducting the long-overdue overhaul and maintenance; (3) resolving the issues of inadequate fuel supply to the power stations, including by gas pipeline system development and/or the construction of liquefied natural gas (LNG) terminals; (4) adopting a zero load shedding target; and (5) improving GECOL's customer service and communications standards, ultimately aiming to build consumers' awareness of their role in helping GECOL achieve the service improvement goals. The government should support GECOL with the necessary funding from its own and external sources.
- Improving GECOL and sector financial sustainability by reducing subsidies on fossil fuel tariffs for electricity generation. This can be achieved, for example, by gradually increasing the tariff to achieve a partial coverage of the cost of fuel subsidies by 2024, while protecting the most vulnerable consumers and educating the consumers on the role of cost recovery for the vital investments and maintenance activities in the sector.
- Imposing cost control and staff reskilling measures—to improve the efficiency of GECOL's workforce at every level of the electricity supply chain.

2. The second stage would strengthen sector governance by introducing an independent sector regulator (the Libyan Electricity Market Regulatory Authority) and starting to introduce significant structural changes, such as (1) increasing competition in generation by opening the sector up for independent power producers; (2) achieving functional separation along the electricity production chain (functional unbundling); and (3) introducing regular tariff reviews.

3. The third stage would elaborate the desired end-state model for the sector. It would include decisions on whether to proceed with the legal unbundling of the functionally unbundled segments and whether to unbundle horizontally into several distribution areas.

4. The fourth stage would consider the evolution into more advanced market models (for example, competitive wholesale market) and sector privatization possibilities to reduce the burden on the state and optimize competitiveness.

It must be noted that implementing power sector reforms in a post-conflict environment entails added layers of uncertainty beyond those found in politically stable environments. The uncertainties increase the need to revisit the initial ambitions and adjust the targets based on the results achieved along the way.

Other country examples to consider

Libya could learn from the experiences of other countries in MENA. Algeria and Tunisia have successfully achieved certain reforms (table 14.3).

The role of natural gas and renewables

Natural gas

Given the economic and environmental advantages of natural gas over liquid fuels, the shortage of natural gas for electricity generation needs to be addressed. In Libya, multiple alternatives exist for increasing supply of natural gas to the power sector, including through reducing or eliminating exports to Italy, increasing domestic exploration and production, reducing associated gas flaring, and importing LNG through multiple entry points (onshore and offshore) (World Bank 2021c). An attractive alternative in the short- to medium term is LNG import through offshore facilities such as floating storage and regasification units.

Renewable energy

Alongside conventional power sources, renewable energy is an important element of power sector development for Libya at every stage. Renewables—especially solar and wind power—could eventually help Libya transition away from its electricity sector's dependence on fossil fuels. Renewables could also help to lower generation costs and the fiscal costs of electricity sector subsidies. The regulatory mechanisms for renewable energy expansion will have to change over time. The current state of development in the field suggests that competitive auctions for renewable energy may be preferable to the more rigid feed-in-tariffs. The end-state model for renewable energy integration would be chosen during the second or third wave of the power sector reform. From a security perspective, the following aspects of renewable energy technology stand out: (1) Concentrated solar power installations, typically comprising a single generator, pose more risk of shortfall if damaged than wind and solar PV, which are inherently scalable, and (2) wind turbines and solar towers are generally easier targets for sabotage or destruction than conventional generation units or decentralized renewable installations.

TABLE 14.3 **Reform achievements in Algeria and Tunisia**

COUNTRY	ACHIEVEMENTS
Algeria	• Successful transformation of Sonelgaz, the state utility, into a holding company and its internal unbundling into production, transmission, and distribution subsidiaries
	• Establishment of the official regulator—Commission de Régulation de l'Électricité et du Gaz
Tunisia	• Early sector opening to private investment in generation
	• Establishment of a clear framework with dedicated commissions to allocate independent power producer concessions
	• Strong emphasis on renewables and energy efficiency

Source: World Bank.

ANNEX 14A: PEAK DEMAND FOR ELECTRICITY IN LIBYA

MAP 14A.1

Peak electricity demand by region

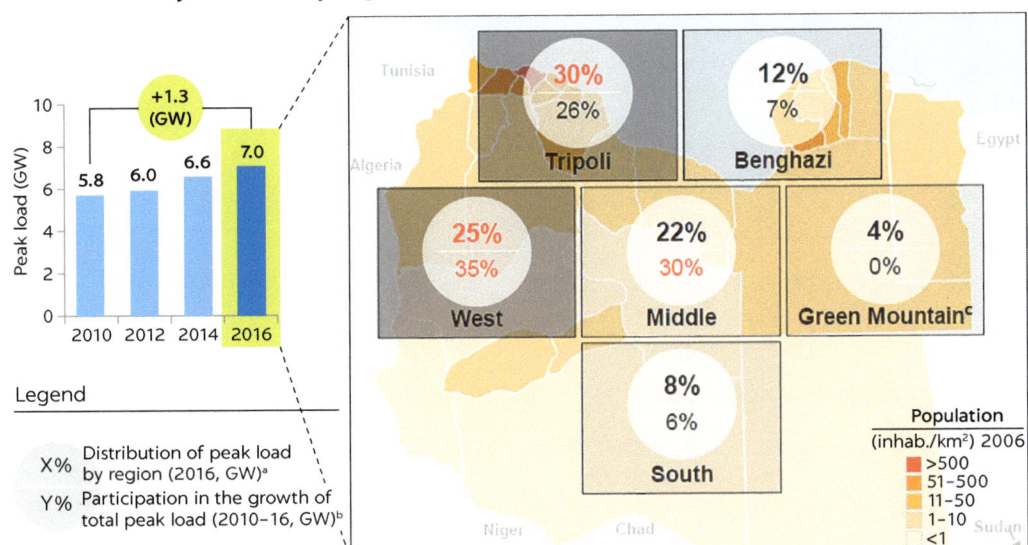

Source: World Bank 2017b, based on General Information Authority of Libya, GECOL data, and Strategy & analysis.
Note: GW = gigawatt; inhab. = inhabitants; km² = square kilometer.
a. [Regional peak (GW)] / [Total peak (GW)].
b. [Regional peak growth (GW)] / [Total peak growth (GW)].
c. No regional growth can be explained by problems with the transmission system (especially in the mountainous region in and around the city of Beida); loads shedding is frequent due to challenging environmental conditions, not yet completed substations and lines, and damages incurred because of clashes.

ANNEX 14B: KEY GENERATION CAPACITY CHARACTERISTICS

Panel b in figure 14B.1 shows no generation in the South. After 2011, this region lacked its own power-generation capacity and faced extensive and prolonged power outages as well as voltage instabilities. In 2019, the long-awaited Ubari power station (640 MW) was commissioned to supply electricity to Libya's Southern and Western regions (Gas to Power Journal 2019).

Generation in the East is limited to two aging steam power plants, both over 30 years old. Their generating units have been severely downrated or put out of service pending major overhauls. The absence of any significant generation in the East and its dependence on the Benghazi North power plant as the sole source of energy when the Eastern and Western power networks were isolated was the major reason for successive blackouts in most of the region. For many years there had been calls and plans for a new power plant in Tobruk, but progress was made only in 2020. Once completed, the plant will have a total power output of more than 650 MW and dual fuel (natural gas or distillate fuel oil) capability (Reuters 2020a). See table 14B.1 for further potential improvements.

MAP 14B.1

Location of GECOL generation assets

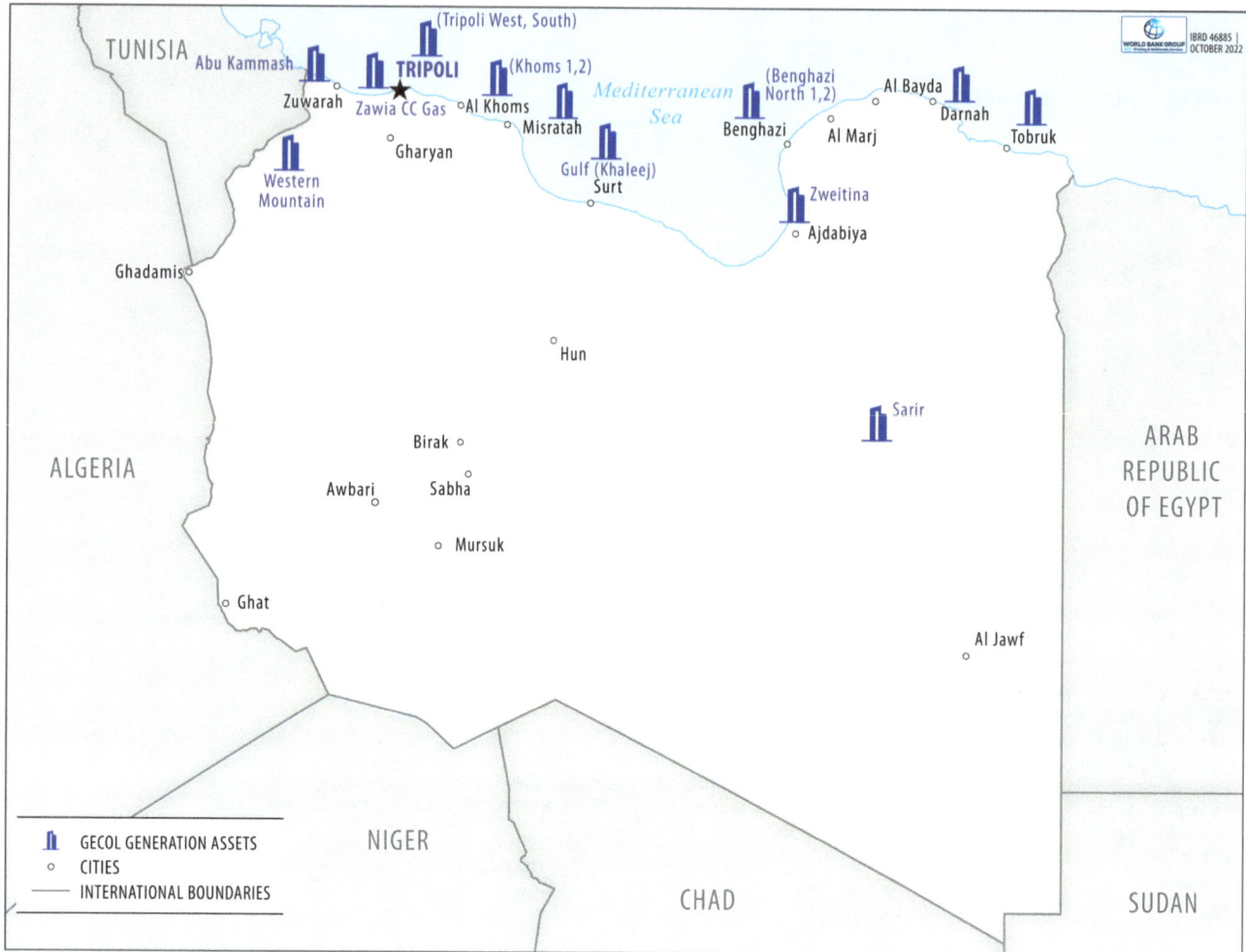

Source: General Electricity Company of Libya (GECOL).

FIGURE 14B.1

GECOL generation assets, by type, age, and region, 2017

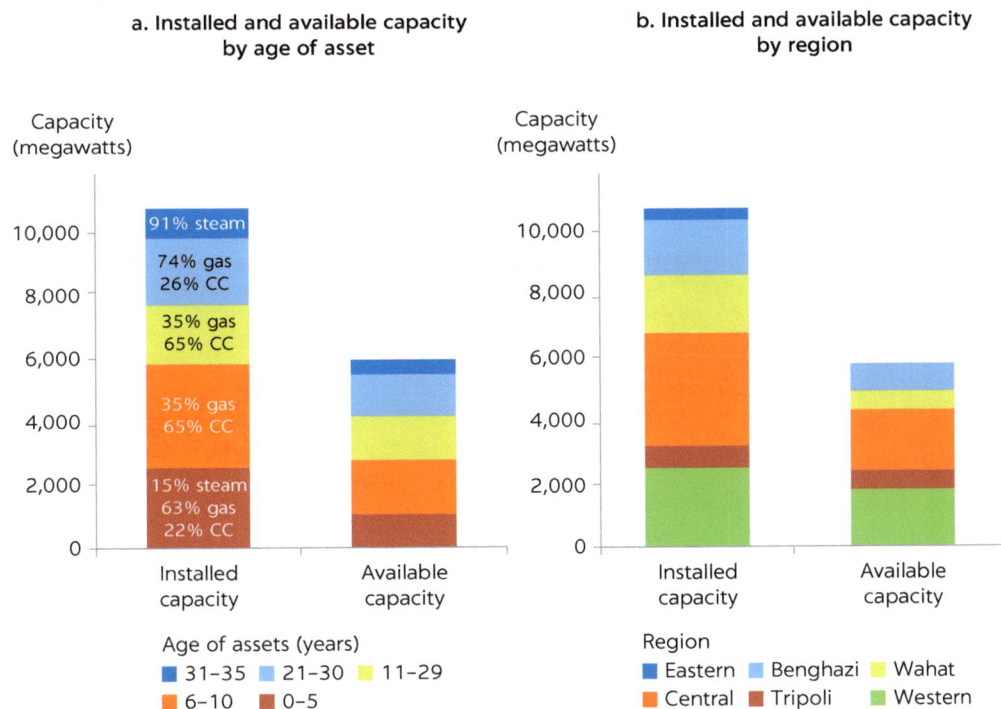

a. Installed and available capacity by age of asset

b. Installed and available capacity by region

Age of assets (years)
- 31–35
- 21–30
- 11–29
- 6–10
- 0–5

Region
- Eastern
- Benghazi
- Wahat
- Central
- Tripoli
- Western

Source: World Bank 2017b.
Note: GECOL = General Electricity Company of Libya.

TABLE 14B.1 **Measures to improve GECOL's performance**

MEASURE	ACTIVITIES
Streamlining (reengineering) processes in the revenue cycle	• Collect data for and maintain a customer master file to include all General Electricity Company of Libya (GECOL) customers connected to the grid.
	• Introduce centralized billing based on advanced monitoring and surveillance technology.
	• Use estimated reading only when the customer's meter is not accessible.
	• Introduce advanced surveillance technology to detect abnormal readings.
	• Conduct systematic field assessments looking for irregular connections and tampered or damaged consumption meters.
	• Introduce penalties for late position settling.
	• Introduce a disconnection policy against nonpaying customers (based on specific criteria and following reminders).
	• Introduce a wider array of billing and payment channels (e-billing via email or text messaging, mobile phone payments).
	• Conduct intensive media campaigns to encourage customers to pay on time.
	• Introduce regular trainings for employees working in cash collection, meter reading, billing, and the accounting system.
Implementing a revenue-protection program	• Install advanced metering infrastructure.
	• Create metering control centers.
	• Introduce state-of-the-art meter data management software and train operators of the metering control centers to systematically monitor consumption by target customers.

continued

TABLE 14B.1, *continued*

MEASURE	ACTIVITIES
Installing smart and prepaid meters	• Identify the customer group for the first rollout with consideration of requirements of the revenue protection program.
	• Pilot test smart-meter technology, data communication technology, system integration requirements, and other technology.
	• Secure client engagement, including commitments from the board and management, on the smart meter rollout plan, financing, and training.
	• Prepare a detailed financing plan, including adequate capital expenditure and staffing.
	• Provide for proper project management and organization, allowing reasonable timeframe for every stage (cost-benefit analysis and regulation from the authorities, tender of the pilot project, pilot and testing by the utility, authorized deployment of smart meters).
Implementing demand-side management (DSM) measures	• Assess the technical potential for DSM.
	• Set DSM objectives, goals, and targets.
	• Identify DSM measures.
	• Design DSM programs and portfolio.
	• Conduct cost-effectiveness analysis and secure DSM funding and board approvals.
	• Develop operational and administrative protocols for selected DSM programs.
	• Pilot test DSM programs.
	• Upscale DSM programs based on results.
	• Conduct evaluation, monitoring, and verification.

Source: World Bank.

ANNEX 14C: ESTIMATING THE LOST VALUE OF ELECTRICITY SUPPLY

Annex 14C quantifies the lost value of electricity from retrospective (backward-looking) and prospective (forward-looking) points of view.

Retrospective analysis

The retrospective analysis relies on data available for 2010–18. It compares recorded data with a counterfactual scenario of political stability. The counterfactual scenario assumes a 6 percent annual growth in electricity supply. This rate of growth is considered realistic given Libya's historical trends (electricity supply grew at an annual rate of 8 percent between 2001 and 2010). The magnitude of the costs of the failure to deliver electricity is assessed as the sum of (1) the value of electricity supply not delivered to meet peak demand (a proxy for the cost of load shedding) and (2) the cost of power outages (blackouts). For both components, a discount rate of 6 percent was used.

For the first component, it is assumed that consumers whose demand for electricity was not met would have been willing to pay the full cost-recovery tariff, estimated at LD 174 per megawatt hour (MWh) for 2021.[5] To be on the conservative side, this figure was reduced to LD 150. At the exchange rate of LD 1.35 per $1.00, the tariff used is $111 per MWh. This cost is not very high for a country in the Middle East and North Africa region once the fossil fuel subsidy component is factored out. However, given the broad base to which this cost was applied—that is, the wide gap between the volume of electricity supplied under normal circumstances and that actually supplied in the conditions of political instability and armed conflict—the total value lost under this component amounts to as much as $8.6 billion in 2018 dollars (table 14C.1).

For the second component, a much higher price ($500 per MWh) was applied. It captures the cost of the inconvenient and urgent alternatives consumers adopted in response to the interruption of power.[6] This rate was applied only to the duration of the blackout time (the number of hours of unplanned power interruptions). Lack of data availability is the greatest constraint for calculations of value lost caused by power outages, as no systematic account of power shortages incidents is available. The estimate—of $7.2 billion—is therefore very tentative and calls for a more detailed look in the future. The total value of the two components is $15.8 billion in 2018 dollars (table 14C.2).

Prospective analysis

The prospective analysis relies on electricity demand projections for 2020–30 from World Bank (2017a) used to develop a least-cost expansion plan for Libya's electricity sector (World Bank 2017e). Scenario A is characterized by continued political instability; scenario B is characterized by political stability. Scenario A is used as a reference scenario to estimate the incremental electricity consumption (scenario B minus scenario A), as a proxy for incremental electricity demand, expressed in gigawatt hours (GWh) per year. Annual growth rates for electricity demand are 4.1 percent in scenario A and 7.5 percent in scenario B.

The incremental demand is then multiplied by a measure of consumers' willingness to pay for it: that is, an electricity tariff fully recovering the production costs of electricity. For 2020, this tariff is assumed to be $116 per MWh, a result of applying a cost escalation factor of 2 percent a year to the 2018 tariff used in the retrospective calculation. The same escalation factor is then used for 2020–30.

TABLE 14C.1 Estimated value of electricity supply not delivered to meet peak demand, 2011–18

Hundreds of millions of US dollars

ITEM	2011	2012	2013	2018	PRESENT VALUE DISCOUNTED BACK FROM 2018 (BASE YEAR) TO 2010
Lost value of electricity	943	241	78	1,903	8,579
Cost of power outages	711	705	780	712	7,189
Total losses	1,654	946	858	2,614	15,768

Source: World Bank.

TABLE 14C.2 Estimated cost of power outages, 2011–18

ITEM	2011	2012	2013	2018
Domestic supply (GWh/year)	25,934	34,322	37,976	34,637
Average domestic supply (GWh/day)	71	94	104	95
Average domestic supply (GWh/hour)	2.96	3.92	4.34	3.95
Incidence of outage (days/year)	20.0	15.0	15.0	15.0
Incidence of outage (hours/year)	480.0	360.0	360.0	360.0
Incidence of outage (hours/day)	1.32	0.99	0.99	0.99
Supply lost (GWh/year)	1,421	1,410	1,561	1,423
Cost of outages (hundreds of millions of US dollars)	711	705	780	712

Source: World Bank.
Note: GWh = gigawatt hours.

Assuming a discount rate of 6 percent, the calculation results in a present value of $9.5 billion over the 10 years from 2020 to 2030. This figure represents the value of electricity supply not delivered to meet peak demand and thus lost to the economy. The cost of power outages was not estimated in the prospective analysis, because of the very high level of uncertainty about the incidence of such events in the future.

ANNEX 14D: ESTIMATED FINANCIAL SAVINGS ASSOCIATED WITH SETTING ELECTRICITY TARIFFS AT COST-RECOVERY LEVELS

Raising the tariff charged by the General Electricity Company of Libya (GECOL) to LD 100 per megawatt hour (MWh) would generate LD 2.6 billion in additional revenue; collections might drop by LD 1.2 billion. The net result would be estimated savings of LD 1.4 billion over 2018–23.

In the report for the World Bank covering all aspects of the Libya electricity sector assessment (World Bank 2017a), PricewaterhouseCoopers considered it prudent to slow the electricity tariff increases (to 63 LD per MWh by 2024, for example) (box 14D.1).

FIGURE 14D.1

Financial impact of tariff increase to LD 100 per megawatt hour by 2023

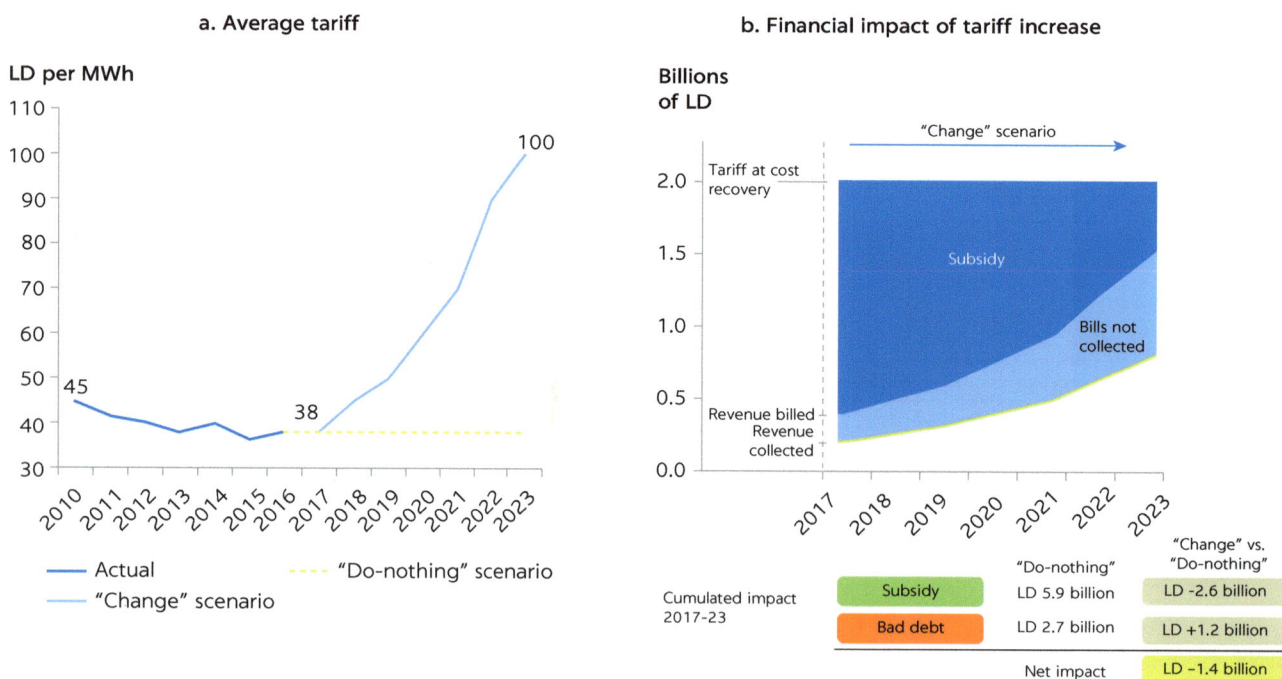

Source: World Bank 2017b.

BOX 14D.1

GECOL's commercial losses from metering, billing, and collection shortfalls

Due to limited metering and billing coverage, GECOL incurred a high level of commercial losses estimated to be LD 2.7 billion during the period from 2010 to 2015.

Metering

- Wide range of nonfunctioning and defective meters within Tripoli and other areas of Libya, causing high-level commercial losses at each voltage level
- Limited meter coverage in other areas compared to Tripoli
- The customers have access to the meters, and the possibilities of manipulations are present
- Widespread illegal connection, which has become a normal habit in Libya
- Inaccurate meter reading due to wide use of estimation
- Location access difficulties that negatively affect meter reading, connection, and disconnection and collections
- Increase of direct cost related to regulate meter reading process (staff, printing, etc.)

Billing

- No regular billing in place for all customer groups
- There are two periods for billing monthly and quarterly for residential customers
- Two billing systems in place (manual and automatic)
- In general, billing process only implemented in Tripoli, while other areas do not have functioning meters nor billing.
- High financial costs of using the traditional method of invoice delivery and print.

Figure B14D.1.1 Commercial losses

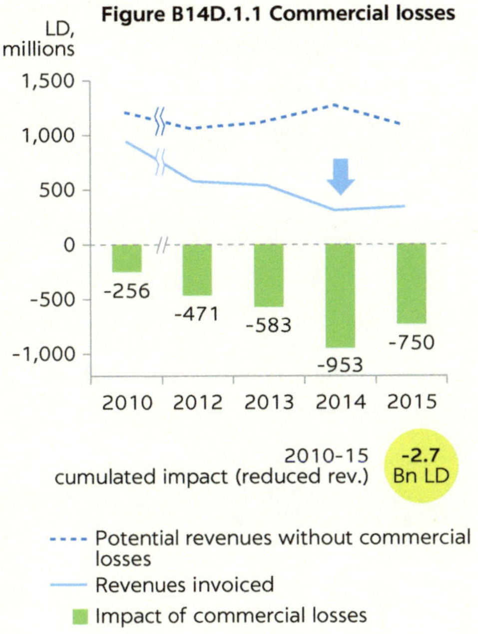

LD, millions

Year	Impact
2010	-256
2012	-471
2013	-583
2014	-953
2015	-750

2010–15 cumulated impact (reduced rev.): **-2.7 Bn LD**

- ---- Potential revenues without commercial losses
- —— Revenues invoiced
- ■ Impact of commercial losses

Due to low collection rates, GECOL incurred an estimated cumulative deficit between invoices and collected revenue of LD 1.6 billion during the period from 2010 to 2015.

Collection

- Each commercial office can set its own ceiling for nonpaying amount. For the last few years, there has been no disconnection for nonpaying clients. Particularly, for individual clients.
- In case of nonpayment, GECOL cuts electricity for institutional clients but for the last few years, it hasn't cut off electricity for individual clients.
- Seven days is the period in which customers are allowed to pay without penalty (but there are no penalties in force).
- Cutting electricity is not currently in force though it is legal as it is stated in the GECOL policy.
- GECOL has no write-offs; it would remain shown in the system, unless a formal resolution is issued to write off those accounts receivable.
- The whole process leads to a high percentage of commercial losses and the difficulty of locating them.
- A Smart Meter pilot project was initiated in 2009 but stopped in 2010 and never continued.

Figure B14D.1.2 Cumulative deficit

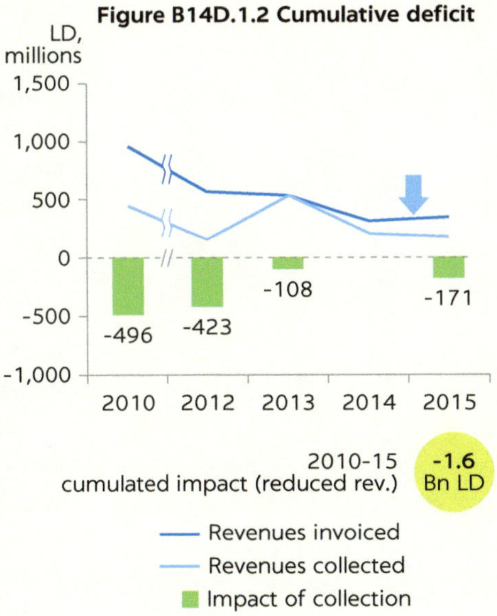

LD, millions

Year	Impact
2010	-496
2012	-423
2013	-108
2015	-171

2010–15 cumulated impact (reduced rev.): **-1.6 Bn LD**

- —— Revenues invoiced
- —— Revenues collected
- ■ Impact of collection

Source: World Bank 2017e.
Note: GECOL = General Electricity Company of Libya.

TABLE 14E.1 Priority interconnection projects

	CAPACITY (MEGAWATTS)			
	INITIAL (AS OF 2018)	ADDED	TOTAL	COMMISSIONING YEAR
Reinforced interconnections				
Libya (Tobruk)–Egypt, Arab Rep. (Saloum Sidi Krir power plant) Stage 1	180	370	550	2025
Libya (Tobruk)–Egypt, Arab Rep. (Saloum) Stage 2		450	1,000	2030
Proposed new interconnections				
Tunisia (Bouchemma)–Libya (Melitia) Stage 1		500	500	2023
Tunisia (Bouchemma)–Libya (Melitia) Stage 2		500	1,000	2027

Source: World Bank.

ANNEX 14E: PRIORITY INTERCONNECTION PROJECTS FOR LIBYA

Libya has been in the orbit of the regional electricity interconnection projects for decades. In 1988, Egypt, Iraq, Jordan, the Syrian Arab Republic, and Turkey initiated an effort to upgrade their electricity systems to a regional standard. They were later joined by Lebanon, Libya, and the West Bank and Gaza, to form the EIJLLPST (Egypt, Iraq, Jordan, Libya, Lebanon, West Bank and Gaza, Syria, and Turkey) regional interconnection (World Bank 2013). Libya was connected with Tunisia in 2002, but the connection is no longer operational, because of stability issues that are under study.

General Electricity Company of Libya (GECOL) management has shown strong interest in the development and growth of the transmission system. Planning was based not just on the requirements to serve the load needs of the Libyan network but also on possible future wheeling of power between Egypt and Tunisia through the Libyan network and wheeling and supply of power to Italy. For these and other reasons, GECOL pushed strongly to introduce a 400 kilovolt (kV) backbone, further reinforcing the 220kV transmission network (World Bank 2017d).

The Value of Trade and Regional Investments study by the World Bank (2021b) identifies priority interconnection projects for Libya. They include transmission capacity reinforcements with Egypt and new interconnections with Tunisia (table 14E.1).

ANNEX 14F: LIBYA'S NATURAL GAS PRODUCTION AND RESERVES

Libya has substantial natural gas production resources along with those of its oil. Map 14F.1 shows the locations of the major oil and gas fields and the related infrastructure.

Libya has been an oil and gas producer since the 1950s. Originally, associated natural gas production represented the bulk of Libya's gas production. Over the past two decades, nonassociated gas fields have come online to support increased domestic demand and pipeline exports to Italy. The advent of the Greenstream Pipeline between Libya and Italy in 2004 led to a large increase in gas export and corresponding growth in production (figure 14F.1, panel a, left-hand axis).

MAP 14F.1

Libyan oil and gas infrastructure

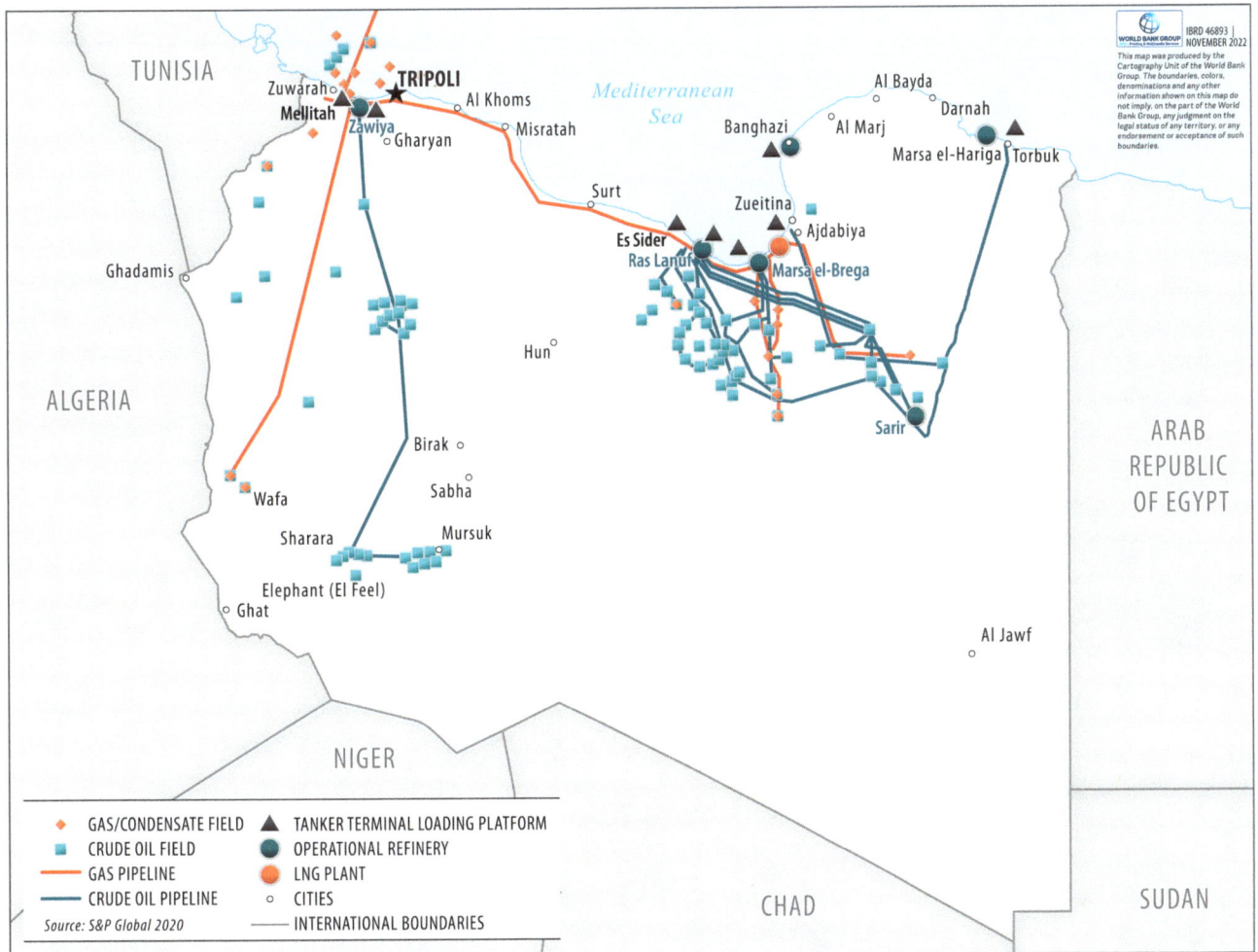

Source: Gupte 2020.
Note: Approximate locations, based on government drawings.

Gas reserves grew steadily from 1980, flattening out in recent years—notably, due to lack of upstream exploration and production in the wake of the 2011 unrest (figure 14F.1, panel a, right-hand axis).

After the sharp decline in 2011, a temporary spike of natural gas production in 2014 was followed by a slight overall downward trend through 2020 (figure 14F.1, panel b).

Gas demand within Libya was relatively limited for many years, with production volumes of 400–600 million cubic feet per day sustaining domestic requirements. Domestic production is expected to grow in the coming years to support new power projects.

Natural gas production and reserves in Libya by 2020

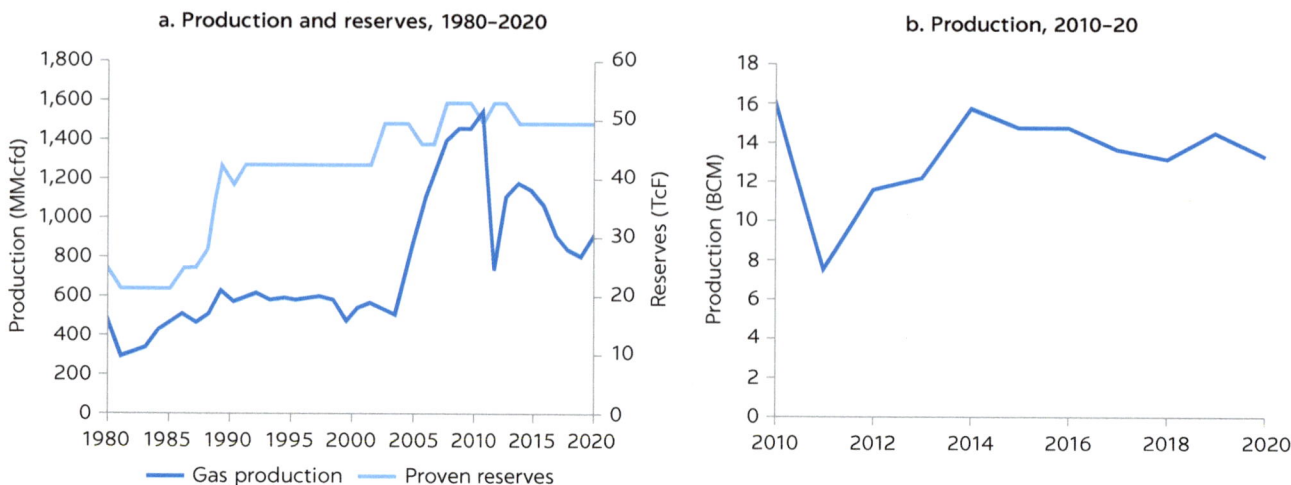

a. Production and reserves, 1980–2020

b. Production, 2010–20

Gas production — Proven reserves

Sources: Panel a, World Bank 2021c; panel b, BP 2021.
Note: BCM = billion cubic meters; MMcfd = million cubic feet per day; Tcf = trillion cubic feet.

NOTES

1. Electricity access rate is still considered close to 100 percent. However, being connected to electricity infrastructure does not guarantee access to electricity at any given moment. Indeed, Libyan consumers have suffered major loss of power in recent years.
2. Based on IEA data. The US Energy Information Administration (EIA) data point to a similar pattern.
3. In addition to the overhead transmission lines, Libya has a growing network of 220kV underground cables, mostly to connect to new 220kV substations located in the heart of its major urban areas such as Benghazi, Misurata, and Tripoli. The underground cable system has been very reliable.
4. A more aggressive assumption would have been a continuation of trend for 2001–10, during which annual growth was 8 percent.
5. The actual tariff during 2010–17 was LD 38–45 per MWh (World Bank 2017f).
6. Using a diesel generator is a typical example of an alternative power supply. When no alternative power supply is readily available, the cost may be even higher (including, for example, the lost income caused by an interrupted business operation, damage to households caused by spoilage of food in refrigerators, and damage to the health of hospital patients).

REFERENCES

Al Jazeera. 2021. "War-weary Libyans Yearn for End to Daily Blackouts." August 29, 2021. https://www.aljazeera.com/news/2021/8/29/war-weary-libyans-yearn-for-end-to-daily-blackouts.

Barltrop, Richard. 2019. *Oil and Gas in a New Libyan Era: Conflict and Continuity*. UK: Oxford Institute for Energy Studies.

BP. 2021. *Statistical Review of World Energy 2021*. London: BP. https://www.bp.com/content/dam/bp/business-sites/en/global/corporate/pdfs/energy-economics/statistical-review/bp-stats-review-2021-full-report.pdf.

Britannica. 2020. "Economy of Libya." In *Encyclopedia Britannica* on-line. https://www.britannica.com/place/Libya/Economy#ref46549.

CNBC. 2020. "Libya's National Oil Corporation Declares Force Majeure on Its Largest Oil Field after Shutdown by Militia." June 10, 2020. https://www.cnbc.com/2020/06/10/libya-state-oil-firm-declares-force-majeure-on-largest-oil-field.html.

EIA (Energy Information Administration). 2020. Database. Washington, DC: EIA. https://www
.eia.gov/international/data/world#/?pa=0000002&c=ruvvvvvfvtvnvv1urvvvvfvvvvvvfvvvo
u20evvvvvvvvvvnvvuvo&ct=0&tl_id=2-A&vs=INTL.2-2-AFG-BKWH.A&cy=2016&vo=0&v
=H&start=2010&end=2017.

Gas to Power Journal. 2019. "GECOL Connects Fourth Unit of Ubari Power Station to the Grid."
July 15. https://www.gastopowerjournal.com/itemlist/tag/Ubari.

Gupte, Eklavya. 2020. "Map: Libya's Oil and Gas Infrastructure." *Insight* (blog), S&P Global,
January 29, 2020. https://www.spglobal.com/commodityinsights/en/market-insights
/blogs/oil/012920-map-libyas-oil-and-gas-infrastructure.

IEA (International Energy Agency). 2020. Data and Statistics (database). Vienna. https://www
.iea.org/data-and-statistics.

IEA (International Energy Agency). 2021. Data and Statistics (database). Vienna: IEA. https://
www.iea.org/reports/sdg7-data-and-projections/access-to-electricity.

Libya Herald. 2021. "Government Approves Electricity Spending on Stations Overhauls."
July 12, 2021. https://libyaherald.com/2021/07/government-approves-electricity
-spending-on-stations-overhauls-40-mobile-generators-and-57000-telegraph-poles/.

Policy Corner. 2021. "Libya—A Potential Powerhouse for Clean Energy." August 16, 2020.
https://www.policycorner.org/en/2021/08/16/libya-a-potential-powerhouse
-for-clean-energy/.

Reuters. 2020a. "Announcement: Mytilineos Relaunching Construction of Power Plant in
Tobruk," November 30, 2020. https://www.reuters.com/article/announcement
-mytilineos-relaunching-cons-idAFL8N2IG220.

Reuters. 2020b. "Protests Flare in Libya's Benghazi over Power Cuts, Living Conditions."
September 10, 2020. https://www.reuters.com/article/us-libya-security-protests/protests
-flare-in-libyas-benghazi-over-power-cuts-living-conditions-idUSKBN2613MX.

UNSMIL (United Nations Support Mission in Libya). 2021. "Economic Working Group
Discusses Plan to Address Electricity Crisis with Libyan Electricity Company Leadership."
Updated October 6, 2021. Tripoli: UNSMIL. https://unsmil.unmissions.org/economic
-working-group-discusses-plan-address-electricity-crisis-libyan-electricity-company.

World Bank. 2013. *Middle East and North Africa: Integration of Electricity Networks in the Arab
World: Regional Market Structure and Design.* Washington, DC: World Bank. https://
openknowledge.worldbank.org/handle/10986/19329.

World Bank. 2017a. *Supporting Electricity Sector Reform in Libya, Task A: Sector Performance and
Structural Sector Reform, Deliverable 2: Rapid Assessment of the Sector Performance.*
Washington, DC: World Bank. http://documents1.worldbank.org/curated/en
/315261527073425670/pdf/01-Task-A-Rapid-Assessment-of-the-Sector-Performance.pdf.

World Bank. 2017b. *Supporting Electricity Sector Reform in Libya, Task C: Institutional
Development and Performance Improvement of GECOL.* Final report December 14, 2017.
Washington, DC: World Bank. http://documents1.worldbank.org/curated
/en/193171527061676535/pdf/08-Task-C-Improving-GECOL-Technical-Performance.pdf.

World Bank. 2017c. *Supporting Electricity Sector Reform in Libya, Task A: Sector Performance
and Structural Sector Reform: Options Study for GECOL Restructuring.* September, 2017.
Washington, DC: World Bank. http://documents1.worldbank.org/curated
/ar/647381527074345716/pdf/task-A-sector-performance-and-structural-sector-reform
-deliverable-4-1-options-study-for-GECOL-restructuring-report.pdf.

World Bank. 2017d. *Libya: Supporting Electricity Sector Reform, Task D: Strategic Plan for
Renewable Energy Development: Least-cost Expansion Plan: Energy Mix and Renewable
Resource Assessment.* Washington, DC: World Bank. http://documents1.worldbank.org
/curated/en/118971537999946577/pdf/02-Libya-LCEP-Final-Report.pdf.

World Bank. 2017e. *Libya: Supporting Electricity Sector Reform: Customer Service Financial
Performance.* Washington, DC: World Bank.

World Bank. 2017f. *Supporting Electricity Sector Reform in Libya, Task A: Electricity Act and
Sector Restructuring.* Washington, DC: World Bank. http://documents1.worldbank.org
/curated/en/509201527048436472/pdf/Task-A-sector-performance-and-structural-sector
-reform-deliverable-3-2-electricity-act-and-sector-restructuring.pdf.

World Bank. 2017g. *Supporting Electricity Sector Reform in Libya, Task A: Sector Performance and
Structural Sector Reform: Project Review and Recommendations.* Washington, DC: World Bank.

http://documents1.worldbank.org/curated/en/647381527074345716/pdf/task-A-sector
-performance-and-structural-sector-reform-deliverable-4-1-options-study-for-GECOL
-restructuring-report.pdf.

World Bank. 2021a. "The World Bank in Libya." Updated October 6, 2021. Washington, DC:
World Bank. https://www.worldbank.org/en/country/libya/overview#1.

World Bank. 2021b. *The Value of Trade and Regional Investments in the Pan-Arab Electricity
Market: Integrating Power Systems and Building Economies.* Washington, DC: World Bank.
https://openknowledge.worldbank.org/handle/10986/36614.

World Bank. 2021c. *Commercial Structuring and Project Development Roadmap for LNG Import:
Supporting LNG Import Facility Project Preparation in Libya.* Washington, DC: World Bank.

Zaptia, Samia. 2019a. "Audit Bureau to Identify Real Causes of Libya's Crippling Power Cuts
within Ten Days." *Libya Herald,* October 2, 2019. https://www.libyaherald.com/2019/10/02
/audit-bureau-to-identify-real-causes-of-libyas-crippling-power-cuts-within-ten-days/.

Zaptia, Samia. 2019b. "GECOL on Defensive in Heated Press Conference to Explain Chronic
Power Cuts." *Libya Herald,* July 16, 2019. https://www.libyaherald.com/2019/07/16/gecol
-on-defensive-in-heated-press-conference-to-explain-cronic-power-cuts/.

15 Degradation of the Water Sector during Libya's Armed Conflict

IYAD RAMMAL AND SIXTO A. REQUENA

World Bank

Water infrastructure in Libya has suffered considerable damage over the past decade because of targeted attacks, impairing its productive and service capacity and increasing water infrastructure operating costs. Before the armed conflict, about 95 percent of the population had good-quality water services; today, only 64 percent of people have access to safe drinking water. In addition, budget allocation for critical inputs, including chemicals and energy, have been significantly reduced, resulting in diminished services and deterioration of infrastructure assets from lack of proper maintenance.

INTRODUCTION

Libya is among the world's most water-scarce countries, with an average renewable water endowment of about 100 cubic meters per person per year—one-tenth the internationally adopted scarcity threshold. The Man-Made River Project (MMRP), which pumps fossil water from southern Libya, provides roughly 60 percent of the country's supplied drinking water; the rest comes from other groundwater sources (30 percent) and desalination (10 percent) (Aldeeb 2019). Network losses were estimated at 35–55 percent in 2012; given that no investments have been made since then, the figure is probably even higher today. Just 54 percent of the population was connected to water and 45 percent to sanitation in 2019 (Elsonni 2019). Most wastewater treatment plants are out of order, with serious implications for public health. All desalination plants suffer acute shortages of chemicals and spare parts. Together with their aging, these shortages mean that they function at less than 25 percent of design capacities (Alrwaimi 2019).

This chapter examines the costs of the armed conflict on the water sector and estimates what it would take to effect recovery. The first section provides an overview of the sector; the second section looks at the economics of water; the third section focuses on water shortages in the context of the financial and economic cots of war; the fourth assesses damage to water infrastructure; the fifth section examines sector recovery and investment; the sixth identifies challenges, opportunities, and recommendations; and the last section offers some concluding remarks.

OVERVIEW OF THE WATER SECTOR

Institutional responsibilities and legal framework

During the armed conflict that followed the 2011 revolution, the General Authority for Water Resources (GAWR) continued to be in charge of overall water resources management, strategic planning, and policy making. Since then, responsibility for executing strategies, plans, and projects has been shared mainly by three state-owned national monopolies: the General Company for Water and Wastewater (GCWW), the authority for the MMRP, and the General Company for Desalination (GCD).[1] Each monopoly has regional subsidiaries and operating units. The institutional framework also includes the Joint Authority for the Study and Development of the Nubian Sandstone Aquifer System (NSAS), which includes Chad, the Arab Republic of Egypt, and Sudan along with Libya.[2]

With the exception of GAWR, whose functions were reassigned to report to the Ministry of Water Resources (established in 2014), the functions and responsibilities of the three executive water agencies are ruled by laws and regulations passed before the 2011 revolution,[3] including the laws that created them.[4] These laws and regulations established them as public utilities, organized as autonomous corporate bodies. Each of the three utilities has had large capital expenditures financed by the national budget for the construction of their infrastructure for service delivery, halted during the armed conflict. They are nevertheless expected to deliver their water supply service functions while covering operations and maintenance (O&M) costs out of revenues collected from end water users.

Key issues in water resources management

To face extreme renewable water scarcity, Libya developed massive underground infrastructure for fossil water source utilization under the MMRP Authority (box 15.1). The significant damage it suffered during the armed conflict has impaired its productive capacity and raised its O&M costs. Water infrastructure, especially under the MMRP, is vulnerable to targeted attacks that could easily disable its production and delivery capacity, as shown repeatedly by shutdowns effected by militia groups. The lack of proper maintenance—the result of unpredictable budget allocations—could also inflict major financial and economic losses.

Amid MMRP water supply disruptions, especially after 2014, water demand resulted in overabstraction of groundwater in the northern coastal aquifers, causing seawater intrusion and degrading water quality and soil fertility. Tariffs paid by the GCWW for water from the MMRP and the GCD and tariffs collected by GCWW for water service delivery to end customers are well below costs, with a large proportion of their budgets subsidized by the National Treasury.

Water sector budgets during the armed conflict

A major effect of the armed conflict has been the suppression of economic growth and the unpredictability of fiscal expenditures because of disrupted hydrocarbon-sector government revenues, whose oil prices have also been worsened by the COVID-19 pandemic. Confronted with slower economic growth and lower government revenue, Libyan Treasury authorities resorted to debt financing and attempted to constrain expenditures as much as possible.

BOX 15.1

Libya's Man-Made River Project

The Man-Made Project Authority (MMPA) was established in 1983 to implement the Great Man-Made River Project (MMRP), which is a big water network pipeline to transfer fresh water from ancient underground aquifers (400–800 meters deep) in the Sahara in the southwest over about 4,000 kilometers to the coast of Libya in the north for domestic use, agriculture, and industry. It was called as the largest irrigation project in the world. The project's total cost until the end of 2017 was reported by the MMRA to be LD 12.4 billion (about $8.9 billion). The completion of Phase 1 was formally celebrated at Benghazi in 1991 and can transfer 2 million cubic meters of water per day through some 1,600 km of double pipeline.

Phase 2 with a design capacity of 2.5 million cubic meters of water a day started supplying western Libya in 1996, while another pipeline goes north and east to the coast and turns west supplying some cities, including Tripoli.

Phase 3, with 1,200 kilometers of pipeline, was divided into two parts: (1) part one was an expansion to phase I with an additional 700 kilometers of new pipelines to increase the daily supply capacity of the existing system to 3.68 million cubic meters.

The project also includes two additional phases (4 and 5). The total capacity of the MMRP with all phases built would be some 6.5 million cubic meters of water per day.

Source: GMR (Great Man-Made River) Water Supply Project. Water Technology. https://www.water-technology.net/projects/gmr.

TABLE 15.1 **Budget approved and authorized, General Company for Water and Wastewater, 2018**

ITEM	BUDGET (MILLIONS OF DOLLARS)		
	APPROVED	AUTHORIZED	PERCENT AUTHORIZED
Salaries and administrative expenses	199.0	190.2	96
Water supply and energy expenditures	50.4	6.6	13
Other operations and maintenance expenses	16.8	5.7	34
Capital expenditures	18.6	1.0	6
Arrears from previous years	74.6	0.00	0
Total	359.4	203.5	57

Source: General Company for Water and Wastewater budget.
Note: Rate of exchange is LD 1.36 per dollar.

For 2018, for example, the budget approved for the GCWW was $359.4 million, and the budget authorized to be actually spent was $203.5 million (table 15.1). Salaries to staff were largely unaffected by cuts (96 percent was authorized for payment); in contrast, just 6 percent of the budget for capital expenditures was authorized. The 2018 GCWW budget authorized only 13 percent of its spending for water supplies (from the MMRP and the GCD) and energy supplies; it authorized 34 percent for operating expenses.

Limited GCWW-authorized payments to third parties for water supply, energy, and other operating expenses have resulted in low capacity utilization of GCWW infrastructure and frequent interruptions. It has also had a domino effect on the performance of the MMRP, the GCD, and the General Electric

Company of Libya (GECOL). Not being paid for the water they delivered to the GCWW, both the MMRP and the GCD had no recourse but to cut their own operational expenses and reduce production well below design capacity; not being paid for the electricity it delivered, GECOL had no recourse but to stop supplying electricity to the GCWW—a crucial input for operating various components of its distribution networks, including pumping stations, tube-wells, and water treatment plants.

Water supply and sanitation

In 2011, about 95 percent of people in urban areas and 90 percent in rural areas had access to adequate drinking water in Libya. Access to sanitation was at 60 percent in urban areas and 40 percent in rural areas. In 2019, only 64 percent of people had access to safe drinking water.[5] Water shortages in Libya's main urban centers, especially Tripoli and its surroundings, became frequent beginning in 2015 and worsened significantly during the spring and summer of 2019, when damage to water supply infrastructure was used to trigger the liberation of opposition prisoners.[6]

Assuming 174 liters per capita per day and 50 percent distribution losses, total water demand in urban areas was about 719 million cubic meters in 2019. To supply this water, every year the GCWW purchases 380 million cubic meters of drinking water from the MMRP (53 percent) and 28 million cubic meters from the GCD (28 percent); it produces the balance of 311 million cubic meters (43 percent) at well-desalination water treatment plants and tube-wells. However, most of the GCWW's desalination water treatment plants are out of use, producing about 3,000 cubic meters a day, a fraction of the total 73,100 cubic meters a day they were designed to produce. Similarly, only 1,591 of GCWW's 2,964 wells are operational; the rest need urgent maintenance.

In 2020, water service provision in major urban centers was limited to 8–10 hours a day, with some episodes lasting just 3 hours.[7] Extreme rationing began in 2015; it became acute in the summer of 2019, when supply from the MMRP stopped flowing to Tripoli for two days.

The rates per cubic meter paid by the GCWW to the MMRP ($0.058) and the GCD ($0.20) are well below their production costs of $0.50 and $0.76, respectively. The rates charged by the GCWW to final customers are also low; revenues from water tariffs paid by end users cover only about 7 percent of the budget.[8] The GCWW collects wastewater in most urban areas through its sewage collection networks. It is supposed to treat wastewater at 75 wastewater treatment plants in main urban centers (CEDARE 2014), but only 10 are reported to be operational (UNICEF 2019). Sewerage networks are old and suffer frequent blockages.

Lower capacity utilization raises unit costs. The costs of production of the three monopolies have been going up while their revenues were going down. Lack of funding for proper maintenance of the distribution network has caused increased physical losses.

Water for irrigation

Libya has about 2.35 million hectares (ha) of arable land and 470,000 ha developed for irrigation, of which an estimated 316,000 ha is actually irrigated (Siebert et al. 2013). Total water demand for irrigation is about 4,961 million cubic meters a year, supplied by groundwater sources (well-fields and the MMRP) (92 percent), surface sources (7 percent), and treated wastewater (1 percent).

More than 85 percent of irrigated lands are located along the Mediterranean Sea, mostly in the northwest, near Tripoli (including the Jefara Plain system) and the northeast around Benghazi (including the Jabal Akhdar system). Both the Jefara Plain and the Jabal Akhdar systems have rainfall and local well-fields, but irrigation demand for water surpasses their supplies. It is estimated that annual demand for water in the irrigation schemes along the Mediterranean is about 4,217 million cubic meters and that the annual local availability of water is about 2,228 million cubic meters (table 15.2). The balance (1,989 million cubic meters a year) is transferred from the distant Mursuk and Kufra-Sarir basins using infrastructure deployed in phases 1 and 2 of the MMRP (see map 15.1). Government-led pilot irrigation schemes are also implemented in the southern deserts.

The well-fields of the MMRP are located 2,820 kilometers away from the irrigation demand centers, in the Nubian Sandstone Aquifer system, the southeast (AlKufra and Tazirbu), and the southwest (Jabal Hassauna well-fields). The MMRP started to suffer the consequences of the armed conflict in early 2014. It suffers frequent interruptions. In the north, irrigation schemes are overextracting groundwater, causing drops in water tables and seawater intrusions.

The water balance

Libya is a desert country that has always confronted water scarcity. Annual water availability rose from about 2.18 billion cubic meters in 1990 to 2.9 billion cubic meters in 1995 and 3.8 billion cubic meters in 2000 (table 15.3). After 2000, no substantive increase in water availability has occurred. Annual demand for water rose from 3.5 billion cubic meters in 1990 to 3.9 billion cubic meters by 1995 and 4.5 billion cubic meters in 2000. In 2020, demand is estimated at about 7. 2 billion cubic meters, and it is expected to reach 8 billion cubic meters by 2025. After improving significantly during the 1990s—thanks to the start-up of MMRP phase 1 in 1993 and MMRP phase 2 in 1996—the water balance has deteriorated every year since 2000, when it was –673 million cubic meters. In 2020, it reached –3.4 billion cubic meters.

Demand for water has increased as a result of population growth and increased economic activity. Per capita income peaked at $12,065 in 2010. To feed such increased population and support increased economic activities,

TABLE 15.2 **Demand for and supply of irrigation water, 2019**

Million cubic meters

SCHEME	DEMAND	SUPPLY			
		LOCALLY AVAILABLE			
		SURFACE	WASTEWATER TREATMENT PLANT	WELL-FIELDS	MMRP
Northern irrigation schemes	4,217	352	47	1,829	1,989
Other schemes, including oases	744	0	0	744	0
Total	4,961	352	47	2,573	1,989

Source: Demand is based on actual irrigated areas reported by FAO 2016.
Note: MMRP = Man-Made River Project.

TABLE 15.3 **Actual and projected supply of and demand for water, 1990–2025**

ITEM	1990	1995	2000	2005	2010	2015	2020	2025
Total supply and demand (million cubic meters)								
Supply	2,178	2,908	3,820	3,820	3,820	3,820	3,820	3,820
Supply excluding MMRP	2,178	2,178	2,178	2,178	2,178	2,178	2,178	2,178
Demand	3,485	3,885	4,493	5,128	5,794	6,495	7,236	8,022
Balance	−1,308	−978	−673	−1,308	−1,974	−2,675	−3,416	−4,202
Per capita supply and demand (million cubic meters)								
Supply	491	588	713	659	616	595	556	526
Supply excluding MMRP	491	440	406	376	351	339	317	300
Demand	786	785	839	884	935	1,012	1,053	1,114
Libyan population (millions)	4.44	4.95	5.36	5.80	6.20	6.42	6.87	7.27
GDP per capita (constant 2010 dollars)	n.a.	n.a.	8,964	10,643	12,065	5,900	6,092	n.a.

Source: Based on information in the presentation by the General Authority for Water Resources (GAWR) to the United Nations Support Mission in Libya, March 2019. Libyan population and GDP per capita are from the World Bank database.
Note: As a result of the armed conflict, actual water supply is believed to be less than shown in this table. GDP = gross domestic product; MMRP = Man-Made River Project; n.a. = not available.

Libya would need about 7.2 billion cubic meters of water a year in 2020, 3.4 billion cubic meters more than it produces.[9] It is estimated that more than 150,000 ha of land prepared for irrigated agriculture in Libya are not in use.

THE ECONOMICS OF THE WATER SECTOR AND THE COST OF WAR

Economic and social development and the construction of water infrastructure

Confronted with water scarcity and the need to increase the supply of water to support economic and social development in the 1970s and 1980s, the government undertook massive water infrastructure investments, estimated at about $41 billion, most of them between 1983 and 2010 (table 15.4).[10] Investments included the MMRP, desalination plants, water treatment plants, water distribution networks in urban centers, and wastewater treatment plants. Most of the investment projects were implemented to increase water supply for irrigation along the Mediterranean coast.[11] The government was able to pay for these investments thanks to the oil and gas boom that began in the 1960s. Implementation of the investment programs in the water sector was halted in 2020.

The Man-Made River Project

The MMRP is a highly complex water transfer system conceived to include 1,300 wells located in the Kufra-Sarir, Mursuk, Al-Jaghbub and Al-Kufra, Hamada, and the extension of the Mursuk basins, to be deployed sequentially in five phases.[12] Each well was expected to produce an average of 8,640 cubic meters of water a day, feeding the water transfer systems illustrated in map 15.1.

TABLE 15.4 Infrastructure investments, production capacity, and capacity utilization of infrastructure built between 1983 and 2010

TYPE OF INFRASTRUCTURE	INVESTMENT (MILLIONS OF DOLLARS)	ANNUAL CAPACITY (MILLION CUBIC METERS)		CAPACITY UTILIZATION (PERCENT)
		DESIGN	ACTUAL 2019	
Man-Made River Project (MMRP)	30,000	2,373	840	35
Desalination plants	1,060	192	56	29
Water treatment plants and distribution networks	8,100	199	100	50
Wastewater treatment plants	1,871	235	47	20
Total	41,031	2,998	1,042	35

Source: Preliminary investment estimates based on information from UNICEF 2019. Capacity and capacity utilization estimates are based on information from the General Authority for Water Resources (GAWR).

MAP 15.1

The Man-Made River Project

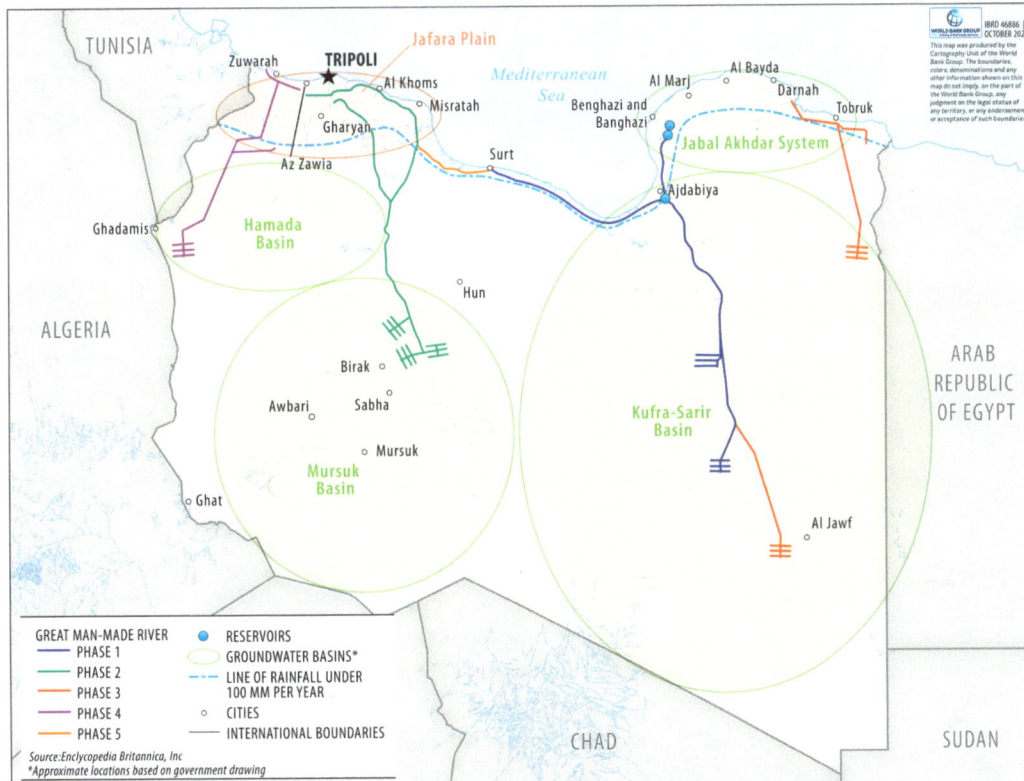

Source: Original compilation of information from the government for this publication.

Powered by energy-intensive pumping stations and aided by state-of-the-art information and communications technologies, water from the well-fields in the desert was expected to travel about 4,000 kilometers, through four-meter diameter pipes, before reaching the demand centers on the Mediterranean coast. The pipes were produced by two factories designed and installed in Marsa-Brega (south of Benghazi) as a subproject of the MMRP.

The factories were expected to continue production of spare pipes. MMRP had a total investment cost of $30 billion, with a design capacity of 2,373 million cubic meters a year. In 2011, capacity utilization was 50 percent. Phases 4 and 5—which are still to be completed—will supply water for other areas in the northwest and northeast areas in Libya.

Desalination plants

Libya was an early adopter of desalination technologies, including multi-effect distillation, thermal vapor compression, and multistage-flash and reverse osmosis. It invested $1.06 billion in these technologies between 1977 and 2010, for a capacity of 192 million cubic meters a year. In 2019, capacity utilization was 29 percent.

Water treatment plants

Water treatment plants and distribution networks for supplying drinking water to the growing urban population, most of which lives on the Mediterranean coast, were put in place between 1977 and 2010, at a total investment cost of $8.1 billion. Total installed capacity is 199 million cubic meters a year. In 2019, capacity utilization was about 50 percent.

Wastewater treatment plants

Confronted with water scarcity, Libya wanted to treat used water in urban centers to be reused in fruit-tree growing. Toward that end, it invested $1.8 billion between 1977 and 2010, building wastewater treatment plants with total installed capacity of 235 million cubic meters a year. In 2019, wastewater treatment plant capacity utilization was about 20 percent.

The costs and financing of water services, 2019–20

In 2019, it cost Libya about $710 million to operate and maintain the water infrastructure described in the previous section. Energy costs were the largest expense, at $338.5 million, most of them accounted for by the MMRP, which used a large amount of electricity to operate the pumping stations of its water transfer systems. The second-largest expense was labor, estimated at $207.7 million, most of it accounted for by the GCWW, which employed more than 15,000 people.[13] The third-largest expense was materials for O&M of the infrastructure under the three water utilities (the MMRP, the GCWW, and the GCD), at $163.9 million.[14]

The government paid for 83 percent of these expenses ($586.9 million); the rest ($123.1 million) was paid for with tariff revenues. As a result of the armed conflict, both water tariff revenues and government support to the companies have decreased, reducing the production of water, which subsequently affected water tariff revenues. The government's contribution has also been reduced, as a result of lower production of oil, the main source of income for the government.

WATER SHORTAGES, UNMET DEMANDS, AND THE FINANCIAL AND ECONOMIC COSTS OF WAR

Water shortages in urban centers have become daily events since the onset of the armed conflict. Water service shortages gradually extended to all main urban areas, including Tripoli and Benghazi, as the duration of water supply service decreased from 24 hours a day seven days a week to 8 hours or less per day in 2020. Tripoli and Benghazi have to go without water every time there is a power blackout, which happens frequently. As water shortages became daily events, urban populations' unmet demands for water forced them to look for alternative sources, including bottled water and bulk water from water vendors.

The supply of water for irrigating farms along the Mediterranean coast has decreased since 2011. At the outset of the armed conflict, agriculture production cost increased, as farmers overabstracted water from their local well-fields to compensate for shortages of water from the MMRP; as a result, water tables fell drastically, increasing pumping costs, creating seawater intrusion, and reducing land productivity.

The production capacity of the MMRP was first impaired by the 2011 bombing of the Brega pipe factory, which produces spare pipes. Later, frequent power blackouts impeded normal pumping operations and forced the MMRP to lower its production capacity. Beginning in 2014, major components of the MMRP started to fail because of limited international expertise for specialized maintenance and software updates.

As a result of unmet demands, urban dwellers and irrigation farmers have incurred financial and economic losses. Financial losses by urban dwellers are the additional expenses they had to incur to get water services from alternative sources. The share of the population affected by extreme rationing is believed to have risen from 5 percent in 2012 to 20 percent by 2019, according to Omar Salem, head of the executive committee of the GAWR. To confront extreme rationing, urban dwellers had to purchase bulk water from private vendors. As the quality of service deteriorated, urban dwellers facing extreme water rationing purchased an average half a bottle of water per capita per day. The financial cost of the armed conflict to urban dwellers is estimated to be at least $1.32 billion since the 2011 revolution, of which $296 million was incurred in 2019 (table 15.5).[15]

The financial losses for irrigation farmers are the additional financial expenses they had to incur to operate local pumps. This expense is the only one included in the estimate of financial losses of about $349 million during the armed conflict in the irrigation sector; farmers may also have reduced their output and sales of produce and hence lost revenues.

The financial losses to the MMRP, estimated at $581 million, are based on the increased unit cost of production and reduced sales of water services to the GCWW and irrigation schemes.[16]

Since 2012, the total financial cost of war in the water sector and from damage during the armed conflict is about $2.25 billion, an average of at least $281 million a year (table 15.5).

TABLE 15.5 **Financial costs of armed conflict in the water sector, 2012–19**

Millions of dollars

LOSS	2012	2013	2014	2015	2016	2017	2018	2019	2012–19
Urban population financial losses	81	102	123	145	167	190	213	296	1,316
Irrigation farmers financial losses	0	12	25	37	50	62	75	87	349
MMRP financial losses	n.a.	25	48	69	87	104	118	130	581
Total financial losses	81	139	196	251	304	356	406	514	2,246

Source: World Bank.
Note: MMRP = Man-Made River Project; n.a. = not available.

The economic cost of the armed conflict for the water sector has not been estimated. It is probably several orders of magnitude greater than the estimated financial losses. The economic cost of the armed conflict for the water sector would include the following:

- Disability-adjusted life years lost to the disease burden (ill health, disability, early death) caused by the proliferation of waterborne diseases because of lack of water; intermittent or low-quality running water; pumping costs; storage facilities; time spent waiting for water vendors to come to deliver water to households; and similar costs
- Degradation of lands because of overabstraction of groundwater, the cost to consumers of higher food prices, and the cost of lost employment opportunities
- Severe damage inflicted to the MMRP by war and the accelerated degradation of water infrastructure because of lack of spare parts and proper maintenance
- Correction for the price distortion of low tariffs and the low cost of inputs (especially the cost of energy at $0.03 per kilowatt hour).

Increases in production and service delivery costs during the armed conflict

The unit costs per cubic meter at market prices of the MMRP rose from $0.21 in 2011 to $0.26 in 2020, an increase of about 25 percent. The increase mainly reflects MMRP's loss of economies of scale by operating at 50 percent capacity utilization.

Desalination plants have decreased production drastically; average capacity utilization of desalination plants is estimated at 29 percent (Alrwaimi 2019). The major cause of increased costs has been the lack of maintenance of distribution networks, which has increaesd the volume of water lost in the distribution network. In addition, in the presence of rationing, frequent stop and start-up of operations causes high pressure in the distribution pipes that has increased the volume of water lost in the network. These losses increase the unit cost of distributed water to final users by about 40 percent (from the GCWW financial statement 2019). This cost increase should be attributed to the armed conflict, because lack of proper maintenance and rationing is one of its consequences.

DAMAGE TO AND DESTRUCTION OF PHYSICAL INFRASTRUCTURE

Water and sanitation facilities have been affected by the conflict, through damage and poor O&M as a result of lack of cash to purchase consumables and spare parts, in addition to lack of local capacity. This section describes these effects.

The Man-Made River Project

Before 2014, the infrastructure of the MMRP was in very good condition (despite the 2011 attack on the Brega Marsa pipe plant), as it was designed and constructed to high quality standards. All imported equipment was almost new and regularly maintained before the 2011 revolution. Some components of the MMRP deteriorated after 2014, as a result of the armed conflict and political and institutional instability. The value of damage and losses is estimated at $422.8 million (table 15.6). This estimate does not include the cost of lack of maintenance, which is likely to be high, as a result of the lack of spare parts and the failure to undertake periodic and emergency maintenance operations.

The General Company for Water and Wastewater

The GCWW and its employees in many areas, especially Tripoli, have been exposed to serious threats. Its infrastructure suffered damage and destruction as a result of several factors, including insecurity (burglary, vandalism, theft, and looting); direct exposure to the armed conflict; and loss of working hours as a result of insecurity at work sites and disruption of service offices. Material losses, itemized in table 15.7, totalled about $36.5 million; other losses are estimated at $73.8 million, yielding a total of $110.3 million. These figures do not include the costs associated with lack of maintenance, which is likely to be high, as the GCWW is experiencing rapid deterioration as a result of the lack of spare parts and the failure to undertake routine and emergency maintenance operations.

TABLE 15.6 **Estimated damage and losses to the Man-Made River Project infrastructure from armed conflict, 2020**

TYPE OF LOSS	ESTIMATED LOSS (MILLIONS OF DOLLARS)
Destruction of the Al-Nahr Company (MMRP), workshop facilities and headquarters, and the Brega pipe manufacturing plant	294.1
Destruction of 150 production wells; tampering with wellhead components, transformers, control units, communications system, and electricity cables	58.8
Destruction of parts of the headquarters building, maintenance workshops, operating and handling mechanisms, and central valve workshops	36.8
Destruction of seven substations and transformers	14.7
Damage to components of the systems, including substations in the well-fields, a result of recurring interruptions to public electricity network	14.7
Destruction of valve chambers, as a result of illegal connections, and damage to vacuum valves	3.7
Total	422.8

Source: Data from MMRP cited in Zaqlai 2020.
Note: MMRP = Man-Made River Project.

TABLE 15.7 Estimated damage and losses to the General Company for Water and Wastewater from armed conflict, 2019

TYPE OF LOSS	ESTIMATED LOSS (MILLIONS OF DOLLARS)
General services material stolen from Thursday market stores	16.9
Damage to headquarters	4.1
Materials stolen from water supply stores at the Thursday market Ameil	3.5
Damaged or stolen Tarhouna Services office vehicles	3.1
Stolen pumps, cables, and operating panels (sewage stations); damaged water wells (Al-Jafara service area); stolen monitoring systems (four district offices); stolen equipment; stolen items from "tourist stores"; and other	2.8
Damaged and stolen vehicles of the Tripoli administration	2.6
Damage to building in the General Administration and the Administration of Employment in Tripoli and levies	2.0
Damaged materials inside storage area of treatment plant (bombed)	1.4
Other, including damage to headquarters, buildings, and stores and the machinery, equipment, vehicles, and equipment they contain; network infrastructure, pumping lines and stations, equipment, electrical appliances, cables, and upper tanks; valves installed on wells, remote control and operations systems, damage to voltage transformers; and other damage	73.8
Total	110.3

Source: Data from GCWW cited in Zaqlai 2020.
Note: GCWW = General Company for Water and Wastewater.

Desalination plants, water treatment plants, and wastewater treatment plants

The cost of damage to or destruction of desalination plants has not been estimated. However, as a result of budgetary limitations, the infrastructure of the GCD has suffered extensive deterioration, forcing eight desalination plants to suspend activities because of lack of critical productive inputs, mainly electricity and chemicals.

Damage from lack of spare parts and inadequate operations and maintenance

Starting from an already low preconflict level of maintenance, infrastructure functionality and water services have gradually declined as a result of the armed conflict; they are now approaching critical collapse levels. Water supply pipelines have been left idle for extended periods, denying major urban centers of potable water. Several wastewater treatment plants remain out of service, and the functioning ones are not working at full capacity. Desalination plants are experiencing serious shortages of chemicals and electricity inputs in addition to not receiving major overhauls; as a result, they are operating far below full capacity, with deleterious effects not only on the water supply but on the infrastructure as well.

The GCWW faces myriad risks. Professional skilled maintenance personnel were foreigners, who left because of the armed conflict; it is difficult to recruit people willing to work in the midst of an armed conflict. The company also lacks sufficient cash flow for basic needs (spare parts, fuel, chemicals for desalination) and electricity to run water pumps and desalination and treatment plants.

TABLE 15.8 **Estimated total financial losses imposed on the water sector by armed conflict between 2012 and 2019**

AFFECTED PARTY OF ESTIMATED LOSSES	ESTIMATED LOSSES (MILLIONS OF DOLLARS)	PERCENT OF TOTAL
Urban dwellers	1,315.9	47
Irrigation farmers	348.8	13
MMRP and GCWW	1,114.3	40
Reduced revenues and higher unit costs of MMRP: $581.2 million		
Damage of MMRP infrastructure: $422.8 million		
Damage of GCWW infrastructure: $110.3 million		
Total	2,779.0	100

Source: Estimates in tables 15.6 and 15.7.
Note: GCWW = General Company for Water and Wastewater; MMRP = Man-Made River Project.

To estimate the financial cost of lack of spare parts and apporpriate O&M, we combined the estimates of financial costs imposed by the armed conflict on urban dwellers, irrigation farmers, and the MMRP and the estimated losses from damage during the armed conflict imposed on the MMRP and GCWW. There was no direct damage on GCD infrastructure or equipment during the armed conflict.

Total financial losses are estimated to be at least $2.8 billion, of which 47 percent is borne by urban dwellers (table 15.8). Other affected parties are the MMRP (36 percent of the total financial cost), irrigation farmers (13 percent), and the GCWW (4 percent). If we assume that the scarcity prices in Libya during the armed conflict represent true economic costs (meaning minimal distortions because of taxes and import duties), then the financial estimates are a close approximation of accounted economic costs.

SECTOR RECOVERY

With a peace agreement, or after the elections, conditions for sector recovery will be in place. Sector recovery planning will include short-, medium-, and long-term planning. The following activities will need to be part of a recovery plan:

- Refurbish the Brega and Sarir pipe factories.
- Restart proper maintenance of MMRP pipe infrastructure, pumping stations, and reservoirs.
- Refurbish and upgrade the technology of the eight active desalination plants and provide them with the chemicals they need to operate.
- Install state-of-the art pressure management equipment at water treatment plants and distribution networks, which can reduce both physical losses and consumption of energy for pumping.
- Assess and then refurbish wastewater treatment plants to comply with environmental regulation and sanitary standards, so that treated wastewater becomes a cost-effective source of water for irrigation.

Before the armed conflict, the World Bank drafted a proposal with the following recommendations, which could serve as a starting point:

- Update the National Water and Wastewater Strategy.
- Build the water database and carry out an infrastructure assessment.

TABLE 15.9 **Preliminary estimate of investment needed to effect recovery of MMRP and GCWW**

ITEM	ESTIMATE (MILLIONS OF DOLLARS)
MMRP losses as a result of damage and destruction during armed conflict	422.8
GCWW losses as a result of damage and destruction during armed conflict	110.3
Engineering studies and assessments, including specification of turnkey contracts	106.6
Transactions costs	51.2
Total	690.9

Source: World Bank.
Note: GCWW = General Company for Water and Wastewater; MMRP = Man-Made River Project.

- Review, revise, and implement appropriate water tariffs and billing.
- Restructure the sector's institutional and legal framework, with a focus on effective coordination.
- Rehabilitate the water infrastructure (much of which is approaching designed life), as appropriate.
- Improve water service access for urban and rural households, with attention to people not connected to the network.
- Use agricultural water more efficiently and improve treated wastewater reuse.

Only phase 1 and phase 2 of the MMRP are in operation. An updated status report on the completion of the remaining phases (3, 4, and 5) needs to be prepared. Based on the findings of this report, preliminary investment estimates can be made. Most desalination plants are nonoperational. An updated report of the status of these plants needs to be prepared. Based on such a report, qualified statements can be presented regarding potential investment needs.

Plans for expanding water production capacity need to be updated. An in-depth assessment of technology options should be conducted and lifetime minimum cost criteria established.

As MMRP capacity utilization goes down, its unit cost goes up. As unit costs go up, unit costs of desalination plants become competitive. A lifetime cost-effectiveness analysis should be undertaken to determine exactly how much capacity of each would need to be in place to reliably supply water to Libya's main urban centers. An analysis of this nature was conducted in the late 1998 (El Geriani et al. 1998). It needs to be updated.

A very preliminary estimate for sector recovery would be the replacement cost of the lost infrastructure plus the engineering designs for refurbishment of damaged infrastructure. This estimate is about $691 million (table 15.9). It does not include the investment needed to refurbish desalination plants. These estimates need to be confirmed by a fact-finding mission to Libya, to confirm the reported damage and losses to the infrastructure.[17]

CHALLENGES, OPPORTUNITIES, AND RECOMMENDATIONS

Challenges

Effecting the recovery of the water sector will require the following:

- Definition of principles, policies, and institutional arrangements
- Planning and execution of emergency rehabilitation of water infrastructure

- Restoration of production capacity of the MMRP
- Refurbishment of desalination plants
- Overhaul of the water distribution networks in Tripoli and Benghazi to restore water service continuity.

Stakeholder groups may need to be established to agree on and implement responsibilities for the emergency rehabilitation of water infrastructure and establish rules and procedures for the various water agencies.

A second challenge will be to define policies to reform state-owned monopolies in the water sector. To manage recovery and return to normality, water sector authorities will need to address concerns about the efficiency of the current sector executive organization under the three national monopolies.

A third challenge is related to the need to establish an economic regulatory agency to manage the monopoly issues of the three national monopolies. The policy making for the regulatory agency needs to try to introduce market-based principles to manage infrastructure efficiently and to balance the interests of end users and the technical, economic, and financial sustainability of the water services provided under natural monopoly conditions.

O&M of Libya's water infrastructure has been financed by fees paid by end users (approximately 17 percent) and the national treasury (approximately 83 percent). Going forward, the government needs to define a more sustainable financing policy, in which user fees could play a more significant role.

Opportunities

Libya is a resource-rich economy. Resumption of activities in the 1.3 million barrel-a-day oil and gas industry will increase revenues very quickly. Libya also has a low level of indebtedness and substantial international reserves accumulated before the armed conflict. Water instituions have extensive experience in planning and implementing competitive procurement of turnkey contracts for highly complex infrastructure projects. Public-private partnerships could be explored to improve outcomes. Once peace is achieved, contractors' costs will fall, as concerns about security fade.

Over the past 20 years, technological innovations have significantly improved energy efficiency in the production of fresh water using desalination technologies. These developments make desalination plants an option for increasing the supply of water for urban centers, freeing up water from the MMRP for irrigation.

Innovation in large-scale wastewater treatment plants has lowered unit costs and improved environmental and sanitation standards. They can make treated wastewater a source of water for irrigation.

Recommendations

Confirm estimates of emergency investment cost for restoring production capacity through a fact-finding mission to Libya. Assess investment needs to restore production capacity of desalination plants to preconflict levels. Understanding the investment purpose and needed budget for investment may help in the prioritization of needed investments for recovery and reconstruction. Water desalination is considered as the potential source of unconventional water resources in Libya, therefore an assessment for the water desalination sector (policies, regulations, investments, conditions of existing plants, and so forth) would be necessary for water sector sustainability and resiliency.

Explore options for reform, with the active participation of Libyan policy makers and stakeholders. International experience offers a menu of options for overhauling institutional and operational arrangements in the water sector. Local water sector policy makers, strategic planners, and senior staff involved in the management of existing infrastructure need to assess them to determine what makes sense for Libya.

Explore the use of public-private partnerships. Financing can benefit from international experience in contractual arrangements that mainstream private sector involvement to bring in technical know-how for infrastructure investments and O&M. The World Bank Group is well positioned to bring in its "from millions-to-billions" approach to finance infrastructure projects in the water sector.

Conduct a financial sustainability roadmap, which shall include a review of the water tariffs and billing linked to ongoing operations and proposed investments, to address water loss and nonrevenue water, energy efficiency, climate change impacts, and so forth.

Strengthen public awareness and outreach on water sector technical and fiscal situations to improve water conservation and sustainability programs and enhance transparency, accountability, and social contract.

The way forward

The water sector should be resilient for the ongoing and future challenges, including the foreseen impact of climate change. The ongoing political uncertainty is affecting the sector development, and therefore, it would be important that the water sector plans its response to the needs following the mentioned recommendations. The recommendations can be grouped in three phases:

Phase 1: Short-term response. Maintain and protect the main service delivery through the rehabilitation of existing facilities, while enhancing capacity building and water sector data. Establish and improve the O&M plan and develop an institutional and capacity-building program, which may include but is not limited to a water policy note, customer relations management and billing system, water data improvement, staff training, strengthening the citizen partnership, exposure to new water and wastewater technology and training, assessments of the desalination and wastewater system for future development and cost-benefit service, and so forth.

Phase 2: Medium-term response. Recover damages and system enhancement. This would focus on repair and reconstruction of the damages that had occurred for the big facilities in the water system that suffered damage during the conflicts, option development for sector reform and verification of the cost-benefit and cost-effectiveness of the water facilities and management, and development planning of the water sector and exploration of options including the involvement of the private sector in the reconstruction and development process.

Phase 3: Long-term response. This would include a water security development program and financial sustainability of the water sector, which may include development of nonconventional water resources (desalination and wastewater treatment and reuse, for example), increasing the water and wastewater efficiency and quality, and so forth.

CONCLUDING REMARKS

Libya's water infrastructure has suffered significant damage and destruction, impairing its productive capacity and raising its unit operating costs. End users of water have suffered losses of about $1.67 billion in 2019, including $1.32 billion by urban dwellers because of rationing of drinking water and $349 million by irrigation farmers.

The MMRP incurred financial losses that are estimated at $581 million, because of lack of payment for the water it delivers and increased unit production costs. Losses from damage during the armed conflict are estimated at $423 million for the MMRP and $110 million for the GCWW. Taken together, the estimated financial cost of the armed conflict imposed on the water sector is at at least $2.8 billion. If distortions from taxes and import duties are minimal, such financial cost could be taken as a preliminary estimate of the economic costs imposed by the armed conflict on the water sector in Libya.

Restoring the capacity of production and delivery of service by the MMRP and the GCWW will cost at least $690 million. This figure needs to be confirmed by a fact-finding technical and economic mission to Libya.

NOTES

1. In urban areas, the Housing and Utilities Project Implementation Authority has jurisdiction that complements that of the GCWW.
2. NSAS is a major fossil aquifer that extends over more than 2 million square kilometers under Chad, Egypt, Libya, and Sudan.
3. Laws were passed after 2011, but they are not in effect. For example, Law No. (59) of 2012 for Local Administration System reform was put on hold by Law No. (9) of 2013, under which other ministries and state-owned enterprises retain their control over municipalities.
4. Laws that were enacted before 2011 include the MMRP Authority Law 10/1983 and Law 11/1983; public companies GCWW, Decree No. 923 of 2007; and GCD Decrees No. 924 of 2007 and No. 250 of 2009.
5. Access figures before and after the armed conflict are from WFP (2019).
6. Most of this infrastructure remained damaged; humanitarian organizations rehabilitated some of it.
7. In some areas and at certain times, supply could not be maintained or kept stable (because of low water pressure caused by poor maintenance, which interrupted pumping; lack of energy; or other reasons). Less water was therefore supplied.
8. Tariffs are as cited in El Geriani et al. (1999).
9. While water consumption behavior changes from country to country, Libyan water experts from different water institutions referred to the need for more water due to high temperatures, mainly in summer; water availability (groundwater, desalination, and so forth) with no dependency on rainwater due to low rainfall average; more water consumption in urban areas where most Libyans are living; the way of life in middle-income countries like Libya accompanied by low water tariff; and no efficient collection and weak services, which do not motivate people to pay. More specific study may be needed to highlight the elements related to water consumer behaviors in Libya while there is water scarcity.

10. The volume of underground water pumped from the Jefara Plains grew by 11 percent a year over 1948–78; the population grew by 3 percent a year over the same period (UNECA 1991).

11. During the 1960s and 1970s, oil and gas industry investors deployed export infrastructure facilities in various Mediterranean ports, including Tripoli (Es Sidra), Marsa Brega (south of Benghazi), and Tobruk/Marsa-Hariga, near the Egyptian border. Later, oil refineries and petrochemical industries were developed to process oil and gas produced in Libya.

12. Phase 1, Sarir-Sirt/Tazerbo Benghazi Systems, comprises Sarir and Tazerbo well-fields with total production of 2.0 million cubic meter per day (MCMD) and 234 wells; 1,926 kilometers of mainly four-meter diameter pipes; and total storage capacity of 54 million cubic meters. Phase 2, Hasouna–Jeffara System, comprises major structures in the east and northeast Jebel Hasouna well-fields; 586 wells, with total of 2.5 MCMD; and 1,732 kilometers of mainly four-meter diameter pipes. Phase 3, Ghadammes well-field, comprises 106 wells, with total production of 90 million cubic meters per year. Phase 4, Al Gardabiya–Assadadah link (not yet completed), comprises 190 kilometers of four-meter diameter pipes. Phase 5 (not yet completed), Kufra well-field, comprises 285 wells. Total expected production: 1.68 MCMD.

13. The MMRP (with 2,472 employees) and the GCD (with 900) have much lower labor costs.

14. Estimates of labor costs are based on average national wages and the number of employees per utility. Estimates of energy costs are based on input-output coefficients and the average tariff of electricity as reported by GECOL. Materials for O&M, including spare parts, are assumed to represent 20 percent of total expenses. Tariff revenues are based on current tariffs times the estimated volumes of water dispatched to customers.

15. Twenty percent of the urban population—about 1.1 million people (270,000 households)—are assumed to confront extreme rationing. If each household purchases two 20-liter containers of bulk water a day at $1 a container, it spends $197 million a year on bulk water. If the containers costs $0.50 a bottle, the total would be $99.5 million.

16. The MMRP Authority reported to the authors that phase 1 is producing 700,000 cubic meters a day and phase 2 is producing 700,000 cubic meters a day. These figures would represent capacity utilization of about 30 percent, rather than the 50 percent assumed in this chapter.

17. The financial losses as a result of damage were taken from the GAWR, the MMRP, and the GCWW.

REFERENCES

Aldeeb, Ahmad Ali. 2019. Presentation to the World Bank mission Tunisia, by members of the executive committee of the Man-Made River Project. Tunisia, June.

Alrwaimi, Abdusalam. 2019. Presentation to the World Bank mission Tunisia, by members of executive committee of the General Company for Desalination. Tunisia, June.

CEDARE (Centre for Environment and Development for the Arab Region and Europe). 2014. *Libya Water Sector M&E Rapid Assessment Report*. Cairo: CEDARE. https://www.humanitarianresponse.info/sites/www.humanitarianresponse.info/files/assessments/libya_water_sector_me_rapid_assessment_2014.pdf.

El Geriani, A. M., O. Essamin, P. J. A. Gijsbers, and D. P. Loucks. 1998. "Cost-Effectiveness Analysis of Libya's Water Supply System." *Journal of Water Resources Planning and Management* 124 (6): https://ascelibrary.org/doi/10.1061/%28ASCE%290733-9496%281998%29124%3A6%28320%29.

Elsonni, Abdalla Taher. 2019. Presentation to the World Bank mission Tunisia, by head of executive committee of the General Authority for Water Resources. June.

FAO (Food and Agricultural Organization). 2016. *Country Profile: Libya*. Rome: FAO.

Siebert, Stefan, Verena Henrich, Karen Frenken, and Jacob Burke. 2013. *Update of the Global Digital Map of Irrigation Areas*. Rome: Food and Agricultural Organization.

UNECA (United Nations Economic Commission for Africa). 1991. "Population Growth, Libya." Addis Ababa: UNECA. https://data.worldbank.org/indicator/SP.POP.GROW?locations=LY.

UNICEF (United Nations Children's Fund). 2019. *Assessment of Water Supply Systems and Institutions in Libya*. New York: UNICEF.

WFP (World Food Programme). 2019. *Libya Interim Country Strategic Plan (2019–2020)*. Rome: WFP. https://www.wfp.org/operations/ly01-libya-interim-country-strategic-plan-2019-2020.

Zaqlai, Nabil. 2020. *The Water Sector in Libya and the Challenges that Face Companies Working in the Sector*. Tripoli: Water Sector Resilience Project.

16 A Health Sector in Intensive Care

**MOHINI KAK, SEVERIN RAKIC, JESSE D. MALKIN, MANSOUR FAISAL
ALRUMAYYAN, DENIZHAN DURAN, MARIAM M. HAMZA, ARIAN HATEFI,
ALMOATAZ BEDIN ALLAH SHIKHY, AND CHRISTOPHER H. HERBST**

World Bank

*The Libyan health sector is in crisis. The conflict has deepened problems that
existed before 2011, including lack of preparedness for a shift toward noncommunicable diseases, poorly functioning primary health facilities that resulted
in an overreliance on hospitals, limited and poor-quality services in remote
areas, weak health information systems, and limited and inefficient use of
health financing. Various international organizations have stepped in to fill
gaps, by helping health authorities carry out timely responses to disease outbreaks, including for COVID-19, and stock essential medicines and medical
supplies. Systematic interventions are needed to improve the primary health
system, the health work force, pharmaceutical and supply chains, and health
financing.*

INTRODUCTION

As a result of the conflict and political instability that have plagued Libya since
2011, many health outcomes in Libya are worse than the averages of Middle
East and North Africa (MENA) as well as upper-middle-income countries.
This chapter provides an overview of the Libyan health sector now in intensive
care, highlighting some of the health systems challenges that require urgent
attention across financing, service delivery, information systems, and governance, to the extent possible given the scarcity of data.[1]

The chapter begins with a discussion of the effect of conflict on health and
the health care system in Libya. It then explores growth of the private sector
and increase in external financing caused by decline in public health care
service delivery. The chapter then reflects on challenges that have emerged
due to secular changes in disease burden, for which the current health system is unprepared. The last two sections provide the recommendations for
reform, including strengthening the primary health care system, governance
of the health sector, pandemic preparedness, the health care workforce,
pharmaceutical supply chains, health financing, and data collection systems,
and concluding remarks.

THE STATE OF HEALTH AND THE HEALTH SYSTEM: THE COST OF WAR

Deterioration and stagnation of health outcomes

Intermittent conflict for over a decade has contributed to a health sector in Libya that is completely discordant with its classification as an upper-middle-income country. In 2011, prior to the conflict, rapid improvements in health outcomes were evident and aligned with other upper-middle-income countries and countries in the MENA region. However, over a decade of instability has led to a stagnation and even declines in key health and nutritional outcomes (figure 16.1).

Life expectancy at birth in Libya has been stagnating around pre-war levels and the mortality rate for adults, particularly men, is above the average in MENA. While life expectancy increased by about 1 year in Libya between 2011 and 2019, the increase in MENA countries was on average over 1.5 years and in upper-middle-income countries over 2 years. The mortality rate is also poorer in comparison. The share of the male population that survives up to 65 years is 6 percent lower in Libya than the average for MENA countries (World Bank 2021c). Premature mortality from the main noncommunicable diseases (NCDs) increased in Libya between 2011 and 2019, while it decreased during the same period in MENA and upper-middle-income countries where the overall burden of NCDs is equivalent to Libya.

Achievements made in reduction of maternal mortality and child undernutrition in Libya were negated by the war. The maternal mortality ratio increased from 56 to over 70 deaths per 100,000 live births between 2011 and 2017, well exceeding averages in both MENA and upper-middle-income countries. In addition, stunting in children under five years, which was high even before the war, increased drastically since 2011, bringing Libya to the first position in the Eastern Mediterranean region and the sixth position in the world. Forty-four percent of children under five years in Libya are stunted (WHO 2021b; World Bank 2021c).[2] Many other countries in the region have been gradually reducing stunting prevalence during the same period.

Deterioration of health systems

Service delivery

The health service delivery architecture remains the same as it was before 2011, although its functionality has been severely impacted by the war. Pre-war achievements in health outcomes were driven by the public health system, which was the main health services provider. Preventive, curative, and rehabilitation services were provided to all citizens free of charge by the public sector. The health care delivery system operated on three levels: (1) the first level consisted of the primary health care units, primary health care centers, and polyclinics, staffed by specialized physicians and containing laboratories as well as radiological services and a pharmacy; (2) at the second level, general hospitals in rural and urban areas provided care to patients referred from the first level; and (3) the third level comprised tertiary care specialized hospitals (WHO EMRO 2007). The same types of health facilities form the basis of current public health sector in Libya but with diminished capacity due to the conflict (figure 16.2).

Almost 300 public health care facilities have closed primarily due to infrastructure damage and security concerns and many remaining facilities are not

FIGURE 16.1

Selected health indicators in Libya, the Middle East and North Africa, and upper-middle-income countries

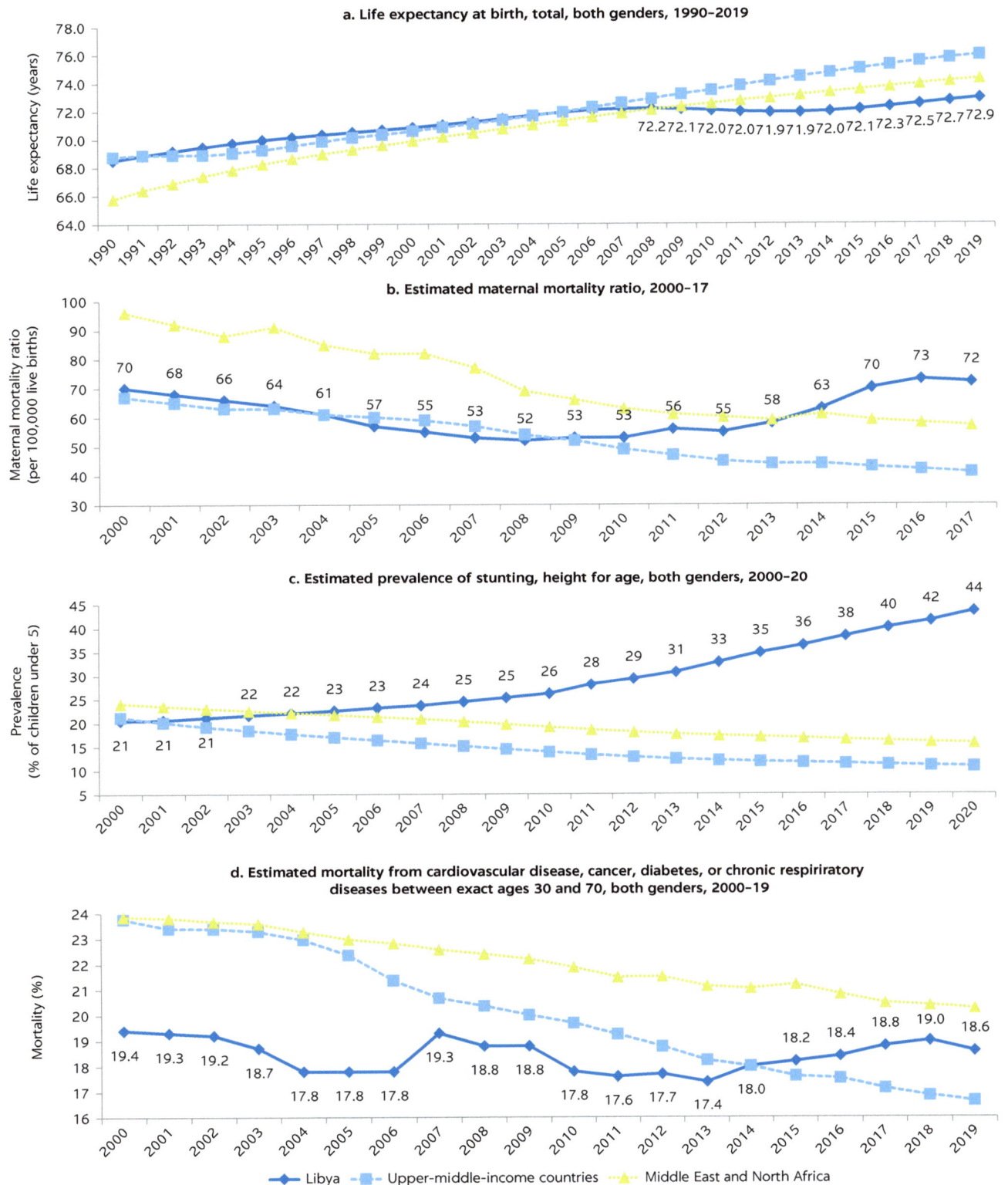

a. Life expectancy at birth, total, both genders, 1990–2019

b. Estimated maternal mortality ratio, 2000–17

c. Estimated prevalence of stunting, height for age, both genders, 2000–20

d. Estimated mortality from cardiovascular disease, cancer, diabetes, or chronic respiriratory diseases between exact ages 30 and 70, both genders, 2000–19

Libya — Upper-middle-income countries — Middle East and North Africa

Source: World Bank 2021c.

FIGURE 16.2

Libyan public health care delivery system in 2016

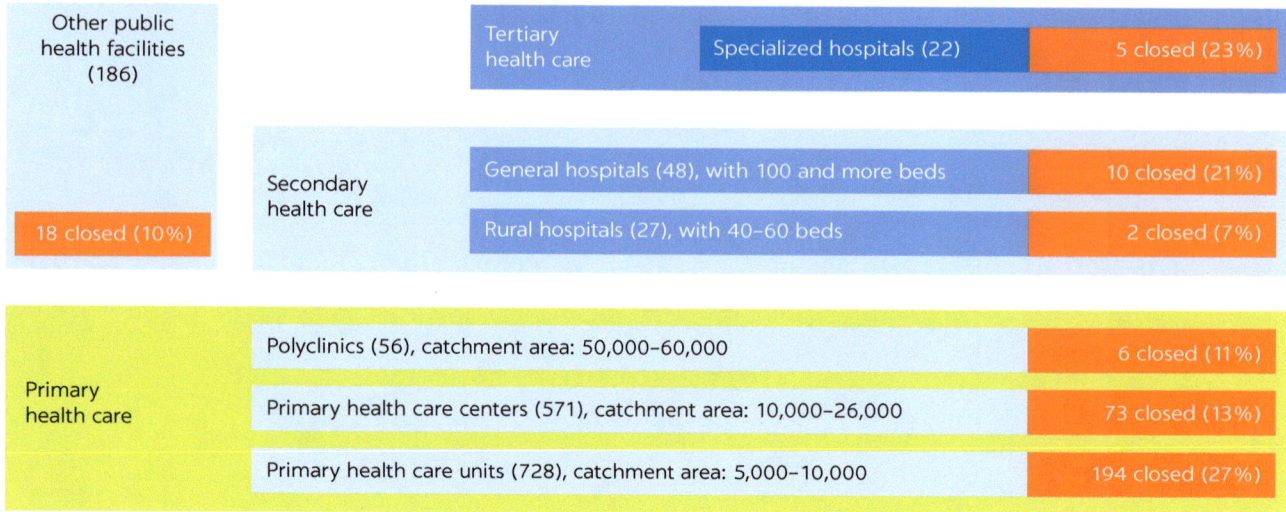

Other public health facilities (186)	Tertiary health care	Specialized hospitals (22)	5 closed (23%)
	Secondary health care	General hospitals (48), with 100 and more beds	10 closed (21%)
		Rural hospitals (27), with 40–60 beds	2 closed (7%)
18 closed (10%)			
Primary health care		Polyclinics (56), catchment area: 50,000–60,000	6 closed (11%)
		Primary health care centers (571), catchment area: 10,000–26,000	73 closed (13%)
		Primary health care units (728), catchment area: 5,000–10,000	194 closed (27%)

Source: WHO and Libyan Ministry of Health 2017.
Note: Other public health facilities include dental clinics, branches of the National Center for Disease Control, dialysis centers, medical supply warehouses, ambulance service centers, referral medical laboratories, blood banks, infertility centers, diabetes treatment centers, oncology centers, mental health clinics, physiotherapy centers, immunology centers, and diagnostics and imaging centers.

fully functional. For example, out of a total of 1,355 primary health care (PHC) facilities, 273 were closed in 2017 because of either a lack of maintenance (51 percent), inaccessibility on account of conflict (20 percent), physical damage (19 percent), or other parties occupying it (11 percent). In addition, according to the 2017 Service Availability and Readiness Assessment (SARA) report, only one-third of the total number of primary health care clinics were fully functional, with the mean basic service provision index for PHC facilities being 45 percent and for hospitals 69 percent. Only about 40 percent of PHC facilities offer basic maternal and childcare, and only about half diagnose and treat diabetes (51 percent), cardiovascular diseases (48 percent), and chronic respiratory diseases (45 percent) (WHO and Libyan Ministry of Health 2017).

Basic infrastructure such as electricity, clean water, sewerage, and telecommunications is also not consistently available for health facilities, in part because power plants and water treatment facilities were subject to frequent attacks by armed groups. In 2016, 86 percent of hospitals had access to sources of clean water, and 64 percent had functional telecommunication equipment. Basic amenities availability was worse in primary health care, where 97 percent of facilities had electricity available, 71 percent had access to clean water source, and 13 percent had functional landline telephones (WHO and Libyan Ministry of Health 2017). Electricity and water outages tend to interrupt the continuity of service provision. The daily blackouts in Tripoli, for example, averaged 12 hours in mid-2020. These frequent electricity cuts[3] have been exacerbated by shortages and high prices of fuel to run back-up generators (WHO Country Office Libya 2020). Further, the frequent droppages of voltage create problems in sustaining operation of the sensitive medical equipment. Electricity cuts also contribute to instability of water supply in the health facilities and poor environmental hygiene in about half of the PHC facilities (Action Against Hunger 2020).

An influx of refugees and migrants has put an additional strain on the already stretched public health care system. More than half a million migrants and refugees currently reside in Libya, according to UN estimates, equal to about 9 percent of Libya's population of 6.9 million (Devi 2021). Some are housed in crowded detention facilities where diseases can easily spread. Few are tested for communicable diseases before entering the country. Cases reported to the National Center for Disease Control show high and increasing numbers of common infectious diseases, such as respiratory infections and diarrheal diseases (National Health Information and Documentation Center, various years), with refugees and migrants tending to make up a large share of infectious disease cases. In 2018, for example, 32 percent of pulmonary tuberculosis cases were migrants.

Access to essential medicines

The pharmaceutical supply chain is weak with severe shortages in availability of medicines across public health facilities, and at the level of medical stores and warehouses. Although medicine registration, selection, procurement, distribution, and use did not meet international standards even before 2011 (Mustafa and Kowalski 2010), the conflict has further weakened the system. Shortages of essential medicines and medical supplies are prevalent across public health facilities in Libya, with the medicine availability index scores being highest for hospitals (41 percent), followed by warehouses (13 percent), and being lowest for PHC facilities (10 percent) (Elfituri et al. 2018; MoH 2019a; WHO and Libyan Ministry of Health 2017). Significant variation exists in availability across medicine categories as well. Over 80 percent of PHC facilities did not have anti-infective medicines used to treat communicable diseases, child health medicines, and NCD medicines in 2016.

Issues exist across all levels of the supply chain. Procurement practices are often opaque, and over the past few years, the Ministry of Health (MoH) has been implementing changes to pharmaceutical procurement shifting between decentralized and centralized systems. Hospital pharmacies and PHC facilities are expected to send their requisitions and receive their supplies through the Medical Supply Organization (MSO) (World Bank 2021b). However, poor logistic information systems for tracking medicines from procurement through dispensing have prevented decision-makers from having access to important information to effectively plan, allocate, budget, and deliver medicines. Resupply ordering times for PHC facilities vary widely with one-third taking less than two weeks and another one-third third taking more than two months, which can lead to stockouts (Çelik and El Taguri 2021). Limited stock management exists at hospitals; 28 percent have computerized systems, 39 percent use stock ledgers, and 51 percent use stock or bin cards. Poor storage and handling practices at district warehouses and dispensing pharmacies, such as poor temperature management, also compromise drug quality (WHO and Libyan Ministry of Health 2017; World Bank 2021b).

More recently, financing for pharmaceuticals has also become an issue of concern. The National Pharmacy Department and MSO received no budget for more than a year (since 2000) for pharmaceuticals and equipment. This is expected to have further contributed to essential medicines stockouts for public health care facilities, which do not have budgets for pharmaceutical expenditures nor the ability to purchase drugs locally. The lack of availability for essential medicines at public health facilities also contributes to increases in out-of-pocket expenditures by households who seek drugs from private health care facilities or pharmacies.

Health workforce

The conflict has impacted the composition, availability, and distribution of health workers. Pre-conflict availability of health workers in Libya was in line with that of MENA countries. There were 13 physicians, 2.5 dentists, 2 pharmacists, 48 nurses, and 23 paramedical staff per 10,000 population, with regional variations (WHO EMRO 2007). Libya was dependent on foreign nurses for all quality and specialized nursing care and for midwifery, while about 16 percent of physicians and 10 percent of dentists were non-Libyans. Many foreign health care workers fled Libya after armed conflict began in 2011. Libyan health workforce shrank by more than 50 percent by 2016 (WHO EMRO 2021). Libya now faces shortages of many types of medical professionals including bachelor-degree nurses, family practitioners, and mental health practitioners, and a surplus of many others, such as dentists. Partly because of security concerns, large cities often have many providers and rural areas few, leaving the needs of rural residents often unmet (MoH 2019a).

Staff shortages in facilities have led to higher patient loads for physicians and nurses, which have adversely affected quality of care. Physicians in clinics with shortages saw an average of 147 patients per month, whereas those in clinics without staff shortages saw an average of 98 patients (World Bank 2018). Similarly, nurses in clinics with shortages saw an average of 329 patients in the month, whereas those in clinics without staff shortages saw an average of 111 patients (World Bank 2018). These higher patient loads could be threatening quality of care and further demotivating health workers.

Health worker motivation and ability to provide care has been affected by violence as well as constrained due to basic shortages at health facilities. A survey of 510 randomly selected primary health care clinic providers in Libya's two largest cities, Benghazi and Tripoli, showed that 25.2 percent of female primary health care workers and 32.9 percent of male primary health care workers had faced security problems at work. This potentially had a significant impact on workers' motivation, with further analysis indicating that more than 80 percent of those who had not faced security problems at work were strongly or somewhat motivated, compared to only about 50 percent for those who had faced security problems at work (World Bank 2022). One-third of providers also reported that their clinic needed infrastructure repairs or rehabilitation. Lack of electricity, heating, and regular water and security issues were cited as major concerns. More than half (57 percent) of providers reported that their duties had been adversely affected by medical supply stockouts in the previous three months. This also impacted motivation. Of those whose duties were *not* affected by medical consumables or supply problems, more than 80 percent reported being strongly or somewhat motivated. However, only about 60 percent of those whose duties were affected by medical consumables and supply problems reported being strongly or motivated (World Bank 2018). Additionally, 88 percent of providers reported that they had been paid late at least once during the previous three months, which was also shown to be correlated with lower motivation levels. The incomplete and late payments were usually attributed to the lack of financial resources at the national level.

Access and quality of care

Patient experience of primary care services point to gaps in quality and access to care. A survey of 1,012 randomly selected patients leaving primary care clinics found that 32 percent went to a clinic other than the one closest to them (World Bank 2018). The most common reasons were not enough doctors or nurses, medication stockouts, and overcrowding in clinics closer to them. Twenty percent of patients reported forgoing treatment because of cost. The need to improve drug stocks was the primary health care concern in both Tripoli and Benghazi. Most concerning was the quality of service provided, reflected by the infrequency of basic procedure provision, such as vital sign measurement or physical examination (figure 16.3).

Considerable variation exists in barriers to access across regions, urban-rural areas, employment, and migrant status. According to data collected by the REACH Multi-Sectoral Needs Assessment from 2017–19, people residing in urban areas are seven times less likely to face access challenges to health services due to shortages in medical staff, and four times less likely to face challenges due to shortages in medicines and supplies, than those in rural areas. Regional variations exist as well. Governorates such as Almarj, Ghat, Derna, and Alkufra, which have been significantly impacted by the conflict, had the highest prevalence of health care access barriers, as well as the highest share of financing barriers. Other factors, such as job status and migrant status, also influence access. While overall 42 percent of all respondents faced challenges accessing care (REACH 2017, 2019), those with permanent jobs were less likely to face finance-related challenges to care, with 10 percent of those with permanent jobs facing finance barriers, versus 60 percent without any work. Migrants also faced greater challenges, with almost 22 percent of migrants facing financial barriers, compared to an average of 17 percent for the remainder of the sample (Duran and Hamza 2022).

Health information systems

Implementation of routine health information systems and periodic health surveys to support decision-making have been disrupted. Health information in the past was received directly from statistical offices in all the hospitals and from the

FIGURE 16.3

Patient recollections of basic procedures performed at primary care appointments

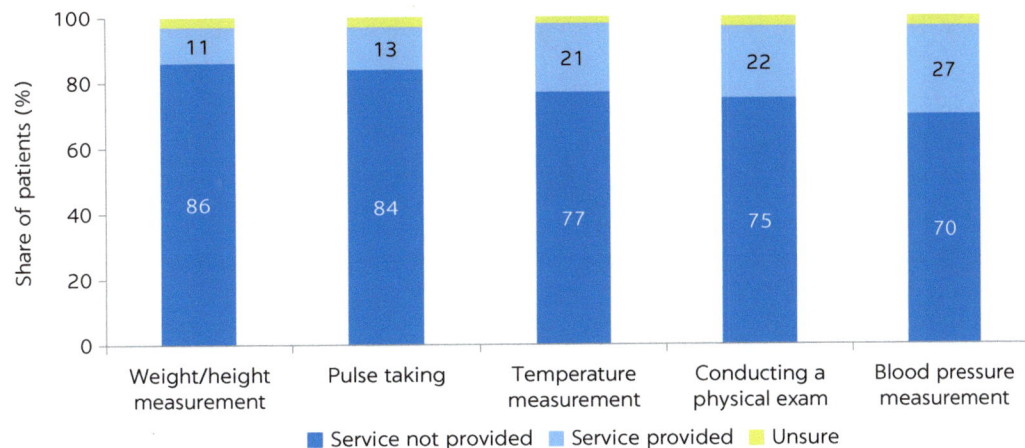

Source: World Bank 2018.

statistical units of the Directorate of Health at the district level. In 2006, the Health Information and Documentation Centre (HIC) was established in the Ministry of Health, with the primary responsibility of collecting routine data from health facilities, conducting health surveys, training human resources for the statistical units, and issuing various statistical reports. Between 2000 and 2010, it coordinated the implementation of several surveys, including the WHO STEPwise Approach to NCD Risk Factor Surveillance survey in 2009; the Global Youth Tobacco Survey in 2003, 2007, and 2010; and the Family Health survey in 2007. However, since then, the HIC's ability to do so has been constrained. The last survey measuring health outcomes was the Family Health Survey in 2014 and the SARA survey, which was conducted in 2017 in collaboration with WHO to assess service availability. While the HIC continues to collect health status and system indicators at a central level, these data are incomplete. The flow of information through routine reporting systems from hospitals and primary health care centers has been disrupted and information of service delivery has become unreliable (WHO EMRO 2020). Libya currently lacks key attributes of a well-functioning platform, such as an integrated web-based health information system, standard operating procedures for data management, data quality assessments, and health sector reviews for effective use of data (MoH, WHO, and EU 2017). In addition, the legislative and regulatory framework required to ensure a functioning health information system is inadequate. While efforts are being made to roll out the District Health Information System-2 (DHIS-2), its full uptake and use is expected to take time.

Health financing

Public health care spending has declined over the past decade with concerns about efficiencies in expenditure. The government's health care budget more than doubled between 2011 and 2012—for reasons that are unclear—before declining sharply between 2012 and 2015 (figure 16.4). More recent data

FIGURE 16.4

Per capita public expenditure on health in Libya and comparative groups of countries, 2006–18

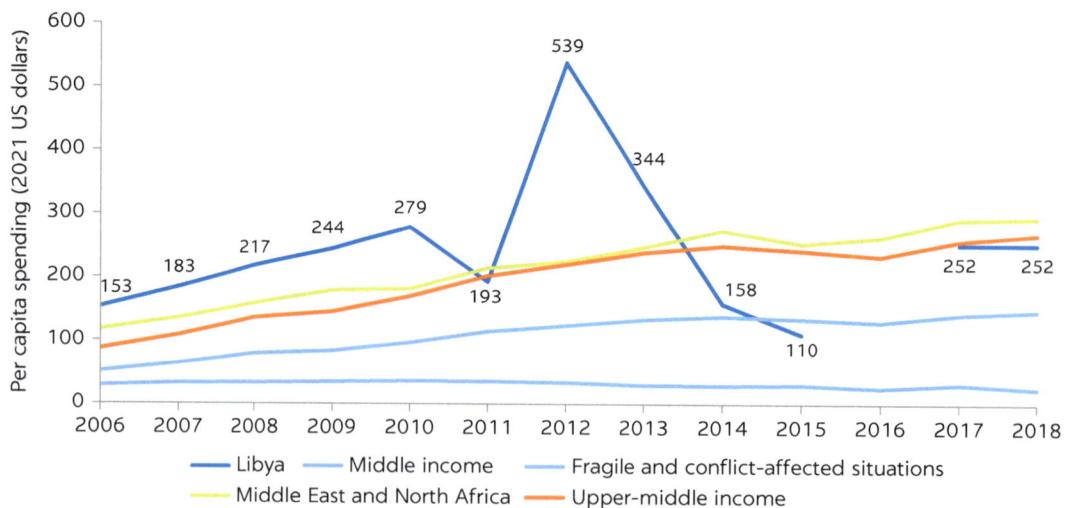

Source: Libya National Health Information and Documentation Center (various years); World Bank 2021c.
Note: Health care expenditures for Libya post-2010 are obtained from the annual reports of Libya National Health Information and Documentation Center.

are unavailable. As of 2015, Libya's public expenditure on health was less than both middle-income-country and MENA averages. Most of the budget is dedicated to salaries. Budgeting and expenditure tracking for health are fragmented, with more than three ministries and five directorates involved. The role of local authorities remains unclear.

Out-of-pocket expenditures for health care have increased. Even as per capita gross domestic product has declined, out-of-pocket health care expenditures nearly doubled during the past decade, reaching $196 in 2019, according to data from a household survey conducted by REACH (2019). In 2019, one-third of the population incurred catastrophic health expenditures, defined as health spending that constituted more than 40 percent of a household's nonfood expenditures. This is a significant increase in comparison to 2006, when out-of-pocket expenditures were 23 percent of total expenditures on health (WHO EMRO 2007). Given the high levels of health care access barriers, it is likely that these expenditures underestimate the true health needs experienced by the population. Catastrophic health expenditure prevalence is high across population groups and higher in areas more significantly impacted by the conflict than elsewhere. Thirty-nine percent of all respondents incurred catastrophic health expenditure at the 10 percent threshold, and more than 23 percent of the population faces catastrophic health expenditure at the 40 percent level (Duran and Hamza 2022).

Health system governance

Governance structures were fragmented even prior to 2011, and the conflict has further contributed to the problem. Oscillating efforts at decentralizing and centralizing the health sector prior to 2011 contributed to early fragmentation. Efforts at decentralizing the health system started in 2000, when the central Secretariat of Health was dismantled in favor of the district level. However, in 2006 there was a return to centralization and the Secretariat of Health was reestablished and authorized to supervise central institutions and district health secretariats. In 2011, the Ministry of Health was established and headed by a Minister of Health. The second round of conflict in 2014, which resulted in competing governments—one in the East and one in the West—further eroded stewardship and governance in the health sector (Çelik and El Taguri 2021).

The roles and responsibilities of the different autonomous institutes, districts, and municipalities is still evolving. The coordination mechanism among the different autonomous centers, offices, and directorates (figure 16.5) is often unclear, limiting alignment of efforts at the national, district, and municipal levels. Additionally, the roles of districts and municipalities are also evolving and not yet clearly defined. Supervision and monitoring systems in the sector are not effective, and the accountability mechanisms and management capacities are weak, which makes overall governance and coordination challenging (Schaeffer, Lassoued, and Ouelhazi 2021).

The recent development of a national health policy document that sets the stage for a health sector strategy and strengthened governance systems is a step in the right direction, but its implementation is likely to require a stable authorizing environment. The National Health Policy 2030 recognizes several key weaknesses in governance of the health sector, including (1) outdated and inconsistent laws and decrees, (2) outdated planning processes that are not consistent with post-2011 developments, (3) unclear institutional cooperation mechanisms

FIGURE 16.5

Structure of Libya's Ministry of Health

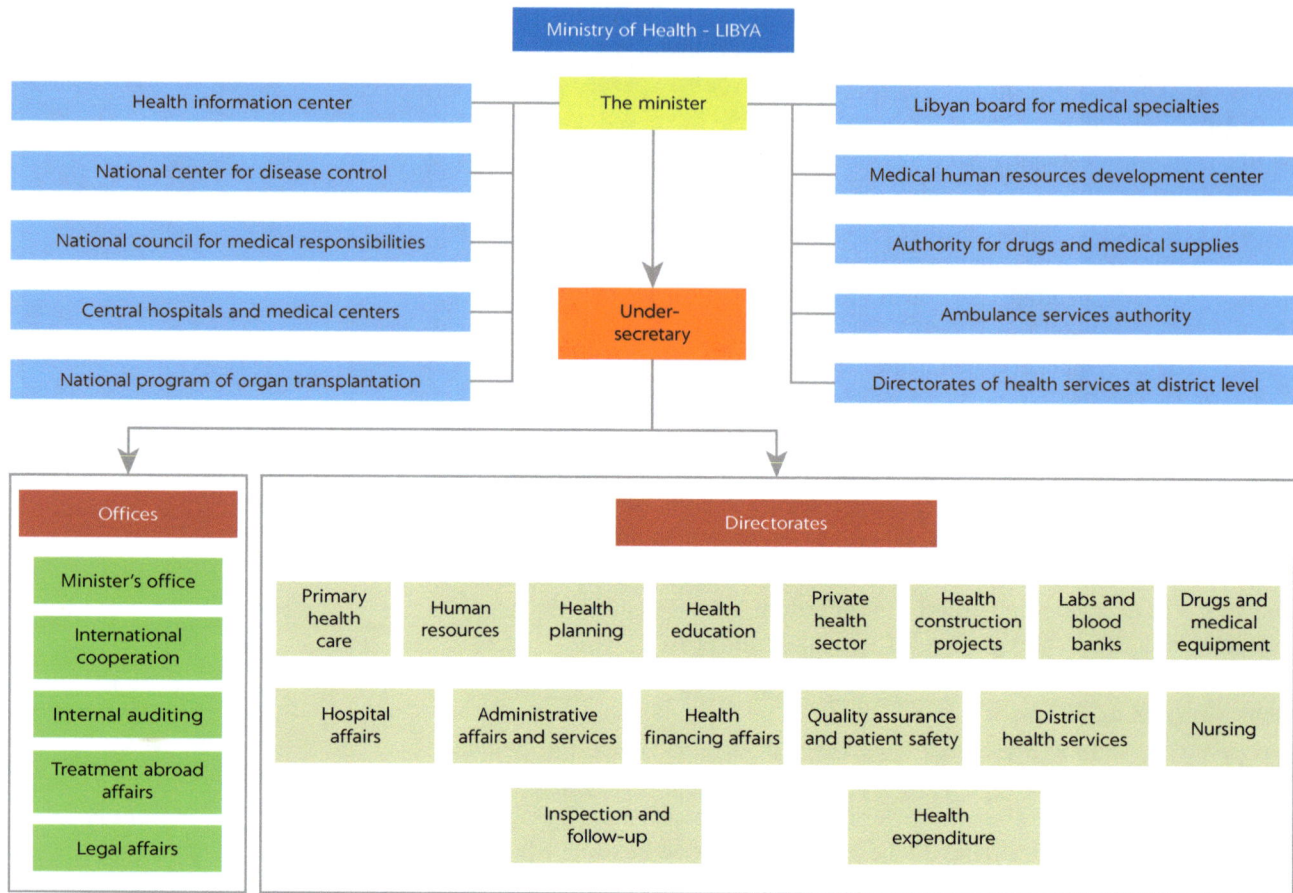

Source: MoH 2019b.

with weak technical and programmatic accountability, (4) excessive autonomy and decentralization beyond intended leading to lack of central control, (5) absence of management boards and centralization of managerial powers in autonomous institutions, and (6) ineffective oversight and accountability (MoH 2019c). The policy intends to redefine health system governance by granting further autonomy to hospitals of reasonable size and devolving powers to regions where a regional health authority may be established (MoH 2019b). It is, however, unclear whether the MoH has the political authority to implement these changes.

THE CHANGING LANDSCAPE OF THE HEALTH SECTOR: GROWTH OF THE PRIVATE SECTOR AND EXTERNAL AID

With the decline of public service delivery due to the war, the private sector has increasingly become a key provider of health care. In 2007, the small private health care sector in Libya mostly provided complementary primary and basic secondary care through 431 outpatient clinics and 84 inpatient clinics, with the bed capacity of 1,361 (WHO EMRO 2007). However, the closure of public health facilities and concerns about security led to substantial growth in the number of private sector health care service providers to meet the demand. Private service providers rely on self-financing and are concentrated in urban areas, driven by demographic concentration and the population's propensity to pay (World Bank 2021a). While most private outpatient clinics were established in the 2000s, other type of private health facilities showed significant growth between 2007 and 2018 (figure 16.6). The number of private laboratories and pharmacies more than doubled between 2007 and 2018, and the number of diagnostic and imaging centers more than quadrupled (MoH 2019a). More than 530 private outpatient clinics, 235 private inpatient clinics, 371 dental clinics, 411 private laboratories, 16 diagnostic imaging centers, and 3,089 private pharmacies provided health services to the Libyan population in 2019. There were far more dental clinics, pharmacies, and diagnostic imaging centers in Libya's private sector than its public sector in 2019. The private sector now constitutes almost a quarter of primary health clinics in Libya. Public sector weaknesses have also allowed the private sector to gain a larger share of the Libyan pharmaceutical market since 2014, despite dramatically increasing prices, which is especially problematic for migrants, who have no access to free care and must rely on the private sector (Elfituri et al. 2018; REACH 2017).

The private sector remains unregulated, limiting its potential to contribute to improved health care outcomes. An inadequate regulatory and control framework exists, with no clear quality of care standards being followed in the absence of an accreditation body. The Directorate of Treatment Affairs in the Ministry of Health contracts for services from private providers for certain conditions, such as cancer treatment, but there is no harmonized fee schedule for private providers or relevant regulations. The private sector depends on out-of-pocket payments because the budgetary health financing system is inefficient at purchasing high-quality health services or offering financial risk protection (WHO EMRO 2014). Private services are therefore accessible only to patients who can pay.

FIGURE 16.6

Growth of private health facilities in Libya between 2007 and 2018

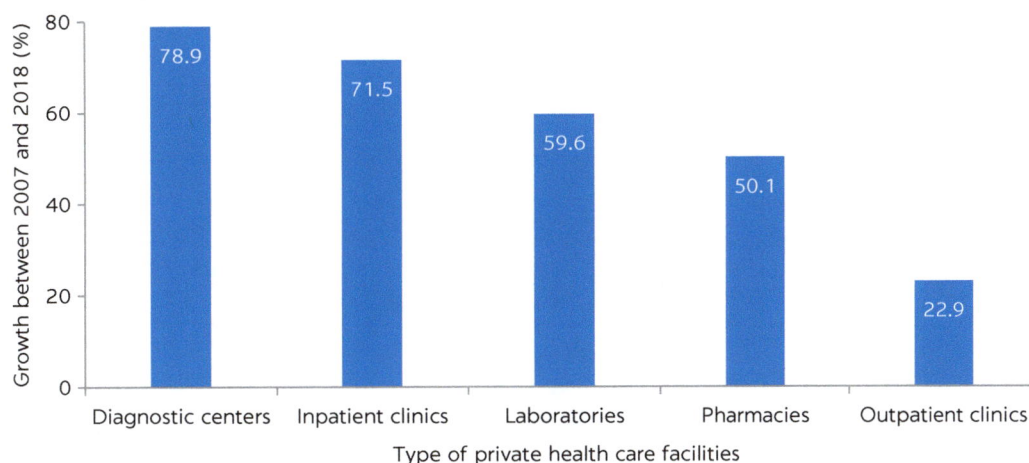

Source: MoH 2019a.

There has also been a significant increase in external financing of the health sector and involvement of international aid organizations in provision of the health services. There were no external sources of health care financing in Libya in the late 2000s (WHO EMRO 2007). Various international organizations have stepped in during the conflict to fill some of the gaps in Libya's troubled public health care system. Humanitarian funding for health has been reported since 2011 (OCHA 2022). However, the available data do not differentiate between direct funding of service provision and external financing of health care (figure 16.7).

The focus of international organizations has been to support Libyan health authorities to carry out timely responses to disease outbreaks, establish health facilities, provide essential medicines, and facilitate access of health care to migrant populations. Turkey and Italy have provided bilateral support, and the World Health Organization has played a major coordinating role in the health sector and provided drugs and medical supplies to public clinics and hospitals (Alharathy 2017, 2018; Assad 2020). The European Union established a health program aimed at improving Libyans' access to health care, launched a project designed to increase access to mental health services in the country's three largest cities, and funded mobile clinics in Eastern Libya (Assad 2017, 2019; Najjair 2018). Doctors without Borders supports the treatment of refugees in Libyan detention centers. It operates mobile health care clinics, provides medicines to hospitals, and provides vaccines to health clinics (Saim 2016). The United Nations High Commissioner for Refugees (UNHCR 2020) opened a clinic that serves both Libyans and migrants in Tripoli while supporting the Humanitarian Response Plan 2020, a plan that provides a shared understanding of the most pressing humanitarian needs and interventions to pursue (Gluck 2020; Health Sector Libya 2020; OCHA 2021). UNICEF is playing a key role in the country's COVID-19 response, among other things, and several other agencies are supporting different aspects of health service delivery. Moving forward, transitioning this support from gap filling to rebuilding and strengthening the public health system will be critical in facilitating sustainable, quality, equitable health services for all.

FIGURE 16.7

Reported humanitarian funding for health in Libya, 2006–21

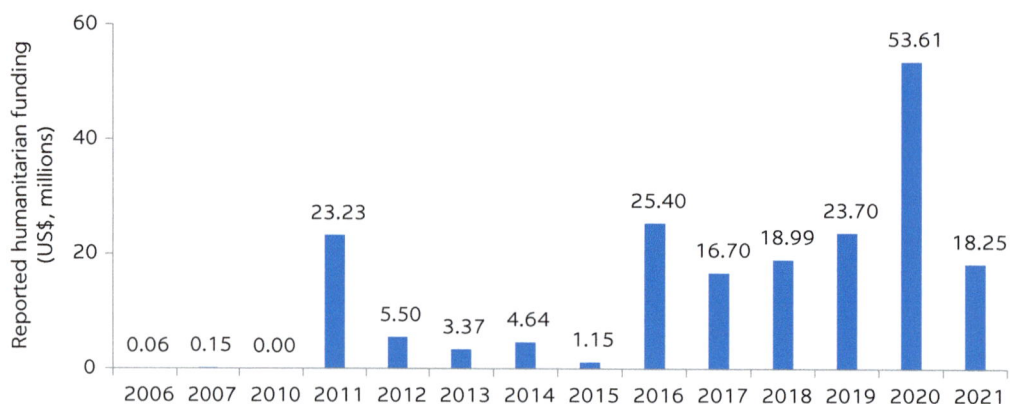

Source: OCHA 2022.
Note: Data for 2008 and 2009 are missing.

EMERGING CHALLENGES: BEYOND THE CONFLICT

Beyond the much-needed repair and renewal efforts to revive the damaged public health services and systems, two new challenges have emerged due to changes in disease burden for which the current health system is unprepared.

First, over time there has been a significant shift in the burden of disease toward NCDs, for which the current health system is unprepared. This had started gaining recognition over a decade ago with the implementation of the STEP survey in 2009, but progress in NCD control was never made due to the conflict. The incidence of major NCDs has increased in Libya since 2011 (IHME 2021), particularly cardiometabolic diseases. The incidence of diabetes mellitus increased by 50 percent between 2011 and 2019, cardiovascular disease rose by 42 percent, cancer by 22 percent, mental disorders by 16 percent, and chronic respiratory disease by 13 percent. Obesity, a key risk factor for the NCDs, more than doubled during the past three decades and has reached "epidemic proportions" (Lemamsha, Randhawa, and Papadopoulos 2019). High blood pressure and high blood glucose are also among the major risk factors that drive development of NCDs in Libya, contributing to the leading causes of death in Libya, such as ischemic heart disease and stroke (figure 16.8). Having a strong PHC system with the capacity to deliver a comprehensive continuum of care package that includes promotion, screening, risk stratification, referral, management, and follow-up care to reduce adverse events caused by NCDs is critical for an effective NCD response. Yet very few primary health care facilities have staff trained to treat NCDs (WHO and Libyan Ministry of Health 2017) and about two-thirds of primary health clinics have no antibiotics, analgesics, insulin, blood pressure

FIGURE 16.8

Leading causes of death in Libya, 2009 and 2019

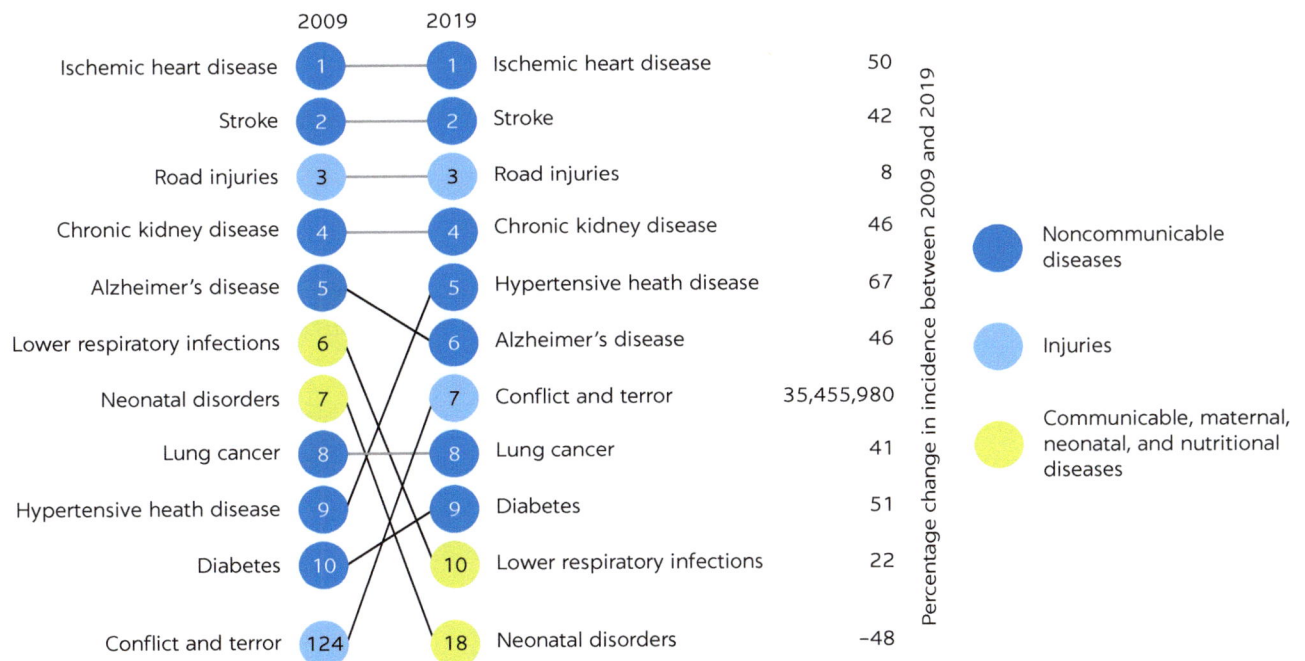

Source: IHME 2021.

medication, or any of Libya's other top 20 essential medicines (WHO Country Office Libya 2020).

Second, the COVID-19 pandemic has imposed an additional burden on the health care system. In the early days of the pandemic, some health care workers had no personal protective equipment and refused to report to work (WHO Country Office Libya 2020). Many hospitals had to suspend services because of infections among their workers. This stretched the capacity of hospitals that remained open. The emergency room at Al-Hawari General Hospital in Benghazi, was one hospital inundated with COVID-19 patients in the summer of 2020 (Golden 2020). The pandemic also revealed the limitations of the current health system to tackle public health emergencies. The rate of positive COVID-19 test results in Libya was as high as 22.7 percent in September 2021, perhaps because of low levels of testing in the country. Clear geographic disparities in response capacity are evident. As of March 2022, testing remained heavily concentrated in the West (96 percent of all tests conducted nationwide), and there were significant deficiencies in surveillance of all municipalities, especially in the South and East (WHO 2022). Libya started vaccinating its population in April 2021. However, even though Libya has been able to secure vaccines, systems to deploy them are constrained, with only around 15 percent of the Libyan population fully vaccinated in February 2022. The country has limited cold-chain capacity, which poses a challenge to both storing and distributing vaccines (WHO 2021a), and vaccine hesitancy is also emerging as a key barrier (NCDC 2021).

THE WAY FORWARD

Systematic interventions are needed to strengthen Libya's troubled health system. These involve not only rebuilding health infrastructure that has been destroyed due to the war but redesigning service delivery, strengthening systems for improved governance, management and monitoring of health services and human resources, and reforming the health financing architecture. Given the fragile context in Libya, consideration will need to be given to actions that are feasible and could be prioritized in the short term and those that are critical for sectoral reforms but are more likely possible in the medium to long term.

Rebuilding health services

Short-term actions: In the absence of reliable and current data, one of the first steps could be to conduct a national service delivery indicators (SDI) survey to take stock of the status of health service delivery to inform reconstruction efforts and provide a baseline for a health sector reform strategy. Alternate models of providing care such as outreach or mobile units in hard-to-reach areas could also be considered in the interim, complementing facility-based care and ensuring access to basic services close to home, particularly as reconstruction efforts may take time.

Medium- to long-term actions: In initiating recovery and reconstruction efforts, it will be important to prioritize investments in health facilities in areas that have been most significantly impacted by the conflict and have the poorest service provision. As demonstrated earlier, people in urban areas face fewer challenges regarding medical staff shortages, medicine shortages, and financing shortages, and regions impacted significantly by the conflict have a much higher share of individuals facing access barriers to health services. Therefore, prioritizing rural areas and conflict-affected districts for rebuilding health facilities and services would potentially have the most benefit.

Redesigning the primary health care system and improving quality of care

Short-term actions: To facilitate provision of an essential and equal package of services across all facilities, a key first step will be to develop national standards for PHC facilities that outline an essential core package of services to be provided covering maternal and child health, NCDs, and infectious diseases, including development of quality standards for delivering these services and updating population, staffing, and cost norms for PHC facilities. This will help build on the existing Primary Health Care Strategy and provide a basis for building a PHC system that provides uniform services and standards of care and is equipped to address the changing profile of disease burden in the country. Staff training, focused on reskilling existing workers to enable them to provide an updated comprehensive and integrated package of services, and the development of digital or paper-based job aids (such as checklists and communication and counseling material) to support capacity building could also be taken up in the short term.

Medium- to long-term actions: The rollout of the national standards will take longer and may need to be implemented in a phased manner keeping the resource envelope in mind. Implementation may include hiring additional specialized staff as needed and financing to ensure facilities are equipped to provide an expanded package of services. Priority during the first phase may be placed on rural and conflict-affected areas. To develop a culture of quality of care, mechanisms to monitor and measure quality will also need to be established. This could include the establishment of resolute quality teams that support achievement, monitoring, and maintenance of quality accreditation or standards (both structural and process quality) in hospitals and PHC facilities.

Strengthening supply chains for pharmaceuticals

Short-term actions: The need to strengthen Libya's pharmaceutical system is clear and critical as it has the potential to improve health care access as well as reduce out-of-pocket expenditures. As this may require systemic reform, an immediate step should be to undertake an assessment of current pharmaceutical financing and budgeting systems. This will help identify potential actions to facilitate demand-driven allocations (and not as a percentage of MoH budget). In addition, an assessment of the distribution systems should be considered to identify root causes of stockouts and quality issues at public health care facilities and to develop initiatives to improve performance. At the same time, steps to develop and publish clear guidelines and procedures for procurement of pharmaceuticals to avoid current opaqueness in the process should be prioritized.

Medium- to long-term actions: A pharmaceutical management information system should be developed and rolled out across facilities to better manage drug and medical supply inventories at the facility level. Such an information system can also facilitate the planning and budgeting for pharmaceuticals at the national level.

Reskilling and building the capacity of the health workforce

Short-term actions: Ensuring health workers are safe in their workplace and are paid fully and on time will be a vital first step toward improved motivation, availability, and performance. Continuous professional development and bridging programs should be considered to increase workers' capacity and reskilling in the short run, particularly for the PHC workforce, which needs to be developed into skilled generalists, working as a team of doctors and nurses trained in basic general practice. To improve distribution and reduce turnover in more remote areas, monetary and nonmonetary incentives should also be considered. Such incentives could improve the motivation and capacity of health workers and can include different mechanisms, including career progression and continued professional development and mentoring.

Medium- to long-term actions: Reforms are needed to improve the availability, distribution, and performance of health workers. To do so, the physical, technical, and organizational capacity of health-training institutions can be strengthened to increase the number of qualified health workers, particularly in nursing given the high number of diploma nurses. Decentralized education strategies, including e-health, could be considered. Strengthening broader regulatory and financing aspects related to workforce development, distribution, and performance is also critical. All these measures should be guided by national-level planning efforts, including the development and implementation of a national human resources for health strategy and the evidence and data needed to support its development.

Rebuilding information systems and enhancing capacity for use of data for decision-making

Short-term actions: Nationally representative data on health outcomes and service delivery in Libya are outdated, and having current data is critical to inform reform and rebuilding efforts. Libya has recently initiated rolling out the DHIS-2 to start collecting routine information from public health facilities on service delivery and has an Early Warning Alert and Response Network for infectious disease outbreaks in place. This is a good start and needs to be supported and continued, including considering interventions such as incentivizing facilities that routinely report through the DHIS-2 to highlight the relevance of data collection and reporting, as current reporting levels are low.

Medium- to long-term actions: Libya should consider reviving the practice of launching periodic DHS, STEPS, and SDI (or SARA) surveys to track changes in population level changes in health outcomes and services over time. This is important for evidence-based decision-making, to monitor and identify the need for reforms, and to report on progress on health-related Sustainable Development Goals. Technical and financial support can be leveraged in this regard from development agencies, both for building capacity of the HIC in the design of information systems and surveys, as well as for data collection and analysis, as needed.

Strengthening health financing system

Short-term actions: Given the extremely high shares of catastrophic health expenditure across all groups, the government will need to prioritize increasing the share of health in the national budget, as well as identify ways to improve the fiscal space. Implementing subsidies for purchase of essential medicines, coupled with increasing fiscal space for health, is among the most significant short-term health financing priorities that could be implemented. Embarking on the national health accounts development process would also help identify areas for improving efficiency of health expenditure and allow generation of additional evidence needed for planning and funding allocation decisions in the Libyan health system.

Medium- to long-term actions: While the full implementation of a national health insurance scheme is likely to take time, in the medium term, Libya could prioritize the implementation of targeted schemes to ensure the poorest and most vulnerable can access health services free of charge in both public and private facilities, including pharmacies. Libya can benefit from the experience of other post-conflict settings in scaling up financial risk protection schemes that target and prioritize the poor and the vulnerable, such as through the removal of user fees for service visits as well as drugs in private facilities.

Improving the governance of the health sector

Short-term actions: To provide a sense of stability, rather than restructuring the MoH governance structure, it may be more helpful to refine the existing MoH structure by clearly defining governance roles and responsibilities and links among the different entities governing the health sector in Libya. This could help generate a shared understanding of roles across institutions and administrative levels minimizing the experience of fragmentation.

Medium- to long-term actions: Further efforts to strengthen the existing governance structure should be based on a systematic institutional capacity assessment of the MoH. This will help identify areas for improving functional and financial efficiency and coordination among the different directorates, autonomous institutions, districts, and municipalities. It will also help develop a capacity-building plan to strengthen governance capacities at national, district, municipal, and facility levels as needed to support implementation of any proposed reorganization of the MoH structure in line with the existing proposals and national policy (MoH 2019b, 2019c). Any effort to restructure or decentralize without first capacitating and empowering the relevant levels and institutions in the health system may otherwise contribute to further fragmentation and dysfunctionality.

Regulating the private sector

Short-term actions: If regulated, the burgeoning private sector could be an effective complement to public health facilities, particularly in Libya's largest cities. Effective engagement of the private sector will require a comprehensive review of the current regulatory and compliance framework for the health care sector and the initiation of a formal public-private dialogue among relevant stakeholders. This will help create an environment of trust and an efficient channel of communication and contribute to the development of a strengthened regulatory framework and the identification of priority areas for public-private partnerships, such as delivery of services through purchase or insurance modalities, including primary care services, clinical support services, specialized clinical services, and managing hospital operations. Building the capacity of the existing private sector unit within the MoH will be key to initiating these processes.

Medium- to long-term actions: To facilitate implementation of the regulatory framework and ensure compliance to defined standards, a single robust accreditation body may need to be established with a governance structure that is able to identify and address current gaps and regional disparities that lead to non-compliances and uncontrolled prices. Standardized frameworks that can be used either centrally, at the district or facility level to strategically purchase services, along with capacity building of staff to manage these service contracts, should be considered. In addition, existing health insurance schemes should be strengthened to enable people to access quality services within the private sector at harmonized prices, creating an enabling financing environment for people and the private sector, contributing to improved access to services (World Bank 2021b).

CONCLUDING REMARKS

Libya's health sector is under extreme stress—with poor infrastructure, attacks on medical facilities, and closures of medical facilities—brought about by years of civil warfare and armed conflict. Policy makers have opportunities to strengthen the health care system, by placing greater emphasis on noncommunicable diseases, prioritizing primary health care, strengthening Libya's health care workforce, improving supply chains for medications and medical supplies, improving information systems and data sharing for evidence-based planning, strengthening health care governance, and financing and leveraging the private sector for improving health care access and quality.

NOTES

1. This chapter draws on several reports on Libya's health care system, including those by the United Nations Support Mission in Libya and the United Nations Human Rights Office of the High Commissioner, the World Bank, the Libyan Ministry of Health, Health Sector Libya, the World Health Organization, and the European Commission. The chapter also draws on publications found in the PUBMED database. Because of the armed conflict and COVID-19 pandemic, few recent household surveys or nationally representative studies have been conducted. As a result of the conflict, and the resultant data constraints, this chapter's data and summary conclusions should therefore be interpreted with a degree of caution.
2. The estimates are based on standardized methodology using the World Health Organization's Child Growth Standards. The United Nations Children's Fund, the World Health Organization, and the World Bank group jointly review available data sources to update the country-level estimates. Each agency uses its existing mechanisms for obtaining data. The stunting prevalence estimates come with levels of

uncertainty due to both sampling error and nonsampling error. The uncertainties are higher for countries where primary data are limited, such as Libya (stunting prevalence among children under 5 years of age was estimated to be 43.5 percent, with uncertainty interval of 36.5–50.8 percent).

3. See chapter 14, "The Electricity Sector."

REFERENCES

Action Against Hunger. 2020. *Multi-Sector Needs Assessment: Libya.* Paris: Action Against Hunger. https://fscluster.org/sites/default/files/documents/libya_aah_msna_2020_final _report.pdf.

Alharathy, S. 2017. "Italy Donates 1 million Euros to Conflict-Ridden Areas in Libya." *Libya Observer,* September 17, 2017. https://www.libyaobserver.ly/news/italy-donates-1-million -euros-conflict-ridden-areas-libya.

Alharathy, S. 2018. "WHO Distributes Essential Medicine to Health Facilities across Libya." *Libya Observer,* September 12, 2018. https://www.libyaobserver.ly/inbrief/who-distributes -essential-medicine-health-facilities-across-libya.

Assad, A. 2017. "EU Launches €10.9 Million Healthcare Program in Libya." *Libya Observer.* December 14, 2017. https://www.libyaobserver.ly/health/eu-launches-%E2%82%AC109 -million-healthcare-program-libya.

Assad, A. 2019. "European Union Launches Mental Health Project in Libya." *Libya Observer.* August 20, 2019. https://www.libyaobserver.ly/health/european-union-launches-mental -health-project-libya.

Assad A. 2020. "Libya's Health Ministry to Probe 'Negligence' at Tripoli University Hospital." *Libya Observer,* August 3, 2020. https://www.libyaobserver.ly/health/libyas-health -ministry-probe-negligence-tripoli-university-hospital.

Çelik, Y., and A. El Taguri. 2021. *Reforming the Health System in Libya.* Ankara: Statistical, Economic and Social Research and Training Centre for Islamic Countries.

Devi, S. 2021. "New Libyan Government Faces Health Challenges." *Lancet* 397 (10281): 1250. https://www.sciencedirect.com/science/article/pii/S0140673621007704.

Duran, D., and M. Hamza. 2022. "Determinants of Healthcare Access and Spending in Libya: A Post-Conflict Analysis." Background paper. World Bank, Washington, DC.

Elfituri, A., A. Almoudy, W. Jbouda, W. Abuflaiga, and F. M. Sherif. 2018. "Libya's Pharmaceutical Situation: A Professional Opinion." *International Journal of Academic Health and Medical Research* 2 (10): 5.

Gluck, G. 2020. "UNHCR Helps Re-Open Health Centre During Lockdown in Libya." July 16, 2020. Geneva: UN High Commissioner for Refugees. https://www.unhcr.org/en-us/news /stories/2020/7/5f0ffb954/unhcr-helps-re-open-health-centre-during-lockdown-libya .html.

Golden, R. 2020. "Patients Suffering from Coronavirus Increase at Benghazi's Al-Hawari Hospital." *Libya Observer,* August 30, 2020. https://www.libyaobserver.ly/inbrief/patients -suffering-coronavirus-increase-benghazi%E2%80%99s-al-hawari-hospital.

Health Sector Libya. 2020. Coronavirus Disease 2019 (COVID-19) Preparedness and Response Plan for Libya (WHO, IOM, UNHCR, UNICEF, UNFPA, UN Habitat, IMC, HI, TDH, MSF-Holland, MSF France, Emergenza Sorrissi-Naduk, IRC, PUI, UN Women). March 26, 2020. Tripoli: Health Sector Libya.

IHME (Institute for Health Metrics and Evaluation). 2021. Global Burden of Disease Compare /Viz Hub database. http://ghdx.healthdata.org/gbd-results-tool, accessed March 30, 2021.

Lemamsha, H., G. Randhawa, and C. Papadopoulos. 2019. "Prevalence of Overweight and Obesity among Libyan Men and Women." *Biomed Research International* 2019: 8531360. https://www.hindawi.com/journals/bmri/2019/8531360.

MoH (Ministry of Health). 2019a. *Mapping of Private Health Facilities of Libya 2019.* Tripoli: MoH Health Information Center.

MoH (Ministry of Health). 2019b. *Reorganized Structure of the Ministry of Health*. Tripoli: National Center for Health Sector Reform.

MoH (Ministry of Health). 2019c. *Well and Healthy Libya: National Health Policy, 2030*. Tripoli: National Center for Health Sector Reform.

MoH (Ministry of Health), WHO (World Health Organization), and EU (European Union). 2017. *Libyan Health Information System: Assessment and Roadmap of Priority Actions—Final Report*. Tripoli: MoH, WHO, and EU. https://reliefweb.int/report/libya/libyan-health -information-system-assessment-and-roadmap-priority-actions-final-report.

Mustafa, A. A., and S. R. Kowalski. 2010. "A Need for the Standardization of the Pharmaceutical Sector in Libya." *Libyan Journal of Medicine* 5 (1). https://www.tandfonline.com/doi /full/10.3402/ljm.v5i0.5440.

Najjair, H. 2018. "WHO Sends Mobile Health Clinics to Eastern Libya. *Libya Observer*, April 25, 2018. https://www.libyaobserver.ly/inbrief/who-sends-mobile-health-clinics-eastern -libya.

National Health Information and Documentation Center. Various years. Annual reports. Tripoli: Ministry of Health, World Health Organization, and European Union.

NCDC (National Center for Disease Control). 2021. *COVID-19 Vaccination Pillar. Libya —Summary of Main Progress Indicators. Campaign Week 3*, November 25. Tripoli: NCDC.

OCHA (United Nations Office for the Coordination of Humanitarian Affairs). 2021. Humanitarian Response Plan 2021. East Jerusalem: OCHA.

OCHA (United Nations Office for the Coordination of Humanitarian Affairs). 2022. Financial Tracking Service (database). https://fts.unocha.org/.

REACH. 2017. *Market Systems in Libya: Assessment of the Wheat Flour, Insulin, Tomato and Soap Supply Chains*. Geneva: REACH. www.reach-initiative.org.

REACH. 2019. *Libya–2019 Multi-Sector Needs Assessment (MSNA): Libyan Population*. Geneva: REACH. https://www.reachresourcecentre.info/country/libya/theme/multi-sector -assessments/cycle/684/#cycle-684.

Saim, M. 2016. "Health System Is in a State of Hidden Crisis." Paris: Médecins Sans Frontières, March 17, 2016. https://www.msf.org/libya-health-system-state-hidden-crisis.

Schaeffer, M. G., M. Lassoued, and Z. Ouelhazi, eds. 2021. *Proceedings of the Libya Local Government Forum, Tunis, Tunisia, September 14–16, 2019 (Revised for Publication: January 2021)*. Washington, DC: World Bank.

UNHCR (United Nations High Commissioner for Refugees). 2020. *Mental Health and Psychosocial Response during COVID-19 Outbreak*. June 2020. Geneva: UNHCR. https:// reporting.unhcr.org/sites/default/files/UNHCR%20MENA%20Mental%20Health%20 and%20Psychological%20support%20during%20COVID-19%20-%20June%202020.pdf.

WHO (World Health Organization). 2021a. "Libya: Health Response to COVID-19." WHO Update 26. Geneva. https://reliefweb.int/sites/reliefweb.int/files/resources/who_libya _covid-19_update_30_april_2021.pdf.

WHO (World Health Organization). 2021b. The Global Health Observatory (database). Geneva: WHO. https://www.who.int/data/gho.

WHO (World Health Organization). 2022. *Libya COVID-19 Surveillance Weekly Bulletin. Epidemiological Week 10 (07-13 March 2022)*. Geneva: WHO. https://reliefweb.int/sites /reliefweb.int/files/resources/covid-19_epi_weekly_libya_13_march_2022.pdf.

WHO (World Health Organization) and Libyan Ministry of Health. 2017. *Service Availability and Readiness Assessment of the Public Health Facilities in Libya*. Geneva and Tripoli: WHO and Libyan Ministry of Health. https://www.humanitarianresponse.info/sites/www .humanitarianresponse.info/files/assessments/service_availability_and_readiness _assessment_final_12-03-2018.pdf.

WHO (World Health Organization) Country Office Libya. 2020. *Annual Report 2020*. Cairo: WHO Regional Office for the Eastern Mediterranean. https://www.humanitarianresponse .info/sites/www.humanitarianresponse.info/files/documents/files/who_libya_annual _report_2020.pdf.

WHO EMRO (World Health Organization Regional Office for the Eastern Mediterranean). 2007. *Health Systems Profile–Libya.* Cairo: WHO EMRO.

WHO EMRO (World Health Organization Regional Office for the Eastern Mediterranean). 2014. *Analysis of the Private Health Sector in Countries of the Eastern Mediterranean: Exploring Unfamiliar Territory.* Cairo: WHO EMRO.

WHO EMRO (World Health Organization Regional Office for the Eastern Mediterranean). 2020. *Comprehensive Assessment of Libya's Health Information System 2017.* Cairo: WHO EMRO.

WHO EMRO (World Health Organization Regional Office for the Eastern Mediterranean). 2021. *Health Workforce Snapshot: Libya.* Cairo: WHO EMRO.

World Bank. 2018. *Libya Primary Health Care Survey Analysis.* Washington, DC: World Bank.

World Bank. 2021a. "Assessment of the Private Healthcare Sector in Libya." Background paper. World Bank, Washington, DC.

World Bank. 2021b. "Pharmaceutical System Strengthening: Global Lessons for Reform in Libya and Fragile and Conflict Countries." Background paper. World Bank, Washington, DC.

World Bank. 2021c. World Development Indicators (database). World Bank, Washington, DC. https://databank.worldbank.org/source/world-development-indicators.

World Bank. 2022. "A Technical Paper on the Availability, Motivation, and Performance of Primary Care Healthcare Workers in the Libyan Regions of Tripolitania, Cyrenaica, and Fezzan." Background paper. World Bank, Washington, DC.

17 Education Reform in the Context of Conflict, Migration, and COVID-19

DONNA ESPEUT, REMY PIGOIS, NARINE ASLANYAN, ANNA RESSLER, IBRAHIM FARAH, AND ERICA AIAZZI

United Nations Children's Fund

The Libyan education sector has been devastated by the conflict and by changing migration flows. The ongoing efforts at decentralizing education reform that capacitates subnational actors, along with effective multistakeholder, multisectoral coordination mechanisms at all levels, must be prioritized. Improving the education sector requires (1) introducing education and learning opportunities for all children in a way that addresses learning interruptions; (2) optimizing the content, structure, and quality of education systems; (3) incorporating psychological-social support, life skills training, and prevention of violence activities; and (4) enhancing the management of qualified, motivated teachers to maximize children's ability to learn.

INTRODUCTION

Before the 2011 revolution, Libya was a positive outlier in the Middle East and North Africa (MENA) on several education indicators. Since then, measures have deteriorated. The impact of the armed conflict on physical infrastructure has been extensive, with at least 37 schools destroyed; 182 partially damaged; and some repurposed as shelters for internally displaced persons (IDPs), military barracks, and field hospitals for armed groups. Reduced school availability and school closures during the spikes of the conflict have led to school overcrowding, compromising the quality of the learning environment.

This chapter synthesizes the evidence and analyzes the impact of the protracted conflict, mixed migration, and the COVID-19 pandemic on Libya's education sector, with a focus on preprimary and formal basic education.[1] It is organized as follows: the first section provides a brief overview of the sector before the 2011 revolution. The second section analyzes the impact of the conflict, mixed migration, and COVID-19 on supply-side and demand-side factors. The third section recommends policy reforms and actions that could support and promote good-quality education and intersectoral synergies for equitable investment in human capital while ensuring that no child in Libya is left behind. The last section provides concluding remarks.

EDUCATION BEFORE THE 2011 REVOLUTION

Policy landscape

Libya acceded to the Convention on the Rights of the Child (CRC) in 1993 and both the Optional Protocol to the CRC on the sale of children, child prostitution, and child pornography (2004) and the Optional Protocol to the CRC on the involvement of children in armed conflict (2004). In Libya, the first nine years of school (six years of primary school and the first three years of secondary school) have been free and compulsory since 1969.[2] Preprimary education, which is provided primarily by private providers (MoE 2012), has not been compulsory until now. Participation in early education remains very low.

Several policies and legislative frameworks have fostered an enabling environment for inclusive education, and legislation outside of the education sector addresses some core drivers of vulnerability. For example, social protection legislation, including Law No. 20 (1998) of the Libyan Social Security Fund, made provisions to support families considered fragile with various forms of social assistance, such as financial support, education, and housing assistance (UNDP 2020).

There have been gaps and bottlenecks related to the implementation and enforcement of policy frameworks, however. For example, Libya approved the Disabled Persons Act No. 5 of 1987, but the existence of a disability policy did not translate into equitable educational access for all children living with disabilities (Abdul-Hamid 2011). There are laws and regulations prohibiting corporal punishment in schools, but various forms of violence in schools are still prevalent.[3]

Governance and coordination

Before the conflict, the Ministry of Education (MoE) was the lead government agency for education. As formalized by the Council of Ministers Resolution 134, it had 18 departments and 4 affiliated bodies (MoE, UNICEF, and European Union 2019). The mandate for teacher development did not reside within a single ministry. The Ministry of Higher Education and Scientific Research offered preservice teacher education through universities and colleges, and the MoE offered in-service teacher training. The National Board for Technical and Vocational Training and Education, an independent administrative authority, was responsible for technical and vocational education and training (TVET). Coordination between the three bodies was limited (MoE, UNICEF, and European Union 2019).

Libya does not have a fully functional routine information system in schools to provide data for effective management of the education system, evidence-based policy, resource allocation, and program decision-making. Consequently, basic education data (for example, the number of students, the number of schools, and the number of teachers) are not systematically tracked or easily available.

Financing and budget management

Before 2011, Libya allocated a larger share of its budget to education than other MENA countries (MoE 2011). Public expenditure on education accounted for 6.3 percent of gross national income in 2009 (MoE 2012). However, shortcomings existed with respect to the financing of different levels of education and building blocks of education service delivery. Like other countries in MENA, for example, Libya underinvested in early childhood care and education (ECCE) (World Bank n.d). The majority of public investment in education was and is still dedicated to salaries. In 2009, 94 percent of the public education budget was allocated to teachers and support staff.

Literacy, enrollment, and attendance

Before the 2011 revolution, Libya was a positive outlier in the MENA region, ranking well on a multitude of education-related indicators. The country met its education Millennium Development Goals (Carter 2018). In 2008, the adult literacy was 88 percent—well above the regional average of 72 percent—and literacy was universal for men and women between the ages of 15 and 24. Between 1973 and 1985, the female student population increased by 130 percent (Ali Elabbar 2017). Gross enrollment rates were near universal for both boys and girls at all levels except preprimary. In 2006, the gross enrollment ratio was 9 percent for preprimary education, with a gender parity index (GPI) of 0.97; 110 percent for primary education, with a GPI of 0.95; and 93 percent for secondary education, with a GPI of 1.17 (MoE 2012).

Disparities existed by household wealth, disability status, and geographical location. Analysis of the 2007 Libya Family Health Survey (Pan Arab Project for Family Health, or PAPFAM]) revealed that a child from the richest wealth quintile was almost three times more likely to attend ECCE than a child from the lowest wealth quintile (14.3 percent versus 4.6 percent) (figure 17.1). No data exist with respect to migrants before 2011.

Despite being an upper-middle-income country, high levels of investment in education did not translate into high education sector performance. Libya ranked 128th out of 139 countries in the quality of its primary education system and 138th out of 139 countries on the quality of its higher education and training. Factors contributing to the education sector's challenges included poor teacher qualification levels, absenteeism, lack of facilities and adequate equipment, and traditional curricula that were oriented only toward preparing students for

FIGURE 17.1

Participation rates in early childhood care and education, by wealth quintile, 2007

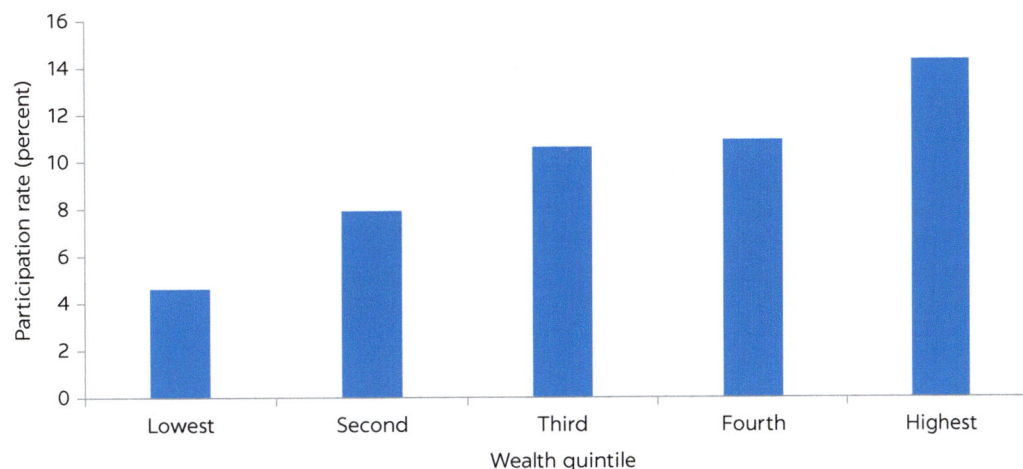

Source: World Bank 2017, based on results of 2007 Pan Arab Project for Family Health.

university studies, according to the 2011 World Economic Forum (2010) survey. Large numbers of inactive teachers remained on the payroll, and shortfalls in the quality of education were reflected in learning outcomes, as evidenced by the high levels of grade repetition (Carter 2018). Poor alignment between the education system and the job market, characterized as a centralized state economy, contributed to high rates of unemployment among women and youth (MoE 2012). Its teaching system centers on core subjects and does not provide recreational activities, life-skills education, or psychosocial support.

The shortcomings of the education system are rooted in suboptimal governance and the quality-of-service delivery. As described in the next section, the shocks experienced by the country since 2011 have placed further strains on Libya's education system.

EFFECTS OF ARMED CONFLICT AND THE PANDEMIC SINCE THE REVOLUTION

A series of events adversely affected education in Libya after 2011 (figure 17.2). The 2011 revolution and mixed migration flows shaped Libya's trajectory over the past decade. Still grappling with protracted armed conflict associated with

FIGURE 17.2

Critical events since 2011 that have affected the education sector

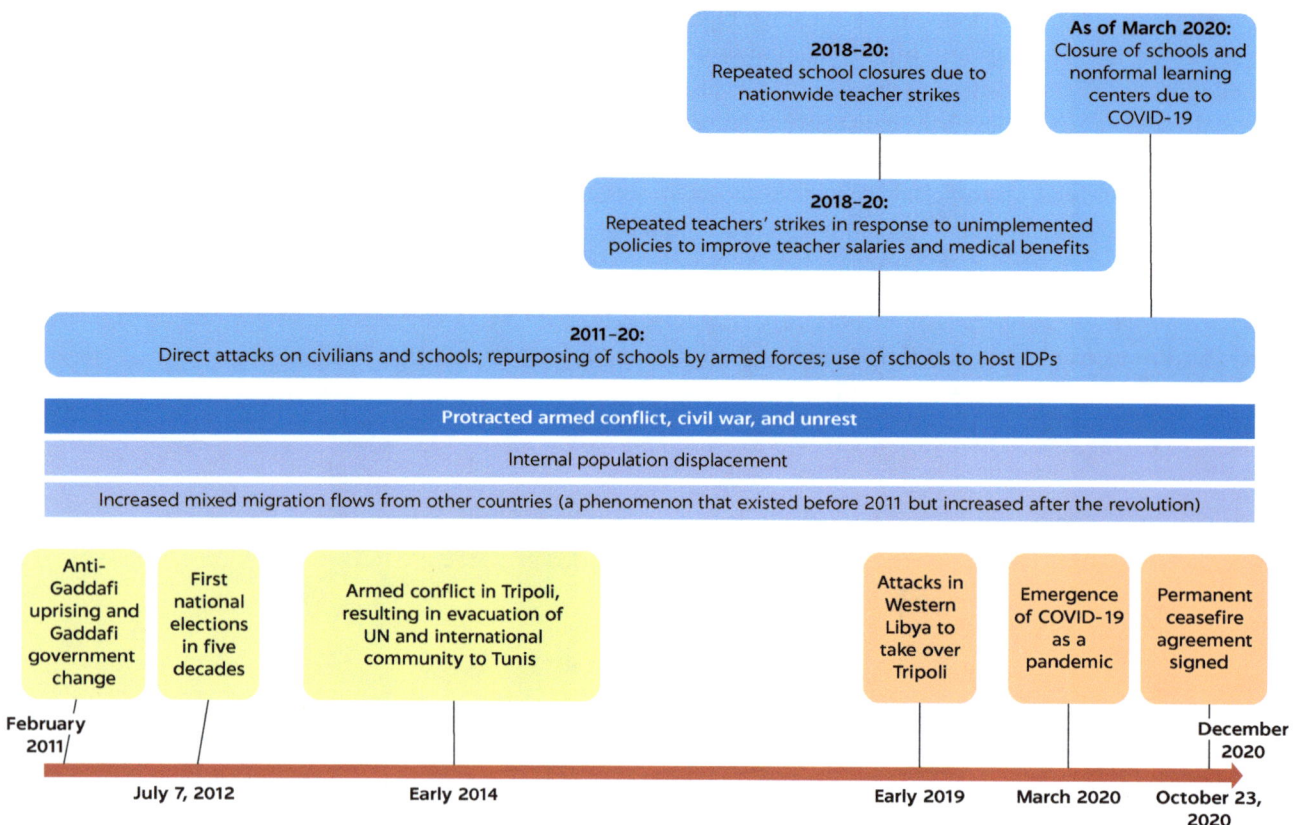

Source: UNICEF.
Note: IDP = internally displaced person; UN = United Nations.

the Gaddafi government change, school-age children in Libya are now contending with education obstacles resulting from the COVID-19 pandemic.

Although data are limited, existing studies suggest that during the past decade, the overall quality of Libya's educational system has continued to deteriorate. As shown in table 17.1, a decrease in the quality of education was noted just a few years after the revolution, even before the internal armed conflict reached its peak and the governance system was fragmented (World Economic Forum 2012).

Impact on supply-side factors

This section provides an analysis of the impacts of the conflict, mixed migration, and COVID-19 on the supply-side factors of the education sector.

Governance and coordination

For a number of years, the governance of the education sector was impacted by the fragmentation of national governance. Parallel education ministries in the East and West complicated administration of schools and reform efforts. The establishment of the Government of National Unity in March 2021 allowed for the reunification of line ministries. Improved coordination at the national and subnational level is essential to future reform initiatives.

Policy landscape

Libya does not have an overarching national education development plan. The quality and timeliness of activities in the education sector have historically been hampered by political fragmentation. The reunification of education line ministries during 2021 is a critical opportunity. The development of a unified policy and a national education development plan is an essential next step.

The Education Sector Working Group (ESWG) was established, with UN support, in August 2015 to coordinate sector policies and the design and implementation of programs, projects, and activities. The group's main objective is to craft a coherent and coordinated education sector response plan, with a focus on emergency and strategic linkages to resilience building and early recovery in Libya. The ESWG is part of the International Technical Coordination Structure of the Government; it reports to the Basic Social Services pillar under the Joint Technical Coordination Committee. The group focuses on policy-level upstream interventions and responds to the humanitarian crisis.

TABLE 17.1 Performance of the education sector just before and just after the 2011 revolution

INDICATOR	2010/11	2012/13
Quality of primary education	128	134
Quality of the education system	138	142
Quality of mathematics and science education	113	135
Internet in schools	129	134
Management of schools	137	144

Source: World Economic Forum's Global Competitiveness Index.
Note: Figures show ranking out of 144 countries.

Infrastructure and supplies

Physical infrastructure in the education sector has been severely affected by the conflict. Between 2011 and 2019, at least 37 schools were destroyed and 182 were partially damaged (OCHA 2020c). In 2020 alone, at least 16 schools had been hit by air strikes, affecting 15,890 students (UNDP 2020).

A 2016–17 nationwide assessment of the water, sanitation, and hygiene (WASH) situation in 140 schools found that 96 percent had limited sanitation services, 67 percent had a limited drinking water source, and 48 percent had no hygiene services (NCDC 2017). The assessment also documented widespread shortcomings related to the maintenance and cleaning of school WASH facilities; the availability of essential WASH supplies, such as soap for handwashing; and drinking water quality.

There has been substantial repurposing of schools. In 2020, 27 schools in 14 municipalities were repurposed to serve as temporary shelters for IDPs (UNDP 2020). The 2019 Multisector Needs Assessment in 18 mantikas (districts) found that schools in mantikas such as Al Jfara and Derna had been repurposed by armed actors as military barracks and field hospitals (REACH and ACTED 2020).[4]

Quality of the learning environment

Humanitarian actors have galvanized support to rehabilitate schools and build additional classrooms to create more learning spaces for displaced children and to rehabilitate and extend WASH facilities. However, the reduced availability of schools has led to school overcrowding, which has compromised the quality of the learning environment (OCHA 2020a). Libya does not have parent-teacher associations or other mechanisms for community involvement in schools, limiting opportunities for communities to work collaboratively with the MoE to address school issues.

The 2019 MSNA noted that school overcrowding was reported in the mantikas of Al Jfara, Derna, Misrata, Murzuq, Sebha, Sirte, Tripoli, and Ubari. Urban areas, where 85 percent of Libya's population resides (UN Habitat 2020), have extremely large school populations, with some primary schools accommodating as many as 2,000 students (MoE, UNICEF, and European Union 2019). Impacted schools have adopted a shift system to accommodate the large numbers of students accessing a reduced number of functional schools. The conflict compounded systemic issues that were already present across the education system; a 2012 nationwide school assessment found that 57 percent of sampled schools held classes in the morning only, 35 percent held classes in morning and afternoon shifts, and 8 percent held classes only in the afternoon (MoE 2012).

Financing and budget management

There is a paucity of financial data on the education system since 2011. UNICEF (2019b) has noted limited investments in the enabling environment, including school infrastructure and teacher professional development. Humanitarian and development partners have filled resource gaps to support system preservation and mitigate education access barriers for marginalized and vulnerable children. Other challenges abound—including outdated curricula, low teacher compensation, and weak procurement and distribution bottlenecks for essential supplies such as textbooks.

Human resources

Evidence on teacher supply is limited. However, it appears that a major surplus of teachers—estimated at 200,000 in 2019—remain on the MoE's payroll despite being inactive.[5] In 2012, the World Economic Forum ranked Libya 140th out of 144 countries in teacher training (MoE 2012). Weakness in teacher management and low sectoral efficiency was already reflected in the MENA region's lowest student-teacher ratios. For instance, in Libya, the student-to-teacher ratio had reached as low as 4.3 students per teacher in 2007 (average in MENA was 20) due to the government policy to boost public sector employment and is anecdotally reported as only increasing slightly during the post-revolution period to the present time.

Although most teachers in Libya meet academic qualifications for entry into the profession, many lack training (MoE, UNICEF, and European Union 2019; United Kingdom Home Office 2020).[6] For example, there are capacity gaps with regards to the instruction of children with special needs, classroom management, and positive discipline (MoE 2012; MoE, UNICEF, and European Union 2019). Lack of gender balance is also an issue; an estimated 85–90 percent of teachers are women, and some schools have only female teachers (MoE, UNICEF, and European Union 2019). The crisis has eroded teacher morale and motivation, affecting the availability and quality of education services. With a monthly salary of LD 680–850 in 2020, teachers in Libya receive far lower salaries than other civil servants, and salaries are sometimes delayed. Since 2018, there have been several teachers' strikes, each resulting in school closure for several weeks.

Data for decision-making

Libya lacks a comprehensive education management information system (EMIS). As a result, there is a dearth of administrative data on levels and trends in various aspects of Libya's education system. With UNICEF support, the Ministry of Education has made progress during 2021 with laying the foundation for the development and rollout of EMIS in the coming years.

Threats of violence

Violence against children in school is prevalent in Libya, despite laws prohibiting corporal punishment in schools. A 2018 study revealed that physical violence is much more prevalent in schools than in homes, with teachers the most frequent perpetrators (NCDC, UNICEF, and Coram 2018). The same study highlighted the elevated risks of physical violence among students with disabilities.

Peer violence is also a problem in Libya, with 36 percent of children reporting being bullied (NCDC, UNICEF, and Coram 2018). Having a disability significantly increases the likelihood that a child will be a victim of bullying: 53 percent of children with disabilities reported that they had been victims of bullying at school, with 18 percent reporting that they were frequently bullied.

Unequal access to the internet

Schools exist throughout Libya, with special outreach programs (such as mobile classrooms) for nomadic children and children in hard-to-reach areas (MoE, UNICEF, and European Union 2019). However, access to the internet is varied, likely exacerbating disparities in educational outcomes. Internet access and access to distance education is impacted by regular power; wide variation in smartphone, computer, and television ownership; and variation in the reliability of mobile network coverage across mantikas and population categories.

Misalignment of education with the labor market

Although the MoE updated standard curricula and textbooks in 2012, the harmonized distribution and use of those materials needs to be optimized. There is weak alignment of the education system to the labor markets. As a result, Libya has high rates of unemployment, despite relatively high rates of tertiary enrollment. The unemployment rate among youth (ages 15–24) increased from 17 percent in 2010 to 48 percent in 2015 (41 percent for men and 68 percent for women) (World Bank 2015).

Since the 2011 Gaddafi government change, the MoE has sought support from the United Nations to expand its TVET program, which is implemented by public and private sector providers. It has introduced regulations to mitigate the effects of the conflict on TVET, particularly given the large numbers of IDP students in institutes of higher learning and technical colleges who were unable to continue their education during the humanitarian crisis (Jurado 2018). According to a new regulation, since 2018, displaced students can register at host institutions for up to three semesters and still receive their final diploma from their original TVET center. Enrollment in TVET is low, however, and the quality is substandard (Jurado 2018).

Impact of COVID-19

To try to contain the spread of COVID-19, Libya closed all its schools on March 15, 2020. The move affected an estimated 1.3 million children (UNDP 2020). Schools reopened in the Western region for the preparation of grade 12 exams on August 31, 2020, and in the Eastern region on September 6, 2020, for the preparation for grade 9 exams. Schools remained closed for all other grades until January 2021. With support from UNICEF, both MoEs introduced distance education via television and digital platforms during school closure. However, according to the 2020 Multi-Sector Needs Assessment (MSNA), only 17 percent of households with enrolled school-age children reported access to education during the lockdown (REACH 2020).[7]

The MoE reports that for the 2019-20 academic year, the primary school certificate pass rate was 62 percent (Libya Observer 2021), and the secondary certificate rate was 44 percent (Libyan Express 2020). These rates are not dramatically different from previous years. However, it is unlikely that they reflect real learning levels for children who were not able to go to school for almost nine months or the fact that remote learning reached a small minority of children.

Data from the international humanitarian community for January–October 2020 reveal several gaps in achieving humanitarian response targets, particularly in relation to (1) the number of school-age children accessing formal and nonformal education (90 percent gap), (2) the number of children accessing psychosocial support in schools and learning spaces (57 percent gap), and (3) the number of teachers and education personnel trained in psychosocial support (99 percent gap) (OCHA 2020b). In contrast, humanitarian partners have been on track in increasing the numbers of children receiving essential learning materials and supplies, accessing rehabilitated and repaired educational facilities, and receiving meals in school (OCHA 2020b).

Impacts on demand-side factors

Eroding participation in education

In 2012, one year after the revolution, there was minimal change in the number of students enrolled across the country, even in provinces with the densest populations and severe humanitarian need (for example, Benghazi, Misrata, and Tripoli). Rural provinces (primarily in the Southern part of the country) accounted for a low number of enrolled students, however. (MoE 2012). According to national estimates, there was a significant decline in enrollment in 2014 and 2015 (21 percent decline for boys, 17 percent decline for girls), directly attributable to the conflict (UNSMIL 2015). In 2017, gross enrollment was estimated at 96.7 percent in primary and secondary school, including displaced Libyan children (Carter 2018). There is no gender-disaggregated data.

According to the 2020 Humanitarian Response Plan, which was finalized before the emergence of the COVID-19 pandemic and subsequent school closures, 127,000 school-age children were in need of support to access safe and quality formal and nonformal education, including 38,500 IDPs, 12,500 returnees, 17,500 migrants and refugees, and 58,500 nondisplaced students.

A multiple overlapping deprivations analysis (MODA) based on data from 2014, profiles children facing deprivations in education (table 17.2). It reveals that Libyan children who suffer from multiple overlapping deprivations are particularly vulnerable to educational exclusion. Children 0–4 who are deprived of early childhood development (ECD) have the highest rate of deprivations that overlap with child protection and health dimensions (18.6 percent of children in this age group are simultaneously deprived of all three dimensions). Children 15–17 who are deprived in education have the highest rate of overlapping deprivation with nutrition, housing, and sanitation dimensions.

MODA findings also revealed that in 2014, one in five children either did not complete basic schooling or was behind in schooling years (figure 17.3). The analysis concluded that schooling quality might keep children from progressing in school, there may be incentives for children to drop out of school early, and/or there may be a lack of support from caregivers or teachers (UNICEF and SPRI 2020).

Gender differences

An assessment conducted in four municipalities (Al Bayada, Sebha, Zintan, and Zwara) found that girls constituted 56 percent of students at the primary school level, 44 percent at the junior-secondary level, and 33 percent at the senior-secondary level (UNICEF 2020b). As a result of conflict-related school

TABLE 17.2 Characteristics of children with highest rates of deprivation in education, 2014

AGE (YEARS)	CHARACTERISTICS
0–4	• Live in rural areas • Live with mother or household head with no education • Live in households that have four or more children or are labor constrained[a] • Often also have deprivations in child protection and health
5–14	• Live in household headed by a woman • Have household head with no education • Have disability • Have household head who works in the private sector
15–17	• Live with household head with no education • Are or were married • Often also have deprivations in nutrition, housing, and sanitation

Source: UNICEF and SPRI 2020.
a. In statistical terms, these households have either no household member who is fit for productive work or they have a high dependency ratio. They are labor constrained.

FIGURE 17.3

Deprivation headcount rate for early childhood development and education indicators, by age group, 2014

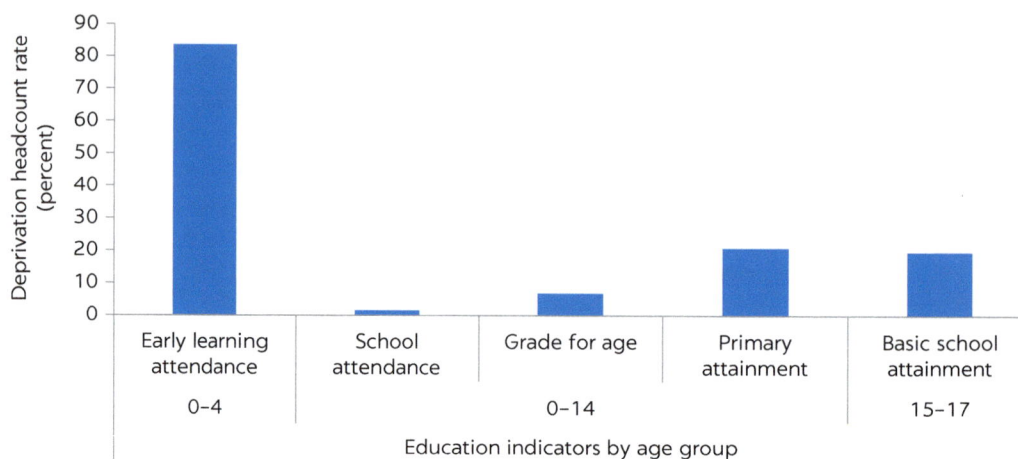

Source: UNICEF and SPRI 2020.

closures, students are required to travel longer distances to go to school, increasing the risks of harassment on their commute (REACH and ACTED 2020).[8] The risk of sexual- and gender-based violence is elevated in times of crisis. It is particularly widespread among migrant women and girls (United Kingdom Home Office 2020).

Gender-related beliefs and norms appear to drive gendered experiences in navigating the impacts of shocks since 2011. For example, although early marriage has declined to extremely low levels nationwide (UNFPA n.d.), indications and anecdotal evidence reveal that early and forced marriage may be increasing (UNICEF 2020b). The December 2019 Libya Joint Education Needs Assessment reports that 20 percent of girls (17 percent in the South and 25 percent in the West) who were not attending school cited marriage as a reason.

Affiliation with armed groups

There is anecdotal evidence that during some periods, high rates of unemployment and the lack of economic opportunities may be pushing some children to join armed groups (UNESCO et al. 2017), diverting them away from the educational system. The proliferation of armed groups limits civic, political, and economic opportunities for youth (United Network of Young Peacebuilders 2020) and fosters disillusionment (UNICEF 2020b). Concepts of masculinity—in particular, the responsibility of men and boys to protect and provide economically for their families—may also be motivating their affiliation with armed groups (UNICEF 2020b).

Household resilience

Weak coping capacity of households reduces educational access. According to the 2020 Humanitarian Response Plan, 35 percent of households with children enrolled in school reported challenges in sending their children to school; many of these households withdrew their children from school as a result (OCHA 2020c). In 2020, the percentage of households reporting that they were unable to cover education-related needs in the 30 days before data collection was much higher for refugee families (almost 30 percent) than for IDP and nondisplaced families (each below 10 percent) (REACH 2020).[9]

Children with disabilities, internally displaced children, and children from ethnic minorities

Stigma and discrimination impede equitable access to quality education. Children with disabilities and children on the move face systemic discrimination and barriers that limit their educational access. According to the MODA, which is based on 2014 PAPFAM data, disability is the most important differentiator among children deprived in education; the rate of education deprivation was 16 percent for children with disabilities, compared with 6 percent for children without disabilities (UNICEF and SPRI 2020). Students with disabilities accounted for 0.84 percent of the school population in 2012 (MoE 2012).

Since 2011, efforts have been made to ensure that IDP children are not excluded from education. Libyan educational institutions have allowed children to enroll in school even when they have lost identity documents normally required for school enrollment (REACH and ACTED 2020).[10] Children on the move still face access barriers, however. A 2016 survey by the International Organization for Migration revealed that almost half of the female migrants interviewed had no formal education. Migrants living in areas affected by conflict or displaced by the conflict continue to face educational access barriers and have a myriad of unmet needs related to their protection, nutrition, health, and security (UNICEF 2020a).

Data on inclusive education for children from ethnic minority groups such as the Amazigh, Tuareg, and Tubu do not exist. However, the 2019 MSNA showed that in places such as Murzuq, discrimination against girls in educational settings is often rooted in tribal discrimination, not gender inequality (Carter 2018; REACH and ACTED 2020).[11] The Tawerghan, for example, have been systematically marginalized. They account for a large proportion of conflict-related IDPs (UNSMIL 2018). Having a physical disability and being from an ethnic minority background are strong predictors of a child's likelihood of reporting physical violence (Coram and UNICEF 2018). Understanding the intersection of traits is critical to addressing education-related barriers for subsets of children.

Large numbers of children on the move who are non-Arab are out of school (UNICEF 2018). In Tripoli, for example, at least 77 percent of migrant, refugee, and/or asylum-seeking children from countries such as Eritrea, Ethiopia, and Somalia were not enrolled in school in 2018. An estimated 35 percent of migrant and refugee children are unaccompanied and/or separated (OCHA 2020c), further limiting their contact with formal service delivery in education and other social sectors.

Violence and threats to safety

Violence and threats to the safety of children (particularly girls) have contributed to the reluctance of some parents to send their children to school (UNDP 2020). The on-going instability and political turmoil since 2011 have taken a toll on the psychosocial well-being of school-age children. Conflict-induced stress is believed to be negatively affecting both school attendance and the ability of girls and boys to learn (UNICEF 2019b). The quality of the learning environment is a demand driver. Various supply-side factors, such as infrastructure (including the lack of separate latrines for girls), teacher and teaching quality, and violence in schools reduce access to education (OCHA 2020a; UNICEF 2020b) (figure 17.4).

FIGURE 17.4

Drivers and determinants of demand for education since 2011

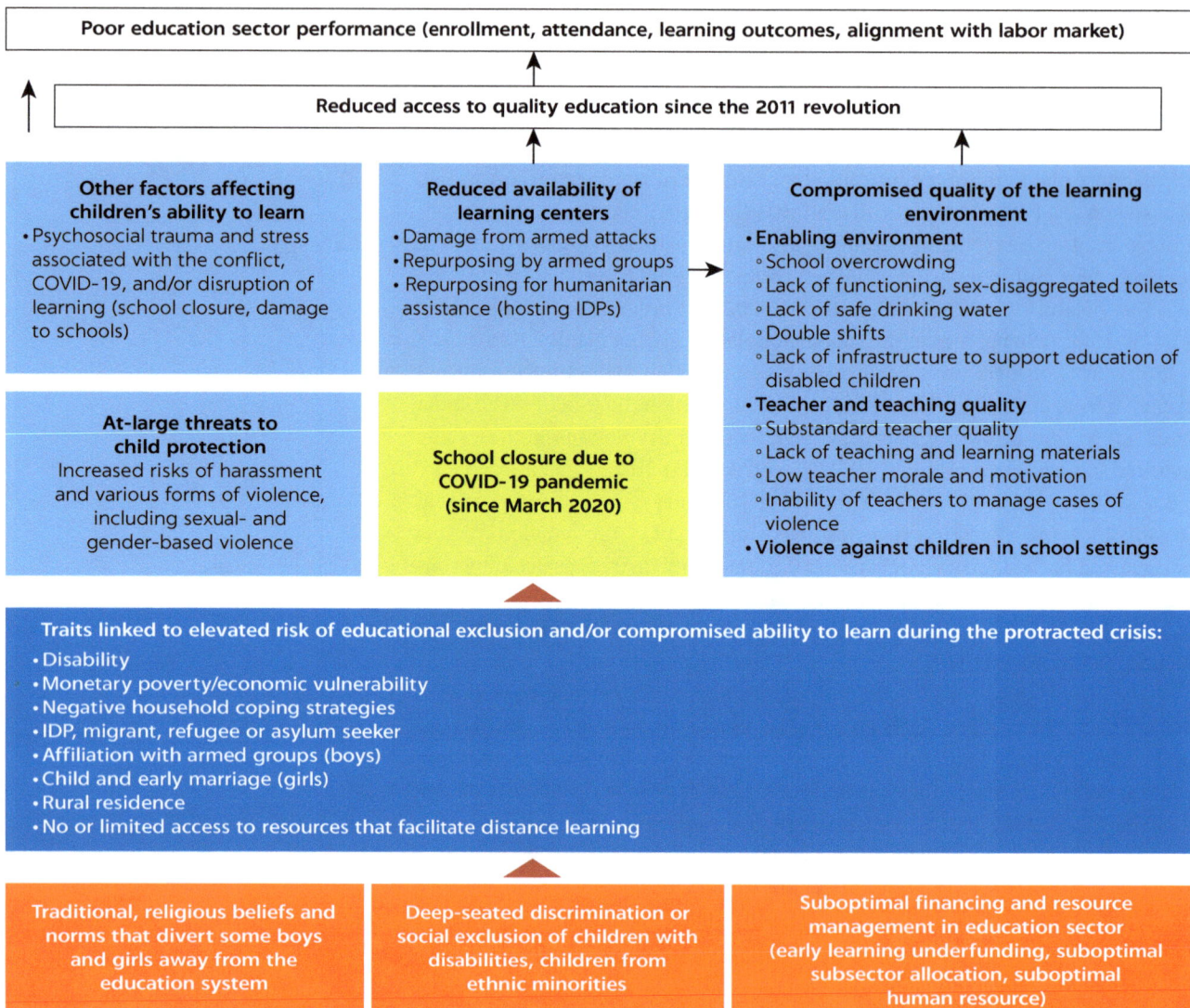

Poor education sector performance (enrollment, attendance, learning outcomes, alignment with labor market)

Reduced access to quality education since the 2011 revolution

Other factors affecting children's ability to learn
• Psychosocial trauma and stress associated with the conflict, COVID-19, and/or disruption of learning (school closure, damage to schools)

Reduced availability of learning centers
• Damage from armed attacks
• Repurposing by armed groups
• Repurposing for humanitarian assistance (hosting IDPs)

Compromised quality of the learning environment
• **Enabling environment**
  ◦ School overcrowding
  ◦ Lack of functioning, sex-disaggregated toilets
  ◦ Lack of safe drinking water
  ◦ Double shifts
  ◦ Lack of infrastructure to support education of disabled children
• **Teacher and teaching quality**
  ◦ Substandard teacher quality
  ◦ Lack of teaching and learning materials
  ◦ Low teacher morale and motivation
  ◦ Inability of teachers to manage cases of violence
• **Violence against children in school settings**

At-large threats to child protection
Increased risks of harassment and various forms of violence, including sexual- and gender-based violence

School closure due to COVID-19 pandemic (since March 2020)

Traits linked to elevated risk of educational exclusion and/or compromised ability to learn during the protracted crisis:
• Disability
• Monetary poverty/economic vulnerability
• Negative household coping strategies
• IDP, migrant, refugee or asylum seeker
• Affiliation with armed groups (boys)
• Child and early marriage (girls)
• Rural residence
• No or limited access to resources that facilitate distance learning

Traditional, religious beliefs and norms that divert some boys and girls away from the education system

Deep-seated discrimination or social exclusion of children with disabilities, children from ethnic minorities

Suboptimal financing and resource management in education sector (early learning underfunding, suboptimal subsector allocation, suboptimal human resource)

Source: UNICEF.
Note: IDP = internally displaced person.

THE WAY FORWARD: POST-CONFLICT, POST-COVID-19 REFORMS

As Libya emerges from the shocks of protracted conflict and the COVID-19 pandemic, ensuring quality education for all will require reform of the education system. The creation of a national development plan, which currently does not exist, is an essential step in facilitating Libya's progress against the 2030 Sustainable Development Goals (SDGs). The future development of a unified national education sector plan (aligned to the national development plan) is paramount to ensuring equitable access to good-quality education and high education sector performance. Several educational reforms in the short and medium term are essential, including the following:

Improving governance and coordination

- Increased coherence and coordination in the delivery of education services across MoE departments and related bodies (MoE, UNICEF, and European Union 2019)
- Maintaining the safe opening of schools in both COVID-19 and ceasefire contexts
- Enhanced decentralized management and delivery of education services while (1) maintaining the core objectives of the national curriculum while allowing municipalities to adapt curriculum activities and modes of delivery and (2) instituting or strengthening mechanisms to support decentralized decision-making and budgeting by municipalities
- Improved sector budget allocation and spending, rationalizing subsector allocation to address all aspects of education service delivery, including ECCE, infrastructure strengthening, human resource management, quality improvement, and alternative modalities for the delivery of education services (such as distance learning)
- Implementation of reforms to improve learning outcomes and align with the labor market

Enhancing human resource development and management

- Enhanced management, capacity building, task-shifting, and deployment of the oversupply of teachers
- Strengthened quality and relevance of pre- and in-service teacher training on core subjects and cross-cutting issues that affect children's ability to learn (including psychosocial stress and trauma, special needs/functional difficulties, classroom management, and violence)
- Expanded professional development of a qualified pool of female and male teachers

Improving the content, structure, and quality of education through a life-course approach

- Preprimary included as a free and compulsory component of basic education in Libya
- Reformed curriculum to (1) align secondary education and TVET with labor market needs to ensure that students have skills that make them employable contributors to labor productivity, and (2) incorporate psychosocial support, recreational activities, life-skills training, and the prevention and responses to violence against children
- Accelerated education and learning opportunities for children who have been excluded from traditional modes of education delivery

Improving accreditation and quality assurance

- Formalized mechanisms for routinely assessing and improving education quality at all levels, including mechanisms for involving community members in quality monitoring and quality improvements in schools
- Strengthened links to the private sector and other employment opportunities by tracking labor market dynamics and sectors with high job creation prospects and aligning skills to support labor productivity and economic participation of young men and women once they leave the education system

Developing routine data and creating an EMIS

- Strengthened availability and access to data as an operational requirement for implementing inclusive educational policies and programs throughout Libya
- Foster acountability across various aspects of service delivery and outcomes

Investing in human capital and demobilization

The historically low level of investment in ECD is an impediment to mitigating the intergenerational effects of the protracted humanitarian crisis on Libya. ECD should be positioned as a foundational component of Libya's future human capital development. Low ECCE coverage continues to place children, especially children from less educated, marginalized, and/or economically unstable households, at a clear disadvantage in terms of holistic development, compromising their potential for full educational, civic, labor, and political participation and productivity across the life course. As Libya advances toward peace, the education sector will need to redouble its efforts to accommodate large numbers of children who are marginalized, overage, and/or out of school.

Ensuring that no one is left behind

Aligned with the "leave no one behind" commitment that underpins the SDGs, Libya will need to refine strategies that address the learning needs of key subpopulations that continue to be excluded from the education system, including children with disabilities, children from economically fragile households, historically marginalized ethnic minorities, and children on the move.

Libya has achieved gender parity in education, but the differential access of girls and boys during the humanitarian crisis requires gender-sensitive monitoring of educational outcomes, as well as age- and gender-disaggregated data generation and analysis. Achieving inclusive education will require short-, medium-, and long-term strategies to expand equitable access to education and learning opportunities, tailor modalities of service delivery, and track learning outcomes—not just school enrollment or attendance—in groups of children that have been underrepresented in the education system.

Promoting and leveraging intersectoral synergies

The multiplicity of factors influencing education supply and demand calls for explicit points of intersection between education and other sectors. Meaningful and sustainable intersectoral action will require clear frameworks for intersectoral engagement as well as child-sensitive financing and resource allocation across sectors. Deep vulnerabilities of key subpopulations of children highlight the link between education and social protection. However, without a child-sensitive, inclusive national social protection policy, and requisite resourcing and data systems for ministries with social protection mandates, synergies will not be fully realized.

Points of intersection exist with child protection (violence prevention and response, supporting children on the move, and preventing child marriage); health; nutrition (school feeding programs); and WASH (facilities for girls and boys and school-based strategies that support menstrual hygiene management). Formal coordination mechanisms are needed at the central/national and subnational levels, with clear and agreed upon protocols and procedures to facilitate multistakeholder, multisectoral action.

CONCLUDING REMARKS

Because Libya lacks a functioning EMIS, the impacts of the protracted armed conflict (particularly its spikes in 2014 and 2019–20) and the COVID-19 pandemic are not fully known. It is clear, however, that governance of the education sector is more fractured than it was before the revolution. The impact of the armed conflict on the physical infrastructure has been extensive. Reduced school availability and school closure have led to school overcrowding, compromising the quality of the learning environment. In addition, violence in schools remains a critical issue.

Ensuring good-quality education for all will require several structural reforms, including harmonization of the coordination and leadership of various entities, a pressing priority. Education reforms will play a crucial role in ensuring an inclusive recovery and supporting access to the labor market for youth. Ensuring fair access to education for all will also be crucial to peacebuilding in the medium term across different regions and groups of population in Libya. A decentralized reform that capacitates subnational actors, along with effective multistakeholder, multisectoral coordination mechanisms at all levels, must be prioritized. Internal MoE reforms are also necessary to harmonize the work of different departments and bodies; to optimize and make education spending more transparent; and to give more emphasis to early childhood education, infrastructure strengthening, and recurrent costs for the maintenance of schools.

NOTES

1. Mixed migration refers to cross-border movements of people, including refugees fleeing persecution and conflict, victims of trafficking, and people seeking better lives and opportunities.
2. The 1969 constitution decreed compulsory free education through the ninth grade.
3. These laws include Law No. 134 of 1970 on Education, which permits the Minister of Education to issue regulations on student discipline; the School Discipline Ordinance for Schools; Regulations Concerning Primary and Preparatory (Basic) Education; Regulations Concerning Secondary (Intermediate) Education of 1979; and Regulation Concerning Student Discipline of 1983.
4. The mantikas were Al Gharbi, Al Jabal, Al Jfara, Al Jufra, Al Kufra, Azzawya, Benghazi, Derna, Ejdabia, Ghat, Misrata, Murzuq, Sebha, Sirt, Tripoli, Ubari, Wadi Ashshati, and Zwara.
5. Some nonqualified teachers are also on the education sector's payroll. They are generally not assigned teaching positions (MoE, UNICEF, and European Union, 2019).
6. MoE, UNICEF, and European Union (2019) was conducted in 2013–14 and updated in 2017.
7. The mantikas were Al Gharbi, Al Jabal, Al Jfara, Al Jufra, Al Kufra, Azzawya, Benghazi, Derna, Ejdabia, Ghat, Misrata, Murzuq, Sebha, Sirt, Tripoli, Ubari, Wadi Ashshati, and Zwara.
8. The mantikas were Al Gharbi, Al Jabal, Al Jfara, Al Jufra, Al Kufra, Azzawya, Benghazi, Derna, Ejdabia, Ghat, Misrata, Murzuq, Sebha, Sirt, Tripoli, Ubari, Wadi Ashshati, and Zwara.
9. The mantikas were Al Gharbi, Al Jabal, Al Jfara, Al Jufra, Al Kufra, Azzawya, Benghazi, Derna, Ejdabia, Ghat, Misrata, Murzuq, Sebha, Sirt, Tripoli, Ubari, Wadi Ashshati, and Zwara.
10. The mantikas were Al Gharbi, Al Jabal, Al Jfara, Al Jufra, Al Kufra, Azzawya, Benghazi, Derna, Ejdabia, Ghat, Misrata, Murzuq, Sebha, Sirt, Tripoli, Ubari, Wadi Ashshati, and Zwara.

11. The mantika*s* were Al Gharbi, Al Jabal, Al Jfara, Al Jufra, Al Kufra, Azzawya, Benghazi, Derna, Ejdabia, Ghat, Misrata, Murzuq, Sebha, Sirt, Tripoli, Ubari, Wadi Ashshati, and Zwara.

REFERENCES

Abdul-Hamid, Yara. 2011. *Situation Analysis: Middle East and North Africa*. Stockholm: Save the Children Sweden. https://bettercarenetwork.org/sites/default/files/Child%20Rights%20 Situation%20Analysis%20in%20Middle%20East%20and%20North%20Africa.pdf.

Ali Elabbar, Ageila. 2017. "National Libyan Public Education Reform: Entire Transformative Strategies, 2020–2026." *American Journal of Educational Research* 5 (10): 1044–57.

Carter, B. 2018. *Girls' Educational Needs in Libya*. Brighton, United Kingdom: Institute of Development Studies. https://assets.publishing.service.gov.uk/media/5bb2236ded915d259 eaa7776/413_Girls_education_Libya.pdf.

Coram and UNICEF (United Nations Children's Fund). 2018. *Study on Violence against Children in Libya*. London: Coram.

Jurado, I. 2018. *Mapping of the TVET System in Libya and Transitional Strategic*. Document 2018/2021. Tripoli: UNICEF Libya.

Libyan Express. 2020. "Secondary Education Certificate Results: Less Than Half Passed Their Exams," September 16, 2020. https://www.libyanexpress.com/secondary-education -certificate-results-less-than-half-passed-their-exams/.

Libya Observer. 2021. "Ministry of Education: 62.4% Pass Rate for Primary School Certificate," January 5, 2021. https://www.libyaobserver.ly/inbrief/ministry-education -624-pass-rate-primary-school-certificate.

MoE (Ministry of Education). 2011. *Statistical Bulletin 2010/2011*. Tripoli: Centre for Information and Documentation.

MoE (Ministry of Education). 2012. *Nationwide School Assessment*. Tripoli: MoE.

MoE (Ministry of Education), UNICEF (United Nations Children's Fund), and European Union. 2019. *Towards a Strategy for Teacher Development in Libya*. Conducted in 2013/2014 and updated in 2017. Tripoli: MoE, UNICEF, and EU.

NCDC (National Centre for Disease Control). 2017. *Libyan Assessment of Water Quality, Sanitation and Hygiene in Libyan Schools*. Tripoli: NCDC.

NCDC (National Centre for Disease Control), UNICEF (United Nations Children's Fund), and Coram. 2018. *Study on Violence against Children in Libya*. Tripoli: NCDC.

OCHA (Office for the Coordination of Humanitarian Affairs). 2020a. *Humanitarian Needs Overview: Libya*. United Nations, New York.

OCHA (Office for the Coordination of Humanitarian Affairs). 2020b. *Humanitarian Response Monitoring Humanitarian Dashboard*, January–October 2020. United Nations, New York. https://www.humanitarianresponse.info/sites/www.humanitarianresponse.info/files /documents/files/20201124_libya_hrp_humdash.pdf.

OCHA (Office for the Coordination of Humanitarian Affairs). 2020c. *Humanitarian Response Plan*. New York: United Nations. https://reliefweb.int/sites/reliefweb.int/files/resources /libya_hrp_2020_english_full_v1.pdf.

REACH. 2020. *2020 Libya Multi-Sector Needs Assessments*. Geneva: REACH.

REACH and ACTED. 2020. *2019 Libya Multi-Sector Needs Assessment*. Geneva: REACH.

UNDP (United Nations Development Programme). 2020. *United Nations Socio-Economic Framework for the Response to COVID-19 in Libya*. New York: UNDP.

UNESCO (United Nations Educational, Scientific and Cultural Organization), EU (European Union), Networks of Mediterranean Youth, and Peacebuilding. 2017. *National Consultation about Youth, Peace and Security: Libya Case*. New York: UNESCO. https://www.youth 4peace.info/system/files/2017-10/2017%20-%20Report%20-%20Libya%20National%20 Consultation%20on%20Youth%2C%20Peace%20%26%20Security.pdf.

UNFPA (United Nations Population Fund). n.d. *The Libyan Youth Today: Opportunities and Challenges*. New York: UNFPA.

UN Habitat. 2020. *Libya Overview*. New York: United Nations. https://unhabitat.org/libya.

UNICEF (United Nations Children's Fund). 2018. *Libya 2018 Humanitarian Situation Report*. New York: UNICEF. https://www.unicef.org/media/76886/file/Libya-SitRep-Dec-2018.pdf.

UNICEF (United Nations Children's Fund). 2019b. *UNICEF Libya Humanitarian Situation Report, January–June*. New York: UNICEF. https://reliefweb.int/report/libya/unicef-libya -humanitarian-situation-report-january-june-2019.

UNICEF (United Nations Children's Fund). 2020a. *Country Office Humanitarian Situation Report No. 3, July–September 2020*. New York: UNICEF. https://www.unicef.org/media /87981/file/Libya%20Humanitarian%20SitRep%20No.%203%20Sept%202020.pdf.

UNICEF (United Nations Children's Fund). 2020b. *2019 Vulnerability Assessment of Young People in Four Municipalities in Libya*. New York: UNICEF.

UNICEF (United Nations Children's Fund), and SPRI (Social Policy Research Institute). 2020. *Multidimensional Child Deprivation in Libya Brief—Education: A Life-Cycle Approach*. New York: UNICEF.

United Kingdom Home Office. 2020. "Libya: Security and Humanitarian Situation," Version 4.0. Country Policy and Information. London: United Kingdom Home Office.

United Network of Young Peacebuilders. 2020. *Beyond Dividing Lines. Youth-led Civic Engagement for Peace in Libya*. The Hague: United Network of Young Peacebuilders. https:// unoy.org/wp-content/uploads/Policy-Brief-Libya-Beyond-Dividing-Lines.pdf.

UNSMIL (United Nations Support Mission in Libya). 2015. *Libya Humanitarian Needs Overview*. September. Tripoli: UNSMIL.

UNSMIL (United Nations Support Mission in Libya). 2018. "UN Statement on Forced Eviction of Tawergha IDPs." August 19, 2018. Tripoli: UNSMIL. https://unsmil.unmissions.org/un -statement-forced-eviction-tawergha-idps.

World Bank. 2015. *Labor Market Dynamics in Libya: Reintegration for Recovery*. Washington, DC. https://doi.org/10.1596/978-1-4648-0566-0.

World Bank. 2017. *Expanding Opportunities for the Next Generation*. Washington, DC: World Bank.

World Bank. n.d. *Early Childhood Development for a Better Chance*. Washington, DC: World Bank.

World Economic Forum. 2010. *The Global Competitiveness Report 2010–2011*. Geneva: World Economic Forum. http://www3.weforum.org/docs/WEF_GlobalCompetitivenessReport _2010-11.pdf.

World Economic Forum. 2012. *The Global Competitiveness Report 2012–2013*. Geneva: World Economic Forum. http://www3.weforum.org/docs/WEF_GlobalCompetitivenessReport _2012-13.pdf.

RELATED READINGS

Capasso, M. J. Czerep, A. Dessi, and G. Sanchez. 2020. *Libya Country Report*. EU-Listco. https:// static1.squarespace.com/static/5afd4286f407b4a0bd8d974f/t/5df25c4673bd39119 31d2927/1576164430045/Libya+-+Country+Report+Final.pdf.

Devereux, Stephen. 2015. *Social Protection and Safety Nets in the Middle East and North Africa*. Institute of Development Studies, Brighton, United Kingdom. https://gsdrc.org/document -library/social-protection-and-safety-nets-in-the-middle-east-and-north-africa.

Government of Libya. 2020. "Attack in Schools 2019–2020." Tripoli.

IPC-IG (International Policy Centre for Inclusive Growth) and UNICEF (United Nations Children's Fund). 2018. *Non-Contributory Social Protection through a Child and Equity Lens in Libya*. Brasília: IPC-IG.

Libya Education Sector. 2019. *Libya Joint Education Needs Assessment*. December 2019. Tripoli. https://educationcluster.app.box.com/v/LibyaJENADec2019.

UN (United Nations). 2020. *Situation of Human Rights in Libya, and the Effectiveness of Technical Assistance and Capacity-Building Measures Received by the Government of Libya*. Report of the United Nations High Commissioner for Human Rights to the Human Rights Council 43rd session, February 24–March 20. New York: UN. https://www.securitycouncilreport .org/atf/cf/%7B65BFCF9B-6D27-4E9C-8CD3-CF6E4FF96FF9%7D/a_hrc_43_75_e.pdf.

UNHCR (United Nations High Commissioner for Refugees). 2020. *Libya Update*, December 11, 2020. Geneva: UNHCR. https://reliefweb.int/sites/reliefweb.int/files/resources /UNHCR%20Libya%20Update%2011%20December%202020.pdf.

UNICEF (United Nations Children's Fund). 2011. *Libya MENA Gender Equality Profile*: *Status of Girls and Women in the Middle East and North Africa*. New York: UNICEF.

UNICEF (United Nations Children's Fund). 2019a. "MENA Generation 2030 Country Fact Sheet for Libya." New York: UNICEF. https://www.unicef.org/mena/reports/mena -generation-2030.

UNSMIL (United Nations Support Mission in Libya). 2020. "UNSMIL Condemns Brutal Attack Against School Children in Al Ajaylat City, Calls for Perpetrators to be Brought to Justice Swiftly." December 3, 2020. Tripoli: UNSMIL.

18 Creating Conditions for Low-Carbon Pathways during Conflict

MATTHEW BRUBACHER

United Nations Support Mission in Libya-United Nations Development Programme

The author examines how even, and in part due to, conflict dynamics, programs and reforms can be advanced that mitigate carbon emissions. It shows that with the requisite technical and political skills, interventions such as subsidy reform, energy transition, and water rationalization are often easier to implement during rather than after conflict. Implemented properly, these interventions can not only mitigate emissions but enhance resiliency and sustainability.

INTRODUCTION

Of all the threats to global security, climate change is the most certain and most impactful (IPCC 2019; WEF 2020). Although climate change poses a threat to all, it does not affect all countries equally, and not all countries are equally prepared. Unfortunately for Libya, it is not highly exposed to its effects, and its ability to withstand the impacts has been eroded over the years as a result of unsustainable natural resource management.

This chapter examines how, even during, and in part due to, conflict dynamics, programs and reforms can be advanced that mitigate carbon emissions. It shows that with the requisite technical and political skills, interventions such as subsidy reform, energy transition, and water rationalization can even be easier to implement during than after conflict. Implemented properly, these interventions can not only mitigate emissions but enhance resiliency and sustainability.

The chapter is organized as follows. The first section examines how conflict affects a country's carbon emissions and why the same principles that underlie "build back better" initiatives to stimulate a low-carbon recovery should be applied to countries in conflict. The second section examines the legacy of unsustainable water management practices in Libya as well as the challenges it faces in modernizing its electricity system. The third section then explains how the impacts of climate change will exacerbate these existing challenges. The fourth section prescribes several strategic interventions that, if implemented during the conflict, could set Libya on a low-carbon recovery pathway and make it more resilient to manage the effects of climate change. The last section provides some concluding remarks.

UNDERPRIORITIZATION OF CLIMATE CHANGE AND THE BENEFITS OF ACTING NOW

Temperatures in Libya are increasing and precipitation decreasing at rates that are faster than global averages (Union for the Mediterranean 2019). Libya's access to fresh water is rapidly depleting, with few readily available alternatives. Despite the gravity of the situation, carbon mitigation and adaptation interventions remain overshadowed by immediate needs, as they are in many countries experiencing conflict. "How can I be concerned with how much fresh water is left in my country when there is a tank going past my door?" said one public employee. The international community also underprioritizes climate change in Libya, finding it too risky and complicated to engage programmatically.

Underprioritizing carbon mitigation during an armed conflict is problematic, as modern conflicts tend to be more endemic, more destructive, and take much longer to resolve. Waiting to engage also misses opportunities created by conflict dynamics themselves. Carbon mitigation enthusiasts have rallied to the slogan of "build back better" during the COVID-19 pandemic. Armed conflict creates similar, albeit more amplified conditions that induce dramatic carbon emission reductions. Just as with countries affected by COVID-19, this unintentional benefit is short lived, as carbon emissions tend to rise rapidly as the economy recovers unless structural changes are implemented.

Understanding these dynamics is important, because the greatest potential for increasing carbon emissions, some 70 percent globally, comes from developing countries (Hatem et al. 2011; World Bank 2010). The developing world has the highest carbon emission growth potential, not only as a result of gross domestic product (GDP), but because the ability of countries to decouple economic growth from carbon emissions tends to increase with economic growth, because of the structural transition of developing economies toward service sector–based economies, and because modes of production tend to become more efficient and cleaner as income rises. As conflict slows economic growth, this decoupling dynamic is delayed, increasing aggregate carbon emissions over time.[1] If the world is to have any chance of stabilizing carbon emissions, all countries must obtain a requisite level of development to begin permanently decreasing their emissions. The challenge is to obtain this growth without irreparably breaking the global carbon budget.

ERODING RESILIENCY: LIBYA'S LEGACY OF UNSUSTAINABLE NATURAL RESOURCE MANAGEMENT

History of water overuse

With no rivers and nearly all its territory composed of hot, arid desert, Libya has historically been sparsely populated, with most of its towns located along the coast. Less than 2 percent of Libyan land is arable—the land in the Jifara Plain, near Tripoli, and the Marj Plain, near Benghazi—and only slightly more is suitable for livestock. For the rest of the country, rainfall is sparse and too low to sustain life beyond the occasional oasis that breaks an otherwise desert landscape.

Despite the lack of precipitation, the Libyan government invested heavily in agriculture, using coastal aquifers to increase production. Production was so intensive that water withdrawn from coastal aquifers exceeded natural replenishment by over 500 percent (Asswad 1995). By the time the government recognized the unsustainability of this venture, in the mid-1970s, vested interests had been established and it was too late to stop. Seawater progressively and irreversibly entered coastal aquifers (Zurqani et al. 2019). Other pollutants, including nitrates, also mixed with the ground water (Alfarrah and Walraevens 2018).

To compensate for the exhaustion of the coastal aquifers, the government built the Man-Made River (MMR) to pump fresh water to the coast from deep fossil water aquifers in the South. Doing so allowed the government to not only continue the same water-intensive agriculture practices but to expand them on an industrial scale. Taking advantage of its capacity to produce ammonia, a fertilizer plant was opened in Marsa al Brega to create fertile topsoil on top of the sand. In combination with the seemingly limitless fossil water, large circular state farms arose in the desert, growing everything from citrus to watermelons and wheat. Nearly all the farms used open irrigation and, as the newly tapped aquifers were pressurized, water poured into the desert.

Muammar Gaddafi proclaimed that there was enough water for 4,000 years, but the reality was more modest. Libya currently derives its water from the Nubian Sandstone Aquifer System (NSAS) in the East and the Murzuq Aquifer in the West. Both of these systems are gifts from a geological age that existed over 100,000 years ago, when the Sahara was not only green but awash with water (Alker 2008). As a result of their current location, however, the recharge rate of these aquifers is negligible, making their water supply finite. While these aquifers have better natural defenses against seawater intrusion, the lower the water levels become, the worse its quality and the higher the chances of intrusion.

Fortunately, the NSAS is vast, covering over 2 million square kilometers. Because of its size, the estimated capacity of the NSAS to deliver water to Libyans is up to 200 years, as long as neighboring states, including in particular the Arab Republic of Egypt, do not increase their extraction rates (Nicholas 2011). The western Murzuq Aquifer, which lies principally in Libya, is much smaller. One study estimates that its lifespan may last only until 2037 (Mazzonia, Heggy, and Scabbiaa 2018). This is the same lifespan, approximately 50 years, that the MMR was engineered to have. MMR engineers state that the lifespan of the MMR was designed to coincide with the exhaustion of the Murzuq Aquifer.

The conflict in Libya may have inadvertently expanded the lifespan of Libya's fossil aquifers. After the revolution, particularly after the civil war in 2014, the heavily subsidized agricultural sector suffered, and production declined. Up to 70 percent of production was lost (30 percent after 2014) from its peak, when 470,000 hectares were irrigated. Despite the drop in production, however, the number of Libyans employed in this sector remained broadly constant, with 6 percent of Libyans nationally and 22 percent of Libyans in the South continuing to claim employment in the agricultural sector (REACH 2018).

The actual drawdown rate from the aquifers is uncertain. While the MMR is estimated to extract 7,000 million cubic meters a year, most agricultural projects and southwestern municipalities operate their own wells autonomously (Tinmore Institute 2012). Despite the uncertainty, however, current extraction rates are estimated to be four to ten times the amount of water that is renewable.[2] With little to no collection of water tariffs and increasing water leakage as a result of poor infrastructure, Libya's rate of water consumption is well beyond what is sustainable. (Of course, Libya could invest in building more desalination plants, but doing so would require significantly huge volumes of electricity.)

An inefficient and eroding electricity sector

Once the envy of the continent, Libya was one of the first countries in Africa to become 100 percent electrified. Despite its vast size, Libya's electrical grid is highly centralized, with 14 large power stations built along the coast near the population centers. It has one of the cheapest prices in the world, just behind República Bolivariana de Venezuela, with a kilowatt costing LD 0.020 ($0.005), well below the global price average of $0.139.[3]

The General Electric Company of Libya (GECOL), the utility company, is a fully integrated state monopoly that manages all aspects of the sector, from production to distribution and retail. There has been a drift toward natural gas, which produced 63 percent of Libya's power in 2020, with Libya's remaining power produced by oil (Almaktar, Elbreki, and Shaaban 2021). Despite efforts, no substantial on-grid renewable capacity exists, as Libya continues to lack several of the fundamental policy aspects, including a feed-in-tariff scheme and the ability to reimburse capital expenditures for private sector investment.

There are also governance problems within the incumbent utility. Given the low tariff rates and the fact that GECOL receives constant subsidy streams regardless of performance, the company has always operated at a significant loss. As long as there was a centralized government, the system was able to provide reliable electricity. The structural weaknesses inherent in the incentive systems in combination with the lack of oversight became evident after the collapse of a unified central government.

In the euphoric chaos that followed the revolution, Libyan consumers stopped paying their electricity bills, and consumption rates soared. Libyan per capita electricity consumption rose from 17 terawatts in 2011 to 30 terawatts in 2013 (IEA 2019). As demand rose, the ability of GECOL to recuperate its operating expenses dropped below 10 percent. GECOL did not help its predicament; instead of cutting costs, GECOL's wage bill soared by increasing its staffing to well over 45,000, even though just a third of this number was required.[4]

This unbalanced system held together for the first few years following the revolution, but it soon started to unravel. As of 2021, only half of Libya's 10,236 megawatts (MW) of installed capacity, some 5,300 MW, is functional. In the summertime, production drops to 3,700 MW, as a result of inefficiencies created by heat. The drop in production during summer coincides with Libya's peak demand, which was 7,500 MW in the summer of 2019 (Almaktar, Elbreki, and Shaaban 2021). With the supply-demand gap nearing 50 percent, blackouts became frequent and long. To make the situation worse, in an effort to demonstrate their value, local militia disabled emergency breaker systems and forced local operators to turn the electricity back on. By the summer of 2020, the stress on the system became too heavy, and grid-wide blackouts started to occur, fomenting civil unrest that often resulted in more damage to electricity infrastructure.

The burgeoning electricity crisis directly affects water security. At the distribution level, Libya has relatively few elevated water reserves, so electricity cuts quickly result in low pressure or empty taps. Upstream, the lack of electricity interrupts the operation of Libya's eight remaining desalination plants, which use the energy-intensive process of thermal evaporation to produce fresh water rather than the more energy-efficient reverse osmosis.

The most significant threat caused by electricity shortages, however, is to the MMR. Both branches of the MMR require significant amounts of power to operate the 1,300 wells pulling up fossil water. As a result, when electricity is scarce, supply preference is given to the MMR over local communities. In the southeast, around Kufra, this is not a problem, as the MMR provides local communities with water. In the southwest, however, particularly in the Brak Valley north of Sebha, local communities operate their own pumps. When electricity is in short supply, these communities are cut off from electricity and therefore their water supply. As the MMR continues to operate, the communities have developed an adverse relationship with the infrastructure; since 2018, when the electricity crisis began, nearly 153 pumps have been destroyed. Given the lack of alternative water sources, the threat to the MMR represents one of the most significant existential threats to the country.

CLIMATE CHANGE: THE GREAT ACCELERATOR

Libya faces significant challenges to make the provision of water and electricity reliable and sustainable. These challenges become significantly more complicated with climate change. Because of its geographical position and arid climate, Libya is becoming hotter and drier. By 2020, global temperatures had already increased 1.02°C above preindustrial levels in 1880 (NASA 2021). Temperatures in the southern Mediterranean had increased by 1.5°C (Union for the Mediterranean 2019). This is faster than the average warming trend is set to continue. By 2040, the increase in the temperature will likely be 2.2°C, reaching approximately 4°C by the end of the century (IPCC 2021).

Higher temperatures do not necessarily reduce precipitation, as warmer climates cause more evaporation and warm air can potentially carry more water, resulting in heavier rains (Abramowitz and Bishop 2015). That said, in the Mediterranean, the temperature differential between a cooler sea surrounded by a large land mass that is warming more quickly leads to a situation in which precipitation decreases more rapidly than in other parts of the world (Tuel and Eltahir 2020). In Libya, precipitation is decreasing at a rate of approximately –1.95 millimeters a year (Ageena 2013). That rate is rising, and Libya may lose another 7 percent of its rainfall by 2050 (World Bank 2018). The decrease in precipitation will be accompanied by longer periods between rains, which will become heavier.

Sea level rise is another concern, as it consumes coastal land and increases the salinity of ground water. Although the deep aquifers in the South keep seawater at bay, there is always a possibility that the water finds its way in—and that risk increases with higher sea levels. Globally, sea level increased by 19 centimeters in the 20th century, with most of that increase taking place in the later part of the century (UN 2018). While the cause of sea level rise globally is the same—namely, the expansion of water when it is warmed plus the additional water from melting sea ice—the pace of its rise varies. Globally, the sea is rising by 2.5 millimeters a year; in Libya, the average annual sea level rise over the past 20 years was 6.8 millimeters.[5] Depending on how quickly climate change occurs, the sea could rise another 2.5 meters by the end of the 21st century (NOAA 2021).

As a preponderance of Libyans live on the coast, most of the population will be adversely affected. Approximately 5.4 percent of urban areas will be under water with a one-meter sea level rise (World Bank 2010). The area's most vulnerable to sea level rise will be the oil crescent and low-lying cities, such as

Benghazi (Raey 2010). A much larger area will be affected by stronger storm surges, which could cause damage, including to Libya's vast network of oil infrastructure.

Estimating the aggregate cost of climate change to Libya is complicated, not least because of uncertainties about how quickly temperatures will rise. This uncertainty stems both from the inability to predict how much anthropogenic greenhouse gases will be emitted as well as a degree of uncertainty as to the reaction of ecosystems to climatic forcing (Stern 2016).[6] However, one economic model for North Africa predicts that countries would lose 2.39 percent of their GDP with a 3°C rise, a figure that rises to a 3.69 percent loss if it rises one additional degree (Kompas, Pham, and Chee 2018).

The rise in temperature will increase national demand for both water and power. Unfortunately, the efficiency of thermal electricity plants, such as those in Libya, as well as transmission and distribution drops in hotter temperatures. The ideal temperature for steam, single-cycle, and combined-cycle turbines, regardless of their fuel source, is 8°C. Starting at 15°C, turbine efficiency drops approximately 0.7 percent with every additional degree Celsius. Similarly, the capacity of power lines drops 1.5 percent and their efficiency another 0.5 percent with every degree (Sen 2018). This is why Libya's power supply declines by as much as 30 percent at the height of summer. As climate change creates longer and hotter summers, Libya's investments will face progressively weaker returns.

USING CONFLICT DYNAMICS TO BUILD BACK BETTER

Armed conflict, like COVID-19, tends to lower carbon emissions, often dramatically, but the benefits are temporary if structural adjustments are not made to allow for a low-carbon recovery. During the peak of the COVID-19 confinement, in April 2020, global carbon emissions fell by 17 percent—approximately the amount of reduction needed every year until 2040 if the world is to avoid reaching 1.5 C° (Le Quéré et al. 2020; UNEP 2019). These declines are temporary, however. The world is expected to rebound by 3.5 percent in 2021 as demand resumes.

The reduction in carbon emissions is even more pronounced in countries experiencing intense armed conflict. As with COVID-19, this reduction generally follows the fall of GDP caused by lower consumption and productivity rates. This was the case for Libya, whose GDP and national carbon emissions were cut in half in the first years after the outbreak of conflict in 2011 (figure 18.1). The Syrian Arabic Republic and the Republic of Yemen experienced the same pattern (Rother et al. 2016). The more intense the conflict, the more dramatic the reduction in GDP and carbon emission (Siddharth et al. 2019).

As with COVID-19, the reduction in GDP and carbon emissions caused by conflict is often short lived. As a country stabilizes, it generally experiences an economic resurgence referred to as the "Phoenix factor," as modes of production and consumption reengage with vigor (Siddharth et al. 2019).

The challenge for countries in conflict is to ensure that this resurgence is not accompanied by a similar increase in carbon emissions. Although its contribution globally is negligible, in 2013, Libya's carbon emissions per capita were among the highest in Africa, at 9.96 metric tons a year.[7] These rates are two to four times higher than other countries in North Africa (World Data Info 2020). To avert a return to business-as-usual model in which GDP and carbon

FIGURE 18.1

Carbon emissions, GDP, and conflict intensity in Libya, 2006–16

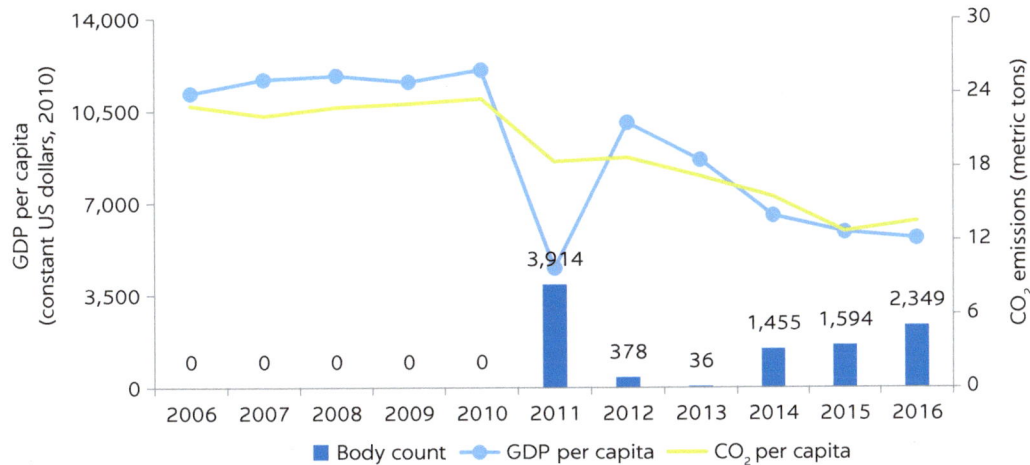

Source: The data used for the body count come from the Uppsala Conflict Data Program (UCDP), which has provided data collection on civil wars for the past 40 years. It is the most utilized dataset by conflict-related studies and has become akin to a global standard on how conflicts are defined and studied. Although there are a variety of datasets for carbon emissions, this study uses the CAIT Climate Data Explorer tool run by Climate Watch, as it uses a composite of multiple datasets. Carbon emissions will be measured in metric tons per capita. GDP per capita data is from the World Bank adjusted to 2010 US dollars.

Note: CO_2 = carbon dioxide; GDP = gross domestic product.

emissions recover in tandem, a basket of interventions is required to decouple economic output from emissions. Several of these "build back better" interventions are most effectively implemented during rather than after conflict. The following interventions are currently being pursued in Libya. Although each intervention could be implemented independently, they are mutually reinforced.

Catalyzing the energy transition during instability

When it comes to mitigating carbon emissions, few areas offer as much opportunity as energy transition. Producing energy, be it for electricity, transportation, or heating, is the single biggest contributor to carbon emissions globally. Energy transition—the transforming of energy systems from fossil fuels to a system that is less carbon intensive—is so important (Sgouris and Csala 2014). The main ways to facilitate the transition are by improving the efficiency by which energy is produced and used or by employing lower carbon-intensive methods of energy generation.

Libya has one of the highest solar irradiation levels in the world. Harnessing only a small fraction of the solar energy reaching Libyan territory would provide the country with all the energy it needs and more.[8] Introducing solar to the grid, however, is complicated by a myriad of vested interests, including sunk costs of the utility company, subsidized energy, and bureaucratic inertia. Technical challenges include grid instability, which impedes absorption, and the lack of metering, which complicates prospective payment for the service rendered. As a result, no on-grid solar exists, and Libya is forced to import rather than export electricity from its neighbors, often accumulating years of unpaid bills.[9]

The root of the problem lies in the fact that Libya, like most countries in the region, developed highly centralized, top-down utilities that controlled all aspects of the electricity system. As demand increased, these state-owned companies found themselves ill-equipped to respond to modern consumer demands. Normally, these pressures are resolved by transforming the centralized monopolies into decentralized systems by breaking them into a myriad of companies, including independent power producers. The rationale for this neoliberal practice—known as *unbundling*—is that by introducing the private sector, the utility will become more efficient and generate power at lower prices. As the global price of renewables has become more competitive, independent power producers tend to gravitate toward renewables, leading the charge toward energy transformation (Foster and Rana 2020).

Libya created the Renewable Energy Authority of Libya (REAOL) in 2007 and many organizations from Deutsche Gesellschaft für Internationale Zusammenarbeit (GIZ) to the World Bank have offered support to introduce on-grid solar. REAOL, however, has struggled to obtain its first project; although it had a mandate, it had no legal personality and GECOL remained a fully integrated monopoly by law. In addition, as Libyans were not paying for electricity, there was little revenue to be made in renewable investments. Although public funds could be used for capital investment and the subsidy regime amended to include a feed-in-tariff scheme, thereby reducing the need for fuel imports, this required high-level policy reform.

This need for high-level policy reform is what distinguishes Libya from lower-income countries, such as the Republic of Yemen. Despite the attraction of off-grid solar, given its relative ease of implementation and its ability to improve resiliency in schools and hospitals, in Libya, these projects do little to incentivize the energy transition and have almost no impact on mitigating carbon emissions.[10]

Libya and the Republic of Yemen have fundamentally different energy systems. While Libya continues to have 100 percent electrification, the Republic of Yemen's national utility company never reached over 40 percent of the population. While electricity in Libya was essentially free, the Republic of Yemen charged and collected a high tariff for its services (Ali, al-Qadasi, and Khoday 2013). As a result, Libyans continue to expect that electricity will return as before, whereas in the Republic of Yemen, people knew they were on their own after the war started and the utility company effectively collapsed (World Bank 2017b).

With the motivation of necessity and the support of entrepreneurs and generous foreign assistance, off-grid solar proliferated, and it is becoming the dominant rather than supplementary energy system in the country (Abdulrahman 2019). This is a significant success and an example of how conflict can incentivize the energy transition in low-income countries. This experience, however, cannot be replicated in Libya as long as its centralized grid continues to operate. When faced with 100 percent electrification and a population that is accustomed to electricity as an entitlement, a policy-based approach is required to shift a country to a lower-carbon pathway.

A utility company that benefits from constant public financing will resist that transition until its rents and business model are disrupted. Armed conflict is one such source of disruption that can alter the interests of the incumbent utility. In Libya, as the electricity crisis deepened and street demonstrations began to create existential threats for the government, the need to reform changed from an option to a necessity. As the heads of the utility company began to lose their jobs, with some facing prosecution, the administration became open to advice.

In 2020, after the worst summer blackouts, a coalition of partners including the United Nations Support Mission to Libya (UNSMIL), the World Bank, the US Agency for International Development, the United Nations Environment Programme, and the United Nations Development Programme, with the support of the European Union, gathered to support GECOL in the crisis, quickly putting together an Emergency Grid Stabilization Program. Although the primary expenditure of the program is to repair Libya's fleet of thermal-powered turbines, the program includes multiple interventions, including energy efficiency and the introduction of on-grid solar. Should the level of cooperation be maintained, and the business-as-usual bloc remain off-balance, this program could not only stabilize the grid but do so in a manner that moves the country toward a better governed, more efficient, and lower-carbon energy system.

Reforming subsidies through subterfuge

One of the most significant opportunities to create the conditions for energy transition is through subsidy reform. Some 13 percent of all global carbon emissions are linked to the overconsumption created by subsidies, and nearly half of those subsidies are in the Middle East and North Africa (MENA) region (World Bank 2017a). Although politically popular, subsidies have very few redeemable qualities. They crowd out innovation and make renewable energy, including rooftop solar, less competitive. They are regressive, amplifying inequalities, and they create distortions and rents exploited by a range of unsavory actors. In Libya, the legal price of gasoline since 2005 is LD 0.15 ($0.03) a liter, making it among the cheapest in the world. As a result, some 30–40 percent of Libya's refined fuel is smuggled, costing the state approximately $750 million annually (Assad 2017). The smuggling rackets are so pervasive that they contribute to domestic fuel shortages, often forcing Libyans to pay well above the legal price (Eaton 2018).

With profit margins of this size, every time there is an effort to cut subsidies, rent seekers mobilize to thwart the attempt. According to international best practice, subsidy reform should involve phased price increases whose cost to the public is offset by social welfare benefits. According to this methodology, the public should be educated about these reforms through public communications before implementation (IMF 2014). While such an approach was discussed and attempted several times in Libya, policy makers always balked at the pressure by rent seekers and the prospect of social unrest (Zaptia 2020a).

To circumvent these pressures, in 2019, the Minister of Economy took advantage of the extreme price distortions to completely cut the subsidies from lubricants and kerosene. As the distortions were so pronounced, these cuts went largely unnoticed by the public, who were accustomed to strong price swings. Although these two fuels are peripheral compared with gasoline and diesel, pursuing subsidy reform by subterfuge has been used in similar contexts beyond Libya and demonstrate why politically difficult reforms might even be easier to implement during conflict than after.[11]

Addressing grievances through flare reduction and solar power

Although most of Libya's population resides on the coast, most of its natural resources including oil and water are in the South. Despite living atop Libya's wealth, the South is economically marginalized. Fuel shortages, including liquefied petroleum gas (LPG) for cooking, are common, and prices are much higher than in other parts of the country. To demonstrate their discontent and compel concessions, turning off the tap along the poorly secured gas and oil lines became common practice.

Instead of repeatedly condemning these acts, the National Oil Corporation (NOC) chose to improve its image with local communities by engaging in numerous social welfare projects. Beyond the usual community development initiative, one of these projects was to capture flared gas to create LPG for domestic consumption, which it implemented in one of its main Southern oil fields and sold on the local market (Zaptia 2020b). The effort not only relieved supply shortages but it also turned a profit.

Operational flaring of gas during the production of oil is a wasteful and extremely harmful practice that contributes some 350 million tons of carbon a year (World Bank 2017b). Despite being decried as both wasteful and harmful, flaring continues to increase. Libya is among the world's worst polluters in terms of its barrel-to-flare ratio, increasing its carbon emissions from flaring from 2.3 to 5.9 million cubic meters per year (GGFRP 2020). Any action to harness instead of burn flare gas is an effective mitigation action. The NOC has communicated its desire to further develop its flare reduction capacities.

Unlike the NOC, which has a significant profit margin, the MMR project has barely enough budget to keep its operation running. As a result, it has not been able to engage in the same community activities as the NOC. In 2019, after repeated sabotage of its wells, the UN and partners launched a project to build distributed solar stations along the southwestern grid of the MMR. The idea was to provide supplementary electricity to both the MMR and local communities. Construction of several modular 5 MW stations would allow more communities to earn livelihoods from maintaining those stations, and the distributed power would help stabilize the grid. Most important, by linking the existential threat of water security to on-grid solar, more political leverage could be mobilized to implement the policy reform required to allow for on-grid solar projects to develop. Although this could also be accomplished through the Emergency Grid Stabilization Program, when dealing with a country in conflict, it is always good to pursue an objective through more than one avenue.

Making Libya's limited water resource last longer

Libya will need to invest much more heavily in desalination and wastewater treatment to survive. Doing so will take time. Until then, its water lifeline is tied to the fossil aquifers that lie 500 meters below the surface in the deep South. To lengthen the life of these aquifers, Libya needs to use less water. While it is always good to reduce water use in households and industry, nothing compares to water use in the agricultural sector, which consumes well over 80 percent of Libya's water. This is where the greatest potential exists to rationalize water use.

Unfortunately, there has been very little investment to improve the efficiency of water use since 2011. The most common form of irrigation, some 40 percent, continues to be open-air sprinkler systems followed by more water-efficient drip irrigation, which represents 26 percent of all irrigation (WFP 2020). The intensive use of water for agriculture partly reflects the fact that the cost of water is not incorporated into its production. Water remains an essentially free resource for most farmers in Libya, providing them little incentive to rationalize water use.

Pressures from the conflict, however, are creating stress and adding significant costs in the agricultural sector. The fertilizer factory in al Bayda has closed, and farmers find it increasingly difficult to get basic supplies, including fertilizers and spare parts. The main purchaser of agricultural products, the Libyan government, arbitrarily switched to imports after 2014, leaving the produce of many Libyan farmers stranded. On top of this, electricity shortages have interrupted production, forcing farmers to operate their own autonomous energy sources thereby increasing costs.

These stresses, caused during the conflict, create new opportunities to reorient Libya's agriculture sector so that it uses water better. Instead of relegating farmers to unemployment, the Food and Agricultural Organization and the General Water Authority, with political support from UNSMIL, initiated a project to survey the use of water in the agricultural sector. The study will not only provide valuable information on how quickly Libya's fossil water supply is being utilized, but it will also identify the most significant opportunities where water can be rationalized. By providing financial assistance or in-kind support, such as solar pumping stations, the government can encourage farmers to adopt more efficient water irrigation techniques or switch to less water-intensive crops. Instead of spreading fertilizers in the desert to grow wheat with open sprinkler systems, for example, farmers can competitively grow dates and melons.

Another opportunity to introduce on-grid solar while conserving water is by covering Libya's open water storage facilities with floating photovoltaic panels. Water brought from the aquifers by the MMR is stored in several large open water reservoirs, where it is treated before use. The level of evaporation in these reservoirs is a function of its surface size and the evaporation rate. Globally, these losses are estimated to be greater than the industrial and domestic water uses combined (Zhao and Gao 2019). In a semi-arid environment in Nevada, for example, open water reservoirs can lose 40–60 percent of their total output (Friedrich et al. 2018). Libya has several open reservoirs. The largest are in Ajdabiya, south of Tripoli, and in Gharyan, Ghardabiya, and the Grand Omar Muktar reservoir, south of Tripoli. Each of these reservoirs has a surface area to generate up to 50 MW of electricity with photovoltaic. The reservoirs have the advantage of being located near major cities, so transmission loss to get the electricity to the consumer is reduced. Covering the water surface reduces evaporation by 5–15 percent; the cooling effect by the water that does evaporate increases the efficiency of power generation.

CONCLUDING REMARKS

For most actors, both national and international, the impacts of climate change remain a distant concern. This is particularly true in conflict zones, where people are forced to focus on immediate needs.

The fluidity and fragmentation caused by the conflict in Libya complicates engagement with national actors, particularly those not based in the country and who are unfamiliar with conflict dynamics. Most climate mitigation organizations, including climate-financing mechanisms, keep their distance from countries in conflict or continue to engage with them through traditional mechanisms that are ill adapted to the context, waiting instead for the patient to stabilize before providing it with assistance.

The problem with this approach is that by the time the conflict subsides, it may be too late to enact the reforms required to set the country on a low-carbon pathway. The fact that conflict reduces carbon emissions and destabilizes actors that would otherwise impede reforms creates opportunities that fade as the economy recovers. Unlike developed countries, developing countries do not have the luxury of exponentially increasing their emissions to grow their economies. The effects of climate change are already being felt, and its impacts will increasingly impede development and exacerbate risks to vital resources such as water.

This chapter shows the links between resource management and climate change in Libya as well as the trajectories and consequences that will result if development continues with business as usual. It identifies opportunities for carbon mitigation that are being implemented by using conflict dynamics. These opportunities can be exploited effectively only if people with technical and financial expertise team up with those involved in political processes. This partnership is vital to navigate the complex decision-making processes in order to make the changes necessary to not only address the impacts of climate change but address the root cause.

NOTES

1. According to the Environmental Kuznets Curve, countries increase their levels of carbon emissions as their economy grows until they reach a level of per capita income that enables them to begin permanently reducing their emissions. The theory attributes the reduction to the public demand for a cleaner environment, the structural shift to a more service-based economy, and the ability to invest in increasingly efficient modes of production and introduce larger proportions of clean energy into their energy mix. If this theory holds and there is a direct correlation between income and pollution, then countries will simply grow out of their polluting behavior.
2. The current rate of abstraction from the various groundwater aquifers is estimated at 7,000 million cubic meters per year. The available water supply of safe yield is estimated at about 3,200 million cubic meters per year from nonrenewable water from the basins; another 650 million cubic meters per year is attributed to direct recharge from rainfall. One report estimates that annual groundwater recharge in Libya is around 250 million cubic meters and consumption is estimated at 1 billion cubic meters. See Al-Khamisi (2015).
3. The tariff has not been raised since 2005. See Global Petrol Prices (2020).
4. GECOL has not been publishing any annual reports since 2010.
5. Seal level increased by 40.92 millimeters between 1993 and 2015 (World Bank 2018). Sea level rise is North Africa is estimated to be 5 and 10 millimeters per year. See Nichols et al. (2021).
6. A climate forcing is an imposed perturbation of Earth's energy balance.
7. World Bank, "CO_2 Emissions (metric tons per capita)–Libya," World Bank Data, Washington, DC. https://data.Worldbank.org/indicator/EN.ATM.CO2E.PC?locations=LY.
8. The average annual solar irradiation is 2,470 kilowatts per square meter per year, whereas the potential of solar energy resource is estimated at 140 × 106 gigawatts per year (RCREEE 2010).
9. Both Egypt and Tunisia each export approximately 200 megawatts of electricity to Libya and are planning to increase that amount. Algeria is also planning to export electricity to Libya through Tunisia. See Africa Oil and Power (2020).
10. In a period of three years, Yemen went from having almost no solar to nearly 50 percent of households in rural areas and 75 percent in urban areas having photovoltaic (PV) solar systems. See World Bank (2017b).
11. This approach to subsidy reform was also used in South Sudan. In December 2017, at the height of the seven-year civil war, the government ended its fuel subsidy program without fanfare at the height of the conflict, when the population was united in facing a common threat rather than criticizing the government for unpopular reforms.

REFERENCES

Abdulrahman. 2019. "Yemenis Go Solar amid War Energy Shortage," Reuters, November 17, 2019. https://www.reuters.com/article/us-yemen-security-energy/yemenis-go-solar-amid -war-energy-shortage-idUSKBN1XR0EL.

Abramowitz, G., and C. H. Bishop. 2015. "Climate Model Dependence and the Ensemble Dependence Transformation of CMIP Projections." *Journal of Climate* 28: 2332–48.

Africa Oil and Power. 2020. "Expanding Libya's Installed Power Capacity." Cape Town: Energy Capital and Power (accessed March 2, 2021).

Ageena, I. 2013. "Trends and Patterns in the Climate of Libya. 1945–2010." Ph.D. thesis, University of Liverpool.

Alfarrah, N., and W. Walraevens. 2018. "Groundwater Overexploitation and Seawater Intrusion in Coastal Areas of Arid and Semi-Arid Regions." *Water* 10 (2).

Ali, W., F. al-Qadasi, and K. Khoday. 2013. *Prospects of Solar Energy in Yemen: A Policy Note.* United Nations Development Programme, New York.

Alker, M. 2008. *The Nubian Sandstone Aquifer System: A Case Study for the Research Project Transboundary Groundwater Management in Africa.* Bonn: German Development Institute.

Al-Khamisi, Ahmad. 2015. "Severe Water Crisis Looming in Libya." NewArab, March 20, 2015. https://www.newarab.com/news/severe-water-crisis-looming-libya.

Almaktar, M., A. Elbreki, and M. Shaaban. 2021. "Revitalizing Operational Reliability of the Electrical Energy System in Libya: Feasibility Analysis of Solar Generation in Local Communities." *Journal of Cleaner Production* 279. https://doi.org/10.1016/j.jclepro .2020.123647.

Assad. 2017. "Audit Bureau: Libya spent $30 billion on fuel subsidies in five years," *Libya Observer*, August 19, 2017. https://www.libyaobserver.ly/economy/audit-bureau-libya-spent -30-billion-fuel-subsidies-five-years.

Asswad, R. 1995. "Agricultural Prospects and Water Resources in Libya." *Ambio* 24 (5): 324–27.

Eaton, T. 2018. *Libya's War Economy: Predation, Profiteering, and State Weakness.* London: Chatham House.

Foster, V., and A. Rana. 2020. *Rethinking Power Sector Reform in the Developing World.* World Bank: Washington, DC.

Friedrich, K., R. Grossman, J. Huntington, P. Blanken, J. Lenters, K. Holman, D. Gochis, B. Livneh, J. Prairie, and E. Skeie. 2018. "Reservoir Evaporation in the Western United States: Current Science, Challenges, and Future Needs." *Bulletin of the American Meteorological Soc*iety 99 (1): 167–87.

GGFRP (Global Gas Flaring Reduction Partnership). 2020. "Global Gas Flaring Data." Washington, DC: World Bank (accessed September 15, 2020). https://www.worldbank.org /en/programs/gasflaringreduction/global-flaring-data.

Global Petrol Prices. 2020. "Libya Electricity Prices." Global Petrol Prices (database). https:// www.globalpetrolprices.com/Libya/electricity_prices/.

Hatem M'henni, H., M. El Hedi Arouri, A. Ben Youssef, and C. Rault. 2011. "Income Level and Environmental Quality in the MENA Countries: Discussing the Environmental Kuznets Curve Hypothesis." Working Paper 587, Economic Research Forum, Giza, Egypt.

IEA (International Energy Agency). 2019. "Libya." Paris: IEA (accessed March 2, 2021). https:// www.iea.org/countries/Libya.

IMF (International Monetary Fund). 2014. *Energy Subsidies in the Middle East and North Africa: Lessons for Reform.* Washington, DC: IMF.

IPCC (Intergovernmental Panel on Climate Change). 2021. "Summary for Policymakers." In *Climate Change 2021: The Physical Science Basis. Contribution of Working Group I to the Sixth Assessment Report of the Intergovernmental Panel on Climate Change*, edited by V. Masson-Delmotte, P. Zhai, A. Pirani, S. L. Connors, C. Péan, S. Berger, N. Caud, Y. Chen, L. Goldfarb, M. I. Gomis, M. Huang, K. Leitzell, E. Lonnoy, J. B. R. Matthews, T. K. Maycock, T. Waterfield, O. Yelekçi, R. Yu, and B. Zhou. Cambridge and New York: Cambridge University Press. https://doi.org/10.1017/9781009157896.

Kompas, T., V. H. Pham, and T. N. Che. 2018. "The Effects of Climate Change on GDP by Country and the Global Economic Gains from Complying with the Paris Climate Accord." *Earth's Future* 6 (8). https://doi.org/10.1029/2018EF000922.

Le Quéré, C., R. B. Jackson, M. W. Jones, A, J. P. Smith, S. Abernethy, R. M. Andrew, A. J. De-Gol, et al. 2020. "Temporary Reduction in Daily Global CO_2 Emissions during the COVID-19 Forced Confinement." *Nature Climate Change* 10: 647–53. https://www.nature.com/articles/s41558-020-0797-x.

Mazzonia, A., H. Heggy, and G. Scabbiaa. 2018. "Recasting Water Budget Deficits and Groundwater Depletion in the Main Fossil Aquifer Systems in North Africa and the Arabian Peninsula." *Global Environmental Change* 53: 157.

NASA (National Aeronautics and Space Administration). 2021. "Vital Signs." Washington, DC: NASA. https://climate.nasa.gov/vital-signs/global-temperature/.

Nicholas, M. 2011. "The Nubian Sandstone Aquifer System: Thoughts on a Multilateral Treaty in Light of the 2008 UN Resolution on the Law of Transboundary Aquifers." *Texas International Law Journal* 46: 379-411.

Nichols, R., D. Lincke, J. Hinkel, S. Brown, A. Vafeidis, B. Meyssignac, S Hanson, J-L. Merkens, and J. Fang. 2021. "A Global Analysis of Subsistence Relative, Sea Level Change and Coastal Flood Exposure." *Nature* 11 (4): 338–42. https://doi.org/10.1038/s41558-021-00993-z.

NOAA (National Oceanic and Atmospheric Administration). 2021. "Climate Change: Global Sea Level." Washington, DC: NOAA (accessed February 22, 2021). https://www.climate.gov/news-features/understanding-climate/climate-change-global-sea-level.

Raey, M. 2010. *Impact of Sea Level Rise on the Arab Region*. Cairo: University of Alexandria, Regional Center for Disaster Risk Reduction.

RCREEE (Regional Center for Renewable Energy and Energy Efficiency). 2010. *Provision of Technical Support/Services for an Economical, Technological and Environmental Impact Assessment of National Regulations and Incentives for Renewable Energy and Energy*. Tripoli: RCREEE.

REACH. 2018. *Libya: Multi-Sector Needs Assessment*. Geneva: REACH.

Rother, B., G. Pierre, D. Lombardo, R. Herrala, P. Toffano, E. Roos, G. Auclair, and K. Manassah. 2016. *The Economic Impact of Conflicts and the Refugee Crisis in the Middle East and North Africa*. IMF Discussion Note, International Monetary Fund, Washington, DC.

Sen, G. 2018. "The Effect of Ambient Temperature on Electric Power Generation in Natural Gas Combined Cycle Power Plant: A Case Study." *Energy Reports* 4: 682–90.

Sgouris, S., and D. Csala. 2014. "A Framework for Defining Sustainable Energy Transitions: Principles, Dynamics, and Implications." *Sustainability* 6 (5): 2601–22.

Siddharth, K., X. Fang, L. Kolovich, and C. McLoughlin. 2019. "The Economic Consequences of Conflicts." In *Regional Economic Outlook: Sub-Saharan Africa*. Washington, DC: International Monetary Fund.

Stern, N. 2016. "Economics: Current Climate Models Are Grossly Misleading." *Nature* 530: 407–409.

Tinmore Institute. 2012. *Water Security and Interconnected Challenges in Libya*. Lakewood, CO: Tinmore Institute.

Tuel, A., and E. A. B. Eltahir. 2020. "Why Is the Mediterranean a Climate Change Hot Spot?" *Journal of Climate* 33 (14): 5829.

UN (United Nations). 2018. Goal 13: "Sustainable Development Goals: Take Urgent Action to Combat Climate Change and Its Impacts." New York: United Nations (accessed February 22, 2021). https://www.un.org/sustainabledevelopment/climate-change/.

UNEP (United Nations Environment Programme). 2019. *Emissions Gap Report 2019*. Nairobi: UNEP.

Union for the Mediterranean. 2019. *Risks Associated to Climate and Environmental Changes in the Mediterranean Region*. Barcelona, Spain: Union for the Mediterranean.

WEF (World Economic Forum). 2020. *The Global Risks Report 2020*. Geneva: WEF.

WFP (World Food Programme). 2020. *Libya: Agriculture and Livelihood Needs Assessment Report. A Study of the Fezzan Region*. Rome: WFP.

World Bank. 2010. *World Development Report 2010: Development and Climate Change.* Washington, DC.

World Bank. 2017a. *Reforming Fossil Fuel Subsidies for a Cleaner Future.* Washington, DC: World Bank.

World Bank. 2017b. *Republic of Yemen Restoring and Expanding Energy Access Power Sector Reengagement Note,* Washington, DC.

World Bank. 2018. "Libya Dashboard," Climate Change Knowledge Portal (database). Washington, DC: World Bank (accessed February 8, 2021). https://climateknowledgeportal .worldbank.org/country/Libya.

World Data Info. 2020. "Energy Consumption in Libya," WorldData.info (database) (accessed February 21, 2021). https://www.worlddata.info/africa/libya/energy-consumption.php.

Zaptia, S. 2020a. "Fuel Subsidy Reform Proposal Presented to Serraj Government," *Libya Herald,* March 3, 2020. https://www.libyaherald.com/2020/03/03/fuel-subsidy-reform -proposal-presented-to-serraj-government/.

Zaptia, S. 2020b. "NOC to Produce LPG in Sharara Oil Field for Local Consumption," *Libya Herald,* May 8, 2020. https://www.libyaherald.com/2020/05/08/noc-to-produce-lpg-in -sharara-oil-field-for-local-domestic-consumption/.

Zhao, G., and H. Gao. 2019. "Estimating Reservoir Evaporation Losses for the United States: Fusing Remote Sensing and Modeling Approaches." *Remote Sensing of Environment* 226: 109–24.

Zurqani, A., A. Mikhailova, J. Post, J. Mark, and R. Elhawej. 2019. "A Review of Libyan Soil GECOLs for Use within the Ecosystem Services Framework." *Land* 8 (5).

RELATED READINGS

Farfan, J., and C. Breyer. 2018. "Combining Floating Solar Photovoltaic Power Plants and Hydropower Reservoirs: A Virtual Battery of Great Global Potential." *Energy Procedia* 155: 403–11.

Geels, F. 2014. "Regime Resistance against Low-Carbon Transitions: Introducing Politics and Power into the Multi-Level Perspective." *Theory, Culture & Society* 31 (5): 21–40.

Konapala, G., K. Ashok, M. Yoshihide, and E. Michael. 2020. "Climate Change Will Affect Global Water Availability through Compounding Changes in Seasonal Precipitation and Evaporation." *Nature Communications* 11 (1).

Lagwali, F. 2008. "Forecasting Water Demand for Agricultural, Industrial and Domestic Use in Libya." *International Review of Business Research Papers* 4(5): 231–48.

Organski, A., and J. Kugler. 1981. *The War Ledger.* Chicago: University of Chicago Press.

Zeleňákoval, M., P. Purcz, I. Gargar, and H. Hlavatá. 2013. "Comparison of Precipitation Trends in Libya and Slovakia." *WIT Transactions on Ecology and the Environment* 172. https://doi.org/10.2495/RBM130301.

19 Social Assistance Programs and Their Effectiveness in Responding to Crises

**CARLO DEL NINNO, AMR S. MOUBARAK, ADEA KRYEZIU,
MATTEO CARAVANI, REMY PIGOIS, AND MAYA HAMMAD**

World Bank, World Food Programme, and United Nations Children's Fund

The authors demonstrate that numerous ongoing and interrelated shocks have adversely impacted Libyan households and the poorest segments of the population, including the displaced. The combination of fuel shortages, significant water and electricity cuts, and economic deterioration in 2020 had devastating consequences for children and households in Libya. Approximately 1.3 million people in Libya—about 18 percent of the population—needed humanitarian assistance in 2019. About 35 percent of the population in need were children, and 371,700 were displaced persons or refugees. The coauthors provide that the major challenge ahead is for the national government of Libya to launch a concerted effort toward expansion and modernization of the current social protection system, as part of its short-term strategy to support the recovery efforts. Reforms of the social protection system, and the social assistance programs, will play a crucial role in providing the necessary support to Libyan households in a more systematic and transparent way.

INTRODUCTION

Several ongoing and interrelated shocks are severely affecting Libyan households and the poorest segments of the population, including the displaced. The combination of fuel shortages, significant water and electricity cuts, and economic deterioration in 2020 and 2021 had devastating consequences for children and families in Libya. Nearly 1.3 million people in Libya—about 18 percent of the population—needed humanitarian assistance in 2019 (OCHA 2021). About 35 percent of the population in need were children (OCHA 2021), and 371,700 were displaced persons or refugees (OCHA 2021; UNHCR 2019).

The team is grateful to the contributions of Hend Irhiam (Operations Analyst, World Bank) for her contributions to country context and political economy analysis of the chapter. The authors are also grateful to the contributions of Sara Hariz (Social Protection Specialist, World Bank); Almoataz Bedin Allah Saleh Ahmed Shikhy (Consultant, World Bank); Haya Abassi (Programme Policy Officer, World Food Programme); Mohamed Aburagheba (Programme Associate, World Food Programme); Grace Namugayi (Vulnerability Analysis and Mapping Officer, World Food Programme); and Charlotte Bilo (International Policy Centre for Inclusive Growth).

This chapter reviews the social protection system, including the universal price subsidy scheme, noncontributory social assistance programs, and its delivery mechanism, utilizing limited available secondary information and in-depth interviews. The chapter then offers a synthesis of findings and identifies policy options and a strategic direction of the reform of the social protection system.[1,2]

The chapter is organized as follows. The first section describes the current context and types of shocks faced by households in Libya. The second provides a brief overview of the social protection system, its evolution, and an in-depth review of the current universal price subsidy scheme in Libya and its lack of adequacy or efficiency in reaching poor households. Section three presents findings from the joint stock-taking exercise on the state of social assistance programs, including coverage, adequacy, comprehensiveness, identification of which programs remained active during the crisis, as well as challenges in the social protection delivery system. The fourth section summarizes key challenges and presents options for reforms to pave the way for modernization and expansion of social protection. The last section covers concluding remarks.

CONTEXT AND EFFECTS OF THE CRISIS

Libya's decade-long crisis is estimated to have impacted 3 million people, about half of the population (UN HRP 2017). As of December 2021, an estimated 803,000 people were in need of humanitarian assistance in Libya. This number is expected to reach 1.5 million in 2022. At the peak of the conflict, nearly half a million Libyans were reported to be displaced from their homes (figure 19.1), with many households experiencing multiple instances of displacement over time. From mid-2020, many internally displaced persons (IDPs) were able to return home, with 640,000 IDPs returning between mid-2020 and mid-2021, reducing the number of IDPs to 212,000 people. Migrants and refugees, for which Libya plays a significant role as a transit and destination country, are also a key humanitarian concern. As of the end of 2021, over 260,000 refugees and migrants were estimated to be present in Libya (OCHA 2021).

FIGURE 19.1

Libya displacement and return timeline, 2014–21

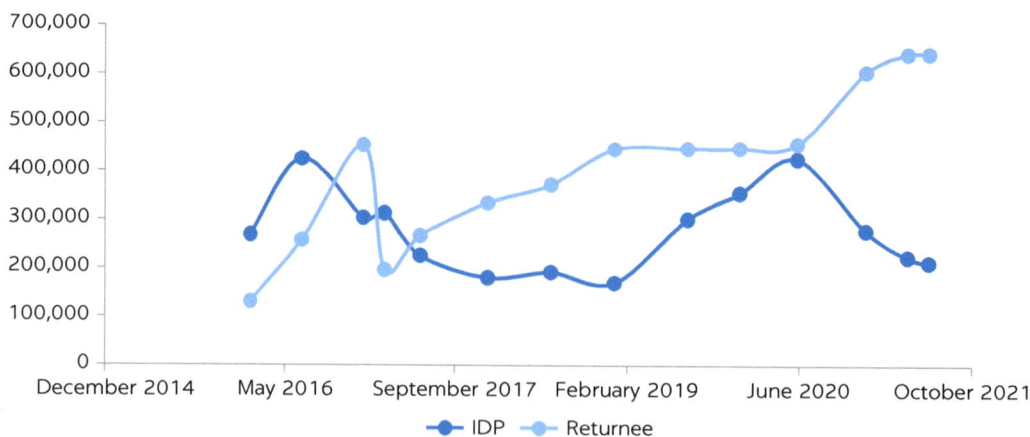

Source: International Organization for Migration Displacement Tracking Matrix Libya dataset, "DTM Libya," https://displacement.iom.int/Libya.
Note: IDP = internally displaced persons.

The economic vulnerability of households grew in 2020. COVID-19 pandemic restrictions compounded the contraction of economic activity, which adversely affected low-income households, which make up most of the informal sector, as well as non-Libyans, who rely more on daily wages and who generally do not benefit from social protection programs. As of the end of 2021, Libya had reported almost 400,000 cases of COVID-19 and 5,700 COVID-related deaths (figure 19.2) (WHO 2021). In parallel, Libya's public health infrastructure, already devastated by the prolonged conflict, was further weakened by shortages of fuel, water, and electricity, with an estimated 1.2 million people in need of primary and secondary health services, including 425,705 children (UN HRP 2021). As a result, the total number of people in need of assistance was projected to reach 1.8 million by the end of 2021 (UNICEF Libya 2020).

Effect on household-level vulnerability, shocks, and coping mechanisms

Overall, the conflict has increased the prices of basic food staples and services, driven largely by scarcity of subsidized fuels and interruptions in the supply chain and import financing in recent years. The average median cost of a household's Minimum Expenditure Basket (MEB) rose 3 percent during the first quarter of 2020. By April 2020, the MEB median cost increased by another 36 percent.[3] Cooking fuel prices increased nearly 30 percent in 2020 (compared to 2019). In the South, these price increases were as much as 50 percent.

According to the World Bank and World Food Programme's (WFP) joint vulnerability assessment of Libyan households (known as the Libya Vulnerability, Shocks, and Coping Mechanisms Survey, or VSCM-S), the security situation in Libya appears to have impacted every segment and population in the country, especially the displaced (World Bank 2020). The crisis displaced about 25 percent of interviewed households. As normalcy gradually comes back to Libya, about 70 percent of displaced households returned, while the remaining (7 percent) are still scattered. More than 75 percent of displaced households are severely impacted by the three-pronged effects (the conflict, the economic shocks, and the COVID-19 pandemic) from the destruction of properties, the loss of savings and assets, and a spike in fuel and food prices to

FIGURE 19.2

Daily cases and deaths attributed to COVID-19 in Libya, March 2020–July 2021

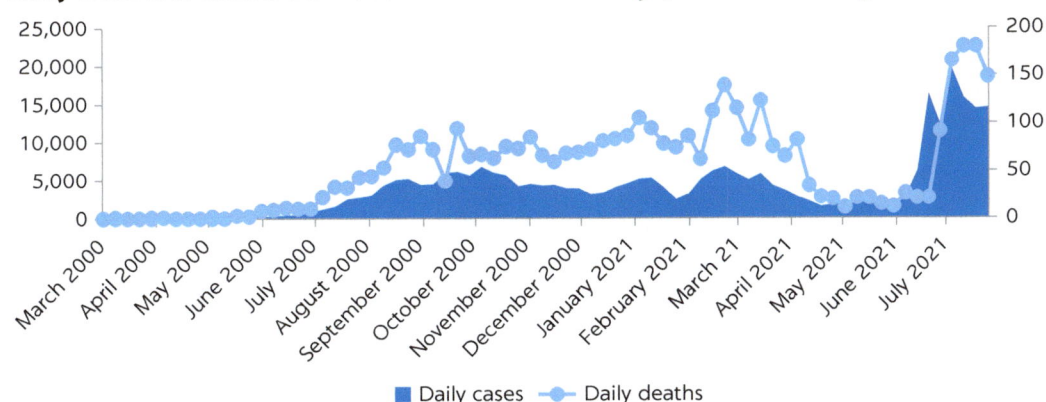

Source: World Health Organization Emergency Dashboard, "Libya," (database), https://covid19.who.int/region/emro/country/ly.

limited likelihood opportunities and interruption of essential services. Furthermore, about 50 percent of the households were food insecure and were not able to cover basic expenses. Displaced households (25 percent) are three times more likely to be food insecure than nondisplaced households (host communities).

Food insecurity

The VSCM-S found 7 percent of households to be food insecure, with an additional 3 percent classified as borderline. However, 42 percent of respondents were found to be only marginally food secure, and average expenditures on food stood at 63 percent of total expenditure, on average, suggesting significant vulnerability among Libyan households. Displaced households were three times more likely (17.7 percent) to be food insecure than nondisplaced households (5.6 percent). Food insecurity among returnee households stood at 9.5 percent. In turn, female-headed households tended to be more food insecure (9.2 percent) than male-headed ones (6.8 percent). Figure 19.3 provides the composition of different categories of food insecure households by gender and residency status.

Household-level shocks

As for shocks experienced by households, one-third of VSCM-S respondents reported experiencing significant shocks within the 12 months preceding the survey. Displaced and female-headed households reported higher rates of shock (45 and 42 percent, respectively) than male-headed or nondisplaced households (30 and 29 percent, respectively). Price fluctuations, death of a working member in the family, and increased fuel or food prices were the three major reported shocks, which together affected about 60 percent of VSCM-S respondents. Displaced households surveyed reported severe economic losses due to the conflict. For 54 percent, houses were either destroyed or seized; 16 percent lost all properties, including houses, animals, vehicles, and firms and 28 percent lost all properties and savings. In turn, 42 percent of returnee household heads report that their houses were seized or destroyed, 7 percent said they lost all their properties and assets (including houses, animals, vehicles, and firms), while 23 percent report that they lost all properties and savings.

FIGURE 19.3

Food insecurity, by gender and residence status

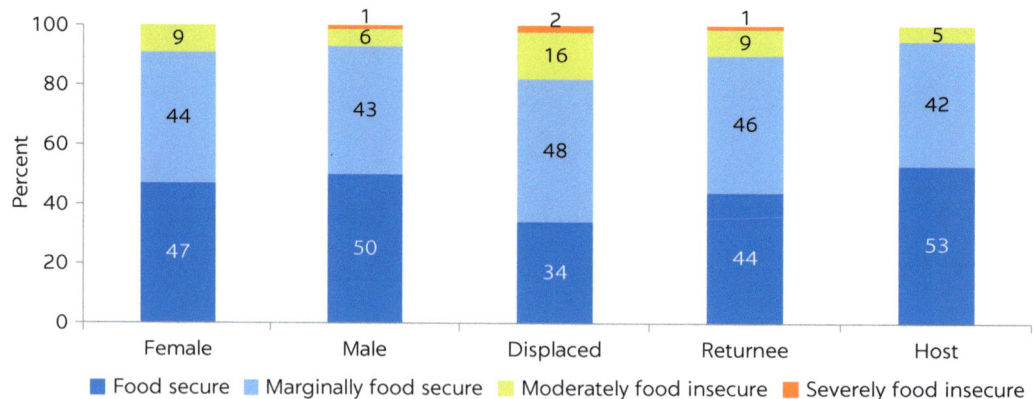

Source: VSCM-S 2021.

Largely negative coping mechanisms are employed by Libyan households, including debt, adjustment of consumption-based strategies, and livelihood-based strategies. These type of negative coping strategies generally affect health and education outcomes of the households in the short or medium term in addition to exposing the household to additional shocks in the future due to depletion of assets or incursion of debt.

Debt is the most common of negative coping strategies employed by households during and after the crisis. Around one-third (29 percent) of the Vital Statistics Cooperative Program's (VSCP) respondent households reported incurring debt in the three months prior to the survey. Almost half the displaced households incurred a debt (42 percent) compared to 25 percent of hosts and 38 percent of the returnee households. Meanwhile, 53 percent of displaced households indicated they had adopted at least one consumption-based coping strategy. The most reported coping strategies were relying on less preferred or less expensive food and restricting adults' food consumption. Households also reduced the number of meals and reduced meal size once a week. Figure 19.4 details these types of coping mechanisms across emergency, crisis, and stress strategies employed by households.

It is important to note that for many households, government-subsidized fuels are not accessible because of capture and illicit shipping (also known as black-market fuel trade) to Tunisia and other neighboring countries. In addition, some parts of Libya saw a 390 percent increase in the price of cooking fuel and a 100 percent increase in nongovernment subsidized gasoline caused by the interruption of the supply chain (REACH 2021). Despite some relief in fuel price pressures during the summer and winter of 2020, the conflict and oil production blockade also interrupted the flow of financing to regional and governorate level units in the South, thus preventing access to public services (health and education) or humanitarian assistance.

Devaluation and liquidity problems

The food and commodities crises have been exacerbated by the liquidity crisis, which makes essential goods prohibitively expensive for low-income households.

FIGURE 19.4

Livelihood-based coping strategies in Libya (percent)

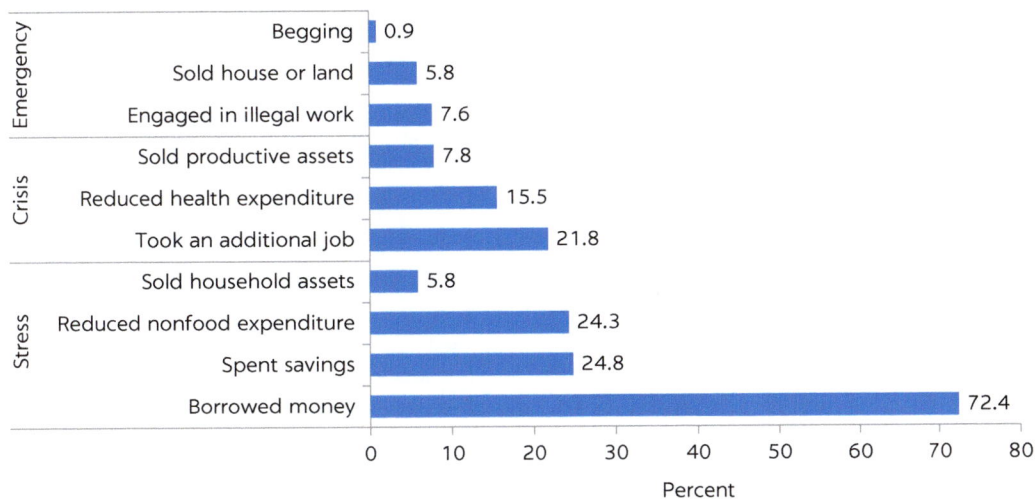

Source: VSCM-S 2021.

The COVID-19 pandemic has compounded the difficulties, resulting in an almost complete halt of economic activity, adversely impacting the limited private sector and devastating the informal labor economy.

Before devaluation in January 2021, the Libyan dinar was highly volatile. This situation exacerbated liquidity problems in the banking sector and demand for import financing. As most food products are imported, the precipitous decline in the Libyan dinar has made the MEB less affordable to low-income households.

To keep up with these price increases, a recent survey shows Libyans, migrants, and refugees have adopted one or more coping mechanisms to maintain some level of food security, including buying less expensive foods, reducing the number or size of meals, and prioritizing children for food with the adults reducing their consumption (WFP 2020).

Breakdown in budget discussions resulted in chronic delay in pay of public sector workers (in mid-2020 and early 2021). Reports of delayed salary payment for public sector workers have corresponded with lack of available liquidity to finance the payments of pensions and social assistance programs including the Social Solidarity Fund (SSF) and Ministry of Social Affairs (MoSA) programs. These trends are especially problematic given strong dependence of large households on single wage earners (who often have a public sector job). In addition, several social assistance programs were suspended (or are currently deemed inactive), which were intended to support the Libya households in mitigating the economic effects of the conflict.

Effect on health care facilities

Access to health care significantly deteriorated, with a grave risk of increased communicable and noncommunicable diseases. In 2021, an estimated 1.2 million people needed primary and secondary health services, including 425,705 children (UN HRP 2020). More than half of the functioning health care facilities in 2019 have closed due to security issues and funding deficits. Those that remain open are constrained by significant shortages of staff, medicines, and supplies. An estimated 70 percent of primary health care facilities do not have the 20 most essential medications. During the first two months in 2020, there was a stockout of essential vaccines, including those that prevent childhood diseases such as measles and polio. An estimated 316,000 children and 10,000 teachers needed education support. Due to COVID-19, schools closed in mid-March 2020 and did not reopen until 2021.

THE EVOLUTION OF THE SOCIAL PROTECTION SECTOR AND THE ROLE OF SUBSIDIES

Libya's social protection system consists of both contributory and noncontributory assistance programs. The system, as designed, is very inclusive, as it is tied to a universal human rights-based approach that responds to everyone's needs across the life cycle. Before 2011, the social protection system was fully functioning, and spending on social protection was estimated at 4.4 percent of GDP in 2010 (IPCIG 2018). Programs were characterized by adequate benefits and a comprehensive set of programs that were tax financed (mostly through oil revenues), government implemented, and grounded in legislation. Before 2011, Libya was the only country in the Middle East and North Africa (MENA) region with a universal child allowance program covered by law. In addition, decades of a socialist system (Jamahuriya) in Libya resulted in solid state and public assistance programs, which have historically provided vast numbers of jobs in the public sector (85 percent of the Libyan workforce is employed in the public sector), universal food and fuel subsidies, and free health care and education.

Libya's current social protection system relies largely on energy price subsidies and cash assistance to households. However, the coverage of social assistance programs in place (both active and dormant), covering a wide range of contingencies and risks, remains limited. Excluding spending on universal subsidies, national social assistance expenditure accounts for less than 1 percent of gross domestic product (GDP) (World Bank 2021). In addition, the existing social protection system in Libya remains fragmented, with the same population groups eligible for and covered under different social assistance programs. Finally, the Libyan government continues to lack a comprehensive social protection response to mitigate the effects of the current crises on households. Libya remains one of a few MENA countries with no new social protection mitigation measure to tackle the effects of COVID-19 pandemic or the increasing burden of the conflict on households.[4]

Current subsidy schemes and their legacy

Like many countries in the MENA region, Libya has a long history of using food and fuel price subsidies as a primary instrument of social protection. Consumer price subsidies covered basic food staples (flour, sugar, and rice) and energy products (gasoline, diesel, and kerosene). These price subsidies make up a significant part of the state's budget. The subsidy schemes date back to 1971 and were introduced through a national price stabilization fund, known as the Compensation Fund. Subsidies and transfers handed out by the Libyan government were estimated at LD 6.7 billion in 2018, or 13.6 percent of overall government expenditure. Figure 19.5 shows the share of subsidies by the general budget disaggregated by type of subsidies.

FIGURE 19.5

Universal subsidies in Libya

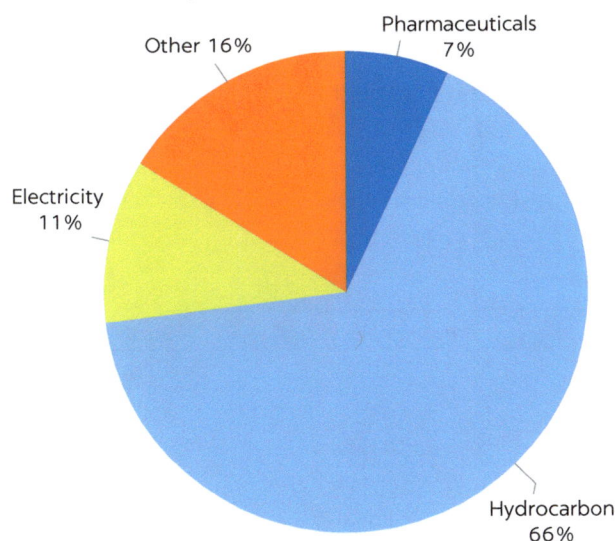

Source: Calculations based on World Bank 2019.

Until 2018, the provision of public services (water, sanitation, education, and garbage collection), medicines, and animal feed was also subsidized under the same scheme. The Compensation Fund determined the domestic prices and paid the difference, with the objective of keeping essential consumption items at affordable prices and protect consumers. As is the case with most price-targeted programs, the fiscal burden of these compensation funds was variable and no targeting or quantity caps in provision of subsidized goods were introduced.

Subsidies on energy (hydrocarbon subsidies)

Table 19.1 shows the percentage of market price subsidies by fuel commodity from the latest available data (2013). The largest increase in energy subsidies occurred during the 2000s and until 2008, when the price of oil in the global market significantly increased while domestic prices remained stable, creating an ever-increasing gap and reaching a peak at LD 12.4 billion in 2014 (World Bank 2018). Despite the precipitous decline in revenues and subsequent reduction in government spending, subsidies continued to occupy a significant share of total expenditures, including for the estimated 2021 budget, which remains unsustainable given current revenues, with subsidies at LD 17 billion. Table 19.1 provides a snapshot of international and subsidized price differentials by type of commodity.

According to a study commissioned by the Committee for Hydrocarbon Subsidies at the Ministry of Planning in January 2017, it is estimated that 30–40 percent of fuel produced and imported by Libya is stolen or smuggled, the economic distortions of which are estimated to cost the economy a loss of US$750 million per year (GoL MoP 2017). Despite the removal of food subsidies, spending on energy subsidies reached 12.5 percent of GDP in 2017 (World Bank 2017).

Although the precipitous decline in revenues had a dramatic effect on government spending, energy subsidies continued to occupy the lion's share of expenditures in Libya's budget. The plunge in revenues in 2019 resulted in the Government of National Accord (GNA, Western Libya) cutting total expenditures by 22 percent from LD 46.1 billion in 2019 to LD 36.2 billion in 2020. However, subsidies remained the lion's share (table 19.2). Subsidies and transfers increased from LD 6.4 billion in 2017 to LD 7.9 billion in 2019, making up over 16 percent of total expenditures. Although expenditures were reduced, subsidies continued to occupy a significant share of total expenditures including in the estimated 2021 budget (at LD 17 billion), which remains unsustainable given current revenues. This is due to Libya's highly rigid expenditure structure that provides little room for a more cost-effective approach to social protection in scenarios where hydrocarbon revenues are volatile.

TABLE 19.1 **Subsidy levels by commodity, 2013**

	SUBSIDIZED PRICE (LD)	MARKET PRICE (LD)	SUBSIDY (% OF MARKET PRICE)
Gasoline (L)	0.15	1.072	86
Diesel (L)	0.15	1.11	86
Electricity (kWh)	0.02	0.156	87
LPG (L)	2	20.939	90
Kerosene (L)	0.09	1.089	92

Source: Araar, Choueiri, and Verme 2015.
Note: kWh = kilowatt hours; L = liter; LD = Libyan dinar; LPG = liquefied petroleum gas.

TABLE 19.2 **Subsidies by type, 2018–20**

LD, millions

	2018	2019	2020 Q1	2020 Q2	2020 Q3	2020 Q4
Total	6,626.8	7,235.0	1,076.1	2,870.8	4,200.0	5,600.0
Fuel	4,370.0	4,200.0	850.0	1,700.0	2,550.0	3,400.0
Electricity and public lighting	820.0	820.0	0.0	360.0	540.0	720.0
Medical	766.8	1,545.0	0.0	495.8	637.5	850.0
Public service (cleaning)	410.0	410.0	168.6	200.0	300.0	400.0
Water and sanitation	260.0	260.0	57.5	115.0	172.5	230.0
Emergency budget	—	—	588.8	1,794.7	2,538.2	4,527.0

Source: Libyan authorities; World Bank 2021.
Note: — = not available.

Subsidies on food staples

Food subsidies were introduced by Law No. 60 of 1976,[5] which envisaged the establishment of consumer cooperative associations across the country, with a view to having these programs managed by citizens to enable the distribution of subsidized food commodities. The subsidized basket of goods would include products ranging from flour, wheat, and rice to pasta, coffee, and milk for children (Araar, Choueiri, and Verme 2015). In 2010, the entire Libyan population had access to the universal food subsidy program. However, national sources report suggested significant leakages and occurrences of double dipping (LOOPS 2015).

Since 2014, most food subsidies were cut or suspended in large parts of the country due to the conflict, and at that time were abolished in key centers such as Tripoli and Sebha, reducing the purchasing power of consumers. While the system remained partly functional in Benghazi, a shortage of funds to pay importers of subsidized commodities, as well as distributors, saw a de facto removal of food subsidies from 2016, and which had fully ceased by 2017 (REACH 2017; WFP 2016; World Bank 2016). This resulted in shortages in food supply and emergence of trade on the black market and a consequent rise of food prices by 31 percent in the first half of 2016.

Welfare impact of subsidies programs

Price subsidies in Libya are inefficient, costly, and not targeted. In addition, a portion of subsides is being smuggled to neighboring countries. In April 2018, the chairman of the National Oil Corporation stated that it estimated that 30–40 percent of fuel produced and imported by Libya is stolen or smuggled.[6]

Energy subsidies are homogeneous across all households. They are heavily consumed by rich households. A World Bank study using 2007/8 Libyan household expenditure survey (the most recent available comprehensive survey of expenditures) highlighted that the richest 20 percent of the population household benefits 3.5 times more from energy subsidies than poorest households in monetary terms. This can be seen in figure 19.6, which shows that richer household receive more subsidies per capita than poorer households. It also shows that the main energy products consumed by household are gasoline and electricity.[7]

FIGURE 19.6

Per capita benefits from subsidies on energy products, 2007/08

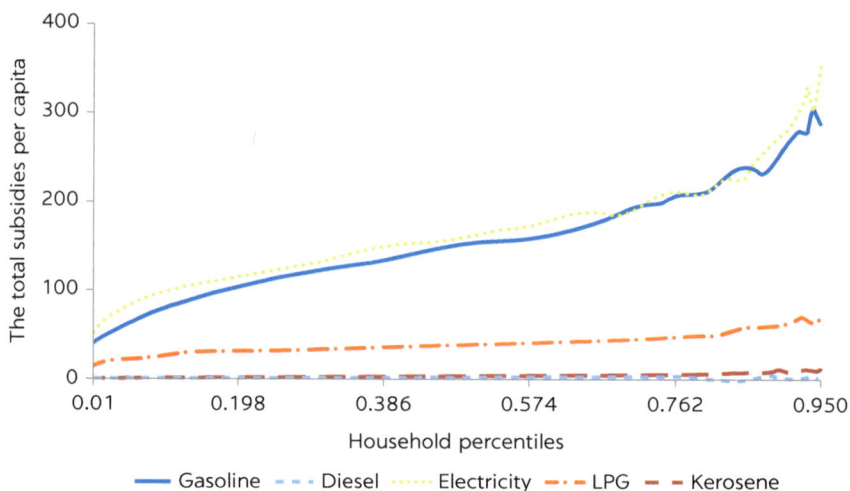

Source: Calculations based on Libyan Household Consumption Survey 2007/8; Libyan authorities; World Bank calculations.
Note: LPG = liquefied petroleum gas.

Some of the largest increases in the total energy subsidy bill occurred over the past two decades due to the increasing volatility of the prices of fuels and lower levels of production in country. This has prompted renewed discussions on reform of energy price subsidies. The main five products (gasoline, diesel, liquefied petroleum gas [LPG], kerosene, and electricity) have driven most of the increases in the overall government expenditures on subsidies. The subsidy gap in Libya (using the price-gap methodology) has significantly increased given the volatility of international prices of fuel. The largest increases occurred prior to the revolution, reaching a peak at LD 12.4 billion in 2014. Highest recorded subsidies were for kerosene and LPG. Many of the products were subsidized at over 85 percent of the products' market value. These increases have become unsustainable and prompted several attempts at subsidy reform before and after the revolution.

A reduction in subsidies would lay the foundations for macroeconomic stability and create the fiscal space for more targeted interventions. In the medium term, the country would need broader and deeper structural reforms to sustain economic growth, including improving tax revenues, enhancing the management of public financial and human resources, launching civil service reform, and promoting the development and diversification of the private sector.

Attempts at reforms

In 2020, the GNA adopted plans to reform the existing fuel subsidy system. These plans were largely unsuccessful. In 2020, subsidies reached LD 5.6 billion or 16 percent of total expenditures. The GNA looked to implement subsidy reform plans that had been previously adopted in 2015 and replace the price subsidies scheme with a universal cash transfer system. Apart from fuel, other items in the subsidy list included electricity, water and sewage, sanitation, and medical supplies. Development expenditures were minuscule for the year, LD 1.8 billion or 5 percent of total expenditures, compared to LD 4.6 billion in 2019. All capital expenditures projects for 2020 were virtually eliminated.

Although the Government of National Unity (GNU) has communicated efforts to launch subsidy reforms soon, it is unclear if the current proposal is still considered.[8] Previous attempts at energy price subsidy reform have failed in Libya, and the current situation in the country offers few options for curbing the rising inflation affecting the prices of fuels and basic commodities due to the depreciation of currency and increasing subsidy bill. To that end, if the GNU decides in the near-to-medium term to go ahead with a subsidy reform program, they should include large-scale cash-transfer mitigation schemes.

The GNU may decide to reduce the subsidies for oil petroleum products and compensate consumers with cash transfers; if so, feasibility studies should be carried out (see box 19.1 for considerations). The feasibility should include the selection of the hydrocarbon subsidies targeted for reduction (gasoline, diesel, or cooking gas). Studying the institutional capacity to implement a compensation scheme would also inform the design of the most appropriate program. Identifying all the steps of the reform process, including well-sequenced mitigation mechanism, will be key to engendering the political will and ensuring buy-in the reform process.

BOX 19.1

Key considerations in setting parameters for subsidy reform

Globally, most governments provide some form of subsidy for energy consumption and use in the form of producer or consumer subsidies. The magnitudes of these subsidies are staggering. Fossil fuel subsidies—defined as fuel consumption times the gap between existing and efficient prices (including environmental costs)—were estimated at $4.7 trillion, or nearly 6.3 percent of global gross domestic product (GDP) in 2015. This increased to $5.2 trillion in 2017, divided almost equally between petroleum, natural gas, and coal.[a] Despite overwhelming international evidence of its fiscal costs, redistributive inefficiency, and climate impact, however, reforming energy subsidies remains a largely unfulfilled agenda.

In a review of over 90 subsidy reform scenarios globally over the past three decades, social protection has been shown as a key driver in supporting gradual reform of price subsidies and ensuring sustainability and buy-in of the general population. In a review of these subsidy reform episodes, the provision of cash transfers to a big proportion of the population—including the poor and vulnerable, and in some instances the middle-class (for social cohesion reasons)—has been predominantly used as the key mitigation mechanism. The steps below provide examples

of how measuring the welfare impact of subsidy reform (and the inherent price hikes) and ensuring institutional buy-in are key to supporting the design, financing, and rollout of a mitigation program. This, in turn, ensures success of the reform (defined by its intended objectives).

The following steps require significant buy-in and an understanding of political economy challenges associated with reform:

- *Deciding key parameters:* The parameters of subsidy reform include the type of fuel to be reformed (for example, octane 95, diesel for commercial, and liquefied petroleum gas [LPG], among others) and the target price or target savings amount (for example, reduction of subsidies to LD 80 per barrel or LD 110 million reduction in subsidies). These reform targets will have to be broadly communicated in relevant government bodies and agencies.
- *Analyzing the welfare impact:* In some settings, the welfare impact of price reform may be minimal, because of high leakage in the current price subsidy scheme (for example, shipment of subsidized fuels to nearby countries) and lack of

continued

Box 19.1, *continued*

a price control or price enforcement mechanism that allows retail sellers of fuel to sell subsidized products at price demanded.

- *Estimating the real fiscal gains:* It will be key to calculate the fiscal gains from the agreed-on reforms, including expected savings and what proportion will be reallocated to compensation mechanisms.

- *Identifying eligible groups for compensation:* It will be necessary to simulate the coverage of the defined target population based on proposed eligibility criteria. Using administrative and reported data, the government can calculate the total "compensation" bill in the immediate term. A second step will be to calculate the impact of transfers on the welfare of households countrywide.

- *Communicating:* Strategic communication, informed by evidence-based opinion polls, qualitative focus groups, and message testing, can have a significant impact on the success of any subsidy reform episode and must be done before reform rollout. This is especially the case in situations where subsidy reform episodes can result in shared gain to the entire population (due to lower information, financing of social protection programs, or human capital investments).

- *Refining program delivery:* Delivery mechanisms should be further defined. Specifically, communication, registration for the informal sector, verification of income and asset information, payment mechanism, and grievance and redress.

- *Linking with expansion of social assistance:* Expansion of social assistance is a key priority, given the type of commodities considered for price reform. To that end, a clear three-year plan for expansion of social assistance should be set in motion, assuming a social protection instrument is already in place.

- *Addressing political economy challenges:* Political economy challenges can be the difference between success or failure of any subsidy reform attempt. A thorough stock-taking can support countries during subsidy reform episodes. These types of political mitigation tools can help policy makers identify whether there are stakeholders with high degrees of interest and disproportionate influence regarding the reform. A matrix approach to winners and losers of subsidy reform can be developed.[b]

Sources: Yemtsov and Moubarak 2018; Gentilini et al. (forthcoming).
a. Coady et al. 2019.
b. Inchauste et al. 2017.

THE STATE OF SOCIAL ASSISTANCE IN LIBYA

This section is based on the findings from the joint stock-taking exercise on the state of social assistance programs including coverage, adequacy, and comprehensiveness (box 19.2). The stock taking completed in Libya helped to shed light on specific program design aspects, as well as delivery aspects per each program that was included in the analysis. The knowledge gained from the stock taking will help inform the choice of policy tools to accompany the intended energy subsidy reform efforts and shape an inclusive recovery plan in Libya. It will also help identify which programs and delivery system aspects can be used to provide Libyan households with the support they need and help enhance access to, and the quality of, essential services under a more integrated approach.

The stock-taking exercise of social protection in Libya

The stock-taking diagnostic analysis of social protection in Libya was a collaborative effort among World Bank, World Food Program, United Nations Childrens Fund (UNICEF), and the International Policy Centre for Inclusive Growth, which used the Core Diagnostic Instrument (CODI) tool (ISPA n.d.). The CODI tool included a questionnaire that helped to collect information on the institutional, programmatic, and delivery system aspects of a country's social protection system. Key delivery aspects of social assistance program reported what exists in the country vis-à-vis the outreach, eligibility, payments, type of benefits, coverage, financing, and overall delivery of benefits and services to the intended populations.

The stock-taking analysis also included a thorough literature review of existing documents such as laws, decrees, policies, reports, evaluations, and official social media websites. The analysis was complemented with repeated key informant interviews with technical focal points under the Social Solidarity Fund (SSF).

The stock taking and literature review also found that the difficulty gathering systematized and updated information was the result not only of the ongoing crises but also the lack of information generally between different line ministries and implementing bodies. In its Sustainable Development Goals *2020 Voluntary National Reviews Synthesis Report* (UN DESA 2020), the government noted that "the weakness and lack of data, information and indicators required for the measurement and evaluation, as a result of current circumstances, also negatively affect the achievements on the Sustainable Development Goals."

Social assistance now consists of the following programs:

- Cash assistance and in-kind transfers to specific categories of vulnerable groups, provided through the SSF, the MoSA, and the General Authority for Sponsorship of Martyrs, Missing Persons and Amputees
- Zakat assistance (with the government having some form of decision-making power or supervision)[9]
- Fee waivers for hospitalization in public and private hospitals, under the Ministry of Health
- Education grants and school support programs for poor households, under the Ministry of Education

Institutional, legal, and policy structure of social assistance

With the exception of the Convention on the Rights of Refugees, Libya has ratified and acceded to most international treaties that create several obligations related to social protection. Generally, the right to social protection as a whole is enshrined in Article 9 of the 1996 International Covenant on Economic Social and Cultural Rights (ICESCR) that "recognizes the right of everyone to social security" encompassing *contributory schemes,* providing protection against a loss of work-related income due to sickness, disability, maternity, work-related injury, unemployment, old age or death, as well as *noncontributory schemes*, such as universal or targeted social assistance.[10] Law No. 13 on Social Security (dating back to 1980) provides the most comprehensive definition of the concept of *social protection* as understood and applied by the Libyan state for the past four decades. In addition, Article 11 reiterates this as it calls for "an adequate standard of living including basic assistance, food, housing water, sanitation and clothing and the continuous improvement of living conditions."[11]

Through its ratification of the Convention on the Rights of Persons with Disabilities in 2018, Libya is obligated to provide persons with disabilities an adequate standard of living as well as social protection and poverty reduction programs, especially assistance to cover disability-related expenses.[12] Moreover, under the Convention on the Rights of the Child ratified in 1993, Libya is obligated to protect children's right to an adequate standard of living by assisting parents and legal guardians through the provision of "material assistance."[13]

Legal and institutional directives related to social protection

In the aftermath of the 2011 ousting of Muammar Gaddafi, a Constitutional Declaration was published regulating the process of electing a Constitution Drafting Assembly (CDA) to replace the old one from 1959. An assembly was elected in 2014. However, it faced numerous challenges, such as being boycotted by the Amazigh community[14] and having its chairman dismissed in 2016 (ICJ 2015; Libya Observer 2016). Nonetheless, the CDA succeeded in producing a draft constitution by 2017, but this has not yet been put to a referendum, nor has it been formally adopted, effectively having the Constitutional Declaration of 2011 yet to be replaced.

Libya has an established and comprehensive social protection system, the rights to which are entrenched in the 2011 Constitutional Declaration. Article 8 indicates that the "state shall guarantee equal opportunity for every citizen and shall provide an appropriate standard of living." In addition to its articulation in Article 8, the right to social assistance is guaranteed and operationalized by several implementing executive regulations. Article 5 stipulates that motherhood, childhood, and old age are to be protected and that children, youth, and persons with disabilities will be taken care of by the state. Law No. 13 on Social Security (1980) stresses the right to social security, especially in the case of loss of income or death of a breadwinner or in the cases of emergencies for Libyan citizens in Article 1 and extends such protections to non-Libyan residents as well. Law No. 13 also established the zakat benefits (Art. 2), social insurance (Art. 3), social care and health care services (Art. 12), basic pension (Art. 22), emergency grants (Art. 27), and the family allowance (Art. 24), which have subsequently been elaborated in their own legal frameworks. Law No. 16, on the other hand, replaced some of the provisions established the Basic Pension Benefit for low-income households (initially created in 1969 and then regulated by Law No. 16 in 1985) and defined basic assistance as the "noncontributory cash assistance guaranteed by the social security system." These legal instruments, as well as others regulating social assistance, are featured in table 19.3.

National stakeholders

The responsibility for the social protection sector in Libya is scattered across several ministries, national direct implementors, and policy-making bodies. Figure 19.7 illustrates the national actors involved in the social protection sector in Libya.

TABLE 19.3 Legal instruments governing social assistance programs

MAIN LEGAL INSTRUMENT	OTHER LEGAL INSTRUMENTS	PROGRAM	OBJECTIVE
Law No. 16 on Basic Pension (1985)	• Law No. 12 Amending Law No. 16 on Basic Pension (2013) • Law No. 1 Amending Law No. 16 on Basic Pension (2017)	Basic Pension Benefit	Financial support to vulnerable groups, (elderly, disabled, widows, orphans) and those unable to work
Law No. 27 on Allowances for Children and Wives (2013)	• Decree No. 565 on Wives and Children's Grant	Wives and Children's Grant	Financial support to all Libyan children and some Libyan married and unmarried women
Decree No. 119 on the Establishment of a Marriage Support Fund (2012)	• Law No. 5 on the Establishment of a Marriage Support Fund (2019)	Marriage Grant	Financial support to poor couples wishing to marry and poor newlyweds
Decree No. 184 on Compensation to Citizens in Cases of Crises and Natural Disasters (2012)	• Law No. 20 on Social Solidarity Fund (1998)	Disaster Compensation Benefit (also known as Emergency Assistance)	Financial support to those experiencing hardship as a result of losses in sources of income due to crises or natural disasters
Law No. 13 on Zakat (1997)	• Executive Regulations of Law No. 13 on Zakat (1997) • Decree No. 30 on Zakat Beneficiaries and Rules of Distribution (2005)	Monthly Cash Assistance[a]	Distribution of zakat one-off benefits based on Sharia principles
Law No. 5 on Persons with Disabilities (1987)	• Executive Regulations No. 41 on Benefits for Persons with Disabilities (PWDs) (1990)	PWD Grant (Part of the Basic Pension benefit)	Cash support to finance caretakers for PWDs not in care centers and unable to care for themselves
Law No. 4 on Permanently Handicapped Individuals as a Result of the Liberation War (2013)	• Law No. 1 on the Care of Families of Martyrs and Missing Persons due to the 17th of February Revolution (2014) • Law No. 7 Amending Law No. 4 (2015) • Decree of the Military General No. 26 (2020)	Families of Martyrs, Missing Persons, and Amputees Grant[b]	Financial support to the categories as well as transportation subsidies, health insurance coverage, and priority in receiving housing and commercial loans

Source: Government of Libya.

a. See https://www.facebook.com/zakatlibya/photos/pb.393963277365445.-2207520000../2880461522048929/?type=3&theater.

b. This program was gathered during the literature review. The stock taking did not include any information on this program. We are not aware if it is still active and if it falls under social assistance. Also, not all programs are included in the stock-taking analysis.

Program-level descriptions

This section provides a brief description of each entity and the key programs engaged in the delivery of social assistance, which were reviewed as part of the program diagnostics carried out by the World Bank and WFP in 2020. At the *ministerial level,* the relevant government entities involved in the provision of social protection (namely noncontributory programs) include the MoSA, the Social Solidarity Fund, the Social Security Fund (SSecF), the Marriage Aid Fund, and the Zakat Fund. At the strategic coordination, policy, and planning level, the Ministry of Finance and the Central Bank of Libya are responsible for social protection programming, together with key interministerial bodies, which include the National Economic and Social Development Board (NESDB) and National Committee for Persons with Disabilities. Figure 19.8 provides a list of key programs and types of benefits and assistance schemes offered.

FIGURE 19.7

National actors involved in the social protection sphere

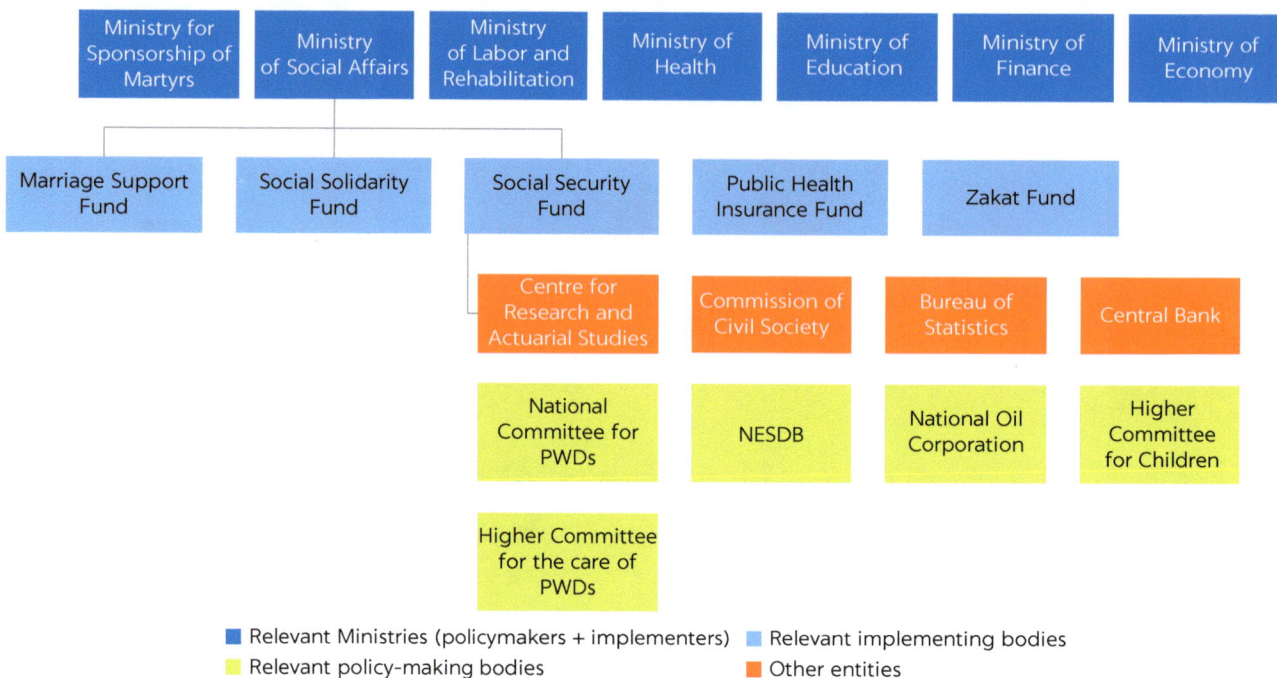

Source: UNICEF 2021.
Note: NESDB = National Economic and Social Development Board; PWD = persons with disabilities.

FIGURE 19.8

Social assistance programs

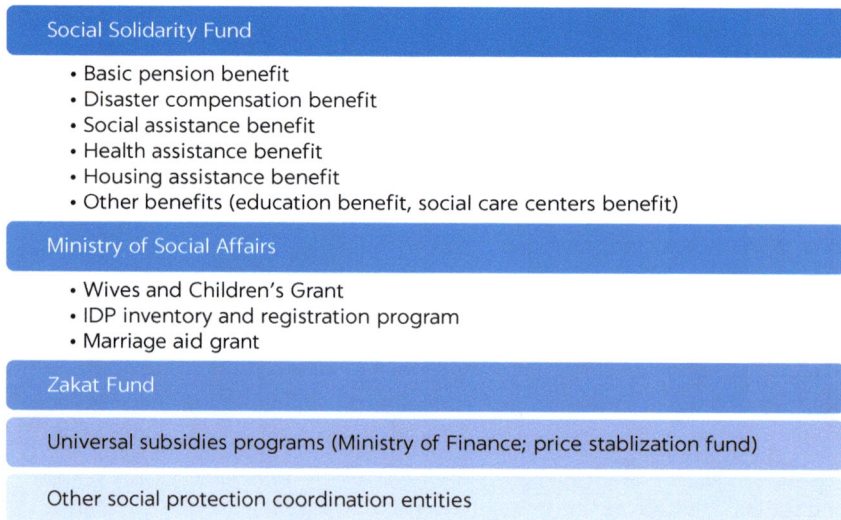

Social Solidarity Fund

- Basic pension benefit
- Disaster compensation benefit
- Social assistance benefit
- Health assistance benefit
- Housing assistance benefit
- Other benefits (education benefit, social care centers benefit)

Ministry of Social Affairs

- Wives and Children's Grant
- IDP inventory and registration program
- Marriage aid grant

Zakat Fund

Universal subsidies programs (Ministry of Finance; price stablization fund)

Other social protection coordination entities

Source: Original compilation for this publication.
Note: IDP = internally displaced person.

Overall, social assistance programs have declined in both number and coverage over the course of the conflict. Programs are now largely limited to the Western part of the country, have seen their funding disrupted and, for some, ceased activity altogether. Important building blocks of the pre-2011 social assistance system, such as education or housing benefits, are inactive. Since 2014, most food subsidies were cut or suspended in large parts of the country, due to the conflict, and at that time were abolished in key centers such as Tripoli and Sebha. Similarly, the Wives and Children's Grant programs were inactive for several years, with recent moves from the GNA in 2021 suggesting reactivation. Similarly, the long-dormant marriage grant made news headlines when the government announced the program's reactivation. However, it remains to be seen, at the time of this chapter's publication, whether these declarations will result in effective reactivation or be limited to supporting short-term political objectives.

Ministry of Social Affairs

According to the Organizational Structure Decree No. 120 (2012), MoSA has three subsidiary autonomous bodies: the SSecF,[15] the SSF, and the Marriage Aid Fund. The MoSA has global oversight of the social protection sector in Libya. The MoSA also directly manages the Wives and Children's Grant, though this program was inactive for several years of the past decade. The main implementation agency for social assistance programs, housed within the MoSA, is the SSF, which manages most of Libya's social assistance programs. The ministry works primarily on supporting women, children, the elderly, and persons with disabilities by developing appropriate policies and legal frameworks and implementing programs such as supporting families to become economically dependent through home projects and providing financial aid for pregnant women (MoSA n.d.[16]), monitoring care homes, and coordinating the efforts of civil society (LOOPS 2016).[17]

There are also a few notable departments within the ministry that are particularly relevant for future engagement in the social protection strategy development process, including the following:

- *Department for Family and Children:* Providing care for women and girls that face gender-based violence, and overseeing the implementation of legislation related to equal opportunities for women[18]
- *Department of Humanitarian Affairs and Assistance:* Responsible for responding to shocks through the provision of emergency assistance equipment and shelter, assessing the number of poor, large, and needy families as well as approximating the value of disaster compensation and monitoring the rapidness of its delivery[19]
- *Department for Affairs of People with Disabilities:* Responsible for health assessments to confirm disability and the issuance of disability cards. Equipping people with disabilities centers with necessary materials, providing housing for people with disabilities[20]

Social Solidarity Fund

The SSF is the main implementing agency in Libya for state-led social assistance programs. SSF is part of the MoSA, established in 1998 through Law No. 20, which regulates the SSF's role in granting one type of pension, called the Basic Pension, for those who do not have contributory pensions, jobs, properties, or any official source of income.

SSF has 26 branches (approximately 60 offices) across the country, 15 in the Western region and 11 in the Eastern region.[21] The SSF has its own operating budget, which is independent from the budget allocated to the MoSA, and it is based on and financed by a 1 percent contribution that is deducted from the total revenues of employees (public and private), self-employed workers, donations, and the Zakat Fund.[22] Within the SSF, there are currently five departments, each with its own budgets and responsible for its respective, dedicated programs.

Following is a description of key functioning programs using the latest available information on program design, coverage, expenditure, and benefit structures.

Basic Pension Benefit

The Basic Pension Benefit is the largest active program under the SSF. First established in 1969 and later regulated through Basic Pension Law No. 16 (1985), it provides eligible beneficiaries with a monthly cash transfer of LD 450 (or US$100), equivalent to the Libyan minimum wage.[23] If potential beneficiaries are assessed as having an income that falls below the Basic Pension Benefit amount, they are eligible to receive a supplementary benefit equal to the difference between their income and the Basic Pension Benefit amount.

The Basic Pension Benefit covers a range of vulnerable categories. This includes persons with disabilities or chronic diseases (representing 66 percent of beneficiaries in 2020), vulnerable women (22 percent), vulnerable children (6 percent), and the vulnerable elderly (5 percent). As of December 2020, the Basic Pension Benefit covered a total of 178,956 individuals (see annex 19A).

Disaster compensation benefit

This benefit is intended to support victims of natural disasters who have suffered physical or material damage. This includes those who have suffered from physical damage to their property. The compensation is also provided to households affected by the deaths of family members caused by accidents. The Disaster Compensation Benefit is activated after the shock has occurred and damages and losses have been assessed. Benefit levels are determined on a case-by-case basis, depending on damages incurred and the specific economic situation of the family.

From its establishment in 2002 to the present day, the compensation benefit has supported around 11,245 households, with the total financial compensation over the period reached being at LD 30.7 million. Cash transfers of some LD 1.9 million were made in 2020, for the Western, Northern, and Southern regions (but excluding the Eastern region), with 75 percent of funds allocated and disbursed to the Western and Southern regions and 25 percent to the Eastern region. The range of cash assistance provided in 2020 ranged from LD 4,000 to 20,000. Figure 19.9 provides an illustration of the program's number of cases (coverage) and total expenditures (in millions of LD) since 2002.

Social services benefit

The program, also under SSF under the auspices of the MoSA, provides cash and in-kind transfers and reaches over 1,009 households with LD 1,000 a year per household. It is important to highlight that, through this scheme, between April 2019 and December 2019, a total of 3 million LD was disbursed for 15,000 IDPs in total, both Libyans and non-Libyans, via in-kind support.

FIGURE 19.9

The disaster compensation benefit, expenditures, and coverage

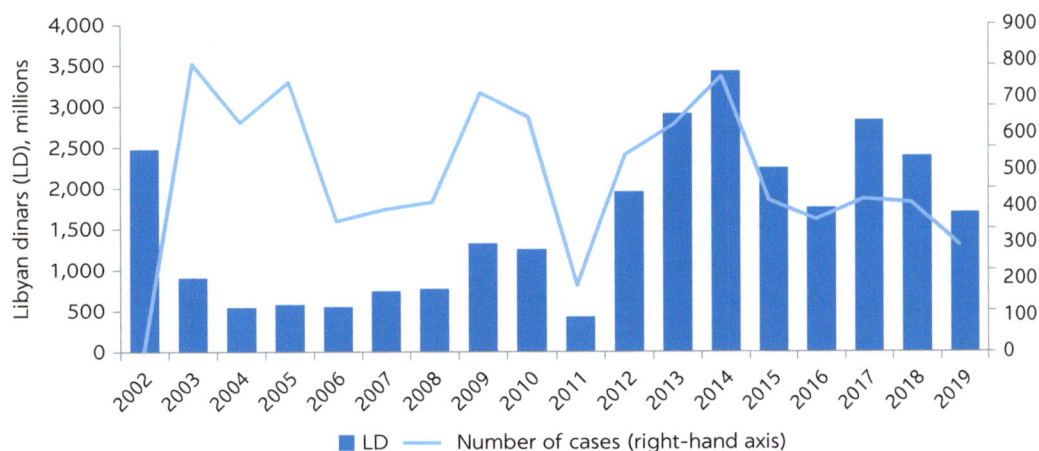

Source: Ministry of Social Affairs, Social Solidarity Fund, Department of Social Development.

Health Assistance Benefit

As the smallest functioning program in SSF, the Health Assistance Benefit has limited funding but provided cash transfers to 1,968 individuals, each receiving a lump sum of LD 1,000 (total budget for 2020 was LD 4 million), even if they are part of the same household.

Housing benefit

The housing is inactive and is expected to remain dormant for the foreseeable future.

Wives and Children's Grant (WCG)

The WCG is a program under the MoSA that has operated largely outside the SSF. The program was launched in 2013, ceased activity in 2014, and recently reactivated in 2021. The reactivated program was allocated LD 75 million transferred to the MoSA for grants in early 2021. In May 2021, the MoSA launched a digital platform to detail the application process, address citizens' issues, and enable beneficiaries to communicate with the MoSA directly, including to inquire about family data, and make sure it is correct. The recommencement of grant was backdated to January 2021, with disbursement commencing in May 2021.

Zakat Fund

Established in 2012,[24] the fund operates autonomously, yet it falls under the General Authority for Religious Affairs and Endowments (GARAE). The fund distributes monthly cash assistance and other cash and in-kind benefits financed through zakat.[25]

Marriage Aid Fund

Established in 2012, the fund operates autonomously but is under the MoSA.[26] It oversees the distribution of financial assistance to couples who wish to marry but cannot afford to do so and also supports them in finding housing.[27]

Social Security Fund

Established in 1980, the SSecF oversees the implementation of *contributory benefits,* such as pensions and total and partial disability insurance in cases of work injuries or occupational illness for all workers, as well as one-off grants for employees and short-term benefits in cases of birth, injuries, or illness for self-employed workers.

Ministry of Finance

As a policy and strategic planning entity, the Ministry of Finance sets the budgets of different entities. The ministry also oversees the implementation of subsidies on fuel, electricity, water, medication, and food (GoL MoF 2020). At the *Institutional level,* there are additional policy-making and implementation bodies that are relevant for social protection programs and policies:

- *The National Committee for Persons with Disabilities*[28] was originally established under the SSecF, 2012. In 2018, the committee had its first meeting, where it discussed the possibility of establishing the Higher Committee for the Care of People with Disabilities, which in 2020 seems to have been established to ensure the health, education, and rights to care for people with disabilities, as well as the provision of cash and in-kind assistance wherever needed. Yet there are no available documents indicating the operational difference between the national and the higher committee.
- *The National Economic and Social Development Board (NESDB)* is placed under the authority of the prime minister (PM) and aims to support the PM in studying the regulatory and policy impact analysis of the economic and social legislations; proposing policy initiatives; contributing to the preparation of studies to build a diversified knowledge base on innovation and partnership between the public and private sectors; encouraging positive dialogue among the political, economic, and social partners; supporting the integration between state and society; and finally, contributing toward establishing the values of justice and democracy and strengthening the notion of decentralization. The NESDB also works on gaining the support of various parties, social and economic institutions, and civil society for the policies and programs of the state.

Need for social assistance programs far outstrips capacity of functional programs

Figure 19.10 shows the extent of financial need both nationally and at the district (baladiyah) levels. In 2016, 60 percent of Libya's population needed financial assistance according to the Multi-Sectoral Household Survey to Assess Family Needs, conducted by the Libyan Bureau of Statistics, United Nations High Commissioner for Refugees, WFP, UNICEF, and United Nations Population Fund (LBS et al. 2016). Only 5 percent of households noted regular social assistance as a main source of income.

Yet according to the low-vision patient questionnaire (LVCS-S) survey, in which patients provided responses during phone interviews with members of the research team, only 4 percent of households reported benefiting from some form of social assistance from the government, nongovernmental organizations (NGOs), or other UN agencies in the six months prior to the survey. About 16 percent of displaced households reported receiving assistance.

Of those who reported receiving assistance, 69 percent of the assistance received was through WFP's General Food Assistance, with only a small share

FIGURE 19.10

Percentage of households in need of financial assistance, by baladiyah, 2016

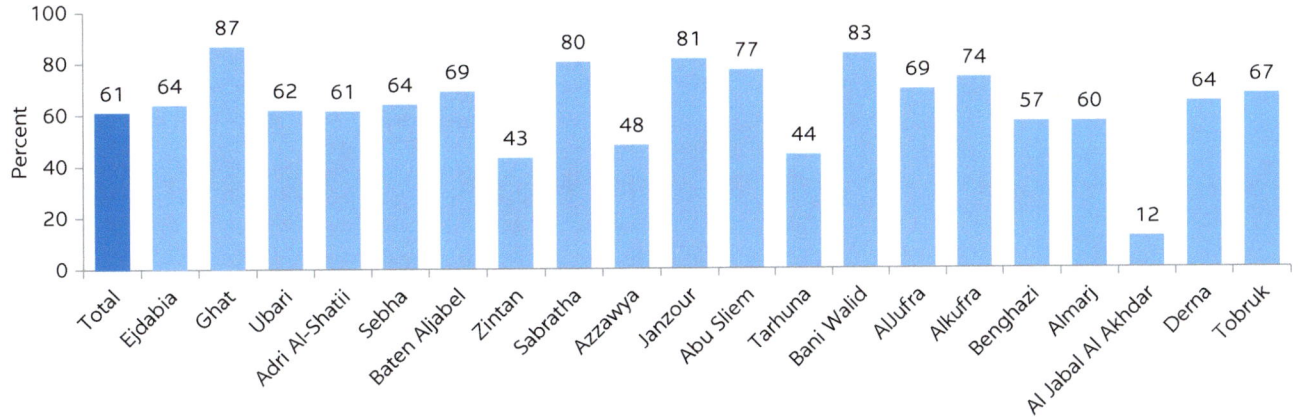

Source: LBS et al. 2016.

FIGURE 19.11

Households receiving assistance, by percentage and type

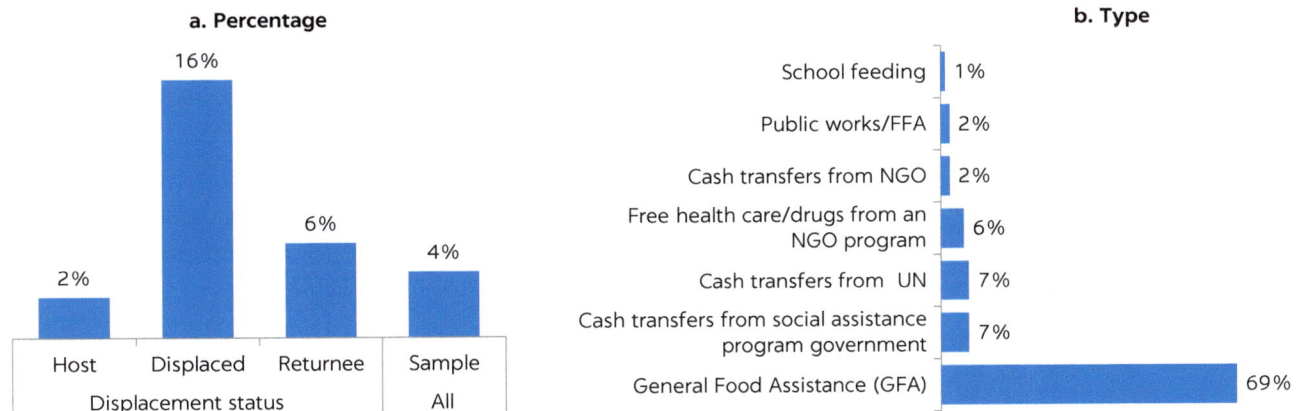

Source: VSCM-S 2021.
Note: FFA = Food for Assets initiatives; NGO = nongovernmental organization; UN = United Nations.

received through national programs (7 percent), the UN, or NGOs (7 and 8 percent, respectively). Only 1 percent reported accessing school feeding (figure 19.11).

Annex 19A lists all the social assistance programs identified and analyzed under the stock-taking exercise. The annex also categorizes and groups programs that are implemented by the SSF (the first seven) and those not implemented by the SSF.

THE SOCIAL PROTECTION DELIVERY SYSTEM

Over the past 30 years, countries have prioritized the development and modernization of social protection delivery systems in the provision of cash and in-kind services and transfers to poor and vulnerable households. The development of these delivery systems has been largely influenced in recent years by the introduction of information technology and related digital solutions that have eased the process of identification and delivery of these services. However, delivery systems components, whether in identification, eligibility verification, enrollment, payment mechanism, grievance and redress mechanisms, monitoring and evaluation or other business processes, are not new concepts. Several countries have successfully taken steps to reform these business processes to ensure more effective and efficient delivery systems in provision of cash, in-kind benefits, and services to beneficiaries.

Globally, the delivery systems of social protection programs constitute the operating environment for implementing social protection benefits and services, with core implementation phases along the delivery chain (figure 19.12). In delivering in-kind benefits or cash to the intended beneficiaries, the social protection programs generally involve some form of outreach to promote awareness and understanding among the intended population. In addition, the chain involves a form of intake and registration to gather information on people's characteristics, needs, and conditions; using that information, the implementers undertake some sort of assessment to profile those characteristics and determine potential program eligibility, assign the appropriate level of benefits and services, take enrollment decisions, and notify and onboard beneficiaries. Once the potential beneficiaries are registered and enrolled into a program, depending on the program objectives, there is the provision of in-kind or cash assistance. After the provision of benefits, the delivery chain concentrates on the management of beneficiaries' data, to ensure that information is accurate and up-to-date and that the offices comply with any co-responsibilities, grievances, and appeals and conduct reassessments and/or accounting for beneficiaries exiting the program(s).

We focus on the following:

- Identification (where we bundle intake and registration, assessment of needs and conditions, and eligibility and enrollment decisions)
- Provision of benefits and/or services
- Monitoring and grievance and redress mechanisms (GRMs)

Libya has many programs in place (some active, others not), and several laws indicate the importance and need for social protection overall. The system is not

FIGURE 19.12

The social protection delivery chain

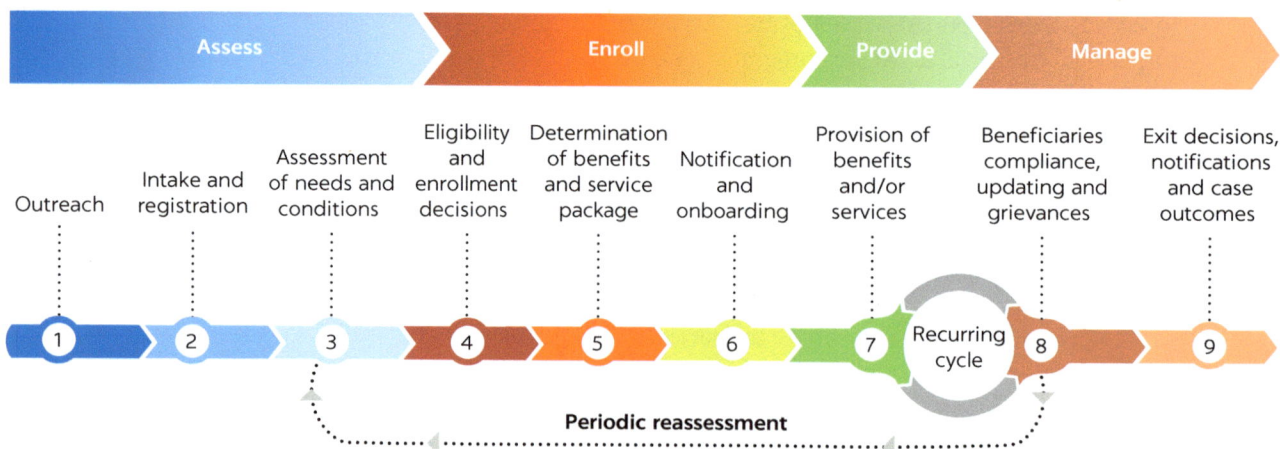

Source: Lindert et al. 2020.

well integrated, however, and it lacks centralized information systems (that is, registries and identification). The mandates of different agencies providing social protection support overlap, and the legal framework behind the social protection programs and policies is confusing. For instance, more than 50 laws, decrees, and executive regulations organize the work of the social protection sector.

The cornerstone is Law No. 13 of 1980, which established the SSecF and provides a comprehensive definition of social protection that includes social assistance measures such as the Emergency Benefit, as well as zakat, social security benefits and social care services for the most vulnerable. Ever since, several laws have been introduced over time, providing a comprehensive legal framework; nonetheless, it remains unclear whether they are in force, or where their accountability begins or ends,[29] leading to confusion with regard to both their individual roles and responsibilities and the inherent lack of integration across and institutions with the objective of protecting those most in need.

The SSF is responsible for implementing the five active social assistance programs. There are also two inactive programs under the SSF umbrella, but our analysis and stock taking concentrate mainly on the active ones, the main reason being that we attempted to extract the most recent and updated information on the overall system, as well as specific program delivery mechanisms in the country. As such, most of the analysis of the delivery chain and delivery system in Libya has to do with SSF, as opposed to many implementing agencies.

The following sections look at the subset of the delivery chain specifically related to the active programs implemented by the SSF. Where possible, we do reference the Wives and Children's Grant, which was very recently reactivated and falls under the MoSA.

Identification phase

The identification phase consists of a number of steps and characteristics:

- On a system level, at present, there is no unified intake and registration system for all social protection programs, implemented by the SSF or other bodies, including the MoSA. Similarly, SSF does not operate an integrated database of program beneficiaries.
- The Basic Pension Benefit has its own database (or data registration platform), which is housed under the Basic Pension Department within the SSF. All the other benefits (apart from the social care centers benefits/services), have their own specific databases under the Social Development Department, which is also under the SSF.
- The Civil Registry is responsible for the provision of identification (birth and death certificates) and validation of residency and citizenship of Libyans. The Civil Registry operates under the Ministry of Interior. Its link to the SSF is through the SSecF.
- The SSecF (the agency responsible for contributory social protection programs and provision of pensions) is linked with the SSF. This link is used to verify eligibility of social solidarity fund applicants. However, all the data sharing and linkages are done manually. Preliminary findings from the stock-taking interviews indicate that the SSF plan for 2022 is to centralize all the databases (or matching platforms).
- It is important to highlight, however, that on a case-by-case basis, the SSF can bundle benefits for a specific household, in addition to the Basic Pension Benefit, provided that they fulfill all the eligibility criteria.

- The intake and registration process, overall and specific to Basic Pension benefit (which falls under the SSF), for instance, is done in-person, and not in a digitized manner. Applicants, before they become registrants or even beneficiaries, have to physically request the application from the relevant office or branch, and they are required to submit the necessary proof and documentation.
- Across these registration and intake channels, little information is available related to the MoSA's use of data available at other agencies. Preliminary stock taking indicates that any validation is done manually (via letters confirming socioeconomic status of households); information on linkage of data and availability of data for eligibility determination was not accessible at the time of writing.
- Going forward, and with the aim of improving and modernizing the identification of potential beneficiaries of social assistance programs, the Civil Status Department (responsible for the Civil Registry) has entered into a memorandum of understanding with the Ministry of the Economy to develop an electronic infrastructure for improving economic and financial services. This included the launch of the Kick-Start Project in 2019, for developing a biometric data system.
- In general, to be eligible for social assistance programs and benefits in Libya (under the SSF), being considered poor is a necessary but not sufficient condition. While eligibility is conditional on program objectives (see table 19.3, with information on program-specific eligibility), the overall eligibility for social assistance benefits necessitates that the applicants and potential beneficiaries cannot be recipients of the SSecF benefits and must provide proof of no registration within the SSecF. In addition, having both an active bank account, as well as providing a photocopy of the most recent Family Booklet,[30] are the main requirements for eligibility purposes.

Social workers across the five implementing departments of the SSF play a fundamental role in the implementation of the program. They are tasked to carry out the surveys and screening of potential beneficiaries, to assess the needs and conditions, and determine eligibility for the program. This includes determining whether the individual is eligible for the programs or has any assets or sources of income to automatically exclude the household from the SSecF benefits.

Box 19.3 illustrates the eligibility requirements for the Basic Pension Benefit, which is one of the largest, active programs.

Provision of benefits and/or services (payment mechanisms)

With respect to the provision of benefits or services (known as the "payments phase," as well), all programs under the SSF follow the same process. Cash transfer benefits are delivered via bank transfers, directly to beneficiaries' bank accounts. Beneficiaries without an active bank account receive a check from the local SSF branch, which can be cashed at local banks. In this respect, it is relevant to note the role digital payments can play in an environment challenged by liquidity constraint. On the other hand, all the in-kind assistance provided by the SSF is delivered by the local SSF branches. An interesting point to note is that, under the MoSA, the recently reactivated Wives and Children's Grants deliver automatic payments based on the civil registry database.

Eligibility for and enrollment in the basic pension program

The following requirements apply for enrollment:

- Applicants, or potential beneficiaries (before they are enrolled and become actual beneficiaries), must provide proof of citizenship, generally in the form of a National ID, as well as the status of residency in the country (that is, legal, national of Libya).
- If potential beneficiaries are assessed as having an income that falls below the Basic Pension Benefit amount, they will receive a supplementary benefit

equal to the difference between their income and the Basic Pension Benefit amount.

- Potential beneficiaries must also show that there is no able-bodied person who is legally obligated to support them, nor that they have assets or capital that could be used or invested.
- Another eligibility aspect is that of disability, proving the inability to work (cleared by health committee).

Source: Based on interviews with Social Solidarity Fund and Libyan government counterparts, 2021.

Monitoring and grievance and redress mechanisms

Monitoring and grievance and regress mechanisms covers the following elements:

- *Overall management:* The Central Management Department, within the SSF, is responsible for the overall management of the social assistance programs. This includes the creation of committees that confirm eligibility, based on program criteria, as well as follow-up at the field level to ensure that benefits have reached the intended beneficiaries.
- *Compliance:* Under the Basic Pension Benefit, implemented by SSF, for instance, a verification is conducted for the "assessment of needs and conditions, and eligibility requirements," in cases when the SSF case workers office receive external/additional information that an applicant owns assets. In such cases, they verify the information by conducting an in-person field visit to confirm eligibility by their field offices or branches. The last check and confirmation are done by the local mayor to prove the residency of the potential beneficiary and reliability of the documents submitted.
- *Case management:* The Basic Pension Benefit (implemented by SSF), for instance, carries out studies and research necessary to develop and update the pension benefits. The Basic Pension Department, in charge of carrying out the pension benefits, undertakes periodic follow-ups of the beneficiary lists to verify eligibility and disbursements. The department also cross-references names of beneficiaries with other social assistance programs.

CHALLENGES AND OPTIONS FOR REFORM

Libya's social assistance programs and social protection system provide some level of coverage for the most vulnerable population throughout the life cycle (including children, people with disabilities, the elderly, and others), supporting a wide range of contingencies and risks. The menu of benefits available under the social protection sphere include cash and in-kind support, universal price subsidies, zakat transfers (although not confirmed), fee waivers, and education grants, and much of it is supported by a robust legal framework for protection of households along the life cycle.

However, Libya's social protection system's main challenge is the fragmentation, duplication of programs, and lack of sustainable financing mechanism within the fiscal budget. The overall system continues to be characterized by an ad hoc entitlement measure, with a number of legacy beneficiary rolls and long waiting lists for programs that lack funding and the ability to reprioritize beneficiaries based on their vulnerabilities and/or needs. This does not bode well for a system that is supposed to be adaptive and capable of responding to shocks. Furthermore, programs work in silos, within their respective implementing agencies, and lack an integrated, coherent, and coordinated approach in the provision of benefits or referral to services.

Challenges

To that end, these challenges can be categorized under the following five main findings:

1. **Energy and other subsidies are inefficient and do not reach the intended populations.** Subsidies and transfers increased from LD 6.4 billion in 2017 to LD 7.9 billion in 2019, making up over 16 percent of total expenditures. Although expenditures were reduced due to drops in prices and overall production in Libya, subsidies continue to occupy a significant share of total expenditures, including in the estimated 2021 budget (at LD 17 billion), which remains unsustainable given current revenues. These subsidies are highly regressive, benefiting higher income households with a larger share of consumption of fuels and who have been better equipped to access other aspects of the consumer subsidies scheme (for example, pharmaceuticals and hospitalization abroad). Finally, the subsidies' structure will continue to be an unpredictable burden on the Libyan economy as international prices of fuel continue to be volatile, rendering a changing total subsidy bill. Thus, a continuation of the subsidy structure will mean that there is little room for a more cost-effective approach to social protection. This comes against the backdrop that the current COVID-19 pandemic (and associated drop in demand and prices of fossil fuels) present a "golden opportunity" for reform.

2. **Libya has a strong constitutional and legal framework that supports the provision of social protection.** Its cornerstone is Law No. 13 (1980). These legal provisions established a comprehensive legal definition and associated institutions for social protection, including the SSF. However, changes in institutional arrangements, introduced over the past few decades but not fully realized, resulted in overlapping mandates of implementing agencies and fragmented programs, thus hampering efficient coordination.

3. **The review of the current available programs shows that many lack clear objectives, they are not systematically evaluated, "right-sized," and they lack the necessary modifications or adaptations based on changing country context, household needs, or evidence.** Many programs remain dormant. The Basic Pension Benefit and the Social Assistance Benefit are two of the largest social assistance programs under the SSF and are currently active; yet they lack clear objectives and design parameters. Since inception, they appear to maintain the same design structure and target mechanisms. The Basic Pension Benefit has a broad reach, with a transfer value equivalent

to the minimum wage. The Social Assistance Benefit and the Health Assistance, on the other hand, support a very limited number of households (or individuals), with low transfer values.

4. **The current delivery system of social assistance programs is largely represented by one implementing agency, the SSF, without clear integration on delivery chain processes with other relevant bodies that implement additional social assistance schemes, including the MoSA.** To offer need-based and relevant assistance to the intended beneficiaries, including a menu of benefits/services per household, delivery systems need to be coordinated and digitized at the central level.

5. **There is no meaningful way to link beneficiaries to social services to maximize the impact of social assistance.** This results from the lack of (1) a system of referral of case management, (2) adequate training of social workers, (3) information of the role of the social welfare worker, and (4) capacity of linking programs that can serve beneficiaries better (for example, education benefits).

Options for reform of social protection sector

Energy subsidy reform plans were reintroduced as a GNU priority under the economic track, together with currency alignment and East-West budgetary unification. The GNU has also adopted the former GNA approach, calling for a well-sequenced, large-scale social assistance mechanism to mitigate the effects of energy subsidy reform and inherent price increases. This approach is considered a cornerstone policy for economic stabilization in Libya—together with monetary and fiscal measures under way—and is expected to continue to be a priority in the coming years.

For social protection system building in the country, these compensatory transfers provide a tangible benefit to individuals and families that can engender buy-in to the reform process itself. They also provide one of the few avenues for creating the fiscal space to expand social safety nets in the country. The cost of these programs varies depending on levels of coverage and compensation, as envisaged by reform objectives. The benefits, however, can be several—lower (net) fiscal outlay, equity in distribution, and better governance, not to mention other spillover effects on climate and carbon emissions. The overall impact, therefore, depends on both the design and delivery of the compensation transfers as they have been experienced, successful or otherwise, in other countries and reform episodes globally.

In Libya, energy subsidy reform and expansion of social protection have taken on an added sense of urgency in the context of the global COVID-19 pandemic, and the incoming GNU has been acutely aware of this opportunity. Policy makers in Libya, as well as in many countries with high energy subsidies, are facing a compelling dilemma: how to maintain fiscal prudence while protecting the lives and livelihoods of their citizens. With lower fuel prices, governments can shift the fiscal resource pendulum. It is arguably evident to the public that the increased health costs and other expenses related to this pandemic are making the existing subsidies unaffordable. The crisis could therefore provide a political window of opportunity for governments to reallocate fiscal means to essential public services. Nevertheless, carrying out these reforms ultimately means that the new GNU ought to undertake significant steps in preparing its social assistance system, to be able to implement such a large-scale mitigation program, in coordination with other programs.

The recent calls for reforms will require advancements in the social protection delivery system and, in turn, improve administrative capacity to implement social assistance efficiently and effectively in a challenging fragility context like Libya. Countries worldwide continue to improve one or more core building blocks of their social protection delivery systems to improve the efficiency and responsiveness of the programs, while taking advantage of advancements in technology and connectivity. For Libya, technology promises an opportunity to reach households when myriad crises can hinder access to benefits and cashless transfers may alleviate the on-going liquidity crises. More broadly, use of technology and user-centric reform of social protection programs can result in the development of more unique IDs for in-take across programs, utilization of social registries, mobile payments, and coordinated bundles of benefits and services under one-stop shops that have become a new goal.

Taking these ideas holistically, Libya's challenge requires a two-phased approach: (1) in the short term, the expansion of programs to support households during the crises (and identifying a way to finance this expansion), and (2) in the medium term, delivering a more modern social protection system to respond to the challenging context.

Short-term reforms

In the short term, the key reforms should focus on the establishment of cash transfer programs to accompany the subsidy reform, mitigate the effects of the crises, support the recovery, build resilience, and strengthen the human capital of the children. The GNU will have the following options: (1) utilization of current programs, such as Basic Pension Benefits and Social Assistance Benefits, while increasing their generosity; (2) reform of current programs, such as the recently reactivated Wives and Children's Grants, and expanding its coverage and increasing its generosity; or (3) the introduction of a new program that can progressively expand its coverage toward a universal cash transfer program. All the reforms envisioned should include special considerations for gender aspects and access to the programs that reflect the rights for women and children.

Medium-term reforms

In the medium term, the key reforms should focus on the following priorities:

1. **Modernization of the Libyan social protection sector is needed to help improve both the efficiency and efficacy of the system.**

   a. Modernizing the social protection system in Libya ought to begin with institutional reforms that aim to promote coordination and efficiency within and across agencies that implement some forms of social protection measure. Overlapping mandates and unclear objectives of separate agencies, often aiming to assist the same targeted population, lead to duplication, redundancies, and reduced impact of program objectives.

   b. Similarly, while the social protection system involves a myriad of contributory and noncontributory measures, the social protection system would benefit from revisions or updates of existing social assistance schemes in place to better respond to a variety of needs across the life cycle. This ought to include recertifications into the legacy programs (that is, legacy beneficiary lists, militia, and so forth), among others.

c. More specifically, modernization of the social protection sector ought to be geared toward specific delivery chain aspects, beginning with the establishment of a social registry and interoperable social information systems and digitization of the payment system following a delivery-chain process mapping to assess end-to-end processes. Overall, before and while undertaking reform efforts, there ought to be a thorough delivery system analysis, a stress test of sorts; the intended reforms, as any other shocks, will affect prices. For delivery systems, dynamism and the ability to provide agile responses are key.

2. **Coordination and integration of the reform process within a social protection policy and a national strategy are essential next steps.** A vision for a national social protection system covering all Libyans with the same rights to access preventive, protective, and promotive schemes is needed to achieve a comprehensive framework within a life-cycle approach.

    a. A legal framework would need to be analyzed and reviewed to support a national sector policy to be comprehensive and integrate a life-cycle approach that will seek to enhance benefits for poor and vulnerable people and protect the welfare of the workers.

    b. The GNU will need to strengthen the leadership of the sector to seek a coordinated approach among national bodies, bilateral donor partners, and international humanitarian actors. It could make use of the Libya National Social Protection Platform, which was established in 2020. It functions as a multistakeholder national forum that can support strategic partnerships and cooperation with national leadership and serve as a forum for organizing analysis and dialogue on policy options.

3. **Libyan institutions will also need to establish the necessarily links across social programs to facilitate reinvestment in human capital post-conflict.**

    a. Social protection can play a crucial role in reducing the depth and severity of multidimensional poverty. The first step is to ensure that no child is left behind from the registration in social assistance programs. In addition, the Wives and Children's Grant will need to seek synergies and complementarity with other sectors for coordinated, multisectoral, and age-specific interventions to improve children's nutritional status; provide access to health care and safe water, sanitation, and housing conditions; protect children from violence and exploitation; and provide opportunities for educational achievement.

    b. For appropriate linkages to social services, the need for coordination and information sharing for intermediation and referrals is very high and will demand interoperable and integrated information systems, and possibly skilled social workers with caseloads that permit significant attention to each client.

    c. Social assistance programs can also play a crucial role in the recovery of hope for youth under 24 years of age, who represent almost 50 percent of the Libyan population, and support their transition to the labor market. The focus should be on linkages with educational and livelihood opportunities and access to recreational and psychosocial support activities. This can help reduce the sense of hopelessness, unnecessary idleness, and frustration at the limited opportunities available to them.

CONCLUDING REMARKS

The establishment of the reconciliatory GNU is a cause for optimism; the government may be able to respond to the current crises affecting households in Libya by reforming the current social protection system. As part of reconciliation efforts, factions representing Eastern and Western Libya have engaged in a multifaceted economic dialogue stemming from the recent political progress with the success of the security track discussions and commitments since February 2021. The economic dialogue has included substantive progress toward the adoption of a single national budget for the first time since 2014, first unified board meeting of Central Bank of Libya since 2014, alignment of the exchange rate across Libya, and restoration of oil production. These major steps may reduce the likelihood of further shocks affecting household welfare and increase the government's fiscal and administrative capacity to mitigate the impact of the crises and support the recovery efforts.

The major challenge ahead is for the GNU to launch a concerted effort toward reforms of the current social protection system, as part of its short-term strategy to support the recovery efforts. Reforms of the social protection system, and the social assistance programs, will play a crucial role in providing the necessary support to Libyan households in a more systematic and transparent way. Those interventions should address the needs of a larger proportion of the poor and vulnerable population and their challenges due to volatility in prices of MEB and the COVID-19-induced economic shutdown, which have left a large portion of the population with fewer assets, less purchasing power, and mounting debts. These government interventions will also be necessary to help cement peace across different regions in Libya.

The government has expressed some interest in introducing reforms that would help consolidate current spending in the social sectors. These reforms should eventually support plans for broader energy subsidy reform, accompanied by large-scale cash transfer programs. The cash transfer programs would help ensure buy-in in the reform process itself, as well as help set the stage for establishing a more adaptive social protection system overall.[31]

The previous GNA announced a few potential programs with enough political backing to be relaunched or adapted, precisely to accompany reform efforts. This includes the Family Allowance Program (a flagship mitigation program introduced in 2019 by GNA prior to the most recent conflict) and introduction or expansion of current social assistance programs, such as the MoSA's Wives and Children's Grants, SSF's Basic Pension Benefit program, or a combination of top-up programs within the SSF.

Reforming, rebuilding, and expanding coverage of the social assistance programs, and an overall system, in Libya will not be an easy task. Despite progress in unifying 80 percent of the government institutions in less than a month since the GNU has taken office, the country continues to face significant political instability at the governorate level, after nearly a year of fragmentation and lack of communication.

ANNEX 19A. BASIC PENSION BENEFICIARIES, 2020

TABLE 19A.1 **Basic pension beneficiaries, 2020**

CATEGORIES OF BENEFICIARIES	VALUE IN LD	NUMBERS TARGETED
Disability		*117,720*
Disabled less than 18 years	345,979,249	70,293
Chronic diseases (including malnutrition)	129,966,282	23,721
Disabled more than 18 years	124,654,507	17,599
Severe mental disability	28,619,156	5,127
Handicapped	2,651,664	602
Vision impairment	1,691,872	316
Amputee	286,100	62
Women		*39,794*
Widow less than 45 years	71,505,420	13,698
Widow more than 45 years	44,117,940	9,035
Divorced but without custody of children	45,209,632	8,708
Divorced with custody of children	37,147,602	7,992
Unmarried mothers	1,789,200	331
Divorced from foreigners	154,320	30
Children		*10,800*
Orphans	26,918,341	5,262
Twins	24,802,274	4,479
Sponsored orphans	4,307,446	949
Minors with separated parents (not living with both parents)	553,994	110
Elderly		*9,740*
Elderly	53,140,225	9,740
Other		*902*
Family of the missing or absent person	2,476,754	483
Patients of social care homes	1,196,850	224
Family of detainee or prisoner	873,304	164
Hospitalized	165,468	31
TOTAL	*948,207,600*	*178,956*

Source: MoSA 2020.

ANNEX 19B: DESCRIPTION OF SOCIAL ASSISTANCE PROGRAMS

TABLE 19B.1 Description of social assistance programs

	BASIC PENSION BENEFIT	DISASTER COMPENSATION BENEFIT	SOCIAL ASSISTANCE BENEFIT	HEALTH ASSISTANCE BENEFIT	HOUSING BENEFIT	EDUCATION BENEFIT	SOCIAL CARE CENTERS BENEFIT	IDP INVENTORY & REGISTRATION PROGRAM	WIVES AND CHILDREN'S GRANT	MARRIAGE AID GRANT	UNIVERSAL SUBSIDY PROGRAM	ZAKAT FUND
Status	Active	Active	Active	Active	Inactive (2010)	Inactive (2008)	Active	Inactive (2019)	Inactive (2014) recently reactivated (2021)	Inactive (2012)	Partially active (no food subsidy)	Active
Responsible implementing agency	Social Solidarity Fund (SSF)	Social Solidarity Fund (SSF)	Social Solidarity Fund (SSF)	Social Solidarity Fund (SSF)	Social Solidarity Fund (SSF)	Social Solidarity Fund (SSF)	Social Solidarity Fund (SSF)	Ministry of Social Affairs (MoSA)	Ministry of Social Affairs (MoSA)	Ministry of Social Affairs (MoSA)	Price Stability Fund; National Oil Corporation	General Authority for Religious Affairs and Endowments
Risk covered/ function	Old age, Disabled, Sick, Orphans, Widows, Divorced women, Unmarried mothers, Family member of missing person	Victims of crises and disasters	Inability to access essential/ social services	Inability to access basic health services	Inability to have a house	Study-related costs of children	PWDs, elderly, juveniles, and women	IDPs	Women and children with no stable source of income	Newly-weds	Poverty and social exclusion	All vulnerable groups
Targeting mechanism	Categorical	Ex-post estimation	Income Means			Categorical	Categorical	Categorical	Categorical / Income Means		Universal	Community based
Objective	Financial support to vulnerable groups, and those unable to work	Cash assistance and in-kind support to those affected by natural disasters such as earthquakes, floods, droughts, fires	Financial support for essential/ social services through cash and in-kind transfers	Financial support to meet basic health needs within specific areas	Financial support to enable the right to affordable housing	Coverage of study-related costs of students		Financial support to those affected by armed conflict	Financial support to all Libyan children and some Libyan married and unmarried women	Financial support to newlyweds (encourage marriage) and existing couples (discourage divorce)	Sets market prices for essential consumption items at affordable rates to protect citizens and residents against global price shocks	Financial support to vulnerable groups

(continued)

TABLE 19B.1 *continued*

	BASIC PENSION BENEFIT	DISASTER COMPENSATION BENEFIT	SOCIAL ASSISTANCE BENEFIT	HEALTH ASSISTANCE BENEFIT	HOUSING BENEFIT	EDUCATION BENEFIT	SOCIAL CARE CENTERS BENEFIT	IDP INVENTORY & REGISTRATION PROGRAM	WIVES AND CHILDREN'S GRANT	MARRIAGE AID GRANT	UNIVERSAL SUBSIDY PROGRAM	ZAKAT FUND
Benefit level and indexation	LD 450 a month (minimum wage)	The value of compensation must not exceed (75 percent) of the total estimated damages and losses; LD 10,000 for each deceased adult member of the household, LD 5,000 for relatives and children	LD 1,000 a year for each household. 300 LD per month for blind university students	Lump sum of LD 1,000 for each individual	LD 250,000 per household			LD 450 a month	LD 100 a month for each child; LD 150 a month for married women		Gasoline, diesel, liquefied petroleum gas, kerosene, and electricity	Monthly cash and in-kind assistance
Geographical areas covered	West, South and North (no data for the East)	West, South and North (no data for the East)	West, South and North (no data for the East)	West, South and North (no data for the East)	All	All	West, South, and North (no data for the East)	West, South, and North (no data for the East)	All		All	
Number of beneficiaries	178,956 individuals (2020)	821 households/cases (2020)	1,009 households + 15,000 IDPs Libyan and non-Libyan (Apr 2019-Dec2019)	1,968 individuals				55,024 households (2019)			Libyan population	
Total expenditure	LD 948 million	LD 1.9 million (2020)	LD 859,900 + LD 3 million	LD 4 million							LD 12.4 billion (2014)	

Source: Compilation based on desk research and consultations, 2020–21.
Note: IDP = internally displaced person; PWD = person with disability.

NOTES

1. Findings in this chapter are based on stock taking, preliminary data collection, and on-going analytical activity aimed at supporting the government of Libya by diagnosing its social protection sector. Sources include secondary information on the current structure of the universal price subsidy system, the state of social assistance programs, the delivery system, and the intersectionality of the social protection system with current humanitarian programs in the country. It offers a way forward for strategic direction in expansion and reform of the social protection system in Libya in view of current crises affecting households and political economy challenges.

2. The World Food Programme (WFP) in Libya and the UNICEF Libya Program contributed to the analytical activity and the writing of this chapter, together with the International Policy Centre for Inclusive Growth.

3. The MEB is developed by the REACH (2020) for the Libya Cash and Market Working Group of the Libya Joint Market Monitoring Initiative and the Libyan Central Bank.

4. With the exception of emergency one-off, in-kind assistance provided by the Zakat Fund to its existing beneficiaries as well new ones, including poor families and IDPs. In addition, the Ministry of Economy adopted a regulation controlling the price of 16 food items such as fruits, vegetables, and meat, to be revised every three months.

5. Law No. 60 of 1976 (dated 10/19/1976) was presented by the minister of economy and approved by the Council of Ministers, and aligns to the Constitutional Declaration (December 11, 1969) and related Law on Cooperative Societies No. 42 of 1956.

6. At an international summit on combating the theft of oil and refined products held in Geneva.

7. The Quest for Subsidy Reforms in Libya 2015, Abdelkrim Araar; Nada Choueiri; Paolo Verme.

8. The Government of National Unity was formed in March 2021.

9. The way zakat is administered differs across the world. In many countries, the state exercises some form of decision-making power or supervision. Zakat collection is legally imposed in a few countries in MENA, such as Libya, Saudi Arabia, Sudan, and Yemen. Five others have structured systems for their collection that are considered voluntary. Zakat is one of the five pillars of Islam and considered a religious duty for wealthy people to help those in need through financial or in-kind contributions. In Muslim-majority countries, it has a long tradition of being part of the provision of social welfare.

10. General Comment No. 19: The right to Social Security (Art. 9 of the Covenant).

11. ICESCR, Art. 11 (1).

12. Convention on the Rights of Persons with Disabilities, Art. 28.

13. Convention on the Rights of the Child, Art. 27 (3).

14. The Berber or Amazigh community is an ethnic group indigenous to North Africa, specifically, Algeria, Libya, Morocco, and Tunisia. Unofficial estimates put the number of Amazigh in Libya at almost 600,000, or about 10 percent of the country's total population.

15. Contested: the Council of Ministers Decree No. 120 on the Organizational Structure and Function of the Ministry of Social Affairs (2012) does not mention the SSecF as one of the autonomous entities under the MoSA. This is also not mentioned in Social Security Law No. 13 (1980). However, the SSecF is listed as one of the entities under the MoSA in its website, and this has also been indicated in LOOPS (2016) and Imneina and Alfarsi (2020).

16. No proof that either of those programs are actually implemented but the MoSA's website mentions them.

17. For a list of its responsibilities see Council of Ministers Decree No. 120 on the Organizational Structure and Function of the Ministry of Social Affairs (2012).

18. Art. 9 Decree no. 120 on the Organizational Structure of the Ministry of Social Affairs (2012).

19. Art. 10 Decree no. 120 on the Organisational Structure of the Ministry of Social Affairs (2012).

20. Art. 13 Decree no. 120 on the Organizational Structure of the Ministry of Social Affairs (2012).

21. Our stock-taking indicates that only 22 branches are currently active, out of 26.

22. Social Solidarity Law No. 20 (1998), Art, 3.

23. In March 2021, the GNU passed a decree to raise the basic pension value to LD 650 ($144) for eligible beneficiaries without family dependents, LD 700 ($155) for eligible families consisting of two individuals, and LD 800 ($177) for eligible families composed of three or more individuals. It was not possible to confirm whether this had been implemented at time of writing.

24. This information was collected through a literature review and is yet to be validated by the government or relevant focal points.
25. Art. 3, Cabinet Decision No. 49 on the Establishment of a Zakat Fund (2012).
26. Art. 1, Council of Ministers Decree No. 119 on the Establishment of a Marriage Support Fund (2012).
27. Art. 2, Council of Ministers Decree No. 119 on the Establishment of a Marriage Support Fund (2012).
28. Article 34 of the Law No. 5 on Persons with Disabilities.
29. The stock-taking interviews have some gaps with respect to holistic comprehension of individual mandates and whether there are any attempts at streamlining.
30. The Family Booklet in Libya is quoted as being the "main proof of citizenship, in which all members of the family are listed and which is presented when applying for jobs, university studies and scholarships, or when taking out a loan from the bank or seeking assistance" (IRBC 2013).
31. For an overview of the adaptive social protection approach, see Bowen et al. (2020).

REFERENCES

Araar, A. N. Choueiri, and P. Verme. 2015. *The Quest for Subsidy Reforms in Libya*. Washington, DC: World Bank. https://documents.worldbank.org/en/publication/documents-reports/documentdetail/344571467980552949/the-quest-for-subsidy-reforms-in-libya.

Bowen, Thomas Vaughan, Carlo del Ninno, Colin Andrews, Sarah Coll-Black, Ugo Gentilini, Kelly Johnson, Yasuhiro Kawasoe, Adea Kryeziu, Barry Patrick Maher, and Asha M. Williams. 2020. *Adaptive Social Protection: Building Resilience to Shocks*. Washington, DC: World Bank Group.

Coady, David, Ian W. H. Parry, Nghia-Piotr Le, and Baoping Shang. 2019. "Global Fossil Fuel Subsidies Remain Large: An Update Based on Country-Level Estimates." Working Papers, International Monetary Fund, Washington, DC. https://www.imf.org/en/Publications/WP/Issues/2019/05/02/Global-Fossil-Fuel-Subsidies-Remain-Large-An-Update-Based-on-Country-Level-Estimates-46509.

Gentilini, Ugo, A. Mukhejre, A. Kryeziu, and Y. Okamura. Forthcoming. "Energy Subsidy Reform and Social Safety Nets: An Overview of Emerging Lessons." Working paper, World Bank, Washington, DC.

GoL (Government of Libya) MoF (Ministry of Finance) 2020. *Financial Report*, March 2020. Libya: MoF. https://finance.gov.ly/pdf/report%20month3.pdf.

GoL (Government of Libya) MoP (Ministry of Planning). 2017. "A Study of Hydrocarbon Subsidy Reform." Tripoli: Ministry of Planning.

ICJ (International Commission of Jurists). 2015. "Libya: Revise Draft Constitution to Ensure Compliance with International Standards." ICJ, Geneva. https://www.icj.org/libya-revise-draft-constitution-to-ensure-compliance-with-international-standards/.

Imneina, Abeir, and Omelez Alfarsi. 2020. "Social Security Laws in Libya: A Gender-Based Perspective." Friedrich-Ebert-Stiftung, Germany. https://library.fes.de/pdf-files/bueros/libya-office/16680.pdf.

Inchauste, Gabriela, and David G. Victor, editors. 2017. *The Political Economy of Energy Subsidy Reform*. Directions in Development series. Washington, DC: World Bank. https://openknowledge.worldbank.org/handle/10986/26216.

IPCIG (International Policy Centre for Inclusive Growth). 2018. *Non-Contributory Social Protection through a Child and Equity Lens in Libya*. New York: UNICEF. https://ipcig.org/pub/eng/OP395_Non_contributory_social_protection_through_a_child_and_equity_lens_in_Libya.pdf.

IRBC (Immigration and Refugee Board of Canada). 2013. "Libya: Identification Documents, Including National Identity Cards (NID) and Birth Certificates; Requirements and Procedures for Obtaining and Renewing Identity Documents, both within the Country and Abroad; Availability of Fraudulent Documents (2011-November 2013)." Ottawa: IRBC. https://www.refworld.org/docid/52cea00b4.html.

ISPA (Inter-Agency Social Protection Assessments). n.d. "Core Diagnostic Instrument (CODI)." Washington, DC: ISPA. https://ispatools.org/core-diagnostic-instrument/.

LBS (Libyan Bureau of Statistics), UNHCR (United Nations High Commissioner for Refugees), WFP (World Food Programme), UNICEF (United Nations Children's Fund), and UNFPA (United Nations Population Fund). 2016. *Multi-Sectoral Household Survey to Assess Family Needs* (Arabic). Tripoli: LBS.

Libya Observer. 2016. Various articles during the year. https://libyaobserver.ly /news?amp%3Bpage=2044&qt-libya_weather=2&qt-sidebar_tabs=2&page=2077.

Lindert, Kathy, Tina George Karippacheril, Inés Rodríguez Caillava, and Kenichi Nishikawa Chavéz. 2020. *Sourcebook on the Foundations of Social Protection Delivery Systems.* Washington, DC: World Bank.

LOOPS (Libyan Organization of Policies and Strategies). 2015. *Policies of Commodities Subsidy.* Tripoli: LOOPS. http://loopsresearch.org/media/images/photolkvz5pp2ye.pdf.

LOOPS (Libyan Organization of Policies and Strategies). 2016. *The Libyan Oil Sector Economic and Social Impacts of Halting the Export of Libyan Oil.* Tripoli: LOOPS. http://loopsresearch .org/projects/view/114/?lang=eng.

MoSA (Ministry of Social Affairs). 2020. Annual Report.

MoSA (Ministry of Social Affairs). n.d.

OCHA (UN Office for Coordination of Human Affairs). 2021. *2021 HPC-Libya Humanitarian Needs Overview (HNO).* New York: OCHA. https://www.humanitarianresponse.info/en /operations/libya/document/2021-libya-humanitarian-needs-overview-hno.

REACH. 2017. *Market Systems in Libya: Assessment of the Wheat Flour, Insulin, Tomato and Soap Supply Chains.* October 2017. Geneva: REACH. https://reliefweb.int/report/libya/market -systems-libya-assessment-wheat-flour-insulin-tomato-and-soap-supply-chains.

REACH. 2020. "Libya Joint Market Monitoring Initiative." August 8–20, 2020. Geneva: REACH. https://reliefweb.int/report/libya/libya-joint-market-monitoring-initiative-jmmi -8-20-august-2020.

REACH. 2021. "Multi-Sector Needs Assessment (MSNA)". Geneva: REACH. https://www .impact-repository.org/document/reach/926f7f36/REACH_LBY_Presentation_2021 -MSNA-Refugee-Migrant-population-and-Libyan-population_February-2022.pdf.

UN DESA (United Nations Department of Economic and Social Affairs). 2020. *2020 Voluntary National Reviews Synthesis Report.* New York: United Nations. https://sustainabledevelopment. un.org/content/documents/27027VNR_Synthesis_Report_2020.pdf.

UNHCR (United Nations High Commissioner for Refugees). 2019. *Global Trends: Forced Displacement in 2019.* Geneva: UNHCR.

UN HRP (United Nations Humanitarian Response Plan). 2017. *Libya: 2017 Humanitarian Response Plan (January–December 2017).* New York: UN Office for the Coordination of Humanitarian Affairs. https://reliefweb.int/report/libya/libya-2017-humanitarian-respons e-plan-january-december-2017-enar.

UN HRP. (United Nations Humanitarian Response Plan). 2021. *Libya Humanitarian Response Plan 2021 (January 2021).* New York: UN Office for the Coordination of Humanitarian Affairs. https://reliefweb.int/report/libya/libya-humanitarian-response-plan-2021-january -2021-enar.

UNICEF (United Nations Children's Fund). 2021. *Country Office Annual Report 2021.* New York: UNICEF. https://www.unicef.org/media/117151/file/Libya-2021-COAR.pdf.

UNICEF (United Nations Children's Fund). 2020. *COVID-19 Behavior Assessment in Libya.* New York: UNICEF. https://reliefweb.int/report/libya/covid-19-behavior-assessment-libya -design-risk-communication-and-community-engagement.

VSCM-S. 2021. "Vulnerability, Shocks, and Coping Mechanisms in Libya." Report, World Bank, Washington, DC. https://documents1.worldbank.org/curated/en/099050406292237714 /text/P1776930a7bdb309092400c964928e24b6.txt.

WFP (World Food Programme). 2016. *Rapid Food Security Assessment, Libya.* Rome: World Food Programme. https://www.wfp.org/publications/libya-rapid-food-security-assessment -september-2016.

WFP (World Food Programme). 2020. *Mobile Vulnerability Analysis and Mapping (mVAM)*, Bulletin no. 4 April–May 2020. Rome: World Food Programme.

WHO (World Health Organization). 2021. *Libya COVID-19 Surveillance Bulletin*. December 26, 2021. Geneva: World Health Organization. https://www.humanitarianresponse.info/en /operations/libya/document/covid-19-epi-weekly-libya-26-dec-2021.

World Bank. 2016. *Libya's Economic Outlook*. Washington, DC: World Bank. https://www .worldbank.org/en/country/libya/publication/economic-outlook-fall-2016.

World Bank. 2017. *Libya's Economic Outlook–October 2017*. Washington, DC: World Bank. https://www.worldbank.org/en/country/libya/publication/economic-outlook-april-2017.

World Bank. 2018. "Libya: Engagement Note on Subsidy Reform." Internal note. Washington, DC: World Bank.

World Bank. 2019. "Libya Subsidy Note." Internal note. World Bank, Washington, DC.

World Bank. 2020. *Vulnerability, Shocks, and Coping Mechanisms in Libya*. Washington, DC: World Bank. https://documents1.worldbank.org/curated/en/099050406292237714/pdf /P1776930a7bdb309092400c964928e24b6.pdf.

World Bank. 2021. *Libya Economic Monitor, 2021*. Washington, DC: World Bank. https://www .worldbank.org/en/country/libya/publication/libya-economic-monitor-spring-2021.

Yemtsov, Ruslan, and Amr Moubarak. 2018. *Energy Subsidy Reform Assessment Framework: Assessing the Readiness of Social Safety Nets to Mitigate the Impact of Reform*. Washington, DC: World Bank. https://openknowledge.worldbank.org/handle/10986/30255.

RELATED READINGS

Gentilini, Ugo, Mohamed Almenfi, Ian Orton, and Pamela Dale. 2020. "Social Protection and Jobs Responses to COVID-19: A Real-Time Review of Country Measures." Washington, DC: World Bank.

International Libya Herald. June 2019, July 2019, May 2020. Various articles. Tripoli: International Libya Herald.

International Summit on Combating Theft and Corruption in Oil and Refined Products in Libya. 2018. Joint Statement. Geneva.

OCHA (UN Office of the Coordinator of Humanitarian Affairs). 2019. Global Trends: Forced Displacement in 2019. New York: OCHA.

OCHA (UN Office of the Coordinator of Humanitarian Affairs). 2021. *Humanitarian Needs Overview–Libya, 2021*. New York: OCHA.

REACH. 2019. "Minimum Expenditure Basket (MEB)." Geneva: REACH.

REACH. 2020. "Minimum Expenditure Basket (MEB)." Geneva: REACH.

UN (United Nations). 2020. Voluntary National Reviews Synthesis Report. New York: UN. https://sustainabledevelopment.un.org/content/documents/27027VNR_Synthesis _Report_2020.pdf.

UNSMIL (United Nations Mission to Libya). 2021. "Humanitarian Response Plan 2021 (draft)." Tripoli: UNSMIL.

World Bank. 2017. *Impact of the Libya Crisis on the Tunisian Economy*. Washington, DC: World Bank.

World Bank. Forthcoming. *CODI Report Libya*. Washington, DC: World Bank.

V Toward New Institutions

20 Equitably Managing Petroleum Resources to Help Resolve Conflict

EHTISHAM AHMAD AND LARS FLOCKE LARSEN

European Union

The authors argue that the development of a system of transparent and fair management of oil revenues will involve significant reforms of allocation of petroleum revenues to ensure adequate levels of public spending on core functions in all parts of the country. This will involve strengthening regional and local governance (multilevel governance). Stronger public finance management systems will be needed to increase accountability and the efficiency of spending and reduce waste and leakages, and greater local accountability will also require own-source revenues and nondistorting transfers. Improving multilevel governance will require an agreement on an intergovernmental finance framework, beginning with an agreed distribution of revenues from the national to regional and/or local levels of government. The intergovernmental finance framework could usefully include a system for distributing a share of oil revenues to oil-producing regions (revenue sharing). It should also include other transfer mechanisms for both producing and nonproducing regions and the development of local own-source non-oil tax revenues at the margin (such as a surcharge or piggyback on a national tax base) for enhanced accountability. Revenue-sharing arrangements have been critical in reducing conflict and creating a national identity in both Indonesia and Nigeria.

INTRODUCTION

The chapter is organized as follows. The first section examines the need for better petroleum management and multilevel governance in Libya. The second section discusses how revenue sharing can help diffuse interregional tensions in oil-producing countries. It clarifies the link between revenue sharing and contractual arrangements in the petroleum sector and draws on the experiences of Indonesia and Nigeria, where revenue sharing helped diffuse centrifugal tendencies. The last section analyzes contracting arrangements in the Libyan petroleum sector and lays out options for potential revenue sharing.

THE NEED FOR BETTER MULTILEVEL GOVERNANCE AND NATURAL RESOURCE MANAGEMENT

Libya's three regions (East, West, and South) date back to Greek and Phoenician (600 BC) times. Under Roman rule, the regions were joined for more than four centuries. The three regions (Cyrenaica, Tripolitania, and Fezzan) were reintroduced during the Ottoman period, maintained during Italian administration until 1937, and then again under British-French rule. The three regions continued after Libya became independent in 1951, until 1963.[1]

Over the next 50 years, Libya's subnational government system was modified no less than 10 times, culminating in the current setup of multiple governorates and municipalities, stipulated by Law 59/2012 and its subsequent decrees (Daoud 2019). Nevertheless, given its long history, the East-West regional split is at the center of the current conflict.

International experience shows that the discovery of natural resources—particularly petroleum, which is typically concentrated in specific regions—can magnify regional imbalances, especially if the benefits are perceived to accrue to elites in the national capital and major metropolitan areas. This perception of unfairness creates resentment and often leads to centrifugal or secessionist tendencies in the producing regions, as seen in Nigeria with the secession of Biafra and the secessionist tendencies in Indonesia following the fall of Suharto.

The same dynamics can be observed in Libya. With the discovery of oil in the late 1950s, Libyans quickly became dependent on oil wealth and rents distributed as salaries and subsidies rather than productive investment. Under the Eastern-based monarchy, Benghazi benefited from its status as co-capital. When Muammar Gaddafi came to power in 1969, he centralized institutions in Tripoli, including the National Oil Corporation (NOC). Since then, differentials in living standards between Tripoli and Libya's Eastern and Southern oil-producing regions have grown, contributing to a widespread perception in those regions of marginalization by central authorities. Inhabitants perceive elites in the capital as profiting from "their" oil wealth without sharing adequate benefits—public services, infrastructure, economic development, and well-paying jobs—with their regions.

Growing centralization, sanctions, and the collapse of public services contributed to the economic roots of the 2011 revolution, which started in Benghazi. It did not diminish the perception of neglect in Libya's oil-producing regions. On the contrary, increased financial crime and corruption since 2011 has reinforced the perception that central authorities in Tripoli are squandering Libya's oil wealth. Political divisions and the inability of democratically elected authorities to improve security and public services across the country led to a political split in 2014.

The parliament (House of Representatives) and the "interim government" established themselves in Eastern Libya; the parliament elected in 2012 (the General National Congress) remained in Tripoli, establishing the National Salvation Government. In 2015, the UN–facilitated Libyan Political Agreement created the Government of National Accord (GNA), as an attempt to unify the Eastern and Western authorities, but the Eastern authorities that remained in place never fully accepted the agreement.

The need to finance the parallel Eastern authorities created a split in the country's financial system and led to several unsuccessful attempts to independently sell oil. Politically, secessionist tendencies have manifested themselves by federalist movements and regular declarations of autonomy by Libya's historical regions (Alarabiya News 2013).

As attempts to gain autonomy failed, Eastern and Southern constituencies resorted to successive blockades of oil production, first in 2013–14, then in 2018, and again in 2020, following a failed attempt to take control of Tripoli. The goal of these blockades was to put pressure on central authorities by cutting off their main revenue stream. Blockades could have been occasions for addressing the demands of fairer distribution of petroleum revenues and improved service delivery; to date, they have resulted in only half-hearted or simplistic solutions. In 2014, protesters were simply placated with salary increases. In 2018, the oil blockade ended after threats of sanctions and a promise to audit the central bank.

The most recent oil blockade was temporarily lifted in September 2020 to allow for better provision of electricity and water to the East. However, the lifting of the oil blockade remains fragile. The Eastern Libyan Arab Armed Forces demanded the deposit of oil revenues in a "special account" out of reach of the GNA in Tripoli, the completion of the central bank audit, and the establishment of a "transparent mechanism for expenditures." To comply with the first request, the NOC has sequestered petroleum revenues in its own accounts and stopped remitting petroleum revenues to the Ministry of Finance account at the central bank. Consequently, central government expenditures have had to be met out of the reserves of the central bank, which is effectively performing Ministry of Finance functions. This arrangement reduces transparency and accountability and breaches the principles of efficient budget management.

Recent economic reforms (unification of the central bank, devaluation, unification of the national budget, and measures to address the banking crisis) have gone a long way to address these concerns and should provide the basis for releasing revenues from NOC accounts. Doing so would help create an integrated and united budget framework for the whole country. For such a framework to be effective, it should be complemented by policies that avoid exacerbating economic imbalances and further degrading public services across the country, particularly in the "aggrieved" Eastern and Southern regions.

In the medium term, the development of a system of transparent and fair management of oil revenues will involve significant reforms of allocation of petroleum revenues to ensure adequate levels of public spending on core functions in all parts of the country. It will involve strengthening regional and local governance (multilevel governance). Stronger public finance management systems will be needed to increase accountability and the efficiency of spending and reduce waste and leakages (Ahmad and Mottu 2002), and greater local accountability will also require own-source revenues and nondistorting transfers.

Improving multilevel governance will require an agreement on an intergovernmental finance framework, beginning with an agreed distribution of revenues from the national to regional and/or local levels of government. The intergovernmental finance framework could usefully include a system for distributing a share of oil revenues to oil-producing regions (revenue sharing). It should also include other transfer mechanisms for both producing and nonproducing regions and the development of local own-source non-oil tax revenues at the margin (such as a surcharge or piggyback on a national tax base) for enhanced accountability. Revenue-sharing arrangements have been critical in reducing conflict and creating a national identity in both Indonesia and Nigeria.

INTERNATIONAL EXPERIENCE USING REVENUE SHARING TO DIFFUSE TENSIONS

Growing centralization, urban concentration, and regional disparities are world-wide phenomena driven by declining employment in agriculture, migrations in search of a higher standard of life, and political decisions, among other factors.[2] They tend to be intensified by highly centralized governance systems and oil rents, as in Indonesia and Nigeria, as discussed on following sections. In oil-rich developing countries, oil reserves are often concentrated in less-developed areas, whereas the financial benefits tend to be concentrated in the capital and major commercial hubs. In highly centralized states, the government often struggles to translate financial gains into high-quality public services in remote regions. This failure contributes to major differentials in living standards and access to public services between producing regions and metropolitan areas, which exacerbate spatial conflicts.

Direct sharing of petroleum revenues with producing regions is important in diffusing tensions and laying the foundations for better subnational governance. It is important that direct revenue sharing be designed in a way that provides incentives for producing regions to maximize production (or, put differently, discourages them from blocking production). The focus on revenue sharing has been seen in Indonesia (post-Suharto) and Nigeria (following the return to democratic rule and the 1999 constitution). The Indonesian case involved successful revenue sharing with municipal and local governments. A revenue-sharing arrangement is merely a starting point in achieving better governance but is not sufficient in itself.

To translate into improved public services and sustainable growth at the local level, a revenue-sharing agreement needs to be accompanied by a functioning multilevel governance system that includes clarity about the number of governments at each level (two or three tiers), the responsibilities for spending and own-source revenue raising for each subnational government, and both ear-marked grants for special purposes (for example, COVID relief) and untied "equalization" transfer mechanisms. This system would form the basis for effective and transparent public financial management (PFM) for the whole country, and a policy framework that should pay adequate attention to income inequalities and the prevention of environmental damage in producing regions.

Indonesia and Nigeria provide good examples of how an agreement on the sharing of natural resource revenues with municipalities and regions diminished secessionist tendencies in producing regions and prevented the countries from breaking apart. Such agreements were part of more comprehensive inter-governmental finance frameworks that also involved equalization transfers to ensure equal levels of public service delivery across regions regardless of their tax base; earmarked transfers for specific purposes (such as infrastructure); and provisions for mobilizing own-source revenues (local taxes, fees, and so forth).[3]

Sharing revenue with only the second/intermediate tier (for example, at the level of Cyrenaica or Fezzan regions) could exacerbate separatist tendencies. When there were only four states in Nigeria, revenue sharing to this level contributed to the outbreak of the Biafran civil war. After the war, more than 30 states were created. After the fall of Suharto in 1999, Indonesia avoided the mistake of sharing revenues exclusively with provinces/regions, focusing principally on the third (municipal) tier. Indonesia provides a good example of revenue sharing together with an equalization transfer mechanism determined by education and health care needs, supplemented by earmarked transfers, especially for public infrastructure.

Revenue-sharing mechanisms need to be linked to the contractual arrangements governing the petroleum sector, usually in the form of exploration and production-sharing contracts (EPSC). The economic content of an EPSC can be replicated in a tax and royalty system and vice versa. A production-sharing scheme, however, allows variation of the economic terms across areas (according to maturity, the extent of geological knowledge, and prior investment) without amendment of fiscal legislation. The production-sharing agreement format allows private investors to participate, while the state retains sovereign rights over petroleum in the ground and remunerates investors with a portion of petroleum produced. The NOC can also participate in such an agreement.

An EPSC is designed to share the risk of exploration and development with a private investor. It allows the private contractor to "book" its potential portion of production as reserves for reporting purposes on stock exchanges. After deduction of royalties (if any), a typical EPSC apportions production between "cost oil" and "profit oil" (figure 20.1). The production-sharing formula should adjust the splits of profit oil between the state and the contractor based on a scale determined by realized overall revenues and costs. The formula should employ the payback ratio (R-factor, or an achieved rate of return calculation [equivalent to a resource rent tax]), not a proxy such as daily or cumulative level of production.

The state/subnational share of oil revenues under an EPSC could come from a share of the royalty, production-sharing revenues accruing to the Treasury Single Account (TSA), corporate income tax, and/or signature and production bonuses. State revenues will also flow from profit distributions by the NOC, from both its sole operations and its participation with private companies in EPSCs.

FIGURE 20.1

Standard production-sharing and tax systems

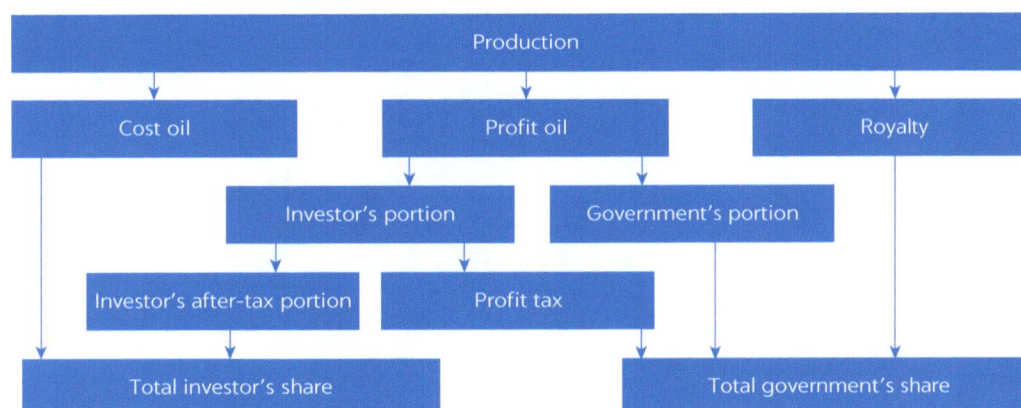

Source: Augustina et al. 2012.

Indonesia's experience

In the wake of the fall of the Suharto regime and the separation of East Timor, Indonesia viewed the sharing of revenues from petroleum and other natural resources as a critical element in responding to the centrifugal forces pulling the country apart. The sharing was based on the standard approach shown in figure 20.1. The focus was largely on the lower or third tier of local governments—municipalities (called districts in Indonesia). The intermediate/second tier (provinces) typically received at most a quarter of the amounts allocated to districts (figure 20.2), in order to avoid the problems experienced in Eastern Nigeria, where the sharing of oil revenues reinforced secessionist tendencies.

The sharing proportions were in line with international best practice—a 15.5 percent derivation sharing for petroleum with subnational governments, which was largely in line with the 13 percent first charge (or expenditure before state-level redistribution) for Nigeria. The Indonesian case is particularly complex, as revenue sharing was based on several types of natural resources, not only petroleum. In addition, there was a set of equalization transfers for education and health, as well as earmarked transfers for capital and infrastructure that added to the significant financing of subnational expenditures.[4]

Aceh and East Kalimantan provinces, which had significant separatist tendencies, refused to accept the sharing proportions under Law 33/2004. After considerable effort and negotiations, an asymmetric arrangement was reached

FIGURE 20.2

Initial revenue-sharing arrangements for natural resources in Indonesia

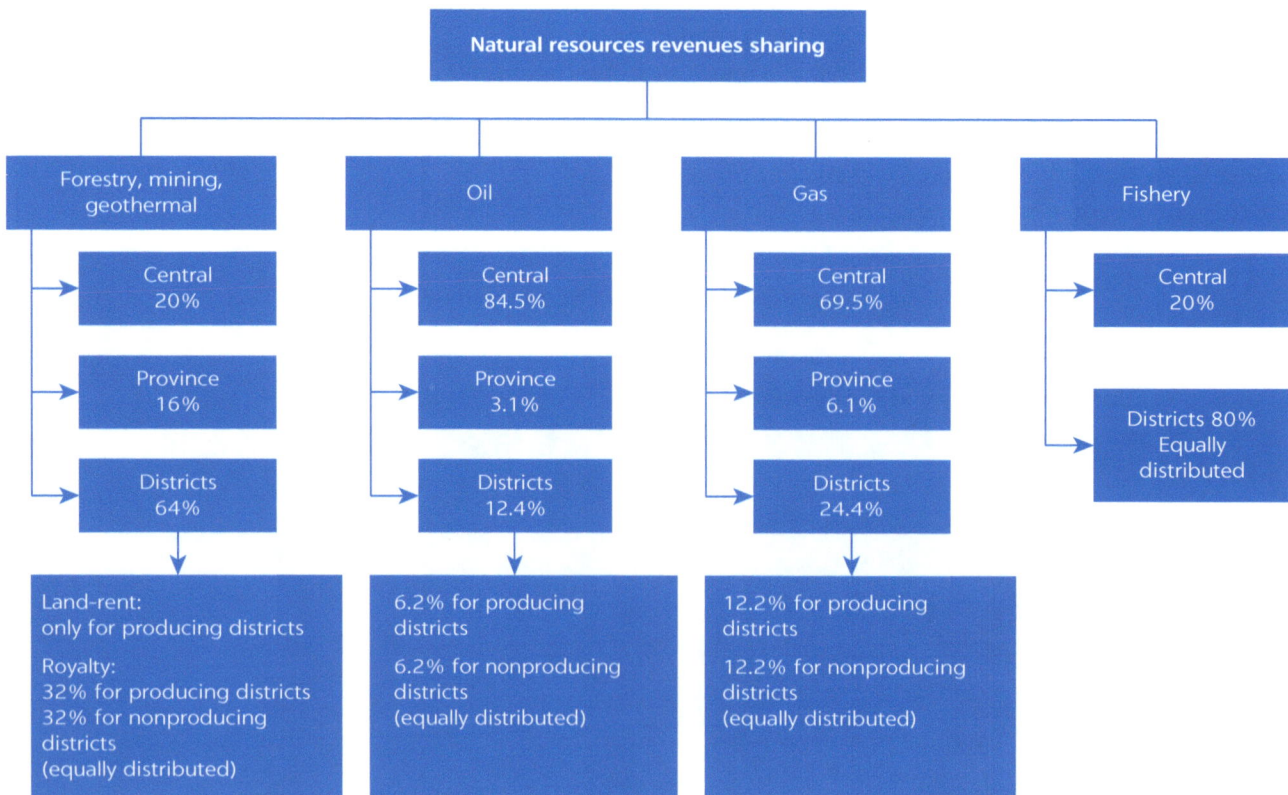

Source: LIU33/2004.

in which 70 percent of revenues went to the producing provinces and districts. This arrangement did not translate into significant improvement in service delivery (Augustina et al. 2012); it is not stable, as it encourages other provinces with natural resources to demand equal treatment, and it can potentially lead to considerable inequalities.

To offset the effects of significant extra funds going to Aceh, the central government amended the equalization formulas to consider additional revenue-sharing transfers. In Canada, the provinces that receive petroleum revenues are completely out of the equalization system. In Libya, the equalization formula itself should not be weakened by the introduction of shared revenues, as doing so is likely to adversely affect the resulting incentive structures (as it has in many Latin American countries that do not have an effective equalization framework).

Indonesia has moved to a simplified gross-split revenue-sharing contract model (table 20.1). It introduces additional difficulties in establishing the true output generated in the oil fields (akin to the Nigerian problem identified by the Ribadu Commission that a significant proportion of oil production was stolen before revenues accrued to the government account to be shared). The problem could be rectified by allowing subnational governments to introduce a quantity-based tax on gross production or transport of petroleum and gas, thereby aligning the incentives for them to ensure proper monitoring of operations. Such a local production-based (carbon) tax could be offset against costs; it would also ensure a sharper focus on environmental sustainability.

Another mechanism that can be used to force producing firms into correctly disclosing information on production/exports is a value added tax (VAT) on all purchases by firms, including capital purchases, with full and immediate refunds on exports. This measure is not designed to generate additional VAT revenues, as most of the VAT collected would be refunded; it is designed to "persuade" firms to truthfully declare outputs and exports. More accurate declarations would have a beneficial impact on all the other taxes along the value chain and the state's total take. China has adopted this approach. It is also part of the design of the Gulf Cooperation Council's VAT, has been implemented in Saudi Arabia and the United Arab Emirates, for example. In Libya, this mechanism would be a medium-term measure.

The Indonesian experience illustrates that although an intergovernmental finance framework can help prevent conflict, it is not sufficient to bring about changes at the local level. Although the agreement on an intergovernmental finance framework prevented the further breakup of Indonesia, or a resumption of the secession tendencies in oil-producing regions, effective decentralization and equitable local service delivery have yet to be achieved, 20 years after the initiation of the revenue-sharing/decentralization reforms. These challenges show the importance of the interactions between policy instruments within multilevel governance and PFM systems.

Options for revenue sharing depend critically on the tax regime and existing contracting arrangements in the petroleum sector, as well as the governance and oversight arrangements associated with intergovernmental functional assignments. The starting point requires a focus on the nature and shortcomings of fiscal instruments currently used or that might need to be developed quickly.

TABLE 20.1 **Indonesia's new approach to revenue sharing**

	COST RECOVERY PSC	GROSS SPLIT PSC
Income tax	The income tax rate is dependent on the date that the government and company signed the PSC. Indonesia's 2015 EITI report details information on changes in the tax rate over time.	The tax rate is currently 25 percent.
Land and building tax	The government applies a tax to land and/or buildings that are in areas used for extractive activities. The basis of charging land and building tax varies depending on the location (onshore or offshore) and phase (exploration or exploitation) of a project.	
Dividend tax (branch profit tax)	20 percent	
Nontax revenue (share of production)	There are six steps involved in determining what share of the total production each party (the government and the contractor(s)) receives: 1) **First tranche petroleum (FTP)** — an initial share of production is divided between the government and the contractor, with the specific distribution stated in the contract. 2) **Investment credit** — an incentive that the government gives in the form of an additional return on capital directly related to oil and gas production facilities. 3) **Cost recovery** — the reimbursement of costs of production, agreed upon between the government and contractor 4) **Equity oil** — the distribution of the remaining oil as stipulated in the contract. 5) **Domestic market obligation** — the contractor is also required to allocate up to 25 percent of its share to fulfill domestic needs in Indonesia. 6) **Domestic market obligation fee** — remuneration from the government to the contractor for the domestic market obligation allocation	Under the gross split PSC. production will be allocated based on the base split formula. The government can adjust it in favor of either party, based on the variable and progressive particularities of the project **Base split** • Government: 57 percent for oil; 52 percent for gas • Contractor: 43 percent for oil; 48 percent for gas Base split can then be adjusted, depending on: **Variable components** 1. Status of the field 2. Location of the field 3. Depth of reservoir 4. Availability of support infrastructure 5. Type of reservoir 6. Carbon dioxide content 7. Hydrogen sulfide content 8. Density of oil 9. Domestic component level 10. Production stages **Progressive components** 1. Price of oil; price of gas 2. Cumulative amount of oil and gas production
Bonuses	**Signature bonuses** — a bonus, agreed upon between the contractor and SKK Migas, is due within one month of awarding of the contract. Historically, these bonuses have generally ranged from $1 million to $15 million with a cap at $250 million. In 2018, the government removed the cap on the size of signature bonuses. **Production bonuses** — a contractor meets a bonus requirement when production exceeds a specified number of barrels per day. The contractor and SKK Migas agree on the specifics of this production limit.	

Source: Malden and Muhammadi 2019.
Note: The process described here differs from the standard practice described in figure 20.1. The mechanism for sharing revenues and the proportions for subnational entities are as in figure 20.2. EITI = Extractive Industries Transparency Initiative; PSC = production-sharing contract.

Nigeria's experience

Before independence, the Hicks-Phillipson Commission (1951) stressed the importance of providing regions with an adequate tax base of their own.[5] Despite this intention, regions remained heavily dependent on shared revenues.

At independence from Britain, in 1960, Nigeria had four regions, which were financed largely by shared revenues. Ethnic and religious differences in the Eastern Province, together with most of the discoveries of petroleum deposits, led to increasing frictions, which culminated in the secession of Biafra and the ensuing civil war. After the fall of Biafra, a period of military rule followed, and the country was divided into 32 states to prevent the centrifugal forces associated with the four-region constitution inherited from British colonial rule.

Nigeria was governed by military juntas in 1966–79 and 1983–99. In 1999, a new democratic constitution was promulgated. It decentralized governance to the more than 30 state and municipal levels that replaced the four regions at independence and shared petroleum revenues on a derivation basis. Balances in the Federation Account (the national TSA, through which all funds flow) are also shared with both state and local governments (see table 20.2). Under this arrangement, the first charges from the national Federation Account include debt service; derivation-based sharing (13 percent of petroleum revenues shared exclusively with petroleum-producing regions); and cash and investment needs of the National Nigerian Petroleum Company. Payments of these first charges on the national Federation Account were to be made before allocation of the balance for other budgetary purposes. The financing of the national budget was made via petroleum revenues, corporate taxes (often linked to the petroleum sector), and customs and excise duties. VAT and personal income taxes were shared separately.

States receiving petroleum revenue shares also receive other transfers, as did other nonproducing states (table 20.2 and figure 20.3). The effect has been reduced conflict over petroleum resources.

TABLE 20.2 **Revenue-sharing mechanisms in Nigeria's 1999 constitution**

MAIN REVENUES SOURCES	BENEFICIARIES
Oil revenues	**First charges:**
Company income tax	External debt service
	NNPC cashcalls
	NNPC priority projects
	13% Derivation
	Judicial council
Custom duties and excise	**Federation account:**
	48.5% Federal government
	24.0% States
	20.0% Local governments
	1.0% FCT Abuja
	2.0% Ecological fund
	0.5% Stabilization reserve fund
VAT	15% Federal government
	50% States
	35% Local governments
PIT	100% States
	Federal (very small)

Source: Ahmad and Singh 2003.
Note: FCT = federal capital territory; NNPC = Nigerian National Petroleum Company; PIT = personal income tax; VAT = value added tax. First charges include priority payments before funds go into the federation account for further sharing and budgetary operations. NNPC cash calls represent the operating expenses of the petroleum company.

FIGURE 20.3

Intergovernmental transfers and revenue sharing to producing states in Nigeria

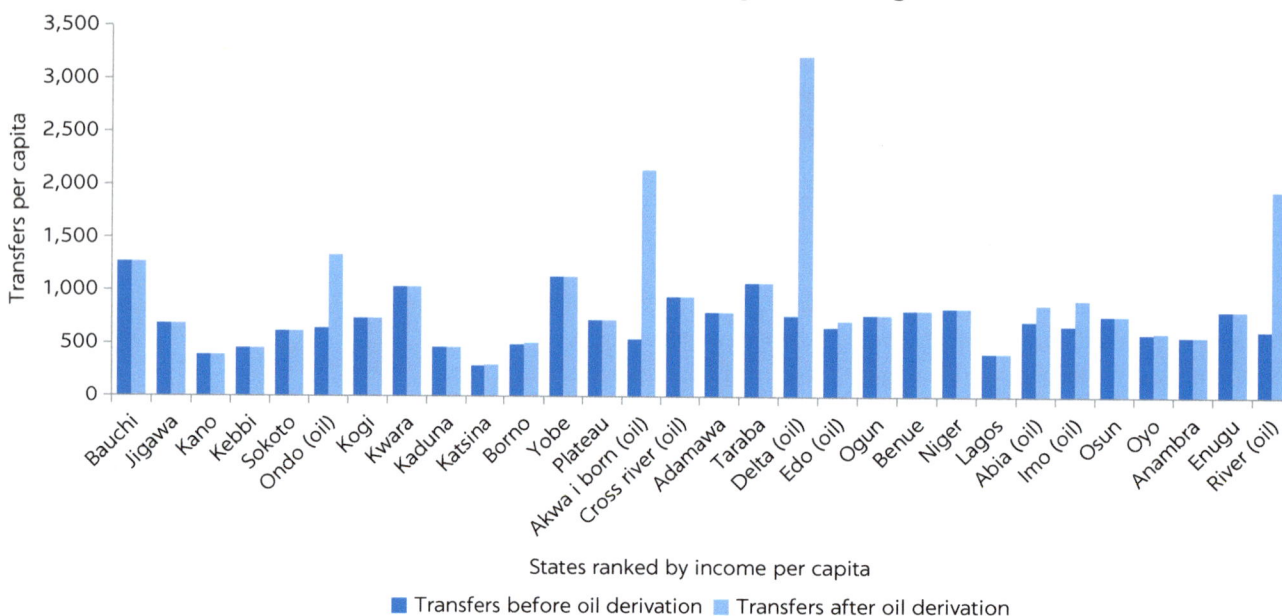

Source: Ahmad et al. 2001, based on data from the Central Bank of Nigeria and World Bank.
Note: Figure includes only 30 states, because data were unavailable for the remaining 6. States are in order per capita income.

Accountability for local spending and investments required allowing for own-source revenues for which the regions could control the rates (by imposing surcharges or "piggybacking" on a national tax). Own-source revenue is essential to establish a link between the financing and the results of spending.

Shared revenues and transfers are not own-source, even if untied, as the recipient jurisdiction cannot increase them. Unclear economic and functional responsibilities, and weak monitoring and PFM mechanisms, led to poor performance on decentralization. It also created leakages in petroleum revenues before they reached the national Federation Account, as documented by the Ribadu Commission (2012) report.[6] Weaknesses in monitoring activities at the local level opened up opportunities for cheating. For every barrel of oil stolen from the official circuit, 100 percent of the revenue remained with local mafias, acting together with influential interests at higher levels. As documented by the thorough petroleum sector audit conducted by the Ribadu Commission, much of the loss of the approximately 250,000 barrels a day came from leakages from the point of extraction to the point of export or before the funds even got to the Federation Account. Cheating on the pricing regime and exchange rates, theft of refined products, arrears on royalties, and loss of the government's share in the production-sharing agreement compounded the problem.

Weaknesses in budget systems and cash monitoring and the lack of an interface between the TSA/budget systems and the systems of the petroleum company contributed to the huge losses. The political economy of multilevel finance probably also had an impact, as local officials and mafia were likely involved and had no incentives to stop the leakages. The Ribadu Commission focused on improving the PFM aspects of monitoring and reporting petroleum operations, including the interfaces of the TSA/Federation Account with improved systems in the Nigerian National Petroleum Company.

In hindsight, assignment of a concurrent tax to governorates/local governments, such as the production excise for environmental damage, could have helped align incentives for the subnational government. In addition to ensuring own-source revenue for local investment, it ensures that the subnational jurisdiction had an interest in stopping any cheating or theft at the local level. This lesson learned could be of relevance for the design of Libya's petroleum taxation and monitoring regime.

OPTIONS FOR LIBYA

Discussions between Western and Eastern authorities within the economic track of the Berlin Process have focused, correctly, on unifying the banking system, the national budget, and public institutions. These are essential first steps in the reunification of the country. However, care must be taken not to focus only on reestablishing the central governance system, without addressing the grievances of Libya's oil-producing regions that led to the fissures in the first place. There is an opportunity to address these grievances once and for all by taking decisive steps toward establishing a multilevel governance system in Libya.

Current contracting arrangements

Libya's petroleum sector is governed under Law No. 25, 1955. The NOC was established in 1970 (Balhassan et al. 2018). Since 1974, EPSCs have been in operation between the NOC and international oil companies; a sophisticated system is in operation. A fourth round of EPSCs has been in operation since 2005, with a 30-year contractual period (5 years for exploration and 25 years for extraction). In accordance with the petroleum law, the tax liability of international oil companies is the gross profit tax rate (set at 65 percent), which includes a petroleum surtax of 41 percent. In addition to a signing bonus, each block on offer includes several production bonuses linked to cumulative production. The NOC is required to pay 50 percent of capital expenditures (capex); as the international oil company does not directly cover exploration costs, it expenses capex as "cost oil" as well as a percentage of operating expenses, depending on the gross production percent for NOC according to the bids.[7] It is estimated that the total government take was about 88 percent of the 2005 EPSC (Bacci 2018); between 2009 and 2014, it was an estimated 76 percent (Rystand and Boston). These shares are more or less in line with the government take from the petroleum sector in Indonesia.

Map 20.1 shows Libya's oil and gas wells, potential areas for additional reserves, and the extensive system of pipelines, which need modernization and repair. Downstream domestic refineries are also in bad shape. (UN Resolution 883, adopted in 1993, banned imports of refinery equipment.) A comprehensive upgrade of the entire refining system is needed.

Budget arrangements, the treasury single account, and the National Oil Company

The NOC's oil comes from its sole operations and its participating interests in EPSCs. Any form of cost recovery, or tax related to profit, requires careful monitoring of allowable costs. Monitoring assumes even greater importance when

MAP 20.1
Libya's oil and gas resources

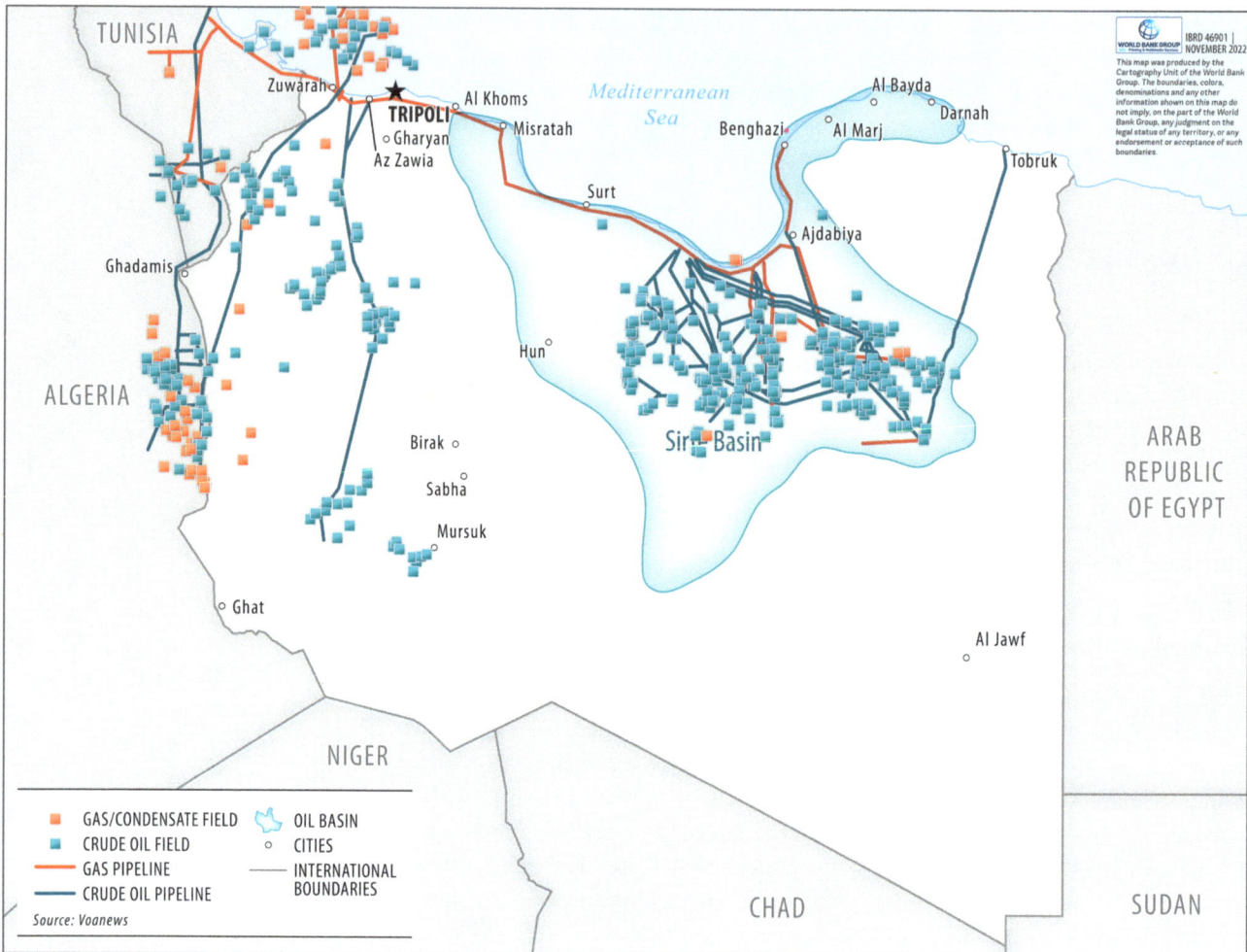

Source: VOA 2011.

there is revenue sharing between levels of government; it is a critical issue in ensuring trust in the overall process. The valuation of production, and the allowable cost rules, should be closely aligned for production sharing and tax purposes, with the full exchange of information between the authority regulating cost recovery and the tax administration.

A corporate income tax on petroleum profits will also usually accrue to the government as part of its take from the petroleum sector; it does not typically go through the NOC. The corporate income tax derived from the contractor's share of production should be designed with international tax considerations in mind. The rate, including on NOC operations, can be higher than the general rate (as in Saudi Arabia); deductions to reach the tax base should be standard, so that the tax paid by foreign companies, including service providers and parties to production-sharing agreements, is eligible for foreign tax credits.

The state's share of production and taxes should flow to the TSA or to a correspondent account of a regional government within the TSA, not to an NOC account. The TSA is normally held at the central bank, as the agent of the government, and is operated on instruction of the Ministry of Finance.[8]

Should petroleum revenues be placed in off-budget accounts rather than the TSA system? The NOC placed oil receipts in its account at the Libyan Foreign Bank during the recent turbulent months following the outbreak of hostilities with the Eastern region, and these funds were not swept into the government's account at the Central Bank of Libya for budgetary purposes. Maintenance of such practices is not advisable if a modern governance system is to be set up, as it creates a parallel administration without adequate oversight. International experience suggests that there is a high likelihood that funds can and will be misused or stolen. Mihalyi, Adam, and Hwang (2020) document such problems at the national level in a range of countries, including Angola, the Democratic Republic of Congo, and South Sudan. In Peru, natural resource shares accrued to local bank accounts outside a TSA. Tracking of public spending at the subnational level suggested that between 2004 and 2011, only 5.3 percent of the transferred resource revenues were spent for public services.

NOC operations and investments should take priority; they should be a prior charge along with revenue sharing and debt servicing before allocations for the annual budget are made. This coordinated system is essential for the orderly running of the budget, which depends heavily on petroleum revenues. It is also important to link the domestic prices of carbon products to world prices plus a carbon tax in order to raise revenues, eliminate waste and smuggling, and lay the basis for financing a sustainable growth path.

The Ministry of Finance is permitted to spend only up to authorized limits in the budget; the balance above the limit normally goes to foreign exchange reserves, to be managed by the central bank or the sovereign wealth fund (SWF). International financial institutions have recommended that SWFs hold only external assets for the benefit of future generations, given the volatility of the market and low interest rates. However, it is rational that in a country with significant reconstruction and investment needs, the SWF should be permitted to invest in national infrastructure. For instance, the Saudi SWF (the Saudi Public Investment Fund) will invest $40 billion a year in domestic infrastructure in 2021 and 2022 to create adequate employment generation hubs. Further, in a period of post-pandemic reconstruction, it makes little sense to borrow externally for building back better investment, when there are Libyan funds potentially available.

Current expenditure patterns and revenue distribution

Some observers have argued that per capita government spending is higher in the East than in the West and that there is no problem with spatial equity in spending, which shows higher aggregate spending in the West (table 20.3).[9] On a per capita basis, spending on chapter 1 (salaries or equivalent) and

TABLE 20.3 Ministry of Finance spending in the West and East, 2019

LD, millions

TYPE OF SPENDING	WEST	EAST
Chapter 1: Salaries or equivalent	19,386	8,046
Chapter 2: Goods and services	4,935	10,233
Total	27,635	13,303

Source: Libyan authorities.

chapter 2 (goods and services) is LD 10,233 in the East and only LD 4,935 in the West. Other government expenditure, such as subsidies (chapter 4) on fuel, electricity, and medicine, are for products or services that should be distributed across Libya and benefit the whole population proportionately.

Looking at revenue distribution solely from this perspective misses several important points. First, averages across regions are not very meaningful, as much of the imbalance is with respect to Tripoli, and there are poor districts and poor people, including in the informal sector, in Tripoli.[10] Furthermore, the disparities are driven by infrastructure gaps and employment opportunities, which are not possible to discern from the broad averages.

Second, the cash releases by the central bank do not reflect total spending in each area, because a significant amount of spending is off budget and nontransparent. In addition, the foreign exchange arbitrage with multiple exchange rates has been responsible for rents that accrue to a privileged minority.

Third, as much of Libya's formal employment is in the public sector, most of the higher-paying jobs and the headquarters of most private firms are in Tripoli.

Fourth, benefits and subsidies are not necessarily uniformly distributed across the country. It is likely that subsidies disproportionally benefit the wealthy, who consume more electricity and gasoline, for example, than poor people.[11] Their distribution is an empirical issue. It should be examined using household survey data when available.

Finally, highly subsidized fuel prices have meant that organized smuggling networks in Libya are reaping major benefits from the smuggling of as much as one-third of some fuels (Eaton 2020). The resulting decrease in fuel distribution via official channels has resulted in higher prices for the wider population and huge benefits for a few people with privileged access, largely in metropolitan areas, adding to political discontent. Although rents are reaped in all regions of the country, Libya's oil-producing regions blame the Tripoli-based government for the situation and perceive individuals linked to the government as the prime beneficiaries.

These dynamics have become key economic drivers of the Libyan conflict. They have contributed to the widespread perception of injustice and marginalization in Libya's Eastern and Southern oil-producing regions.

Options for revenue sharing and transfer design

Perpetuating the three-region model would likely accentuate centrifugal forces in the medium term, without ensuring an improvement in living conditions and public services in the East or other regions. Given the extensive experimentation with subnational administrations since the 1960s—governorates (baladiyah) and municipalities (sha'biyat)—it would make sense to start with the lowest-level governance structure (municipalities), as reforms in administrative arrangements will take time to work out.

The revenue base to be shared with subnational entities needs to be determined. It could include the total government take, including the corporate (profit) tax, as well as the government's share of profit oil or just the royalty (see figure 20.1).

Public funds are typically used to unlock private sources of financing, including bonds, for investment in public infrastructure, including at the subnational level, because infrastructure lasts a long time and provides benefits to future generations; it is not reasonable to expect the current generation to bear the full burden of the financing. Indeed, using natural resources can and should be used to leverage investments for the future (see Collier 2010).

As part of the overall package, the following set-up could be envisaged:

- Ten percent of revenues would be distributed through a revenue-sharing mechanism to municipalities, to be distributed in the ratio of 2:1 across producing and nonproducing municipalities.
- National objectives for country-wide standards for health care and education would be met by special-purpose transfers (typically, associated with common rights and obligations in many constitutions). Such transfers could cover the salaries of workers in education and health care. (Other staff would need to be financed under the revenue-share and other own-source revenues.)
- An own-source revenue handle for local governments could be in the form of:
  - A production excise tax.
  - A piggyback on a national carbon tax on the production or transport (through pipelines) of petroleum/gas products: This tax is essential to ensure that the incentives of local governments are aligned with those of the national administration and that both have an interest in stopping cheating, concealment, or diversion of production, as seen in both Indonesia and Nigeria.
  - A local beneficial property tax could be developed quickly on the basis of occupancy, area of properties, and location. A cadaster and valuation would be needed for a traditional property tax on businesses and all property sales.
- Some countries (such as Indonesia) also maintain earmarked transfers for infrastructure needs and gaps. Public investments, even at the subnational level, need to be determined using consistent design and supplemented by adequate public services.[12]
- National funding of a development bank could be devoted to meeting subnational infrastructure requirements.

Origin-based revenue sharing of natural resources can create considerable spatial inequalities. It would therefore be useful to establish an equalization transfer system in conjunction with revenue-sharing arrangements. Care has to be taken in designing such systems to ensure that they do not create negative incentives for local governments.

It is a mistake to design equalization transfers on the basis of differences in actual spending or poverty levels, as many Latin American countries do. Such a design increases the incentives for local governments to avoid narrowing gaps, as it is in their interest to maximize the size of the deficit under their control to increase the level of transfers.

A simple mechanism for fiscal equalization could be based on "incentive-neutral differentials" between standardized expenditure needs and revenue capacities, a system used by several Scandinavian countries, Australia, and China (see Lou 1997). Such a system would remove the disincentives associated with gaps in service delivery and revenue-raising differentials. Although many countries used complex cost estimates, the tendency is to use simple factors on which information is readily available, including population and demographic data (even Australia has moved to simplify its system). (Annex 20A briefly describes fiscal equalization transfers.)

These measures would have to be complemented with other measures, such as subnational PFM procedures to ensure transparency in the management of petroleum funds; streamlined treasury procedures to prevent the build-up of unused cash balances; and the monitoring of both sources and uses of funds to ensure efficiency in cash management and full information on the sources and uses of public funds. These measures will be critical in establishing trust in the unified budget/treasury system.

CONCLUDING REMARKS

Although a transparent and efficient revenue-sharing system is essential to create a unified and post-conflict system of multilevel governance, it is far from sufficient. It will have to be supplemented with a focus on emergency relief for the pandemic and restoration of basic services. A sustainable growth strategy would depend critically on coordinated national and subnational investments, as well as a non-oil national and local tax system to generate appropriate incentives and accountability. A nondistortionary system of special purpose and equalization transfers will also be needed.

A revenue-sharing arrangement (intergovernmental finance framework) is *not sufficient* to translate into improved development at the local level, but it is a *starting point*. For example, a system of direct revenue sharing (although only one piece of a larger package), whereby producing regions receive a fixed percentage of revenues up front, would be an easily understandable *political win* for producing regions. One would have to accept that such funds would be channeled to municipalities that likely do not yet have the capacity to manage them correctly. Nevertheless, if such a deal can prevent further armed conflict, the net result for the country's development would be positive.

In conclusion, an intergovernmental finance framework should be seen as a starting point, but PFM reforms and capacity building for improved multilevel governance will still be needed for such a framework to translate into improved development at the local level. New information technology opens possibilities for the development of cutting-edge fiscal institutions that better integrate the revenue and spending circuits and payment systems. Many of the options require further work that could enable the incoming administration in 2022 to take informed decisions.

ANNEX 20A: THE DESIGN OF EQUALIZATION TRANSFERS

In most multilevel countries, an equalization transfer system is the glue that holds the country together. It is based on the simple proposition that all people in a country are entitled to a reasonably similar standard of government services. Equalizing the level of services is a critical part of the multilevel health care system that needs to be created in response to COVID-19. Doing so would strengthen national identity.

A common goal of an equalization system is to allow subnational governments to provide access to equal—or at least comparable—levels of public services, taking account of the capacity of those governments to finance services. The capacity to finance similar levels of services is a function not only of the level of revenues. It also depends on the cost of producing the services as well as differences in demand for them. Two local governments with the same per capita revenue may not have the same capacity to satisfy the service needs of their population if their populations have different needs—because of differences in the proportions of young or old people, for example, or differences in the costs of providing these services as a result of different population density or climatic conditions.

Attenuation of the most blatant disparities across jurisdictions requires narrowing inequalities in infrastructure and capital stock, including hospitals and other types of basic infrastructure that were destroyed in Benghazi and elsewhere. The latter is more appropriately determined through capital transfers or investments financed through national resources.

A well-designed grant system should also be based on a transparent formula, and the indicators used in the assessment should not reflect discretionary policy choices made by recipient governments. For example, the total amount of salaries paid to local employees should not be considered an indicator of need, because considering them as such would induce beneficiary governments to increase their wage costs in order to obtain a larger share of the grant.

The expenditure-needs and revenue-capacity approach has many advantages. It allocates the total amount of transfers across subnational governments in a way that promotes efficiency and accountability, provides a known basis for the vertical allocation of national revenue across levels of government, and stimulates accountability by providing yardsticks against which stakeholders (including citizens, auditing bodies, and the upper levels of government that provide finance) can evaluate subnational performance. Several political and technical issues have to be addressed before such a system can be implemented, and its financial sustainability has to be assessed against the number of resources available.

One key question will be whether to assess absolute or relative needs. In many countries, the determination of equalization grants is a relative process. In Australia, for example, the capacities of the states are equalized to the average level (per capita) of service provision, assuming the application of average effort to raise revenue. If sufficient resources were available, it might be possible to equalize to an absolute or minimum standard (such as the provision of nine years of education) that all regions should aspire to achieve, but it is usually more practical to use tied grants to raise standards where they fall short of national minima.

There is also the question of accountability. Equalization systems enable local governments to develop different methods of service provision to best suit their circumstances and the aspirations of their people. Questions concern the operation of accountability mechanisms, including when information on what has been spent is weak, and outputs or outcomes difficult to monitor. However, similar objections could be raised about a grant system based on special-purpose grants, with limited information on what has transpired. Typically, special-purpose grants require stronger information and reporting mechanisms, and if these are weak, a simple equalization framework might be preferable.

The grant systems of many countries rely on the identification and estimation of disabilities (influences beyond a government's control that affect what it needs to spend on providing services or can raise from a particular type of taxation). However, many factors or indicators are likely to reduce the transparency of the system; they could also erode the acceptability of a "black box" approach, including in developed countries. A simple set of options is recommended as the starting point. Use of a few simple indicators (such as the proportions of relevant populations such as school-age children or the elderly) is likely to be all that is feasible; they can help governments provide adequate redistributive transfers. Such systems can be elaborated over time, with the development of databases, administrative capabilities, and technical expertise.

An equalization transfer system can come into play once there is clarity about spending functions and own-source revenues. It would be useful to include it as part of the design of the overall multilevel fiscal system that short-term measures would be designed to achieve. Interactions with earmarked transfers for centrally determined standards, or deconcentrated functions, would need to be dovetailed with the development of the PFM system, although the policy design issues are equally important.

NOTES

1. There were 46 governorates/districts (baladiyah) in 1963; their number was reduced to 25 in 1987. Fifteen municipalities (sha'biyat) were created in 1995; this number increased to 32 plus 3 administrative regions in 2001 before being reduced to 25 in 2007. In desert areas, the municipalities have large areas and low populations and are centered on oases.
2. Ades and Glaeser (1994) and Davis and Henderson (2003) argue that urbanization occurs mainly in response to the shift out of agriculture. Urban concentration in one or two large cities is much more directly affected by policies and politics, such as whether or not investment in interregional infrastructure, adequate local service delivery, and local economic development facilitate more even development across a country.
3. Farvacque-Vitkovic and Kopanyi (2019) provide a useful overview of different types of local government revenue sources, which can be combined to constitute an overall "intergovernmental finance framework" for a country.
4. There was a tension between the untied nature of equalization transfers and the health and education basis for estimating spending needs, on the one hand, and the wage determination for functions that had previously been financed by the central government, on the other hand. This tension may have relevance for Libya's sequencing of the decentralization process.
5. See the Revenue Allocation and Fiscal Commission (the new name of the Revenue Mobilisation Allocation and Fiscal Commission), Presidency Abuja, for details of all the revenue-sharing arrangements. https://rmafc.gov.ng/.
6. The lack of accountability for local operations, together with weak monitoring mechanisms, generated incentives for local governments to facilitate cheating on petroleum production and exports, even before the funds reached Nigeria's foreign bank accounts and the Federation Account.
7. The cost of oil is the part of an oil field operator's entitlement to revenue as compensation for incurred exploration and production costs.
8. The World Bank and the International Monetary Fund did substantial work in Libya establishing a TSA, which was integrated as part of the Ministry of Finance's 2014–15 strategy. Because of the institutional split and ensuing conflict, the work was never finalized. Future efforts should build on this work.
9. Chapter 1 is mainly for wages, but wage elements can also be found in chapters 3 and 4. Allocations for operations and maintenance of infrastructure are typically in chapters 3 and 4. To increase transparency, Libya needs to adopt a proper budget classification and chart of accounts, aligned with international standards. The World Bank has already provided substantial assistance to the Ministry of Finance in this respect.
10. In Chile, the largest number of poor people live in the richest region (the capital and surrounding metropolitan areas).
11. Reviewing evidence on the welfare impact of energy subsidy reform across 20 countries, Arze del Granado, Coady, and Gillingham (2012) find that the top income quintile captures six times more in subsidies than the bottom, in absolute terms, with subsidies on gasoline the most regressive. A study by the International Energy Agency (IEA 2011) finds that the

poorest 20 percent of households receive only about one-tenth of natural gas and electricity subsidies.

12. The IMF and the World Bank recommend that a national body evaluate projects in a consistent manner, using uniform methodology. At a later stage, such a national body could help formulate and manage the contracts needed for public-private partnerships, which can be quite complex and difficult for subnational jurisdictions to handle.

REFERENCES

Ades, Alberto F., and Edward Glaeser. 1994. "Trade and Circuses: Explaining Urban Giants." NBER Working Paper, National Bureau of Economic Research, Cambridge, MA.

Ahmad, Ehtisham, Giorgio Brosio, Alemayehu Dana, Lubin Doe, Stuti Khemani, Victoria Kwakwa, and Tej Prakash. 2001. "Nigeria: Options for Reforming Intergovernmental Fiscal Relations." Fiscal Affairs Department, International Monetary Fund, Washington, DC.

Ahmad, Ehtisham, Lubin Doe, Tej Prakash, Stuti Khemani, Victoria Kwakwa, Raju Singh, Giorgio Brosio, and Alemayehu Daba. 2001 *Nigeria: Options for Reforming Intergovernmental Fiscal Relations.* Washington, DC: International Monetary Fund.

Ahmad, Ehtisham, and Raju Singh. 2003. "Political Economy of Oil-Revenue Sharing in a Developing Country: Illustrations from Nigeria." IMF Working Paper WP/03/16, International Monetary Fund, Washington, DC. https://www.imf.org/external/pubs/ft/wp/2003/wp0316.pdf.

Ahmad, Ehtisham, and Eric Mottu. 2002. "Oil Revenue Assignments: Country Experience and Issues." IMF Working Paper WP/02/203. International Monetary Fund, Washington, DC. https://www.imf.org/external/pubs/ft/wp/2002/wp02203.pdf.

Alarabiya News. 2013. "Libya's Southern Fezzan Region Declares Autonomy," September 26, 2013, updated May 20, 2020. https://english.alarabiya.net/News/middle-east/2013/09/26/-Libya-s-southern-Fezzan-province-declares-autonomy.

Arze del Granado, Javier, David Coady, and Robert Gillingham. 2012."The Unequal Benefits of Fuel Subsidies: A Review of Evidence for Developing Countries." IMF Working Paper WP/10/202, International Monetary Fund, Washington, DC. https://www.imf.org/external/pubs/ft/wp/2010/wp10202.pdf.

Augustina, C., E. Ahmad, D. Nugroho, and H. Siagian. 2012. "Political Economy of Natural Resource Revenue-Sharing in Indonesia." Working Paper, LSE Asia Research Center, London School of Economics.

Bacci, A. 2018. *Algeria's and Libya's Petroleum Fiscal Frameworks.* London: Energy Council.

Balhassan, S., B. Misbah, M. Omar, I. Musbah, and B. Khameiss. 2018, "Impact of Proposed Changes to Libyan Oil Taxation System." *Journal of Engineering and Applied Sciences* 13 (15): 6085–90.

Collier, Paul. 2010. *The Plundered Planet: Why We Must—and How We Can—Manage Nature for Global Prosperity.* Oxford: Oxford University Press.

Daoud, Rani. 2019. "The History and Evolution of the Sub-National Government System in Libya." *Proceedings of the Libya Local Government Forum.* Tunis: World Bank.

Davis, James C., and Vernon Henderson. 2003. "Evidence on the Political Economy of the Urbanization Process." *Journal of Urban Economics* 53 (1): 98–125.

Eaton, Tim. 2020. *Libya: Rich in Oil, Leaking Fuel.* London: Chatham House. https://chathamhouse.shorthandstories.com/libya-rich-in-oil-leaking-fuel/index.html.

Farvacque-Vitkovic, Catherine, and Mihaly Kopanyi. 2019. *Better Cities, Better World : A Handbook on Local Governments Self-Assessments.* Washington, DC: World Bank. https://openknowledge.worldbank.org/handle/10986/32120.

IEA (International Energy Agency). 2011. *World Energy Outlook 2011.* Paris: IEA. https://www.iea.org/reports/world-energy-outlook-2011.

Lou, Jiwei. 1997. "Constraints in Reforming the Transfer System in China." In *Financing Decentralized Expenditures,* edited by Ehtisham Ahmad. Cheltenham, UK: Edward Elgar.

Malden, Alexander, and Fikri Zaki Muhammadi. 2019. *Indonesia's Oil and Gas Revenues: Using Payments to Governments Data for Accountability*. New York: Natural Resource Governance Institute. https://resourcegovernance.org/sites/default/files/documents/indonesia-oil -and-gas-revenues-using-payments-to-governments-data-for-accountability.pdf.

Mihalyi, D., A. Adam, and J. Hwang. 2020. *Resource-Backed Loans: Pitfalls and Potential*. New York: Natural Resource Governance Institute.

Ribadu Commission. 2012. *Report of the Petroleum Revenue Special Task Force*. Abuja, Nigeria: Federal Ministry of Petroleum Resources.

VOA (Voice of America). 2011. "Some Looking Forward to Recovery of Libyan Oil Production." Voice of America News, August 23, 2011. https://www.voanews.com/a/companies -countries-look-to-oil-production-recovery-in-libya-128353708/144279.html.

RELATED READING

Wehrey, Frederic. 2018. *The Burning Shores: Inside the Battle for the New Libya*. New York: Farrar, Straus and Giroux.

21 Subnational Governance

ANDREW CHEATHAM, DANIEL STROUX, AND MOHAMED FORTIA

United Nations Development Programme

The authors argue that 10 years after its revolution, Libya is still struggling to transition to a functioning democracy with local governance systems and administrations that meet the needs of the population. One of the major frustrations that brought about the revolution was the heavily centralized rule of the Muammar Gaddafi government. Since 2011, successive interim governments and legislative bodies have tried to remedy the problem with legal reforms that set out a decentralized authority that shared competencies and responsibilities among central, provincial, and local authorities. In practice, a few responsibilities have been transferred to local municipalities. Legal ambiguity has caused confusion between the central authority and the local administrations, leaving room for lasting concentration of power at the national level. Mayors and local councilors have been extremely frustrated by the complete failure to transfer responsibilities and distribute budget allocations, as prescribed by law. The authors provide that there is a real risk of repeating and relying on technocratic approaches that are delinked from, and do not fully recognize, the political economy of engagement in Libya. Mechanistic interpretations of the principles of national ownership were at the center of international support in 2011–20 and have failed the international community. It is essential to integrate political economy considerations in a manner that begins to understand the prevailing economic incentives and helps to address the tensions and unresolved conflicts.

INTRODUCTION

In 1932, the great American jurist Louis Brandeis described local governments in a federal system as laboratories of democracy. At its best, a functioning decentralized state can ensure that the needs of people are met in a way that prioritizes and accounts for local customs and practices without contravening national principles. As a practical matter, local officials are better placed to service the public goods and respond quickly to dynamic demand than administrators far from the scene. Barber (2013) describes the qualities that city administrations now share worldwide: pragmatism; civic trust; participation; indifference to borders and sovereignty; and a democratic penchant for networking, creativity, innovation, and cooperation. Mayors are responding to transnational problems more effectively than nation-states, which are stuck in domestic political squabbles and geopolitical disputes. For Libya, effective decentralized governance systems are key to ensuring long-term peace and stability.

The chapter examines subnational government in Libya. It is organized as follows. The first section describes the methodology. The second section describes the imperfect legal frameworks in Libya and the divide between theory and reality. The third section examines the obstacles to holding elections, which are hindering the effectiveness of local institutions. The fourth section discusses challenges for women. The last section provides some concluding remarks.

METHODOLOGY

Much has been written about the structural and political challenges to successful decentralization in Libya since 2011 as well as the centralized state under Muammar Gaddafi (Zougagh, Romanet Perroux, and Andrieu 2020). This chapter focuses on local governance concerns as of 2021. It approaches the subject of subnational governance and decentralization from a practical perspective. Information was gathered through key informant interviews to determine the most pertinent technical and practical issues. Long-form discussions were conducted with mayors and municipal council members from across Libya. The key informant interviews were complemented by a survey of the literature and news reports.

Facilitators of the key informant interviews deployed a conversational approach, intended to gather in-depth qualitative information about the professional experience of informants and the regular experiences of their day-to-day duties and responsibilities. Each respondent was asked the same series of questions in order to be able to compare and contrast experiences across locations. Interview subjects came from diverse geographic (origin of the family) and ethnic backgrounds. Half of them were women. The high female participation provided in-depth insight into the practical challenges faced by female councilors within their municipalities.

IMPERFECT LEGAL FRAMEWORKS AND THE DIVIDE BETWEEN THEORY AND REALITY

This section examines the legal and policy texts that make up the framework for decentralization in Libya. It analyses the de jure and de facto elements and makes recommendations for the way forward.

The decentralization of governance functions in Libya has been fraught with challenges for decades. In 1951, Libya's first constitution created a federal state that was administratively divided into three equally represented provinces based on the historic regions under Ottoman rule, which continued during Italian colonization. Authority was divided between the central government and the provinces.

In 1963, constitutional amendments abolished the federal government structure and established 10 governorates. These governorates/provinces (muqat'at, later muhafadat) were subdivided into districts (mutasarrifiyat), each of which was further split into subdistricts (mudiriyat). Large cities were organized directly as municipalities, headed by mayors, and subdivided into wards.

When Gaddafi took power in 1969, he replaced systematic subnational governance and established ambiguous, overlapping, and contradictory patronage networks of competing population groups, including tribes and municipalities (Pickard 2013). After the revolution to overthrow Gaddafi, the National Transitional Council (NTC) issued Law No. 59 of 2012 on the Local Administration System. The spirit of Law No. 59 was to establish, as part of the vision for the new Libya, a governance system through elected councils on a municipal and provincial level that worked to represent voices and needs of their constituents. These elected bodies were to be assigned tasks and competencies that flowed effectively from the national to the provincial and local levels. Law No. 59 supported power sharing, with institutionalized mechanisms for regular communication through consultative structures allowing the three tiers to operate cohesively (Mikaïl and Engelkes 2019).

Although Law No. 59 prescribed roughly a general geographic boundary of decentralized administrative units beneath the national government, subsequent (in)action continued the legacy of ambiguity and dominance by central authorities. The law divided local governance structures into provinces (muhafadat), municipalities (baladiyat), and neighborhoods/localities (mahalla).

In 2013, post-revolution Libya's first parliamentary body, the General National Congress, passed Law No. 9, which amended portions of Law No. 59 of 2012 and effectively suspended the declaration of provincial units. Under the current constitutional framework, the 2011 Constitutional Declaration, and current legislation, there is no recognition of defined (Western, Eastern, Southern) "regions" as they pertain to subnational governance.

Taken together, Law No. 59 and Law No. 9 provide some clarity for the geographic divisions for decentralized local administrations. Starting in 2013, successive administrations defined the boundaries of the municipalities, reaching a total of 126 in 2017 (Zougagh, Romanet Perroux, and Andrieu 2020). As of 2020, the Government of National Accord (GNA) recognized 116 municipalities. The unofficial total of municipalities operating as such is unclear, as some were created in the East in recent years by the parallel (unrecognized) Interim National Government (ING).

Nonetheless, Libyan governance processes, to the extent that they are decentralized, flow directly from the executive branch institutions directly to the municipal authorities. As a legal matter, the creation of provinces in Libya, as envisaged in Law No. 59, has yet to occur.

Beyond the geographic units, local governance bodies have also varied for decades, with Gaddafi regularly changing the structure and personnel of the appointed institutions, mostly underneath a narrative of his 1969 revolution and/or the Jamahiriya ("state of masses"). This aspect of local governance has also evolved since 2011. During the revolution, communities spontaneously formed "local councils" to administer their territory and address the needs of citizens (Zougagh, Romanet Perroux, and Andrieu 2020). Libya also has a rich tradition of socially established consultative and leadership bodies, including tribal councils, which have handled a variety of local matters from justice and dispute resolution to basic service delivery. These bodies, such as social councils, still play a significant role today. Some of these local institutions have state sanctions in law, but none has been empowered directly to carry out state functions.

Municipal Council structures were established by Law No. 59; their detailed composition was stipulated under Decree 130 of 2012, which states that each municipality shall be composed as follows: 5 members for municipalities that have a population of 250,000 or less; and 7 members for additional people. Of these members, there should be at least one woman member. The requirement for a member from the revolutionaries was later changed to include any citizen with special needs (Bylaw of Law No. 59 of 2012 on the local administration system attached to Cabinet Decree No. 130 of 2013). Under Law No. 9, until provinces are created by legislative action, the powers of provincial councils are redistributed to Municipal Councils, except as indicated in Paragraph (C) of Article (12) and Paragraph (B) of Article 13 in Law 59, which provide for powers to be transferred to the central government. Paragraph (B) of Article 13 is of particular importance, as it pertains to the endorsement of the municipal budget, which under Law No. 9 is vested in the central government. Therefore, municipal councils and municipal staff, collectively as bodies (as opposed to geographic units) are referred as "the municipalities" and are the only subnational institutions with state authority in Libya.

Key informants representing municipalities indicated that the heart of the issue was not the confusion over the geographic units or the nature of the municipal bodies; the primary issue, in the view of all municipal officials, was the transfer of power and competencies (including fiscal control) to subnational bodies. As part of a decentralization regime, the most relevant transfers of power, in both law and fact, have been related to fiscal and administrative matters. (Political matters are largely seen to be best kept to national actors.) For years, mayors and council members have demanded allocation of fiscal control over prioritized demand-driven budgets to maintain, operate, and develop local facilities and functions to serve the public. They believe that logical, practical, and efficient assignment of administrative decision-making is crucial for the delivery of public goods, which is particularly important for stabilizing their conflict-affected communities.

Article 25 of Law No. 59 addresses the role of municipalities mandating them with "execution of municipal regulations, and with the establishment and administration of public facilities relating to urban planning, organization, buildings, health and social affairs, water utilities, lighting, sanitation, roads, squares, bridges, local transportation, public hygiene, gardens, public recreation areas, shelters, real estate, spaces, public markets, and construction permits for tourism and investment projects within the boundaries of the municipality." The article gave municipal councils primary authority in six areas:

1. Civil registration
2. Control of the municipal guards (health and safety), local markets, and slaughterhouses
3. Management of local transport infrastructure
4. Issuance of licenses at the local level
5. Monitoring of environmental and health issues
6. Following up on projects launched at the local level in cooperation with ad hoc specialized administrative units.

Law No. 9 increased the responsibilities of municipalities (as bodies) by legally transferring several provincial powers under Law No. 59 to municipal councils. None of these powers has been transferred. Mayors and councils are caught up in an inefficient struggle to serve the growing needs of their citizens through ad hoc personal initiatives to garner support from patrons inside or outside the central government.

During interviews, councilors and mayors were clear that no competencies outlined under the legal framework have been officially delegated. One mayor from the Southern region stated that even the most basic municipal duties, such as water and sanitation services, needed to be conducted physically, administratively, and budgetarily through the central government. He mentioned that he would regularly travel to Tripoli for months at a time to meet with ministries requesting support. These cumbersome endeavors are a regular practice for most mayors. They are particularly taxed as mayors must pay for their own travel and accommodation.

Other key informants told similar stories. The mayor of Zawiya explained that being only 30 kilometers from Tripoli he felt lucky that his trips were less burdensome. However, he was incensed at the general principle that such trips were required. He lamented that municipal councils must gain permission from central authorities even to plant trees in their communities.

Closely connected to the failure to transfer technical roles and responsibilities as prescribed by law were respondents' passionate complaints over failures to make adequate budget allocations to municipalities. Chapter 6, Articles 49–51 of Law No. 59, structures portions of the local governance financial administration scheme. Of the 15 revenue sources cited in the law, respondents claimed that the treasury has failed every quarter to provide what is due. All key informants agreed that a severe lack of funding from the central government has plagued local governments and been a major obstacle to providing basic services.

Law No. 13 2014 (On Adopting the State's General Budget) provides the most recent outline of the chapters of the Libyan budget. Those most applicable to local governance include chapters 1–3, which allocate funds for state salaries, operational expenses, and development projects, respectively. According to key informants, municipal councils never officially received funding geared for municipal development (chapter 3). The only funding received to date has been for salaries (chapter 1) and operational costs (chapter 2), which are centrally paid and administered. Even then, funding has been extremely limited relative to needs, late, and inconsistent. A municipal councilor for Misrata stated that he and his councilors in the municipality had not received their salaries for the past eight months, that the city had to resort to donations from its residents and informal agreements with businesses in the city, such as the Libyan Iron and Steel Company and the municipality's Free Trade Zone to receive some funding for service delivery.

To address some of the developmental issues, many municipalities have resorted to using the limited funds they receive from chapter 1 and chapter 2. The mayor of Zawiya noted that he is supposed to be allocated LD 500,000 every quarter from chapter 2 but claimed that he had received the funds only one quarter each year since 2014. The budgetary issues are worse for areas under the control of the Khalifa Haftar, the commander of the Eastern-based Libyan National Army (LNA) (or those deemed to be susceptible to his influence). A mayor from one such municipality, Bent Baya, stated that when he went to Tripoli to gain access to funds and services for his residents, he was met with great opposition. The GNA would not give him access to the funds and services, he claimed, because they feared he would redirect the funds to Haftar and his forces in the region.

The central government claims that lack of adequate controls and oversight are the main reason for not delegating portions of the budget for development projects. It fears widespread corruption if it grants fiscal control to the municipalities. One mayor pushed back saying that the government had never even tried a minimal pilot approach of allowing the municipalities to deal with the development budget. "Let us try for just one year and see what happens," he said.

What is clear is that there remains great confusion between the municipalities and the central government as to where the boundaries of their fiscal responsibilities should be—and there does not seem to have been much progress in the first 100 days of the GNU's work. Respondents felt that the GNU must consider immediate executive action to "activate" Law No. 59 by transferring the administrative authority outlined under the law and successfully allocating budget for chapters 1–3.

All respondents agreed that careful legislative reform must be addressed in the medium term to specify the transfer for administrative and fiscal authority to decentralized institutions. Mayors and councilors demanded some legislative certainty under a framework that delineates administrative and fiscal competencies through internationally recognized principles of deconcentration, delegation, or devolution of authority.

Deconcentration relocates decision-making and financial and management across levels of the central government physically to the geographic subunit; there is no real transfer of authority between levels (Gregersen et al. 2004). *Delegation* features a principal–agent relationship in which the central government delegates power and responsibilities for various public functions to another level of administration while maintaining some control (Pickard 2013). *Devolution* transfers specific powers entirely from one level to another (another level of government or entities of civil society).

Article 23 of Law No. 59 has led to some delegation of powers (in theory) through somewhat of a principal–agent relationship, between the Ministry of Local Government and municipalities (Pickard 2013). Under the law, the minister reserves the right to issue decisions and instructions, to oversee the work conducted, and to approve or reject decisions made by the municipal council in accordance with executive regulations (Pickard 2013). Respondents from all regions, but particularly the East and the South, agreed that the relationships between the new minister of local government and councils have been extremely troubled.

The failure to fully implement Law No. 59 has caused great dysfunction and hardship within municipalities and their councils, slowing or preventing the provision of basic state services. The mayor of Abu-Wanis noted that the roads in his municipality are known as "death roads" because of their severe state of disrepair. He stated that the central government has neglected its duties by leaving the municipality without funding or authority to save lives by repairing the road. Respondents from municipalities across Libya echoed his views about the inoperative law.

Formally and informally, Eastern and Southern municipal officials have complained that the minister has failed to formally recognize local authorities by handing over official seals and stamps. They have also repeated calls for budget allocations and administrative authority, which they had hoped to receive from the new government. Eastern and Southern municipality respondents implied that the new minister along with other parts of the GNU was working to maintain a hold of their centralized authority for the medium and long term. Many Eastern and Southern municipalities had de jure and/or de facto arrangements that aligned them solely or partially with the ING/LNA, providing a partial justification for why some municipalities had received less recognition from the central authorities.

Immediate institutional arrangements are needed to remedy the problems raised. The GNU has proposed a plan to establish provinces and directly appoint governing bodies. The division would reportedly include 13–14 groupings of municipalities across the country, based on population. The groups of municipalities would then hold all the competencies of the "provinces," as provided for in Law No. 59. This executive action would bypass the legislature's mandate to determine the geographic scope and manner of selecting provincial councils by law. The unelected governors and councils would be a clear departure from the democratic frameworks in place for the implementation of decentralized government. Interviewed respondents voiced unanimous and adamant opposition to the GNU proposal, which was widely perceived as a move by the central government to maintain full control over local governance competencies and resources.

A member of the House of Representatives (HoR) and Libyan Political Dialogue Forum (LPDF) representative, Mohammed Al-Raeid, proposed another idea, that "the country should be divided into 12 districts, each two of which should form a financially independent economic region with a budget as per the population and geographical location," adding that going on with this stream of actions would "increase corruption and make government expenditure control difficult" (Assad 2021a). It is not clear what the means of selecting "district" councils and "governors" would be in the proposal. Whatever is agreed to by the legislative and executive branches, activating the provincial level is a crucial institutional arrangement for effective subnational governance.

Another set of recommendations was provided by the chairman of the Central Commission of Municipal Council Elections (CCMCE), Salem Bentahia, in 2020. The institutional process he proposed includes a Decentralization Process Organizing Committee (DPOC) composed of six nominated mayors representing the 116 (GNA-designated) municipalities, the last three former ministers of local government before the political split, and CCMCE representatives (Bentahia 2020). Among other things, the DPOC would convene to nominate members and define the roles for and actions of the Supreme Local Administration Council (SLAC)—a body to implement the decentralization process as per Article 42 of Law No. 59 (Bentahia 2020). Bentahia suggested that the top priority for the SLAC should be determining municipalities' budget allocations based on predefined and agreed criteria (such as population and geographical area).

Some of his recommendations were added during the municipal subtrack of the LPDF conducted at the start of the dialogue process in October 2020, in which mayors and heads of local councils provided recommendations on how to improve subnational governance in Libya. The mayors echoed the need for the full implementation of Law No. 59, demanding that it be achieved in less than a year. They also recommended that some core competencies be transferred within four months. The mayors agreed that there should also be an immediate transfer of responsibilities and an immediate interim budget for urgent matters for a period of four months.

An association of 40 mayors from all over Libya gathered on April 8, 2021, in the municipality of Wadi Al-Buwanis to discuss the challenges they face in their municipalities. During these discussions, the mayors made recommendations on how to alleviate many of the challenges. The main recommendation was the full implantation of Law No. 59. The mayors also demanded the issuance of the funding for municipalities from chapters 2 and 3 of the national budget.

TABLE 21.1 Opportunities to bridge the gap between legal theory and reality in the immediate, short, and medium terms

TIME FRAME	OPPORTUNITY
Immediate	• Issue chapters 2 and 3 of a rapidly approved 2021 national budget that prioritizes municipalities.
Short term	• Implement institutional communication/coordination mechanisms for mayors and municipal councilors to discuss needs, including planning priorities and budget requirements with the central government, including the bodies mandated under chapter 5 of Law No. 59, the High Council of Local Administration and Supreme Council of Regional Planning. In the short term, these bodies must bridge directly between the municipal and national levels (to include provincial councils when appropriate). • Transfer competencies for the health sector, solid waste management, and water and sewage to the municipalities, as stipulated in law No. 59.
Medium term	• Fully enact Law No. 59, ensuring the transfer of all relevant competencies to municipalities. • Pass all associated legislation envisioned under Law No. 59, including the laws on the provinces and provincial councils.

Source: Original table developed for this publication.

They discussed how holding regular, plenary meetings between all municipal heads and the prime minister could help define priorities, address urgent bottlenecks, and formulate unified development policies for improved local governance. One major concern of the mayors was the possibility that the GNU might create unelected counterpart bodies with authority and control over municipalities. Table 21.1 highlights the opportunities to bridge the gap between legal theory and reality in the immediate, short, and medium terms.

OBSTACLES TO HOLDING ELECTIONS, WHICH HINDER THE EFFECTIVENESS OF LOCAL INSTITUTIONS

This section illustrates the challenges faced by the CCMCE, the main electoral body charged with holding municipal elections. It offers considerations for strengthening the body's institutional capacity.

The already challenging environment for subnational governance has been made more complicated by the difficulties Libya has encountered in holding democratic elections. Following the 2011 revolution, the CCMCE worked for years to galvanize local democracy under the most challenging conditions. For various reasons, the CCMCE could not conduct elections in a timely manner. A series of delays reduced the effectiveness and legitimacy of local institutions.

Between 2013 and 2016, Libya held its first 92 elections for local councils, following the creation of the municipalities under Law No. 59. The processes, known as the first generation of local elections, were perceived as largely successful. However, with the start of the 2014 civil war, many municipalities found it difficult to operate, as political divisions and governing paralysis at the national level left local administrations to fend for themselves. When the councils' four-year mandates ended, the Libyan state was too engulfed in conflict to implement the second round of municipal elections nationwide (Talbot and Denehy 2018).

Following the last first-generation election in Sirte in December 2016, in late 2018 the CCMCE resumed council elections under the newly appointed chairman, Salem Bentahia. All 116 officially recognized municipalities had to be considered. These municipalities could be divided into three groups: (1) 92 municipalities in which first-generation council elections were held between 2013 and 2016, (2) 6 municipalities in which security problems prohibited elections in 2014, and (3) newly created municipalities, mainly in the Eastern part of the country. Because of the political split, the CCMCE was able to conduct only 43 elections as of April 2021. Other factors—including funding issues, security, legal challenges, and the COVID-19 pandemic—also made it difficult to hold elections.

In 2018, the CCMCE was able to hold only three elections, in Bani Waleed, Derj, and Zawia (three of the six municipalities with security problems). The same year, mandate renewal was due in over 60 municipalities, all having had elections in 2014.

The elections for councils with expired terms were delayed by the late arrival of government funding in September 2018, which also overlapped with a GNA decision to change the executive regulations governing municipal council elections, including the change from a single nontransferable-vote system to a party block vote system. This change made by the GNA executive regulations was issued in haste and was not subject to consultations with key electoral stakeholders, greatly affecting the orderly continuation of mandate renewal of the municipal councils. In November 2018, the CCMCE did initiate, post facto, a consultation process on the newly issued regulation. A few important recommendations from this process were accepted by the GNA, but the contested party block vote system remained in place for general lists.

The GNA's new regulations negatively affected the CCMCE's capacity to run elections in the East. Until then, local elections had been conducted under a legal framework elaborated by the ING during its official term (before 2014). Eastern factions took issue with the government's unilateral changes to the process. Despite support from the Tobruk-based HoR, the ING opposed the CCMCE's attempts to run the second-generation electoral processes in the East (as noted in a letter from HoR speaker's office to the CCMCE chairman). The Easterners not only rejected the regulations passed by the GNA; the acting minister of local government designated the CCMCE chairman as a persona non grata in the Barqa region. Following these events, the CCMCE was forced to freeze plans for approximately 20 elections in the East.

In 2019, the CCMCE's complications deepened, as the LNA moved to Southern Libya and initiated attacks on Tripoli on April 6. Despite these new challenges, the committee was still able to conduct 22 elections in the Southern and Western regions; elections were postponed in only 11 municipalities because of security and political obstacles. Some elections in the South (Qatrun, Sharghia, and Traghen) scheduled for 2019 were halted for legal reasons, following a June ruling by the Tripoli Administrative Court to annul the executive regulations governing local elections.

An amendment to the regulations, No. 6/2020, and its approval by the Presidency Council, finally allowed the CCMCE to resume electoral processes in March. However, the COVID-19 pandemic and heavy fighting in and around Tripoli hindered a quick turnaround of electoral processes. The LNA eventually withdrew from the area on June 3, 2020. The post-war burden of divided communities imposed a since of urgency for the CCMCE, which ran 18 more elections, including in Ghat, Misrata, and several municipalities of Greater Tripoli by April 2021.

The CCMCE adjusted to the difficult circumstances, including extremely challenging security threats, but the unstable legal framework remains a core problem. Great instability has flowed from the 2018–19 changes in regulations and the electoral system. Globally, the party block vote system, which the GNA introduced, is rarely used in democratic elections, and it has been subject to profound criticism by many stakeholders in Libya. It allows the winning list to gain all seats with a simple majority, meaning that even if a list wins by only one vote it takes all posts on the council (except the two reserved seats, one for a woman and one for a person with a disability). The motivation of the GNA was to allow mayors to give councils a stable majority during their four-year mandate. This motivation was reasonable, but the system potentially leads to great exclusion of key groups and opinions within a municipality.

Disagreement about the regulations and electoral systems has been expressed through numerous legal complaints since 2019. One challenge to the regulations raised in the Zawara election resulted in a decision to remove the elected council and replace it with the predecessor group. This case is one of many that demonstrate the need to reform the legal framework and introduce a more comprehensive law on council elections. In the meantime, however, the second generation of elections must proceed until a legislature can pass more functional and appropriate election laws.

Low voter turnout characterized the elections in 2020–21 in larger municipalities in and around Greater Tripoli. Focus groups conducted by the UN electoral team supporting the CCMCE revealed a mix of reasons, including limited knowledge about the work of municipal councils, citizen frustration with the perceived incompetence of elected institutions, lack of knowledge of candidates and lists, and hesitation to go to polling stations out of fear of COVID-19. The intervention and intimidation by armed groups in electoral processes in the municipalities of Hay Alandalus, Swani Ben Adam, and Tajoura, as well as the viral mis/disinformation on social media about cancellation of two elections, also contributed to citizens refraining from participation (Assad 2021b).

Despite all the issues surrounding the ability of the CCMCE to hold elections, it has made progress toward full mandate renewal for municipal councils. In order to conclude the second-generation elections, the committee must still conduct 70 elections across Libya. Some will be difficult, for a variety of reasons, including security issues (for example, in Murzuq) and issues or irregularities with geographic boundaries, which must be clarified by the Ministry of Local Government (MoLG).

Under the leadership of both chairmen, Otman Gajjji (2013–18) and Salem Bentahia (2018–21), the CCMCE has been able to operate independently and gain the trust of Libyan citizens as a professional and competent electoral management body, under the umbrella of the MoLG. The CCMCE has fulfilled its responsibilities in preparing and conducting more than 130 municipal council elections, taking special care at each stage of the process, from voter registration to the announcement of the final results. In 2018, the Presidential Council, through Decision No. 496/2018234, strengthened the independence of the institution by designating the CCMCE as the authority for council elections with a legal personality with financial autonomy.

Despite this decision, the status of the CCMCE has remained that of a "committee" with ad hoc status and limited financial liabilities. It continues to receive only chapter 2 (operational) budget allocations and no chapter 1 (salaries) or chapter 3 (development) allocations, despite its right to financial transactions and full public budget, restricting the CCMCE's capacity to exercise its mandate. Internally, the CCMCE has functioned with constant instability, in large part because staff salary payments can be drawn only from the operational budget. No budget has been available for paying salaries for several months each year. Under these conditions, the CCMCE has hardly been able to keep its core team working. In addition, there has been a continuing risk that qualified personnel will leave for other national institutions or international organizations.

Both Chairman Bentahia and his predecessor have been able to shield the committee from interference, which could have compromised its independence with political pressure. To maintain these important achievements for Libya's democratic processes, it is crucial that the GNU continue to respect the independence of the CCMCE and help protect its credibility and public trust. It is equally crucial that the CCMCE board members continue to protect the integrity of the institution against interference, which could easily compromise the reputation it has built since 2014.

The CCMCE's future institutional status will also need consideration. The draft constitution—created by the Constitutional Drafting Assembly in 2017 and likely to be considered for referendum—proposes that just one national electoral authority conduct all elections. The preparation and conduct of local elections would therefore come under the responsibility of the High National Election Commission (HNEC), or an equivalent body (Pickard 2020). Chairman Bentahia has suggested moving in this direction by integrating the work of the CCMCE and the HNEC. Integration of the CCMCE's tasks would need an adaptation of legislation, including Law No. 59, that puts the CCMCE under the umbrella of the MoLG (and the executive branch) rather than the HoR, where the HNEC is administratively anchored. Table 21.2 highlights the opportunities to improve the electoral framework in the immediate, short, and medium terms.

TABLE 21.2 Opportunities to improve the electoral framework in the immediate, short, and medium terms

TIME FRAME	OPPORTUNITY
Immediate	• Ensure that the CCMCE has the necessary funding, human resources, and political support to finish the second generation of elections.
Short term	• Protect the CCMCE's independence to preserve the trust in and the reputation of a democratic institution with a record of having conducted over 130 credible council elections since 2013. • Strengthen campaigns to raise awareness among citizens regarding democratic participation through elections, and initiate campaigns to raise awareness about voting and local elections. These campaigns should explain the duties and responsibilities of municipalities to serve citizens (highlighting the social contract).
Medium term	• Review the electoral legal framework concerning the third generation of municipal and provincial elections, including the electoral system. A new comprehensive legal framework should be elaborated to protect electoral integrity including relevant civil and criminal laws. • Establish the CCMCE as a more permanent entity in law, possibly with statutory integration into the national commission, anticipating new institutional arrangements following a constitutional referendum.

Source: Original table developed for this publication.
Note: CCMCE = Central Commission of Municipal Council Elections.

CHALLENGES FOR WOMEN

This section looks at the role of women in local governance and the challenges they face in conducting their duties as elected representatives.

Women have long played a significant role in Libya, having gained the right to vote in 1964. However, 40 years under Gaddafi's government has caused the perception of women in political office to be considered tokenism. During the Gaddafi era, the government selected women based on Gaddafi's interests rather than merit (Doherty 2013). Coupled with Libya being a patriarchal society, this practice made it difficult for the gender norms in the country to be shaken off. Libyan women were active in the 2011 uprising, providing medical aid to the revolutionaries on the front lines and organizing international awareness campaigns (Omar 2012).

After 2011, the NTC's 40-member body included just two women—not a positive sign for the newly formed government. The NTC tried to amend the underrepresentation by stipulating in Law No. 4 (On the Election of the General National Congress) that all parties wishing to compete for the 80 seats must include women. Decree 13 states that the councils of all provinces and municipalities should include at least one woman (Cabinet Decree No. 130 of 2013 regarding Law No. 59) (UNICEF 2011).

This legal scheme has had unanticipated consequences, according to respondents, who indicated that it has been interpreted not as a minimum requirement but as a maximum. As part of separate research conducted by United Nations Development Programme in 2018 and 2019 for the Stabilization Facility for Libya (SFL), over 50 municipal official respondents expressed an understanding that only one woman could be a member of each council (for reasons not specified).

The lack of female representation has caused practical difficulties for councilwomen across Libya, who find themselves the sole female representative in what is a traditionally male-dominated field. The councilwoman for Ghat stated that if she had another female colleague, she could rely on her support for her projects and initiatives, many of which regard issues faced by the female residents of her municipality and do not seem to be of great concern to her male colleagues.

Although the laws governing the composition of municipalities did not exclude women from running for all seats on the main list, the quota installed a perception that a woman could not run for a separate seat, as prescribed by the law. All but one of the female members currently serving in Libya's municipal councils was elected as a separate "woman's" seat. The municipality of Abu Wanis is the only exception, with two female members. However, the second woman was elected as part of the quota system for the revolutionary disabled (the other seat that is mandated).

Libya's traditionally patriarchal society has been one of the biggest challenges faced by councilwomen. Sirte is heavily influenced by male-dominated tribal institutions, which has caused many problems for the municipality's sole female member. The councilwoman for Sirte stated that it was the first time in the history of the city that a woman had been elected or appointed to a senior political position. At first, she said, it was very difficult for her to carry out her duties. Many of her colleagues did not accept a woman as their equal.

To address these challenges, she relied on her tribe for support. Over time, her colleagues treated her more as an equal member of the council. Other women echoed her comments.

Another major issue raised by most of the councilwomen was the "boys' club" culture within the municipalities. The councilwoman for Misrata mentioned that male members would host council meetings outside of normal working hours and give her very short notice of them.[1] Such practices, which appear to be widespread across the country, reduce the participation of women in council affairs. The councilwoman for Zawara said, "They would make plans to meet at 10 p.m. and give me very short notice." She also reported being given no prior notice when ministers from the central government visited the city.

The placement of councilwomen into gendered roles based on patriarchal stereotypes was another major complaint from key informants. The councilwoman for Zawara said that her colleagues assigned her only files they deemed "suitable for a woman." This type of discourse is consistent with Section 24 of the Libyan Labour Relations Act (2010), which states that "women workers shall not be employed in types of work that are unsuited to their nature as women." Respondents explained that "women's portfolios" in municipal councils have included areas such as education, "woman affairs," and "social affairs." The councilwoman for Zawara complained that such practices are "wrong and sexist."

All of the councilwomen in the study believed that the MoLG should play a large role regarding the roles of female council members. The councilwoman for Abu Wanis said that it was the duty of the MoLG to oversee the operations of municipalities and correct any irregular and discriminatory practices. Many saw the limited mechanisms available to them to contact the MoLG as a major problem. The councilwoman for Tripoli Center stated that she had been trying to contact the ministry for over a month with no success despite being a member representing the capital. The councilwoman for Ghat stated that she was also unable to get access to the ministry, even though it was her right as an elected member of the council. She stated that all contact with the MoLG had to first go through the mayor, preventing her from airing her grievances independently to her central government counterparts regarding the actions of her colleagues. "The MoLG should be supporting women in municipal councils," she said.

The situation of Libyan woman in political positions has been precarious. The tribal and patriarchal social structure of the country has posed a challenge to increased and effective female political participation. This is particularly the case in subnational governance, where ill-defined laws and regulations have caused confusion about the duties and responsibilities of the municipality and its members (especially its female ones). The MoLG has a duty to correct the operations and administrative irregulates found within the municipalities, including investigating all claims of gender-based discrimination.

One solution is to ensure that the democratic process is upheld through credible, inclusive, and peaceful municipal council elections. Table 21.3 highlights the opportunities to expand and deepen women's roles in local governance in the immediate, short, and medium terms.

TABLE 21.3 **Opportunities to expand and deepen women's roles in local governance in the immediate, short, and medium terms**

TIME FRAME	OPPORTUNITY
Immediate	• Arrange meetings between the MoLG and all municipal councilwomen, so that the ministry hears concerns. • Create dedicated impartial complaints procedures that protect women councilors and guarantee a response from the MoLG. • Enact regular oversight mechanisms for municipalities to ensure that there is no discrimination or toxic and oppressive work environments. • Ensure that the rights, duties, and responsibilities of mayors and councilors are clearly explained to municipal councils.
Short term	• Allow councilwomen to create collaborative groups for joint projects and initiatives for their municipal councils (city twinning). • Create a formal forum or union where councilwomen can meet and collaborate. Such an effort could build on the recommendation of city twinning. This forum/union should have direct meetings with the MoLG to ensure attention and support for proposals. • Provide dedicated trainings for councilwomen. Training workshops could be extended to the wider public to increase female participation in local governance.
Medium term	• Establish a dedicated budget for each municipality for women's empowerment initiatives. • Increase the quota for women councilors ("30 percent + initiative"). • Create a quota to increase the number of female general staff within the municipal government.

Source: Original table developed for this publication.
Note: MoLG = Ministry of Local Government.

CONCLUDING REMARKS

Ten years after its revolution, Libya is still struggling to transition to a functioning democracy with local governance systems and administrations that meet the needs of the population. One of the major frustrations that brought about the revolution was the heavily centralized rule of the Gaddafi government. Since 2011, successive interim governments and legislative bodies have tried to remedy the problem with legal reforms that set out a decentralized authority that shared competencies and responsibilities among central, provincial, and local authorities.

In practice, only a few responsibilities have been transferred to local municipalities. Legal ambiguity has caused confusion between the central authority and the local administrations, leaving room for lasting concentration of power at the national level. Mayors and local councilors have been extremely frustrated by the complete failure to transfer responsibilities and distribute budget allocations, as prescribed by law. Consequently, mayors and other municipal officials have been forced to set up personal ad hoc arrangements with national officials and other powerful figures to meet the demands of their constituents. The situation has severely impeded the delivery of state services to communities in desperate need of recovery after repeated cycles of violence and severe fragility.

Although the first generation of municipal elections, held in 2013–14, was ostensibly successful, elections have been hindered by the long-standing crises across Libya. Expired municipal mandates have led to community frustration and challenges to the legitimacy of local administrations. Demands for new elections must be met to secure the foundations of representative democracy.

Women's representation in local governance has also been dismal since the 2011 revolution. On paper, steps have been taken to promote the participation of women in local governance. In practice, women struggle every day to be heard and to fulfil their roles as local leaders and representatives.

NOTE

1. Across Libya, it is widely perceived as inappropriate for women to travel around the city alone in evening.

REFERENCES

Assad, A. 2021a. "Al-Raeid: HoR Budget-Review Sessions Were 'Shameful.'" *Libya Observer*, May 26, 2021. https://www.libyaobserver.ly/economy/al-raeid-hor-budget-review-sessions -were-shameful.

Assad, A. 2021b. "North Tripoli Court Approves the City's Municipal Elections." *Libyan Observer*, February 22, 2021. https://www.libyaobserver.ly/inbrief/north-tripoli-court -approves-citys-municipal-elections.

Barber, B. 2013. *If Mayors Ruled the World: Dysfunctional Nations, Rising Cities*. New Haven, CT: Yale University Press.

Bentahia, S. 2020. *Stability through Local Elections and Local Administration: Local Administration Path Decentralization Process (DP)*. Tripoli: Central Committee for Municipal Council Elections.

Doherty, M. 2013. *Women's Political Participation in Libya: Quotas as a Key Strategy for States in Transition*. Washington, DC: National Democratic Institute.

Gregersen, H., A. Contreras-Hermosilla, A. White, and J. Phillips. 2004. *Forest Governance in Federal Systems: An Overview of Experiences and Lessons*. Washington, DC: CIFOR. https:// www.cifor.org/publications/pdf_files/interlaken/interlaken_pre-paper.pdf.

Mikaïl, B., and S. Engelkes. 2019. *Piece by Piece: Solving the Libyan Puzzle through Municipalities*. Libya Brief 8, Regional Program on Political Dialogue South Mediterranean, Konrad Adenauer Stiftung, Bonn.

Omar, M. 2012. "Women in Libya and the Arab Spring," *Huffington Post*, January 4, 2012. https:// www.huffpost.com/entry/arab-spring-libya-women_b_1076873.

Pickard, D. 2013. "Decentralization in Libya." October 1, 2013. Washington, DC: Atlantic Council. https://www.atlanticcouncil.org/blogs/menasource/decentralization-in-libya/.

Pickard, D. 2020. *Libya: Comparison of Two Constitutional Text According to International Standards of Democracy*. Washington, DC: Democracy Reporting International.

Talbot, F., and D. Denehy. 2018. *Is It Time for Municipal Elections in Libya?* Rome: Italian Institute for International Political Studies. https://www.ispionline.it/en /pubblicazione/it-time-municipal-elections-libya-21779.

Zougagh, H., J. L. Romanet Perroux, and K. Andrieu. 2020. *Decentralizing Democracy: The Legal Framework of Local Governance in Libya*. Chicago: American Bar Association.

www.ingramcontent.com/pod-product-compliance
Lightning Source LLC
Chambersburg PA
CBHW061134030426

42334CB00003B/27